Zbigniew Brzezinski

Zbigniew Brzezinski

AMERICA'S GRAND STRATEGIST

Justin Vaïsse

TRANSLATED BY CATHERINE PORTER

Harvard University Press

CAMBRIDGE, MASSACHUSETTS · LONDON, ENGLAND

2018

Printed in the United States of America
SECOND PRINTING

This book was originally published in French as
Zbigniew Brzezinski. Stratège de l'empire,
copyright Odile Jacob, 2016.

Library of Congress Cataloging-in-Publication Data

Names: Vaïsse, Justin, author. | Porter, Catherine, 1941– translator.
Title: Zbigniew Brzezinski : America's grand strategist / Justin Vaisse ;
translated by Catherine Porter.
Other titles: Zbigniew Brzezinski. English
Description: Cambridge, Massachusetts : Harvard University Press, 2018. | "This book
was originally published in French as Zbigniew Brzezinski. Stratege de l'empire, copyright
Odile Jacob, 2016." | Includes bibliographical references.
Identifiers: LCCN 2017039431 | ISBN 9780674975637 (cloth)
Subjects: LCSH: Brzezinski, Zbigniew, 1928-2017. | Statesmen—United States—Biography. |
Polish Americans—Biography. | National security—United States—History—20th century. |
United States—Foreign relations—20th century. | United States—Strategic aspects.
Classification: LCC E840.8.B79 .V3413 2018 | DDC 355 / .033073092 [B]—dc23
LC record available at https://lccn.loc.gov/2017039431

Contents

Introduction   1

1 A Brilliant Young Man in the Cold War University   15

2 A Political Adviser Is Born   67

3 The Rise of a New Foreign Policy Elite   117

4 From the Trilateral Commission to the White House   157

5 Portrait of an Academic in Politics   213

6 In the White House   271

7 The Age of Authority   359

Conclusion   403

Notes   413
Acknowledgments   479
Index   481
Publications Index   501

Zbigniew Brzezinski

Introduction

In September 1938, a ten-year-old boy named Zbigniew Brzezinski arrived in New York by boat from Poland with his family. He was not fleeing persecution or poverty; his father had been appointed as Poland's consul general in Montreal, and the boy spent his adolescence in Canada, sheltered from the turmoil of the Second World War. Still, he kept his ears tuned to the radio and his eyes fixed on a map of battle sites, as his heart was with the Allied armies. He watched helplessly as Nazi Germany and then the Soviet Union subjugated Poland and the rest of Eastern Europe. These years shaped his vocation; he went on to become an expert in the international politics that had deprived him of his birthplace. His admission to Harvard in 1950 made him more than a specialist in the communist world; it made him an American, by inclination and by conviction, long before he became a US citizen in 1958.

In the 1960s, the young immigrant with the unpronounceable name became a respected professor and made his mark in his field with several important books; his media appearances familiarized the public with his accent. He was also an influential adviser whose opinions were sought by political decision makers and candidates for elected office; he was consulted on the Vietnam War, on the conflicts in the Middle East, and on policies related to Europe and the USSR. In the 1970s, he took an interest in a Democratic governor named Jimmy Carter, an outsider like himself, a relatively unknown figure who wanted to become president of the United States. This gamble propelled Brzezinski to the command center of the American empire in the middle of the Cold War. His role as Carter's national security adviser allowed him to fulfill his vocation; in it, he was able to influence the course of international politics and chip away at the Soviet Union. But his story did not end when he left the White House in 1981. During the decades that followed, he asserted himself as one of the most respected voices on international matters. He became a geopolitical authority whose influence was felt on all the issues that marked our times, from the Gulf War to the Iraq War, from the fall of the Berlin Wall to the rise of China. In other words, he was a strategist for the American empire.

Zbigniew Brzezinski's story deserves to be told because it is more than the success story of a talented, tenacious, and hard-working immigrant. His life is striking in what it illustrates about America and its relation to the world, from the confrontations of the Cold War to the disorders of the present day; in what it reveals about the transformations, over several decades, of the men and women who were responsible for conceiving and directing American foreign policy; and finally, in what it suggests about the fundamental relations between thought and action. Like Henry Kissinger, Brzezinski was a pioneer, an early exemplar of a now-familiar model—that of the political strategist, the academic who becomes counselor to the president.

One legendary scene can serve as a touchstone for understanding the revolution Brzezinski embodied. One day in December 1960, banker Robert Lovett's car stopped in a snow-covered street in Georgetown, the chic neighborhood in Washington, DC, where the newly elected president of the United States, John Kennedy, lived. Lovett, a sixty-five-year-old man, personified the WASP elite. The son of the head of the Union Pacific Railroad, and a Yale graduate, he had led the first American Air Force squadron in World War I. In 1940, he had left behind his business interests in New York to serve as deputy to Secretary of War Henry Stimson in Washington, where he had overseen the formidable expansion of American air power. After the war, he had been secretary of defense under President Harry Truman. Lovett was a Republican, but his aura was such that the Democratic president-elect Kennedy offered him on that day in December not one ministerial portfolio but his choice of three: defense, foreign affairs, or treasury. The banker declined all of them, claiming poor health. In his place, he recommended Robert McNamara for defense, Dean Rusk for foreign affairs, and Douglas Dillon for treasury. Soon afterward, Kennedy made all three appointments.[1]

Such was the prestige and power of the Establishment, a caste of elder statesmen who had defended the United States against totalitarianism and built the American world in the mid-twentieth century. This group is the focus of *The*

Wise Men, a book by Walter Isaacson and Evan Thomas in which Lovett appears alongside Averell Harriman, Dean Acheson, Charles Bohlen, George Kennan, and John McCloy.[2] These men, most of them from patrician families, tended to be educated in the same institutions—boarding schools such as Phillips Academy or Groton, then Harvard, Princeton, or Yale at the university level—and as students, to belong to the same clubs, like the Skull and Bones secret society at Yale. They went to work in industry and banking, but they put their knowledge and international networks at the service of the nation. Profoundly affected by the First World War and by the crisis of the 1930s, they were resolutely internationalist and lived in an Atlantic universe centered on Europe—a world in which America was obliged to exercise its leadership without hesitation but with discernment. They were men who, present at the creation of the American world and its institutions in the 1940s and 1950s, would see their consensus gradually broken by the Vietnam fiasco in the late 1960s.[3]

Another type of foreign policy elite was emerging, consisting of university graduates, often with Ph.D.s, for whom international affairs were the principal occupation and the exercise of political power was an explicit quest.[4] This new elite was much more diversified in terms of social standing. WASPs were no longer in the majority, and wealth was less abundant. The new group included academics, journalists, researchers in think tanks, employees of major philanthropic foundations, assistants to members of Congress, the occasional diplomat, and often men who had occupied several such posts in turn. They were also more politicized, increasingly so during the decades that followed. On the left, for example, were Richard Holbrooke, Anthony Lake, and Leslie Gelb, and on the right, Richard Burt, Elliott Abrams, and Richard Perle. But the two pioneering figures who opened the way to this new elite, those whom all the ambitious young figures wanted to emulate, were Kissinger and Brzezinski.

Eight years after the Georgetown episode, to widespread surprise, Kissinger was named national security adviser by President Richard Nixon. Eight years after that, Brzezinski reached the White House. Neither one belonged to the Establishment, neither was WASP, neither was a wealthy banker or a New York lawyer. Both were naturalized European immigrants, the first a Jew of German origin, the second a Catholic of Polish origin. Both spoke with foreign accents and bore exotic names, even if Heinz Kissinger had chosen to change his first name to Henry.

A Product of the Cold War University

If the new foreign policy elite seemed to come in large numbers from university campuses, it was because during the 1950s and 1960s universities had acquired unprecedented preeminence. To be sure, Harvard had already been interested in international affairs, starting with the war of 1898, and Woodrow Wilson, himself a scholar, had launched "The Inquiry," a project in which he brought together experts to conduct research on the First World War and its aftermath and advise him on foreign policy. But it was the Second World War that really brought the government into close touch with universities, most notably on weapons development (as in the Manhattan Project for the atomic bomb), the economy, and education. With McCarthyism behind them, academics increasingly collaborated with Washington. This was the phenomenon known as the Cold War University, from which Kissinger and Brzezinski emerged, along with Walt Rostow, Stanley Hoffmann, Samuel Huntington, Thomas Schelling, and many others.

As America achieved durable prosperity and took on global responsibilities, a virtuous circle was established. On the one side, the government's needs for expertise were increasing exponentially, in foreign policy as well as on domestic issues. Insight was required from specialists on the workings of the international system; on the processes of economic development in Third World countries; on regions that were not well known up to that point, such as Southeast Asia or the Middle East (hence the effort to develop area studies); on the principles and practices of nuclear deterrence; and on other topics. On the other side, universities were developing at a rapid pace, swollen by the baby boom generation and the GI Bill of Rights' financing of college studies for veterans. During the 1960s and 1970s, universities gained an eminence they had never before enjoyed in American society.

Within this general atmosphere, the academic discipline of international relations was gradually asserting itself, carving out a specific identity within the rather chaotic field of political science. When Brzezinski arrived at Harvard in 1950, the Department of Government he joined awarded only "political science" degrees. But the department was sharply split into at least four fields of specialization: comparative politics, political theory, domestic politics, and international politics. From the latter, the further subfield of international relations had begun to emerge, shaped by Hans Morgenthau in particular; his *Politics among Nations* was published in 1948.[5] Morgenthau was determined to liberate the newly hatched discipline from the dominion of history and international law.

In this development, the major American philanthropic foundations—above all, Carnegie, Ford, and Rockefeller—played a key role, building the intellectual cadre that was to support American foreign policy. Whereas in 1945 only a small number of universities had programs in international affairs, in 1965 such programs, along with area studies, existed in the major university centers from New York to California. This was thanks mainly to funding by the big foundations and by the CIA and other federal agencies, which provided massive financial support to research in the social sciences as well as in the hard sciences. Indeed, government support became a target of protests in the 1960s. Student demonstrators denounced what they saw as compromises with power— particularly by academics at Harvard—and condemned the idea of knowledge being instrumentalized to serve imperialist or even genocidal policies.

At Harvard in the 1950s, Brzezinski worked at the Russian Research Center established in 1948 by a grant from the Carnegie Corporation. Efforts to create a center dedicated to international affairs began in 1954 with the support of the Ford Foundation. The idea took concrete form in 1958 when the dean of the faculty of arts and sciences, McGeorge Bundy, inaugurated the Center for International Affairs (CFIA), with Robert Bowie as director and Kissinger as associate director. It was this network that was later invited to work closely with John F. Kennedy, through the intermediary of Bundy, then Kennedy's national security adviser. Kissinger and Brzezinski, along with Thomas Schelling, contributed to these efforts in different ways. Although Kissinger did not find his experience as a consultant to the Security Council very satisfying (he had no say in decisions), Brzezinski, who worked in the Policy Planning Council under President Lyndon B. Johnson, flourished in that role. These early developments created the pathways into the 1970s, which saw both men reach the highest level of political decision making, and become leading symbols of a broader renewal of the talent pool devoted to American foreign policy.

But the ascent of these new experts did not go unnoticed by the Establishment, or fail to elicit a reaction from it. A letter sent by Brzezinski to Averell Harriman in June 1974 makes clear that concerns were being voiced:

Dear Mr. Harriman: I have been told by some friends that you expressed the view that my Polish background somehow disqualifies me from dealing objectively with the US-Soviet relationship. Accordingly, I hope you will glance at the two enclosed items which speak for themselves. Since you are a blunt man, let me also say quite bluntly that I do not feel that Henry Kissinger's background disqualified him from dealing effectively with the Middle Eastern problem, nor do I think that your background as a millionaire capitalist prevents you from dealing intelligently with the Soviet communists.[6]

When he wrote these words, Brzezinski was still only a rising figure—a Columbia professor and director of the Trilateral Commission (a nongovernmental organization founded by David Rockefeller to convene the power elite of the United States, Europe, and Japan). Harriman meanwhile was a political giant. Eighty-three years old, he was heir to the immense fortune accumulated by his father in the railroad industry and an international investor in his own right, especially in Russia. He had served as Franklin Delano Roosevelt's special envoy to Europe and Moscow, and attended the major international conferences held in Tehran, Yalta, and Potsdam, eventually with the status of ambassador to the Soviet Union (in the years 1943 to 1946). After the war, he had served two years as Truman's secretary of commerce, been elected to one term as governor of New York (1955 to 1959), and run twice (unsuccessfully) for the Democratic presidential nomination (for the 1952 and 1956 presidential races). He retained considerable influence under the Kennedy and Johnson administrations.[7]

Brzezinski's letter to Harriman illustrates the clash between two generations of elites. Even Brzezinski's affronted and somewhat impertinent tone—it is clear that he felt cut to the quick—is revealing in this respect. But there were two more immediate causes for the antagonism: Harriman had imputed Brzezinski's "hawkish" positions to his Polish origins, and the reason behind that imputation was his fundamental disagreement with the policy Brzezinski favored toward Russia.

In his reply of July 2, 1974, Harriman denied the statements attributed to him. These, he insisted, were willful distortions of comments he had made in a discussion about the composition of the Democratic Advisory Council's Russian Study Group. His reason for rejecting Brzezinski's participation in that meeting, he recalled, was because of their earlier encounter at a Council on Foreign Relations meeting in 1961, where he deemed Brzezinski's position too hawkish—and because he preferred to include Marshall Shulman, another Columbia-based expert on the Soviet Union. But his letter also thanked Brzezinski for the articles sent, with which Harriman said he broadly agreed. He made a further gesture of reconciliation, writing "I am quite ready to drop the past if you are." He even offered a little flattery ("I would be fascinated to hear about the Trilateral Commission") and invited Brzezinski and his wife for a visit to one of his homes in New York State, where they might talk about Russia and the state of the Democratic Party.[8]

Although that visit did not take place (the Brzezinskis always spent the summer at their vacation home on Mount Desert Island in Maine), the exchange of friendly greetings continued; reconciled, the two men corresponded and met in person on several occasions. Harriman contributed to the Carter campaign, for which Brzezinski was the principal foreign policy adviser, and when Brzezinski was named national security adviser, Averell and Pamela Harriman offered him temporary lodging in Washington during the six months before his family arrived from New York in 1977. (Marshall Shulman, Richard Holbrooke, and others benefited similarly from the Harrimans' largesse.) Nevertheless, the relationship between the two men was to become strained again. Harriman worried about what he viewed as the administration's clumsiness and its overreactions toward the Soviets, especially in 1978. Unsurprisingly, Harriman was much closer to Secretary of State Cyrus Vance, to whom he had been a mentor—and whose Establishment-aligned thinking and manners put him at odds with Brzezinski, especially regarding the USSR. But what was really at stake was access to the president. Now, every time Harriman saw Carter at the White House, Brzezinski managed to be present; participating in such conversations was one of Brzezinski's crucial privileges.[9]

Thus hostility between Harriman and Brzezinski resurfaced and, despite his earlier denials of any qualms about Brzezinski's ethnicity, Harriman expressed them now. It was a fundamental mistake, he told others in his circle, to choose a Pole to handle relations with the Soviets.[10] Lovett went even further in his scorn for Brzezinski: "We shouldn't have a National Security Adviser like that who's not really an American. . . . I can't imagine anyone negotiating with the Russians with his loathing and suspicion."[11]

The Origin of Brzezinski's Political Thought

Was Brzezinski an anti-Soviet hawk and cold warrior just because of his Polish origins? This would be too simple an explanation. After all, as he himself pointed out, many WASP Americans shared his opinions, and he also defended détente with the Soviet Union. Yet in studying Brzezinski's positions and academic work on the USSR and Eastern Europe, it is hard to set aside his situation as a Polish Catholic immigrant, and recently minted American, and to view him as an ordinary hawk. Indeed, that would be astonishing, given his personal history. Brzezinski's diplomat father, prior to being assigned to Montreal, had served in Germany at the beginning of the Nazi regime, and then in the USSR during Stalin's Great Terror. From Canada, his family had experienced the annexation of Poland as profoundly traumatic. How, under these conditions, could the son have become anything but anti-communist and anti-Russian?

In fact, Brzezinski's Cold War career was studded with battles and provocations against the communists and the Soviet Union, in which he employed means that grew exponentially over time. In Montreal in 1947 and 1948, he used his rhetorical talents against the communist students in McGill University's "Parliament." A decade later he engineered an infiltration of the 1959 World Youth Festival in Vienna, helping to stage a counter-propaganda stunt against an intended showcase for Soviet communism. As national security adviser (from 1977 to 1981), he pursued policies of harassment of the Soviet empire, including increased propaganda aimed at "nationalities" and dissidents; reinforcement of American radio services (Radio Free Europe and Radio Liberty), which he supported enthusiastically throughout his life; and support of the mujahedeen in Afghanistan, ranging from nonlethal support before the 1979 Soviet invasion to more robust support in 1980, via Pakistan, initiating the policy that would be followed by the Reagan administration. He was also in frequent contact with Pope John Paul II (a Pole, born Karol Wojtyla) starting in late 1978, especially regarding efforts to prevent the military intervention of the Warsaw Pact forces in Poland on December 5, 1980. More generally, his support for détente was either instrumental (a matter of multiplying people-to-people exchanges to pull Eastern Europeans out of Moscow's orbit), or else very limited. Given that he never believed the Soviet Union could last forever, any such accommodation could be made as a purely tactical maneuver.

But to what extent can these moves be attributed to his origins, his identity, his family history, his hope to see Poland freed from the communist yoke during his lifetime? Compare him with his Harvard contemporaries, immigrants like himself, and things appear more complicated. Stanley Hoffmann, born to a Jewish mother in Vienna but taken to France as an emigrant in early childhood, had fled to Nice during the Occupation, then hid in Lamalou-les-Bains, a village in Languedoc, when the Germans invaded the free zone. From this background he retained not only very liberal, anti-totalitarian tendencies but also a realist streak (including a conviction that, in certain situations, only force can defeat force) and a particular concern for human beings caught up in the turmoil of broad political currents—hence his writings on the ethics of international relations. Henry Kissinger, born under the Weimar Republic, left Fuerth in 1938 at the age of fifteen. He was deeply affected as a youth by a context turned so anti-Semitic that his father, a high school teacher, could no longer find work. He came away with a mistrust of the weaknesses of democracy and a fear of extreme-right resurgence that influenced his vision of America. From his academic work, he also concluded that the best way to keep peace was to maintain a balance of power, which implied coming to terms with nondemocratic regimes. In short, it may be that "the child is father of the man," but the child is not necessarily the father of the strategist or the thinker. No straight line can be drawn from personal history to political opinions or expressions.

This last example, of Kissinger, points to the approach of the present work. Rather than focusing on Zbigniew Brzezinski's Polishness, as Harriman did, this biography aspires to a broader assessment of his political thought. It examines how Brzezinski's ethnic and religious identity interacted with his political opinions, with his academic and intellectual agenda, and with the small-scale and large-scale events of history and the stuff of daily life. In short, this book traces the evolution of a complex personality over seven decades of activity, paying particular attention to the four years Brzezinski spent at the White House exercising responsibilities at the highest level of government.

This line of thinking opens up a still broader question, by way of Brzezinski's work, related to the subject of the Cold War University and its key role in prompting the United States to take on global responsibilities. What has been the real impact of the academic work of social scientists on American national security policies? Much has been written on the social sciences' bearing on nuclear strategy (and the influence of strategists such as Albert Wohlstetter,

Kissinger, and Bernard Brodie), applications of game theory (Schelling), and models of economic development (Rostow, Huntington).[12] Kissinger's diplomacy has likewise been read as an application of his own scholarly writings on Metternich, Bismarck, and the balance of powers in Europe. Brzezinski's case, too, has been examined in this light. But if we consider the social sciences in a narrow sense—that is, if we focus on the original theories, frameworks, and concepts developed by political scientists and historians, and exclude those that merely confirm common sense—we are faced with a striking conclusion. There seems to have been no impact whatsoever. Brzezinski the academic and Brzezinski the strategist stand as two different men. To be sure, the latter benefits from the knowledge stored up by the former. But he is not indebted to the former for the most salient components of his art. In fact, we must move to a less elevated level of abstraction to look for what differentiates a Zbigniew Brzezinski from a Richard Allen, his successor in the White House, who was not an academic: we must turn to the level of thought patterns, intellectual reflexes, representations of history and international relations—ingredients that can be traced only indirectly to academia. In the end, we are left with the unsatisfying sense that Brzezinski's academic past, while it played a certain role in his exercise of power, did not furnish him with strategic visions that were ready-made and relevant to his work.

Brzezinski's Importance

There are numerous books about Henry Kissinger, including more than a dozen serious biographies. Yet there is only one about Brzezinski, published originally in Polish.[13] Beyond this, one must look to diverse testimonies in collective works, and one shorter book suggesting that it was Brzezinski who won the Cold War.[14] This gap can be explained in part by the relative importance of the two men: Kissinger maintained his position of responsibility for eight years (1969–1977), and he was named secretary of state in 1973; Brzezinski was national security adviser, for only four years (January 1977 to January 1981), and under Carter, whose presidency is commonly written off as a failure, its foreign policy included (a very debatable judgment). Kissinger was also a more active player than Brzezinski, traveling throughout the world to bring about his diplomatic coups, from the opening to China to the "shuttle diplomacy" in the Middle East, and from the Paris Peace Accords negotiations to the

Moscow accords containing nuclear arms. Brzezinski generally stayed at the White House, traveling only occasionally—to China, Algeria, Pakistan—and as part of the president's entourage. Kissinger took great pains to cultivate his own legend and to maintain good relations with the press, whereas Brzezinski, although his media presence was considerable, never managed to win favor with journalists. His treatment by the media, fueled by leaks from the State Department, was often brutal—although more favorable portraits came along once in a while to soften his image. While Kissinger's memoirs ran to some 4,000 pages, Brzezinski's totaled a much more modest 573.

Still, whether the spotlight is on the trajectory of his career, or on his academic output, or on the influence he wielded in diplomatic debates from the 1950s through the first decade of the twenty-first century, Brzezinski stands as a giant on the stage of American foreign policy. Only consider that, on December 7, 1956, Senator Hubert Humphrey consulted him about the political developments arising in the USSR.[15] And fifty-four years later, on March 24, 2010, President Barack Obama consulted him about Middle East policy.[16] Across the half-century following Kennedy's inauguration, Brzezinski advised, in one way or another, nine American presidents (the sole exception was George W. Bush), and dozens of other high-ranking American leaders. He worked actively for the presidential campaigns of Kennedy (1960), Johnson (1964), Humphrey (1968), Carter (1976), George H.W. Bush (1988), and Obama (2008). He founded the Trilateral Commission in 1973, and decades later was still playing an important role in public debates—in the 1990s, for example, concerning the expansion of NATO, and in 2003, on the war in Iraq. Perhaps it is no surprise that conspiracy theorists came to portray him as a shadowy operator, pulling strings from backstage.

This is all the more the case in that, as Carter's national security adviser, he left his mark on essential developments in American diplomatic history. Some of these have been haunting the United States ever since (such as the Iranian revolution, the failure of the hostage rescue attempt in 1980, and the support of the Afghan mujahedeen) while others were controversial or incomplete (including progress on human rights policy and the SALT II agreement). Several, however, were undeniable successes, including the Torrijos-Carter treaties on the Panama Canal, the Camp David accords and peace treaty between Israel and Egypt, and the normalization of diplomatic relations with China.

Brzezinski authored or coauthored (with Samuel Huntington or Carl Friedrich, in particular) a dozen books and hundreds of articles and columns that have shaped US foreign policy debates, including in academic circles, about the nature of totalitarian regimes, US-Soviet relations (in particular regarding Eastern Europe), the impact of economic and technological changes on international relations, America's geopolitical priorities, and more. He also created the Research Institute on Communist Affairs at Columbia in the early 1960s, and was one of the most frequently cited Sovietologists of his era.

The biography that follows is organized chronologically, but each epoch allows us to explore a different theme that also provides the context for understanding Brzezinski's trajectory. Thus the first chapter deals with Brzezinski's youth in Europe and in Canada, and time at Harvard, but it also brings to light the contours and the content of the Cold War University through Brzezinski's highly successful path within Harvard during the 1950s. The milieu was highly conducive to his ambitions, offering advantages from the Russian Research Center to the CFIA, and from contacts with Washington to trips behind the Iron Curtain.

The second chapter focuses on the transformation during the 1960s of a solid academic, who was nevertheless attracted by the sirens of power, into a "political animal." The several milestones along the way include his appointment at Columbia, his rise in social power and media prominence, his first stint in government under Johnson, and finally Humphrey's 1968 campaign, which could have propelled him to the White House or State Department had Nixon not won the election.

Chapter 3 contextualizes this rise, describing how new mechanisms for selecting the American foreign policy elite came into being in the 1960s and illustrating, against the background of the Vietnam War, the traditional Establishment's replacement by a professional class. Through Brzezinski's example, with occasional comparisons to Kissinger (the other master strategist who fully exploited the new rules), this chapter explores in depth the new social system that was being created.

The next chapter looks at events unfolding between 1970 and 1976. During these years, Brzezinski broadened his field of intellectual and political expertise beyond the Atlantic world, in part by researching and writing a book on the "technetronic age" and in part with a stint in Japan. Above all, this period saw his influence take on new dimensions with the creation of the

Trilateral Commission—in which his founding role is obvious, and attested by the archives—and especially with a development that stemmed directly from the Trilateral Commission, Jimmy Carter's presidential campaign in 1976.

Chapter 5 offers a pause in the biographical narrative, painting a mid-career and mid-life portrait of Brzezinski that offers a reflection on the origin of his political thought. The chapter reviews his childhood, his Polish-American identity, his moral values, and his political convictions—but also his academic intellectual baggage and the areas in which he was influenced by other thinkers—in an attempt to understand what counted most in Brzezinski's image of the world.

The sixth chapter deals with Brzezinski's four years in the White House. Given the abundance of the sources, an entire book could be devoted to his role as national security adviser in the Carter administration during those rich years of rapid change; other writers have focused on this period, beginning with Brzezinski himself.[17] Alongside the foreign policy story, this book provides a perspective in light of what came before; in other words, it examines how Brzezinski's concepts, ideas, and convictions played out when they were confronted with the harsh realities of bureaucracy and of international politics. The chapter ends with an attempt at summing up the "Brzezinski administration," assessing his political judgment and measuring his achievements against his ambitions.

The final chapter covers the subsequent decades until his death on May 26, 2017. For Brzezinski, these years constituted the age of authority. To be sure, he did not go back to the White House, but as a tutelary figure of American foreign policy he has influenced the most important debates in Washington—in the 1980s, for example, on the Gorbachev phenomenon and the end of communism, and soon afterward on the question of the post–Cold War period in not only Europe but the Persian Gulf. In the 1990s, he played an active and influential role in the extension of NATO to Poland and other Central European countries, while also intervening forcefully in the debate over the Israeli-Palestinian peace negotiations, and, of course, in the debate over the wars in the Balkans. A fierce opponent of the Iraq war in the early years of the twenty-first century, he spoke out vigorously against George W. Bush and finally found a new Kennedy in Obama, although the latter ended up, inevitably, disappointing him.

Taken together, the chapters of this book aim to remember Brzezinski as he should be remembered. He was a thinker who changed, with his opinions and his predictions, America's relation to the world—most notably to Europe, Russia, and China. And he was a political actor who established himself as America's grand strategist.

1

A Brilliant Young Man in the Cold War University

Early in the morning of July 20, 1977, Zbigniew Brzezinski, who had been national security adviser to the American president for six months, left his office in the White House and headed across the street to Blair House, the Pennsylvania Avenue residence for guests of the president. He was scheduled to have breakfast with the Israeli prime minister, Menachem Begin, who was visiting Washington shortly after the historic victory of the party he had created, the Likud.[1] When Brzezinski arrived, he was surprised to see an array of photographers and TV cameramen waiting for him in front of the building. A few seconds later, Begin walked down the Blair House steps and ceremoniously presented him with a folder. Opening it, Brzezinski found that it contained archival documents attesting to the role his father, Tadeusz Brzezinski, had played in saving German Jews, providing them with visas for Poland while he was serving as consul in Leipzig—so effectively that he was recalled at the insistence of the German authorities in 1935.

For Begin, this was a way of getting into the national security adviser's good graces. But for Brzezinski, it was both a personally moving moment and a significant gesture of support. During the campaign and since his arrival at the White House, attacks against his Middle East views had proliferated. His position, developed with colleagues from the Trilateral Commission and a group from the Brookings Institution, in favor of an overall peace settlement that would include self-determination for the Palestinians and would result either in an independent Palestinian state or in a federation with Jordan, had made him many enemies in the Jewish community.[2] He was accused more than once, most notably by CBS reporter Marvin Kalb, of being anti-Israel, and behind the political question obviously lurked the suggestion that, as a Polish Catholic, he might well be anti-Semitic (an unfounded insinuation, as Chapter 5 shows). The public gesture by the Israeli hawk made it clear to all that the national security adviser should no longer be harassed on these grounds.

The initial surprise behind him, Brzezinski sat down to breakfast with Begin— the conversation took place in Polish—and it was his turn to surprise his interlocutor with his detailed knowledge of the ideology, organization, and struggles of the Haganah (Defense), the Zionist militia in Palestine (from 1930 to 1948) and especially its secessionist branch, the Irgun. This group, inspired by Vladimir Jabotinsky and led by Begin since 1944, had spearheaded the violent insurrectionist movement against the British in Mandatory Palestine. This familiarity with the Irgun was not an isolated instance. Since the 1940s, Brzezinski had been interested enough in armed movements of national resistance to develop in-depth knowledge on the subject; the same interest led him to follow other movements, including those of the Palestinians and the mujahedeen.

In the early 1950s, Brzezinksi had occasion to explain this lifelong preoccupation. He was a student at the time, and had spent only three years of his life in Poland. When he met Jan Nowak, the head of the Polish branch of Radio Free Europe in Munich and a hero of the Polish Home Army during the Second World War, Nowak, too, was struck by Brzezinski's detailed familiarity with the history of the various movements of Polish resistance to the Nazis and to the Soviets, and by the student's numerous well-informed questions. Seeing Nowak's astonishment, Brzezinski explained that he had belonged to the Polish Boy Scouts during the 1930s, and that later, under the Occupation, the Scouts had contributed to the struggle against the occupiers by carrying out acts of sabotage against the Germans. He was sorry that he had not been able to participate.[3] He had compensated for his absence by taking an avid intellectual interest in the matter.

These episodes from Brzezinski's youth are reminders of the rather extraordinary environment in which he grew up. His father was born in 1895 into a family from Galicia with ties to nobility, studied law at the University of Vienna, then joined the army of the newly reconstituted nation to fight the Bolsheviks in the Polish-Soviet War of 1919–1920. In 1921, he joined the diplomatic service, representing his country in Lille (from 1921 to 1931), Leipzig (1931 to 1935), and Kharkiv in the Ukrainian section of the USSR (1936 to 1937) before he was posted to Montreal as Poland's consul general in 1938. After that, he was to see his cherished homeland only once more. In 1924, he married Leonia Roman, who was also a descendant of Polish nobility, and who already had a son from a first marriage that had ended in divorce. Zbigniew was born to the couple on March 28, 1928, in Warsaw.

Zbig, as he was nicknamed by his family and friends, spent the first three years of his life in France, and the following four in Germany. When his father was declared persona non grata by the Third Reich for supplying exit visas to Jews fleeing the growing persecutions, he had to leave Leipzig. Zbig was only seven years old then, but he remembered seeing Nazi parades and torch-lit marches; indeed, they left deep impressions.[4] Anti-Semitism did not spare Poland. Although Marshal Joseph Pilsudski's authoritarian regime protected minorities, especially the Jews, strong anti-Semitic tendencies persisted nonetheless. Brzezinski also remembered how angry his father became on one occasion, when he witnessed a demonstration by anti-Jewish Polish students in the Polish capital. They were chanting, "Warsaw and Krakow to the Poles! Let the Jewish pigs go live in Palestine!" Tadeusz attacked the students with his cane.[5]

From 1936 to 1938, a delicate mission was entrusted to Tadeusz Brzezinski. He was sent to represent Poland in the Soviet Republic of Ukraine, as consul in Kharkiv (the capital until 1934)—fifteen years after the Polish-Soviet War split the Ukrainian territory into a Polish sector and a Soviet Russian sector. Prudently, Zbigniew and his mother stayed behind in Warsaw; these were the only years the boy lived in his native country. But when his father returned, he had terrible stories to tell. After the great Ukrainian famine, there were the years of the Great Terror, Stalin's purges in the USSR. There were frequent massacres, and members of the Polish elite whom Tadeusz had received at dinner could disappear a few weeks later, executed by the regime. These stories made an enormous impression on the young boy.[6]

Just as Adolf Hitler and Benito Mussolini were signing the Munich Agreement with French and British prime ministers Édouard Daladier and Neville Chamberlain that would send Europe sliding into war, the Brzezinski family was preparing to move to Quebec, where Tadeusz was to assume his responsibilities in November 1938. One of the reasons for this choice was Zbigniew's half-brother's illness, which led the family to seek out a treatment site; there were thermal baths nearby. Along with a tutor, governess, attendant, and even the family dog, they sailed on an ocean liner and landed in New York a few weeks later. But the Brzezinski brothers barely had time to see the Statue of

Liberty and take a quick tour of Manhattan before they had to head to Penn Station and get on a train to Montreal.[7]

As his father began his new assignment, Zbigniew was enrolled in Saint-Léon, a Catholic school in an upper-middle-class environment, in a city where Polish émigrés were scarce. Once the pleasure of novelty wore off, adaptation proved difficult. The boy was homesick; he missed Poland. The political climate was ominous, and the Brzezinskis did not go back for their summer vacation in 1939. It was the right decision; Hitler's troops began to invade Poland, and Warsaw was bombed on September 1.[8]

For the eleven-year-old boy, it was the beginning of a period of anguish and intense excitement. He had clear memories of the impressive Polish military parades and of the grandiose funeral services for Marshal Joseph Pilsudski. Poland's victory over the Red Army had made him optimistic. He did not want to believe that Poland's defeat by the Nazis was inevitable. The news was wrenching, especially on September 17, when the Soviets invaded the country, in keeping with the Nazi-Soviet pact, and on September 28, when Warsaw had to capitulate.[9] Because he could not join the fight himself, Zbigniew kept a detailed diary of the war's daily developments, which he followed through newspaper and radio accounts and discussed at length with his father. During the next six years, no significant incidents escaped his journal. Those frantic weeks in September 1939 marked the beginning of his passion for international affairs.

In 1943, Radio Berlin announced that four thousand bodies of Polish officers had been discovered near Smolensk; the broadcast attributed the killings to the Soviet secret police (the NKVD). In fact, it turned out that the mass graves found by the Germans dated to the summer of 1940 invasion, and contained more than 20,000 victims. For Zbigniew, then a fifteen-year-old adolescent, the massacre in the Katyn Forest, which had decimated the Polish military and civil elite, was a shock. For once, neither he nor his father doubted that the Nazis were telling the truth: the Soviets were indeed responsible. He was furious at the Americans, who turned a blind eye and, rather than displease Stalin, refused to support the request of the Polish government in London to allow the Red Cross to investigate. Stalin accused the Americans of peddling Nazi propaganda and took advantage of the occasion to break off all relations with them.[10]

The discovery of the Katyn massacre and Roosevelt's abandonment of Poland in favor of relations with the allies remained sources of anger for

Brzezinski throughout the decades that followed. In 1952, when he was twenty-four and still working on his doctoral thesis, he wrote to the Select Committee of the House of Representatives to contribute to the investigation undertaken by the Madden Commission (named for its director Ray J. Madden); the investigation established the responsibility of the Soviets but did not lead to international action.[11] When the truth finally emerged in 1989, Mikhail Gorbachev authorized an association of Polish families to visit the Katyn Forest and agreed that Brzezinski could be part of the delegation. Brzezinski laid a bouquet of roses with a signed message written in English and in Polish: "For the victims of Stalin and the NKVD." He underscored the fact that among the victims were Russians as well as Poles, and asserted that recognition of Stalin's crimes would open a path to reconciliation, not more hatred. He also asked Moscow to recognize its responsibility officially, and Gorbachev did so the following year.[12] Later, when revisionist temptations began to surface in Moscow, Brzezinski supported the researchers working to establish the definitive history of the massacre.[13]

In 1945, Brzezinski enrolled at McGill, the top Anglophone university in Quebec. He received his undergraduate degree in economics, with distinction, four years later, and was awarded a Master of Arts in political science in July 1950. When he was still quite young, he had begun to teach himself Russian by reading Pushkin's *The Captain's Daughter*.[14] At McGill, taking full advantage of his gift for languages, he was able to consult original sources to write his master's thesis on Russo-Soviet nationalism, under the direction of Frederick Watkins, who left to teach at Yale a few years later.[15]

The thesis, a solid and well-informed study of over a hundred and fifty pages, began with the observation that nationalism had played an essential role in international relations from the early nineteenth century on; the author focused on its manifestations in the Soviet Union, and on its significance for the future and for the viability of what Lenin had built. There was an acknowledgment of the unifying roles played by Marxism, centralization, and Soviet patriotism in the context of the Second World War. But the conclusion from closer examination was that local strains of nationalism were alive and well within the Soviet republics, and constituted a real powder keg for Moscow. Moreover, the policy of Russification had been intensified under Stalin, with mass deportations, and the economy had been reorganized to avoid autarchy among the nationalities and to encourage their structural dependence—a sign that the Kremlin took the problem seriously. The Soviet leaders faced a dilemma: if they went too far in checking local nationalism, they risked blowing up the whole edifice. But if the republics were too free to indulge local nationalist sentiments, their centripetal tendencies would increase and gradually crack the structure from within.

According to Brzezinski's analysis, Russo-Soviet nationalism at the time was still powerful enough to prevail. But if there were a crisis, the centripetal tendencies would assert themselves quickly. The text concludes as follows:

> The Western world has at its disposal all the means to create a multi-national anti-Soviet version of the Comintern [Communist International]—and its appeal would be exceedingly powerful. . . . The reliance within the USSR on the Russian community indicates the lack of reliance on the non-Russian communities and the intense assertion of Russo-Soviet Nationalism could possibly be more than national pride—it could be an indirect indication of internal, but it must be emphasized latent, dissension.
>
> Russo-Soviet Nationalism and what we believe to be true Freedom will clash someday—and understanding the component elements of Russo-Soviet Nationalism may help a great deal the cause of Freedom.[16]

This conclusion is noteworthy in that it offers a succinct version of the "Brzezinski approach" as early as the summer of 1950, a tight summation of his stance regarding academic research and international politics. To be sure, Brzezinski began his thesis with the ritual language in which a scholar rejects prejudices and proclaims objectivity. But the text is actually a militant document. It suggests that while it might not be possible to defeat the Soviets today, it is possible to understand their system well enough to identify its weaknesses and increase the likelihood of its succumbing to them. His precise and rigorous study of the various nationalities within the USSR led to a nuanced conclusion: the Soviet Union has a growing problem of unity but can still deal with it. This in turn set up a political recommendation: the West should create a sort of inverse Comintern that would accentuate the dilemma of the nationalities and fuel the internal frictions that could cause the Soviet bloc and the Union itself to implode.

There was no detour through the realm of pure scholarship, then, for Brzezinski. From the outset, he put knowledge at the service of a real-world objective: the victory of freedom in general, and the liberation of Poland in particular. The descriptive part of the document had to be of the highest possible scholarly quality because that would allow the prescriptive part to hit its target, and yield a policy with real potential to be effective. Here already, he was staking out a position within the Western academic debate and combating the experts he saw giving too much credit to communist claims—in this case, the claim that the cement holding the communist bloc together was solid, and its unity would only endure.

During his time at McGill, the young Zbigniew did not hide his anticommunist views; a friend described him during those years as "religious and hawkish."[17] Though he was not a militant in a political organization, he put his oratorical skills to work in "Student Parliament" debates staged as part of the university curriculum on the model of the British Parliament. Zbig naturally represented the center-right Progressive Conservative Party (known for centrist views on social questions), using his considerable talent as a polemicist on international affairs against the crypto-communist students of the Progressive Party. Any opponents who have debated against Zbigniew Brzezinski can attest to the imperious energy he brought to the task. But even by his standards, he recalled being a "very vociferous debater" at McGill—a phrase sure to induce a shudder in those who knew him.[18]

He had little patience with student militancy, keeping his eyes fixed on the future and on "history writ large." But occasionally he channeled his anticommunist views into direct action, however futile. When Hewlett Johnson, "the Red Dean of Canterbury"—known for his pro-Soviet sympathies from the 1920s on—visited McGill, Brzezinski, who called him Stalin's mouthpiece, wanted to sabotage his talk. After a discussion with his accomplices, he rejected the idea of cutting his microphone, which would look too much like a communist tactic. Instead, they convinced the housekeeping staff to skip the room where the prelate was to speak, claiming that others were in charge of cleaning it. When Johnson arrived to give his talk, thanks to the efforts of the conspirators, the room was littered with trash.[19]

Tackling Harvard, 1950–1960

Brzezinski quickly came to see his McGill years as merely a transitional phase, a launching pad for continuing his studies in the United States. After winning a fellowship to study at Oxford, an award ultimately denied him because he was not yet a Canadian citizen, he was accepted by Duke and most importantly by Harvard. This opportunity gave his life a different direction, toward academia but also increasingly toward politics. Brzezinski felt at home at Harvard, which provided a solid foundation for his personal and professional development, unlike Kissinger, whose move to Harvard left him with mixed memories.[20] If it was military service that Americanized Kissinger, it was Harvard that Americanized Brzezinski. Here is how he himself summed it up: "Harvard and I clicked. I did very well in my studies after an initial uncertain beginning, when they couldn't promise me anything because they didn't know me and I took a chance on it. But then Harvard started offering me things. So I was easily assimilated into Harvard, and through Harvard also into America, and then very quickly I began to feel like an American, and, even more striking, to be treated like an American."[21]

By saying that Harvard could not "promise anything" to him, Brzezinski referred to his having been accepted into the International Studies Program, but without a fellowship from the Government Department. According to a letter dated July 30, 1950, his professor Frederick Watkins, during a visit to Cambridge, tried to intercede on his behalf with Merle Fainsod, the great specialist on the USSR. Fainsod was pessimistic about the chances of getting a fellowship, but promised to inquire at the Russian Research Center whether anyone there might need some help.[22] This is what seems to have opened the door: three weeks later, the director of Harvard's Extension School told Brzezinski that he could begin a trial period serving as research assistant to Alex Inkeles, an important figure in the Russian Research Center, with a stipend of $500 for the year. By combining this with his fellowship from McGill, Brzezinski concluded that he could manage.[23]

This was the beginning of a ten-year association not simply with Harvard but also with the university's Russian Research Center, where Brzezinski rose quickly through the ranks. Starting out as a research assistant, he became a graduate student fellow while working on his doctoral thesis, which he completed in 1953; he then became a research fellow and, finally, a research associate.[24] During this period he participated in a number of the Russian Center's research projects and in all of its debates. When he left Harvard in 1960, it was to become the director of Columbia's Research Institute on Communist Affairs, linked to that university's Russian Institute, which paralleled Harvard's

Russian Research Center. To be sure, Brzezinski took an interest in other sectors of academe: he taught during all his years at Harvard and in 1958 he was one of the first research associates to join the new Center for International Affairs (CFIA), created at the behest of Dean McGeorge Bundy and directed by Robert Bowie and Henry Kissinger. But the place where he found his stride and earned his stripes was the Russian Research Center.

When he arrived in Cambridge from Montreal in September 1950, Brzezinski lived in Kirkland House, one of the student residences located alongside the Charles River; he soon became a tutor, to supplement his meager resources. The friendships he formed there—especially with Samuel Huntington and Henry Rosovsky, both a year older—remained among the strongest of his life.[25] Brzezinski worked seriously and systematically, never earning a grade below A-. But he was far from being a workhorse like Huntington (who finished his thesis in four months); he spent his weekends enjoying free time, going out, and dancing.[26] A few years later, when his financial situation had become less precarious, he even drove a used Jaguar, showing the extroverted, flamboyant side of his character.[27]

Above all, he spent endless hours discussing current events with other students, among them Paul Sigmund, James Schlesinger, Judith Shklar (who had also come from McGill), Albert Mavrinac, Stanley Hoffmann (who had come to Harvard in 1951), and Inge Schneier, who later became Hoffmann's wife. Kissinger, too, despite being five years older, was involved with the younger group because the war years had delayed his studies. During the group's discussions, it was not unusual for Brzezinski and Sigmund to constitute the "Catholic clan." Recalling this, Hoffmann later gave the mischievous report that, if certain Catholics had doubts about what should be done in the case of nuclear war (Could the bomb be used again? What does the Pope say?), Brzezinski had none. As for domestic political issues, they proved less divisive. Like most of his cohort, Brzezinski was a Cold War liberal; situated on the left of the political spectrum, he looked favorably on Adlai Stevenson (even if he mistrusted Stevenson's idealistic leanings vis-à-vis Stalin). He was anti-communist and anti-McCarthy.[28]

It was his friend Sam Huntington who introduced Brzezinski to Wellesley College student Emilie Anna Benes, nicknamed Muska. In addition to being young and attractive, on her way to a degree in studio art, Muska was the grand-niece of Edward Benes, the last president of free Czechoslovakia. Her father, like Zbigniew's, had been a consul general—in his case in San Francisco—until the coup in Prague. Brzezinski and Muska were soon engaged, and they were married on June 11, 1955, at St. Ignatius, a Catholic church on Boston College's Chestnut Hill campus.[29] The couple's resources were limited; they left for their honeymoon in Italy with $800 between them. They crossed the Atlantic on separate ships, as Zbigniew had arranged to give onboard lectures to pay for his trip, but were reunited as soon as he landed. They discovered Italy together, crisscrossing Rome on a scooter. During the 1960s, they had three children, and Muska kept up her sculpting. Her artistic career flourished especially during the 1990s and 2000s.

When Zbig had crossed the American border in September 1950, he had not been a Polish citizen but a Canadian, and for the first four years he remained a foreign student. He was granted permanent resident status on October 7, 1954, with Harvard's support. His marriage to Muska (born in Geneva in 1932 but already an American citizen) accelerated things; he was naturalized at age thirty on December 22, 1958, without having to wait the customary five years as a permanent resident.[30] Taking the oath of allegiance during a ceremony arranged by the Daughters of the American Revolution was a moving experience for him. "Yes, I had a sense of real pride that day. I remember laughing, because the Daughters of the American Revolution were greeting us, the new citizens, and sticking pins of American flags onto our lapels, and the one who did that to me was very enthusiastic and drew blood. So I felt I was already shedding blood for America."[31]

Even though he retained—and indeed never lost—a slight Polish accent, Brzezinski was a very popular lecturer at Harvard. His presentations were always rich, structured, and clear. They were also lively and original. Once he went to class in disguise, sporting a fake mustache and a counterfeit Russian accent. Seeking to get a reaction from the students to force them to refine their arguments, he posed as a Soviet guest speaker who had come to defend Marxism and Leninism at Harvard. After a time, he threw off the costume and fervently defended the liberal capitalist model. On another occasion, Rosovsky recalled, Brzezinski borrowed the billy club Rosovsky had brought back from his military service; he threatened the students with that disturbing accessory during a comparative totalitarianism course.[32] His talent as a professor and a speaker, which continued to grow, would prove very useful later. In May 1978, for example, at the beginning of his historic trip to Beijing, he gave a presentation to the Chinese Minister of Foreign Affairs Huang Hua that lasted no less than three and a half hours (in part because of the need for translation). His magisterial overview, complete with multicolored maps and charts, was delivered in an intimate setting. The professor succeeded in convincing his interlocutors that America's intentions were serious, and the visit opened the way to normalization of diplomatic relations.[33]

Brzezinski's time at Harvard gave him the opportunity to perfect his talents as a lecturer. As early as February 18, 1952, when he was not yet twenty-four years old, he gave a presentation on his favorite topic at a Simmons College Forum in Boston. Later, he received a thank-you letter from the organizer; she was so enthusiastic that she enclosed ten dollars, insisting he accept it as his fee, even though that had not been part of the original agreement.[34] Two years later, Brzezinski gave another evening lecture at the same forum, and left its director astonished. The latter knew that his audience members tended to eat and drink too much before the presentation and were inclined, as a result, to be ungracious if not hostile to the lecturer, in their impatience for the talk to be over. This time, the moderator had to cut off the question-and-answer session. "Your material was excellent," he wrote to Brzezinski, "but even good material won't hold that group. It was your intense and lively presentation which did it."[35]

In the mid-1950s, then, Brzezinski was already a sought-after speaker in the Boston area and even beyond—as far as West Point, for example. Notes from Brzezinski's hosts in the archives spanning the 1950s through the 1970s make clear their enthusiasm, even allowing for the American tendency to exaggerate. Typical among them: "You were terrific! Faculty and students were equally delighted." "Nothing less than brilliant." "Splendid presentation." "I can't remember when so many people came up to ask for a copy of the talk." "You scored a great hit." "It was a treat to hear you." In these notes, too, are phrases that—while certainly intended as positive observations and always accompanying complimentary remarks—speak to the steelier aspects of Brzezinski's style: "rapid-fire delivery," "machine gun tactic," "impatience with vague questions."[36]

Brzezinski's popularity as a lecturer also sprang from his accumulation of a spectacular knowledge base that he knew very well how to mobilize. In just a few years he had become a specialist on the USSR and the communist world—indeed, become one of the first scholars identified as a Sovietologist.[37]

There were many eminent figures at Harvard during the 1950s—among them, Arthur Schlesinger and Arthur Schlesinger Jr., William Yandell Elliott, Samuel

Beer, McGeorge Bundy (who became dean in 1953), Barrington Moore, Wassily Leontief, and Alexander Gerschenkron—but three in particular inspired Brzezinski and played major roles in both his intellectual development and his academic career. They were Carl Friedrich, Merle Fainsod, and Robert Bowie.

Friedrich was one of the most influential professors in the Harvard Government Department, and his rivalry with Elliott in the 1940s remains legendary. Friedrich was liberal by temperament. A German who had come to the United States as an exchange student, he had chosen to remain when Hitler rose to power. As a professor of constitutional law, he was meticulous and rational; he was wary of concentrations of power. When Huntington was a candidate for tenure in the department in the late 1950s, Friedrich voted against him, basing his judgment on Huntington's book *The Soldier and the State*. He had not escaped Nazi Germany, he declared, only to put a militarist on the Harvard faculty. Elliott was his opposite. A force of nature, he was a veteran of the First World War and a former football star. He was also from the South, and a poet, who had enjoyed a moment of glory in the 1920s for his thesis on pragmatism. The course he taught on classical political philosophy was deemed superficial by some of his colleagues. While Friedrich played the cello, Elliott, by contrast, organized cockfights on the plantation he still owned in his native Tennessee. He was also an adviser to politicians, and had had his eye on Washington, to Friedrich's disapproval. The two men remained courteous in their interactions, but they disliked each other. Friedrich was Brzezinski's mentor; Elliott was Kissinger's.[38]

In 1953, Friedrich had already come to appreciate the intellectual qualities and the knowledge demonstrated by his student Brzezinski, having directed the young man's thesis on purges in the Soviet system. When Friedrich reengaged with a project he had begun in the 1930s but abandoned when the Second World War broke out—a comparison of the Nazi and Soviet regimes under the unifying heading of totalitarianism—he invited the young Brzezinski to work with him on the book. Friedrich was well acquainted with Nazi Germany; Brzezinski contributed his knowledge of the USSR, and more broadly his dynamism. Friedrich was a demanding professor and known, according to Stanley Hoffmann, as someone who "exploited" his students.[39] Indeed, his affect toward Brzezinski was more like a schoolmaster's than a coauthor's. Shortly before their book appeared, for example, he scolded Brzezinski in writing for failing to take care of footnotes and cross-references—in response to which the young man pointed out that he had been unable to complete the task because, when he should have been dealing with them, Friedrich's chapters had not yet been drafted.[40] For Brzezinski, the fact remained that he was writing a book with a "big name." Coauthoring with someone as prestigious as Friedrich would quickly bring higher name recognition to himself.[41]

Although Friedrich was an intellectual guide for Brzezinski and a providential coauthor, he was not a specialist on the Soviet Union, the subject that most interested the younger man. After their book's publication, correspondence between them was cordial but not at all intimate. All of Brzezinski's inspiration and admiration seemed to be reserved for Professor Merle Fainsod. The latter had moved back and forth between studying the United States, especially the New Deal administration (he had also worked in the Office of Price Administration during the Second World War) and studying the USSR, where he had spent a year doing research in 1932. After the war, he had turned resolutely toward the East, helped set up the Russian Research Center, which he headed from 1959 to 1964, and gained recognition as one of the most eminent specialists of his day on the Soviet Union.

In 1953, Fainsod published *How Russia Is Ruled,* a text that stood as the most authoritative book in the field of Sovietology for the next twenty years. Then Fainsod, helped by Brzezinski and several other young researchers, plunged into the archives of the Communist Party in Smolensk. More than two hundred thousand pages had been seized by Nazi intelligence services in June 1941, sent to the United States by the US Army in 1945, and finally made available to Fainsod (via the US Air Force and the RAND Corporation) in 1954. The resulting book, *Smolensk under Soviet Rule* (1958), was a history of the Soviet regime as "seen from below." It helped in particular to relativize the vision of a centralized and omniscient totalitarian power that Fainsod himself had described earlier—as had Friedrich and Brzezinski, in even more detail.[42]

Merle Fainsod was a source of inspiration and a model for Brzezinski, who was both his research assistant and his teaching assistant (for his course on politics in the Soviet Union). When Fainsod died in 1972, Brzezinski was shocked, as he wrote to a friend, also describing the funeral oration he himself had delivered before the entire Harvard community.[43] In this moving eulogy, he declared, most notably: "He was my teacher. What I learned from him goes beyond Soviet studies—for Merle Fainsod had a way of sharing his commitment to a scholarship that was pure, of generating an enduring enthusiasm for one's work, of setting a personal example for one's conduct. . . . His scholarship was very much a part of my own growing up as an academic. . . . He was easily available to his students. . . . He also played an active role nationally, consulted frequently on Soviet affairs with the Government and the mass media."[44]

The third figure who counted for Brzezinski, especially in the late 1950s, was Robert Bowie. This lawyer and law professor was close to Lucius Clay and John McCloy, with whom he had worked during the occupation of Germany. He was not a scholar but rather a sage, a counselor who became the third director of the Policy Planning Staff at the State Department, in 1953, succeeding George Kennan and Paul Nitze. Given his connection with Harvard and his own high profile, McGeorge Bundy had asked him to create the Center for International Affairs. Brzezinski admired Friedrich and Fainsod for their scholarly expertise, but he gravitated quickly to Bowie's practical approach to foreign affairs.[45] Bowie in turn was struck from the start by the young man's originality and sharpness of mind, and considered him a stronger analyst than Kissinger (his associate director, with whom, to be sure, he had bones to pick).[46] He drew Brzezinski toward the CFIA starting in 1958, and went to some lengths trying to keep him at Harvard in 1960. Their friendly relations continued through the following decades. Bowie was part of the small group that created the Trilateral Commission in 1972, and was called back into action under Carter to occupy the number two spot in the CIA, which was then under the tight bureaucratic control of the national security adviser—namely, Brzezinski. In February 1952, Brzezinski gave up his first idea for a thesis project, which had been to focus on the control of the Communist Party within the Soviet army. Nevertheless, the early research he had done on that topic yielded his first professional publication.[47] For his dissertation, he decided to study the purge as a phenomenon in totalitarian systems, drawing on Soviet sources, émigré testimony, Trotsky's archives, and thousands of accounts collected in the context of the Refugee Interview Project. He defended his thesis before Fainsod and Friedrich in April 1953, and published it under the auspices of the Russian Research Center in early 1956.[48] It is worth recalling the mark left on the young Zbigniew by stories told by his father, the Polish consul in Kharkiv at the time of the Great Terror. In *The Permanent Purge,* Brzezinski advanced the thesis that the purges were not an irrational aberration—a bout of bloodthirsty madness by mankind. On the contrary, they were endemic to totalitarian systems, with the USSR offering the best example. Purges were logically justified in such systems by the need to "find a substitute for the restraints of the constitutional system it [the totalitarian system] has destroyed."[49] A struggle over succession is obviously what leads to use of the purge mechanism, but that use does not occur, as one might imagine, in the struggle's early stages. While of course the struggle is aimed at wiping out the competition, physically if need be, a certain balance of forces imposes moderation and prudence at the outset. Only later do purges come to be deployed, as instruments of political control. The victor must be assured that his entire hierarchy is faithful to him, and this implies that any subaltern figures who supported his rival must be eliminated. Moreover, pressure for a purge often comes from the lower ranks, as local officials strive to consolidate their positions and eliminate their own rivals by denouncing them. Typically, then, a purge coincides with a moment of stability in a regime, when the regime is in full control and can exercise its power without restraint. "The purge is an expression of the regime's power," Brzezinski argued, "not an effort to achieve it. A purge is thus the supreme example of totalitarian success."[50]

To explore his line of thinking a bit further, a purge represents more than a tool for purifying the party. It does not touch the masses; often, it even accompanies a loosening of controls. Nevertheless, it has an educational function, for the public at large engages with it by way of spectacular trials or through the customary means of propaganda. In particular, a purge reaffirms the gap between the elite and the general population, since it settles everything inside the hierarchy, and eliminates any lingering notion that spontaneous leadership might arise in response to an appeal for new ideas. It reinforces the perception of an anonymous, implacable organization of interchangeable party managers. In sum, despite the mad chaos that purges seem to unleash, they perform quite useful functions in a totalitarian state: they reinforce the security of the leadership while keeping the enemies of the regime permanently on guard and periodically eradicating them; they provide a way of getting rid of accumulated tensions; they renew and stimulate internal activity, eliminating stagnation; they direct the inevitable dissatisfactions toward guilty parties that are not part of the regime. Brzezinski concluded with a prediction that the purges in the USSR, being consubstantial with the totalitarian regime, were not going to disappear. They might, however, take gentler, somewhat less bloody forms. Rather than repeats of Stalin's Moscow trials, Brzezinski predicted "quiet purges" that would essentially meet the same goals—especially given the abasement of the population, which had learned its lesson.

Brzezinski's book was well received. Commentators declared themselves in agreement with its major conclusions and praised Brzezinski's work, although some regretted the omission of the East European regimes, the study of which would have enriched the analysis. Edward Taborsky, in the *American Political Science Review,* endorsed the analysis for the most part and, in a paraphrase of many of his colleagues' assessments, praised its "solid foundations of carefully selected and properly analyzed facts."[51] Other commentators had a fundamental criticism: the book placed too much emphasis on the concept of totalitarianism. Empirical studies, they noted, appeared to undermine the abstract theory that there were such thing as centralized, omniscient, and omnipotent regimes, and especially to contradict the idea of a nature that was essentially immutable. In the *Journal of Politics,* for example, John Gillespie characterized Brzezinski's text as "a valuable little book," but claimed that Brzezinski's own description of the evolution of the forms and function of purges was proof that the concept of totalitarianism, on which the author relied a great deal, was inadequate.[52]

The debate was important considering that between 1953 and 1956, while Brzezinski was writing the book drawn from his thesis, he had simultaneously been working with Carl Friedrich on their coauthored book on the concept of totalitarianism. That book was also published in 1956, as *Totalitarian Dictatorship and Autocracy.*[53] Friedrich had returned to his idea of comparing the Nazi and Soviet regimes in 1953, two years after the publication of Hannah Arendt's celebrated work, *The Origins of Totalitarianism.*[54] In that work, Arendt, after a historical examination, offered a definition of the totalitarian state emphasizing the dissolution of the social structures inherited from the nineteenth century—hereditary classes, political parties, nation-states, and so on—to the exclusive benefit of an all-powerful state dominating a society that had been atomized especially through the use of terror. Friedrich sought to give the concept of totalitarianism a more scientific turn. In an irony of history, the day he brought a group of researchers and intellectuals together at Harvard to discuss his theory was the very day when American newspapers announced Stalin's death.[55] He subsequently revised the theory with Brzezinski's help; the two of them drafted the bulk of their joint manuscript in 1955, and it was published the following year—a year that began with the Twentieth Congress of the Soviet Communist Party, which accelerated the process of de-Stalinization.[56]

In *Totalitarian Dictatorship and Autocracy,* Friedrich and Brzezinski insisted on the uniqueness of the totalitarian form of power, as distinct from classical authoritarianism, Oriental despotism, and absolute monarchy. As case studies, they took Italian fascism (which Hannah Arendt had not included), Nazism, and Russian communism, adding incidental explorations of Mao's China, Eastern European satellite governments, and even Argentina. They proposed to define totalitarianism by six characteristic features: an official ideology, a single party directed by a single man, a police force based on terror, a monopoly over communications and the rewriting of history, a monopoly over violence and weaponry, and a centralized economy. Brzezinski later said that the theoretical framework came essentially from Friedrich, but that he himself had added ideology—the element that became most important in the book—as the factor that integrated the whole: totalitarian policy is energized by the objective of revolutionary social change (the prospect of remaking mankind and remodeling society while eliminating pluralism).[57] In the process, the two authors did not go quite as far as Arendt in abstraction (she saw the driving force of totalitarianism in the megalomaniacal political will to prove that everything is possible). They shared the approach of other researchers such as Merle Fainsod, Barrington Moore, and Sigmund Neumann. Friedrich and Brzezinski concluded that totalitarian regimes, by their very nature, do not tend to soften—and that they are solid. They offer no way for a revolt to succeed.

When it came out, the book was welcomed as an important contribution to the debate. However, as had been the case three years earlier when Friedrich tested his hypotheses on Harvard colleagues, the concept was contested. Historians in particular (Michael Karpovich, for example, and Geroid Robinson, the head of the Russian Institute at Columbia) reasoned that the characteristics identified by the authors might have applied to Nazi Germany, but they mapped only imperfectly to the recent past and present reality of Russia. George Kennan accepted the book's point of departure—that the Nazi and communist regimes each represented a newly evolved political form—but rejected the proposition that one concept could encompass them both. Alex Inkeles saw in the USSR a more fluid and more complex society than the one described by Friedrich and Brzezinski. Meanwhile, it was all too easy for commentators to emphasize the many developments in the direction of softening and de-Stalinization that had been taking place in 1956, after the book had gone to press.[58]

Friedrich rigidly continued to defend his concept and his vision of the USSR for a long time afterward. By contrast, Brzezinski demonstrated a certain flexibility in his use of the concept over time, and in the mid-1960s he finally abandoned it as a tool for analysis and description in favor of a more complex view of the realities of the Soviet Union that stressed in particular the "degenerescence" of the regime. Several factors came into play in this relativization. For example, Brzezinski's work on the Smolensk archives with Merle Fainsod had revealed the breadth of the resistance to the central Soviet power, and the fact that the communist regime in Smolensk constituted more of a powder keg than a model of totalitarian discipline. The system was rife with struggles: Smolensk versus Moscow, peasants versus the party, workers versus overseers, the party versus the police, and so on. In short, the idea of a total, omniscient, centralized control did not hold up.[59] The events of 1956 (de-Stalinization and insurrection in Budapest) and their aftermath surely affected Brzezinski's thinking. Throughout his intellectual career, he took care to respect the facts, never imposing a static, ready-made vision on a political situation—which is not to say that he had no biases or that his vision was necessarily accurate. In 1956, in "Totalitarianism and Rationality," he acknowledged that after Stalin's death the regime went through a stage of rationalization. But the totalitarian revolution was far from over, and he refuted the predictions of scholars such as Isaac Deutscher who believed that rationalization, which could be explained by the Soviet Union's status as a modern industrial society, would turn it into a democracy.[60] His travels in the countries of the communist bloc may have played a role, as well. The result of these various influences was that, in 1957, without giving up the concept of totalitarianism itself, he indicated in an article published in *Problems of Communism* that Poland was no longer a totalitarian country, by virtue of the relative freedom of expression that reigned there, the vitality of the Catholic Church, the absence of slogans and flags, the divisions between the leadership and the police, and a generalized pragmatism. But Poland was not a democracy; it was an authoritarian regime that was based on Władysław Gomułka's popularity and rejection of Russia.[61]

The Cold War University

The particular milieu that allowed Zbigniew Brzezinski to flourish was that of the Cold War University. The phrase denotes the phenomenon by which, from the 1940s to the 1960s, American institutions of higher education, especially the most prestigious ones, reoriented their programs toward the production of knowledge directly useful to the federal government in its effort to deal with the global responsibilities it had taken on in 1945, or even in 1941. Washington offered universities massive funding for the pursuit of knowledge that was urgently needed in areas as varied as foreign languages, social and political information about the regions in the world where American power was to be exercised from then on, social psychology, the economics of development, strategy in general and nuclear strategy in particular, weapons, technology, materials science, the space race, and more. The interpenetration of Cold War objectives with academic production unsettled the American academic landscape. On the one hand, it favored the emergence of new fields of knowledge, and also new products; it allowed the United States to catch up with European universities, and even to gain a decisive lead that has been maintained throughout the decades. On the other hand, it raised questions about the impartiality of academic knowledge and it corrupted research processes. These negative effects were noisily and sometimes violently denounced during the student revolts of the 1960s.

A subject of interest for historians since the 1990s, after having been a target of protestors, the Cold War University remains an evolving historiographic field, as research continues to reveal the profound effects of this interpenetration.[62] The theme is of interest here because no university embodied the phenomenon better than Harvard, because few fields were more thoroughly transformed than Russian Studies, and because Brzezinski was among the many beneficiaries of the Cold War University. Indeed, he was a preeminent embodiment of its spirit, exemplifying the goal of putting the most advanced knowledge at the service of a political cause—that of freedom.

University professors had already been of assistance to Washington on international matters from time to time. The group of thinkers brought together starting in the fall of 1917 by President Woodrow Wilson to help him with his foreign policy, christened "The Inquiry," included many academics, along with lawyers and journalists.[63] The idea was to accompany the American war effort, formulate policies for the postwar period such as the Fourteen Points, and prepare for the peace negotiations at Versailles. In the 1930s, by contrast, Franklin D. Roosevelt's "brain trust"—the team of intellectuals, including professors from Columbia and Harvard, who helped him conceptualize the New Deal—concentrated primarily on domestic affairs.

The Cold War University had its real origins in the Second World War: America found itself once again, in a few short years, at the head of an empire that it did not know very well, and it had to confront enemies about which it knew next to nothing. Mars (god of war) approached Minerva (goddess of wisdom) as a matter of urgency, above all on the question of weapons systems, including nuclear weapons (as in the Manhattan Project) and the formation of civil and military occupying forces, but also on research into various parts of the world—vanquished ex-enemy realms that had to be administered, allies that had to be protected from various threats including internal subversion, adversaries whose plans had to be countered and whose regimes deserved to be destabilized. There was an immense need for capabilities in what now would be called nation-building, which encompasses all the functions from providing security to constructing an administrative apparatus. To meet the need, it was necessary to draw on existing national resources. Thus, for example, the Wartime Commission of the US Office of Education launched a campaign to mobilize all educational institutions, from primary schools to private universities, to meet the needs of the armed forces and of industry.[64]

For international affairs, the exchanges were most intense in the Office of Strategic Services (OSS), the intelligence service created hastily in June 1942 to coordinate the previously disparate espionage efforts of the various agencies and armies. The research and analysis branch of the OSS, nicknamed the "Chairborne division" because it had so many professors in its ranks, was the ancestor of the CIA's Directorate of Intelligence; its mission was to learn as much as possible about allied and enemy countries alike, in order to guide the war effort.[65] It was in part from this service that area studies emerged. Thus, after the war, Geroid Robinson, who led the research and analysis branch's Russian division, created Columbia University's Russian Institute, one of the two great research centers focused on this region, the other being Harvard's.

Beginning in late 1941, research came into great demand. The effort was only superficially reduced in 1945–1946, and it was intensified thereafter with the deterioration of US-Soviet relations. The construction of tools for the Cold War, especially from 1947 through 1950 (the NSC, the CIA, the Air Force, the Defense Department, and so on) was accompanied by a major intellectual effort within universities, helped by massive financial support, which went almost exclusively to the hard sciences, which were the most costly. Among the holes that urgently needed to be filled, knowledge of the USSR and its allies had priority. "Never before," as one observer summed it up, "did so many know so little about so much."[66] Until then, Washington's eyes and ears on

Soviet political society were concentrated in the embassy in Moscow, with its limited means; any understanding was thanks to the perceptive skills of diplomats such as George Kennan. The latter, skeptical about the massive effort undertaken by the universities, wrote to a friend in 1950: "The judgment and instinct of a single wise and experienced man whose knowledge of the world rests on the experience of personal, emotional, and intellectual participation in a wide cross-section of human efforts are something we hold to be more valuable than the most elaborate synthetic structure of demonstrable fact and logical deduction."[67]

But demonstrable facts and logical deductions were exactly what Washington was looking for at the time—it wanted solid, stable knowledge about the Soviet Union. The need was twofold: it was essential to create a discipline and acquire knowledge that could be supplied directly to federal agencies, and it was essential to produce qualified specialists that those agencies could recruit as staff members. From the start, one of the explicit missions of the major research centers at Columbia and Harvard was to train young people in Sovietology through Master's and Ph.D. programs. Some 40 percent of the scholars who graduated from Columbia's Russian Institute between 1948 and 1952 went on to work in federal agencies.[68] The CIA, created in the meantime, was a major recruiter; moreover, it put together its own team of economists who specialized in the USSR, and those experts were in frequent contact with their university colleagues throughout the Cold War. The stakes were high: it was critical to assess the size and growth rate of the Soviet economy and thus the scale of its defense efforts.[69] The CIA also commissioned a great deal of work from academia. For example, Walt Rostow, an economist at MIT and later President Lyndon Johnson's national security adviser, received a contract for work carried out jointly with Harvard that was published in book form in 1953 as *The Dynamics of Soviet Society.* It hardly mattered that Rostow was not a recognized specialist in the region.[70]

The CIA was not the only source of federal funding. As is often the case in US federal bureaucracy, centralization was nonexistent, coordination was minimal, and the competition was ferocious. Every agency and every service in the Pentagon or the State Department had its own research policy. Thus the young Air Force, which had been created in 1947, supported many innovative projects undertaken by different institutions, from RAND in Santa Monica to Harvard and MIT, in varied realms, such as Russian studies, strategic studies, social psychology, brainwashing and conditioning, radars and missiles, and war games.[71] It was only in the late 1950s, for example, after the Sputnik episode, that somewhat more centralized federal funding was directed toward area studies, but a number of additional sources remained available as well. By the early 1960s the federal government was supporting research programs at the level of roughly $1.5 billion a year, essentially devoted to area studies.[72]

Philanthropic foundations, too, operating alongside the federal government, were essential players in the creation of the Cold War University. According to the Gramscian analyst Edward Berman, "the Carnegie, Ford and Rockefeller foundations have consistently supported the major aims of United States foreign policy, while simultaneously helping to construct an intellectual framework supportive of that policy's major tenets."[73]

The role of foundations was not limited to financial support. They served as intermediaries between the needs of the federal government and the intellectual resources of the universities, and they helped shape the new American university.[74] In the first few years, through the early 1950s, the Carnegie and Rockefeller Foundations were the principal operators in the realm of institutional creation. Thus in 1946 Columbia University was chosen as the recipient of Rockefeller Foundation support, with initial funding of $250,000 for the creation of a research center to be known as the Russian Institute. When the Ford Foundation joined in, it adopted a different approach. Organizing an annual nationwide competition, offering individualized fellowships, the Foundation let the recipient choose the university to which he or she would be appointed. This made it possible to attenuate the concentration somewhat: between them, Harvard and Columbia had monopolized funding for work on the USSR. According to one estimate, Berkeley, Stanford (through the Hoover Institution), Dartmouth, and Bryn Mawr combined received only 10 percent of the amounts that went to the Harvard-Columbia axis.[75]

The philanthropic foundations also played a notable role in the advent of area studies in the United States, a field that focused multidisciplinary attention on particular regions. Even before the war, the Rockefeller Foundation worked together with the American Council of Learned Societies to create pilot programs in integrated studies. When the war broke out, bringing an urgent appeal for information in its wake, the US Navy and then the Army borrowed this model in a large-scale effort to train their personnel to take on the responsibilities of occupation and contact with foreign regions. At Harvard, for example, military training programs were set up and the best professors were called upon to contribute. Adam Ulam (who was teaching at the University of Wisconsin at the time) was a "drill instructor" in the Army Specialized Training Program, which was split between language instruction (60 percent) and course work in culture and politics (40 percent). Carl Friedrich directed the Civil Affairs Training Program for Army officers; it offered instruction in a wide range of disciplines (languages, economics, history, and so on) focused on specific countries.[76]

The OSS was another important incubation site for the area studies model, which owes its success to the integrated response that it could offer to meet the needs of the political authorities. Regarding the Soviet Union, for instance, the questions of American civilian and military leaders were not limited to foreign policy; they also bore on many other crucial aspects. Was the regime stable? Would Soviet society accept the war effort? Would the Red Army be able to stand up to the assault by the Wehrmacht? Was Moscow in a position to profit from the Lend-Lease Act? Could the USSR make good use of American economic aid? This is how the pluridisciplinarity that underlay area studies (a composite field that historian Barry Katz has called "social science in one country") developed in response to specific requests from political and military authorities.[77]

Beyond this new field of study, the philanthropic organizations also supported the creation of international relations as a discipline—one that gradually acquired autonomy within departments of government and political science. International relations began to nourish the many schools that were created from the 1930s to the 1950s, often thanks to impetus from a foundation or enlightened donor. Examples include the School of Advanced International Studies at Johns Hopkins, the Fletcher School at Tufts and Harvard, and the School of International Service at American University. These schools trained generalists who could fill positions in the many Washington agencies with an international orientation. The Ford Foundation, moreover, approached fifteen universities, including Harvard, in 1953 for the purpose of creating five research centers on international affairs—this was the origin of Robert Bowie's CFIA.[78] The Ford Foundation also helped finance the travels of young scholars. Brzezinski, too, benefited from the generosity of these foundations, directly and through academic and research institutions.

The universities in question were inevitably affected by the massive influx of new funding from federal agencies or philanthropic foundations, whose influence helped shape the Cold War University. Although a few institutions resisted at least certain aspects of the transformation, universities most often welcomed and even actively solicited these complementary revenues, setting themselves up as an academic lobby. The historian Rebecca Lowen gives the example of Stanford, which, short of money during the Depression, had already had to accept New Deal financing, going against its own pro-business ideology. When the Second World War came along, Stanford saw its revenues decline further, and several members of its faculty left to work in Washington. The university was thus quite happy to recuperate funding tied to the expansion of America's international activities; in 1947, external financing covered more than 25 percent of its instructional budget.[79] Such developments created internal tensions between the new elite of the Cold War University, the "star" professors who could attract the funding that had become essential for the growth of institutions, and the traditionalists (or protestors), who often had more trouble finding jobs in the most prestigious universities.

The very mission of the university was in question—a reorientation that Clark Kerr, chancellor of the University of California, Berkeley, summed up in the early 1960s under the name "multiversity." As he saw it, universities had several missions, and in particular they had to serve society through their research for the benefit of science, industry, and the federal government (he used the term "federal grant university").[80] Research was increasingly becoming the primary activity of the most prominent professors. The creation of research centers and schools that specialized in training professionals to respond to the needs of the federal government left little room for the traditional curriculum— and for the undergraduate students who had earlier been at the heart of the university's mission. Thus, the 1960 student revolt can be analyzed in part as a cry of protest by a constituency neglected by the Cold War University. According to the psychologizing terminology of the time, the presumed "apathy" and "anguish" on the part of undergraduates were analyzed as symptoms of a failed "adjustment" to their new milieu, whereas in reality, universities had stopped paying attention to these students (although they were much more numerous than ever before).[81]

The student revolt brought to the surface many other tensions that had been building up around the Cold War University. For example, in 1965, a scandal broke out in Chile. An American scholar had concealed the military funding behind a project as he sought the collaboration of Chilean colleagues.

But the truth soon came out. As part of something called Project Camelot, the US Army had commissioned a research office at American University to try to develop a model for predicting and influencing politically significant social change in other countries. A team of leading sociologists was financed by a six million dollar budget over three years. When the scandal reached the United States, Defense Secretary Robert McNamara immediately put a stop to the project.[82] This revelation was accompanied by many others during the same period, particularly exposing the CIA's financing of academic studies, other intellectual activities (the Congress for Cultural Freedom, for example), and even student projects, as we shall see in the case of Brzezinski and the Independent Research Service in 1959. What was at stake was the neutrality of academic work; there would be a lingering suspicion that research and knowledge were being exploited and manipulated by Washington. This theme was developed in several books, including one by Noam Chomsky and colleagues about the Cold War University, one by Sigmund Diamond on "the compromised campus," and one by Ron Robin on the "military-industrial complex."[83]

The latter expression was borrowed from Dwight Eisenhower's famous farewell speech pointing to the dangerous dynamic between the military and its industrial suppliers. In the same January 1961 speech, the Republican president also warned against the excesses of the Cold War University:

In this [technological] revolution, research has become central; it also becomes more formalized, complex, and costly. A steadily increasing share is conducted for, by, or at the direction of the Federal government. Today, the solitary inventor, tinkering in his shop, has been overshadowed by task forces of scientists in laboratories and testing fields. In the same fashion, the free university, historically the fountainhead of free ideas and scientific discovery, has experienced a revolution in the conduct of research. Partly because of the huge costs involved, a government contract becomes virtually a substitute for intellectual curiosity. . . . The prospect of domination of the nation's scholars by Federal employment, project allocations, and the power of money is ever present and is gravely to be regarded.[84]

In his *Compromised Campus,* Diamond recounted that the first director of Harvard's Russian Research Center, Clyde Kluckhohn, had routinely encouraged his students to write their master's or Ph.D. theses on topics on which the State Department was requesting information.[85] Even area studies, a field that had been largely invented in the context of the war, was criticized for being subject to conditions that, de facto, led researchers to do work of direct use to the US government. The field was also accused of reflecting an essentialist and, to put it bluntly, racist view of the world—as if a region had to be reduced to its peculiarities, following the pattern of Orientalism.[86] After reaching their peak during the 1960s, area studies programs tended to stagnate. Later, after the fall of the USSR, the Ford and Andrew W. Mellon foundations announced they would favor global rather than regional studies—a shift that led to a loss of specialized knowledge about the various regions of the world.

The historian David Engerman rejects some of the accusations that have been made against the Cold War University. He reminds us that its founders created an academic field, not an office of consultants indentured to Washington, and that the studies undertaken extended far beyond the needs of the federal government. "While the government agencies and foundations that supported Russian Studies had created the field to learn more about the Politburo," he writes, "they also created experts on Pushkin."[87] He concedes, nonetheless, that during the 1960s the very broad way in which, at the outset, federal agencies had thought about their return on investment tended to shrink. The fact remains that the tremendous increase in resources devoted to international affairs created a body of knowledge that had been virtually nonexistent in the 1930s, and this had positive impacts in a variety of domains. Studies in Sovietology, for example, brought advances in the measurement of economic growth, and in the understanding of power diffusion in industrial societies (totalitarian or not), the impact of language on mental structures, and interactions among cultures.

The Cold War University had another positive aspect: it caused the academic world to be enriched by the immigration of intellectuals from Europe, and in turn to assimilate them.[88] The joke is often shared that American universities' two greatest benefactors of the twentieth century were Adolf Hitler and Margaret Thatcher, since both pushed so many fine scholars and experts to American shores. (They did it in very different ways, to be sure—Thatcher by making deep cuts in higher education budgets.) What is certain is that the Cold War University offered a particularly favorable context to academics who were refugees from Europe. Jeremy Suri refers to the Jewish academic community of Walt Rostow, Daniel Ellsberg, Henry Kissinger, and others as the "connective tissue" of the Cold War University.[89] At Harvard, this was not only a Jewish phenomenon. In the Russian Research Center, for example, scholars of many origins contributed their knowledge: Friedrich, of course, but also Alexander Gerschenkron, Wassily Leontief, and, not to forget the Poles, Richard Pipes, Adam Ulam, and Zbigniew Brzezinski.

Harvard embodied the Cold War University more than any of its peers; the man identified most with its development was Harvard's president from 1933 to 1954, James Bryant Conant.[90] A chemist by training, he was also a public figure—a patriot, an internationalist, an anti-communist—convinced of the role that universities had to play in the life of the nation. He participated, for example, in the Committee to Defend America by Aiding the Allies (also known, after its founder, as the William Allen White Committee). Starting in May 1940, under the discreet inspiration of Franklin D. Roosevelt himself, this group mobilized to sway public opinion in favor of going to Great Britain's aid.[91] Once America had entered the war, Conant—along with his friend Vannevar Bush (vice president of MIT and president of the Carnegie Foundation)—was one of the architects of the Manhattan Project, working to build the atomic bomb. Secretly involved in the project from late 1941 to 1945, Conant contributed to major decisions and witnessed the nuclear test at Alamogordo.

Beyond his personal involvement, Conant, who introduced the Scholastic Aptitude Test (the SAT, designed to enable a greater degree of meritocracy) into Harvard admissions, also put the resources of his university at the service of the war effort. He helped the White House draw up the framework of the military draft, and he opened his campus to the Army and the Navy for intensive training programs in foreign languages and knowledge of specific regions, as well as math and science instruction. Responding to requests from the military, he modified Harvard's academic calendar and admissions process, and a large number of his professors enrolled in the OSS. The university received enormous sums of money during this period—totaling some $31 million—for research programs tied to defense, in such areas as computer science, radar, and the development of napalm.[92] The Cold War only accentuated the interpenetration; Conant himself was convinced of the Soviet danger. In December 1950, again along with Bush, he was one of the most prominent figures on the Committee on the Present Danger, which sounded the alarm, as the NSC-68, a particularly gloomy National Security Council Report presented to the president (on which Conant had served as a consultant) had done eight months earlier. One of the causes Conant got behind was the institution of universal military service (to replace the partial service system set up in 1948).[93]

It is hardly a surprise, then, that Conant welcomed the idea of a Russian Research Center at Harvard. Columbia had set up its Russian Institute in 1946, and now the Carnegie Corporation was considering Harvard, Columbia, and Stanford as alternative choices for a research and teaching program to concentrate on social psychology and cultural anthropology. Harvard won out, for a few reasons. Palo Alto was too far from Washington. Geroid Robinson, the head of Columbia's institute, did not look favorably on behavioral studies (a fuzzy blend of social psychology, cultural anthropology, and sociology). Harvard already had good research scholars motivated to catch up with Columbia.[94] And, as Sigmund Diamond details, no one seemed to mind that the connection with federal agencies, via the Carnegie Corporation, would by necessity limit the political activities of the scholars at the Center.[95]

The Russian Research Center came into being in early 1948, upon receipt of a Carnegie Corporation check for $100,000, with its objectives clearly spelled out: to inform the federal government (in particular the CIA and the State Department) of research results, particularly concerning the application of behavioral studies to Russia; to create a unit for the analysis of Russian media; to collect testimony from refugees and defectors; and to send scholars behind the Iron Curtain.[96] The Center pursued this multifaceted mission faithfully during the years that followed. During the 1950s Brzezinski participated in all four objectives to varying degrees. Gradually, Harvard's Russian Research Center acquired greater prestige than Columbia's, being more oriented toward research. Between 1945 and 1955, Columbia and Harvard produced 75 percent of the Ph.D.s in the field of Russian studies, but Columbia had twice as many as Harvard, and had awarded many more masters degrees.[97] The Carnegie Corporation, satisfied with the performance of Harvard's center, decided to give it $150,000 a year for five years, starting in the academic year 1952–1953.[98]

Carnegie was not the only source of the Russian Center's funding: the US Air Force and the State Department also participated, and, indirectly, so did the CIA. A good example of how the federal government's intervention worked can be seen in the request addressed by the State Department to MIT, asking if the university could improve the Voice of America radio broadcasts to

Eastern Europe and the Soviet Union by cutting through the static introduced by Moscow. MIT wanted to go much further and work on the *content* of the broadcasts. For what would become Project Troy, MIT, which specialized primarily in engineering studies, needed Harvard and the resources of the Russian Center. The Project Troy report, completed in mid-February 1951, went well beyond technical questions to address political matters including problems facing the Soviet population, policies toward defectors, and planning for the post-Stalin era.[99]

Caught up in the game, Harvard and MIT together developed two more programs along the lines of the first—Troy Plus, and the Soviet Vulnerability Project—this time under the control of the CIA, probably to avoid Congressional investigations. Rostow directed the first of these projects, even though most of the expertise came from the Russian Center scholars—Clyde Kluckhohn, Alex Inkeles, Barrington Moore, Richard Pipes, and Adam Ulam. Its goal was simple: to develop a strategy for weakening the Moscow government's control over its population and its territories, through a combination of diplomacy and propaganda (including radio broadcasts, appeals to the various nationalities, and more). The report was published in 1953 as *The Dynamics of Soviet Society*.[100] But none of these reports had solid scientific foundations, and their recommendations, often vague or conventional, were not anchored in firsthand knowledge of the USSR. As a result, they were not very useful.[101]

The Refugee Interview Project (RIP) undertaken by the Russian Center during its early years was quite another matter. Since scholars were denied direct access to Soviet territory, the best alternative sources of information about it were refugees who had reached West Germany. With massive support from the Air Force, the Russian Research Center sent several specialists, including Merle Fainsod in 1949, to conduct systematic interviews. The project produced a huge amount of material (by early 1952, while the work was still under way, there were already 30,000 pages of data), making it possible both to understand better what was going on in Soviet society and politics (with the organization of factories, family structures, the delivery of medical care, political controls, and so on) and to provide young scholars—such as Brzezinski, who was writing his thesis—with high-quality source material.

The report produced by RIP's directors for the Air Force was, with one chapter removed, published as a book.[102] *How the Soviet System Works* has since been criticized, most notably by Daniel Bell, for taking a purely sociological approach and dismissing the central question of power.[103] Indeed, the approach its authors took was sociological. They described an industrial society undergoing modernization; it was a dictatorship but, most important, it was an imperfect, dysfunctional social system. In it, discontent was widespread—although it had not reached the stage of antagonism or revolt. Citizens and local centers of power could escape the demands of the central authorities by hedging and refining their "techniques of accommodation."[104]

The tens of thousands of refugees questioned by the RIP had placed less emphasis on individual freedoms than was expected, and they had expressed appreciation for the social benefits of the Soviet Union, especially in the areas of education, health, and job security. Many had also mentioned their pride in the military and economic accomplishments of the USSR. More striking was the fact that, while their attitudes differed by social class (peasants were the only ones uniformly hostile to the regime), local nationalism was a less important factor than had been anticipated. Even though 35 percent of the refugees interviewed were Ukrainian, the idea that Ukraine was a "powder keg" had to be relativized. As for the chapter of the report not included in the book, it focused on the armed forces. Here again, the interviews revealed that there was broad support for the Soviet socioeconomic system. In short, the report presented serious challenges to the approaches that certain American strategists had proposed (including the young Brzezinski, even if his proposed course was cautious and nuanced) to bring down the Soviet Union by precipitating either a revolt of the nationalities or a military coup.

Beyond the Russian Center, there were other prominent symbols of the Cold War University in the Harvard world Brzezinski joined in 1950–1951. One was the International Seminar created that year by William Yandell Elliott, with special help from his student Henry Kissinger. Initially known as the Harvard Summer School Foreign Students Project, it was designed to convene promising figures first from allied or neutral countries, beginning with Europe and Asia and then expanding from there. The program's descriptive materials attest to its hope of countering communism's powers of seduction (which were partly poetic and spiritual).[105] The ideological objective of the International Seminar was perfectly clear: it was to provide a more accurate image of America and to cultivate a network of pro-American alumni. It was also to encourage intellectual dialogue, and thus the journal *Confluence* was launched in 1952, with Kissinger as the lead editor, to publish articles on political and cultural topics by prominent academics and intellectuals (among them, Reinhold Niebuhr, André Malraux, Richard Rovere, Walt Rostow, J. K. Galbraith, Bertrand de Jouvenel, and Hannah Arendt).[106] The seminar and the journal were core components of the Cold War University's ideological and intellectual offensive, along with the Congress for Cultural Freedom, the Salzburg Seminars, and the Fulbright grant program.[107] They were made possible by financing by the CIA through "front" foundations—arrangements that did not become public knowledge until 1967.[108]

The summer seminar gave young people, some of them with left-wing sympathies, access to lectures, debates, and discussions with Harvard professors such as McGeorge Bundy, Robert Bowie, Raymond Vernon, and Arthur Schlesinger Jr., plus a few field trips in the Boston area and to Washington, DC, to discover the reality of America. In the early 1960s, some would even get the opportunity to meet Kennedy in the White House. At the outset, in 1951, there were only about twenty participants, all Europeans already studying in the United States. In 1952, twenty-two students from Asia made the trip in addition to twenty-one Europeans. Subsequently, some forty young people participated each year. Each new cohort increased the size of the far-reaching alumni network—a network that formed the basis of Kissinger's contacts abroad in later years. Whenever Kissinger planned a trip in the 1960s and even in 1970, he had his alumni roster close at hand.[109] All the participants in the International Seminar valued it as a unique experience, so much so that Kissinger received countless recommendations from friends and colleagues on behalf of particular applicants. Brzezinski, for example, brought two Polish candidates to his attention. In 1956, he recommended Adam Ciolkosz, a strongly anti-communist socialist he thought would provide useful perspective at a time when the USSR was launching a propaganda offensive on the theme of the German threat (because of Germany's integration into NATO). And in 1957, he recommended the author Gustaw Herling Grudzinski, a Polish émigré—but heard back from Kissinger that it was hard to include someone already making a home in the United States.[110]

Kissinger's and Brzezinski's work intersected again at another prominent Harvard Cold War site: the Center for International Affairs (CFIA, later the WCFIA). Kissinger became the CFIA's associate director, and Brzezinski was one of the first research associates to join. As noted already, it was the Ford Foundation that spurred the creation of the CFIA when it solicited proposals for several international affairs centers in 1953. The process got off to a slow start, but the newly appointed dean McGeorge Bundy exerted considerable effort to bring the center into being. For its director, he was insistent on having Robert Bowie, who refused the initial invitation in 1956—he wanted to remain on the Policy Planning Staff—but ended up accepting. Bowie arrived at Harvard on June 1, 1957.[111]

Despite Bowie's deteriorating relations with Kissinger, the center prospered rapidly, building up a remarkable team.[112] In the early 1960s, the CFIA scholars also included Raymond Vernon, Stanley Hoffmann, Thomas Schelling (a future Nobel Prize winner in economics), Samuel Huntington, Joseph Nye, Morton Halperin, Karl Kaiser, and associate members such as Robert Jervis and Kenneth Waltz. A program for American and foreign fellows was introduced, along a different model than Kissinger's summer seminars. The fellows were professionals, most often mid-career diplomats, who came for a year and were seen as colleagues by the CFIA scholars; each had an individual research project. While surely they absorbed something of the American ethos, the foreign fellows above all brought perceptions of their own countries to the CFIA. It was an enrichment welcomed by all the researchers, Brzezinski among them.[113]

The latter, who quickly became close to Bowie, was one of the first contributors to the center. The CFIA avoided addressing issues in which existing region-focused centers (such as the Russian Research Center) specialized, and instead focused on Eastern Europe. Thus Brzezinski served as a sort of bridge between the two organizations, owing to his research on the relations among Communist countries. His 1960 book *The Soviet Bloc: Unity and Conflict*, which he dedicated to Fainsod, included a preface by Bowie and was published under the joint auspices of the Russian Research Center and the CFIA, "the oldest and the youngest of such centers at Harvard." In it, Brzezinski thanked the CFIA, which supplied "a unique forum for testing my hypotheses against the judgment and experience of senior foreign-policy officials from a variety of countries," the famous Fellows.[114] (The second book published under the auspices of the CFIA was Kissinger's *The Necessity for Choice*, the following year.)[115] The CFIA also produced, under Brzezinski's direction, *Ideology and Foreign Affairs,* a report requested by the Senate Commission on External Relations, whose president at the time was William Fulbright. It included contributions from researchers at the center and elsewhere, including Merle Fainsod, Stanley Hoffmann, Carl Friedrich, William Elliott, and Walter Laqueur.[116] Brzezinski was thus the author of the CFIA's first two publications.[117]

Like the Russian Center, the CFIA embodied the Cold War University by also engaging in a constant exchange of ideas, information, advice, and talents with the nation's capital. Experts came and went along the Northeast Corridor connecting Boston, New York, and Washington, offering their knowledge to those responsible for American foreign policy. These ties had been established as early as the Second World War, but it was in the 1950s that Harvard became an epicenter of cooperative exchange between researchers and politicians. It was an ideal ecosystem for Brzezinski; he flourished, and in turn, productively served the system.

A Committed, Peripatetic, Activist Academic

I became a scholar simply because Harvard gave me the opportunity to be a scholar, and I became serious about trying to be a decent scholar. But there was always something within me that drew me to action, influencing events, impacting. And then as I began to feel my oats, I began to crystallize my ambition, which was nothing less than formulating a coherent strategy for the United States, so that we could eventually dismantle the Soviet bloc.

—Zbigniew Brzezinski (2010)

The years between 1956 and 1960 saw a shift in Brzezinski from exclusively academic preoccupations—his thesis, his first publications, teaching—to a new interest in exploring, however modestly at first, the world of politics. He began to write for more popular, nonspecialist journals, and to respond to solicitations from highly placed political figures. He contributed to John F. Kennedy's 1960 electoral campaign. During those years, he began to travel widely, especially behind the Iron Curtain. In 1959, for example, his travels took him to Vienna to sabotage the Youth Festival organized by the communists. At the end of the decade, when he learned he would not be offered a tenured position at Harvard, he seems to have handled the disappointment with equanimity. In any case, it led him to New York, that is, halfway to DC and that much closer to the center of power.

Even in his earliest work, Brzezinski situated his analyses in an explicitly political context. It was a desire to familiarize himself with the enemy's weaknesses that made him want to explore a theme like nationalities within the Soviet empire, or the loyalty of the Red Army, or the dynamics of purges. Starting in 1956, once his first two books had come out (his thesis and *Totalitarianism and Dictatorships*, with Carl Friedrich), he began publishing in less scholarly journals, so that his analyses could have more influence in public debates—and to raise his profile as a specialist in the Eastern bloc.

Journalists frequently sought commentaries from Harvard experts, especially those at the Russian Research Center, and Brzezinski, a voracious consumer of news (as he had always been, since the outbreak of the Second World War), kept watch for the slightest developments. When America learned of Stalin's death on the night of March 5, 1953, the importance of the event moved him to pick up the phone and call Fainsod, even though it meant waking him up. His rationale was that journalists would start calling at dawn: Shouldn't Fainsod prepare himself to react? After the news had been shared, there was an awkward silence. Then, still half-asleep, Fainsod responded: "Zbig, do you know what time it is? Don't you think he would still have been dead by tomorrow morning?"[118]

Stalin's death led to a series of political developments in the Soviet bloc, developments that reached a turning point with the Twentieth Congress of the Communist Party of the Soviet Union in February 1956. Brzezinski offered his analysis of de-Stalinization in an article for *The New Republic* in June 1956, his first piece for the mass-market magazine that was the mouthpiece of modern internationalist liberalism at the time. "Shifts in the Satellites" showed how the countries of Eastern Europe were caught off guard by de-Stalinization and were uncertain about what course to follow in response to the denunciation of Stalin's excesses, whose political lessons they had incorporated (elimination of deviations, personal selection of the entire leadership, a Russian-style model for economic development, political formulations that conformed to Stalinist dogma) into their own regimes. "The present situation is plainly embarrassing to the satellite rulers who are attempting to conform to the new line without destroying the fundamental patterns of their rule. In such periods of transition even the unforeseen can happen."[119]

Given the repeated outbreaks in Poland, the insurrection that followed in Budapest and its crushing by Soviet tanks (in late October and early November of 1956) were probably not unexpected events, but they shook Brzezinski's convictions: "My views in the 50s were focused on foreign affairs, and they were rather hard-nosed—that is to say, I really wanted a confrontation with the Soviet Union, because I felt the Soviet Union was weak. For me, the major turning point was '56, when it became clear—during the Hungarian crisis, as well as the Suez crisis—in America's conduct, that the policy of liberation was a sham, was essentially a slogan of convenience of domestic type for American politics, and not a serious reflection of American commitment."[120]

Brzezinski had been sympathetic with the rollback doctrine preached by Eisenhower and the Republicans during the 1952 electoral campaign, a doctrine designed to exploit anti-communist sentiments and appease the McCarthyites. Now, with no American support being offered to the insurgents in Budapest despite the implicit encouragement that doctrine had given them, he was able to assess its full hypocrisy. This was one reason for his later decision to side with the Democrats, most notably as a Kennedy supporter.[121] In early 1957, in the *Journal of International Affairs*, he launched a bitter attack on Eisenhower's foreign policy, calling it "A Study in Contradiction."[122] Tracing the evolution of American attitudes toward Eastern Europe, he argued that the policy of Yalta, which was content to leave Eastern European countries "free but friendly" with the USSR, had been deftly exploited by Moscow, so that the United States had had to adopt a policy of containment—in other words, to accept the status quo. The limits of the policy of "liberation" pursued in the aftermath of the Korean War had been revealed as early as 1953 in Poland; that policy was buried in 1956 by Secretary of State John Foster Dulles's message reassuring the Soviets that the United States would not intervene in the USSR's crackdown on the insurrection in Hungary. America had a foreign policy that was both unacceptable to the Soviet Union and completely discredited. In other words, it had no foreign policy.

Brzezinski's suggestion was to democratically neutralize Eastern Europe. Washington would guarantee the existing borders, but would put both NATO and German rearmament back on the table in exchange for an evolution of the satellite countries toward a neutral status comparable to Austria's or Finland's, and the United States would remain ready to intervene militarily if Moscow continued its "saber rattling" in the region. Such a situation could offer the Soviet Union hope, given the developments observed in Asia, that political and economic developments would ultimately push these neutral countries, and even perhaps some parts of the West, into the Soviet orbit. But Europe and America had no reason to fear this peaceful competition, and could approach it with complete confidence, provided that their determination and their red lines were clearly established. At that point, America would have a real policy at last.[123]

The article is interesting in two respects. First, it shows the mix of creativity and approximation that often characterized Brzezinski's political recommendations. His proposal was at once logical, bold, and unrealistic. How could it be imaginable that Moscow would suddenly accept neutral status for the satellite countries and democratic elections in Budapest, Warsaw, and Prague? How could America ensure this neutral status and contain the USSR if NATO were dissolved and Germany disarmed? Second, it shows him making a first step toward the great political cause he would take up in the 1960s and beyond: peaceful engagement with Eastern Europe. With these satellites, achieving neutrality was not enough; it should be a matter of reducing tensions and gradually increasing economic and cultural exchanges, to begin to influence the Eastern European societies and in the long run encourage their independence from Moscow. Brzezinski's proposed path diverged dramatically from Dulles's supposed policy of liberation, Kennan's excessively passive and static policy of containment, and Kissinger's policy of mutual accommodation to achieve a détente based on acceptance of the status quo.

Over the next few years, Brzezinski focused on relations within the Soviet bloc and the tensions between Moscow and the satellites, a line of work that produced multiple articles and culminated in the 1960 book *The Soviet Bloc: Unity and Conflict*.[124] The book was met with mostly positive reviews. The *New York Times* declared it to be "outstanding" and the *Russian Review* praised it for adding a new dimension to the understanding of Soviet foreign policy.[125] It became a standard resource on the complex relations Moscow had maintained with its satellites since "communism in one country" had given way to an empire theoretically unified by Marxist-Leninist ideology but whose cracks were becoming more and more apparent. These cracks, while known to specialists, had not yet been subjected to systematic study or to a presentation accessible to a broader audience. Brzezinski demonstrated both in-depth knowledge of the various countries of Eastern Europe, where he had traveled several times between 1956 and 1960, and a degree of clarity in his historical and conceptual analysis that allowed his readers to grasp complex developments, especially concerning interactions between power and ideology, a theme to which he returned often. Still, this did not prevent several commentators from criticizing his sometimes jargon-laden writing.

The approach was historical. Brzezinski saw the oscillations between uniformity and diversity as the key to the postwar history of the Eastern bloc, a history he presented in four phases. During the first phase, from 1945 to 1947, the various communist parties attempted to seize power without provoking the West at a time when Stalin was embroiled in treaty negotiations. In this context, the "People's Democracy" was the ideological slogan and the political tactic (building a broadly leftist front) used in place of the dictatorship of the proletariat and of a one-party state.[126] In the second phase, in 1947, once the power of the communists had been strengthened, Stalin could impose more uniformity on the bloc, notably through the creation of the Cominform bureau to convene the communist parties from all across Europe.[127] This phase saw the imposition of controls by Moscow, and the purging of men who had struggled to achieve communist victory—with the exception of the too-powerful Tito. He was able to flourish outside the block where rigid Stalinist uniformity became the rule, and where a forced march was underway towards Soviet industrialization, designed to increase dependency on the center. By 1953, the tensions that built up during this second phase burst out, especially in East Germany and in Poland, and a third phase began in which greater diversity was accepted in the form of the "New Course" preached by Georgy Malenkov.[128] But the crisis was too serious to be settled by half-measures, and the 1956 uprisings in Poland and Hungary forced Moscow to reset its course toward unity. In this fourth phase, Nikita Khrushchev fought against the idea defended by Tito, as well as Polish and Chinese leaders, that there could be different routes toward socialism.[129] (It should be noted that the Sino-Soviet schism, so important in the early 1960s, had not developed far yet. Brzezinski would add a new chapter to subsequent editions of the book addressing it. Indeed, he became an expert on the topic, even though he had not anticipated the schism and had tended to downplay its importance at an earlier stage.)

Brzezinski concluded with the possibility of ideological erosion, recalling the crucial importance of this factor above and beyond the economic interdependence fabricated by Moscow and even beyond the use of force. "The Communist camp is at one time an empire and a church . . . The closest analogy to it is the Islamic world," he explained.[130] A rejection of its common ideology, which might well result from repeated failures to keep economic and social promises, could thus be fatal for the Soviet bloc. It could disintegrate, like so many former empires, or it could be emptied of its substance even while remaining a formal reality, as had been the experience of Islam and Christianity as state systems. He noted, however, that for this to take place, "the ideology must first be denied both victories and enemies, a difficult and paradoxical task since denial of one can be construed as the manifestation of the other."[131] In other words, it was necessary to keep the USSR from winning material and symbolic victories, but also to avoid aggressive confrontation, which would reinforce the bloc's unified opposition to the West.

This work to reveal the internal tensions within the Soviet bloc was a manifestation of a development in Brzezinski himself: his field of interest and expertise was broadening, in a pattern of concentric circles. He began with the Red Army and the Communist Party (1952); then he became interested in the political system of the Soviet Union as a whole (1953, with his work on purges); next, he added a comparative dimension (totalitarianism, 1956); and then went on to study the Eastern bloc and relations among communist countries, especially those of Eastern Europe (1956–1960). The expansion of Brzezinski's focus is evident in an article on the East-West confrontation in the Third World.[132] Called "The Politics of Underdevelopment," it is striking for its uncharacteristic pessimism. Brzezinski saw America in an unfavorable position in Asia in relation to the USSR. Democracy, he explained, is harder to defend than a closed and coherent ideology such as communism. Democracy is founded on a lengthy tradition and on the existence of a bourgeoisie that often does not exist in Asian countries, where the capital needed to support entrepreneurs is often lacking as well. As the elites of developing countries became attracted to the Leninist themes of imperialism and capitalist oppression, they also saw in the Soviet system a credible and speedy path to industrialization. In short, Russia and China had the advantage.

What could America do, then, in a developing Asia? First, avoid doing the wrong things, such as providing military support to conservative forces and setting up pro-Western dictatorships; these steps would alienate younger generations in lasting ways and would be held up by the communists as proofs of Western malfeasance. A less damaging solution might be to offer financial support for industrialization, to give the moderates a chance to win out—but this option was not realistic, as American taxpayers would not want to give money to ostensibly neutral but actually hostile regimes, and the private sector would not run the risk of investing. In the end, the best strategy to adopt was minimalist. It entailed, above all, doing nothing that might precipitate a massive shift toward communism in those countries. The United States should simply improve aid policies, basing them more on business and getting rid of all relations of dependency—and more broadly, shift from a policy of action (on the model of the Marshall Plan) to "a policy of sympathetic observation and disengagement," which could "do much to eradicate the hatred of colonialism and the suspicion of imperialism which even our present actions breed."[133]

In the second half of the 1950s, as he began to make his analyses and his political recommendations known to a broader public, Brzezinski attracted the attention of various elected officials and politicians. His earliest foray into American political life as an expert on the Soviet bloc was in late 1956, when Hubert Humphrey, who headed the Senate Foreign Relations Committee's subcommittee on disarmament, asked him for an evaluation of Soviet strategy and the possibility of reaching an arms limitation agreement. This consultation took place by mail, since Humphrey was unable to organize hearings. Brzezinski's responses show the scholar's familiarity with Soviet debates and the Russian literature on nuclear issues. The Soviet Union, he thought, might sign agreements to limit nuclear weapons if its conventional superiority in Europe were maintained. However, the likelihood that the Soviets would agree to inspections or an independent agency was minimal. Finally, Brzezinski shared his impression, formed during recent travels, that in all the nations of the Soviet bloc, the possibility of German rearmament weighed heavily on people's minds.[134]

In 1957, Brzezinski provided help to then Senator John F. Kennedy through the intermediary of his graduate school classmate Fred Holborn (son of German historian Hajo Holborn), who was a Kennedy adviser. In the middle of a crisis, Gomułka's Poland had asked America for financial aid ($100 million in credits and $200 million in grains and various goods, to be paid in Polish currency). In a speech to the Overseas Press Club on May 6, 1957, Kennedy criticized the administration for its timid response.[135] Although no definitive record of the exchanges has been found in the archives, Kennedy's arguments are, as Patrick Vaughan has noted, strikingly similar to Brzezinski's.[136] Both men asserted that to refuse aid would reinforce Warsaw's dependence on Moscow, would give ammunition to the Stalinist Poles, and would present a bad example for the other countries of Eastern Europe.[137] Identifying "the so-called satellite nations" as "the Achilles heel of the Soviet empire, . . . the potential source of an inflammation that could spread infectious independence throughout its system," Kennedy called for a different policy toward the region, one that would go beyond black-and-white simplicity and beyond the non-credible politics of liberation; it would recognize that the growing differences among the regimes of the Eastern bloc offered America new possibilities.[138] During the summer, Fred Holborn came back to Brzezinski for help with a speech Kennedy was to give in the Senate on August 21, an extension of the May speech concerning assistance to Poland. In a personal letter written two days after the speech,

Kennedy thanked Brzezinski for his "ideas and criticisms," which had allowed the senator to "sharpen the speech considerably."[139]

Brzezinski's contacts with Kennedy extended into 1960, during the presidential campaign. His role remained modest, to be sure. He is mentioned in articles about the "brain trust" Kennedy gathered around him.[140] But he was not in the inner circle—and in any case the brain trust, the largest prestigious academic assembly that had ever been brought together by a presidential candidate, was also intended for public display. Kennedy used it to project an image of modernity and especially to appease the liberals. Still, Brzezinski seems to have played a significant role on two occasions. In May 1960, after the incident of the U-2 spy plane shot down while flying over Soviet territory, Brzezinski was consulted by Kennedy's team. Khrushchev had dramatically walked out of a Paris summit with Eisenhower in protest of the U-2 incident—but there were rumors at the time that Khrushchev was in trouble internally, leading many observers, including some within the administration, to attribute Khrushchev's behavior to his political situation.[141] Brzezinski's information contradicted this view, and led Kennedy to adopt a hard line in his speeches about the performance of the Eisenhower administration. On October 1, Kennedy gave a speech in Chicago, outlining a program of "peaceful engagement" with the satellites, Poland in particular, as a more effective way to counter the USSR than the politics of liberation pursued by the Republicans. Here, Brzezinski's positions are clearly recognizable.[142]

An article by Robert Novak, who was at the time a reporter for the *Wall Street Journal,* portrayed Brzezinski as an essential player in Kennedy's operation, but it resulted from a sort of prank by Kennedy's adviser Ted Sorensen.[143] Here is Brzezinski's account: "I was not seeking a position in the Kennedy campaign, but Sorensen showed up to Cambridge one day and it was a luncheon. Sorensen was then the policy advisor to Kennedy. And the luncheon included Galbraith, Leontief, and William Langer, who was to be deputy head of CIA, a professor of history. Probably one more person, but I don't remember. And me. I was an assistant professor, and they were all full professors—fifteen, twenty years older. And that was a foreign policy consultation. I don't know why I was invited."[144]

Some two months later, Brzezinski saw the front-page story in the *Wall Street Journal.* Its large-type headline and stacked subheads read as follows: "Kennedy's Brain Trust: More Professors Enlist But They Play Limited Policy-Making Role. They Supply Technical Data, Help Overcome Distrust of Senators by 'Liberals.' " And the last subhead was "Aid from Zbigniev Brzezinski"—as if Brzezinski were playing a major role that warranted a page-one headline. The article identified Sorensen as the key operator, and described the lunch he had set up to consult the Harvard brain trust shortly before a major foreign policy address Kennedy was scheduled to give on June 11. It added that the only really useful advice the candidate gained from the lunch concerned Khrushchev's situation during the Paris summit, and was provided "by a Harvard professor with the incredible name of Zbigniev Brzezinski [who] reads *Pravda* with his morning coffee and revels in the intrigues of the Kremlin." Brzezinski's recalled later how he reacted: "I couldn't believe it when I read that. I phoned up Sorensen, and I said 'Mr Sorensen, I read this story about me being the chief of this advisor group—what is it about?' And he says, 'Don't take it seriously. When we did have this meeting with you and the senior professors there, the newspapers learned about it somehow. They phoned me up—and I thought you had such an exotic name that I would name you as the head of the group!' "[145]

Zbigniew and Muska Brzezinski were personally involved in the Kennedy campaign. Muska was active at the campaign headquarters, and during the weekend of October 29–30, 1960, Zbigniew gave a talk on foreign policy issues in a campaign meeting at the Empire State Building, along with Senator Herbert Lehman, who spoke about questions of integration. In a letter to Hoffmann, Brzezinski wrote in a joking tone that this was a real introduction to politics for him and he was learning fast; by observing Lehman, he had concluded that the secret of a successful campaign speech was (1) to speak loudly, (2) to shake one's fist while speaking, and (3) to convey personal conviction. He tried to do all three at once, and was not unhappy with the result.[146]

The most accurate part of Novak's description in his *Wall Street Journal* article is the bit mentioning *Pravda*—more generally speaking, the reference to the high-quality information Brzezinski used to nourish his erudition, aided by Harvard's Russian Center. But knowledge acquired through books, newspapers, and radio broadcasts was not enough, and Brzezinski filled in the gaps, during the 1950s, with several significant trips to Europe and behind the Iron Curtain; visits that were only a prelude to his ceaseless crisscrossing of the globe in the 1960s and 1970s. In particular, he traveled to Munich in 1953 and to Western Europe in 1955.[147] He also traveled to the USSR in 1956; to Poland in 1957, 1958, and 1959; to Austria, Czechoslovakia, and East Germany in 1959; and to Yugoslavia, Bulgaria, the USSR, Mongolia, and Japan in 1960. The notes he took reveal an alert gaze, attentive to details that informed his understanding of the societies he was analyzing. He struck up conversations easily (in English, Russian, Polish, or French) with ordinary citizens, students, intellectuals, military personnel, even political leaders. The preface to *The Soviet Bloc* (1960) includes an ironic acknowledgment: "I am also grateful to several officials of various communist states for their willingness to discuss matters they should not have discussed with me."[148] Many residents of the countries he visited came to see him. Besides conversing with the public, he often went to see movies and plays, and visited universities, courts, collective farms, and, of course, tourist sites.

His trip to the Soviet Union in 1956 is undoubtedly the most interesting. Entries in his personal diary offer arresting glimpses of Russian society:

August 29th

In train, still Finland. New, big green cars, compartments for 2 people only, radio, table, old-fashioned fixtures such as lace curtains, Persian rugs in the corridor covered with a green roll-over.

7 P.M. am now in the Soviet Union: young MVD frontier guard took my passport away. Another registered currency. Now we have just stopped in Luzhaika where a big flowered sign in Finnish and Russian says "Veemu miru mir" ["world peace"]. Another sign says "We are living in an age in which all roads lead to Communism."

Nice Russian woman with whom I had my first Russian conversation (about architecture—she is returning from the Atomic exhibition in Sweden) gave me a caviar sandwich.

. . .

Sept. 6 [Moscow]

. . .

Evening: sat in restaurant with four students—most critical of lack of travel, freedom, standard of living. Exempt from milit. service as students. Still thought we started the Korean war. Molotov quite popular—not crude or vulgar. Another mentioned race riots in Kazakhstan. One belong to Komsomol but another said that this doesn't mean much. One of them live in one room with his mother: 45 r. per month. Armenian hates Georgians.

Sept. 8th (Sat.)

Flying to Odessa via Kiev. Old plane, half cargo, but trip so far o.k. At the Vnukovo airport saw the new jet transport TU 104 take off for

Irkutsk. Terrific plane with a slow take-off. Flights, an official said, are still irregular—only special flights.

Spread out some old NYT magazines in the plane—passengers came up and borrowed them.

9th [with fellow student Mark]

Afternoon: drove to a sovhoz, good soil, lots of corn planted, another beach and the museum of the defence of Odessa (quite interesting, many weapons, captured flags, etc.).

talked to a Jewish engineer, till 52 a lecturer in the university but thrown out during the anti-Semitic season. Can't get job back. Not party member.

Evening: sat on the boulevard facing the sea. Mark asked someone for a match and we started talking. Soon someone pressed unto a political subject and a huge crowd gathered. About 100–150 people pressed on us, sitting, leaning right in our faces. Asked us to criticize socialism— whether we agree with the French socialists' critique, etc. We pointed to inequality here and some people immediately left. Others talked about capitalism. Only two classes here they said. Two types in crowd: friendly and curious on the one hand, and cocky and somewhat aggressive on the other. Followed by a procession to the hotel.

Evening: beautiful boat "Lensoviet," luxurious cabin (no. 108). Made in East Germany last year. Met on deck with a party member who readily admitted social inequality in the USSR . . .

11th [at Yalta]

. . .

—4 pluses that the people mention often: education, pensions, medicine, vacations—

11th

. . .

—my answer to Negro question: much like your anti-Semitism. Usually stops them—[149]

When Brzezinski returned and reported on his travels to his students and colleagues at the Russian Center, his descriptions were less anecdotal, more analytical, and above all more political.[150] He was struck by the bureaucratic inefficiency and the weak productivity that reigned in the USSR. The living standard was low, but the citizenry was not aware of this, even though there was more social inequality than in America, he believed. What struck Brzezinski as a scholar was the gulf between everyday life and the political process; the two spheres appeared to be entirely separate. This was a paradox, since the concept of totalitarianism presupposed precisely a fusion of the two, an extensive control of social activities. Brzezinski gradually abandoned the use of the concept in the years that followed. But ignorance of the political system on the part of the public was also a source of the regime's solidity; no one seemed to know who was on the Central Committee or what changes in its composition might signify. The population was indifferent, even if Khrushchev seemed less popular than the others. In the end, the reforms carried out by the regime after Stalin's death made it possible to alleviate certain tensions. The Ministry of Internal Affairs (MVD) was less obtrusive, whereas the party's role and its recruitment increased—another source of stability.

In 1957, for the first time since 1938, Brzezinski went to Poland for several weeks. Unfortunately, no notes on this visit have survived. On a personal level, he had the opportunity to visit sites he had known in childhood, and he seems to have been struck by the fact that he was no longer Polish, and felt himself to be an American. This was a year before he was naturalized.[151] He drew on this trip to write "Poland—A Political Glimpse," an article in which he asserted that Poland was no longer a totalitarian regime but an authoritarian regime based on Gomułka's popularity and on anti-Russian feelings.[152] The following year, Brzezinski had the opportunity to return to Poland for a week, this time with a delegation including Eugene Rostow, then a dean at Yale, and Milton Katz, a professor of international law at Harvard. Brzezinski's impression of a regime in which ideology no longer played much of a role had been reinforced: the prevailing inefficiency tempered the dictatorship; the Poles were demoralized and skeptical.[153]

The group had the opportunity to "drive out in two taxis to the monument dedicated to the ghetto fighters who perished in 1943," Brzezinski noted in his diary, referring to the Warsaw Ghetto uprising. He described the scene: "The large, simple, block-like monument with a few striking figures of Jewish martyrs standing out sharply in contrast to the severe and immobile surface. It is night, and the monument, with the surrounding destruction, makes an eerie impression—one thinks of the 300,000 Jews massacred on the spot. I have the taxis line up in front of the monument and illuminate it with their headlights. There isn't much that anybody can say."[154]

A few days later, the group went to Lublin and visited the Majdamek concentration camp, where two million people had died.

We are shown tiny gas chambers in which 150 to 300 people were gassed at a time; we are shown the little peep-hole through which the ss man could watch this operation. We visit the barracks: in one, the teeth and the hair of the victims is on display; in another, 820,000 pairs of shoes from the victims are gathered—high-heel straps, sandals, men's work shoes, peasant boots, even children's shoes, are lying together in mute testimony. In a corner, on top of one of the piles, there's a small bouquet of fresh red roses. The impact of this is so overwhelming that we all walk out of the barracks shaken. We drive to Kazimierz, a picturesque ancient city overlooking the Vistula.[155]

A few weeks before one of his trips, probably in 1956, Brzezinski was approached by the CIA and asked whether during his travels he could make notes, on behalf of the agency, on a certain type of railway freight car produced by the Soviets. During the conversation, an agent mentioned, in passing, the application for naturalization that was waiting at a bureau in Boston. Despite the implicit threat, Brzezinski refused; the trip was for academic purposes, and he had the feeling that it would not be appropriate to accept a mission from the CIA to be carried out during his travels. But he added that he would be prepared to keep his eyes open, and if he observed something that might interest the agency he would report back. The men contented themselves with this promise, and did not insist.[156] In fact, during the trip, a student with whom Brzezinski had a lengthy conversation confided that he could give him details about his father, who headed a secret weapons factory. Not knowing whether the student was a sincere dissident or an agent provocateur, Brzezinski did not follow up on the offer.[157] His refusal to turn himself into a CIA agent must not be misconstrued. When not on an academic mission, Brzezinski had no principled scruples against cooperating with the agency—as he showed during a somewhat unusual trip in 1959 to Vienna.

From July 26 to August 4, 1959, the World Festival of Youth and Students was held in Vienna. This large international gathering, organized for the seventh year by Moscow, featured performances, debates, exhibits, and the like. The previous festival, held in Moscow itself in 1957, had been very successful, with more than 34,000 young people attending from 131 countries. To a great extent it achieved its propaganda aims; even the American delegation had been receptive to the themes of the communist message communicated during the various events. On the basis of this popular success, the organizers had decided to take the risk of scheduling the next festival in Vienna—that is, for the first time, on the other side of the Iron Curtain. The stakes were so high that the head of the KGB, Alexander Shelepin, personally oversaw the preparations.[158]

On the American side, the State Department was wary.[159] It officially discouraged young people from participating in this "trap for young tourists," but it soon began to direct those who insisted on going toward an information group called Independent Service for Information on the Vienna Youth Festival (ISI). The CIA was also mindful of this propaganda operation. Via the National Student Association, an organization founded in 1947 (and partly funded by the CIA between 1952 and 1967), the agency had tried to disrupt the 1957 Moscow Festival by rather pathetic means (stink bombs, fake invitations to supposedly official cocktail parties, and so on). Now ISI was one of its instruments. In the fall of 1958, two former members of the National Student Association (who had attended the earlier festivals) had created this new structure and found a dynamic young leader for it in Gloria Steinem, who would later become a charismatic figure in American feminism. ISI went to work at once. It published a guide and information sheets for interested students, designed to prepare them to respond to communist propaganda and particularly to the questions and criticisms of their third-world peers. It organized practice dialogue sessions with pretend foreign students, on issues such as the race question in the United States or the intervention in Libya.[160] And it recruited non-communist students for the official delegation, which was dominated by communist sympathizers.

Certain students were too clearly identified as anti-communists to be included in the ISI group; this was the case for the man Steinem considered the star of her group, Zbigniew Brzezinski. Separate funding allowed them to buy plane tickets for these students.[161] While the organizers knew that the CIA was behind ISI, the students involved did not. The intellectual Michael Harrington, situated decidedly on the left but also very anti-Stalinist, had a suspicion that the State Department was funding ISI. Hesitant to accept the free plane ticket, he only agreed on the condition that he would go as an independent delegate, free to criticize capitalism as well as communism—a demand that put an end to the matter. Had he known that the funding source was actually the CIA, he would never even have considered participating.[162] For Brzezinski, there was no such issue. He was well aware of the situation, and fully subscribed to the project concocted in the office of CIA agent Cord Meyer.[163] "I certainly did not initiate it," he later recalled, "but I had friends who were involved in it, like Paul Sigmund [who] used to be a professor at Princeton. And through them I got sucked into it, and we were all some kind of social friends, and it seemed like a great adventure." He went on to explain:

> A lot of it was planned in advance, in the way that we decided to be a participatory kind of group of some sort. I forget how that was contrived, but we decided to publish some kind of a newspaper for the young participants, and gain access to its proceedings, and then engage in debates within the Communist Youth Festival with those who were susceptible to debate, such as some Poles, Czechs, and so forth. But we also decided to give ourselves a very deliberately kind of quasi-revolutionary flavor, by embracing strongly the Algerian cause against the French—in order to legitimate the cause of Hungarians whom the Soviets had crushed, to get across the message that Soviets were reactionary and imperialistic and so forth. . . . [The idea was to] sow confusion. Sow ideological confusion. Play the game.[164]

When the American students—for the most part "real" students, younger than the thirty-one-year-old Brzezinski—arrived in Vienna, they found an atmosphere of intense ideological rivalry. The participants from the Eastern bloc, most of them making their first trip outside the Iron Curtain, were shielded from contamination. They were kept together, for example, and always accompanied. Silence was imposed on the waiters who served the Chinese delegation. Through its Austrian network, the CIA counterattacked by organizing bus trips to the Hungarian border to see the barbed wire and the watchtowers, and by having banners with messages such as "Remember Hungary" or "Remember Tibet" pulled by planes flying over the city.[165]

ISI lost no time entering the fray, with the result that the official American delegation to split up. To counter the festival's official newspaper, Steinem ran an International News Bureau that became the main source of information for foreign journalists, and so irritated the Soviet ambassador that he complained to the Austrian government. To stir up trouble among the communist delegations, Brzezinski slipped into the living quarters reserved for the Soviets and, brushing against some students there, spat out in Russian with a strong Polish accent: "Out of my way, Russian pig!"[166] It was a student prank, but one very much informed by the Master's thesis on nationalities he had written ten years earlier. The ISI group got together in the evenings to plot their next moves: "I remember Gloria lying in bed in a sort of frilly robe while the rest of us sat around the bed strategizing. I thought it was kind of an amusing, and slightly eccentric, scene."[167]

But Brzezinski's finest move was made with his buddy Walter Pincus, who later became a celebrated journalist with the *Washington Post*. At the end of the festival, the two friends found their way onto the roof of a building over-looking the square and hung two flags, one Algerian flag and one Hungarian, each with the middle cut out (this was the symbol of the October uprising in Hungary), along with a banner spelling out "Peace and Freedom" in German. The organizers reacted quickly; they turned off the spotlights and tried to catch the troublemakers. Brzezinski and Pincus made their escape by crossing a plank that led to another building.[168]

In the end, the festival was a failure for the Soviets. Most of the events were of poor quality and poorly attended (they had to bring in audiences from Hungary and Czechoslovakia to fill the auditoriums). More than that, with so many feisty Americans on the scene, they lost control of the discussions. One East German defected; the Italian delegation decided to leave in reaction to the obvious manipulation of the discussions; the Indian, Chilean, and Brazil-ian delegations were divided.[169] A few months later, a critical internal report (it led to the firing of several of the organizers) pointed out certain failures: the neutral countries did not go along with the project, indoctrination was minimal, or even negative, and the effectiveness of opposition groups—both in influencing delegates and criticizing the festival—had been underestimated.[170] In short, the ISI wager had paid off. The organization evolved into the Inde-pendent Research Service and went into action again for the Helsinki festival in 1962; Robert Kennedy personally followed the preparations and invited the students to a debriefing in his office when they came back.

When the CIA's funding was revealed in the press several years later, Gloria Steinem took full responsibility for her acts.[171] She recalled her own anti-totalitarian ideals, described the convergence of her views with the agency's, and clarified that the CIA's role had been limited to financing ISI. It was certainly true that during the 1950s the agency was more in tune with the internationalist liberals than it was later on. The break—which did not trouble liberals like Brzezinski—came about in the 1960s and 1970s—during the Vietnam War, the time of "dirty tricks." Colorful as it was, the Vienna episode should not be overdramatized. Pincus referred to it as "a college weekend with Russians," and Brzezinski commented: "Yeah, not terribly serious, to be completely frank. Youthful exuberance."[172]

On February 3, 1960, Zbigniew Brzezinski wrote to Dean McGeorge Bundy to announce his resignation from Harvard, having just accepted an offer from Columbia University. He was to become an associate professor of public law and government in the Department of Political Science and in the Russian Institute, beginning June 30.[173] This letter brought to an end a little drama that had gone on for two years, during which, after many discussions and hesitations, the Harvard Government Department had decided to promote two internal candidates, Henry Kissinger and Stanley Hoffmann, and had hired an external candidate, Edward Banfield. This was a disappointment for Brzezinski, but he accepted the decisions gracefully and took advantage of the opportunity to work in New York, then the center of gravity of American foreign policy.

It should be acknowledged that the situation Dean Bundy faced at the end of the 1950s was not a simple one; he suffered from an oversupply of talent. He had promoted many formidably gifted young people in recent years, and they had reached the age when they might aspire to tenure in the Government Department; among them were Henry Kissinger, Samuel Huntington, Zbigniew Brzezinski, and Harry Eckstein. But the number of positions was limited. Huntington was the first to be denied tenure, after a long and painful series of interviews; he accepted a position with tenure at Columbia. For Brzezinski, paradoxically, it was the creation of the CFIA that struck the fatal blow destroying the prospect of getting tenure. The Government Department had opposed the creation of the center, which it saw as a distraction and an insufficiently scholarly enterprise. The financial plan for the center included a tenured position for Robert Bowie, who was thus appointed to a professorship without encroaching on the department's budget. A half-time appointment was reserved for his associate director, Kissinger, with the understanding that the department would cover the second half of his salary. But the Government Department faculty balked—so Bundy and Bowie, who needed Kissinger, agreed to a compromise. The department voted to promote Kissinger to the status of associate professor, which conferred on him the sought-after tenure. In exchange, the CFIA would support another half chair—an opportunity the department took advantage of by promoting Hoffmann to the rank of associate professor, thus acquiring two new tenured faculty members in international affairs at once.[174]

Harry Eckstein and Brzezinski were not in the running for these positions, since they had different areas of specialization. But their progress was nevertheless blocked, all the more so because the department had reinforced its strength in domestic politics by hiring Edward Banfield. In short, Brzezinski's path at Harvard seemed cut off for the next four or five years, and Eckstein decided to leave for Princeton. "I am naturally a little disappointed but, I suppose, it was in the books," Brzezinski wrote to his friend Albert Mavrinac.[175] Over the next few weeks, Hoffmann expressed his sympathy to Brzezinski, and his regret that they had not been promoted together, while Brzezinski's two protectors, Bowie and Fainsod, made strenuous efforts to find a solution. They had both been taken by surprise by the deal made between the department and Bundy, and neither had realized what it implied for Brzezinski. By contrast, Brzezinski's coauthor Carl Friedrich remained passive.[176]

The solution that took shape during the winter of 1959 came from Bowie. He was prepared to pay Brzezinski's entire salary from the CFIA's fund for five years if the department voted to appoint him, which would mean increasing the number of tenured positions. But Brzezinski said he was uncertain about having the support of three faculty members: Samuel Beer, David McClosky, and Adam Ulam.[177] By April, he was even more skeptical that Bowie's maneuver could succeed, and in any case he did not want a halfway solution that would have him stay on without a promotion to associate professor—that is, without tenure. When he intensified his search for a position elsewhere, he received an offer from the University of Chicago, where he went for interviews, and also an offer from Berkeley.[178] He continued to describe himself as disappointed, but he was less affected than he had expected; he felt ready to leave, without any sense of failure, and he was appreciative of the efforts his mentors—at least Bowie and Fainsod—had made to keep him at Harvard.[179]

Later in the year, Bundy finally made the decision to create an additional tenured position in the Government Department for Brzezinski, but he wanted a unanimous vote of approval from the department members. A single professor refused to go along; ironically, it was a professor of Polish origin, Adam Ulam. Brzezinski's fate was thus sealed. He would not remain at Harvard.[180]

> There were other people there, I won't mention their names, but what I do remember is that they were so visibly unhappy and kind of crushed, and whined and complained. And I remember my wife and I, when I was told we would have to leave, gave a party, which we called "a shipwreck party," and everybody had to come in costume. And we had the wildest party, probably, that Cambridge has ever had—everybody in costumes, dancing like crazy, lots of drink, vodka, champagne. We invited everybody, including people who were against me. And there was one only reason: to show that "Je m'en fiche."[181]

Following Huntington's example, Brzezinski accepted an offer from Columbia. Berkeley's offer was more lucrative, but Brzezinski had a good reason to choose Columbia: its position on the East Coast, along the corridor of power. Did he regret leaving Harvard? Just two years later, in May 1962, he received the exceptional offer from Harvard's Government Department of a full-time tenured position with only half-time teaching responsibilities, leaving considerable time for research.[182] After a month and a half of soul-searching and weighing the options, he rejected the offer. "I must say I reached [that] decision with many hesitations, misgivings, and conflicting pulls," he wrote to a friend. "In many ways, I was very attracted and it would have been the fulfillment of an old ambition, all the more satisfying because it would have ironically [been] much earlier than if I had stayed at Harvard. . . . In addition, I want to shape my own life and not have Harvard shape it for me. I want to stay; they make me leave. Two years later they want me back, and should I drop everything and just run back?"[183]

Although Harvard's offer was tempting, he saw the decision to stay at Columbia to develop the research potential of the Russian Institute and the Research Institute on Communist Affairs as a kind of validation of the choice he had made two years earlier: "I can now let off steam because I have made an honest woman of Columbia and what was a shotgun wedding has now been legitimized by my own independent decision."[184] Incidentally, Harvard's Government Department also tried to bring Huntington back, and in that effort was successful; he returned to his alma mater in 1963 and remained for the rest of his career. In the spring of 1965, Harvard tried one last time to recruit Brzezinski; the details of the offer remain unknown, but once again he refused.[185] His destiny was no longer in Cambridge but right where he was, in New York, halfway between Cambridge and Washington.

2

A Political Adviser Is Born

When I went to Harvard I didn't have a clear notion that I wanted to be an academic. I wanted somehow to influence events, that I remember. But whether that would be by joining the foreign service, or dealing with foreign affairs in some capacity, or being an academic—I hadn't really thought that through. But then Harvard started getting me things. That kind of pushed me in one direction, that direction took off and then I began to be noticed, first as an academic, a promising one, I guess, and then as one with a policy orientation. And at Harvard I noticed that academia and policy intermingled, and that began to attract me more and more. So by the end of that decade and the beginning of the next one, by 1960, it was clear to me that I wanted to combine the two. And by the 70s, it was clear that I wanted the second more than the first.

—Zbigniew Brzezinski (2010)

The offer Brzezinski accepted at Columbia, although less financially appealing than the one from Berkeley, was still advantageous. He was appointed associate professor with the prospect of tenure, with an annual salary of $9,000 plus $500 contributed by the Russian Institute. Furthermore, the Institute financed his first year entirely, which meant that he did not have to teach in the 1960–1961 academic year.[1] He took advantage of the situation by undertaking, with support first from the CFIA (where he ran a seminar in the spring of 1960) and then from Columbia's Russian Institute, a series of trips: to Mongolia and the Soviet Union in May; to Yugoslavia, Bulgaria, and the Soviet Union again in July and August; and in the fall to Japan, where he took part in the third international conference on Sovietology.[2] In 1962, when Brzezinski decided to resist the sirens of Cambridge, geographical location was not the only factor. He explained it this way: "I thought if I went back to Harvard I would still have my former professors, as colleagues, but still my former professors. Whereas at Columbia in some way I was a top dog."[3] He became a full professor at Columbia in 1962, at the age of thirty-four. With this choice he put himself in prestigious company, among the small club of stars who had said no to Harvard's attempts to seduce them, choosing instead to stay at Columbia. The group included, most notably, the literature professor and critic Lionel Trilling, the historian Richard Hofstadter, and the Nobel Prize-winning physicist Isidor Rabi.

In late 1961, Columbia's president Grayson Kirk (who had filled in for Dwight Eisenhower in 1951 and succeeded him in 1953) announced the creation of a new research center and made Brzezinski its director. Funded by the Ford Foundation, the Research Institute on Communist Affairs (RICA) had a primary mission to study relations among the communist countries, above all, those involving China, on which Brzezinski was increasingly focused. The new center was made to order for him in the wake of his book *The Soviet Bloc: Unity and Conflict.* He knew he could count on the cooperation of his colleagues at Columbia, especially those from the Russian Institute, such as Henry Roberts, its director; Alexander Dallin, a friend who had paved the way for Brzezinski's move to Columbia; Martin Wilbur, a specialist on East Asia; and Schuyler Wallace, an internationalist.[4]

As the first of the major research centers on Russia, created in 1946, Columbia's Russian Institute had dominated the field for a time, along with its counterpart at Harvard, founded in 1948. But in the early 1960s, the Institute seemed to be in a stagnant phase. This at least is what can be gleaned from the exchanges between Alexander Dallin and Brzezinski during the summer of 1962. As Brzezinski described the scene to Dallin:

> When I go to Bowie's outfit or to RRC [Russian Research Center at Harvard], I always get a feeling of a vibrant, energetic environment, of people working and turning things out, of students always somehow in a state of animation and competition. The RI really needs a big kick in the pants; this includes the secretaries, for one often has to wait and fuss to get one's things typed, as well as the staff which is nice and

friendly but perhaps it ought to be a touch less nice and friendly and
more productive. . . . If we want to make an impact and really shape the
thinking of people, and not merely contribute material useful to others
for footnoting, then we ought to bear this in mind in our hiring, and
in inviting people.[5]

Dallin agreed: the scientific standards of the Russian Institute were too
low, the curriculum needed to be revised, and the level of publications—
essentially theses, especially in Russian history—had to be raised. Perhaps,
he suggested, RICA could generate the energy that was lacking in the Russian
Institute.[6] Clearly, RICA was to become a more modest and more agile center
than the Institute; it would go on to generate a great deal of energy around
its indefatigable director and would serve as a platform for receiving scholars
and training students. In 1975, under Brzezinski—who had just returned from
nearly two years away, some of which time was spent managing the Trilateral
Commission—the Research Institute on Communist Affairs changed its name
to the Research Institute on International Change, suggesting a viewpoint that
was now global rather than regional.

In the early 1960s, Brzezinski was still a bona fide academic, a scholar who
specialized in communist affairs. The professor of the Columbia years was no
longer the very young, slightly eccentric lecturer who threatened students with
a billy club to teach them what a totalitarian regime was like in the 1950s. His
courses scored very good reviews, according to the available records. As a teacher
he was described as clear, exciting, and tuned in to current events, yet display-
ing a high level of erudition. He was also seen as demanding and sometimes
acerbic. He made an impression, as evidenced by this recollection by one of
his students, a certain Madeleine Albright, who was to become President Bill
Clinton's secretary of state:

> I first met Brzezinski when, as a young Harvard professor, he had come
> to give a lecture at Wellesley. In the interim he had published *The Soviet
> Bloc,* a perceptive analysis of how Stalin had put together his empire.
>
> He was still only in his mid-thirties but was already being quoted every-
> where and was increasingly visible in policy circles. I thought it essential
> to get into a seminar he was offering on comparative Communism, itself
> a novel idea. With all respect to my other former professors, I judged it

the best course I took in graduate school. The professor was challenging, the material totally new, and the students all thought they were the best.

Brzezinski assigned lengthy readings in Russian without questioning our ability to understand them. Because he was a good friend of my friends the Gardners and I was older than most students, I was able to see his human side. To most of his students, however, he seemed unapproachable. He was brilliant, did not put up with blather, and while he spoke with a Polish accent, he did so in perfect, clear paragraphs. Even at this time there was little doubt he was going to play an important role in US foreign policy.[7]

The Brzezinski of the 1960s was still a true scholar, an erudite researcher who was noted in his field of study, and someone around whom certain structuring debates were organized. The documentary resources of Columbia's Russian Institute replaced those of Harvard's Russian Center, and Brzezinski was able to go on keeping himself remarkably well informed about what was happening on the other side of the Iron Curtain. A self-portrait from 1963 gives an idea of his work rhythm and his intellectual (and social) life:

> Each day I devote a fair amount of my time to keeping up with Communist literature. Usually I begin my morning by reviewing the latest Communist press, various reports and digests. The rest of my morning is normally spent on my own research and further reading and writing. The afternoons are spent in seeing students, in conference, seminars, classes. The evening, when not absorbed by some social event (both my wife and I enjoy plays, dinners, and formal balls) is usually devoted to the perusal of some lengthy Soviet or Chinese statement, on plowing through one of their theoretical or political magazines, or sometimes to listening to Radio Moscow.[8]

This meticulous attention to developments in the USSR provided him with material for several articles on the relationship between ideology and power in the Soviet Union; these were collected in a book published in 1962.[9] Brzezinski's in-depth and constantly updated knowledge also influenced his position on the concept of totalitarianism, and especially the way the concept applied to the contemporary Soviet Union. As noted previously, after the publication of *Totalitarian Dictatorship and Autocracy*—the book he wrote with Carl Friedrich—and in particular after his extended visit to the USSR, Brzezinski had shown more flexibility than his professor in the use of the concept, even as he defended its validity. In October 1961 he spelled out his thinking in "The Nature of the Soviet System" in *Slavic Review.*[10] To define totalitarianism, he chose not to revert to the six characteristics he and Friedrich had enumerated. He argued that totalitarian regimes were distinguished by their politicization of the masses: instead of manipulating social pluralism for their own benefit as authoritarian regimes did, they destroyed that pluralism in order to construct a new society that reflected their ideology. Thus, there were three characteristics of totalitarianism: (1) an ideology based on refounding society and humanity; (2) the absence of moral, legal, or traditional restraints on the exercise of power; (3) a logic of action and destruction or absorption of all the other social groups.[11] Other elements—the single party, the policy of using terror, the monopoly on violence, and the centralized economy—were thus relegated to the background or reformulated as part of one of these three pillars.

The evolution and, in a certain way, the softening of the Soviet regime after de-Stalinization clearly called for a reformulation of the concept of totalitarianism, as Brzezinski saw it. He judged that the roles for terror and secret police corresponded to a specific phase—Stalinism, or a totalitarian breakthrough—but that those instruments, even if they continued to exist, had become much less important under Khrushchev. The Soviet regime had moved on. Yet the next phase did not bring the USSR out of totalitarianism; "the almost frenetic effort of the regime to indoctrinate the masses" and the revitalization of the role of the Communist Party had replaced terror as the means for achieving the changes targeted by the ideology, and it was the determination to change that counted.[12] Moreover, economic modernization, rather than necessarily having a liberalizing effect, was entirely compatible with indoctrination, as demonstrated by the example of Czechoslovakia, in contrast to Poland and Hungary.[13]

It is not surprising that, when Carl Friedrich got in touch with his young coauthor a few weeks after the appearance of Brzezinski's article to propose an update to their book, he expressed some perplexity: "Reading you, and more especially *The Soviet Bloc,* I get the feeling that you have moved somewhat away from our joint position. Is this true?"[14] Brzezinski replied that indeed he had the same concern, and regretted that their geographical separation made it difficult to have the type of prolonged exchanges of views that would allow them to resolve such differences. He added that while the conceptual framework proposed in their 1956 book seemed remarkably well suited to grasping the original features shared by the Nazi regime and the USSR in 1953, the evolution of the Soviet Union and its satellites since then required a serious revision of that framework.[15] This was particularly the case for Poland. As early as 1957, Brzezinski no longer viewed Poland as a totalitarian regime. He described it as resembling Fascist Italy: a totalitarian leadership that was completely ineffective at wielding power, a great deal of residual pluralism, and a national conspiracy to manifest a hard-line discourse with nothing behind it. He indicated that it would also be necessary to add a section on quasi-totalitarian regimes such as those of Cuba and Guinea and another on the relations among totalitarian states, while completely rewriting the sixth chapter, on the pockets of resistance to totalitarianism.[16] In early 1962, Brzezinski and Friedrich finally decided that, for practical reasons but also for more fundamental reasons involving the content, Friedrich would revise the book on his own; it was to be published in 1965 under both of their names, but with a notice indicating that the revisions had been made by Friedrich, who would receive all the royalties for the new edition.[17]

If Brzezinski could not or would not agree to revise *Totalitarian Dictatorship and Autocracy*, it was also because he was overburdened with work. He was without question extraordinarily productive, but in the early 1960s he had made more commitments than he could keep. With his friend Samuel Huntington, who was his colleague at Columbia until 1963, and with the help of a fellowship from the Guggenheim Foundation, he undertook a vast comparison of the American and Soviet system; he and Huntington published their *Political Power: USA / USSR* in 1964.[18] Their goal was to study the theory of convergence, that is the idea, widespread throughout the world and especially in Asia, that the difference between the American and Soviet sociopolitical systems would gradually shrink, with the USSR becoming wealthier and more liberal. The logic underlying this convergence would be that of industrialization, which would be in some ways more determining than the political logic of differentiation. It would lead the two systems to adopt the same types of structures, priorities, and mentalities (bureaucratic organizations, economic efficiency, productivism).[19]

The book had two distinct parts. Huntington and Brzezinski began with a comparative description of the political systems of the two countries, and focused particularly on the role of ideology, on the way the top leaders were selected, and on decision-making mechanisms. They then offered case studies to show how the two systems responded to specific challenges, such as agricultural production (surplus on the American side, deficit for the Soviets), civilian-military relations (General Douglas MacArthur and Marshal Georgy Zhukov), relations with satellite countries (Cuba and Hungary) or with allies (France and China). Ultimately, the authors rejected the theory of convergence, dismissing not only what both of the countries in question understood it to mean (the inevitable absorption of the other system), but also what the rest of the world, including serious scholars, meant by the term. The theory of convergence was based on a single factor, industrialization, whose effects it exaggerated while it neglected the differing national experiences of the United States and the Soviet Union. Moreover, the theory did not take the political factor into account: the sociocultural attitudes of Detroit and Sverdlovsk, two urban centers of auto-mobile construction, were no more likely to converge than those of Detroit and Essen under the Nazis; ideological mobilization and political control would win out over the emergence of common features. In short, in the authors' refutation of convergence, one can find the totalitarian factor between the lines, even if it is not cited as such in the book.

Nevertheless, by the time Friedrich's revised edition of *Totalitarian Dictatorship and Autocracy* appeared in 1965, Brzezinski seemed to be distancing himself increasingly from the concept of totalitarianism and leaning toward that of "degeneration." The Soviets, as he explained in May 1966 in a letter to Friedrich, were not actually exiting from totalitarianism: "I would rather put it that in my view their totalitarianism is decaying. In other words, I do not subscribe to the notion of liberalization of totalitarianism but, on the other hand, I do not believe that it is an immutable and eternal system. My own feeling is that the Soviets have not succeeded in keeping their totalitarianism vital but at the same time the leadership is unwilling to make the necessary adjustments. The consequence is a degenerative process, with the likelihood of a permanent political crisis setting in."[20]

A few months earlier, in *Problems of Communism,* he had published an article that became the point of departure for an animated debate that took place over the next couple of years.[21] In the article, he raised the question of the transformation or decay of the Soviet system, and he spelled out his definition of degeneration, which could apply to tsarist Russia, France under the Third Republic, or the China of Chiang Kai-shek. The issues he listed included standardized and uniformly mediocre leadership; persistent divisions over secondary issues, in the case of the USSR, and no longer over the meaning of history: "a regime of the clerks [who] cannot help but clash over clerical issues."[22] He also noted a certain instability; an inability to define the chief objectives of the political system; and, finally, the participation of groups that had not previously been active in politics (for the USSR, this meant economists, scientists, regional powers, military strategists), which added to the confusion and the impossibility of introducing reforms. He concluded that this was indeed the state of the Soviet system under the ultra-conformist leaders Leonid Brezhnev and Alexei Kosygin, and only bold reforms could relaunch the Soviet political system.

The journal *Problems of Communism* invited Sovietologists, including several foreigners such as Michel Tatu in France, to indicate their positions with regard to Brzezinski's article, and over the next two years twenty-one specialists contributed to the discussion. Brzezinski published a collective response in May 1968 and proposed to represent their positions on a spectrum that went from the evolution of the regime (renovation or gradual adaptation) to revolution (degeneration or even collapse).

As for Brzezinski, he reiterated his conviction that the Soviet Union had entered into the degenerative phase, meaning that those in power were unable to respond to the challenges posed by society, nor could they attract skilled leaders. The Communist Party was no longer a source of innovation but an obstacle to social progress and to growth, owing to the bureaucratic and dogmatic constraints it had put in place, and this opened up an ever-widening gap between society and the political system. The intervention of new groups made the system still more confused and paralyzed, while the aging leadership could neither revert to terror under a single all-powerful dictator nor undertake the necessary reforms. Brzezinski suggested that the USSR would not be capable of sustaining its economic and technological development without major internal changes (a conclusion that the Czechs, he noted, had already reached—Prague Spring was at its peak), and in the long run it would be unable to withstand the economic competition of the West, especially that of the United States. At bottom, he remarked, this was doubtless the expression of a classic cycle of Russian history in which fossilization and stagnation followed periods of activism and modernization driven by the central authorities. But, he added, it would be a mistake to rejoice in such a situation. The modern world, he wrote, was on the eve of a fantastic transformation, the passage to the post-industrial era, which he identified in other texts as the technetronic era. Thus, he warned:

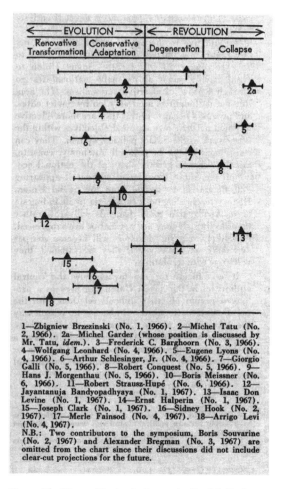

1—Zbigniew Brzezinski (No. 1, 1966). 2—Michel Tatu (No. 2, 1966). 2a—Michel Garder (whose position is discussed by Mr. Tatu, *idem*.). 3—Frederick C. Barghoorn (No. 3, 1966). 4—Wolfgang Leonhard (No. 4, 1966). 5—Eugene Lyons (No. 4, 1966). 6—Arthur Schlesinger, Jr. (No. 4, 1966). 7—Giorgio Galli (No. 5, 1966). 8—Robert Conquest (No. 5, 1966). 9—Hans J. Morgenthau (No. 5, 1966). 10—Boris Meissner (No. 6, 1966). 11—Robert Strausz-Hupé (No. 6, 1966). 12—Jayantanuja Bandyopadhyaya (No. 1, 1967). 13—Isaac Don Levine (No. 1, 1967). 14—Ernst Halperin (No. 1, 1967). 15—Joseph Clark (No. 1, 1967). 16—Sidney Hook (No. 2, 1967). 17—Merle Fainsod (No. 4, 1967). 18—Arrigo Levi (No. 4, 1967).
N.B.: Two contributors to the symposium, Boris Souvarine (No. 2, 1967) and Alexander Bregman (No. 3, 1967) are omitted from the chart since their discussions did not include clear-cut projections for the future.

Fig 2.1 The Views of Sovietologists on the Possible Evolution of the USSR, 1968.

"It is in the interest of all mankind that the second major nuclear power does not remain an increasingly antiquated despotism, a vestigial remnant of 19th-century ideology and of early industrial bureaucratism, committed to domestic and international goals of fading relevance to the new realities."[23]

Brzezinski was sometimes mistaken in his predictions of the future, but was also often right on target, and his characterization of the evolution of the Soviet system belongs to the second category. Moreover, during the years that followed his 1968 article, he shifted his focus away from the USSR and other communist regimes; their unending stagnation made them less interesting. In fact, Sovietology in general declined along with the Soviet Union during the 1970s and 1980s, but Brzezinski had already jumped ship. In the meantime, the concept of totalitarianism as a tool for analyzing the contemporary Soviet Union was abandoned once and for all.

While the academic Brzezinski continued to assert himself as a professor and a scholar during the 1960s, the political Brzezinski—who had earned his first stripes, as we have seen, toward the end of his Harvard years—was gradually coming to the fore. For Brzezinski, it was out of the question to spend his entire career as a professor, however talented he might have been: "Had I been given tenure at Harvard, I would have been delighted and I would have stayed. But then I was forced to think, what do I really want to be? I said to myself I don't want to be crossing the Harvard yard year after year carrying a folder, lecture number 7, 'joke used last year,' 'class reaction,' tweed jacket. I want to influence the world, shape American policy. And New York is better for that."[24]

Brzezinski had been drawn to the political world since childhood, but, just as eating whets the appetite, the attraction became more pronounced in proportion to the degree of success he encountered. In New York, success was not slow in coming, and the key role was played—as it was for Kissinger a few years earlier—by the Council on Foreign Relations (CFR). It was because he published a number of articles in *Foreign Affairs,* the council's journal, that Brzezinski began to be known beyond academic circles. And it was through his connections in the CFR rather than through his contacts at Harvard or Columbia that he was invited to serve on President Lyndon Johnson's Policy Planning Council from 1966 to early 1968.[25]

The editor of *Foreign Affairs,* Hamilton Fish Armstrong, took Brzezinski under his wing. Armstrong was a legend of the Establishment, a gentleman of the old school married to a German woman (his third wife; his first had run off with the journalist Walter Lippmann in the 1930s). Armstrong invited Brzezinski to his elegant receptions and made him one of the most frequent contributors to the journal.[26] Brzezinski even boasted to Robert Bowie, in May 1961, that he had been the first author in *Foreign Affairs* to appear in two issues in a row. In the same letter, more humbly, he thanked Bowie for the recommendation the latter had written in support of his membership in the CFR. During that period, in order to join the CFR one had to be recommended in writing by several current Council members.[27]

Once the formalities had been completed, Brzezinski participated in the Council's activities, in particular in a series of studies on transatlantic relations. The Council asked several experts to lead seminars on the relations between the United States and Europe in 1964, and to turn their talks into publications the following year. Several important books resulted from this initiative: Kissinger's *Troubled Partnership,* which emphasized Western Europe; Brzezinski's *Alternative to Partition,* with a focus on Eastern Europe; and Timothy Stanley's *NATO in Transition,* which offered the US-centric strategic point of view.[28]

His participation in the Council helped make Brzezinski better known, and journalists began to take note of his ability to present complex situations in a synthetic way and to offer trenchant analyses and memorable formulas, all the more so in that he published with increasing frequency in nonspecialist media, most notably in *The New Republic* (nearly an article a year during the 1960s). In 1962, he began to publish op-ed pieces in the *New York Times* and the *Washington Post.* In 1961, for instance, when he published an excerpt from a new chapter of *The Soviet Bloc* devoted to the beginning of the Sino-Soviet schism in *The New Republic,* the well-known journalist Joseph Alsop contacted him enthusiastically to set up an interview.[29] Two weeks later Alsop wrote: "The *New Republic* article has made a useful stir. Mac Bundy [at the time Kennedy's National Security Adviser] was talking to me about it at luncheon."[30] But the journalists did not always play along. In 1964, Brzezinski suggested an analysis to Roscoe Drummond of the *New York Herald Tribune,* who used it as the basis for an entire article: the risk of an accidental or impulsive firing of a nuclear weapon might well exist, but it was greater on the side of the USSR, with its leaders always described by their successors as "irresponsible" and "paranoid." Drummond thanked Brzezinski warmly and promised to give him credit in the future; the latter replied: "And I am not against getting credit."[31]

During this period, Brzezinski also began to appear on radio and television, from the BBC News to *Meet the Press.* In these contexts he was very much at ease, capable here too of summarizing things in a concise and striking way—a talent that drew the attention of another category of actors, politicians seeking analyses of international affairs. In fact, Charles Bartlett, a celebrated journalist at the time (he had received a Pulitzer Prize in 1956 and was close to Kennedy), invited Brzezinski to lunch in August 1961 and assured him that he could be more directly useful in the White House. Brzezinski thanked him for his suggestion and said that he would be prepared, if asked, to serve as a consultant on Sino-Soviet questions, but that the academic context gave him a detached perspective that he did not want to give up. Bartlett promised to pass on to the president a memorandum on the aftermath of the Berlin crisis in which Brzezinski suggested that America propose to the Soviets and to Western Europeans that they jointly launch a program for economic development in Eastern Europe. Such a collaboration would serve to embarrass the Soviets by capitalizing on the Berlin Wall, and in the long run it would attract East Europeans toward the Western orbit by improving their standard of living (yet another scenario aimed at fostering "peaceful engagement").[32]

But the surest channel of communication with President Kennedy remained McGeorge Bundy, the former Harvard dean who was now Kennedy's national security adviser. As early as February 1, 1961, Brzezinski wrote to him to criticize—politely—the reference to Poland in Kennedy's State of the Union address (the president had offered to fund and explore common projects). It would henceforth be more difficult for Warsaw, according to Brzezinski, to accept Washington's overtures publicly.[33] A few months later, he told Bundy about a sensitive conversation he had had with the Polish ambassadors to the United States and to the United Nations about the Berlin Wall crisis, and he offered to follow up on those contacts if Bundy deemed them useful. Bundy replied that it was always good to listen to the Poles but that, "for serious bilateral communication," he had more channels than he could use.[34]

Brzezinski kept sending information to Mac Bundy anyway, especially during the 1962 Cuban Missile Crisis. With Richard Pipes at Harvard, another Pole (the duo was sometimes called the Polintern), he pressed Bundy to treat the situation as strictly an American-Cuban affair and to act firmly with Castro before the Soviets declared officially that they had troops on the island and intended to keep them there. That way Khrushchev would not be able to do very much and the matter would be quickly swept under the rug.[35] As we know from history the crisis developed differently, and Brzezinski sent another letter of advice to his former dean. This time he suggested that the United States should take advantage of the fact that Moscow had announced that the bombers present on the island did not belong to the Soviets. Such action would allow the United States to complete the naval "quarantine" by taking control of Cuban air space via an operation of the Organization of American States; a patrol—it could be called the Cuban Air Space Peace Patrol—could be authorized to shoot down Castro's planes if necessary. That would obviously give the United States a lasting strategic advantage and would weaken both Castro's regime and the image of the USSR as Castro's protector. This action would send a message of firmness along the lines of Kennedy's October 22 speech, when the president denounced the Soviet missile buildup as unacceptable and announced a "quarantine" of Cuba on military equipment to Cuba. Finally, Brzezinski warned Bundy against the temptation to soften the American line and treat Khrushchev with kid gloves to protect the Soviet leader's position vis-à-vis the Politburo's "hard-liners." On the contrary, Brzezinski indicated, the United States had to show that adventurism did not pay, and that Khrushchev had pulled back in the face of a real danger—a tactic accepted in communist doctrine—and not an imaginary one. No response to this letter from Bundy has been found in the archives.[36]

In contrast, Brzezinski was delighted when he received a letter signed by President Kennedy congratulating him on his opinion piece in the *Washington Post,* immediately after the Cuban Missile Crisis had been resolved (November 4, 1962).[37] In that text, Brzezinski emphasized in particular how important the effect of surprise had been in Kennedy's October 22 speech. If he had followed the reasonable recommendations of some of the observers and warned the Soviets of the quarantine in advance, Khrushchev would have been able to accelerate matters and gain the diplomatic upper hand, or else he would have had to prove by force that the blockade had not been a bluff.[38] Brzezinski had his colleague Richard Neustadt authenticate the signature (it was indeed Kennedy's, even though it didn't look like his official signature) and hung it on the wall of his Columbia office.[39] Clearly, Brzezinski's channels of communication with the Kennedy White House were limited.

By contrast, under the Johnson administration, before he was called to the State Department, Brzezinski had more direct relations with the vice president. He met with Hubert Humphrey in the White House in 1965 and followed up on their discussion by sending a memorandum on the US policy toward Europe—with particular attention to the challenge posed by French president Charles de Gaulle—in which Brzezinski promoted his policy of peaceful engagement.[40] In addition, Brzezinski was sometimes asked by the Senate Foreign Affairs Committee to comment on Soviet matters, or, in 1965, on transatlantic relations,[41] and also by the CIA: he participated in sessions devoted to analysis, most notably concerning the Sino-Soviet schism in 1962.[42] All this activity put him in a marginal position with respect to power, up to 1966, but his networks were expanding and his reputation increasing.

Brzezinski continued to accumulate marks of recognition and social ascension. In 1963, he was selected as one of the "Ten Outstanding Young Men" of the year by the Junior Chamber of Commerce; he had been nominated and supported by Representative John Brademas.[43] He was also becoming a celebrity in Polish-American circles, where he was a frequent guest. In May 1962 he participated in an American-Polish roundtable organized by the Ford Foundation; it was held near Warsaw and included Polish authorities and other leading figures. On the American side, among others, there were Hubert Humphrey, Shepard Stone (director of international affairs at the Ford Foundation), and the presidents of several companies such as McGraw-Hill.[44] Four years later Brzezinski received the Alfred Jurzykowski Foundation prize (the "Millennium Award") for his "creative work"; subsequently, he used his influence with that group in seeking support for various projects.[45] Going beyond the Council on Foreign Relations, he was also invited to the Bilderberg Group meetings (as of 1966 if not earlier), and sometimes to the Wehrkunde Transatlantic Conference.

This rapid social ascension was accompanied by an improvement in his material circumstances. The young man of limited means who had arrived at Harvard in September 1950 and the young bridegroom who had set off on his honeymoon with a meager student budget had become an established professor with a good salary from Columbia ($19,000 in 1966, $29,000 in 1971), he was receiving significant royalty payments, plus honoraria for his lectures and consultancies.[46] He and his wife, childless for ten years, had a son, Ian, in 1963; then another one, Mark, in 1965; and a daughter, Mika, in 1967. Their comfortable financial situation allowed them to buy a vacation home in Northeast Harbor, on Mount Desert Island in Maine, through the intermediary of William Burden, an entrepreneur friend. Zbigniew regularly spent the month of August there, and he often socialized at the Seal Harbor Club with prestigious summer residents such as David Rockefeller. The Brzezinskis came close to losing their house during their housewarming party in October 1967. Because the weather was dreary, they decided to make a fire. But the chimney caught fire and the blaze began to spread; a visit from the fire department put an end to the "housewarming."[47] A few years later, the journalist Robert Scheer had the opportunity to see Brzezinski at his Mount Desert property. Scheer observed:

"Vacationing at his Northeast Harbor, Me., summer home, [Brzezinski] proved to be an interested father to his three children and almost boyish himself as he raced about at excessive speeds in his powerboat and his Mercedes. . . . Seeing him in Maine, one has the sense of a man who is enormously pleased with the upward mobility of his life and deeply grateful for the opportunities this country presents to its immigrants."[48]

From the late Harvard years on, Brzezinski looked beyond the USSR toward Eastern Europe, but also toward the Third World. This tendency increased considerably during the 1960s, with articles and books that covered a much broader spectrum than before. His field of expertise was the starting point, but these publications took on the whole world: Sino-Soviet relations, Africa, transatlantic relations, and the hot topics of American foreign policy in Cuba, for example, and especially the war in Vietnam. His texts were based on knowledge of the world that his travels continued to enlarge. In 1963 he took a sabbatical year and traveled around the world, visiting the Far East, including Kemoy and Thailand, the Middle East, Russia, and Western Europe.[49] If he was clairvoyant regarding Africa and the communist world, he was both subtle in the broad outlines and unrealistic in his recommendations when he dealt with Europe. But it was his steadfastly hawkish position on Vietnam that remains the most controversial.

In 1962, Brzezinski spent a month and a half traveling on the African continent, seeking to supplement his scholarly knowledge of a subject on which he was editing a book, *Africa and the Communist World*.[50] He by no means claimed to be an Africanist, but, following RICA's mission, he claimed to be shedding light on the relations between communist countries and Africa, and on the relations among communist countries on the subject of Africa. The various chapters examined the political and economic initiatives of the major actors: the USSR (Alexander Dallin, Alexander Erlich, and Christian Sonne), Eastern Europe (Robert and Elizabeth Bass), Yugoslavia (William Griffith), and finally China (Richard Lowenthal). Brzezinski, for his part, offered an introduction and a conclusion that opened up future perspectives on the subject.

The communist countries' interest in Africa, he noted, had begun in 1956, as they became fully cognizant of the ideological stakes represented by the Third World. But penetrating Africa was not simple, first owing to the lower level of development in the communist world as compared to the West, a lag that was a handicap for external economic assistance, then because of the conditions of decolonization (the colonizers had departed voluntarily, a pattern that did not conform to communist predictions), and finally because the Soviets, the Europeans, and the Chinese were unfamiliar with African practices and customs. Of course, they were helped by the connection that had been established between capitalism and imperialism thanks to elites often trained in left-leaning European universities, and also by the concept of neocolonialism. But the communists from the north bumped up against an old problem: the articulation between communism and nationalism, the latter being highly developed among the elite that emerged after independence. The concepts of Negritude or the African personality, Brzezinski noted, left the communists perplexed. In his conclusion he offered the following prognosis: "There is at present little likelihood that any of the new African states will espouse Communism or even associate itself fully with the Communist bloc. The desire to be independent and non-aligned is so strong, so intense, and so widely shared that any move in that direction, either through local initiative or under Communist pressure, is likely to result in a strong counterreaction."[51]

He was more pessimistic as to the long term, judging that the new countries would have trouble modernizing quickly in the absence of a dictatorial regime, and that liquidation of the remaining pockets of white supremacy risked supplying the Soviets with an ideal opportunity to get involved in Africa. More generally, Brzezinski predicted that, despite their official support of continental unity, the communists would favor the Balkanization of sub-Saharan Africa, which would offer a better context for their maneuvers. In the end, he recommended to the Western democracies, and especially to the United States, that they be sensitive to the importance that the Africans attached to the liquidation of the last vestiges of colonialism: "American neutralism on this subject cannot help but produce something less than African neutralism in the East-West conflict."[52]

Brzezinski was on target with regard to Africa, as his predictions came to pass, by and large. Concerning the division of Europe, he developed an analytic framework that history has tended to justify in its broad outlines, but in slightly different forms: Östpolitik and détente rather than the "peaceful engagement" he advocated. We have already seen the first act of the reflection that led to the 1961 *Foreign Affairs* article, "Peaceful Engagement in Eastern Europe," and then to his work for the Council on Foreign Relations, which was published in book form as *Alternative to Partition* in 1965: It was the Budapest uprising, or rather America's passivity, that led him to conclude that neither containment preserving the status quo nor the rhetoric of "liberation" were serious policies, and that a radical change of approach was necessary. Thus he defended the idea of democratic neutralization of the countries of Eastern Europe. In a 1961 article he wrote for *Foreign Affairs* with his friend Bill Griffith (another specialist in Eastern Europe, from MIT, who had worked for Radio Free Europe in the 1950s), he had formulated his ideas differently.

The policy of peaceful engagement was based on an analysis of the weaknesses of the Soviet regime, which was incapable of responding to the aspirations of the populace in terms of economic progress or political liberties. Peaceful engagement meant embracing Eastern Europe as closely as possible in order to transform it gradually and tug it away from Moscow's orbit. Since the West was not ready to commit fully to a strategy of support for uprisings, it needed to stop claiming that it had such a strategy, that it envisaged a possible victory in those terms. Instead it should pursue the same objectives—increasing diversity within the Soviet bloc and loosening the ties between the countries of Eastern Europe and Moscow—through a different and more effective policy. Thus America and the Western European countries should significantly increase their economic exchanges with Eastern Europe rather than leaving the region in relative stagnation on the assumption that doing so could lead to discontent and regime toppling (the politics of "the worse the better"). On the contrary, economic development of the region, binding it to the West, would encourage the desire for independence. More generally, Western Europeans should make their Eastern counterparts political and cultural partners rather than adversaries, while multiplying educational, scientific, intellectual, and artistic exchanges among civil societies in order to expose populations to their power of attraction.

The Federal Republic of Germany in particular was encouraged to abandon the Hallstein Doctrine that forbade it to have relations with countries that recognized East Germany, at least where nations that had no real choice were concerned (constrained as they were by Moscow); that would enable it to make its influence freely felt in the region. It should also accept the Oder-Neisse line more unequivocally, for the prevailing uncertainty allowed the communists to maintain Poland in a state of hostility in that regard. All this should be accomplished, Brzezinski and Griffith noted, while the ideological struggle would continue, chiefly through radio broadcasts. The aim was still the constitution of a belt of neutral states on the model of Finland, not via an explicit demand addressed to the USSR, but as the result of an internal process in the Eastern countries; the West would guarantee not to exploit those states and would respect Moscow's strategic interests. One cannot rule out the possibility that what Brzezinski had in mind, with this policy, was to pave the way for a more traditional and less unrealistic outcome, namely, insurrection, a revolt against the Soviet yoke—but this time a more massive and successful insurrection. This hypothesis was of course not spelled out, because a certain consent from Moscow, a certain détente, as it were, was required for the policy of peaceful engagement to be possible, setting in motion, theoretically, a virtuous circle between the two superpowers. "In the long run," Brzezinski and Griffith wrote, after making specific recommendations for each country in Eastern Europe, "a gradual change in Eastern Europe which neither challenges Soviet security nor abandons the area to the Soviets, may also help to improve American-Soviet relations."[53]

Three years later, at the Council on Foreign Relations, Kissinger and Brzezinski delivered concurrent lectures on transatlantic relations; both appeared in book form in 1965. For the most part Brzezinski's *Alternative to Partition* pursued the themes of his 1961 article. Contrary to other observers such as George Kennan, for whom a certain disengagement from Europe, including military disengagement, was the prerequisite for an East-West rapprochement, Brzezinski insisted on the key role of the United States. On the one hand, the United States had to keep a standing military presence in Europe that would be powerful enough to contain the USSR. On the other hand, it needed to take the initiative toward the goal of transforming relationships and offering an alternative to the partition of Europe (the first imperative being the condition of possibility for the second). Europe could not do this on its own, if only because it needed an easing of US-Soviet tensions in order to succeed. America needed to invite its Western European partners to come together and formulate "a joint all-European economic development plan" that would be addressed to the East.[54] In Brzezinski's subsequent texts, this idea became that of a "community of the developed nations" that would include both Western and Eastern Europe and in the long term, potentially, the USSR. In Brzezinski's thinking, the countries of Eastern Europe, some of which were farther along than others on the path to modernity, could have a moderating influence on Russia's political and ideological development. Trade could serve as a tool to encourage or punish good or bad pupils, provided that the US Congress agreed to leave more freedom to the executive branch. Multilateral organizations such as the Organization for Economic Co-operation and Development (OECD) could also contribute to socializing the Eastern Europeans.[55]

This stance on the part of an America that would take the initiative also corresponds to a desire to counter Charles de Gaulle. Brzezinski was not fundamentally hostile toward the general; he approved of the latter's aspiration to move beyond the logic of blocs, but he judged that de Gaulle could not succeed in this effort on his own. "Isolated from the US and Germany," Brzezinski wrote in 1964, "France can only obstruct, not construct."[56] This is because France had to contend with suspicion on the part of the other Europeans, who did not want to see a Franco-German condominium, and there was skepticism even on the part of the Germans, for whom the United States remained the closest ally. In short, the Europe that would extend from the Atlantic to the Urals could only be built in partnership with Washington. De Gaulle's policy ultimately risked driving America out of Western Europe without driving the USSR out of Eastern Europe, and it risked encouraging other nationalisms.[57] Brzezinski, although he was close to Robert Bowie, was not a particularly ardent defender of the multilateral nuclear force (MLF, a joint force entailing submarines equipped with nuclear weapons maintained by NATO allies). In 1963 he wrote to congratulate Bowie on an article that had just come out, which he described as "the most persuasive case yet made on behalf of the multilateral force"—but with no indication that he agreed with it.[58] He found the idea interesting as a way of defending Western Europe robustly while avoiding the multiplication of national strike forces, but he remained skeptical. And in any case he condemned Moscow's knee-jerk rejection.[59] Although his approach was not that of a fierce Atlanticist, he saw American leadership in Europe as a necessity.

The vision proposed in *Alternative to Partition* was attacked on three points. First, its grand plan for economic development seemed inordinately sweeping. Next, the Soviet Union and even Eastern Europe would not necessarily be receptive to the initiatives Brzezinski was suggesting. He gave many logical reasons why Moscow had nothing to fear from his proposals, as these were in conformity with the declarations of the Soviet leaders about peaceful coexistence, the necessity of economic development, peace and security, and so on. But there is a big difference between saying and doing, and the Soviets also knew how to read between Brzezinski's lines. Finally, his recommendation in favor of opening the flood gates in relations with Eastern Europe while continuing to isolate the German Democratic Republic (GDR)—which, in Brzezinski's view, was an anachronism to be resolved—was met with a good deal of skepticism. To Pierre Hassner, a French specialist in international relations he had befriended at Harvard, who pointed this out, Brzezinski replied that his position entailed a certain logic of communication (it would be easier to sell the plan to the Germans) and of long-term reassurance (the Germans must not be able to reproach the Americans later on for having signed off on the division of their country).[60] Nevertheless, Brzezinski was on target with his prognosis regarding the logic of détente and the way it would work (exposure of the Eastern European populations to the magnetic attraction of the West), but he failed to see the key role that the two Germanys would play.

A doubt persists, nevertheless, as to Brzezinski's underlying intentions. Did his long-term strategic calculation consist in detaching the countries of Eastern Europe from Moscow's orbit on the strength of their economic development and their exposure to contacts with the West? In other words, did it consist in creating the conditions for breaking up the Soviet bloc? Or or did it rather consist in diffusing the tensions of the Cold War and in creating an environment that would make it possible to achieve, in the long run, a sort of softening or humanizing of the communists throughout the Soviet bloc, including the Russians? In July 1967 he sent Vice President Humphrey a memorandum summarizing a discussion they had had, and here he seems clearly to lean toward the second option:

> The one issue on which there was a sharp division of opinion concerned the problem of our attitude toward Eastern Europe. Should we try to do in East Europe what the Soviet Union is trying to do in Western Europe—i.e. try to fragment it and to detach it from the respective major alliance system? In my view, while we ought to try to increase East European independence as a *tactical* goal we should not lose sight of our major *strategic* objective—namely, the creation of a broader framework of stability that eventually includes both the Soviet Union and Eastern Europe.
>
> Our goal should therefore be different than that of the Soviets in Western Europe—because we are stronger, because we are less ideological, because we have a broader global perspective.[61]

In any case, in *The Troubled Partnership,* Kissinger took a different approach. Primarily, his book was focused on Western Europe and dealt essentially with military questions, nuclear weapons in particular (an entire chapter was devoted to a systematic refutation of the MLF advocated by Kissinger's "intimate enemy" Robert Bowie). Kissinger stressed the divergences of historical perspective between Europe and the United States and the need to allow the allies a degree of autonomy, the importance of making joint decisions. His views were based above all on a conviction that the Alliance had to be revitalized so it could stand up to the USSR, with an underlying assumption that the status quo would have to be accepted; he expressed no hope for change. But the difference between the two authors goes even further. Brzezinski, optimistic about the chances that the West would win out in the peaceful competition he was proposing, envisioned a fluid, open situation. Kissinger, by contrast, was consistently pessimistic, especially about Germany, which he thought might be vulnerable to sweet talk from Moscow, and about the potential for détente; far from facilitating the eventual reunification of Germany, détente might well lead Moscow to conclude that the separation could continue at no cost. Between Brzezinski and Kissinger, whose personal relations were good (they exchanged friendly remarks and jokes by mail), this was the first serious public debate on international issues.

While Brzezinski looked rather dovish toward Europe, with his policy of peaceful engagement (which is obviously not a policy of accommodation designed to last), he often took a harder line on other topics, such as the Cuban Missile Crisis. Moreover, a few days after that crisis, he examined the implications of the new situation and set forth his perception of US-Soviet relations. Kennedy's reaction made it possible to thwart Russia's plans to acquire an immediate nuclear advantage and to benefit from a favorable strategic uncertainty in the person of Fidel Castro. But it was necessary to go beyond a merely defensive approach, for America would find itself in a structurally unfavorable position if it did not display its resolve firmly.

> There would be no Berlin problem if the Soviet Union was a status quo power. It could then allow the reunification of Germany under explicit guarantees for Soviet security. But the Soviet Union is not a status quo power; it is a revolutionary one. Moreover, it is an increasingly self-confident revolutionary power. . . .

Because we are the status quo power, we cannot afford a strategic
parity and must always strive for both nuclear and strategic superiority.
The automatic and fashionable equivalents [*sic*] of our bases and theirs
simply ignores the intellectually more difficult problem of assessing who
is trying to expand and who is primarily favoring the status quo.[62]

In other words, Khrushchev's gamble must not lead the United States to
negotiate an aspect of the relationship that had not been at stake before (such
as the US military bases in Turkey or in Berlin). Otherwise, America's strategic
superiority would crumble little by little under Khrushchev's continued bluff-
ing. In the negotiation, the United States had to put existing Soviet interests
such as their presence in Berlin and in East Germany in the balance; this was
the only way the USSR would come in its turn to appreciate and to defend the
status quo. In the short run, according to Brzezinski, Washington could not
tolerate a Cuban threat. If it became clear that the missiles already present in
Cuba were equipped with nuclear warheads, if the military sites were expanded
and if training of Cubans continued despite the naval blockade, "then we may
have no choice but to destroy this threat before Castro is capable of forcing us
to take the measures the President pledged would follow the firing of a single
missile from Cuba [that is, a nuclear attack on the USSR]."[63]

In strategic terms, whether the USSR should be viewed as an essentially
defensive power or, on the contrary, as evolutionary or revisionist (in relation
to the international order defended by the US) was a central question in American debates throughout the Cold War. It came up again to haunt the Carter
administration in 1978 during the debate over the Horn of Africa, where the
Soviets and the Cubans had established a military foothold. A constant element
in Brzezinski's discourse was the representation of the USSR as an "expansionist opportunist" that had to be contained with great firmness. Allowing the
Soviets, in a spirit of accommodation or détente, to rack up advances here and
there, turning a blind eye to their support for Cuba or, during the 1970s, to the
Cubans' actions in Africa, would end up reinforcing rather than softening
the hard-liners in the Politburo. Thus in 1962 Kennedy had to react firmly, not
gently, if he wanted to reinforce Khrushchev's internal position; the hard-liners
would never forgive him for yielding to anything but a real risk.

More generally, good Soviet-American relations could only be based, as
Brzezinski saw it, on respect for the status quo. That is why he insisted on the

fact that détente had to be balanced, reciprocal, and inclusive of all aspects of the relationship, rather than allowing the Soviets to advance their pawns in the Third World while the European situation remained frozen. This argument formed the core of his criticism of Kissinger in the mid-1970s. The domestic facet of that argument was the risk of a nationalist American backlash if Washington allowed Moscow do as it pleased; this would lead to an even more tense situation, and perhaps even to a crisis. This was Brzezinski's interpretation of what took place between 1978, when he preached in vain for a strong reaction to the Soviet advances in the Horn, and the nationalist wave of 1980 accompanied by a rejection of détente and by a new Cold War. In short, Brzezinski's vision borrowed a great deal from the Munich analogy: Russia was an expansionist totalitarian power that had to be contained with great firmness.

The pitfall, for this vision was Vietnam, and this was the area in which Brzezinski's hard-line was to be the most clearly expressed. His support for a firm stance in Vietnam can be explained by three general geopolitical considerations: the domino theory, the fear of emboldening China and allowing it to upset the relatively stable strategic equilibrium that had been achieved between the USSR and the United States, and, finally, the latter's credibility. In March 1964, Brzezinski reacted to the press conference during which General de Gaulle suggested a "neutralization" of South Vietnam by reading the proposal as a reproduction of de Gaulle's Algerian strategy. Rather than immediately announcing a withdrawal, de Gaulle thought it would be better to use an intermediate formula more acceptable to all parties; in Vietnam's case, this could be the formula of neutralization. Brzezinski argued that de Gaulle was mistaken in perceiving neutralization as a viable option. South Vietnam would not be neutral for long; it would fall into China's lap, transforming the entire region into a Chinese zone of influence without any counter-power, thus leading to the domino effect ("A Row of Dominoes" is a subhead given to Brzezinski's opinion piece in the *Washington Post*).[64] Thailand would become increasingly unstable; so would Malaysia, where communist uprisings were already threatening, and so would Burma. The fall of those Southeast Asian regimes, accompanied by China's increasing power, would have destabilizing effects reaching from Indonesia to India.

In Brzezinski's view, "just as the aggressors have been contained in Europe and countervailing forces have been developed, so in Asia the Chinese should and can be contained, thereby giving a breathing spell to the emerging and developing nations."[65] He added that, if America allowed China free rein and if China succeeded in its support of revolutionary wars, it would win a level of prestige that would place the USSR under enormous pressure in the eyes of the world, and Moscow would then be tempted to follow Beijing's example, a posture that it had been tending to abandon up to that point. Finally, in America, a Chinese victory could reawaken a phase of McCarthyist reaction, with the far right seizing the theme of treason once again. Brzezinski sent a copy of his article to Robert Bowie, along with a memorandum detailing the suggestions he had made in his 1963 article in *Foreign Affairs* on ways to contain Ho Chi Minh.[66] He did it so that Bowie could transmit it to the White House, which he did.[67]

Brzezinski's vision of China was doubtless exaggerated, even more so in that support for North Vietnam was increasingly coming not from its hereditary Chinese enemy but from the USSR. Brzezinski attributed the intensity of Peking's revolutionary engagement to the fact that China was undergoing three revolutions simultaneously: Communist, nationalist, and industrial. This situation made it difficult to reach an understanding with a regime in constant flux or to advance the cause of regional stability.[68] In any case, he was convinced that American involvement in the region was justified by the need to counter Beijing's radicalism and to prove to the Soviets that their restraint, since 1962 in any case, constituted a better policy. In 1965, he did not think a massive intervention on the part of the Soviets was probable, as Moscow would not want to bail China out.[69]

The third element that counted in Brzezinski's position was that of American credibility. Here, it may be that his travels fed into a sort of imperial logic, owing to his vivid perception of the expectations on the part of the rest of the world that America would play an active role. After all, many high-ranking political leaders and other elite figures whom he had met were allies of the United States who had an interest in increasing the protection offered by the big brother. In July 1963, after his grand tour of Asia, he confided that he had been struck by the way his interlocutors, especially in the Far East, expected America to play the role of leader in international affairs.[70] He had also benefited from support from the Thai government to visit the northeastern part of the country where a communist uprising was being hatched (and he had made an additional incursion into Laos).[71] In his *Washington Post* opinion piece the following year, he specifically mentioned this northeastern region as a weak point that could bring down the Thai domino, and he mentioned local politicians who were "already fearful that American commitments are not to be trusted."[72] But it was America's credibility in Europe that counted the most. In October 1965, he wrote to Hassner, disagreeing with him on the subject: "As far as Asia is concerned, my view is that American engagement there is absolutely necessary, for psychological and political reasons, to sustain also an American engagement in Europe. Europeans are wrong to think that they can force us out of Asia but keep us in Europe. As I said, both for psychological as well as political reasons, disengagement in one would lead to disengagement in [the] other."[73]

Until 1968, Brzezinski maintained the same arguments, in his public discussions as well as in his private conversations. Early on, he was optimistic about America's chances of success in Vietnam. Writing in May 1965 to an Indian friend, he used the domino theory and the need to contain China as the chief justifications for the war, and added in a jovial tone: "At the time of writing your letter you were quite concerned about the effect on the future of the policies recommended by the 'Hawks.' As you well know, hawks are clean-cut birds, unlike doves (which is merely a polite word for pidgeons [sic]). That is why I am on their side, and so far I am quite optimistic about the consequence of what's being done."[74]

A few months later, writing to one of his doctoral students, he noted that the policy of intervention, designed to avoid contagion, had proved successful quite recently, when the Indonesian army had put down the communist rebellion, and he maintained that the regional effects of that policy counted more than what was happening in Vietnam. Two years later, the same student questioned him again, and Brzezinski confided that he still held the same view, but that he was more pessimistic than before.[75] This indicated a change of opinion that dated from late 1967 and early 1968. Prior to that point, however, Brzezinski was personally involved with American policy in Vietnam, through his work for the State Department's Policy Planning Council.

On Lyndon Johnson's Policy Planning Staff

Brzezinski's membership in the Council on Foreign Relations and his frequent contributions to *Foreign Affairs* and other publications led directly to his first actual involvement in international policy making, from July 1966 to January 1968. After he had served as consultant to the State Department on several occasions, he received a telephone call from Henry Owen, asking him on behalf of Walt Rostow whether he would like to join the Policy Planning Staff (PPS) as a full-time member.[76] Known at the time as the Policy Planning Council, the organ of the State Department charged with thinking strategically over the long term had been created in 1947 by George Marshall and led first by George Kennan, followed by Paul Nitze and Robert Bowie, then (after two less noteworthy directors) Walt Rostow (1961–1966) and Henry Owen (1966–1969).

By the time Brzezinski joined the PPS, it had lost its original splendor. Under Kennedy, Secretary of State Dean Rusk used it somewhat less than his predecessors had; under the Johnson administration, the center of gravity of decisions about foreign policy shifted unmistakably toward McNamara's Pentagon and even more toward the White House, thus to the National Security Council (NSC) and other presidential advisers, particularly when Rostow replaced McGeorge Bundy as national security adviser. Looking back, Brzezinski added that Rusk did not think in strategic or political terms; he saw himself more as an adviser charged with reflecting the president's preferences rather than suggesting policies. In addition, he did not like to see the administration's strategic options cast into doubt by his troops, especially his subordinates. Finally, the Vietnam question had a powerful tendency to override all other subjects and any efforts at planning.[77]

In a first phase, then, Brzezinski found himself isolated and without real intermediaries, since even the then director Owen, to whom he was close, did not often have the administration's ear. Brzezinski had only limited access to the sources, and had to fight to be put on the distribution list for the issues that interested him: primarily American-Soviet relations. Under these circumstances, if he wanted to have an impact he had to go beyond his marginal institutional position and bypass the State Department, which was itself increasingly marginalized during the final years of the Johnson administration. Not being a professional diplomat or a foreign service officer, he could to some extent get around the hierarchical rules and establish contacts apart from the flow charts without putting his career at risk. He became an independent entrepreneur whose base was the PPS, but whose antennae were in the White House. As he himself put it, he short-circuited the hierarchical paths and passed contraband notes of analysis and recommendations directly to Johnson's advisers, many of whom he knew personally; for example, Harry McPherson, Bill Moyers, Hayes Redmon, and John Roche. It is revealing that all these men were advisers concerned primarily with domestic affairs (McPherson was a special adviser, Moyers the press attaché, Roche a personal adviser), and none of them belonged to Rostow's NSC, where the person in charge of Europe was Francis Bator.[78]

Thanks to these contacts, on several occasions Brzezinski was able to see the president directly and discuss US-Soviet relations with him. He found that, contrary to his reputation, Johnson listened attentively to what was being said. But Brzezinski's success in bypassing the hierarchical structures was not appreciated by everyone. Thus, countering the views expressed by Secretary of State Rusk and by Averell Harriman, Brzezinski presented directly to the president his opinion that the Soviets, despite their declarations, were in no way helping the Americans in Vietnam. Quite the opposite. According to Brzezinski, they were surreptitiously acting to prolong the war, which benefited them on every level, including that of Chinese-American relations, which were made more difficult. Johnson then asked him for a memorandum on the subject, which Brzezinski wrote and Johnson later read to the National Security Council, to Harriman's fury. Because Harriman's own interests were at stake, given the role of intermediary that he could play, he was less well disposed toward Brzezinski than ever. Fortunately, Brzezinski had taken care to leave a copy of the memo on Rusk's desk, and thus did not find himself in a compromised position when the secretary of state summoned him the next day and called him to account.[79]

But Brzezinski's main accomplishment came about a few months after he joined the PPS in the summer of 1966; his influence was perceptible in the speech Johnson gave on October 7, 1966, to the National Conference of Editorial Writers. The talk is sometimes identified as "East-West Discourse," or the "bridge-building speech," or even, tellingly, the "peaceful engagement" speech.[80] In it, Johnson discussed US relations with Western Europe, Eastern Europe, and the USSR, and introduced two noteworthy developments in American policy: German reunification was no longer a prerequisite for easing the tensions with the East; on the contrary, it would be a result of reduced tension. America was shifting from a policy of coexistence with the USSR to a policy of peaceful engagement; this would entail a massive increase in exchanges, especially with Eastern Europe. In short, Johnson adopted two ideas that Brzezinski had been defending since 1961. It is true that the administration had already taken steps in that direction. For example, in a speech delivered in May 1964, Johnson had brought up the need to "build bridges" with the East

in order to wear away the Iron Curtain, and the idea of no longer making German reunification a prerequisite had gained support within the administration,
even if it had not been expressed officially for fear of offending Bonn. But the
October 7 speech marked a real political turning point.

In his widely respected book on Johnson's European foreign policy, subtitled
In the Shadow of Vietnam, Thomas Schwartz does not mention Brzezinski's
role.[81] The reason for this is that Bator, who contributed a great deal to the
book, denied that Brzezinski had had any role at all in the speech. According to Bator, the starting point was a memo written jointly with Rostow on
May 18, 1966, suggesting that the president give a speech on the American
policy toward Europe. This idea was taken up again in the report made by the
Acheson group, which met with the former secretary of state in June to bring
up the question of NATO. Then the National Security Action Memorandum of
July 8 (NSAM no. 352), emanating from the NSC, instructed the secretary of state
to propose to the president concrete acts of cooperation with Eastern Europe
and the USSR in order to create a favorable context for peaceful resolution of
the division in Germany and in Europe. On these bases, Bator indicated, he
himself had produced a memo in August that was transformed by one of his
associates into a draft speech, then into a speech. In other words, there had
been no intervention from outside the NSC.[82]

It is difficult to agree with Bator and conclude that Brzezinski played no
role at all. The speech had three parts: the modernization of NATO, European integration, and East-West relations, with the innovations and political
shifts discussed in the third part. And this third part closely resembles all that
Brzezinski had written since the *Foreign Affairs* article, "Peaceful Engagement
in Eastern Europe," most notably in his *Alternative to Partition* (which had
come out the previous year, in 1965). Johnson declared, in particular: "We
must improve the East-West environment in order to achieve the unification of
Germany in the context of a larger, peaceful, and prosperous Europe. Our task
is to achieve a reconciliation with the East—a shift from the narrow concept
of coexistence to the broader vision of peaceful engagement."[83]

This is followed by a list of concrete actions that had already been carried out and an announcement of new measures, many of which had been
recommended by Brzezinski (facilitation of economic exchanges, easing of
Poland's debt burden, liberalization of regulations governing travel to the
East, and so on). In addition, an agreement with Western European countries

to develop this policy of extending a hand had to be reached—yet another aspect that is found in Brzezinski. Johnson declared, too, that "the OECD can also play an important part in trade and in contacts with the East. The Western nations can there explore the ways of inviting the Soviet Union and the Eastern European countries to cooperate in tasks of common interest and common benefit."[84] *Alternative to Partition* presents precisely the same idea: "Consideration could be given to special arrangements providing for the accession of communist states to some sort of association with OECD, at least to the extent of inviting them to participate in particular phases of the work that concern them."[85]

In interviews, here is how Brzezinski has described the genesis of the speech. He explained that he cooperated closely with Henry on the speech, starting from ideas he had already expressed in *Alternative to Partition.* "We got the speech into the White House, and there, both Walt Rostow and Francis Bator worked on it."[86] When a documentalist from the LBJ Library questioned him in 1971 about his memories, she gave priority to this speech, reflecting the widespread opinion that Brzezinski had influenced it. She asked him whether "50 to 70 percent of the words" had come from him, as she had heard, and Brzezinski answered in the affirmative, although he corrected the proportion: "Well, certain words. Yes, that's true."[87]

Two things are certain. First, Brzezinski sincerely believed that he influenced the speech. Thus, two weeks later, he confided in a personal letter to Daniel Bell: "I am glad that you read right Johnson's speech. The European reaction to it has so far been excellent. Also, because of it, my stay in Washington is proving to be much more fruitful and exciting than I ever dared to anticipate."[88] Second, he was widely credited for it. A profile in *Newsweek* dated November 14, 1966, pointed out that the expression "peaceful engagement" came from his book.[89] At the State Department, Brzezinski's colleagues held him responsible—jokingly— for the fall of Chancellor Ludwig Erhard, which took place a few weeks later (it was in fact accelerated by Johnson's speech, which came across as a snub vis-à-vis the German position on reunification).[90] Raymond Garthoff, for example, in his classic book *Détente and Confrontation,* indicated that it was Brzezinski who wrote the draft of the speech.[91] And even Bator said that a Soviet diplomat whom he asked, a year later, why there had not been more of a response to the idea of peaceful engagement, answered that, as the idea had been Brzezinski's, the Soviets had immediately mistrusted it.[92]

Johnson's speech coincided perfectly with the political line Brzezinski had been defending since 1961, or even 1957, and especially in his 1965 book. At a minimum, Brzezinski influenced the speech indirectly, since he had helped fashion the intellectual environment in which it was produced, and had also supplied one of his key formulations, "peaceful engagement." In the end, if he in fact had no part in writing the speech, as Bator asserted, the misattribution is easy to understand. A secondary point also that needs elucidation: Johnson's attitude toward the shift in the US position on German reunification. Brzezinski suggests that the president had not been fully aware of the scope of this shift and had been surprised by the violence of the reactions on the German side.[93] Bator, on the contrary, asserts that the change had come from LBJ's personal convictions.[94]

As for the effects of the speech, they were mixed: a political leap was indeed made on the question of German reunification, which became officially a goal for peaceful engagement and no longer a prerequisite. But a number of the concrete measures proposed were held up by a Congress reluctant to build bridges with regimes that were supplying material and political aid to North Vietnam.[95] Brzezinski, for his part, has indicated that the reactions of the East were less important than those of the allies; a change in their attitude was the primary goal.[96] It is fair to say that this speech helped increase American pressure on Germany in favor of a revision of the Hallstein Doctrine, opening the way to a revision of Östpolitik, three years later, in a spirit close to Brzezinski's but following different paths.

The events surrounding Johnson's speech reveal a new facet of Brzezinski's personality: his skill at playing the bureaucracy. He had navigated between Harriman and Rusk to defend his own viewpoint to the president without getting into trouble for violating the principle of hierarchy; in connection with the speech, he succeeded in two similar bureaucratic maneuvers. First, during the summer, he managed to bypass the State Department and transmit his draft to Bator, taking advantage of a moment of hierarchical confusion caused by the replacement of the under secretary of state, making it possible to evade the usual controls. Then, once the speech was ready, Brzezinski worried that it would just sit in a drawer. To force the decision, he telephoned one of his contacts in the White House (Moyers or McPherson) and claimed that he had learned from a friend working for Bobby Kennedy that the latter was going to use the anniversaries of the Berlin blockade and the Test Ban Treaty as an opportunity to make a speech critical of the president in the area of East-West relations. Thus the speech had to be taken out of the drawer quickly to pull the rug out from under him. This accounts in particular for the context chosen by the president, a not-very-important meeting of editorial writers: Johnson had to act fast.[97] The precocious bureaucratic skills deployed in this context prefigured the mastery with which Brzezinski would defend his interests as national security adviser under Carter, ten years later.

During the year and a half that he spent at the State Department, Brzezinski was also involved in the formulation of a proposal that originated with the PPS: the creation of a sort of university or foundation that would study the problems common to the industrialized societies of the West and the East alike (the organization of large companies and distribution networks, management techniques, modern agriculture, and so on). The initiative, which was taken up in the June 1966 report of the Acheson group, was not announced in the October 6 speech in New York, but it was adopted and evoked briefly in Glassboro in June 1967. After a number of political setbacks, it led to the creation of the Institute for Applied Systems Analysis, which opened in Vienna in 1972 and brought together countries from East and West, including the USSR.[98] Brzezinski noted later on that President Johnson had very much liked the idea and had remained in contact with him on that question as well.[99]

Brzezinski had no influence beyond the area of East-West relations, but that did not keep him from being interested in other subjects. After the Six-Day War, he pushed the idea that there should be swift and strong action in favor of a peace agreement: he believed that the Arabs had been unsettled by their defeat, and their trust in the USSR had been shaken. A generous Israeli stance, supported by American guarantees of security, would offer a possible solution. However, while he was suggesting an activist American policy that would entail exerting pressure in favor of an agreement, a more cautious attitude prevailed in 1967, consisting in letting the dust settle, which would allow the Soviets, Brzezinski judged retrospectively, to get back onto the playing field, and would eliminate any chance for an agreement. President Johnson, although tempted by the political line suggested by Brzezinski and others, preferred to keep all his internal political capital for Vietnam (a significant proportion of the Jewish community was pressing for withdrawal) and not spend it on the Middle East (a significant proportion of the Jewish community was pressing for intervention).[100]

It is certain that Vietnam required the full attention of the Johnson administration, especially in the later years of the war. Toward the end of 1967, not
long before his departure, Brzezinski judged that it was necessary to make a
symbolic gesture indicating that America did not intend to remain in Vietnam
indefinitely, by withdrawing 50,000 troops, for example. But he also considered, retrospectively, that in the context of the mid-1960s it was impossible to
stay uninvolved, or, once committed, to pull out precipitously.[101] Vietnam was
to put a negative stamp on Johnson's foreign policy, creating a "shadow," to
use Schwartz's term, over the president's other accomplishments, most notably
in East-West relations. This same curse of Vietnam soon struck the electoral
campaign of his vice president, Hubert Humphrey, whose principal adviser on
foreign policy was none other than Zbigniew Brzezinski. Although the two
men had known each other for years, Brzezinski's stint in the State Department
had given him the opportunity to see Humphrey on several occasions and to
exchange opinions on international issues. Thus the two men had a wide-
ranging conversation in July 1967 on which Brzezinski followed up by sending
a memorandum summarizing their points of agreement and disagreement, as
Humphrey was not a passive interlocutor.[102]

1969: Coming Full Circle

In early 1968 Brzezinski decided to leave the administration. He had the impression that he had done everything he could and that he could no longer learn or
contribute much if he remained in his subaltern position in the PPS. Rostow's
team did not really need him, despite Bator's departure from the NSC, and
no other opening was available with the State Department or the Pentagon.
Brzezinski wrote to Johnson to let him know that he was preparing to leave
the administration, and the president showed him particular respect, by inviting him for a conversation in his office. Brzezinski left feeling confident; his
relations with Johnson were good, so that if the president were reelected in
November there was a likelihood that he would be called back to be in the thick
of things.[103]

But history dictated otherwise. On March 31, 1968, two months after
the Tet Offensive, which had given the lie to the administration's optimistic
announcements, and in a speech that surprised even those close to him, Johnson
announced that he would not stand for reelection and that he was suspending

the bombing north of the 20th parallel (in other words, over the bulk of North Vietnamese territory) in order to be able to undertake peace talks, which began in Paris in mid-May. For the next three weeks, Humphrey hesitated over presenting his candidacy,[104] as the presidential campaign was looking challenging. To Humphrey's left, Eugene McCarthy, a senator from his own state, Minnesota, was campaigning against the war in Vietnam and was consolidating the protest movement among liberals. McCarthy lost to Johnson in the New Hampshire primary on March 12, but, with more than 42 percent of the votes, the defeat resonated like a victory. Robert Kennedy, seeing this as proof that Johnson could be toppled, threw his hat in the ring a few days later, presenting himself as a more acceptable anti-war candidate than McCarthy. On the right, Alabama governor George Wallace threatened to siphon off the conservative Democratic votes that the candidate from the White House needed to be sure of winning.

Humphrey nevertheless decided to run, and began to accumulate delegates via surrogates, when the campaign was once again thrown into turmoil by the assassination of Robert Kennedy—who had become Humphrey's principal rival—in Los Angeles on June 5, 1968. Shocked, Humphrey interrupted his campaign for two weeks; he was again in the grip of doubts. Most of Kennedy's delegates shifted to Humphrey, and McCarthy was not in a position to contest the nomination. But the Democratic Convention, held in Chicago from August 26 to August 29, was marked by extreme tension within the party and by street demonstrations that were violently suppressed by Mayor Richard Daley's police force. Humphrey won, but the party was profoundly divided over the Vietnam War. Johnson had refused, since the spring, to allow his vice president to deviate from the political line he had set forth, and he did not want to change that line to help Humphrey win—at least not until late October 1968, a few days before the election.

It was thus a campaign like no other that Brzezinski rejoined in the spring of 1968. He even mulled over the possibility of accepting the offer of a political rival, the Republican candidate in the New York primary race, Nelson Rockefeller. It was Emmet Hughes, another intellectual serving as adviser to Rockefeller, who courted Brzezinski over several weeks, for he was more and more infuriated by Kissinger's behavior: Kissinger took up all the air in the room and played the prima donna. According to David Halberstam, Kissinger declared to a press liaison in the Rockefeller organization who wanted to revise one of his speeches: "When Nelson buys a Picasso, he does not get a housepainter to go and retouch it."[105] Hughes thus brought up the idea of Brzezinski, which appealed to Rockefeller; he invited Brzezinski to lunch, making the possibility of a job offer suddenly more imminent. Brzezinski, who had always been a Democrat, nevertheless had a great deal of respect for Rockefeller, whose liberal Republicanism suited him. Kissinger of course was outraged, and protested. In the end, that "Polish card" was not played, for in the meanwhile Brzezinski responded in the affirmative to Humphrey's appeal.[106]

If he was chosen to play an important role in the campaign, that of foreign affairs adviser, it was because there was a certain rivalry between John Rielly and Ted Van Dyk, two of Humphrey's assistants, and each recommended that Humphrey name Brzezinski.[107] The latter's mission was to coordinate all the general political issues having to do with international affairs, while Rielly followed the candidate, ensuring the daily coordination of foreign policy.[108] Brzezinski was even paid by the day to play his role.[109] He brought together a tightly knit group of experts; the composition of the group showed the persistent influence of the Harvard network and the rise in power of the Columbia equivalent, along with the growing importance of academics, including Robert Bowie, Ray Vernon, Sam Huntington, and Thomas Schelling, all from the CFIA, but also Bill Griffin from MIT, and Marshall Shulman and Richard Gardner from Columbia.[110] During the brief campaign, Brzezinski supervised the regular production of analytic notes produced by his experts and task forces. He took the lead especially on questions involving his candidate's positioning, and he was attentive to the ethnic lobbies (the Poles in particular) and to what was being said about Humphrey in the press, especially to highlight the differences between Humphrey and Nixon during the last two months of the campaign.[111]

A closer look makes it clear that Brzezinski went beyond his foreign policy role and made recommendations on electoral strategy. For instance, on July 19, 1968, he addressed a note to Humphrey that he titled "Teddy Kennedy for Vice President: 'Heads You Lose, Tails He Wins!'"[112] In this very brief memo, he advised the candidate not to offer Ted Kennedy the second slot on the ballot, an option that Humphrey was seriously considering in order to curry favor with the liberals. His argument was simple: Kennedy would have the upper hand whether the Democrats lost (he would regain leadership of the party) or won, given his political heft. Thus, he would be a politically independent vice president, capable of weighing in on presidential decisions. "In either case, you will not be running as your own man. The inevitable impression will be created—however erroneously—that HHH has moved from LBJ's shadow to the Kennedy magic carpet."[113] He even averred that some of Rockefeller's advisers (he was most likely referring to Kissinger or Emmet Hughes) had confided that the choice of Kennedy would reinforce the likelihood that Rockefeller would win the primary, which would not be in Humphrey's interest. The offer was finally made, and it was Ted Kennedy who refused—a fact that did not keep Humphrey from replying to Brzezinski on August 6: "I tend to agree with your memorandum of July 19. Thanks for your advice. It is well taken."[114]

In September, Brzezinski ventured forth again into presidential campaign issues with another memo to Humphrey, a longer one in which he offered an overall strategy and showed with what subtlety he perceived contemporary and possible future developments within the Democratic Party. The conceptual framework of his analysis, an analogy between the Great (economic) Depression of 1932 and the great (political) depression of 1968, with FDR as savior in the one case and HHH in the other, is not very convincing. Moreover, the slogan he proposed for domestic policy, "the humane way to renewal and reconciliation," was not very catchy. But the rest of his analysis and his proposals ("moral leadership and a steady hand") were more striking and coherent, even if not innovative. He concluded with the fact that "winning" presidents had campaigned on a strong theme, FDR on the financial crisis and the New Deal, Ike on change, and Kennedy on youth and the future. Brzezinski believed it was possible to present Nixon's theme, "law and order," as inadequate and retrograde (he did not say that it was a bad theme), and he advised Humphrey to use the crisis in the political system to impose himself as a wise reformer who would know how to adapt America to modern times and prepare it to confront the challenges of the future. Above all, he made an astonishingly accurate prediction about the fate of the Democratic Party in the years to come: "Nixon's victory would mean the disintegration of the Democratic Party. The Democratic Party would become a minority party, with internal frustration pushing it left. Its remnants are likely to be captured by the more radical elements; an extreme left equivalent of Goldwater would probably get to lead the defeated party at least once."[115]

The core of Brzezinski's advice during those months had to do with foreign policy. It is not surprising that Humphrey's first declaration, on July 12, concerned the desirability of a diplomatic shift from containment and confrontation toward reconciliation and peaceful engagement toward Eastern Europe and the USSR (but also the reestablishment of more normal relations with China, a theme that appeared here for the first time in Brzezinski's advice).[116] When Brzezinski sent him suggestions on foreign policy for his acceptance speech at the convention in Chicago, he proposed international reconciliation as an overall theme, as much to make Humphrey's advantages over Nixon stand out (given Nixon's image as excessively anti-communist) as to bury the issue of Vietnam within a broader context (reconciliation between the United States and the USSR, the "community of the developed nations," and so on). Above all, he advised Humphrey never to be defensive on the subject of the previous four years, and indeed to speak only of the future.[117]

To reinforce the vice president's stature as a man of peace, Brzezinski advised him to propose setting up informal but regular summits, two-day meetings to be held twice a year, These meetings would take place outside of the capitals and would not produce a final communiqué. Their regularity and their discretion would enable them to avoid the excessive expectations and disappointments to which the major ad hoc summits gave rise. The plan would be a response to the nuclear age and to the evolutions of the international system, and it would show Humphrey's wisdom and the ability to formulate strong proposals. Coming after a declaration on Europe, this suggestion could not worry the allies.[118] The vice president did not adopt this proposal (for which Brzezinski advocated tirelessly with all his protégés over the next ten years); yet he approved the report of his task force on Europe at the beginning of October. The report recommended annual summits bringing together the United States and Western Europe (a European caucus within NATO), along with initiatives aimed toward ending the partition of Europe, especially by using international organizations. The New York Times pointed out that the report was remarkably similar to a speech delivered in New York by President Johnson exactly two years before—a speech in which "Zbignieu [sic] Brzezinski" had played a certain role.[119]

At this juncture, in the face of the Soviet repression of the spring uprising in Prague, Brzezinski advised Humphrey to strike a balance. On the one hand, it was necessary to express unequivocal moral condemnation: "There is simply no excuse for this kind of barbarian onslaught by a major power against a peaceful people whose only aspiration was greater internal freedom."[120] He recommended evoking the "magnetic of attraction of freedom," which had been demonstrated yet again by this episode. He even recommended suggesting implicitly that he would have done more than Johnson to prevent the Soviet invasion ("it would not do any harm").[121] On the other hand, the invasion confirmed Brzezinski's long-term analyses concerning the evolution of the communist societies in Eastern Europe, and it was indeed necessary to pursue "peaceful engagement" to encourage other spring uprisings. It remained in America's interest to avoid burning bridges and returning to a Cold War approach, which would risk reinforcing reactionary Soviet elements who could proceed to close the borders again and isolate Eastern Europe (and also the USSR), slowing down the developments favorable to the West that had been observed. Brzezinski thus advised the candidate to adopt the stance of a responsible and shrewd leader while avoiding overreaction, and Humphrey followed his advice.[122]

The biggest question of the electoral campaign was Vietnam, where 550,000 American soldiers were stationed during this period of peak intervention. Although Brzezinski had not changed his opinion on the principle of the war itself, starting in late 1967 he had begun to believe that the United States should send pragmatic signals of disengagement in order to seek a political way out. In mid-March, when he had already returned to Columbia, he wrote a memo addressed to the White House advancing the idea of "de-Americanizing" the war, in clearer terms than those of the policy Johnson announced on March 31.[123] In particular, when he began to work seriously on Humphrey's campaign three months later, he tried to encourage the vice president to distance himself from the administration's policy to avoid pushing more anti-war liberals to vote for Eugene McCarthy. At this point Brzezinski was no longer described as a "hawk," but rather as having "become at least mildly critical" of the administration's war policy.[124]

Herein lay the tragedy for Humphrey; Johnson did not tolerate any deviation from his political line, believing that that would send contradictory signals to the North Vietnamese and would endanger the power relations in the negotiations. And during the next few months he decided to intensify or slow down the bombings according to that criterion alone. Had he not dropped out of the presidential race in order to free himself from all political constraints?

The announcement made by Humphrey's former press adviser Bill Moyers, the owner of *Newsday* who had returned to journalism after his stint in the White House, indicating that Humphrey was getting ready to break decisively with Johnson on Vietnam, aroused a burst of optimism in Humphrey's camp that was quickly quenched when the statement was subsequently retracted.[125] At most, Humphrey was able to send out a call for a joint cease-fire in order to create a better atmosphere in the Paris negotiations—an appeal rapidly rejected by Hanoi a few days later.[126]

In mid-July, Brzezinski sent Humphrey an analysis according to which the negative feelings of the population toward the war were in the process of spilling over from the president to Humphrey. His rivals had all stated their positions on Vietnam; it was urgent to set forth a "Humphrey position" that would distinguish him from the White House. Brzezinski suggested phrasings that would accomplish this balancing act: "I do not—and will not—opportunistically disown the past. But neither do I believe that the past should govern the future. Our policies must reflect current needs and times—and also be true to the fundamental reasons for our commitment."[127] American soldiers would have died in vain if Washington imposed a coalition government on the South Vietnamese. Alternatively, there is no reason they could not decide on such a government by themselves: self-determination ought to prevail. To encourage such an approach and create a more favorable climate, Humphrey could propose an immediate cease-fire combined with a plan for gradual de-escalation, which would leave time for the South Vietnamese to prepare to take over their own defense. Washington could thus work toward a plan for reinforcing governance in Saigon (younger leaders, decentralization) and economic reconstruction. In short, Washington could and should act without waiting for the results of the Paris negotiations, but without compromising those negotiations.[128] Everything had been weighed with extreme care to distance Humphrey from the White House, but within acceptable limits. And the outcome convinced no one.

This memorandum presumably served as the basis for discussion during the work of the campaign task force devoted to the Vietnam War. This group met several times over the summer in the presence of Humphrey and regional specialists such as Edwin Reischauer, most notably on July 26.[129] That meeting led to a draft declaration advocating not just a reciprocal cease-fire but a complete suspension of the bombing in North Vietnam; thus completely breaking with the administration's position at the time. In a 1971 interview, Brzezinski recalled that during a later meeting with Humphrey, the vice president agreed that that was a satisfactory formula. The declaration would come at the right moment, it did not contravene American interests, and it met the demands of both the domestic and the international situations. "I remember saying to the Vice President, before he went to see the President—I did not go with him—that he should make it clear to the President that he's showing him the statement not in his capacity as a Vice President but as a presidential candidate for the Democratic Party."[130] According to Van Dyk, Humphrey asked for and was granted a meeting with the president, but his proposal was rejected. Johnson told him that he was doing his best to negotiate peace, that Humphrey's declaration would complicate things, and could even put the lives of American soldiers in danger. Subsequently, Humphrey was unable to get Johnson to budge.[131]

Despite the urging of his team, above all Brzezinski's, the vice president could not make his position public before the Chicago convention.[132] Not until September 30, a month before the election, did he finally announce, on television, his wish for a unilateral cessation of the bombing. At that time the announcement did not have the desired effect, inasmuch as it retained a conditional element that confused the message: Washington would stop bombing unilaterally if Hanoi behaved "responsibly"—a codicil that was never explained.[133] In the end, Brzezinski noted, "he didn't gain the support of the doves and yet he alienated some of the hawks," as he projected the impression that he "was hesitant and couldn't make up his mind."[134] This did not prevent Brzezinski from continuing to offer his candidate a number of different ways to appear more responsible than Richard Nixon (whose peace plan for getting America out of Vietnam remained secret); for example, by announcing the creation of a commission headed by a moderate Republican (William Bundy), which would be charged with presenting a de-escalation plan in time for the inauguration.[135]

It was on October 31, just a few days before the election, that Johnson ordered a suspension of all bombing in North Vietnam, to encourage the Paris negotiations and give his vice president a boost. Brzezinski and Rielly immediately prepared a declaration designed to set their candidate apart from Nixon and George Wallace, who was running as an independent.[136] In fact, that decision, combined with stronger and more explicit support from Eugene

McCarthy, allowed Humphrey to narrow the gap in the polls, trailing Nixon by just two points. But it was too late. Among other factors, the division in the Democratic Party over Vietnam was too much for Humphrey, and Nixon won a decisive victory in the Electoral College (301 votes vs. Humphrey's 191, and Wallace's 19), although the popular vote count was much closer: 43.70 percent to 42.44 percent. This put an end to Brzezinski's hopes.

Less than a month after the election, Brzezinski participated in a colloquium at Princeton organized by the Paris-based International Association for Cultural Freedom, set up at the request of the Congress for Cultural Freedom. The goal of the meeting was to understand the rapid developments that had marked the United States in recent years, along with the transformation of its image and its relation to the world: modernization and postindustrial society, racial issues, the new left and the student revolt, Vietnam and the worldwide anti-war protests, anti-Americanism, and so on. Brzezinski was of great help to the association's secretary general, Constantin Jelenski, and its president, Shepard Stone, in organizing the event during the spring.[137] The program of this Princeton Seminar, which brought together nearly a hundred intellectuals from December 1 to December 5, 1968, reads like a *Who's Who* of the transatlantic intellectual and artistic elite. Its co-presiders were Karl Kaysen of Princeton and Jean-Jacques Servan-Schreiber, editor-in-chief of *L'Express* and author of *Le défi américain*.[138] Attending on the American side were Daniel Bell from Columbia, Norman Podhoretz of *Commentary,* Irving Howe of *Dissent,* John Kenneth Galbraith, Stanley Hoffmann, Arthur Schlesinger, Henry Kissinger, and Martin Peretz from Harvard, but also George Kennan and Saul Bellow, without counting more political figures such as George Ball and McGeorge Bundy (Ford Foundation). There were a number of French participants, including Simon Nora, François Furet, Manès Sperber, François Bondy, and also Michel Crozier (Pierre Hassner was attending a conflicting conference at Princeton). They were joined by other Europeans, including Andreas Papandreou, Günter Grass, and Alastair Buchan, and a few participants from Eastern Europe, Asia, and Africa.

The Princeton Seminar was a huge success. The *New York Times* published daily coverage, and many other newspapers, including several from Europe, described its lively debates.[139] Brzezinski himself reported on the conference to

Shepard Stone, a month later: "I very much enjoyed the seminar, even though I feel it turned into a bit of a 'circus.' . . . I never attended a conference which has been so widely discussed by people outside. Wherever I go, people ask me about the Princeton seminar."[140]

Brzezinski's description of the "circus" does not seem to be an exaggeration, given the vigor and intensity of the debates. George Ball (at the State Department under Kennedy and Johnson) and Andreas Papandreou clashed over the responsibilities of Washington and the Greek elite in the 1967 generals' coup d'état. Brzezinski and Hoffmann, who introduced the session on foreign affairs, crossed swords over America's role in the world. The former, even if he was advocating selective disengagement, insisted on the fact that the United States had global responsibilities and could not ignore them, notwithstanding the recommendations of Europeans such as Servan-Schreiber that the United States pull back. "We cannot play the role of cosmic Metternich," Hoffmann retorted.[141] Brzezinski reproached him for his critical outlook, accusing him of being a Luddite, quick to seize on the defects of a policy but slow to propose political solutions: "For me, you're only a modified version of Morgenthau"—the father of the discipline of international relations, strongly opposed to the Vietnam War by virtue of his classic conception of national interest and geographical spheres of interest. In response, Hoffmann attacked Brzezinski's hawkish tendencies: "For me, you're only a modified version of Walt Rostow"[142]—Johnson's national security adviser. Steeped in the social sciences, Rostow had intensified the war to the point of organizing the Phoenix operation of assassinations targeting the Vietcong infrastructure. The two men then participated—along with Karl Kaiser and others—in a radio debate transcribed and published by the *New York Times,* in which the tone was more civil.[143]

But the most vigorous controversies had nothing to do with international affairs; they concerned the student protests and domestic developments in the United States. Kennan opened the seminar with a diatribe against the student protesters, denouncing "the extremely disturbed and excited state of mind of a good portion of our student youth, floundering around as it is in its own terrifying wilderness of drugs, pornography and political hysteria."[144] Kennan expressed hope for the Nixon administration, but he was rapidly contradicted by Stanley Hoffmann and Arthur Schlesinger. Most important, the conference gave the floor to representatives of the protesters. The Black Power movement was represented by the academic Howard Cruse and the civil rights activist Roy Innis, who advocated the establishment of two parallel societies in the United States, one black and one white—to which John Oakes, the editor of the op-ed pages in the *New York Times,* responded that the proposal was in essence racist.

Sam Brown, at age twenty-five the coordinator of the student campaign in favor of Eugene McCarthy, retorted that racism in America was white—this was at a moment when the Ocean Hill-Brownsville confrontation between the black and Jewish communities was at its height.[145] He denounced the liberal intellectuals who were participating in the conference, describing the event as a failure, and he appealed for more emotion in the approach to social issues. He earned a harsh response from Schlesinger: "Reason without passion is sterile, but passion without reason is hysterical . . . I can imagine nothing worse for our society than the rejection of reasoned analysis by the young."[146] Martin Peretz, age twenty-nine, the future owner of *The New Republic* and a leader of the student protest movement, accused the professors and the experts of not addressing more normative, moral questions to American society, and chastised them for their inclination "to build roads no matter where they take us, to build weapons no matter what values they defend or attack."[147] He also demanded more transparency about the ties between the big corporations and the men who were influencing American policy; for example, in the case of the intervention in Santo Domingo in 1965.

In the turbulent America of the 1960s, professors like Kissinger, who had just been named Nixon's national security adviser and who attended the Princeton seminar only for an after-dinner debate, fresh with the glow of his nomination, stealing the spotlight from the others, and Brzezinski, who had just had to give up hope for a position in a possible Humphrey administration, were both admired and challenged, reflecting the ambiguous legacy of the Cold War University. A month earlier, Brzezinski had had to face a demonstration of boisterous students at Columbia. A chapter of Students for a Democratic Society (SDS), the large student organization created in the early 1960s by Tom Hayden and others, announced its intention to enter the offices of the School of International Affairs to demand the closing of this den of imperialism that harbored various regional institutes, including Brzezinski's Research Institute on Communist Affairs (RICA). But the university administration had gotten wind of the project; it closed the building and posted six security guards at the entrance.

Some hundred students pressed against the doors, and the assistant dean offered to set up a debate between them and professors who agreed to participate: Alex Dallin, Roger Hilsman (who had resigned from the Johnson administration in 1964 to protest against its Vietnam policy), and Zbigniew Brzezinski, a much more interesting target given his role in the State Department and alongside Humphrey.[148] Brzezinski, picking up an apple in his office to look relaxed and detached, went downstairs and engaged in conversation with the students on American foreign policy in general and Vietnam in particular. The conversation became heated, and several demonstrators began to insult him: "War criminal! Imperialist!" In the end, Brzezinski replied: "Look, I hope you have no more questions, because I have to go back and plan some more genocides."[149] The group ended up dispersing.

A year later, in 1969, a more serious matter arose. The Revolutionary Youth Movement at Columbia, a faction of SDS, again went after the School of International Affairs and its director, accusing RICA of collecting vital information for the American government and the military, for example, the names of six thousand Chinese political leaders, information that could be used one day by the Taiwanese government for the purpose of political assassination. The students wanted a complete shutdown of the School of International Affairs; its building could be turned over, for example, to the community.[150] To dramatize their grand gesture, at noon on November 6 the students arranged to bring in a thirty-pound piglet nicknamed "Little Zbigniew" and present it to Brzezinski; in the 1960s protest universe, the pig represented a tool for delegitimizing the elite. In an interview, Brzezinski recalled the incident:

> They arrived, dragging a pig on a rope chanting: "A pig for Professor Zbig." And I knew by then that they had sort of smashed up the Dean's office or something, but I didn't want them to come into my office, in this building, where I had my office, with this pig. So I phoned up, I forget who answered, who, I guess, the President's office? And I said: "Send some police officers because this is going to be ugly." And they said: "Oh we can handle that, we can handle that." So I didn't know what to do, I was thinking, watching them out the window: "What should I do?" when all of a sudden I see the police pulling up, and policemen jumping out of police cars, and kind of circulating, not fighting but there were some threats obviously, and finally the kids pick up the pig,

turn around and go away. So I said "Gee, the administration finally got some guts." Heavens no! What happens is that a lady was walking down Amsterdam avenue about Broadway and she saw this pig being dragged on a rope, so she phoned up SPCA (Society for the Prevention of Cruelty to Animals) and I guess filed a complaint or something. The cops came, to save the pig.[151]

Other less dramatic and less amusing confrontations followed this one, for the students had identified Brzezinski as a hawk and associated him with the Johnson administration. For example, in October 1972, when he went to give a lecture at McGill, his alma mater, activists from the McGill Student Movement stood up in the first row, waved red flags, and tried to keep him from speaking, for he was "stained by the blood of the Vietnamese people." They denounced him as a CIA agent and yelled "Death to imperialism!" But the room soon began to chant a slogan demanding that Brzezinski be allowed to speak, and he joined in. In the aftermath, the students were suspended and barred from access to the campus.[152]

Like many of the old-school liberals, Brzezinski reacted negatively to the student revolt. There are several possible explanations for his attitude. First, he found the agitation of the young Americans futile, especially when he compared it to the role played by students in the Budapest uprising or the Prague Spring, against real dictatorships. It is also possible that his patriotism as an immigrant may have been shocked by the expression of violent complaints against America. In addition, the students lashed out against the university itself, as an institution, and even against the Cold War University, which had been the vehicle for Brzezinski's social and political ascension—the context that allowed his patient and intensive work to pay off, the context in which his particular talents could be expressed. A third explanation is much simpler: Columbia was one of the epicenters of the student revolt, and the site where it took a bad turn. During the spring of 1968, specifically to protest the construction of a gymnasium in Morningside Park (next to the university, against the wishes of the black community in Harlem) as well as the university's ties (and those of president Grayson Kirk personally) to a think tank connected to the Pentagon called the Institute for Defense Analyses, students occupied five university buildings in addition to the president's office. The New York Police Department (NYPD) laid siege, while a group of professors attempted to mediate. In the face of their failure, one thousand police officers invaded the premises and evacuated the students, several of whom were wounded. A month later, the protests resumed, forcing President Kirk to resign. During the years that followed, Columbia suffered from a decrease in external funding, and underwent a pronounced liberal turn.

When Brzezinski wrote to Alistair Buchan on May 1, 1968, a few days after the NYPD assault, to apologize for the fact that the events on campus had prevented him from going to London, he analyzed the situation in terms of a typical revolutionary dynamics. He explained that the university administration was inclined to act decisively in response to the earliest acts of occupation, but that a group of professors had intervened, imposing its mediation and leading the administration to accept more and more concessions without obtaining any in exchange from the extremist students. Thus what had begun as provocations by some fifty students turned into building occupations on a large scale, forcing the police to intervene—and it was not over yet. The administration should have used force right away or else or else should have given in, but above all it should have avoided the stalling and mediation attempts that actually made the situation deteriorate more quickly.[153] This way of schematizing a revolutionary situation surfaced again in Brzezinski's approach to the events in Iran in 1978–1979, when he defended (in vain) the option of military action before it was too late.

Brzezinski was particularly severe in his judgment of those colleagues who were closer to the students or offered to mediate. A week later, he wrote to Sam Huntington—who shared his approach to the student protests—that the April events had "proved, if proof was needed, that that in a moment of crisis intellectuals use their intellect solely to rationalize their emotions and passions."[154] The following year, after the troubles at Harvard in April 1969 and the occupation of University Hall, he sent Huntington a humorous article by Art Buchwald and commented: "Did you know that Stanley Hoffmann was interviewed about the recent crisis?"[155] The article was a pastiche of an interview with a fictional professor whose nose is bleeding after students have thrown him down a flight of stairs. The journalist expresses indignation and exclaims that this was a terrible thing, but the professor explains that the incident has to be seen from the students' point of view and that one has to think hard about the university's failings. Then the students burn down the philosophy department: this is certainly illegal, but they must have had reasons, and sometimes illegal actions lead to just reforms, the professor rationalizes. At the end of the interview, he is seized by the students and hung.[156] It must be said that during Harvard's troubles Stanley Hoffmann, always close to the students, was among the professors who maintained contact and, with Michael Walzer, tried to mediate. Many professors, most notably those of the Russian Center (Richard Pipes, Alexander Gerschenkron) resented him for this and turned a cold shoulder for years, Huntington included.[157] The latter replied to Brzezinski that he had already read the article and even posted it in the Political Science Department at Harvard. And he added, lapidarily: "If this assault on the university accomplishes anything else, it certainly makes one disgusted with the spinelessness of large numbers of one's colleagues."[158]

But Brzezinski was also interested in what the students represented, and since he was increasingly focused, in the second half of the 1960s, on the analysis of social change, in 1970 he proposed a comprehensive interpretation of student revolts in various countries. In "Histrionics as History in Transition," an article published that year, he suggested that the revolt was a symptom of the difficulties encountered in the shift to the "technetronic" era, that is, to a postindustrial society marked by the importance of communications and technology.[159] He began by making a distinction between the students of Mexico City, Madrid, Prague, or Warsaw and those of Berkeley, New York, Paris, or Berlin; the former were oriented toward the concrete goal of liberation from political oppression, while the latter were politically superficial, artificially cemented together by their opposition to the war in Vietnam, and they exalted emotion and action above all, even as they offered a pastiche of past revolutions. In Brzezinski's eyes, they were the product of a gap between disruption of the material context: the revolution in communications and technology, on the one hand, and mentalities that were not yet accustomed to the new age and looked to emotion and action for a meaning that eluded them, on the other. Moreover, he noted, it was not astonishing that students in America—the society that had been the first to enter the technetronic age—should play a pioneering role in the student revolt. In the final analysis, he predicted that these rebels would not become revolutionaries and would end up rejoining society, even if some might be radicalized.

There was no room in Brzezinski's analyses for taking into account the students' political perspectives or complaints; the protestors were objectivized, reduced to a social phenomenon or, more precisely, to an epiphenomenon.

Brzezinski rarely expressed any doubt about the well-foundedness of his approach to the functions of the university or about the questionable interpenetration of politics and academics. He also—and the two things are linked—did not explicitly question the moral dilemmas involved in the military intervention in Vietnam or American foreign policy in general. Still, it is important to note that Brzezinski's political evolution on the question of Vietnam, begun in 1967 and amplified in 1968 when he was working for Humphrey, continued through 1969 and led to active lobbying in favor of putting an end to the fighting and reaching a negotiated solution.

To that end, he joined a citizens' committee called the National Committee for a Political Settlement in Vietnam / Negotiation Now![160] The group had been formed two years earlier under the leadership of Clark Kerr, chancellor of the University of California, Berkeley. In mid-1969, when Brzezinski joined the committee, it had become critical of the strategy followed as of May 1968, which consisted in negotiating with North Vietnam in Paris while continuing to fight in order to do so from a position of strength. That strategy had shown its limits, since twelve thousand American soldiers had been killed since the start of negotiations, which seemed to be going nowhere. The committee wanted to replace that strategy by offering a cease-fire with a freeze on the positions currently occupied, along with a strong signal of America's intentions, such as a sharp reduction in troops, and also free elections under international supervision. The committee also insisted on the importance of democracy in South Vietnam, so that the regime would be reformed. Its function would be to protect minorities, religious rights and union rights; it would introduce agrarian reforms, free political prisoners, and so on. The committee enjoyed the support of a large number of prominent figures from the spheres of academia, religion, and labor; these were often resolute anti-communists who were not doves (they did not defend the idea of a unilateral cease-fire or a sudden, massive retreat), but they considered that the war had gone on long enough, that it was costly on the moral level and a source of deep divisions in the United States. The other members included Daniel Bell, John K. Galbraith, Michael Harrington, Normal Podhoretz, Bayard Rustin, Arthur Schlesinger Jr., Penn Kemble, Tom Kahn, Seymour Martin Lipset, Walter Reuther, Saul Bellow, Reinhold Niebuhr, and some bishops and rabbis.[161]

In early September 1969, Brzezinski, who had become one of the key activists in the group, traveled to Saigon for discussions along with other committee members: Clark Kerr, Roy Prosterman, Milton Sacks, Robert Kleiman, and Mary Temple.[162] The group met with all the important players, notably the American ambassador Ellsworth Bunker, General Creighton Adams, and President Nguyen Van Thieu, on September 4. Brzezinski suggested the idea of taking advantage of the death of Ho Chi Minh, two days earlier, to take the initiative, in particular on the much-discussed cease-fire. He noted that the United States had played a waiting game after Stalin's death, only to learn long afterward that they could have pressed their advantage, given the divisions in the Soviet leadership. The Vietnamese president was interested, but he was not in favor of proposing a cease-fire to Hanoi; he did not trust the Vietcong, and emphasized the lack of a plausible verification mechanism. He also complained about the proposed American aid as too conditional.[163] Brzezinski considered the trip's outcome positive, on balance, and he felt that he had advanced his ideas, broadened the debate, and reached new audiences. But he also noted the negative points: the conservative elements of the Saigon regime were being reinforced to the detriment of democracy and civil liberties; political unity was weak; the American authorities in Vietnam were not aware of the extent of the decline of support for the war in the United States; the policy of Vietnamization was obvious, but its prospects were poor.[164]

Nevertheless, Brzezinski and the committee organized a press campaign to mobilize public opinion.[165] Above all, Brzezinski supported his cause in direct contact with Henry Kissinger; on October 3, he sent Kissinger a memorandum directed to the attention of President Nixon in preparation for speech that the latter was to give on Vietnam.[166] The proposals came from the committee, but Brzezinski added an introductory note that is worth citing: "I write this letter as one who has staunchly supported our involvement in Vietnam. I believed, and I do believe, that this involvement was necessary largely for international reasons. I also do believe that, by and large, most of these international objectives have now been accomplished. At the same time, an entirely new factor has entered the picture: the bitter division at home which is threatening to undermine not only our foreign policy but to split our national life."[167]

From the position of committed hawk that he had held until late 1967, by 1969 Brzezinski had moved to the point of defending an active search for a political solution that would allow America to disengage from Vietnam in order to maintain its domestic unity as well as its image and its power. For that, he would have to wait four more years. But when he thought back on those years, he did not view Vietnam as a mistake. By contrast, he was mistrustful of those who, having learned their lesson too well, replaced the Munich syndrome by the Vietnam syndrome. That group included a number of people who belonged, as he did, to the new elite in American foreign policy.

3

The Rise of a
New Foreign Policy Elite

In '68, I worked for Hubert Humphrey. I was his principal FP advisor . . . but to give you a sense of how realistic and modest my expectations were, I thought maybe I might become an assistant secretary of state for European affairs. Well, it may be strange, but I wasn't ready, and what made my sense of what I can do rise, is Henry. Nixon won, he made Henry. It never occurred to me he would get that. It never occurred to me when I was Humphrey's principal advisor that I could be NSA. It was not in my sense of what is feasible in America. And I was conscious that some people like Harriman and Bohlen publicly used my Polish background to kind of argue against my notion of peaceful engagement.

—Zbigniew Brzezinski (2011)

In the 1950s, when Zbigniew Brzezinski was at Harvard, he found himself in an environment that was unique owing to the constant exchange, almost osmosis, between the university and the American foreign policy elite. But the rules for membership in the leading elite remained quite rigid. Academics served as experts and consultants, not decision makers. Policy decisions were still made by lower-level diplomats in the State Department and, ultimately, by the Establishment elite at the top. The situation began to change, slowly, under President John Kennedy, and over the next fifteen years it was disrupted by the rise to power of what was sometimes known as the "professional elite," consisting of individuals who had imposed themselves at all the decision-making levels of American foreign policy.[1]

In this respect, Brzezinski stands out as a pioneer. His surprise at Henry Kissinger's nomination as national security adviser should not surprise us. In 1968, the new rules for selecting the elite were just beginning to change. Brzezinski did not hesitate to exploit them to his own benefit; he became a symbol of this historical process. Between 1968 and 1976, his trajectory was guided by a single goal: to occupy a position of responsibility. This chapter and the next place his career within the context of the renewal of the American elite.

The Wise Men

Sociologists and historians working to interpret social, political, and intellectual movements have long been used to the notion of generation as an aid. As early as 1928, Karl Mannheim established the contours: one can speak of a generation when men and women born during the same period are "exposed to the social and intellectual symptoms of a process of dynamic de-stabilization," disturbing their environment (war, economic crisis, decline or rise, and so on).[2] This does not mean that the members of a given demographic cohort are necessarily prone to react in the same way to such stimuli; they may even develop radically opposed opinions. Moreover, the worldview formed by a generation, by a group within a generation, or even by a few individual precursors, may be transmitted to subsequent generations that have not experienced the same events; this is the case with the American foreign policy Establishment. The fact remains that this concept may help us decipher the development of the attitudes and approaches of a portion of the elite.[3]

In an article on the "transatlantic American foreign policy elite," the historian Priscilla Roberts, applying this generational approach, proposes to distinguish four generations of decision makers in the twentieth century.[4] First, there were the founders of American internationalism at the turn of the century—Theodore Roosevelt, Alfred Thayer Mahan, Henry Cabot Lodge, John Hay, and Elihu Root—whose formative experience was the Civil War, and who were responsible for turning the United States into an international power. Then there was the generation converted to internationalism and an overture toward Europe owing to the First World War—Henry Stimson above all, but also lawyers Paul Cravath and John Davis as well as businessmen Henry

Davison and Thomas Lamont. These were men who, under the patronage of the first generation (especially Elihu Root), created the Council on Foreign Relations (CFR). The third and most important generation was that of the "Wise Men," whose formative experience often entailed military service during the First World War. This group included such figures as Averell Harriman, John McCloy, Robert Lovett, James Forrestal, and also Dean Acheson—men marked by the double dangers of Nazism and communism during the 1930s who gravitated toward a patriotism tinged with realism and moderation. (Hans Morgenthau and Reinhold Niebuhr were among the sources of inspiration for this group.) Finally, there was the Second World War generation, men who for the most part had served in Europe or in the Pacific: the Bundy brothers, George Ball, Cyrus Vance, Dean Rusk, George H.W. Bush, and Douglas Dillon. Roberts also includes Walt Rostow, Robert McNamara, Kissinger, and even Brzezinski, although the latter was too young to have served during the war. This fourth generation had as its frame of reference the victorious struggle of the United States during the Second World War and the construction of the American world. This was the generation that would lead America into the disaster of Vietnam, supported with more or less enthusiasm by the elders of the third generation, the Wise Men.

Roberts notes that that fourth generation was much less socially and intellectually homogeneous than the preceding ones. She concludes that the generational approach is fruitful leading up to the Second World War and its immediate aftermath (in other words, leading up to the generation of the Wise Men) but that generalizations in terms of shared perceptions and a common approach to the world lost validity when the foreign policy consensus began to splinter over the Vietnam War. "From the 1970s onward," she concludes, "the concept of a continuing American foreign policy Establishment had become so diffuse as to make any generational analysis of it almost meaningless."[5] According to Roberts, there were three Establishment generations over some sixty years, then a new, post-Establishment generation.

For anyone interested in Zbigniew Brzezinski's career, the generational approach is potentially useful on two levels. Over the long run, Brzezinski embodies the rise to power of a new type of elite that brought an end to several generations of the Establishment. His rise, his social profile, and his approach to foreign policy introduced a break with the experience of the earlier elite. It might be tempting to place him in the huge post-Establishment generation that was characterized by a greater diversity of trajectories, more modest social origins, and a much more politicized or even ideological relation to international affairs. It seems that, on a shorter time line and a smaller sociological scale, Brzezinski can be seen as representative of a distinct group, the particular intellectual generation that gravitated toward Harvard or MIT in the 1950s—the Cold War University.

At the heart of this group, in addition to Brzezinski, were such men as Henry Kissinger (born in 1923), Samuel Huntington (1927), Stanley Hoffmann (1928), but also Thomas Schelling (1921), Lucian Pye (1921), Lincoln Bloomfield (1920), and even Walt Rostow and Raymond Vernon (both born in 1913). All these men were marked by the Second World War, sometimes because they had been its victims (three of them were born in Europe), and their professional milieu was a university largely oriented toward the service of power. Their interactions took place within institutions in Cambridge, Massachusetts, especially at the Center for International Affairs created by Robert Bowie in 1958 (Kissinger was its associate director, Brzezinski wrote the first monograph published under its auspices, and Hoffmann led its first research seminar, focusing on France), but also in the Harvard-MIT Joint Arms Control Seminar, the journal *Daedalus,* the Ford Foundation seminars at Bellagio, and so on. It is arguable that this group stood out as distinct both from the Establishment and from the "professional elite," or else that it constituted a precursor or first version of that professional elite, as a group more centered on universities and, most importantly, less ideological and less politicized.

This last element is crucial. Kissinger was close to Nelson Rockefeller, the embodiment of a centrist Republican, and he worked for the Kennedy administration. Brzezinski, a lifelong Democrat, was neither an ideologue nor a sectarian. He was guided by his ideas about foreign policy, he refused to support George McGovern in 1972, and he came out in favor of George H.W. Bush in 1988. Both Kissinger and Brzezinski differed from younger players who could not shift from one camp to another—the Vietnam generation, identified with the left (for example, Morton Halperin, Richard Cooper, Richard Holbrooke, Anthony Lake, and Leslie Gelb) and the generation of those reacting to the Vietnam syndrome, identified with the right (for example, Richard Perle, Paul Wolfowitz, Elliott Abrams, and Richard Burt).

Whether or not the generation or microgeneration to which Brzezinski belonged was distinct from the "professional elite," the massive break was no

doubt made possible by the foreign policy Establishment that had been dominant in America from the 1900s to the 1960s. Here the distinction is primarily
sociological. The British journalist Henry Fairlie was the first to popularize the
term "Establishment," applying it to the English elite in a 1955 article published
in *The Spectator*.[6] He was not targeting simply high society or the rich in general;
he was pointing to a network of men who occupied high positions in British
society (the Archbishop of Canterbury, the editor-in-chief of the *Times*, certain
City bankers, certain highly placed personalities in Whitehall). These men knew
each other, shared the same worldview, and were able to exercise serious power
outside of the political and constitutional frameworks (they could promote
or block nominations, political initiatives, and so on). They themselves were
pragmatic and nonpartisan, or rather above party politics.[7]

In 1962, the journalist Richard Rovere imported the concept into America
and offered a description of the networks that really counted, according to
him, in the political society of the United States.[8] He recounted a discussion he
had had with John Kenneth Galbraith, who was also interested in the subject,
and who, half-jokingly, had Rovere guess who might figure as the CEO of the
Establishment.

> I thought hard for a while and was on the point of naming Arthur Hays
> Sulzberger, of the New York *Times*, when suddenly the right name sprang
> to my lips. "John J. McCloy," I exclaimed. "Chairman of the Board of
> the Chase Manhattan Bank; once a partner in Cadwalader, Wickersham
> & Taft, and also in Cravath, de Gersdorff, Swaine & Wood, as well as, of
> course, Milbank, Tweed, Hope, Hadley & McCloy; former United States
> High Commissioner in Germany; former President of the World Bank;
> liberal Republican; chairman of the Ford Foundation and chairman—my
> God, how could I have hesitated—of the Council on Foreign Relations;
> Episcopalian. "That's the one," Galbraith said. He congratulated me
> for having guessed what it had taken him so much patient research to
> discover.[9]

Rovere certainly did not limit himself to foreign affairs, but he showed that
the presence of the Establishment was especially important in that realm.[10]
He thus considered that "the directors of the Council on Foreign Relations
make up a sort of Presidium for that part of the Establishment that guides our

destiny as a nation."[11] Let us recall that Brzezinski himself was established as a member of the CFR in 1961, and that that institution, then at the peak of its influence, served as his springboard, offering him both visibility (articles in *Foreign Affairs,* the book *Alternative to Partition*) and contacts. Yet Brzezinski's evolution was not that of a classical Establishment figure. To understand the differences, it is useful to look at the group of influential figures nicknamed the Wise Men—a group that embodied the Establishment until the 1960s.

The anecdote recounted in the introduction about the December 1960 meeting between John F. Kennedy and Robert Lovett is telling. Kennedy had just been elected president; he offered Lovett, another potential candidate for the title of "president of the Establishment," a ministerial position of his own choosing. Kennedy may have surrounded himself with intellectuals, but he still "believed in the Establishment mystique," as David Halberstam noted.[12] Four years later, Lyndon B. Johnson had to campaign for the November 1964 presidential election. He too sought the benediction of the Establishment. He charged McGeorge Bundy, one of their own, with assembling a panel (called President's Consultants on Foreign Affairs) that would advise him— and would make the front page of the *New York Times.* Bundy, who made fun of journalists who used the term "Establishment" (according to him it did not correspond to any reality), wrote a memo to the president titled "Backing from the Establishment," and shortly afterward he referred to the individuals whom he persuaded to join—such as McCloy and Lovett, but also Harriman, Acheson, and Dillon—as the Wise Men.[13]

Four years later, on March 25, 1968, the atmosphere was entirely different. Johnson expanded the group by adding Clark Clifford, McGeorge Bundy (who had by then left the White House), Henry Cabot Lodge, George Ball, Robert Murphy, and also a younger man who had just left his position as number two in the Pentagon, Cyrus Vance. The news was not good: the Tet Offensive had demonstrated that the war was not about to be won; the losses had been heavy and public opinion was growing impatient. This "knighthood of the Cold War," as Walter Isaacson and Evan Thomas called it, advised the president against military escalation. The Wise Men now viewed the war that the Establishment had supported as lost, and recommended disengagement. A week later, President Johnson announced that he was suspending the bombing and wanted to begin negotiations—adding on his own initiative that he would not run again for the presidency. Rostow, Johnson's national security adviser and a tenacious hawk, was stunned by what he heard during the March 25 discussion: "As Rostow, who had come to the dinner as Johnson's emissary and observer, listened to the downward drift of the discussion, he sensed the demise of an institution he had long yearned to join, and now felt bitterly disappointed in. 'I thought to myself,' he recalled, 'that what began in the spring of 1940 when Henry Stimson came to Washington ended tonight. The American establishment is dead.'"[14]

The Establishment actually came into being prior to 1940. It can be traced back to the first decade of the twentieth century, when a network that connected Wall Street elite, banks, clubs, and foundations with the sites of power in Washington. That network grew in part out of The Inquiry, the large assemblage of gray matter around Woodrow Wilson and Colonel House (for more on this, see chapter 1). The handful of thinkers who accompanied Wilson to Paris on board the USS *George Washington* for the 1919 peace conference came back convinced that it was essential to keep America engaged and active in the world. They promised each other that they would create an institution to that end, paired with a parallel institution to be created in London—Chatham House.

But as early as June 1918, a first version of the Council on Foreign Relations had already been formed by a group of internationalist bankers, industrialists, and lawyers who were preoccupied with the future of the international system in relation to their business dealings after the war. This first CFR operated under the presidency of Elihu Root, secretary of war and then secretary of state under William McKinley and Roosevelt (Root received the Nobel Peace Prize in 1912). Finally, the scholars in The Inquiry agreed to join their efforts with those of this group and to combine their activities in a new version of the Council on Foreign Relations in 1921. A number of Establishment figures, including Harriman and McCloy, were among the founding members.[15] The following year, the journal *Foreign Affairs* was born. In short, from the outset, the CFR brought the American business community, broadly understood— industrialists, bankers, and lawyers, mostly from New York—together with those who thought about and practiced international affairs, and the journal quickly imposed itself as the beating heart of the Establishment.

During the 1920s and 1930s, the CFR's orientation was clearly internationalist—anti-isolationist—to such an extent that a banker from

J.P. Morgan, a committed isolationist, was almost prevented from giving a talk at the CFR. And the question of American military intervention, in the late 1930s, divided the leaders, even if they were brothers; thus, while Allen Dulles supported intervention, his brother John Foster defended the policy of appeasing dictators. In the 1920s, the CFR, like the journal *Foreign Affairs,* opened up to all regions of the world, including Africa and Latin America. But the world of the Establishment remained strongly Eurocentric, if only because the industrial and financial interests in New York were focused on Europe.[16]

During the Second World War, and then the Cold War, many New York lawyers and bankers—especially those from the CFR—contributed to the administration of the war effort and of major programs such as the Marshall Plan (when someone was needed for the War Department, John McCloy explained, "we thumbed through the roll of Council members and put through a call to New York").[17] The person who figured as titular head of the Establishment at that point was Henry Stimson—himself a disciple of Elihu Root, according to the logic of transmission from generation to generation; he was the touchstone for his adjuncts McCloy and Lovett along with many others. Stimson, a wealthy Wall Street lawyer, a Republican from high society (Phillips Academy, Yale and its secret society Skull and Bones, Harvard Law School), had been secretary of war under William Howard Taft and secretary of state under Herbert Hoover. He agreed to return to Washington in July 1949, at age seventy-three, to lead Franklin Roosevelt's war effort; he was charged with mobilizing thirteen million men, as well as an important portion of American industry and the scientific community, most notably for the Manhattan Project.[18]

The Establishment dominated the 1940s and 1950s, and its influence was still considerable in the 1960s up to the Vietnam fiasco, when Rostow wrote its death notice. What disappeared at that point was a veritable ecosystem with an original and remarkably consistent shape that had lasted half a century—a social milieu with shared values, characteristic attitudes, and a particular approach to international questions.[19]

The Establishment consisted primarily of bankers, lawyers, and industrialists, all with international horizons and all from a narrow social base. For the most part, they were well-to-do men from the East Coast shaped by the same institutions and groups: the boarding schools Groton or Phillips, Skull and Bones or Scroll and Key at Yale, Ivy or Cap and Gown at Princeton, Porcellian or Fly at Harvard. In New York, they belonged to the same clubs and practiced the same sports (tennis or sailing, not baseball or basketball).[20] Their social values had an aura of "noblesse oblige": they exercised self-control and did not seek the limelight; they never boasted—not even of their successes—and adopted a self-effacing, detached, modest posture. They avoided fashion trends like the plague, and were suspicious of ideas that were too brilliant, too original: better to be wrong than to rush ahead.[21] For that reason, they were often conformists responsive to pressure from their peers, who were often their friends, thus giving rise to the impression that they all thought alike.[22]

It is not astonishing, then, that the men of the Establishment were eminent pragmatics, fiercely nonpartisan moderates. Most of them were liberal Republicans, owing to their social milieu and their professions. Like Stimson, almost none of them hesitated to go work in an administration of the opposing party. "Damn it, I always forget." Roosevelt exclaimed when McCloy reminded him that he was a Republican—just like Stimson and Lovett.[23] Having public service in their bones, they could not imagine partisan differences prevailing over good sense, Realpolitik, and pragmatism. "These men did not adhere to a single ideology, nor was ideology a driving force in their lives—except insofar as an instinct for the center can be called an ideology. They were equally opposed to the yahoos of the right and softies of the left. Ideological fervor was frowned upon; pragmatism, realpolitik, moderation, and consensus were prized. Nonpartisanship was more than a principle; it was an art form."[24]

With its position above party loyalties, its distrust of popular movements, and its rejection of elected office—with the exception of Harriman, who was governor of New York from 1955 to 1958—the Establishment cultivated discretion and confidentiality. They served the government only within the executive branch, where Establishment members were called on the basis of their reputations and their networks. It is thus not surprising that the tradition of the Establishment was regularly attacked by populists from both the right and the left in every era. The new left of the 1960s and the new right of the 1970s let loose against this undemocratic and supposedly apolitical Establishment, this private club that operated away from public scrutiny and imposed its choices on the nation. The Council on Foreign Relations in particular was at the center of all sorts of conspiracy theories, as was the Trilateral Commission later founded by Brzezinski and David Rockefeller.

But what were the choices of the Establishment in international matters? Many of these have already been mentioned: internationalism, along with polarization toward the Atlantic world: "a special kinship with England, a vague tolerance—and certain irritability—toward France, and a wary acceptance of Germany" after the war.[25] To this was added a certain American ideology tying together various freedoms—free exchange, free market, human rights—tinged with moral considerations, something John Kenneth Galbraith called "the Groton ethic" (a sense of honor and duty, noblesse oblige, Christian values). Containment as defined by George Kennan sums up the preferences of the Establishment fairly well: it combined anti-communism with the defense of democracies, not through an ideological and militaristic crusade, but through the controlled use of force and Realpolitik when necessary.

This came to be precisely the drama of the Establishment: its firm but moderate and pragmatic position on the containment of the USSR in Europe, a well-known terrain, led to support for American intervention in a more remote Asia, first in Korea, with mixed results, then especially in Vietnam, with disastrous results. Did the fault lie in the conformist spirit of the Establishment, or even in its lack of knowledge of the region? For there is no doubt that, if the Wise Men were all excellent managers of public affairs and were quite familiar with Europe, and sometimes with other regions where they did business, they were not specialists in international affairs properly speaking. Kissinger emphasized this in his 1961 *The Necessity for Choice,* as well as in his discussion of the relations between political decision makers (who often came from the Establishment) and intellectuals in foreign policy. He also pointed out the inherent limitations of the Establishment figures: "In a society that has prided itself on its 'business' character, it is inevitable that the qualities which are most esteemed in civilian pursuits should also be generally rewarded by high public office. As a result, the typical Cabinet or sub-Cabinet officer in America comes either from business or from the legal profession. But very little in the experience that forms these men produces the combination of political acumen, conceptual skill, persuasive power, and substantive knowledge required for the highest positions of government."[26]

It was precisely in these terms that Brzezinski saw his colleague, Secretary of State Vance, an Establishment figure. But in the meantime the Establishment had imploded, opening the way to such figures as Kissinger and Brzezinski.

John Kenneth Galbraith, whom David Halberstam interviewed for his book *The Best and the Brightest,* suggested to Halberstam that he should change his title, and instead call his book "The Establishment's War."[27] In fact, the chief responsibility for the involvement in Vietnam doubtless lay more with the Wise Men than with the "whiz kids" around McNamara in the Pentagon or with the intellectuals around Kennedy and Johnson, such as Arthur Schlesinger and Rostow.

McGeorge Bundy is an interesting figure in this regard, for he belonged to both worlds.[28] He was incontestably a man of the Establishment: from a patrician family in Massachusetts known as the "Boston Brahmins" (hence the nickname he was given in college: "Mahatma Bundy"), he went to Groton and Yale (where he was a member of Skull and Bones), and then, before he turned thirty, he was drafted by Henry Stimson to help him write his memoirs.[29] He served in the ground forces during the war, helping to plan the Normandy Landing with General Omar Bradley. After the war, he worked on the Marshall Plan in the Council on Foreign Relations, wrote speeches for the senatorial campaign of John Foster Dulles (he was a Republican), then went to teach at Harvard. In 1953, he was named dean of Harvard College—the faculty of Arts and Sciences—when he was only thirty-four years old.

He did not succeed James Conant as president, but his position allowed him to pursue the latter's work: to make Harvard a great research university at the service of the country. In particular, he helped create the Center for International Affairs (CFIA). He promoted Bowie, Kissinger, and Hoffmann,—and he tried to promote Brzezinski. He was thus a facilitator, an incubator, as it were, of the "professional elite," without really being part of it himself. After all, he had no serious book to his credit (at least before the end of his active career), and he did not have a Ph.D. or even an M.A.

Bundy may be seen as a representative of the Establishment or of the brilliant intellectuals of Kennedy's brain trust, but the fact remains that the Establishment for the most part supported involvement in the Vietnam War up to 1968. Still, this support did not come about without hesitations, reservations, and ruptures. The subject quickly became so sensitive that the Council on Foreign Relations did not put together a working group on Vietnam between 1964 and 1968—the crucial years of American involvement. Feelings were so strong that the CFR's directors could no longer count even on the social codes of good conduct that had made it possible to preserve civilized debates in the heated 1930s. These codes may also have been weakened under the impact of the opening of the CFR to a larger and more diverse membership, so that it had come to embody a much broader and more heterogeneous Establishment.[30]

Moreover, at the heart of the government as well as in the group of Wise Men, if there was a majority position, there was no unanimity—if only by virtue of the priority granted to Europe, so that the war in Asia was perceived as a distraction. Writing in 1973, Godfrey Hodgson summed up the situation by characterizing a spectrum of ornithological positions, going from hawks to doves, among the leading figures of the period. The real hawks (Rostow and Rusk) thought that the war in Vietnam was necessary and that America had not made a mistake it could have avoided. The skeptical hawks didn't go quite that far: they thought that the war was justified but that serious mistakes had been made; this was Bundy's position. Repentant hawks such as Clark Clifford came around to admitting that the war was an error, and thus joined the doves; the latter incriminated not only this war but also the whole policy of containment in Asia that led to it; this was Paul Warnke's view. Finally, the most committed doves considered the Vietnam War worse than an error: it was a crime (this was the position of Daniel Ellsberg, for one).[31]

Among the Wise Men, Acheson described himself, around 1964–1965, as pessimistic about the situation, and he first supported the position of Under-secretary of State George Ball, who warned Kennedy and then Johnson against getting bogged down. Acheson considered that outcome probable, and he tried to propose alternatives. But once American troops were involved, he became more hawkish, reflecting a sacred union of the Establishment around the flag.[32] In fact, throughout the many meetings of the Wise Men, the Establishment supported Johnson's action, most notably in November 1967; the turning point came only in 1968 with the March 25 meeting—after the Tet Offensive.

In the interim, however, the Establishment was not only being torn apart from the inside, it was also losing prestige. It had lost the trust of Americans, trust based on the idea that the elite knew what it was doing, that it had unique knowledge that equipped it to guide the country in a dangerous world. The Establishment, in other words, was caught demonstrating flagrant incompetence on multiple issues: the events in Vietnam, the complex ties between nationalism and communism, the capacities of the army and of American technology.[33] It was no accident that criticism of the CFR as an antidemocratic political organ and even conspiracy theories involving it began to flourish around this time.[34] Thus it was a symbolic turning of the page when Kissinger arrived in the White House in 1969 and took over American foreign policy, at the expense of Secretary of State William Rogers, an Establishment figure. During the years that followed, it was the White House that dominated American foreign policy; instead of turning to a learned assembly of now largely discredited Wise Men, it now relied on a "professional elite."

In the Council on Foreign Relations, two episodes illustrate the end of the consensus. They occurred just a few months apart, in 1971, and they involved the Bundy brothers. In May, McGeorge Bundy gave three talks on the lessons of Vietnam. He acknowledged errors but continued to think that it had been imperative to prevent a communist victory in 1965. After the third talk, he was forcefully challenged by certain members, who considered that, as a "mea culpa," his speech had not gone far enough. Above all, during the following summer, when he was thinking about publishing his talks, a contact at the *New York Times* advised him against it, for he knew the contents of the *Pentagon Papers,* which were to be revealed shortly afterward. In fact, these documents shone a much harsher—and more honest—light on the war. Bundy never published his talks.[35] That same summer, his brother William, assistant secretary of state for East Asia in the Johnson administration and thus closely involved in the war, was named editor of *Foreign Affairs.* But David Rockefeller, the president of the Council on Foreign Relations, had to face an unprecedented rebellion on the part of certain members, who during a meeting treated Bill Bundy as a war criminal, while his supporters retorted that these were "McCarthyites from the left." Rockefeller came out on top, but only with difficulty.[36]

These episodes illustrate the rapid dissolution of the Establishment, with its influence and its social codes. As Isaacson and Thomas wrote:

> For two decades, the Establishment had held sway by sitting squarely astride the middle ground of "informed" public opinion. But by the seventies, the center no longer held; Vietnam had shattered the post-World War II consensus. Power swung to the extremes. The right was just as noisy as ever, but the left began to shout too. . . .
>
> Vietnam forced nearly everyone, even the old guard, to choose sides between "hawk" and "dove." In the fifties, though they differed over method, the "hard" and "soft" camps did not quarrel over the fundamental assumption that the U.S. had a dominant world role to play. But now liberals had become quasi-isolationists; they argued that the U.S. was badly overextended and had to pull back, that Communism was not monolithic and that its threat had been grossly overstated.[37]

The Establishment was fraying for more than one reason; the political factor—the Vietnam War—was not the only factor responsible for its decline. While New York remained the economic capital of the United States and the world, competing centers of power and wealth were beginning to assert themselves, especially in the South (Texas, Georgia) and the West (California); in other words, the Sunbelt. This migration threatened the social preponderance of the northeastern elite and upset the internal political equilibrium in the Republican Party.

The centrist wing of the GOP, which was the Establishment's center of gravity in its natural habitat, was dealt a symbolic blow in 1964 when Barry Goldwater won out over Nelson Rockefeller in the Republican primaries.[38] But it was truly overshadowed when, in the aftermath of Richard Nixon's southern strategy, the power within the party migrated decisively toward the South and toward the right. It was not long before Jesse Helms, the ultraconservative senator from South Carolina, during confirmation hearings on Reagan's nominees for foreign policy positions, began to ask the following question systematically: "Are you a member of the Council on Foreign Relations?"—an obvious reminder of Joseph McCarthy's "Are you now or have you ever been a member of the Communist Party?"[39] This line of questioning was instrumental in bringing about a sort of anti-Establishment cleansing.

In short, behind the gradual fading away of the old Establishment, a shift that had been precipitated by the war in Vietnam, a deeper process of social and political upheaval was under way in America, one that brought a new type of foreign policy elite to the fore: Kissinger and Brzezinski were its precursors.

The Emergence of the New Professional Elite

"Until Kissinger," Leslie Gelb wrote in 1976, "universities and think tanks were appendages of the Establishment, places to get ideas and faithful subordinates. To be sure, the appendages gained a firm foothold in the Establishment in the Kennedy Administration with men like McGeorge Bundy and Walt Rostow. But with the ascendency of Kissinger, they moved into the very heart of the Establishment and took over."[40]

The logical sequel to the Cold War University, with its fantastic intake in terms of intellect and expertise aroused by America's rise to a position of global responsibility, was the arrival in the foreign affairs marketplace of men specifically trained to deal with international relations—and who would soon find themselves at the helm. "The new class . . . was created not to wrest power away from the older, more traditional Establishment, but ostensibly to serve it," Halberstam recalled, thinking perhaps of the way James Conant or McGeorge Bundy sought to train, one after another, the best possible specialists in area studies and international relations.[41]

The rise of this new class to positions of power was accompanied by a gradual shift in the center of gravity of the foreign policy elite from New York toward Washington, where the Council on Foreign Relations opened a branch office in 1972. The federal capital, which up to then had looked like an intellectual desert, began to acquire a critical mass with stronger universities nourished by foreign affairs practitioners, more and more think tanks, important newspapers and magazines, and so on. The renewal of the foreign policy elite was accompanied above all by a pronounced social change: lawyers specializing in business, businessmen themselves, and Wall Street bankers were being replaced by professors, think tank experts, Congressional assistants, staff members of major foundations, lawyers, political activists, and journalists, all of whom were reaching the very highest levels of decision making in American foreign policy.

This evolution also marked the triumph of meritocracy. The 1944 G.I. Bill of Rights had opened the way: after transforming the composition of university student bodies, it had begun to make its effects felt in American society at large. With new recruitment policies, Harvard, Yale, and Princeton were no longer reserved to the sons of the well born; they were broadly opened up to new populations from the middle or even lower middle classes, including immigrant populations with unfamiliar names such as "Heinz Kissinger" or "Zbigniew Brzezinski." The family name no longer sufficed to guarantee a career; as Halberstam wrote, "it was harder for the children of bygone glories to assume command, for they were often outstripped in college by the hungry, driven children of the meritocracy."[42] Brzezinski himself has often stressed how different he felt from the WASP elite, and how clearly he had perceived the passing of the torch to more diverse populations.

Wall Street bankers were WASPs, and they were influent in the Council on Foreign Relations, they represented this dominant view of America's role in the world, going all the way back to the 30s, even the 20s, Wilson, even going back to Roosevelt, I think that has sociologically changed

America, it has become fragmented, eclectic; other groups, Jews, Central Europeans, Eastern Europeans and now Asians and Hindus have increasingly became part of the game, in a way, I was symbolic, Henry was particularly symbolic because he was among the first, and very visibly so. . . . I remember Carter writing a hand-written note to the entire staff, learning how to spell and pronounce Zbigniew Brzezinski, but that was revolutionary. But now, you have Asian names, Hindu names, all sorts of names.[43]

The passage from one elite to the next did not take place overnight, nor was it all amicable. During the 1970s, two famous incidents of friction emblematized the difference in values between the Establishment and the professional elite: these were clashes between Kissinger and Brzezinski with their respective secretaries of state, William Rogers and Cyrus Vance—two heirs of the Establishment, two men of the old school. Very quickly, Rogers was pushed aside by Kissinger, who centralized American foreign policy in the White House with Nixon's approval, and literally pushed the State Department into the shadows—even as he centralized the operations of a very well-staffed National Security Council (NSC) around himself. But it was not only a classic situation of bureaucratic domination: between the two men there were also different codes of conduct, different values. Rogers's personal discretion, modesty, integrity, and loyalty were in striking contrast to Kissinger's orchestrated self-promotion, his seduction of journalists and his art of calculated retreat, his brusque and often deceptive or devious modus operandi, even toward his own advisers.[44]

Brzezinski, for his part, explained his relations with Vance and Warren Christopher, deputy secretary of state, in terms of sociological differences. In *Power and Principle,* a memoir of his service as national security adviser, he classified both men as representative of a "once-dominant WASP elite" to which he did not belong any more than President Jimmy Carter did, and to which "it was not easy for [him] to relate."[45] He noted, in this context, that the decline of the WASPs in America coincided with a decline in Anglo-American hegemony in the world. Brzezinski also saw Vance and Christopher as embodying the virtues and limitations of the legal profession (both were lawyers), ready to negotiate interminably, even when the intricacies of legal argument ought to give way to the use of force in an international environment much more violent than that of the world of American business, and in which not all problems could be solved by negotiation. Brzezinski deeply regretted that Vance's values as a "gentleman" led him to refuse to consider espionage directed at foreign embassies, and he added that, "like Secretary Henry Stimson earlier, he seemed to feel that one should not read other people's mail," whereas he himself recommended to Carter that microphones be placed in the cottages of Camp David in 1978 to listen to the internal deliberations of the Israeli and Egyptian negotiators (Carter rejected the idea).[46] The Wise Men, especially Averell Harriman, who had been Vance's mentor, returned the compliment, depicting Brzezinski as a dyed-in-the-wool anti-Soviet "who's not really an American."[47]

This confrontation between Vance and Brzezinski—a real one, but considerably exaggerated by the press and thus in the collective memory—was also interpreted as a clash between Establishment values and those of the "new professional elite," by the very authors of the concept of this new elite, Leslie Gelb and Anthony Lake. They depicted the uneven confrontation between Vance, a gentleman operating according to the principle of noblesse oblige (and who, for example, once reprimanded a subordinate for a calumny leaked in the press against the national security adviser) and Brzezinski, who was represented as a cynical operator who would stoop to anything in order to prevail and who used the press freely to destabilize Vance. In reality, the confrontations came about primarily among members of the "professional elite": under the Carter administration, Gelb, a *New York Times* journalist, and Lake, a diplomat who had worked for the Carnegie Foundation, were two of Vance's key lieutenants at the State Department. They were the ones to whom Brzezinski later attributed the flood of leaks directed against him, leaving him to think that the anecdote about Vance's reprimand addressed to "one of his subordinates" was a firsthand account.[48] In short, the real sociological break doubtless ran between Vance, a relic of the former era, and the rest of the administration, rather than between the State Department and Brzezinski's NSC.

The sites of power of the foreign policy Establishment, all located in New York, had been the banks, the major business law firms, the boards of big businesses, clubs, and of course the Council on Foreign Relations. Men left Wall Street for Washington to serve in the government for a few years, then returned to the private sector in order to manage their businesses again. As for the academics from Harvard and MIT who were called on as experts, they generally made the Cambridge-Washington round-trip on a weekly basis, while maintaining their university positions. But in the 1960s, the situation began to change. A between-two-worlds zone developed and expanded, giving experts the opportunity to continue to work on foreign policy after completing stints in positions of responsibility, in a fast-growing network of benevolent universities, think tanks, foundations, newspapers, consultancies, political action committees, and so on. This material infrastructure was what made the rise of the new professional elite possible; the enlightened dilettantism of lawyers and bankers was becoming a thing of the past. "The other pleasant surprise" of those years, Brzezinski has explained, "is discovering that you can be outside of government without having—in my case—to go back to academia 100%, but to use the academic connection to remain relevant to the policy-making process."[49]

Paradoxically, the Council of Foreign Relations remained one of the new professional elite's most important sites of power. The CFR, Root's institution, served both Kissinger and Brzezinski as a springboard from the mid-1950s to the mid-1960s. In the 1970s, as a consequence of the divisions provoked by the Vietnam War, the Council began to lose some of its preeminence, because it was no longer able to co-opt the new elite: whether on the right or the left, these newcomers preferred to criticize from the outside rather than to fall in with the Establishment and respect its rules of low-key debate. In addition, and more important, other comparable organizations, located closer to the center of power in Washington, were on the rise.[50] Nevertheless, the CFR remained a preeminent institution, and it continues to flourish to this day; many members of the new "professional elite" have been groomed there.

The 1970s saw a blossoming of think tanks. The Brookings Institution is one of the most powerful and the earliest, created in 1916. It played a role in the conception of the United Nations and the Marshall Plan, but its foreign policy program was not really fleshed out until Henry Owen, who had been Brzezinski's patron on the Policy Planning Council, became its director in 1969.[51] Owen expanded the activity at Brookings in this area, focusing on concerning defense issues; he recruited a number of experts who had worked in the Johnson and Nixon administrations, such as Edward Fried and Morton Halperin, and he launched numerous task forces to produced new ideas and offer alternatives to the administration's positions. Brzezinski participated in one of these in 1975, on the Middle East, and the experience influenced him so much that in *Power and Principle,* his memoirs devoted to the Carter administration, he reproduced the outlines of the plan for Israeli-Palestinian peace—including the idea of a Palestinian state—that the Brookings group had recommended (one of its members was William Quandt, who later worked with Brzezinski at the NSC).[52]

Positioned to the left of the Brookings Institution, the Carnegie Endowment for International Peace New York was founded in New York in 1910; this group too had Root as its first president. In 1971, pressed by its newly elected president Thomas Hughes, the Endowment decided to relocate from New York to Washington and to work on American foreign policy rather than focusing on the United Nations; it thus provided a home for the new quarterly journal *Foreign Policy.* Much further to the left—indeed, on the margins— was the Institute for Policy Studies (IPS) founded in 1963 by Richard Barnet and Marcus Raskin; the IPS was the voice of anti-imperialist protest. On the right, during the same period, a number of think tanks were also speaking out. The Center for Strategic and International Studies (CSIS), founded in 1962 at Georgetown, a hawkish and conservative Jesuit university, was close for example to the group around Henry "Scoop" Jackson in the Senate and on the Reaganian right; it concentrated on strategic analysis, following the example of Britain's International Institute for Strategic Studies (IISS).[53] Later, in the 1980s, the CSIS become more bipartisan; it welcomed Brzezinski, Kissinger, and James Schlesinger into its ranks in order to balance its political line. The Heritage Foundation, created in 1972 to concentrate entirely on Congress, and the American Enterprise Institute (AEI), created during the Second World War, responded to the challenge posed by Brookings by paying more and more attention to international affairs. The AEI in particular provided a platform for the growing neoconservative movement: its members included Irving Kristol, Jeane Kirkpatrick, and Michael Novak. Finally, moving beyond Washington to the West Coast the Hoover Institution at Stanford continued to welcome experts and thinkers on the right.

But the between-two-worlds zone that offered the new professional elite the possibility of continuing to work on foreign affairs while shifting from one set of responsibilities to another also encompassed other types of institutions: nongovernmental organizations such as Freedom House, charitable foundations (Ford and Carnegie, for example), hybrids such as the Atlantic Council (1961), or the German Marshall Fund of the United States, created in 1972 by the German government thanks to the activism of Guido Goldman (who had studied with Kissinger, Brzezinski, and Hoffmann at Harvard). It also included political groups and "citizens' committees" such as the Trilateral Commission organized by Brzezinski and David Rockefeller, the Coalition for a Democratic Majority, the Committee on the Present Danger.[54] It even included Congress, where congressional assistant positions were becoming more and more specialized.

There remained, of course, the universities and their research centers, such as Brzezinski's Research Institute on Communist Affairs at Columbia, along with schools of international relations (SAIS, the Fletcher School, the Elliott School, and so on), which offered great latitude to their faculties. Brzezinski, for example, was granted frequent sabbatical leaves—for his tour of the world during the academic year 1962–1963, for his stint on the Policy Planning Council from July 1966 to early 1968, for his residency in Japan in 1971, for his work on the Trilateral Commission in 1973–1975, and so on.

For the members of the new professional elite who remained in university positions, however, the articulation between the academic world and the political world was not necessarily easy to manage. This was Brzezinski's case, with the student revolt. But several professors who had taken part in the Vietnam War experienced much more serious misadventures. The offices of John Roche (a personal adviser to LBJ) at Brandeis and those of Ed Gullion (ambassador to the Congo) at Tufts' Fletcher School were bombed, and Walt Rostow lost his position at MIT; his colleagues refused to take him back, and he had to go into "exile" at the University of Texas.[55]

Brzezinski too sometimes found himself squeezed in the uneasy articulation between his university colleagues and the policy he was defending—even if his vision of "peaceful engagement" with the communist bloc compensated somewhat for his position on Vietnam.[56] When he worked in the Policy Planning Council, he tried to improve relations between the academic community and the Johnson administration and even with the president himself. In May 1967, Johnson brought together those of his advisers who were also academics, and Brzezinski tried to explain to the president that his communication problem with the professors resulted from his personal style. Silence fell in the room; no one breathed. Johnson replied that he had taken all the social reform measures the professors had wanted, but that he could not change his style, and he asked all the advisers present to pick up their pilgrim's staffs and go off to defend the administration.[57]

Shortly afterward, Brzezinski received a letter from a Columbia colleague, William Fox, who had been infuriated by the account of that meeting in the *New York Times*. The article described the objective as an attempt on the administration's part to understand "what ailed some of their distinguished colleagues in the intellectual community"—as if the administration were infallible and the problem necessarily lay with the professors.[58] Fox took particular issue with the fact that moderate critics like himself had been ignored and treated as enemies. Brzezinski replied that the article did not accurately report the goals of the meeting, which was supposed to have remained confidential, but that he accepted the criticism and would share it with his colleagues. He added that he was sorry that within academia only the unconditional supporters and the hysterical opponents of the Vietnam War were making themselves heard, for he was in agreement with Fox's reasoned arguments (Fox had stressed that, from Thailand to Indonesia, the dominoes hadn't fallen, a fact that gave the United States some room to maneuver).[59] A little later, contrary to Francis Bator's hopes, Brzezinski advised Johnson against meeting with a group of professors at Harvard: he thought that the faculty had made up its own mind and that a meeting would be of no use (Johnson ended up following Brzezinski's advice).[60]

If the university offered the new professional elite a sometimes ambivalent base, that elite found itself welcomed with open arms by the media, which were experiencing a continuous expansion (in the case of television) and a golden age (in the case of the press). This additional transformation of American civilization contributed to the decline of the old Establishment in many different ways. For one thing, the credibility of Establishment discourse on Vietnam was collapsing, while that of the media was rising. Journalists felt less and less in thrall to politicians, less obliged, for example, to keep state secrets (as they had done with respect to the Cuban missile crisis), while pressure in favor of leaks—a cardinal sin, for the old school—was regularly increasing, first with Vietnam and then with Watergate.[61] More generally, information was spreading, and the major networks, supported by their own networks of correspondents and, before long, by their own media experts, could claim at least as much knowledge of international events as the Wise Men had.

The latter, as Isaacson and Thomas note, "abhorred publicity."[62] By contrast, under the operating rules of the new elite, visibility was a major asset. It was important to publish not in dusty academic journals but in places where the writing could influence the public debate and make authors known at the same time. Two types of publications counted: the journals that focused on international affairs (*Foreign Affairs, Foreign Policy, The New Republic, Commentary,* and the like), and the press that addressed a truly broad audience: the three major publications were the *New York Times, Time Magazine,* and *Newsweek,* but the *Washington Post* (especially in the federal capital) and the *Wall Street Journal* (especially on the right) were also widely read. The opinion pages of the *New York Times* dated from 1970, whereas in many journals the habit of soliciting opinions from experts or publishing their public presentations had already been established. Brzezinski benefited from this privilege starting in the 1960s, especially in the *Washington Post.* From December 1969 to September 1970, Brzezinski even had a regular column in *Newsweek* that was almost always reproduced in the *Washington Post,* a situation that contributed considerably to his reputation.

As for the specialized press, in late 1970, as it happened, Brzezinski participated in the adventure of launching *Foreign Policy,* a magazine created by his friend Sam Huntington along with Warren Demian Manshel (another Harvard alumnus who made a fortune on Wall Street and had already financed the launching of *The Public Interest* in 1965). The idea of *Foreign Policy* was to offer a platform for new and original ideas after the hawk / dove split over Vietnam, in a livelier style than the staid and boring *Foreign Affairs.* The journal was intended to be "post-birds and anti-sacred cows."[63] Its intent was to explore a topsy-turvy world that did not consist exclusively in bipolar confrontation— even if *Foreign Policy* took that situation quite seriously—but also encompassed new developments and new forces: multinational firms, interdependence, the media, technology, oil, North-South relations, the environment, and so on. The quarterly publication, with an original format, quickly took over as the organ of the new elite, and it published several articles that became classics, such as the one by Stanley Hoffmann on the Algerian solution to Vietnam (cited by McGeorge Bundy during his talks at the CFR in May 1971), and texts by Albert Wohnstetter, Paul Warnke, and Paul Nitze on the arms race, Godfrey Hodgson's piece on the end of the Establishment (no surprises), and Brzezinski's articles on the Nixon administration, especially his famous report assigning letter grades to the administration at the half-way mark, in 1971.[64]

Foreign Policy has often been accused of purveying a left-oriented partisan line, the one expressed in Carter's foreign policy, at least within the State Department. It is undeniable that the journal was one of the sites where reconstruction of liberalism took place after Vietnam, and that a number of those who would later work for Carter were published in that journal—Richard Holbrooke, the future deputy secretary of state for Asia, was even its editor from 1972 to 1976. However, the political diversity of the writers was such that the accusation is by and large inaccurate. Moreover, Huntington and Brzezinski were hawkish Democrats, different from the generation of Democrats affected by the Vietnam syndrome (Gelb, Lake, Halperin, Holbrooke, and others), as they proved in the political battles of the Carter administration. And, even with a powerful personality such as Holbrooke in charge, they retained ultimate control over the editorial line of *Foreign Policy*. The archives reveal, among other things, that Brzezinski played an active role in the journal and gave his opinions about proposed members of the editorial committee and potential authors.[65] Thus Charles Gati—a specialist in Eastern Europe and one of Brzezinski's protégés at Columbia—recalls that his article "The Forgotten Region," which suggested that the Ford-Kissinger policy led to neglect of Eastern Europe, was imposed on Holbrooke by Brzezinski, who disagreed completely with Gati.[66]

Brzezinski also proved early on to be a star on television, as much at ease under the camera's eye as he was drafting an op-ed column, and his on-screen performances contributed to his notoriety. As early as 1962, he was chosen to inaugurate the series of televised presentations for five commercial networks that the School of International Affairs at Columbia was negotiating with the Metropolitan Broadcasting Company (in these performances, he evoked the consequences of tensions within the communist bloc).[67] The most important televised debate in which he participated during those years was unquestionably the one on Vietnam, which pitted National Security Adviser McGeorge Bundy supported by Brzezinski and an expert from RAND, against Hans Morgenthau, the father of the discipline of international relations at the University of Chicago, supported in his fierce opposition to the war by two other experts.[68] Brzezinski defended his vision of falling dominoes, warning, as he had done in his *Washington Post* article against the consequences of Chinese hegemony, which would be felt in Asia but would also influence the attitude of the Soviets. During the years that followed, and indeed for the rest of his life, he continued to frequent the New York studios of the various television networks, particularly, from 2007 to his death ten years later, for the *Morning Joe* program on MSNBC on which his daughter Mika was a cohost.

But the depiction of power centers and the operating rules of the new professional elite would be incomplete without the crucial link of presidential campaigns, which have tended to serve as ladders leading toward power.

The "marketplace of experts" in international affairs that can be observed at the beginning of each administration is based on a long period of advance preparation, which decides who will be placed where in the hierarchies of the State Department, the Pentagon, and the NSC. It is not enough for the experts to make themselves attractive by their production of op-ed columns and reports, their knowledge and their original ideas, their institutional positions; they must also commit themselves to the team of a particular presidential candidate—and they must choose the right one, the one who has the greatest chance of winning while being receptive to the message of the expert. If this candidate loses in the primaries, it is always possible to join the team of his victorious rival, but in a subordinate position with respect to other experts. The actual work, moreover, is limited; only a small group of individuals do the bulk of the work, which consisted in drafting speeches, preparing for the debates, and orienting the candidate while reconciling foreign policy with the electoral imperatives.

Brzezinski occupied a subordinate position in the 1960 Kennedy campaign. He also did not play a major role in Johnson's 1964 campaign (he was a member of the orientation council of the committee of young citizens for Johnson).[69] In 1968, by contrast, he was Humphrey's principal foreign policy adviser. A close look at Kissinger's itinerary as adviser in 1968 and Brzezinski's in 1972 will make it clear how electoral campaigns work and highlight their significance. But first, it will be useful to review some of the controversies and challenges that came to the fore as the new professional elite was edging out the old Establishment.

From the mid-1970s on, the idea of the emergence of a new elite was challenged from the left and even more from the right. Conservatives and neoconservatives viewed the new elite as neither more nor less than an avatar of the old Establishment—but a degraded avatar with depleted virility and strength of character; it had abandoned the worldview that had prevailed since 1945 and had lost its faith in America. Carl Gershman, the future president of the National Endowment for Democracy, in a still-famous article in *Commentary,* explained that the liberals had succeeded in distancing themselves with respect to the Vietnam War, for which they were nonetheless responsible. Helped by the eight years under Nixon, to whom moral responsibility for the war had been transferred little by little, they succeeded in restoring their virginity, as it were, and they reinvented a new form of liberalism in foreign policy for which the journal *Foreign Policy* became a primary outlet.[70]

This "Foreign Policy Establishment," according to Gershman, comprised members of the old elite (including Warnke, Hughes, and Vance), young diplomats of the Vietnam generation (Holbrooke, Gelb, Lake, and others), and various experts or theoreticians such as Stanley Hoffmann, Zbigniew Brzezinski, and Marshall Shulman. In the new liberal doctrine, a central place was occupied by the lesson of Vietnam and the blindness to which anti-communism led (Carter, in a speech at Notre Dame on May 22, 1977, evoked "the inordinate fear of communism"[71]). In particular, Gershman stigmatized the five liberal ideas at the heart of that elite's new consensus: military strength was outmoded; the North-South axis had replaced the East-West axis; economic interdependence and third-world nationalisms were creating a world in which America must no longer intervene; the peoples of the world were more interested in equality than in freedom (hence an attitude of moral relativism with regard to sociopolitical systems); and the USSR was above all a defensive power—an idea supported in particular by Kennan. In his conclusion, Gershman declared that "the new Establishment never spoke for the country as a whole but for a narrow if influential sector of the elite which had ceased to believe in America after Vietnam, and which despite its proclaimed optimism seems to have resigned itself to the forward momentum of political forces in the world committed to America's defeat."[72]

Other authors emphasized, as Gershman did, the continuity between the traditional Establishment and the new liberal elite. Thus, far from fading away, the Council on Foreign Relations continued to exercise persistent influence and remained at the heart of the networks that really counted. Richard Perle, for his part, underscored the uniformity of thought that continued to characterize the new elite, along with its gregarious aspect: "There is a tendency to pursue the fashionable. If you asked them to rate national security problems now and five years ago, you would get startlingly different results. They're all drinking from the same intellectual well. They're all living off the same foundations and institutions."[73]

These critiques are partly justified, but the overall approach is erroneous. First, *Foreign Policy* was much more diverse than its critics on the right acknowledged. Of the five pillars of the new liberalism denounced by Gershman, Brzezinski, for example, can be identified with only one—the idea that the world's peoples seem more interested in equality than in freedom; he further developed this position in an article in *Foreign Policy*.[74] But far from drawing a relativist or pessimistic conclusion, he asserted that America must maintain its values, practice "capitalism in one country"; he criticized the country's introspective, even isolationist climate, but he declared his optimism about the future of America. Beyond that, he certainly did not contest the importance of military strength or of the Soviet challenge: he simply tried to incorporate the North-South dimension into his vision.

But even if excessive generalizations were set aside and the validity of the criticisms that Gershwin and Perle addressed to the new Establishment were acknowledged—the fashion effect, the lesson of Vietnam taken too far, and so on—it is the overall framework of the critique that poses a problem. For the idea is not that a leading foreign policy elite has disappeared; it is rather that its sociological profile and operating rules have been overturned. Moreover, the victorious attack of the neoconservatives on the liberals confirms this thesis. The neoconservatives are not Wall Street bankers either; they are foreign affairs professionals. Perle, for example, worked for a citizens' committee—the Committee to Maintain a Prudent Defense Policy, led by two members of the Establishment, Nitze and Acheson—before rejoining the team of Senator Scoop Jackson, who was in charge of international affairs; Gershman was a political activist (with Social Democrats USA) who worked at Freedom House. In other words, though they could stigmatize a faction of the new "professional elite" in power under Carter, they could not deny that they themselves belonged to it—they rose to power under Reagan, relying on their own network of foundations and think tanks, a network that Sidney Blumenthal has called the "counter-Establishment."[75] The tone used in their ideological attacks reinforced the idea that the gentlemen of the Establishment, for their part, belonged definitively to the past.

This controversy underlines an important characteristic of the new professional elite. Undeniably, the 1970s were a decade during which foreign affairs became much more politicized than they had been, the period in which expertise was immediately analyzed as coming from the right or from the left. If think tanks were multiplying, it was because a number of them had a pronounced ideological orientation and had to respond to the political demands of their financial supporters. Moreover, Destler, Gelb, and Lake began their study of the new professional elite with the observation that Carter, and then Reagan four years later, had filled all the higher echelons of the Pentagon, the State Department, and the National Security Council with their own partisans, and that no one remained in place from one administration to the next, so far apart were the two groups in terms of their worldview.

Still, this central characteristic of the new professional elite does not apply to Kissinger or to Brzezinski. Their trajectories do not stand out by virtue of their membership in a camp, a school of thought in foreign policy—liberal, realist, neoconservative, or the new right—but by virtue of the fact that they had gone through the Cold War University and had been pioneers in terms of the new rules for selecting members of the elite, quickly attaining high positions of authority despite their social origins. Left-right polarization came after they had already begun their careers, and neither one was ever driven by ideology; each has always developed his own ideas even to the point, in Brzezinski's case, of not supporting the Democratic candidate in certain instances (1972 and 1988), and to the point, in Kissinger's case, of looking like an opportunist, passing himself off (unconvincingly) as a supporter of the new right in the 1980s and then, later, as a partisan of Bush and the invasion of Iraq. This distinction is what makes it possible to call them precursors—rather than archetypes—of the professional elite, and it reinforces the idea that they indeed belonged to the microgeneration at Harvard that could no longer be characterized as part of the Establishment but was not quite yet part of the professional elite.

Kissinger 1968 / Brzezinski 1972: Two Revealing Electoral Campaigns

Kissinger and Brzezinski were at once precursors and masterminds of the new elite, in the sense that they had learned more quickly but also put into practice more energetically and more successfully than anyone else the new recipes for access to power. One of the keys of their success was the art of putting the capital they had accumulated in one of the four areas that counted—academia, the media, society, and politics—to work in the other areas; in other words, they were able to set up virtuous circles entailing their intellectual standing, their visibility, their networks, and their status as political advisers, so that each advance in one field opened new doors and possibilities in another.

Kissinger benefited early on—starting with his 350-page master's thesis on the direction of history—from a well-deserved image of intellectual brilliance that he maintained through his numerous publications. That image had been his principal asset in the effort to get the attention of people who counted: professors such as William Yandell Elliott, businessmen such as Nelson Rockefeller, journalists, and politicians. In 1951, with the help of Bill Elliott, Kissinger created the International Seminar at Harvard, which gave him an exceptional network of acquaintances, not only abroad but also within the aristocracy of the transatlantic "Republic of Letters," through the journal *Confluence*—and this network opened up new horizons that reinforced his intellectual panache. It was precisely because Nelson Rockefeller found him brilliant but also enterprising, thanks to the summer seminar, that he hired Kissinger in 1955 to run special projects for the Rockefeller Brothers Fund, bringing Kissinger material comfort and greater visibility.[76]

That same year, a certain Arthur Schlesinger Jr., who also admired the young man's intellectual capacities, sent his contacts at the Council on Foreign Relations a copy of the remarks Kissinger had made on one of Schlesinger's papers about nuclear deterrence.[77] That led to Kissinger's first article in *Foreign Affairs* in April 1955.[78] More important, it led to the invitation to become director of a CFR study group on nuclear weapons, a (collective) project that was the basis for his (personal) 1957 best-seller, *Nuclear Weapons and Foreign Policy.*[79] That book really launched Kissinger's public career and gave him enviable visibility. But it also conferred such status that Harvard could no longer deny him a university position, and McGeorge Bundy installed him as deputy director of the CFIA and extracted a tenured position for him in the Government Department. To be sure, these successes were followed by failure when he sought to convert this intellectual and social capital to political capital: he was indeed invited to work for the White House, which wanted to keep his competencies for itself and not let Rusk's State Department put them to its own use, but his relations with Bundy were not good, and Kissinger's first experience in Washington was a failure.

That fact in no way kept him from continuing to move his pawns forward on various chessboards—book publications, interviews and opinion pieces, consultancies for the State Department or RAND, work for Nelson Rockefeller's campaigns, and so on; every move brought him additional experience and supplementary contacts that enhanced his reputation and that he could put to use elsewhere. Then came the 1968 electoral campaign, the high point of a strategy of omnipresence taken to the extreme, and a critical moment in which the capital he had accumulated in his various fields (academia, media, society, politics) could be transformed into the only currency that counted: power. Because the stakes were so high, Kissinger took enormous risks and came close to being ruled out, before ending up with the highest prize in the race, an office in the White House.

To summarize a bit simplistically, Kissinger played the role of double if not triple agent during the campaign, in order to maximize his chances of being part of the team that would finally be in charge. In the beginning, he worked for his patron Nelson Rockefeller, but, once Rockefeller's defeat by Nixon in the primaries was accepted, in March-April 1968, Kissinger offered to inform Humphrey's camp about Nixon—and then to inform Nixon's camp about the progress in the Paris negotiations with North Vietnam.

Ted Van Dyk recalls in his memoirs that he visited the Rockefeller head-quarters in Manhattan around 1965 and was impressed by the documentation, some of it negative, that had been collected about Nixon, a huge "black book" of sorts. When Rockefeller was defeated, Van Dyk remembered that mine of information, thinking that it might be of use to the Humphrey campaign, for which he was an adviser. He then asked Brzezinski to ask his buddy Kissinger for this document, and Kissinger agreed.[80] In his biography of Kissinger, Walter Isaacson added that the offer to show the files to Humphrey's camp was also made directly to Kissinger by Sam Huntington, one of Brzezinski's acolytes during the campaign, at the end of the summer at Martha's Vineyard, where they were both vacationing.[81] There was nothing suspect about this, moreover: until mid-November, Kissinger shared with many people, including Brzezinski, what a poor opinion he had always had of Nixon, even his hatred for the individual. Weeks went by, however, and Kissinger put off keeping his word. Finally, the day when Brzezinski was preparing to go get the dossier in person, Kissinger's secretary called him up to cancel the appointment, for Kissinger had become Nixon's adviser.[82]

Nine years later, in 1977, when Brzezinski had just arrived at the White House, he attended a reception at the Senate in honor of Hubert Humphrey, who had been diagnosed with cancer. During his remarks, Brzezinski declared to Humphrey: "The greatest opportunity in my life was to serve in your 1968 campaign." Then, singling out Kissinger in the audience, he tossed out a barbed remark that was intelligible to only a few insiders: "And I want to publicly thank Dr. Kissinger for the assistance he offered during that campaign."[83]

But the story does not end there. At the beginning of September, Nixon's foreign policy adviser Richard Allen received a phone call from Kissinger, who offered to supply Nixon with information about the Paris peace negotiations with North Vietnam—a crucial factor for the final two months of the campaign, since the announcement of a peace agreement or even of decisive progress could affect the results of the election. Kissinger had refused an offer, made by Allen a few weeks earlier, to become an official adviser to Nixon, saying that he would be more useful if his role were not made public.[84] And with good reason: he had worked as a consultant for the Johnson administration, had excellent contacts within the delegation led by Harriman, and he mentioned to Allen that he was leaving for Paris a few days later.[85] Allen eagerly accepted, and Kissinger—who did indeed have access to information about the peace talks (as was later confirmed by members of the on-site negotiating team, Holbrooke in particular)—had the information transmitted to Nixon, who corroborated this in his memoirs.[86]

In the end, the material transmitted was not crucial. Kissinger did in fact keep Nixon informed about the progress of the negotiations, and warned him in advance about the agreement that allowed the suspension of bombing on October 31. On the one hand, Nixon had another source of information on the negotiating team, a fact of which Kissinger was unaware; on the other hand, it seems that Kissinger may have overreached when he arranged to send an implicit message to the South Vietnamese president Nguyen Van Thieu, that he would obtain a result more favorable to his own interests if Nixon won the election, thus depriving Humphrey of an agreement that would have been highly advantageous for his campaign.[87]

But the result of this transmission of information, which has been denounced as a betrayal by some, was that it enabled Kissinger to attract Nixon's attention and confidence; for multiple complex reasons, Nixon ended up inviting him to become his national security adviser, with the primary task of bypassing the State Department and centralizing foreign policy in the White House. For Kissinger, this was more or less a "mission accomplished," at the price of a few sharp turns and a rapid reversal of his personal opinion of Nixon. "Kissinger's capacity to be all things to all campaigns," Halberstam comments, "an overt Rockefeller man, a semi-overt Humphrey man, a covert Nixon man—reflects the emergence of the rootless operator in the modern superstate."[88] We are undeniably far removed from the Wise Men of the Establishment, whom presidents almost had to beg to get them to agree to go to Washington to serve the country.

Brzezinski provides another example, both of the way successes in various fields of activity were mutually reinforcing, and of the importance of presidential campaigns, even if he falls short of the level of suppleness in maneuvering achieved by Kissinger in 1968. Just as was the case for Kissinger, Brzezinski's greatest asset at the start lay in the intellectual brilliance that drew the attention of his professors and protectors, and that he gradually managed to transform into visibility via the media, into useful social relations, and into an influential political role.

Carl Friedrich, for example, offered to coauthor the book that Brzezinski had in mind on totalitarianism, and this helped make the young Brzezinski known in the university milieu starting in 1956. Then Bowie welcomed him to the CFIA and encouraged him to write *The Soviet Bloc,* which launched his career as a recognized specialist in an important and innovative subject. Paradoxically, it was his failure to achieve a tenured position at Harvard that accelerated his career. As he himself had suspected, New York was an ideal platform for his social and political advancement. His insertion in the networks of the Council on Foreign Relations, his greater media visibility, and his position taking led to the offer of a slot on the Policy Planning Council. From there, he extended his influence toward the White House, and in particular toward the vice president, who turned out to be the Democratic candidate for 1968 and who invited Brzezinski to become his chief adviser on foreign policy. The electoral defeat temporarily broke this virtuous circle, but Brzezinski soon rebounded.

To flesh out the paradigm of the rise of the new elite, it will be useful to take a quick look at Brzezinski's trajectory beyond 1968. He continued to publish, but he extended his realm of expertise toward international affairs in general (*Between Two Ages: America's Role in the Technetronic Era,* 1970), and then toward Japan (*The Fragile Blossom,* 1972), in order to become a more complete, more "universal" expert.[89] His good relations with McGeorge Bundy, who had become president of the Ford Foundation, along with his image as an influential intellectual, allowed him to get funding for a period of residency in Japan. His stint there reinforced his idea that it was essential to privilege ties among developed nations: this was the origin of the Trilateral Commission, which David Rockefeller (Nelson's brother) agreed to fund. Brzezinski became its director, further expanding his networks and his influence. In fact, it was through the Trilateral Commission that he met Jimmy Carter, who found Brzezinski's analytic notes and his advice so fruitful that he named him his principal foreign policy adviser in 1976. Carter's victorious presidential campaign, unlike the one in 1968, finally opened the White House doors to Brzezinski.

If Brzezinski is viewed as a representative or simply a precursor of the new professional elite, then the 1972 campaign is most revealing as far as its functioning and its new rules were concerned. In 1968, and especially in 1976, Brzezinski occupied a central place on the team of the Democratic candidate who won the primaries: the situation was thus clear, and those campaigns, however interesting they may be in themselves, do not contribute much to our understanding of the new mechanisms for selecting decision makers in the realm of American foreign policy. The 1972 campaign, by contrast, allows us to penetrate the workings of the new elite and allows us a better grasp of the conditions of Brzezinski's political rise.

Two weeks after Humphrey's defeat in the 1968 election, responding to a letter of thanks from Humphrey for his services,[90] Brzezinski wrote to thank Humphrey in turn for having entrusted him with an important role in his campaign and for having embodied a humanistic alternative to Nixon. Above all, he shared once again his fears for the Democratic Party: Humphrey had become its political conscience, and he needed to prevent it from deviating toward ideological extremism. To that end, Brzezinski suggested using the network of task forces that had been set up during the campaign.[91] In other words, he offered to continue to advise Humphrey during the years to come. And this is in fact what happened, at Humphrey's urging, most notably in the run-up to the 1972 primaries.

On several occasions in 1969 and 1970, Brzezinski sent advice in response to specific requests by Humphrey.[92] Thus, for the latter's planned trip to the USSR in mid-1969, Brzezinski recommended a program of meetings (and tourism), and he indicated the best way to keep Moscow from instrumentalizing the trip—in particular by spending a couple of days in Prague at the end of his travels to meet the Prague Spring leaders, Alexander Dubcek and Ludvik Svoboda, as well as Gustav Husak, the figure of normalization, and by visiting the village of Lidice, which had been destroyed by the Nazis, to keep things in balance. He also advised Humphrey to go see the "nationalities"—Ukrainians, Georgians, and so on—and to read Aleksandr Solzhenitsyn's latest book to prepare for the visit.[93]

In the course of 1970, Brzezinski and Humphrey began to address each other in their letters as "Dear Zbig" and "Dear Hubert." By contrast, in 1956, Humphrey was "Senator Humphrey"; then throughout the 1968 campaign and in 1969 he remained "Mr. Vice President." This evolution is not simply a reflection of American informality: it marks both Brzezinski's maturation and his rise to a more elevated status, less subordinate to Humphrey; in a more general way, he was acceding to the more egalitarian relationship that can develop between politicians and their foreign policy advisers in a more complex world, one in which the adviser's role has increased in importance. Moreover, as he did during the 1968 campaign, Brzezinski went beyond foreign affairs and sent his reflections and recommendations to Humphrey on two other subjects dear to his heart: the evolution of the Democratic Party and that of American society.

> As I see it, the country is becoming increasingly polarized, with Nixon obviously basing its strategy on the more conservative elements in society, weaning over to his side some of the Democratic party's traditional support from the blue-collar, lower urban middle class. In so doing, he stands a good chance of making the Republican party a truly majoritarian party.
>
> At the same time, the Democratic party seems to be moving to the left, responding to the more extreme and more noisy elements among the well-to-do upper middle class liberals, who enjoy being vicarious radicals, and to the more frustrated and alienated college activists. As a result, the Democratic party seems to be sliding down the same path as the Republicans did in the early '60s: towards increasing rhetorical extremism, with the result that it begins to be more and more distrusted by the mainstream of American life. What happened to the Republicans with Goldwater in 1964 could easily happen to Democrats in 1972, if present trends continue.[94]

The only hope, according to Brzezinski, was to "pre-empt the vital center" by bringing about a clean break with the extreme left. Brzezinski's analysis was not entirely original—Kevin Phillips in 1969 and then Richard Scammon and Ben Wattenberg in 1970 also exposed the growing breach between the Democrats and ordinary Americans, "the mechanic's wife in Dayton, Ohio"—but it was clearly prescient, and it came after a similar warning written two years before, in 1968.[95] It comes as no surprise that Humphrey shared Brzezinski's viewpoint: "Keep writing; I need to hear from you."[96] The latter did not need to be asked twice, and for Humphrey he developed his ideas on the neglect of the middle class, in particular from his own observation post, the university. "One of the reasons for student extremism is that the extremely rich kids don't give a damn because they know that they cannot lose anyhow, while the poorer don't give a damn because they have nothing to lose."[97]

On May 25, 1970, Brzezinski undertook to analyze the American crisis in depth. The diagnosis of loss of confidence was clear: the Establishment, which had held onto America's tiller up to that point, was divided and in the process of dissolving as WASPs were losing their influence, without anything coming in to take its place. The cracks in the Establishment provided a sort of legitimacy to the revolt of young people, pushing them to go too far. It would not be easy to win them back for the American system, so deep was their alienation; new forms of participation would have to be invented to bring this about. Above all, it was essential to reassure the middle class that the situation was not prerevolutionary: "America is neither France of 1789 nor of 1958." In order to discuss the defects and problems of American society, it is necessary to admit that the 1960s "probably saw more positive change than any other decade in this century, whether in regards to race relations, or the war on poverty, or the general development of social consciousness."[98] Of course, this rapid change came at a cost: it created difficulties and anxieties. But perhaps it was possible to counter the revolutionaries on the left and the prophets of misfortune on the right, while creating safety valves for the young activists (such as civil service in underprivileged neighborhoods).[99] If this could be done, the Democratic Party could regain the upper hand.[100]

"I like your positive up-beat. You will be hearing me speak out in that vein," Humphrey replied.[101] The exchanges between the two slowed down during the following year, partly because Brzezinski was living in Japan. But in late 1971, when the campaign started to speed up, Humphrey and his closest adviser, Max Kampelman, got back in touch with Brzezinski. Humphrey asked Kampelman to organize his council on foreign policy, primarily to help him position himself within the complicated environment on the Democratic side: he had to adopt a firm international posture but he must not appear complicit with the military-industrial complex; he had to defend the arms-control agreements but not the abandonment of America's assets, and so on—all this while he remained obliged to make simplistic choices in the Senate when he voted. In short, he needed help, and he added: "Our friend Brzezinski is good at this. I have watched his writings in Newsweek, and I like what he has to say. Also, Henry Owen is pretty good. But I'm sure there are others. Marshall Shulman might be helpful. Max, it is imperative that we get somebody working on it."[102]

The mention of Brzezinski's articles in *Newsweek* is noteworthy, for it highlights the role of media visibility in the choice of political advisers. Yet another transfer of influence from one domain to another: replying on November 24, 1971, Brzezinski said that he would gladly agree to help, and he recommended using the operational conclusion in his book *Between Two Ages: America's Role in the Technetronic Era,* especially the idea of strengthening relations with the traditional allies, Europe and Japan, relations that had been neglected by Nixon.[103] As these exchanges were taking place, Brzezinski was simultaneously discussing his idea for a Trilateral Commission with some close friends.

In the end, Humphrey lost to McGovern in the primaries, and that defeat was confirmed at the Democratic Convention held July 10–13 in Miami. One of the reasons is that this convention contributed to reforming the rules for delegate selection. To correct the deficit of democracy in the process, the McGovern-Fraser committee stressed the role of the primaries and that of minorities (blacks, women, young people, and so on), and McGovern exploited the new procedures to the fullest, thereby gaining a decisive advantage. McGovern ended up carrying the day, even though Humphrey had won more popular votes. The ephemeral "Stop McGovern" movement failed to block the candidate's path, and McGovern headed into his historic defeat by Nixon, as Brzezinski had predicted in 1968. On July 17, Humphrey again thanked "Zbig" and expressed his regret that he had not been able to make more use of the notes and advice that the latter had supplied—but that was the way the primaries worked; they precluded in-depth discussion of foreign policy. "Well," he wrote in the end, " 'your candidate' put up a fight, and in retrospect I think it was a good fight, but lost."[104]

In reality, the situation was a little more complicated than that: Humphrey was not the only one of Brzezinski's candidates who lost. If it was normal for candidates to maintain a stable of advisers, in 1972 it was Brzezinski who gave the impression of maintaining a stable of candidates. Thus, on May 26, 1970, he sent Senator Edmund Muskie—of Polish origin like himself, and Humphrey's running mate in 1968—an in-depth analysis of the American crisis.[105]

The diagnosis of loss of confidence was clear: the Establishment, which until then had had its hand on America's tiller, was divided and coming apart as WASPs lost their influence, and nothing was coming in its stead. The situation supplied a sort of legitimacy to the young people's rebellion, pushing them to up the ante. If that analysis seems familiar, it is because it reproduced word for word the one mentioned above that Brzezinski had sent to Humphrey the day before. And a week later, he wrote to Edward Kennedy that he had been struck by the latter's discussion, during a recent television program, of the problems of contemporary America, and he shared some of his ideas.[106] The diagnosis of loss of confidence was clear: the Establishment, which until then had had its hand on America's tiller, was divided and coming apart as WASPs lost their influence, and so on. So Kennedy, too, benefited from Brzezinski's insights—he thanked him, moreover, soon afterward, with a formula close to the one Humphrey used: "Your letter was most complete and has given me a great deal to think about. From time to time you will find that my public statements reflect the emphasis you suggest."[107]

Two years before the election, it is not surprising to see that Brzezinski sent his ideas to several political figures; what could be more natural when one wants to weigh in on the national debate? But the practice of cutting and pasting continued in 1971 and 1972, simultaneously reflecting Brzezinski's uncertainty as to the ideal candidate that year, the absence of a strong link with a partic- ular candidate who would demand an exclusive right to his insights, and his popularity rating—the fact that he was personally solicited by a number of candidates, and that he could at most personalize his recommendations, but not invent a new foreign policy for each one. Actually, in the course of 1972 Brzezinski plagiarized himself for only two candidates, Humphrey and Muskie. Scoop Jackson was a minor candidate, too far to the right to have a chance to win, and he asked for Brzezinski's advice less regularly than did the two candidates from the center. But Brzezinski did not hesitate to send the same letter to Humphrey and to Muskie, changing only the name of the candidate or of the adviser to whom he addressed them: Kampelman for Humphrey, Lake for Muskie.[108]

As early as December 1970, just before he left for his long stint in Japan, Brzezinski agreed, along with his colleague and friend Richard Gardner, to join a group of advisers working for Muskie under Vance's leadership.[109] As he confided in a letter, he was hopeful that Muskie would prove adept enough to avoid any slippage toward the "extremist" positions of the left, while being a candidate acceptable to a large swath of the Democratic Party.[110] After Brzezinski returned from Japan, he contributed actively to the work of the advisers who were guiding Muskie: in addition to the sketch of a speech that he sent Muskie on August 1, 1971, he sent critical and constructive remarks on the draft of a speech about Asia in September, and on October 14 he shared with Muskie the impressions he had retained from his trips to Europe and Japan, reminding him to use the draft he had sent on August 1.[111] Muskie thanked him, and in fact one of his advisers wrote a text for him to use as a speech or an article based on Brzezinski's ideas; Brzezinski offered his comments on the text and on another contribution to the campaign by Tony Lake.[112]

From January to the end of April 1972, Brzezinski contributed to Muskie's campaign, but he was not in the inner circle; from a distance, he tried to prevent the candidate from veering toward the left. As he explained to a friend: "Muskie, who is basically very moderate, seems to be pulled leftward by the general forces (as well as by some of his advisers). I am trying to keep in touch with him and occasionally do some work for him but it certainly is not easy. My impression is that as he gets stronger, the somewhat left-of-center group around him will congeal more and more strongly and it will become more, rather than less, difficult to get through to him. But I am going to do my best to try, even though I certainly have no personal stake in this whatsoever, except in a broader sense as a citizen of this country."[113]

At the same time—mid-January 1972—Muskie had to deal with an offensive from the left on the part of George McGovern, who proposed a plan for significant reductions in military expenses. Brzezinski pressed Muskie not to let himself be dragged onto that terrain; for example, he should refrain from giving figures and should refer the decision to a bipartisan commission of experts after the elections.[114] He was concerned with preserving Muskie's moderate liberal line, and he was suspicious of the lengths to which the group of advisers put together by Lake (in particular Morton Halperin, Peter Scoville, and Paul Warnke, figures clearly identified with the left) might be tempted to go.[115] Despite his fears, his relations with the group of advisers and with Senator Muskie remained good. A number of his suggestions were adopted—on the defense program (Muskie did not put forward any figures), on funding for Radio Free Europe-Radio Liberty (he defended it), on recognition of Bangladesh (he advocated it early), and so on.[116]

Unfortunately, this candidate acceptable both to Brzezinski and to the left wing of the Democratic Party, who was ahead of Nixon in the polls and easily outstripped his Democratic rivals in the primaries, began to waver on February 26, 1972. That day, in Manchester, New Hampshire, speaking to a crowd as snow was falling, he defended himself against false accusations, which had been made against him and his wife in the local newspapers (and which came directly from the White House—one of Nixon's "dirty tricks"). Visibly upset, he had to interrupt himself several times, and some journalists claimed he was crying—Muskie himself said that it was the snow. Regardless of the reason, his presumed emotional instability was a hard blow to his image from which he never managed to recover. On May 8, 1972, Brzezinski evoked Muskie's withdrawal, announced a few days earlier, and judged that his defeat had been made inevitable by the necessity of attracting the left, where McGovern's dominance was in any case too strong. He predicted McGovern's victory in July, for he thought the Democratic Party was on a suicidal track, and Ted Kennedy encouraged that tendency in order to be able to take advantage of the situation in 1976. Nevertheless, Brzezinski intended to help Humphrey as much as he could before the convention.[117] On August 10, 1972, Muskie thanked Brzezinski for his "contribution to our common effort."[118] The two men met again in 1980, when Muskie replaced Vance in the State Department—but at that point their effort was much less unified.

In mid-July, then, only George McGovern remained on the Democratic side. It was at this point that the classic dilemma of the new professional elite arose for Brzezinski: was he going to join McGovern's team in order to increase his chances of getting a position in a possible McGovern administration, or was the candidate too far removed from his own convictions to make that possible? In 1968, Kissinger would have gladly taken a position in a Rockefeller or a Humphrey administration, and, despite his "hatred" for Nixon, he did not seem to have any trouble adapting to a Nixon administration. But, in 1972, the distance between Brzezinski's convictions—which he was not prepared to compromise—and McGovern's was too great. He dipped a toe in the campaign waters, but pulled it out almost at once.

On August 18, 1972, he responded to the request of a working group on Japan in the McGovern camp. Brzezinski sent them his usual ideas (on the inadequacy of the balance of power that Nixon had advocated, on the need for a community of the developed nations, and so on) but he took the occasion to write to his former colleague Ted Van Dyk to clarify his status—and his position. "I think my contribution would be more worthwhile in regards to the larger issues of foreign policy which McGovern is yet to spell out. The need right now is for an alternative concept to Nixon's balance of power and not for specifics on Japan. If I can be of help in directly shaping McGovern's thinking on these larger issues, for example through you, don't hesitate to call me. But in the meantime I do not want to be listed as part of a study group when I still do not know what McGovern's foreign policy is likely to be."[119]

Brzezinski must surely have been in contact with Abram Chayes, Van Dyk said in his reply on August 25, for Chayes—McGovern's chief foreign policy adviser—had announced that very morning that Brzezinski was officially part of his group of foreign policy advisers. He added, as if to soften things, that they needed Brzezinski's support, that the latter would surely be satisfied with the speech that the candidate was to give soon, and that "the candidate's instincts [were] right, and he [was] further educable."[120]

In reality, there had been no contact between Chayes and Brzezinski, who had not been consulted before being put on the list. Even though he had sent a paper to the working group on Japan, it was obvious that this inclusion was unjustified, and that hidden political stakes were involved: having Brzezinski's endorsement, with his image as a hawk, would show that McGovern benefitted from the support of a large part of the new foreign policy Establishment, and not only from the left, and that he was thus "acceptable," less extremist than his detractors claimed. Moreover, other experts had similarly agreed to help the McGovern campaign from afar, although without giving him their support, and an article by columnists Evans and Novak picked up on Brzezinski's protests and those of others who, contrary to Chayes's claims, had not offered their political support along with their expertise. Brzezinski wrote a clarification, in a letter to the editor of the *Washington Post,* specifying that he did not share McGovern's vision.[121] This was thus the end of his contacts with the McGovern team. To his correspondents, Brzezinski confided that he found the candidate very poor, "a disaster in more ways than one," and that he was expecting a Nixon victory—the least bad of the alternatives, he thought. But he also worried that too large a win by Nixon might reinforce the conservative element in the Republican Party, with potentially worrisome implications for 1976.[122] Even though McGovern was roundly defeated (he came out ahead in only one state), this prediction was not realized, for in the meantime came the Watergate affair, which destroyed the Republicans' credibility and allowed the Democrat Jimmy Carter to win the presidency in 1976. Carter brought with him a number of representatives of the new elite, with Brzezinski among those in the first rank. He had profited from the intervening years by continuing to publish and by creating the Trilateral Commission: his star was continuing to rise.

Photographed here (with his cane) in 1930 welcoming a Polish delegation to Lille, where he was serving as consul general, Tadeusz Brzezinski, Zbigniew Brzezinski's father, went on to represent Poland in Nazi Germany and then in Soviet Ukraine during Stalin's purges.

All photographs reproduced with the permission of Zbigniew Brzezinski except where noted otherwise.

Brzezinski as a young foreign student, hitchhiking in 1950. After moving in 1938 to Montreal, where his father had been named consul general, Zbigniew Brzezinski was admitted to graduate study at Harvard in 1950, at age 22. He fleshed out a scholarship awarded by McGill University with a position as research assistant in the Russian Center, but his resources remained limited.

Brzezinski during a transatlantic crossing, 1953. A popular speaker, Zbigniew Brzezinski taught classes to Harvard students and gave lectures everywhere he was invited, including on ocean liners during transatlantic crossings, which often helped pay for his ticket.

The Center for International Affairs team in 1959–1960. Founded in 1958, Harvard's Center for International Affairs drew Harvard's finest minds on international questions. Robert Bowie is in the center, flanked by Thomas Schelling on his right and Henry Kissinger on his left; behind Kissinger, on the right, is a smiling Zbigniew Brzezinski. Photograph: Weatherhead Center for International Affairs, Harvard University.

Brzezinski in his office at Columbia University. With no prospect of a tenured position at Harvard, Brzezinski accepted a professorship at Columbia in 1960. There he quickly became a star on the faculty—a Sovietologist recognized by his peers. This photo from March 1965 shows him in his Columbia office. Photograph: University Archives, Columbia University in the city of New York.

Brzezinski and Kissinger at the Council on Foreign Relations, 1965. In 1965, the Council on Foreign Relations published several works on transatlantic relations simultaneously, but the two that received the most attention were Henry Kissinger's *The Troubled Partnership* and Zbigniew Brzezinski's *Alternative to Partition*. From *Continuing the Inquiry* by Peter Grose. Copyright ©2006 by the Council on Foreign Relations Press. Reprinted with permission.

Brzezinski on *Meet the Press*. As at ease on screen as in a classroom, Zbigniew Brzezinski was a pioneer among media experts on international affairs. In this *Meet the Press* program from 1965, he defended US intervention in Vietnam against Hans Morgenthau, the father of the realist school of international relations, who criticized the intervention. NBC's *Meet the Press*, 1965, © National Broadcasting Company/NBC Universal.

To Professor Zbiguiew Brezezinski
With appreciation and best wishes,

Brzezinski and President Lyndon Baines Johnson, 1967. Brzezinski's first experience in a position of responsibility was in the Johnson administration, from 1966 to 1968. He did not play a prominent role, but he did have the president's ear. The mistake in the spelling of his name in the dedication of this photograph was typical.

Brzezinski and Vice President Hubert Humphrey on an airplane, 1967. While he was working for the Johnson administration, Brzezinski was in contact with the vice president. He became Humphrey's foreign policy adviser when the latter sought to succeed Johnson in the 1968 presidential campaign. However, with the Vietnam War as background, Humphrey lost to Richard Nixon.

COLUMBIA DAILY SPECTATOR

FOUNDED 1877

Vol. CXIII—No. 25   NEW YORK, N.Y., FRIDAY, OCTOBER 25, 1968   Copyright 1968, by the Spectator Publishing Co., Inc.   TEN CENTS

CU Urban Center To Provide Funds For Nursing Home

By ROBERT HARDMAN

A $3 million, 124 bed nursing home for low-income Harlem residents partly funded by a grant from Columbia's Urban Center will soon rise on a site near Harlem Hospital.

According to Preston M. Lewis, the development administrator for the Central Harlem Nursing Home Company, Columbia provided the initial equity of $85 thousand necessary to start the project, and several members of the group's board of directors are on Columbia's staff at Harlem Hospital.

The initiative to start the center came from a Harlem group concerned with the lack of nursing home facilities in Central Harlem, Mr. Lewis said.

Elderly Harlem people who need nursing home services currently must resort to large wards in municipal hospitals, according to Mr. Lewis. He said that the new nursing home will be the first to serve low-income people in that area.

The facility will be predominantly financed by the state, which recently passed a law providing for assistance to non-profit voluntary nursing homes.

Most of the patients will be re-

DIALOGUE: What started out to be a "tour" of the School of International Affairs and by Students for a Democratic Society turned into a discussion on the steps outside McVickar about the school's ties with the government. Participants are from left to right: Professors Zbiniew Brzezinski, Roger Hilsman, University Proctor William E. Kahn, and SDS leader Stu Gedal.

Hilsman Supports Vietnam Pullout By All U.S. Troops

SDS Confronts Faculty At Door to McVickar

By ROBERT B. STULBERG

Professor of Government Roger Hilsman yesterday told a group of one hundred students demonstrating outside the School of International Affairs that the United States should "withdraw all its troops from Southeast Asia."

"I don't think the United States should ever intervene in an internal struggle like this," he said. "There are no dominoes over there."

The former Assistant Secretary of State who left his government post a few years ago, spoke to the crowd on the stoop in front of the school after the demonstrators were refused permission to "tour" the building.

The protesters, led by members of Students for a Democratic Society, initially planned to march into the school at McVickar Hall on 115th St., but when they arrived at the building, the doors were locked and about six campus security guards stood inside the entrance.

An assistant dean of the school offered to allow the students to enter in groups of five to tour the building, but SDS leaders in-

CU Students Teach in City Schools

By JON GRONER

The Columbia-Barnard Citizenship Council is sending several Columbia students to teach as substitutes in New York public schools during the current teacher's strike.

Teachers. The project was officially approved at a meeting of the Cit-Council Governing Board last night.

At that meeting, the Governing Board approved the following statement:

action has political implications since it supports one side in the bitterly contested dispute. In taking its position, Cit Council was guided by the conclusions of the New York Civil Liberties Union report on the Ocean Hill-Browns-

---

Brzezinski in a dialogue with students. In 1968, to prevent an occupation by student protesters accusing Brzezinski of supporting American imperialism, Columbia University briefly closed the School of International Affairs, where he taught. Faculty members went out to meet the students, but what transpired was a dialogue of the deaf. Reproduced with permission from *The [Columbia Daily] Spectator*, October 25, 1968. © Spectator Publishing Company, Inc.

Appointed to the White House as National Security Adviser in January 1977, Brzezinski occupied an important position in Jimmy Carter's inner circle from the outset; he briefed Carter on the international situation in a private meeting every morning. Jimmy Carter Presidential Library and Museum, Atlanta, GA. White House staff Photographers' collection, US National Archives and Records Administration/NARA.

Menachem Begin and Zbigniew Brzezinski playing chess at Camp David. During the Camp David negotiations (September 5–19, 1978), which concluded with a peace treaty between the Egyptians and the Israelis in 1979, Brzezinski relaxed by playing chess twice with Prime Minister Begin. They each won a game. Jimmy Carter Presidential Library and Museum, Atlanta, GA. White House staff Photographers' collection, US National Archives and Records Administration/NARA.

Deng Xiaoping dines with the Brzezinskis. During his historic trip to the United States in January 1979, Deng Xiaoping went to the Brzezinski home in McLean, Virginia, for dinner. Seated at the table from right to left: Brzezinski, Deng Xiaoping, Cyrus Vance, Zhuo Lin (Deng Xiaoping's wife), and Richard Holbrooke. The hostess, Muska Brzezinski, is seen in the mirror. Jimmy Carter Presidential Library and Museum, Atlanta, GA. White House staff Photographers' collection, US National Archives and Records Administration/NARA.

Jogging in Jerusalem with Jimmy Carter. President Carter appreciated Brzezinski: "Next to members of my family, Zbig would be my favorite seatmate on a long-distance trip; we might argue, but I would never be bored." They occasionally played tennis or went jogging together, as seen here in Jerusalem's Old City in 1979.

Brzezinski at the Khyber Pass. In February 1980, Brzezinski visited a Pakistani outpost at the Khyber Pass to support the Afghani mujahedeen resistance against the Soviet invaders. Picked up by the press, the photo showing him inspecting a Chinese version of the AK47 rifle was interpreted as a bellicose gesture toward Moscow.

Zbigniew Brzezinski and Pope John Paul II, 1980. Soviet propaganda suggested that Brzezinski had worked behind the scenes to get John Paul II, the first Polish pope, elected in 1978. The rumor was unfounded, but the two men got on well personally (two of Brzezinski's children, Mika and Mark, are seen in this photo), and they exchanged views on international issues, Poland in particular.

The Brzezinski family tracing Mao's path. During the summer of 1981, invited by Deng Xiaoping, the Brzezinski family made an extraordinary trip in China along the route taken by Mao Zedong and the Chinese Red Army in 1934–1935. From right to left: Zbigniew, Mark, Muska, Mika, and Ian Brzezinski.

Zbigniew Brzezinski and Ronald Reagan, 1984. Brzezinski was critical of the Reagan administration's foreign policy, but he appreciated Reagan's firm stance toward Moscow. He would be
much harder on George W. Bush, with whom he had no relationship at all; by contrast, Reagan
consulted him occasionally.

Brzezinski and Gorbachev, 1987. When Gorbachev took power in 1985, Brzezinski did not recognize his potential as a reformer right away. Once he was convinced that reforms were under way, he accurately predicted the resultant implosion of the Soviet system.

Brzezinski and George H.W. Bush, 1987. A Democrat from the start, Brzezinski endorsed the Republican candidate George H.W. Bush in 1988, against the Democrat Michael Dukakis (even though Madeleine Albright, one of Brzezinski's protégés, was among Dukakis's foreign policy advisors). Brzezinski deemed Dukakis too left-leaning in foreign policy.

Zbigniew Brzezinski with Lech Wałesa and Muska Brzezinski. Brzezinski energetically supported Poland's transition to a market democracy; some even hoped that he would be a candidate for the presidency. In this photo from 1995, Lech Wałesa was presenting him the insignia of the Order of the White Eagle (the most prestigious honor in Poland), with Muska watching the ceremony. Photograph by Andrzej Iwańczuk/Ageneja Gazeta.

Zbigniew Brzezinski and Barack Obama discuss the Middle East during a meeting in the Situation Room in the White House. "The brightest candidate on the intellectual level since Kennedy" is how Brzezinski described Barack Obama after their first meeting. As president, Obama consulted Brzezinski several times, as on this occasion in 2010. Despite some disappointments, Brzezinski supported him again in 2012. Photograph by Pete Souza/Official White House Photo.

Both born in Europe, both speaking accented English, both graduate students at Harvard, Brzezinski and Kissinger pioneered a new model of foreign policy expert—and both reached the White House as national security advisers. While there was a dose of professional rivalry between them, they remained friends, as demonstrated in this last encounter at the Nobel Peace Prize Forum in Oslo on December 11, 2016. Photograph © Ken Opprann.

4

From the Trilateral Commission
to the White House

On December 15, 1976, when President Jimmy Carter called Brzezinski to offer him the position of national security adviser, he began by saying: "Zbig, I want you to do me a favor."[1] For an instant, Brzezinski feared that Carter was going to ask him to become deputy secretary of state, or simply under secretary of state. In an earlier conversation about the position he would like to have, he had suggested that he could be useful to Cyrus Vance as a thinker, a source of conceptual propositions in the State Department. Happily, the position he was offered was the one he really wanted.

Between Kissinger's nomination to the White House in 1968, which had surprised him, and the offer he himself received in 1976, Brzezinski had come a long way, and his career had taken on an additional dimension during the first half of the 1970s. The university specialist in the communist bloc and in Eastern Europe, brilliant but somewhat limited by his field of expertise, had become a theoretician of worldwide social change and an expert on Japan. Above all, in collaboration with David Rockefeller, he had founded the Trilateral Commission, a private organization that brought together American, European, and Japanese elites; it flourished remarkably during its early years, making Brzezinski an important figure in the new Establishment.

It was this triple diversification—from international relations to sociological reflection, from Europe to Asia, and from the academic world to global political networks—that elevated Brzezinski to Kissinger's level and allowed him to be a candidate for the position of national security adviser in 1976. Moreover, it was also through the Trilateral Commission that he met Jimmy Carter and contributed to his education in international affairs.

In the Technetronic Era, a "Year" in Tokyo

In 1967, while Brzezinski was working on the Policy Planning Council, the second edition of his book *The Soviet Bloc: Unity and Conflict* came out, revised to include the Sino-Soviet schism.[2] The book had already become a classic in Soviet studies, and because of it Brzezinski was viewed as one of the top academic experts in the field. It also gave Brzezinski his image as a pioneer; his seminar on comparative communisms at Columbia was a conceptual innovation that aroused interest among his colleagues as well as among students. From the mid-1960s on, Brzezinski's reflections led him beyond the Eastern bloc, beyond political science as a disciplinary approach, and even beyond the strict academic canons—as he had shown with his essay on Europe for the Council on Foreign Relations, *Alternative to Partition* (1965).

In 1970, he published *Between Two Ages: America's Role in the Technetronic Era*.[3] This book explored the implications of the passage to the post-industrial era for advanced societies (primarily the United States and the USSR), for Third World societies, and for international affairs in general. It was in effect an essay in global sociology, accompanied by geopolitical reflections and recommendations to American decision makers. In his preface, Brzezinski referred to the book as an "essay" or a "think piece" based on solid arguments (and tables, statistics, and so on) rather than as a work in the social sciences with an orthodox methodology.[4]

The trajectory that led to this book had begun in 1966. In an article for *Foreign Affairs* that year, he had suggested that the ideological confrontation between East and West was in some sense an outdated battle. The importance of the Cold War certainly could not be denied or ignored, but the real questions regarding the future lay elsewhere. For the developed societies, and especially for America, which played the role of guinea pig in this context, it was a matter of managing the social impact of the upheavals brought about by the scientific age—automation, computers, the advances of certain sciences such as molecular biology. For the Third World, questions of underdevelopment, overpopulation, and instability were the ones that would dominate. In order to face up to these problems, Brzezinski recommended the creation of a community of developed nations.[5] This basic conceptual framework was by and large that of the book published four years later, with the incorporation of other elements that had appeared in other publications in the meantime, in particular in a widely noticed article in *Encounter* in 1968.[6]

Just as the world had shifted earlier from the agrarian to the industrial age, Brzezinski argued in *Between Two Ages,* it was now shifting from the industrial to the postindustrial age. Sociologist Daniel Bell saw science taking the place of industry as the most decisive element in power and social relations.[7] By contrast, Brzezinski insisted on its concrete applications, especially in technology and electronics, information science, and communications; hence his neologism, the "technetronic" age. The problem was that that age had not fully arrived, and the crisis of modern societies could be explained by the in-between situation, the passage from one to the other, which was quite far along in the United States, less so in Europe and Japan, and even slower to reach the Soviet Union. The technetronic age was upsetting social hierarchies and the established order of the industrial era. Now services were replacing industry; computers and automation were replacing workers; workforce qualifications and also leisure time were getting more attention than unemployment; membership in the dominant class was no longer based on capital but rather on knowledge and the mobilization of talent, the latter having become a source of power. Further, problems of education were arising at the higher levels than in the early years; universities were think tanks that played a direct and central role in society; totalizing ideologies were becoming obsolete at a time when audiovisual information was proliferating; television with its universal images was replacing print, which remained national. Finally, the issue of citizens' participation in complex technical decisions was replacing that of the right to vote, just as the issue of women's equality was replacing that of political rights per se. The psychological effects of these upheavals—dispossession, depersonalization, and loss of meaning—were intense.[8]

America was at once the pioneer and the disseminator of the technetronic age, being the first society to enter the postindustrial era. It was also the best equipped to face it, having embraced the benefits of industrial progress. It thus could be viewed as a laboratory for this new age, especially because it set ambitious goals for itself, such as racial integration on the basis of equality.[9] The world was watching intently to see whether America would be able to respond to the challenges of the new age by increasing participation and pluralism, and by reconciling equality and freedom. By contrast, the USSR had been bogged down since Lenin and Stalin, having institutionalized Marxism. Ideology and bureaucracy created a straightjacket that discouraged flexibility and innovation, and the country was becoming petrified, preferring to repress the societal demands of the new era, such as improved quality of life and better opportunities for self-realization. All this was leading to a loss of legitimacy for the leadership and to the likelihood of gradual decline; in short, the USSR was missing the train of the technetronic age.[10]

For Brzezinski, the Soviet failure to adapt provided a context for understanding the phenomenon of the New Left in the West. This movement sought to bring about a utopia that would meet the demands of the technetronic age (equality but also humanism, self-affirmation, democratic participation, and so on), contrary to the models offered by the USSR and the other communist regimes. Despite its idealistic aspirations, the New Left was not an avant-garde but rather a symptom of a crisis, a reaction born of frustration that failed to offer a constructive response to the ills of the society it described. As for American liberals, many had become "statist establishmentarians," increasingly sure of themselves. The pragmatic liberal of the 1930s and 1940s had given way to the dogmatic and doctrinaire liberal of the 1960s, hostile to business and always ready for more social engineering.[11]

At the international level, the effect of the technetronic revolution was contradictory. On the one hand, this revolution was shrinking the planet into a "global village," as Marshall McLuhan had shown ("a global city," Brzezinski countered, an edgy and agitated city), and it was pushing the planet to become a more integrated community endowed for the first time with a "global consciousness." On the other hand, the revolution was fragmenting the planet, by intensifying the gap between the First and the Third Worlds ("global ghettos") in terms of material conditions, even as it made that gap more visible and better known, thus less tolerable.[12] In the process, it favored instability, and revived nationalism, in reaction, as a fallback value. The Third World, according to Brzezinski's analysis, was at risk of being left behind by that revolutionary wave, and of remaining unstable. This situation could multiply occasions for territorial disputes between the United States and the USSR, on the model of the Fashoda clash (when French-British colonial rivalry in Africa in the nineteenth century almost caused a war). In the technetronic age, the rivalry between the two powers should be less ideological (this was no longer the industrial era), but also more widely extended geographically and more dangerous (owing to the higher level of weaponry and the strategic parity between them).[13]

What was to be done, then, to respond to the challenges that awaited both the Third World and the developed countries? Only America, as the first technetronic society and the world's social laboratory, could avoid the fragmentation of the world, by taking the initiative to forge a community of developed nations. This community had to begin with Europe and Japan, as these two regions were also at the peak of scientific and technological innovation. The creation of the community would be an ongoing process with two phases: the first would be trilateral, and the second would include certain of the most advanced communist countries. It would not be a matter of envisaging a homogenous organization like the European Economic Community. Rather it would be a grouping that could have as its initial expression "a high-level consultative council for global cooperation, regularly bringing together the heads of governments of the developed world to discuss their common political-security, educational-scientific, and economic-technological problems, as well as to deal from that perspective with their moral obligations toward the developing nations. Some permanent supporting machinery could provide continuity to these consultations."[14]

Published in 1970, *Between Two Ages* was very well received. Of course, certain academics criticized the occasional shortcuts, the absence of in-depth analysis—for example, analysis of the complex links between technological change and social change—or the author's fondness for formulas and neologisms like "technetronic," which according to one reviewer "smacks more of Madison Avenue or possibly of Wall Street than of Morningside Heights" (the neighborhood around Columbia University).[15] In addition to Daniel Bell's inspiring work, other books in the late 1960s also explored technology's impact on society, by authors such as Alvin Toffler, Nigel Calder, and Victor Ferkiss.[16] But Brzezinski's was not journalistic, as another reviewer remarked; it was much more thoughtful, better documented, and "brilliant."[17] The *New York Times* used the occasion to offer a portrait of Brzezinski, in addition to a review article that included several other books.[18] *Foreign Affairs* characterized *Between Two Ages* as a "seminal work" on "global society in transition," one that was "bound to elicit major controversy" and would be "difficult to ignore."[19]

Readers do sometimes lose the thread set down at the outset—the impact of technologies on social change—when Brzezinski shifts from "global ghettos" to the student rebellion, from the necessity of Stalinism to rational humanism, and from the New Left to the community of developed nations. This impression is reinforced in the fifth section, a sort of geopolitical essay in which "technetronic" considerations supply only a minor part of the inspiration. Nevertheless, the book represents an intellectual tour de force, if only by virtue of the multitude of facts and figures cited by the author in support of his analyses; these are integrated into a vision that remains coherent and offers new keys for deciphering the world. On the essential points, Brzezinski's intuitions are good; a number of them have been verified, sometimes a little later than he anticipated (the advent of information technologies in the 1990s and 2000s, for example). He certainly did not invent everything, but he deserves credit for presenting a convincing picture of the changes that were underway, and for relating them to the evolutions of the international system—his main contribution lay here, rather than in the sociological description itself (the neologism "technetronic" clearly did not take hold). And that is what allowed him most notably to go beyond the limited framework of the Cold War and bring a remarkable sociological dimension to his vision of international relations, a dimension that was lacking, for example, in Kissinger's work.

However innovative it may have been, *Between Two Ages* comes across as a book profoundly anchored in the intellectual approach to the world that Brzezinski had been developing since the early 1950s, under the influence in particular of a Marxist analysis of history, with the US-USSR rivalry as background.[20] With the internal troubles of the 1960s and the Vietnam War, America was prey to doubt and pessimism, whereas the Soviet Union—which was on the decline, undergoing "petrification," as Brzezinski saw it—still benefited from the image of a rising power. *Between Two Ages* made it possible to reverse that impression and to justify Brzezinski's fundamental optimism in a way familiar to Soviet intellectuals even more than to Americans. It was because America had reached a more advanced historical stage in its development, because it was already between two ages (and not stuck in the industrial age) that it ran into turmoil. But that phase was only transitory: there would soon be as much distance between the United States and the USSR as there was between industrial societies and agrarian societies. Historic inevitability, in other words, was switching sides. What was inscribed in material and social reality was not the Soviet Union catching up with and overtaking the United States (Nikita Khrushchev's "we will bury you"), but the Soviet Union's bogging down with a promise of implosion.[21] On that point, too, Brzezinski was right, even if the ultimate fall of the USSR was as much impelled by failures proper to the industrial age as by its incapacity to adapt to the "technetronic" age.

The surprise of seeing Kissinger appointed national security adviser and the prospect of obtaining a similarly high-level position himself later on incited Brzezinski to complete his education in international affairs through an opening to Asia. To this end, he came up with the idea of spending a year in Japan, not to learn Japanese and immerse himself in the culture, but to observe Asia and the world from Tokyo. He presented his proposal to McGeorge Bundy, then head of the Ford Foundation; Bundy agreed to finance his stay, while Columbia gave him another sabbatical.[22]

Brzezinski chose Japan because the Japanese archipelago appeared to be a rising power in the early 1970s. He did not share Herman Kahn's view that Japan would become a "superstate" and the leading economy in the world in the 1990s.[23] On the contrary, in the book that grew out of his stay Brzezinski stressed the fragility of Japan's growth. However, he was attracted by the country's rapid ascension to modernity and advanced technologies, and by its impressive economic development. His stay in Tokyo roughly corresponded to the spring term of 1971—from January to early June.[24] During his time in Japan, he benefited from the support of the international bank Nomura, which gave him office space in its headquarters in Tokyo and facilitated his meetings with prominent figures in the Japanese economic and political world, including the prime minister and the minister of foreign affairs. He also met a variety of Japanese people whom he questioned about their perceptions of the changes underway in the country, in particular its democratic system, and on Japan's regional and international role. He profited, too, from the opportunity to travel in Indonesia and Korea—China remained closed—and his wife Muska joined him for part of his stay.[25]

In *The Fragile Blossom,* a book based on his impressions and his conversations published in 1972, Brzezinski stressed the personal, even subjective, character of his observations, along with the fact that he was not an expert on Japan.[26] However, the reviews in the press all emphasized the subtlety of his intuitions: they were "penetrating and well-founded," according to the *Journal of Politics.*[27] The *New York Times* compared it to another book written by a specialist on Japan, and concluded that Brzezinski's was much better. The review added that "the brilliance of his intuitive judgment permits him to leap to conclusions which invariably seem the right ones (with the exception of his projection of Japanese nuclear ambitions, which are far greater than he allows)." History proved Brzezinski right: in fact the Japanese were not going to develop the atomic bomb.[28]

If Japan's blossoming was fragile, Brzezinski explained, it was because the pace of its economic development could not remain elevated forever. Of the twenty drivers of development that he identified, only four remained in 1971 (a strong internal demand, the positive role of the state, a banking structure and strict control of exchanges). It was reasonable to expect that the rate at which it was catching up with Western economies would slow down. But Brzezinski was primarily interested in Japan's place on the international stage; with prosperity, the country was ready to play a more important role, although it did not know what that would be. "The growing sense of, and satisfaction from, national greatness clashes with the persisting—perhaps in some respects even heightened—sense of national insecurity, which complicates Japanese vision and causes further uncertainty in goals."[29] This uncertainty was accentuated by an uncomfortable geographic position, which—unlike Germany's—did not make the question easier to answer, and by an elite that, far from being internationalist, were on the contrary "inward-oriented" in addition to being anxious. For these reasons, as Brzezinski saw it, Japan was not a superpower and probably did not wish to become one.[30]

This situation did not facilitate Japan's relations with America. The Japanese knew that good relations with the United States were more important for them than for the Americans, and they did not like this dependency. Conversely, economic and commercial relations were shifting increasingly in favor of the Japanese, which bothered the Americans, who felt Washington should play a pragmatic card. In other words, it should not push for a Japanization of Asian security, which no one in the region wanted; it should encourage Tokyo to invest overseas (in peacekeeping operations, for example); it should help Japan in its quest for a seat on the United Nations Security Council; but it should remain strictly neutral on the question of access to nuclear weapons. Brzezinski recommended going beyond one-to-one discussions with Tokyo and putting all these dilemmas into a broader framework, thus making it possible to reduce tensions. He envisaged a "Pacific maritime triangle" (Japan, Indonesia-Korea, Australia), and then—no surprise here—a community of the developed nations with Europe.[31]

In 1971, at the time Brzezinski was writing his book, Japanese-American relations were undergoing considerable turbulence; this gave him the opportunity to put his new expertise to the test. Since the summer of 1969, the Nixon doctrine (international disengagement on America's part and reliance on regional allies) had created an element of uncertainty as to whether the United States could be counted on to guarantee Japan's security. The uncertainty was accentuated by the US opening to China; Nixon's Beijing visit in February 1972 had been announced the previous July. An added irritation was triggered by the "Nixon shock," the decision to put an end to the Bretton Woods monetary framework (August 15, 1971); the convertibility of the dollar to gold was suspended and tariffs were increased by 10 percent. Brzezinski was well aware that the Japanese were disturbed by this move ("We first struck at Japanese pride and now at their pockets!"[32]). This situation opened the way to a critique of the Nixon administration. On August 20, Brzezinski recommended to Humphrey that he attack Nixon on the grounds that the president was downgrading the traditional allies—Japan and Europe—in favor of the opening to China and negotiations with the USSR. Humphrey used Brzezinski's remarks word for word in the days that followed, most notably in a speech he gave in Alaska. He called for a clarification of the administration's policy toward Japan and enjoined Nixon to stop in Tokyo on his way to Beijing in early 1972.[33]

Brzezinski did not limit himself to offering political advice. It was during the summer and fall of 1971, while he was digesting the lessons of his stint in Japan and writing *The Fragile Blossom,* that he came up with the idea of a private initiative that would bring America closer to Japan and Europe: the Trilateral Commission.

The Creation of the Trilateral Commission

Official historiography designates David Rockefeller as the creator of the Trilateral Commission, and it often leaves the impression that Rockefeller recruited Brzezinski for this enterprise.[34] In reality, it was the other way around. Upon his return from Japan, in the second half of 1971, Brzezinski came up with the idea of a committee that would bring together American, European, and Japanese elites, and he worked out the details of the project with his friends Robert Bowie and Henry Owen. In the spring of 1972 he suggested the idea to David Rockefeller, in whom he found fertile soil for such an enterprise. Rockefeller indeed contributed the financing and the networks necessary to create the Commission, which finally saw the light of day in July 1973. Brzezinski and Rockefeller were the only two indispensable people in the Commission's creation: the first as the principal author of the scenario and director of the film, and the second as producer.

Some of the ideas that led Brzezinski to conceive of this tripartite United States-Europe-Japan dialogue can be identified in his earlier work, but his thinking underwent a pronounced shift after 1968. His ideas on "peaceful engagement" in Europe, which go back to 1957, are reaffirmed in the 1961 *Foreign Affairs* article and in the 1965 book *Alternative to Partition;* they led him to advocate the creation of a "community of the developed nations" for the first time in early 1966, in "New Guidelines for the West."[35] At this point, Japan was called to be part of the new community. But during the years that followed, the message became somewhat blurred. Thus, in Brzezinski's 1967 articles, Japan is mentioned only as a supplement to the principal pillars, which were the United States, Western Europe, and Eastern Europe, and sometimes the USSR.[36] The reason for this was simple: the community of developed nations had two distinct goals. It was to be, on the one hand, an instrument for peaceful engagement with Eastern Europe, and, on the other, a means for reinforcing ties among allies and for facing in common the challenges of the technetronic age, in particular in the Third World. The second objective gradually became paramount, especially after the Prague Spring repression. In his "America in the Technetronic Age," published in *Encounter*, Brzezinski portrayed Japan as one of the pillars of that community, which continued to include the most advanced of the communist nations. By 1970, in *Between Two Ages*, the latter were relegated to a hypothetical "second phase" of construction, and excluded from the "high-level consultative council for global cooperation."[37] In October 1970, in the article "America and Europe" in *Foreign Affairs,* they had totally disappeared.[38]

Brzezinski's stay in Japan reinforced his interest in trilateral cooperation. Then the tensions between the Nixon administration and its European and Japanese partners during the summer of 1971 added a political angle, and almost a sense of urgency, to the goal of tightening links with the allies—as seen from the correspondence between Humphrey and Brzezinski in August 1971. During this same late summer period Brzezinski also introduced a change of scale, shifting from a general political recommendation (regular meetings between American, European, and Japanese heads of government) to the more modest project of creating a network for exchanges among the elite of the three regions. On September 29, he explained to a correspondent that "the most desirable initiative to be taken is a tripartite American—West European—Japanese dialogue. I propose something along these lines in my forthcoming report on Japan. Moreover, more important, a group of my friends (Robert Bowie, George Ball, Henry Owen, and others) and I are attempting to organize more formally a Tripartite American—West European—Japanese Committee."[39]

In an April 26, 1972 communication with Rockefeller's office, Brzezinski sent a memorandum dated November 1971 that did not include an author's name but appeared to have come from the group of friends that had conceived the tripartite committee during the fall.[40] This memorandum is important because it traces with precision, in just three pages, the contours of the Trilateral as it was conceived during the summer of 1972 and as it came into being a year later. The first section explored the "problem": the United States, Western Europe, and Japan were facing the same challenges, those of postindustrial society, but also the degradation of the environment and problems of security. These countries were the only actors who could contribute economic and technological responses to the global problems. Therefore they had a special responsibility, even if their cooperation was hampered by frictions that often had to do with commercial considerations and domestic politics. Their cooperation was thus difficult but necessary, not in order to create a worldwide super-government or an anti-communist alliance (the most advanced states of the Eastern bloc might even, in the future, choose to participate), or a club of the rich (assistance to the developing countries would be, on the contrary, a central objective of the committee), but in order to avoid the vicious circle of unilateral decisions and recriminations that had been seen between the two World Wars.

This cooperation rested above all on the political decision makers, but, as the memorandum states, "private groups [could] play a part." Unlike government leaders, private groups risked nothing by exposing problems and coming up with ambitious proposals: "A committee of prominent American, European, and Japanese private citizens should be formed to this end. It should meet periodically to discuss common concerns, to seek common conclusions, and work to make these conclusions politically acceptable. Its aim should be to put forward imaginative forward looking proposals which could capture the imagination of public opinion in the three areas."[41]

The committee would be strictly independent of the governments in place; otherwise it would lose credibility, even though it should be in a position to put pressure on those governments. It would be made up of business and union leaders, politicians, and intellectuals; in the long run, it would constitute a bloc in support of enlightened, cooperative policies. It would deal simultaneously with economic, political, and security issues, without separating them: that would be its particular contribution. After examining the potential difficulties that such a committee might encounter, the memorandum ends by defining the following stage: it would entail bringing together prominent Americans, Europeans, and Japanese to discuss the proposal and make a decision about launching the group.

The project remained at a standstill until the Bilderberg Group gathered the following spring, at a meeting to which Brzezinski was invited. From the mid-1960s on, he had occasionally attended these meetings of the transatlantic elite, but not as a member, for he found that the group took itself too seriously and that the debates were often boring and predictable. Rockefeller offered to take him to the meeting in his private plane, and it was during the flight that Brzezinski's project was discussed. The two men first became acquainted through the Council on Foreign Relations, and later through their proximity on Mount Desert Island, where Zbigniew and Muska had been vacationing regularly since the early 1960s, and where they had bought a summer home in 1967. They became friends with the Rockefellers; the two couples even went on cruises together. At the time, Rockefeller was working to bring more young people into the social network of vacationers centered on Seal Harbor and its club, which, with older figures such as Walter Lippmann, was beginning to show its age. The relations between Rockefeller and Brzezinski became even closer with the Trilateral adventure, which was also, for David, a way of asserting himself in contradistinction to his brother Nelson.[42]

In his memoirs, Rockefeller recalled that plane trip to Belgium; it was on that occasion, he explained, that he shared with Brzezinski his idea of creating an organization that would bring together representatives from Europe, Japan, and the United States. For several years, he said, he had been urging the Bilderberg Group to invite Japanese participants, but to no avail. He tried once again at the April 1972 meeting in Belgium, but another refusal led him, with Brzezinski's encouragement, to create the Trilateral Commission.[43]

Brzezinski, while refusing to engage in an argument on the subject, recalls that discussion on the plane differently. He was the one, he explained later, who mentioned to Rockefeller the project that he had developed in the fall with Bowie and Owen. Rockefeller was enthusiastic, "very receptive and very much inclined to do it so maybe it was his idea at the same time." At the Bilderberg meeting, both men defended the idea of opening the group to Japanese participants. "Of course," recalled Brzezinski, "his [Rockefeller's] doing it was much more important than my doing it, since I was just a young participant there." The Bilderberg Group's categorical refusal led Brzezinski, Bowie, and Owen to approach Rockefeller once he was back in New York, and propose that he create a new entity. Brzezinski began, through several meetings and exchanges of letters, to sketch out the proposal for Rockefeller, along lines corresponding exactly to those of the "committee" evoked in the November 1971 memorandum.[44]

The precise paternity of the Trilateral is not especially important, and it is certain that both Rockefeller and Brzezinski were indispensable to its creation; the latter, moreover, insists on the roles played by Bowie and Owen alongside his own when the original idea was conceived.[45] Nor were Rockefeller or Brzezinski and his group of friends the only ones who had concluded that a reinforcement of the ties between America and its European allies and Japan was a necessity in the early 1970s. The "Nixon shock," the spectacular "New Economic Policy" announced on August 15, 1971, pushed the president's domestic popularity back up, but many specialists in Japan and international economics were skeptical. Philip Trezise, assistant secretary of state for the economy, and C. Fred Bergsten, in charge of economic affairs on Kissinger's National Security Council, had not even been consulted; they resigned, and both joined the Brookings Institution. Other observers, such as Richard Gardner (at Columbia, one of Brzezinski's close associates) and Richard Cooper (at Yale) strongly criticized the administration's unilateralism.

At the Brookings Institution, Owen and Trezise, along with Max Kohnstamm from the European side and Saburo Ikota from the Japanese side, launched the "tripartite studies" in 1971, a series of economic studies carried out jointly with the Kiel Institute for World Economics and the Economic Research Center of Tokyo; the first studies were published in 1972. Another example was that of Ambassador Gerard C. Smith, the principal negotiator of the SALT agreements starting in 1969, and David Rockefeller's brother-in-law; concerned with interdependency and the convergence of supranational problems and the like, Smith had launched the journal *Interplay* (1967–1971), which was initially focused on transatlantic matters but quickly opened up to Japan. In late 1972, Smith joined the group that created the Trilateral and became president of the American branch.[46]

Although the idea of the Trilateral Commission was not especially original, its creation, organized chiefly by Brzezinski, was a model of institutional construction. In an April 26, 1972, letter to Rockefeller's assistant, Brzezinski recommended that the latter try to recruit George Franklin as the group's secretary. A meeting of the principal collaborators—most notably Rockefeller, Bowie, Owen, McGeorge Bundy, George Franklin, and of course Brzezinski—was set for May 9 to choose the Europeans and Japanese to be contacted; an expanded meeting was to be held in late June or early July, another in September; and so on.

Things unfolded more or less as Brzezinski had recommended. The May 9 meeting launched the "Commission for Peace and Prosperity." Rockefeller disclaimed credit for the original idea of creating the commission and said he did not seek to be its president, but Bowie (who, along with Brzezinski and Owen, mentioned their fall discussions), spoke for everyone in expressing the opinion that he would be the ideal leader. Brzezinski suggested that the Commission could combine the best of Bilderberg and the London-based International Institute for Strategic Studies (IISS), while being more oriented toward action. Then the group discussed procedural issues and the size of the Commission, and suggested names of possible European and Japanese representatives to be invited to the decisive meeting set to take place on July 24 at Rockefeller's luxurious property in Pocantico Hills, New York.[47] On June 10, Brzezinski summed up his progress in a memorandum to Rockefeller, with "Tripartite Commission" as the subject. He had sounded out a number of Japanese men he knew, and if the responses were favorable the organizers would have to be careful not to present the project as a sort of "made in USA" conspiracy. Hence the importance of the July 24 meeting, where their foreign partners would be given the impression that they were helping to shape the organization from the outset.[48]

This effort to create an impression of full involvement is what is striking in the minutes of the meeting at Pocantico Hills, which is sometimes presented as the decisive moment when the Trilateral Commission was conceived. A few adjustments were made and a definitive name was found for the commission; here again, Brzezinski played a key role. A discussion arose around the swimming pool. "Tripartite Commission," he noted, was too reminiscent of the

Tripartite Pact, and "that would be a terrible analogy." But David Rockefeller did not much like "Commission for Peace and Prosperity," which "had the wrong ring." "Then . . . why don't we use the word 'trilateral'?" Brzezinski suggested. "It has a semi-official ring, which is good, since we were not official." The name Trilateral Commission was then adopted unanimously.[49] On the very day of the meeting at Pocantico Hills, *The New Leader* published "Japan in a Trilateral World," an article under Brzezinski's byline in which he expressed his wish for the creation of nonofficial organizations similar to those of the transatlantic world but that would cover the three regions.[50]

The eight Americans present at Pocantico Hills (Fred Bergsten, Robert Bowie, Zbigniew Brzezinski, McGeorge Bundy, George Franklin, Bayless Manning, Henry Owen, and of course David Rockefeller) finally brought together five Europeans (Carl Carstens, Guido Colonna Di Paliano, François Duchêne, René Roch, and Max Kohnstamm) and four Japanese (Kiichi Miyazawa, Kinhide Mushakoji, Saburo Okita, along with Tadishi Yamamoto as an observer).[51] In their discussions, they insisted on the necessity of making concrete recommendations and on watching to make sure these were acted on by the governments of the three regions or by international organizations. They also debated the appropriateness of integrating representatives of communist or developing countries (the idea was rejected, except for the possibility of accepting observers), or Canada (this idea was adopted), and they decided on the themes of the first working groups (the new economic system and the implications of the change in political values). Finally, they defined the structure of the organization: there were to be thirty-one members (fourteen Europeans distributed according to the quota system of the European Community, ten North Americans, including two Canadians, and seven Japanese), a president (David Rockefeller, provisionally), two regional copresidents, and an executive director—Brzezinski. As for the financing, it was supposed to come from the three regions in equal amounts, but everyone knew that the Americans, in particular David Rockefeller and McGeorge Bundy would supply what was needed at the outset.[52] The Europeans and the Japanese wondered whether they were going to be in some sense employed by Rockefeller.[53]

The fifteen months that elapsed between the Pocantico Hills meeting and the first Trilateral conference in Tokyo in October 1973 were devoted to the institutional maturation of the project. The Commission's founding corresponded to a moment of relative decline in American hegemony over military (including nuclear) and economic planning, thus to a moment of re-equilibration and turbulence in America's relations with Europe and Japan.[54] Trilateralism appears in this sense as an American attempt to reconfigure the transatlantic world by including Japan, in order to invent a new, more stable, and more cooperative relation. Moreover, Brzezinski and the other founders explicitly gave the Commission the assignment of easing the frictions between the United States and its allies, tensions that tended to accompany this phase of re-equilibration, especially on the commercial and financial levels. "If war were still possible, we would probably still be at war," Jean Monnet said in May 1974, regarding the disruption of the Western order.[55]

The Commission thus went to work in four directions at once. Toward Europe, it aimed to create a less paternalistic and "more equal" approach than the post–Cold War network of transatlantic relations had achieved (the Bilderberg Group, the Atlantic Council, the Salzburg Seminars, the Aspen Institute, and so on). At the same time the Commission would encourage Europeans to reject de Gaulle-style nationalisms, to become unified (most participants were aligned with Jean Monnet), and to open up more to the rest of the world, beginning with Japan, and to the global problems for which America needed equal partners.[56] In the same spirit, the Trilateral sought also to socialize Japan into the world of the great powers, while escaping the bilateral head-to-head encounters, which only amplified commercial and political frictions. Japan constituted the Trilateral Commission's most important "mission," as Brzezinski suggested in *Between Two Ages*.[57] He confirmed this in an internal memorandum about the Commission's real targets as seen by Gerard Smith in April 1973. Three of the seven announced objectives concerned Japan alone: encouraging Tokyo to play a more active role in the world, achieving a better distribution of the burden of security, reducing the nuclear temptation, and, finally, promoting a direct European-Japanese dialogue. To the goals of rationalizing commercial and financial relations among the three regions and coordinating policies concerning the Middle East, Smith added another, that of influencing American decision makers at the highest level, but he doubted that that goal was achievable.[58] He was proven wrong on the last point, as the Carter administration would be administered almost exclusively, in its upper ranks, by trilateralists.

The Commission also sought to influence American foreign policy more broadly. The elite needed to be encouraged to turn away both from the unilateralism of the right (the Nixon-Kissinger version) and from the isolationist temptation of the left (as reflected in the failed Mansfield amendment mandating that US military presence in Europe be cut by half) in favor of a more responsible approach to global problems. The Trilateral's last implicit goal, or more precisely the background for that goal, remained America's rivalry with the USSR. For Brzezinski and his colleagues, the dominant idea was that the international system had become more complex than it had been during the Cold War, with the appearance of new actors and new global problems, and that America could no longer ensure a satisfactory worldwide order on its own. It needed partners: for fostering development in the Third World, for example, or for managing rare resources and cross-border challenges (raw materials, oceans, the environment, and so on). It was thus less a matter of repairing the Cold War anti-communist alliances as of ensuring the continuity of a world order that the USSR was sufficiently powerful to challenge, but insufficiently powerful to replace.

The Trilateral Commission did not get off to an easy start. The organization was built on solid foundations, but it faced a certain skepticism, especially among the European and Japanese allies. In a first phase, it struggled for recognition, so much so that at the end of 1974 the glass still looked half empty. It was only over the next couple of years that the Commission became a real presence on the American and international landscape, owing especially to its association with leading figures in the Carter administration. This was also the moment when it began to be the object of sharp criticism from both the right and the left—a sure sign of its success.

During the year that followed the Pocantico Hills meeting, Brzezinski was deeply involved in building the organization, in addition to his work at Columbia. Then, starting June 1, 1973, when the Trilateral officially came into being, he obtained a sabbatical year to devote himself to it full-time, followed by an additional sabbatical semester from July to December 1974, and he resumed his academic work at Columbia only on a half-time basis in the spring term of 1975.[59] Scarcely two days had passed after the Pocantico meeting when he and Henry Owen wrote a dense memorandum for David Rockefeller defining the next steps to be taken.[60] During the fall, the group recruited Ambassador Gerard Smith, who would become the president of the American branch, as Rockefeller did not want to take on that role. On January 8, 1973, a core group of organizers—George Franklin, Smith, and Brzezinski, accompanied by Max Kohnstamm, the future president of the European branch and a close associate of Jean Monnet's—traveled to Japan. There they met with their Japanese contacts to define the composition and financing of the Japanese branch, as well as to recruit its president, Takeshi Watanabe, a former director of the Asian Development Bank.[61]

Since the Trilateral Commission was intended to be a network of elites closely associated with powerful figures, particular attention was paid to contacts with leaders at the highest levels. During the first months of 1973, Smith and Rockefeller presented the project to prominent individuals concerned with foreign affairs, such as Senators Mike Mansfield, William Fulbright, and Charles Percy, and also Douglas Dillon, Robert McNamara, and Vice President Spiro Agnew, soliciting their opinions about possible members. The project was uniformly well received.[62] European and Japanese leaders were also made aware of the project: on May 15, 1973, Rockefeller met with Georges Pompidou and Antoine Pinay at the Élysée Palace and talked to them about the Trilateral Commission.[63] On March 2, 1973, an article very favorable to the project appeared in the *New York Times*. Echoing the frustrations of Japan, which continued to feel excluded from the circle of the great powers despite its remarkable economic development, the article described the Commission that would soon be launched, evoking its objectives and its structure.[64]

The year 1973 was not an ordinary one for relations between America and its allies. It was "the year of Europe," as proclaimed by Kissinger, who had become secretary of state, in an attempt on the part of the Nixon administration to redefine transatlantic relations and pay more attention to its allies, including Japan, after four years of focusing on the Soviet Union, China, and Vietnam. Kissinger had been kept informed, most notably by David Rockefeller, about the Trilateral Commission project from its inception, and he encouraged it, offering advice, for example, on the choice of president for the American branch.[65] On April 17, 1973, Brzezinski had lunch with Kissinger at the Sans-Souci Palace near Berlin. Their discussion touched on many topics, from relations with the USSR and China to the financing of Radio Free Europe; Kissinger specifically insisted on being brought up to date on the proposals for the Trilateral.[66]

Less than a week later, on April 23, 1973, Kissinger delivered his the "year of Europe" speech, in which he depicted a world profoundly transformed since the end of the Second World War. He proclaimed the urgency of inventing new forms of cooperation with Europe that would respond to the challenges of the day—energy, for example—and would include Japan, which had become a first-rate power. Stressing the contrast between a Europe with regional interests and an America with global interests, he proposed to the Europeans a new Atlantic charter that "creates for the Atlantic nations a new relationship in whose progress Japan can share."[67]

At first glance, this speech seemed to pull the rug out from under the Trilateral, since it was based on the same observation and pointed in the same direction. The Commission's idea of supplementing a deficiency on the part of governments and creating a new awareness seemed henceforth pointless. In fact, just the opposite was true: the speech offered the Trilateral Commission legitimacy on two counts. It validated the Commission's basic approach even as it offered it a formidable space for critique, given the degree to which it seemed to relegate the allies whose cooperation it purported to seek to a secondary and dependent status. Thus, Europe was reduced to its limited regional horizon, and Japan looked like a fifth wheel, a foreign body to which a place in a preexisting transatlantic framework must be offered. Brzezinski did not hesitate to underline the contrast with the Commission: "We are offering," he explained to *Newsweek,* "a truly trilateral approach on the basis of equality from the start."[68] And shortly after the speech, Brzezinski wrote to Smith that, if the Trilateral's inaugural meeting in Tokyo, which was to present the Commission's declaration of principles to the public, took place before Nixon's trip to Europe and the publication of the new Atlantic charter, it could attract considerable attention. As it happened, because of the European opposition, the Atlantic charter never saw the light of day.[69]

All this did not mean that things went smoothly for the Trilateral Commission. After a trip to Europe in early June 1973, Brzezinski drew up a harsh balance sheet for the Nixon-Kissinger foreign policy, which was rejected almost unanimously by the Europeans. He also emphasized that the Europeans did not have an overall vision of the transatlantic relation, that they were essentially critical and negative; above all, they showed no enthusiasm whatsoever for the idea of developing cooperative projects that would include Japan.[70] The Commission nevertheless continued to forge ahead, and it finally went into operation on July 1, when Brzezinski set up his office in the Chase Manhattan Bank at 30 Rockefeller Plaza and began to use stationery inscribed with its letterhead. To prepare for the inaugural meeting, the first two working groups were set up, one on political matters (the designated rapporteurs were Max Kohnstamm, François Duchêne, Henry Owen, and Kinhide Musakoji), the other on monetary issues (Takeshi Watanabe, Motoo Kaji, Richard Cooper, and Claudio Segre). The rapporteurs on this latter task force, who met in Washington in June, met again in Anchorage with Brzezinski at the beginning of August in order to advance their work; they were to meet in mid-September in Rome for a plenary session with the other members of the team. Brzezinski also announced the working groups to come: trade, energy, development, the oceans, East-West relations.[71] This gives a sense of the Trilateral's activities in those years—solid and serious work, authentically trilateral, with abundant financial support.

As if to emphasize that Japan was the principal stake of the Trilateral Commission, the group's inaugural meeting was held in Tokyo on October 22–23, 1973. It was a meeting of the executive committee (thirty-four people from the three regions), paralleled by work sessions devoted to the two reports, with all the Japanese members. Following the meeting, the group's declaration of principles was distributed at a press conference, and Prime Minister Kakuei Tanaka came to give a talk before the Commission members.[72] However, not everything went according to plan. The meeting was more or less successful, yet the *New York Times* stressed the controversies that marked the occasion. Unexpectedly, the ordinarily placid Japanese members criticized certain passages of the declaration of principles. In particular, the goal of formulating political recommendations; they would have preferred more neutral studies on long-term trends and developments. Further, they objected to the Commission's procedures—only the executive committee was systematically consulted on the publications, rather than the entire membership—along with its "rich man's club" aspect.[73]

The Japanese were not the only ones to criticize the Commission. A number of Europeans, in 1973–1974, suspected the Americans of having creating a new structure—this time multilateral—to indoctrinate them and get them to subscribe to policies that they did not want to adopt. This was the case with Pierre Hassner, even though he could not seriously be suspected of Gaullism; he warned Brzezinski against temptation toward "missionary zeal" on the part of the Trilateral, for that would be the surest way to alienate the Europeans.[74] A few months later, Michel Tatu published a critical article in *Le Monde* suggesting that the Trilateral, which was the private counterpart of Kissinger's initiatives, was only a new instrument of American hegemony. Ironically, Brzezinski wrote to Kohnstamm to suggest a response that would come from Europe, stressing the role Europeans and Japanese members played both in the creation of the Trilateral (at Pocantico Hills) and in its development (the three regional presidents were on equal footing).[75] But he did not want to wait, and since he knew Tatu well—the latter had come to Columbia to study Sovietology in 1965—he wrote him directly a few days later to complain about his article and to stress the relations of equality that prevailed within the Commission, without neglecting to mention his disagreements with Kissinger's approach.[76]

Japanese reservations and European sensitivities were not the only challenges facing the Commission. Even as the initial meeting was taking place in Tokyo, the international context was complicating things: the Yom Kippur War (October 6–25, 1973) and then the oil crisis that heightened diplomatic tensions between Americans and Europeans. On November 2, 1973, Brzezinski wrote to the three presidents of the Trilateral, suggesting a common declaration on Middle Eastern issues that could emphasize the need for consultations among the three regions as a supplement to, or a replacement for, the purely American-Soviet management of the conflict.[77] Despite Brzezinski's persistence, the disagreements were so profound that the Trilateral did not manage to produce such a declaration. In fact, when Kohnstamm presented a summary report on the Trilateral Commission the following month, he stressed the deterioration of the relations among allies that had accompanied the group's first steps (the Middle East, but also the financial crisis, tensions in the grain markets, Watergate, and so on).[78]

Nonetheless, 1974 saw the Trilateral pursue its plan of action. The task forces, after some intensive organizational efforts, regularly produced its scheduled reports starting in the summer of 1973. These were distributed to a carefully selected elite and to the press; in June 1974, for example, the *New York Times* took up the Trilateral's recommendations on international development aid policy.[79] The American branch published the newsletter *Trialogue* every two or three months. The executive committee met for the second time, in Brussels, with all the European members, while the regional branches met separately at regular intervals.[80] At the end of the year, a successful meeting took place in Washington, during which the executive committee had the opportunity to have dinner with Kissinger at the State Department and to meet President Gerald Ford and Vice President Nelson Rockefeller in the White House (December 8–10, 1974).[81]

A few days later, Brzezinski sent his colleagues a memorandum titled "Some Brutal Reflections on the State of the Commission."[82] He shared the majority view that the Washington meeting had been a great success, and he did not challenge the idea that it had marked a kind of symbolic takeoff for the organization. One year and a half before its planned extinction—it had initially been programmed to last three years—its weaknesses were numerous and significant. One of the greatest concerns had to do with Japan; that group was not at a high enough level and was not very dynamic; the reports were not well distributed and not adequately read. In Europe, German participation left something to be desired, and Italian participation was weak—Giovanni Agnelli, one of the founding members, had not attended a single meeting. The impact of the Trilateral in Europe was negligible, and Kohnstamm would have to be replaced; he was leaving his position to direct the brand new European University Institute in Florence. As for the budget, the Japanese and European contributions remained minimal; the Trilateral remained an unbalanced initiative, financed by the Americans. Above all, its impact was insufficient: each member was going to have to make an effort to distribute the group's reports, otherwise the Trilateral would become "a trilateral Bilderberg, providing an ego trip for a few key individuals who enjoy going to international conferences where they are provided with an opportunity to shake hands with the 'big wigs.'"[83]

Although the Trilateral Commission did not achieve all its goals, Brzezinski was excessively tough in his evaluation, and seemed determined to see a glass half empty. During its first year and a half of existence, the Trilateral was mainly in a construction phase. Its underlying influence was increasing, and during the next phase (1975–1976) it gained a privileged place in the global high-level dialogue on international affairs. It even had a certain political impact on specific decisions, or at least on the orientations and reflections of the leaders involved. These results were largely attributable to Brzezinski himself.

On February 8, 1975, when the North American group met, several members tempered Brzezinski's concerns; Edwin Reischauer, for example, considered the Japanese situation quite satisfactory. For Peter Dobell, from the Canadian group, the Commission's real problem was that it was less trilateral than unilateral, relying disproportionately on "the intellectual and physical energy provided by Brzezinski." In fact, one of the questions that arose, on the assumption that the decision to extend the life of the Commission would be made, concerned Brzezinski's replacement, as he was resuming his work at Columbia on a half-time basis that spring, then full-time starting in the fall of 1975.[84] After his departure, the Commission's operations were largely decentralized: he was actually replaced by three people: three regional directors coordinated by George Franklin were chosen to oversee the progress of the working groups.[85]

Brzezinski's image as the battery behind the Trilateral Commission seems quite apt. From 1973 to 1975, he unquestionably ensured the coordination and activity of the network in all three regions, each of which he knew very well, but he also supplied a significant portion of the Commission's political and intellectual strategy; for example, in choosing the working groups. Not all of his enterprises succeeded; the declaration on the Middle East, for example, never came to fruition. There was also the political timidity of the three Trilateral presidents; Brzezinski would have liked to see them take clear public positions on the major issues of the day. This would have helped the group acquire greater political impact and avoid falling back into the discussion model of the Bilderberg group, or the research institute model of the IISS. He recalls those two years as a thrilling period.

> I decided early on that it was something for me to do, that it would give me a new range of experience, and I thought that George Franklin would be very pleasant to work with because he was a gentleman and a very nice human being; and at the same time an intimate of David Rockefeller, they were roommates at Harvard. [We also appointed Gerard Smith] because Rockefeller didn't want to be the American chairman. But Rockefeller was in fact the chairman, and so Gerard Smith was difficult, because he in effect saw himself as the head of the whole thing, and there was always some sort of stickiness about that.[86]

The Trilateral Commission gained a certain public notoriety in 1975, owing to the controversy surrounding one of its reports, that of Sam Huntington and Michel Crozier on the governability of democracies. As early as April 1973, Huntington had suggested to Brzezinski that the Trilateral should look into the transformations of domestic policy in the developed countries, and Brzezinski had indicated that he wanted to include this insofar as possible in the Commission's activities.[87] No sooner said than done, and in June 1974 this was the working group that generated the most interest among members of the Commission, so much so that Brzezinski asked Huntington to come present the report that was being prepared to the executive committee in Washington in December.[88]

The report prepared by Crozier, Huntington, and Joji Watanuke, *The Governability of Democracies,* was finalized in the spring of 1975 and presented to the Trilateral members at their meeting in Kyoto on May 30–31. It immediately set off a heated controversy and even gave rise to requests that the organization officially repudiate it.[89] The authors' thesis, documented especially for America and Europe (the part on Japan was considered less valid and less convincing) was simple. The 1960s had witnessed a revival of the democratic spirit and of political passions that had led to increased activity on the part of nations but a concomitant decline in their authority. In the 1970s, that evolution raised concerns about the governability of democracies, since all systems of hierarchy and authority were being called into question. In the United States, for instance, the power of the president had diminished in favor of Congress, the press, and the bureaucracy, institutions that could not supply substitute leadership. What was required, then, in a way, was less democracy, especially in the areas where it should not rule (in universities, for example), and more concentration of power in the hands of governments, more restraint on the part of civil society in the demands it made of democracies.[90]

Coming from a relatively secret group of private individuals connected with the business world, this report was understandably explosive—oil poured on the fires of conspiracy theorists both on the left and on the right. Far from rejecting the report, Brzezinski was delighted by the controversy it was generating and by the notoriety it was bestowing on the Commission. On June 18, 1975, he came up with a compromise formula to use when the report was published as a book: the controversial recommendations were relegated to an annex and "buried" in a report on the Kyoto discussions.[91] A week later, and again at the end of August, he put forward the idea of a colloquium centered on the report, soliciting written reactions from intellectuals and political figures. He even suggested the idea of a colloquium in each region, with the proceedings published in a common volume: "The debate begun at Kyoto on the governability of democracies should not be allowed to lapse . . . this proposal would have the great advantage of keeping the debate alive on a subject which is both important and a distinctive contribution by the Commission; of involving a wider range of people, including some younger practitioners, in what the Commission has been doing; and of contributing further to the Commission's general impact."[92]

Although that proposal led nowhere, Brzezinski pursued his efforts. He authorized Irving Kristol to publish the American chapter in *The Public Interest,* and he disseminated the complete book, published by New York University Press, very broadly, from Raymond Aron in France to Kissinger and to Cyrus Sulzberger of the *New York Times.*[93] He was thrilled when Japanese prime minister Takeo Miki used the report and then the book to prepare for his discussions with President Ford.[94]

This controversy, which contributed to the notoriety of the Trilateral Commission must not be allowed to conceal the success of the Kyoto meeting at the end of May 1975. The group decided to renew the Commission's mandate for three years, with particular support from the Japanese members—who had been the most hesitant two years earlier.[95] This meeting and the one that followed in Paris in early December 1975 were described by the generally moderate Brzezinski as "spectacular successes." He cited a particularly surprising element, the full and complete cooperation of the French government, which was unexpected.[96] The *New York Review of Books* examined the Trilateral's work and gave the group credit for influencing the State Department to move forward on aid to developing countries.[97] Meanwhile, the Commission launched new working groups; George Berthoin (another associate of Jean Monnet) succeeded Kohnstamm on the European side, and the three-year renewal was definitively approved in December.[98]

In 1976, the Trilateral received another mark of success: the trilateralist Jimmy Carter won the Democratic nomination, then the presidential election, and he named some twenty trilateralists to key positions in his administration, including Brzezinski, Walter Mondale, Cyrus Vance, Harold Brown, Michael Blumenthal, and Warren Christopher. This success was not the sign of excessive politicization. The men in question were immediately replaced on the Commission by former members of the Ford administration such as George Bush and Henry Kissinger, but also by Republican elected officials such as William Cohen and John Danforth, with Democrats such as Paul Volcker and Alan Cranston also named.[99]

It is all the more understandable, then, why the Trilateral became the object of virulent criticism from both the right and the left. It was, in a sense, even more elitist than the Council on Foreign Relations, by virtue of its international character, and it was less concerned with social issues. When President Carter received the Trilateral's executive committee in June 1978, he began with flattering comments, suggesting that if the Trilateral had existed after the First World War, the world would have been able to cancel the Second. He also reproached its members for their elitist and capitalist image, and he complained that his interlocutors, especially those from the Third World, gave him a hard time about his earlier participation and described the Trilateral as a "rich man's club."[100]

The organization thought up by Brzezinski and his friends in the fall of 1971 had thus not avoided certain criticisms they had anticipated and dismissed in advance. But more than the "rich man's club" theme, it was the theme of elitism that fed conspiracy theories and the suspicions of populists on the right and on the left. After all, the Trilateral had been conceived as an instrument for encouraging leaders of the three regions to go beyond domestic considerations in order to cooperate and find solutions for international problems.[101] It is clear what Brzezinski, Bowie, and Owen were targeting: unilateral decisions based on short-sighted political considerations that offered only a limited advantage to one country while making it impossible to cooperate with others in order to solve the most enormous problems posed to the human race; in short, the dilemma of collective action. But the risk of this enlightened supranationality was that popular preferences expressed by democratic mechanisms would be ignored. The Trilateral's definition of national interest was rational and remarkable, Irving Kristol explained in 1980, but that is not the definition given by the public. How could one be certain that the internationalism of the elites was a better guide than the nationalism of Americans, and what legitimacy did it have?[102]

The question was raised all the more acutely in that those elites were the same ones encountered in the Council on Foreign Relations or the Bilderberg Group, a multinational establishment drawn from the "corporate-academic complex," which recommended putting democracy on hold (the Crozier-Huntington report).[103] The role of the Rockefeller brothers was subject to particular scrutiny; they seemed to be behind all the organizations of the elites, and seemed to be promoting men such as Kissinger and Brzezinski, who guaranteed them permanent access to political power. The internationalist vision that was developed by Brzezinski in *Between Two Ages* and that was embodied most notably in the Trilateral Commission had run into the suspicions of public opinion jealous of its own sovereignty. Fortunately for him, in 1976 this criticism was not yet fully developed, so that his advice to Governor Jimmy Carter did not constitute an obstacle to the latter's success. On the contrary, it was largely from the work of the Trilateral that Brzezinski drew his recommendations for the future president.

Jimmy Carter's Presidential Campaign

From the 1950s on, it was Brzezinski's fate to be compared to Kissinger, who was five years his senior.[104] The similarities in their trajectories were so numerous that the parallel seemed to come naturally: two men born in Europe, each retaining the accent of his mother tongue, both finding the springboard for their careers at Harvard during the Cold War years—careers that in both cases began in the intellectual realm and quickly extended into the political. The same stages seemed to follow in sequence, with a gap of just a few years. Both were recognized in the academy; were members of the Council on Foreign Relations; had a first article published in *Foreign Affairs* (at age thirty-two for Kissinger, thirty-three for Brzezinski). Further, both had an initial experience on the margins of power around age thirty (Kissinger was a consultant under Kennedy, Brzezinski served on Johnson's Policy Planning Staff); and had the support of a powerful patron, more precisely a Rockefeller (Nelson for Kissinger, David for Brzezinski). Each man developed the construction of a network (Kissinger's International Seminar, Brzezinski's Trilateral Commission). Finally, both enjoyed the importance of their publications and visibility in the media, and both rose to the position of national security adviser to the president (at age forty-six for Kissinger, forty-nine for Brzezinski).

These similarities were striking at the time, and they sometimes led people to see Brzezinski, because he was younger and more ambitious, as engaged in a sort of competition with Kissinger. They also led certain observers to take the presumed rivalry as a key to understanding Brzezinski, attributing to him what could be described as an obsession, a "Kissinger complex," and even suggesting that there was a fundamental antagonism between the two men, that they were in a sense enemy brothers motivated by mutual loathing.[105] Yet testimonies from the 1950s and the correspondence between the two from the 1960s and 1970s tell a different story, that of a cordial, almost friendly relationship, in which competition is not excluded as a background motif—no more than differences of opinion, one might add—but does not appear excessive or predominant. Kissinger insists on this: "Look, some of the so-called competition was built into the system, in the sense that I was two or three years ahead of him as a graduate student and in every job I got. So I got the jobs that he wanted and deserved—I didn't get them at his expense, but that sort of put him in an inherently competitive position with me and imposed the need to come up with some differences."[106]

It was imperative for Brzezinski to distinguish himself, particularly in 1976, when a certain tension reigned between the two men. What is important to note is that no personal attacks or exchanges of disparaging comments can be found in the press or in the archives. On the contrary, the similarity of their career paths often provided them with occasions for good-humored joshing, such as an incident related by Brzezinski that took place on December 6, 1973. That day Kissinger had invited nine university professors to lunch at the State Department. Having depicted a somber prospect for an America isolated in an international system that was hostile for the near term, especially for the years 1976–1980, "[Kissinger] added that this will happen when I inherit his job, with his having established the precedent of foreign born holding this job. I responded by saying 'I hope this has become a firm tradition.'"[107] Brzezinski, too, expressed slight resentment toward Kissinger in 1977 over the latter's failure to help during Humphrey's electoral campaign ten years earlier.

Starting with their first meeting at Harvard in 1951, Kissinger and Brzezinski maintained good relations. Without being close friends, they saw each other regularly.[108] At that time, Brzezinski was an extrovert and at ease in society, whereas Kissinger was a long way from having acquired the seductive charm and magnetism that characterized him later on, especially in the 1970s.[109] But Kissinger's star was rising, and Brzezinski contacted him in 1956 and 1957 to recommend potential participants in his summer seminar. When Brzezinski saw his chances for a tenured position at Harvard vanish, in early 1959, because Bowie, Kissinger, and Hoffmann had been promoted, he felt no resentment, since those promotions were in international studies and not in area studies, his own field of specialization.[110]

During the 1960s, the two men maintained a regular and cordial exchange of letters. When Brzezinski sent his articles to Kissinger, he always received thanks and most often compliments in exchange. "I thought it admirable," Kissinger wrote him, for example, referring to Brzezinski's 1961 article in *Foreign Affairs* about the centripetal dynamics in the Soviet Union. "I think you will find that the basic strategy that you recommended is being adopted," he added by hand in a thank-you note for the article "Peaceful Engagement in Eastern Europe," at a time when he was still serving as consultant to McGeorge Bundy.[111] An amusing exchange took place in 1963:

> [Kissinger to Brzezinski] I understand from the New York educational station that you recommended me to be on a program with you as a proponent of the 'hard' line. I am flattered, of course, that you should think of me. But I loathe labels, and I was not aware of the fact that you were notoriously more moderate than I am. Moreover, how can I get a reputation for being wize [*sic*] if you will not let me pretend to be of the middle road?
>
> [Brzezinski's response] Since some Eric Fromm type wax [*sic*] to be the "soft," you were only natural as the exponent of the "hard-headed," statesmanlike, realist approach. I was only to make a middle of the way [*sic*] opening statement to set up the "softie" for decapitation. So your reputation for being "wize" (at Columbia we spell it with an "s," like in "Soviet" and "Stalin") would not have been impaired.[112]

In the same vein, some months later, Kissinger congratulated Brzezinski on his nomination as one of the ten exceptional young men of 1963. "No wonder Muska prefers you to me."[113] He added congratulations on the birth of Ian, and asked Brzezinski for his views on the recent evolution of Germany. The latter replied with this opener: "Dear Outstanding 58" (Kissinger had indeed received the same distinction at the same age), and said that he had stopped to see him in Cambridge the evening before to discuss world affairs, but without success. In short, if there was a rivalry between the two men, it in no way prevented a real camaraderie.[114]

The fact that in early 1968 Kissinger blocked Emmet Hughes's attempt to hire Brzezinski for Nelson Rockefeller's team does not seem to have affected their personal relations; Brzezinski, after all, was not especially attracted by that prospect. Moreover, it was Brzezinski whom Ted Van Dyk asked to take possession of the "black book" on Nixon that Kissinger proposed to transmit to Humphrey's campaign team. If Brzezinski was surprised by Kissinger's nomination to serve at the White House in November 1968, he does not seem to have reacted with particular jealousy. This is despite that at the Princeton colloquium,

Kissinger caused a sensation when he arrived in the glow of his nomination, and stole the spotlight from his former colleagues Brzezinski and Hoffmann, both specialists in foreign affairs.[115]

A new phase in the relations between the two men began when Kissinger reached a position of power. Brzezinski naturally found himself in the opposition. This created a situation of structural tension that increased during the 1972 campaign, and especially during the 1976 campaign, when he was the chief adviser to the Democratic candidate who was trying to defeat the Ford-Kissinger team. Kissinger, who had taken on increasing importance since Watergate, represented the continuity of the Republican Party's power. That situation strained the relations between the two men somewhat, although it did not lead to a break. It is important to understand their interaction in detail in order to grasp Brzezinski's position when he arrived in the White House in January 1977, for that position was in part shaped by his opposition to Kissinger.

During the years that the latter spent in the White House (1969–1973), the dialogue between the two men remained ample and cordial, despite Brzezinski's sometimes critical comments about the Nixon administration's foreign policy. When Kissinger invited several academics to come engage in dialogue with him, in the spring of 1969, he also sent a personal letter to "Zbig."[116] The latter was unable to attend the meeting, but the two agreed to have dinner together on July 14, 1969. According to Brzezinski's notes, they talked about the administration's foreign policy—from China (Kissinger said that the reengagement was going to intensify) to the USSR, from Romania to Vietnam (the question "What to do?" was raised several times), as well as personnel matters.[117] Brzezinski, who wrote to Kissinger the next day to say that the dinner had made him nostalgic for Washington, sent—at Kissinger's request—an article on his idea for a community of developed nations, along with a draft of an almost philosophical speech on the "meaning of peace" intended for use by Nixon, who was about to leave for India. Peace was not just the absence of hostilities, Brzezinski maintained, but a process of ongoing progress, at the national and international levels. As it happened, not only did Kissinger thank him warmly for it, but Nixon used Brzezinski's wording on the topic when he toasted his hosts in New Delhi on July 31, 1969.[118]

In October 1969, anticipating a speech that Nixon was scheduled to give, Brzezinski sent him a memorandum on Vietnam with Kissinger as intermediary, suggesting a strategy of cease-fire and negotiation; but he took care to have the memo sent through additional channels.[119] This did not seem to bother Kissinger, who encouraged him to keep on sending suggestions, said that he was glad to have seen him recently, and expressed the wish to see him again.[120] On May 23, 1970, the two men had a long discussion in the wake of the extension of the Vietnam War to Cambodia, which had unleashed a wave of protests, especially among students. Kissinger confided that he was very concerned about the divisions in the country—less the agitation of the left than the possibility of a sudden swing to the right, encouraged by Nixon, whose instincts pushed him in that direction. He criticized the divisions within the Establishment and the irresponsible conduct of professors who were stoking the anger on campuses. He confided to Brzezinski that he thought he would resign from his position before the end of the Nixon administration—even though he predicted a Republican victory in 1972—but that he would not return to Harvard. The two men also spoke about the Middle East, Germany (both predicted that Östpolitik would not go very far), and the situation of Radio Free Europe and Radio Liberty (RFE-RL), whose activity Bonn sought to reduce.[121]

Two days later, Brzezinski sent Kissinger a one-page memorandum, titled "The Cambodian Crisis," which explained that the right way to temper the anger aroused by the operation in Cambodia was to show that it had been fruitful, not militarily but politically, in the Paris negotiations. Nixon should thus propose a cease-fire that would either make it possible to throw the responsibility for the war onto Hanoi, if the proposal were rejected, or else to progress toward peace, if it were accepted—and in either case it would attenuate the criticism.[122] Kissinger wrote back thanking him for the memo and added a handwritten note saying that he was "keeping a sharp eye on the RFE matter."[123]

What is interesting in this exchange is that it took place just as Brzezinski was issuing harsh public criticisms at the Nixon administration. For instance, on May 24, 1970, the day after his conversation with Kissinger and the day before he sent Kissinger his memorandum on Cambodia, Brzezinski published an article in the *Washington Post* titled "Cambodia Has Undermined Our Vital Credibility." He drew up a negative balance sheet of the decision and refuted the comparison made by some "Nixon assistants" with Libya in 1958 or Cuba in 1962 (there, too, it would have been necessary to defend American credibility), for the United States and the USSR had now achieved parity, so that the same actions no longer had the same significance. In sum, he said, "the situation is infinitely more complex and calls for a much more subtle appreciation of international realities."[124] This direct attack does not seem to have troubled Kissinger very much.

This type of relationship, which combined direct discussions between Kissinger and Brzezinski with public criticism by the latter of the Nixon administration's foreign policy, continued through Nixon's first term in office and even beyond. There seems to have been a sort of modus vivendi between the two men, or perhaps a simple calculation: Kissinger gave Brzezinski access and listened to him, or assured him that he was listening, so that the latter would remain moderate in his criticisms, whereas Brzezinski moderated his criticisms so as not to compromise his access to the administration. Kissinger could benefit from his discussions with Brzezinski, by gleaning general information or sometimes by getting his help with a particular issue. For his part, Brzezinski could hope, if not to have an impact on policy decisions, at least to see certain of his specific concerns taken into account, like the defense of RFE-RL.[125]

These varying dynamics were illustrated in 1971 and 1972. For example, Brzezinski published two overall critiques of the Nixon administration: in 1971, a grade report that was not superb but not disastrous, either (the average grade awarded was a B), and in 1972 he published a critique of the concept of balance of power as Kissinger used it. He underlined all the characteristics of Europe under the Congress of Vienna that were lacking in the contemporary international system: military equilibrium between several powers, control of the status quo through diplomacy, ideological consensus. He also criticized the Nixon administration for being interested only in the triangle of rivalry (US-USSR-China) to the detriment of triangular cooperation (US-Europe-Japan), whereas the system ought to create a community of developed nations. He also stressed the prevailing ignorance of new problems, such as those of the Third World.[126]

But during this same time the dialogue with Kissinger continued. Thus, in April 1972, Brzezinski sent him recommendations on the subject of Japan, where Kissinger was planning to travel, and a month later on the subject of Nixon's trip to Poland, offering specific—and in both instances very well informed—advice. On each occasion, the national security adviser wrote a letter thanking Brzezinski, typically adding that he hoped he would see him soon.[127]

Nixon's reelection and then Kissinger's appointment as Secretary of State in September 1973 had no effect on these practices. In October 1973, the brand new Secretary of State assured Brzezinski that he would continue to receive his remarks with interest: "One always learns more from 'friendly critics' than from uncritical friends. We must continue to keep in touch." And he added: "It was good to see you at the UN Dinner."[128] In fact, the two men had lunch together in December and exchanged assorted information in the weeks that followed.[129]

In 1974, however, the relationship seemed to grow strained, as Brzezinski became increasingly critical of détente. It must be noted that his March 1974 article in *Foreign Policy*, "The Deceptive Structure of Peace," did not spare Kissinger. It was less the new grade report showing a decline (C+) that hit home than the concentration of criticism on Kissinger's particular contributions. Brzezinski condemned the administration's triple predilection for "the personal over the political," "the covert over the conceptual," and finally "acrobatics over architecture."[130] All this depicted a diplomacy ill adapted to the new challenges, such as the passage from international to global concerns, North-South relations, or the risk of social and political fragmentation. More seriously still, the administration had ignored the nation's allies to the benefit of its adversaries (Brzezinski detected a "fascination with enemies and ennui with friends" in Kissinger), and its policy of détente was limited, unstable, and unbalanced in favor of the USSR, whether it involved SALT, the Middle East, or trade agreements.[131] The imbalance, as Brzezinski explained to the Senate in July, came from the fact that the Soviets saw détente as compatible with the pursuit of ideological hostilities, because it did not encompass human rights; it was taking place in secret; it was accompanied by indifference to planet-wide problems; and above all it was not reciprocal in terms of openness or technological and commercial advantages.[132]

Kissinger was very unhappy with this article; his three-page response begins this way: "Dear Zbig: I have just read with interest, if also amazement, your *Foreign Policy* article. Since I will be leaving for Moscow this evening to continue the pursuit of a detente which you either support or decry (depending on which Brzezinski you read), my thoughts will necessarily be both hasty and brief. I find it difficult to accept that the author of *Peaceful Engagement in Europe's Future* can now claim that we were too soft in the Strategic Arms Limitation Agreements we have thus far reached."[133]

Kissinger reproached Brzezinski for relying on facts and figures whose validity Kissinger challenged, point by point. In particular, he thought that Brzezinski was taking at face value the Europeans' jeremiads on the lack of consultation, and that he exaggerated the American-Soviet "condominium" at the conference on the Middle East held in Geneva in December 1973. He pointed out that the Soviet sphere of influence in Eastern Europe had been legitimized by Östpolitik, not by the Nixon administration. He corrected Brzezinski's arguments on SALT, and on the trade advantages supposedly won by the Soviets. What he found most shocking was that Brzezinski, after having defended the idea of peaceful engagement, of eased tensions, contacts among civil societies, and so on, should switch sides and adopt, de facto, the critique of the far right.

Kissinger concluded by expressing a desire to meet upon his return from Moscow for a detailed discussion of the subjects on which they "seemed" to disagree. He used the closing formula that was customary between them ("With warm regards"). Although Brzezinski opened his reply with a little joke (since Kissinger had had enough of his criticism, why not appoint him under secretary of state to shut him up?), he noted that Kissinger had made several journalists aware that he was not pleased with the *Foreign Policy* article. But he defended the text in a brief response, especially on the key point: "In regards to detente, which I continue to favor, let me turn the tables around by citing Kissinger to Kissinger: You have said to me more than once that linkage is not a theory but a fact, and I agree with you. What bothers me is that I do see the Soviets getting most tangible benefits in trade (not to speak of the so-called space cooperation) while the returns to us are not so clear-cut, especially in such matters as strategic relations or closer East-West ties, to which trade concessions ought to be linked."[134]

The fact that the letter addressed to Kissinger was sent via Lawrence Eagleburger, and that there are no traces of further contact between Brzezinski and Kissinger in the archives until December 1974, may indicate that this cooling-off phase in their relations was serious. Their contacts, according to the archives in any case, only resumed on the occasion of a Trilateral Commission dinner in Washington (December 8 or 9, 1974). Brzezinski thanked Kissinger warmly for receiving the group, and even asked him for an autograph for his sons Ian and Mark, who were collectors ("You may be amused that following request comes from me . . . I never thought at Harvard that someday I would be asking you this!!!").[135]

In 1975, their relationship seemed gradually to return to normal, and even to take on greater density. Thus, in February, Brzezinski relayed to Kissinger an opening from the Yugoslavs that he had received in a message. In April, just as the South Vietnamese and Cambodian regimes were about to fall, he pressed the secretary of state to finalize an evacuation plan for the allies and their dependents. He also urged Kissinger to make a public announcement spelling out the parameters of a final peace settlement in the Middle East, since the parties involved were not willing to budge.[136] The secretary of state replied that his problem was indeed that of inciting them to budge, even after having announced a plan for the final status. He added: "Even for those of us who live in Newcastle, coals are important, especially when they come from long-tested purveyors such as yourself. Your observations are always welcome; keep them coming as the spirit moves you."[137] In May, Kissinger tried to reassure Brzezinski, William Griffith, and Richard Pipes, who had written him a joint letter expressing their concern about the future of the RFE-RL broadcasts, which were facing budget cuts and political pressures from the East European countries.[138] In September, Brzezinski congratulated Kissinger for his presentation to the United Nations General Assembly.[139] Next month he wrote again, this time with his Columbia colleagues Seweryn Bialer, Richard Löwenthal, and Donald Zagoria, to put Kissinger on the alert. According to their sources, Mao's imminent death was being seen by Moscow as a possible occasion for renewing ties with Beijing, and the new Chinese leadership might be sensitive to the charm offensive being prepared by the Soviets, thus endangering the Washington-Beijing connection. The Columbia professors thus exhorted the secretary of state to consolidate that relationship by taking preventive measures and offering the Chinese an attractive diplomatic, technological, and commercial package in order to ward off such a development.[140]

These recommendations and exchanges became rarer toward the end of the year, and they disappeared almost entirely in 1976. In the meantime, Brzezinski had become Governor Jimmy Carter's chief foreign policy adviser. Kissinger at this time was the key player in Ford's electoral strategy—he projected an image of seriousness, success, and, above all, continuity, after Nixon's resignation. It becomes clear why the relation between Kissinger and Brzezinski began to fray after reading the advice the latter gave to Carter in a letter dated October 28, 1975:

> At some point it will be necessary to take the Kissinger foreign policy head-on. Blaming its shortcomings on Nixon or on Ford will not do, while

Kissinger is likely to become one of the major pillars of the Republican pitch for re-election. Accordingly, Kissinger's foreign policy ought to be attacked directly, and his personal role in shaping it and giving it its somewhat dubious moral-political outlook ought to be the major focus of such a speech. Moreover, this should be done fairly soon and not during the actual Presidential campaign, for at that time, the credibility of some of the criticisms is going to be necessarily reduced. Finally, given the fascination of the mass media with Kissinger, an attack directly on his foreign policy is likely to provoke a great deal of attention.[141]

The background for 1976 was thus in place. Brzezinski could not advise candidate Carter without attacking Kissinger's foreign policy—that electoral necessity would influence his analyses, moreover. After examining Brzezinski's relationship with Kissinger, then, it is time to look at his relationship with Carter.

It was through the Trilateral Commission that Brzezinski not only met Jimmy Carter but also had ongoing privileged access to the ambitious Democratic politician, four years his senior, who served as governor of Georgia from 1971 to early 1975. In April 1973, the principal leaders of the Trilateral had met to select members on the American side, in order to be ready for the launching of the Commission a few months later. They had chosen Daniel Evans, a moderate Republican governor from the West (Washington State) who had connections with Japan, and they wanted to balance the list with a Democratic governor, preferably from the South, which was undergoing rapid industrialization.[142] Jimmy Carter of Georgia had been recommended over Florida governor Reubin Askew; Carter seemed more promising, and he had opened offices in Brussels and Tokyo for trade representatives of his state. Even though it turned out later that the international initiative had originated with his predecessor, its trilateral character was obviously a drawing card.[143]

Carter became an assiduous member of the Commission, and this allowed him both to familiarize himself with international affairs and to reinforce his image in that area in view of the 1976 presidential race. He seems moreover to have fully subscribed to the project of the Commission. On December 15, 1973, he wrote Brzezinski to suggest that he apply the trilateral approach to the problem of energy: "Because of the reluctance of some to deal now with oil because of political considerations, how about exploring the long-range development of other energy sources in concert with Japan & the European countries?" Brzezinski replied to that handwritten letter, signed "Jimmy," that the Commission had already programmed a working group on that question, but he thanked Carter for the suggestion and encouraged him to contact him again whenever he felt that something needed to be done.[144]

Carter was present at the Trilateral meeting in Washington in December 1974, even though he did not stay for the encounter with President Ford. Brzezinski thanked him for his participation and, for the first time in writing, offered Carter his services, in the name of an "us" that designated the Trilateral Commission:

> Dear Jimmy: . . . I watched you on "Meet the press" on Sunday and I thought that you did extremely well. If you need any help on foreign policy, do not hesitate to let me know and maybe we could be of some help. I do think that a serious discussion of foreign policy alternatives to present foreign policy is increasingly needed. The fact of the matter is that the United States is becoming increasingly isolated in the world, and that is really a serious problem. In a nutshell, the threat is not isolationism but isolation, and for that we have to blame our present policy makers.[145]

The governor, who was then in the final weeks of his mandate and preparing for a two-year presidential campaign, responded positively. On December 31, he asked Brzezinski to meet him to discuss foreign affairs and to send him his articles in the meantime.[146] Brzezinski quickly complied, in early January, specifying that his texts offered a general approach, but that precisely for that reason they made it possible to pin down a conceptual framework from which specific policies could be derived. "The problem with most politicians," he added, "is that they lack such a framework, and this tends to give their foreign policy prescriptions a rather shallow character."[147] During the spring of 1975, Brzezinski sent him other articles along with the texts of talks he had given.

The following phase included a key moment in the relation between the two men, in the context of the Commission meeting in Kyoto in May 1975, and more specifically at the press conference Carter gave there, having announced his candidacy for the Democratic nomination some time earlier. During this period, the governor of Georgia was still so little known that the International

Press Association had rejected him as keynote speaker for its lunch in Tokyo on the occasion of the meeting; they wanted someone of higher stature.[148] Carter asked Brzezinski to be at his side during the press conference, in order to show the journalists that recognized specialists in foreign affairs took him seriously.

Brzezinski was struck by the quality of Carter's performance. The latter had remained calm and even managed to come up with amusing answers to the journalists' ironic questions about his campaign, stressing his lack of public recognition and suspecting that what he really sought was the vice presidential slot.[149] Carter did not give any ground. He predicted that he would win the Iowa caucuses—where he had already begun an intensive campaign—but that the press would ignore him. Then he would win in New Hampshire, where he said he had shaken more hands than all his adversaries combined; here the press would highlight the surprise victory of a Southerner in the North. Next, he would beat George Wallace in the South, thus ridding the Democratic Party of that scourge—and only then would the journalists recognize him as a serious candidate and declare him the favorite.[150] For the most part, this is what actually happened during the 1976 primaries. Brzezinski was impressed; here was a candidate who had chutzpah and was not to be dismissed.

The other element that pleased him was Carter's insistence on the fact that the American national interest lay in actively promoting peace between Israelis and Palestinians, and that both sides needed to make compromises—a bold position for a Democratic candidate at the time. In short, Brzezinski returned from Tokyo seduced by Carter. This was the time for the Democratic candidates to recruit their foreign policy advisers. Brzezinski was attracted by Edmund Muskie, owing to his Polish background, but Muskie decided not to run. He was attracted by Scoop Jackson, owing to his hawkish approach to the USSR, but as a candidate Jackson was lacking in charisma. He was attracted by Ted Kennedy, who had great electoral potential, the inverse of Scoop Jackson, but he did not like the idea that the "Camelot Crowd" would return to Washington. He was skeptical of Morris Udall, who struck him as too similar to George McGovern and at risk of repeating the failure of 1972.[151] The other Democrats with whom he was in regular contact in 1975 (Walter Mondale, Joe Biden, and John Brademas, among others) were not running.[152] In the end, it was his wife who advised him to follow his instinct and support Carter, since he appreciated him, despite his lack of public recognition (no more than 2 percent at the national level). Brzezinski acted accordingly and on June 17, 1975, he sent

Carter his thanks for coming to Kyoto and a check for $25 toward his campaign expenses, "meant for good luck."[153]

This did not mean that he cut off all contact with other politicians. His relations with Hubert Humphrey, in particular, continued. Humphrey, without declaring his candidacy for the 1976 elections, never announced that he would not run, which bothered Scoop Jackson in particular, as he occupied the same position on the political spectrum. The possibility that Humphrey would enter the race came up regularly until the Democratic Convention held in New York on July 12–15, 1976. In 1974 and 1975, at Humphrey's request, Brzezinski sent him a good deal of advice on foreign policy, which the senator used amply in his speeches.[154] In January 1976, when he was officially designated as Carter's adviser, he continued to supply Humphrey with phrasing about détente.[155] But this time Brzezinski did not become the sort of poly-adviser he had been in 1972; it was Carter whom he had chosen, and who relied on him in return.

During the second half of 1975, Brzezinski sent Carter advice on the big issues of the day, for example on détente, following a trip to Moscow that convinced him that America was on the losing end of that policy and that détente was simply further whetting Moscow's appetite. He also offered advice on China, forwarding a November memorandum to Kissinger he had coauthored with colleagues about Mao's successor; he even offered to organize a seminar at Columbia on the topic.[156] In December, he brought up various aspects of the East-West relationship. He followed a consistent line of attack on the administration, criticizing not détente itself, which remained desirable, but the way Kissinger was handling it, the excessively personal role he was playing. Above all, he criticized the increasingly unbalanced character of détente: the Soviets were piling up tangible gains, while the Americans were not getting the moderation they had a right to expect; Moscow continued to advance its pawns, in Angola, for example.[157] He also offered his help on the electoral level, indicating that he was ready to campaign for Carter in the Polish-American community, especially in Illinois, where he was relatively well known.

By the end of 1975, Brzezinski had succeeded in officially becoming Carter's foreign policy adviser. In late December, the candidate asked him to begin to lay the foundations for a foreign policy speech that would establish an overall framework for his campaign. Brzezinski worked on it in January 1976 with Richard Gardner, a law professor at Columbia, another trilateralist. The three priorities were reinforcing ties to Europe and Japan, shaping more stable North-South

relations, and promoting détente with the USSR while making it more reciprocal and while also courting China.[158] It is interesting that, in an exchange
with Gardner in January 1976, Brzezinski stressed that the order of priorities,
approved by Carter, reflected the one developed in the Trilateral discussions in
Kyoto eight months earlier.[159] Brzezinski confirmed this retrospectively: "From
the standpoint of substance, there was a symbiotic relation between Carter's
campaign and the Trilateral Commission."[160] As for Carter, he said that, when
he had to accelerate his education in international affairs, "I turned to people in
whom I had confidence to help me. These included people in foreign / defense
fields that I had known, primarily in the Trilateral Commission and many of
whom later became members of my administration, such as Harold Brown,
Dr. [Zbigniew] Brzezinski, Jerry Smith, Cy Vance and others. It was an educational program on a crash basis."[161]

In *Why Not the Best?*, the book he wrote for the campaign and published in
1975, Carter cited his membership in the Trilateral Commission, explaining that
it had given him both high-level training in international affairs and the opportunity to meet foreign leaders.[162] But this was a paradoxical association, for the
central theme of Carter's campaign was precisely the rejection of Washington, of
the established elite, the "professionals." "There is one major and fundamental
issue," he asserted in one of his campaign commercials. "And that is the issue
between the insiders and the outsiders. I have been accused of being an outsider
and I plead guilty."[163] That outsider was advised and "educated" in foreign policy
by the Trilateral Commission, David Rockefeller's creation, and especially by a
man who embodied the new Establishment, Zbigniew Brzezinski. It is important not to overlook the role of representatives of the traditional Establishment,
for example Cyrus Vance. The disconnect could hardly be greater.

This paradox of a populist campaign assisted by members of the top-level elite
was summed up in a famous remark made by Hamilton Jordan, one of Carter's
advisers from Georgia, on the composition of the administration, shortly after
the election: "If, after the inauguration, you find a Cy Vance as secretary of
state and Zbigniew Brzezinski as head of national security, then I would say we
failed. And I'd quit."[164] This "failure" was verified on all counts. Carter named
only trilateralists to the key positions in his administration (and Jordan did not
resign). In 1976, it was most important for Carter to establish his image in the
international realm, and the Trilateral was not sufficiently known to the general
public to be a millstone. Things would go very differently for George Bush in

1980, who had to resign quickly from the Commission and face devastating campaign messages like this one: "The people who brought you Jimmy Carter now want you to vote for George Bush."[165]

The 1976 election campaign is important not only for Brzezinski's personal story but also because, even more than the 1968 campaign, it was a key moment in the new foreign policy system that was emerging after the Vietnam War. The 1976 campaign also shaped the policy of the Carter administration, at least in the early years, and it offered a foretaste of the debates, both internal and public, that were to influence the administration, and of the role Brzezinski would play in these debates.

McGovern had succeeded in turning the new rules for nomination to the Democratic candidacy to his advantage in 1972, but Jimmy Carter was even more skillful in 1976, profiting from the growing number of primaries (fifteen in 1968, twenty-three in 1972, and thirty in 1976). Carter was even more attentive to the imperative of creating momentum that would flow from one primary to the next, beginning with Iowa (January 19) and New Hampshire (February 24), as he had said he would at the Trilateral meeting in Kyoto. He campaigned vigorously in all the strategic primary states to compensate for the fact that he was not widely known; in January 1976 he was the choice of only 4 percent of Democratic voters.[166] But the post-Watergate atmosphere favored the outsider. Carter's electoral strategy, worked out by Hamilton Jordan and Stuart Eizenstat, was brilliant; and his accumulated victories forced his adversaries—George Wallace in North Carolina, Morris Udall in Wisconsin, and Scoop Jackson in Pennsylvania—to give up, so that in late April 1976 he appeared certain to come out ahead at the Democratic Convention. He could thus devote himself to the general election, where he was to face Gerald Ford. Carter seemed to be ahead by a wide margin during the summer, although on November 2 when he finally won it was by a hair (50.1 percent of the popular vote versus 48 percent, 297 votes in the Electoral College versus 240).

In foreign policy, the campaign was punctuated by noteworthy stages: Carter's first speech in Chicago on March 15, 1976; a more important one in New York on June 23; another at the Convention; finally, the televised debate with Ford on October 6 in San Francisco. At each of these stages, Brzezinski served as Carter's chief foreign policy adviser. He combined the campaign with his own activities at Columbia and with the Trilateral Commission (which he was still heading), and he continued to travel at the usual pace: Latin America in January, Tokyo in March, Europe at the beginning of June, Israel in late June and early July, and so on.

The first speech, to the Chicago Council on Foreign Relations in March, was rather general. Carter attacked Kissinger's foreign policy, which he accused of having been conducted in secret, hidden from the American public, whereas the great diplomatic successes (generally Democratic) had been carried out in broad daylight, with a concern for popular support—from the American entrance into the Second World War under Roosevelt to the creation of NATO and, later, the Peace Corps. The speech was well received; the *Boston Globe* reproduced excerpts, while a *Washington Post* commentator devoted a column to it, deeming it the best presentation of foreign policy to date. Only James Reston at the *New York Times* criticized the speech as naïve, insufficiently presidential, and unjust toward Kissinger, adding that this was not really Carter's speech; Carter "was the speaker, but Zbigniew Brzezinski was the principal writer."[167] In his report to Carter, Brzezinski added that a *New York Times* editor had told him that Kissinger had discreetly suggested the critical article to Reston, who was well known to be close to the secretary of state, and Kissinger had good reasons for wanting to defend himself.[168] It is in this context that one finds the only recorded example of a personal attack on Brzezinski by Kissinger. On the occasion of a small NSC committee meeting on oil issues, in the presence of Brent Scowcroft and after new attacks by Carter in the press, the secretary of state exploded: "Brzezinski is a total whore. He's been on every side of every argument. He wrote a book on *Peaceful Engagement* and now that we are doing most of what he said in the book, he charges us with weakness."[169]

After a few less important speeches (in New York on April 1, for instance, about Israel, and at the United Nations on May 13, about nuclear issues), Carter's other major public address took place on June 23, 1976. It was on a wholly different scale: organized by Brzezinski in New York, with the Foreign Policy Association, it was staged before more than two thousand guests at the Waldorf Astoria, and the goal was to help Carter shed the image he had acquired as a primary candidate.[170] He made a trilateral speech, devoted to the reinforcement of ties with Europe and Japan; he also evoked the need to extend a hand to the Third World and help in its development. The speech proclaimed the candidate's optimism about the future of America and of democracy: "We seek not a condominium of the powerful but a community of the free."[171] The contrast with the Ford administration's "amoral" foreign policy was also underlined by a personal attack against Kissinger in a formula that caught on and was widely repeated in the press: "Under the Nixon-Ford Administration, there has evolved a kind of secretive 'Lone Ranger' foreign policy—a one-man policy of international adventure."[172] Contrary to what one might think, it was George Ball, not Brzezinski, who suggested the formula to Carter; the latter even seems to have suggested eliminating any reference to Kissinger, before finally reaching a compromise with Carter, who wanted to keep the reference; there would be a single mention of the "Lone Ranger." The reactions to the New York speech, on the international as well as the national level, were positive. The *New York Times,* for example, published a front-page report, including excerpts from the speech, and also offered an analysis by Reston, who defended Kissinger.[173]

The Democratic Convention confirmed the choice of Carter, and the Democratic foreign party platform was robust, chiefly influenced by the centrist wing of the party rather than by the wing close to McGovern.[174] It was Pat Moynihan, the former ambassador to the UN, a member of the Coalition for a Democratic Majority, and close to Scoop Jackson, who was in charge of the foreign policy section. Even if the platform was a document that did not tie the administration's hands, Brzezinski made sure that its positions were compatible with the positions of candidate Carter.[175] During the summer, the campaign team prepared a speech on East-West relations that was intended to complement the trilateral speech given in New York. This new speech was the object of many internal debates, which were made more urgent owing to information transmitted by a congressional assistant, Brian Atwood. On September 16, Atwood informed Brzezinski that Donald Rumsfeld and James Lynn, Ford's secretary of defense and his budget director, respectively, were preparing to publish a report that would create difficulties for Carter.—After having hidden an alarming report on the degradation of the military balance of power with the USSR in Europe during the primaries—in order to avoid attacks on Ford by Reagan—they were ready to release it. Carter, who had announced cuts of five to seven billion dollars in the defense budget, would be hurt by the report's publication.[176] Brzezinski pressed for a strong line, but ultimately the East-West speech was not delivered.

The last important stage of the campaign was the televised debate on October 6, focused on international affairs. Two weeks earlier, the first direct confrontation, on domestic affairs, had not gone well for Carter, who had been put on the defensive. Now he had to do something to regain the upper hand, especially since Ford had moved up ten points in the polls in the aftermath. During the morning of October 6 in San Francisco, where the broadcast was to take place, Brzezinski spent two and a half hours giving the candidate an intensive briefing. That evening, as Brzezinski had recommended, Carter attacked President Ford at the outset for his absence of leadership. "As far as foreign policy goes, Mr. Kissinger has been the president of this country. Mr. Ford has shown an absence of leadership, and an absence of a grasp of what this country is and what it ought to be."[177] Contrary to expectations, Carter seemed more at ease in this area than Ford.

The president made a mistake that has remained famous, affirming that "there is no Soviet domination of Eastern Europe and there never will be under a Ford administration." When the presenter gave him a chance to correct himself, he made it worse, asserting that neither the Yugoslavs nor the Poles nor the Rumanians considered themselves under the domination of the USSR: "Each of those countries is independent, autonomous: it has its own territorial integrity."[178] Carter was slow to react at first, but he finally exploited Ford's blunder by wondering ironically whether Ford could convince Polish-Americans that Poland was not under the domination and the supervision of the USSR behind the Iron Curtain. Pollster George Gallup designated this blunder as the "most decisive moment in the campaign."[179]

With this last boost from Ford, the Carter campaign came out ahead in foreign policy; the candidate had managed to establish his credibility in this area thanks in particular to his exceptional cognitive abilities. His team, too, played a key role, with Brzezinski at the center of the foreign policy group, in collaboration with campaign coordinators Hamilton Jordan, Stuart Eizenstat, and Jody Powell (Carter's press liaison). Brzezinski was surrounded by experts who contributed to the speeches and to his analytical notes[180] Further, his experience working for Humphrey during the 1968 campaign allowed him to be an effective and experienced coordinator. He was endowed at once with acute political sensitivity and with an administrative ability that rarely missed a beat; memoranda and comments arrived on time, according to an established process, despite his constant travels and his multiple activities.

Starting in early March, Brzezinski urged Carter to organize his team of advisers and publish an official list of names, in order to avoid confusion and to appease the critics of the "Washington establishment."[181] At the end of the month, he explained that international affairs were going to be increasingly important in the campaign, and he stressed the necessity of organizing. Brzezinski insisted that it was important to define the procedures for supplying the candidate with notes, to avoid the cacophony he had experienced in 1968 when all Humphrey's advisers were talking to him at the same time; it was essential to designate a liaison with the White House, and so on.[182] This was the point at which Brzezinski really took control of foreign policy issues in the campaign; he played a dual role as both political driving force and control tower. He exerted partial control over access to the candidate, and he imposed an organizational structure that would be reproduced essentially intact in the Carter administration, after the bureaucratic tour de force in January 1977 that conferred a central role in the formulation of foreign policy on the national security adviser. Both during the campaign and throughout Carter's presidency, Brzezinski supplied a foreign policy organization that was both rational and comfortable and that corresponded to Carter's preferences (a lot of substance, transmitted through an orderly process), but that relied for the most part on the work of a single man—Zbigniew Brzezinski.

In April, the official membership list of the Foreign Policy and Defense Task Force that Carter had asked for was published by his campaign, and ten names were added on May 11.[183] It was by and large this team, led by Brzezinski and Gardner, that met at the Century Club on May 24 to finalize procedures, launch the production of the three types of notes Brzezinski envisaged, and define the speeches to come—on the topics of trilateral relations, then food, "values and foreign policy," East-West and North-South relations, and defense. It is noteworthy that none of these, except for the trilateral speech, became the subject of a formal address.[184] This activity was complemented, starting in July, by specific briefings prepared for the candidate on various international topics, and in September and October by preparations for the transition phase, should Carter be elected.[185]

The administrative side of the campaign had to work smoothly in order to score political points. The dilemma was well known to presidential candidates who were not already in the White House. It was easy to lose votes with international affairs, hard to win them, because voters primarily made up their minds based on domestic issues, except in unusual years such as 1968 or 2004. Conversely, they could become fearful if a candidate appeared irresponsible in his foreign policy orientations, as happened with Barry Goldwater in 1964 and George McGovern in 1972. There were two ways of attracting voters with foreign affairs: by using them to create an image of the candidate as responsible and admired abroad, and by playing on the ethnic preferences of certain voting blocs.

In the spring of 1976, a memorandum written by Richard Holbrooke (after its content had been discussed with Brzezinski) set forth the political framework for Carter. Ford had the advantage of being the commander in chief on duty, but Reagan had pushed him toward the right. Ford had an additional advantage in Kissinger, who remained popular and appeared often on television, without actually campaigning; thus, Kissinger had to be attacked. Moreover, three foreign nations sought to influence the result of elections. The USSR had chosen Humphrey in 1968 and Nixon in 1972, and had helped both candidacies, for example by exerting pressure on the South Vietnamese in the 1968 Paris negotiations, although that was not enough (Nguyen Van Thieu preferred Nixon), then again in 1972, and then by accepting the Moscow summit in May. In 1976, the Soviets, happy with Scoop Jackson's failure, seemed to hesitate. It was essential for Carter to avoid being perceived as seeking their approval, thus he should not meet Soviet ambassador Anatoly Dobrynin too soon; and should do so, when the time was right, in a neutral location. In 1972, Israel had also for the first time preferred the Republican candidate, and Carter's campaign had to avoid repeating McGovern's failure at all costs. Defending a peace agreement was acceptable, but it had to be made clear that doing so would in no way reduce US support for Israel and that Washington would supply "everything Israel needs." China had played a role for the first time in 1972, but was not likely to do the same in 1976. Ultimately, Holbrooke recommended that the campaign avoid making any overly precise declarations or suggestions, something that experts advising a candidate generally tend to do.[186]

Brzezinski, for his part, was more specific. He suggested that Carter wait for the Democratic Convention to accept Dobrynin's invitation, and in any case that he begin by meeting leaders or ambassadors from Europe, Japan, or Israel, in order to avoid contradicting his own discourse and to avoid sending a negative signal to those countries, or to China. More generally, he suggested that Carter should not rush; he should maintain a certain mystery, which could improve his power relations internationally.[187] When the *New York Times* reported on Moscow's curiosity about and interest in Carter's candidacy, Brzezinski was worried that conservatives would exploit the theme; he advised Carter to announce officially that he would meet with no foreign leaders before the nomination, and that his foreign policy views would not be influenced by anyone abroad.[188] In June, he advised Carter to agree to see the German chancellor Helmut Schmidt immediately after the convention, as the two men already knew each other from the Trilateral Commission; that would help him appear to the public as a leader of the free world.[189]

Brzezinski was simultaneously working to burnish Carter's image in the international press. He was well equipped to do so; he had contacts with numerous journalists throughout the world, and he himself had been the subject of countless news articles and reports. In April, he explained the stakes both to Carter and to Powell. He stressed that international coverage did not really count for the primaries, but it was important for the general election, because there was an echo effect; positive portraits of the candidate that appeared abroad ended up influencing the national press when the stature of the candidate was in question. For that reason, he urged Carter and Powell not to ignore requests from foreign correspondents, especially those from Europe.[190]

The most direct way to attract voters was to respond to their specific expectations in the realm of foreign policy. In the briefing book produced to prepare Carter for his televised debate with Ford, the stakes were explained even more directly. The debate would not be a foreign policy debate, but rather a debate about domestic policy with regard to foreign affairs. The candidate must not be irresponsible; he must keep in mind the possible reactions of other countries, but he must target specific sectors of the electorate: "Greeks, Eastern Europeans, Irish, and Jews."[191] That is in fact what happened, with Carter's attack on the Sonnenfeldt doctrine and with Ford's blunder on the absence of Soviet domination of Eastern Europe; on each occasion, additional votes fell to Carter, in Chicago and elsewhere.[192] It was all the easier in that Carter, following Brzezinski's advice, had prepared the ground starting in the spring by denouncing the policy of spheres of influence and its consequences for East Europeans.[193] Under the circumstances, Brzezinski recommended that Carter exploit Ford's gaffe lightly, expressing sadness rather than indignation. "Carter should speak more out of sorrow than anger; we regret that the President is either ignorant of an important problem in international affairs or is indifferent (perhaps under Kissinger's and Sonnenfeldt's influence) to the fate of a large number of people who have kin in this country."[194]

This ethnic positioning, important for East Europeans, was crucial where Israel was concerned, and that was one of the most sensitive issues of the campaign. On April 6, less than a week after Carter expressed himself on the subject in New York in a well-received speech, and the very day of the New York primary, Brzezinski wrote him to say that he had made a mistake in taking the position reported in that morning's *New York Times*. Brzezinski did not approve Carter's comment when the latter said that if he were the Israeli prime minister, "he would not return the Golan Heights to Syria nor the holy places of Jerusalem to Jordan."[195] Such a position limited his room to maneuver, if he were elected; it reinforced the Arab radicals, weakened the advocates of compromise among the Israelis, and made it harder to reach a settlement based on the principle of peace and recognition as opposed to territories and demilitarization. Then he urged Carter to limit himself to what he had said in his speech on April 1: the United States does not dictate peace to Israel, it encourages discussions between Arabs and Israelis on a final settlement and not on an interim arrangement; without progress, the Arab nations will become more radical, and the Soviets will come back to the region.[196]

The pro-Israeli milieus did not know what to make of Carter, who evoked his deep religious attachment to the land of the Bible, on the one hand, but who worried about the fate of the Palestinians, on the other hand, and expressed his conviction that a peace settlement was crucial. The April 6 *New York Times* article reflected that ambivalence: it indicated that Carter was sending all the right signals, according to Israel's supporters, but that at the same time, "many of his closest advisers [were] on record as favoring Israel's returning all of the occupied territories."[197] Brzezinski was unquestionably among them. As early as January 7, 1974, in an article in the *New Leader,* he had laid out a position that he maintained until his death. He maintained that the Arabs should seek restitution of the lands seized in 1967 rather than the destruction of Israel, while the Israelis should seek security and accept the creation of a Palestinian state associated with a Jordanian federation, including the Gaza Strip and the West Bank. Jerusalem would be unified but under a hybrid administration allowing it to be the capital of both states, all this backed by strong American military guarantees and a United Nations peace mission to protect the borders.[198]

The following year, Brzezinski participated in a Brookings Institution task force on the Middle East; the more nuanced and more concrete proposals it produced had the merit of coming from a decidedly bipartisan group. The Brookings report recommended that America play an active—almost an activist—role (cooperation with the USSR could be envisioned if Moscow were ready to interact constructively); the United States ought to work toward a final settlement negotiated between the parties. Such a settlement would include, perhaps in stages, a return to the 1967 borders except for mutually agreed-on modifications, and, ultimately, self-determination for the Palestinians, as long as the latter accepted Israel's sovereignty and the integrity of its borders; self-determination might lead either to a Palestinian state or to an autonomous state within a Jordanian federation.[199] Brzezinski sent Carter the executive summary of this report on January 6, 1976, and then again on May 18, as a reference document, advising him to cite it and to stress that it had been developed by a group that included some very prominent American Jews, such as Philip Klutznick, a Democrat, and Rita Hauser, a Republican.[200]

As if to underline the sensitivity of the subject, in May and June 1976, the campaign team spent a good deal of time answering a request for an interview by the popular Israeli newspaper *Maariv*. Brzezinski had advised Carter to accept, but then changed his mind, because he was too worried that distorted citations might be excerpted from Carter's remarks. He recommended that, at a minimum, the interview be recorded and an adviser be present, although he would have preferred to see the interview canceled.[201] Ultimately, the team decided to proceed through correspondence. Brzezinski wrote the interview, then had it checked by Stuart Eizenstat. The answers he gave were lapidary, and laid particular stress on Carter's personal attachment to Israel: "Israel is the fulfillment of Biblical promise. Our heritage derives from your Law and your Book. That to me has special meaning, which reinforces my own political conclusions regarding the close linkage between our respective national interests."[202]

Throughout 1976, Brzezinski took care to connect directly with Jewish organizations. He also made a brief but intense trip to Israel.[203] During the three days he spent there, he met everyone who counted, in particular Prime Minister Yitzhak Rabin, Foreign Minister Yigal Allon, his predecessor Abba Eban, as well as Shlomo Avineri and Moshe Dayan. General Avraham Tamir took him to see the Golan Heights, a visit that convinced him definitively, and contrary to the goal sought by his hosts, that Israel could not hope to guarantee its security by acquiring more territories. He also had dinner with Shimon Peres, who was Israel's defense minister at the time, while Palestinian and German terrorists were taking hostages on an Air France flight between Tel Aviv and Paris diverted to Uganda. Always in favor of changing the givens of a problem and never frightened off by a power play, Brzezinski asked Peres: "Why don't you send some commandos down to Uganda and storm the damn airport terminal?"[204] Two days later, he learned of the success of the Entebbe raid by the Israeli commando force led by Yonatan Netanyahu. Finally, Brzezinski met Menachem Begin in the very apartment where Begin hid from the British when he was heading the Irgun—a subject that fascinated Brzezinski.[205]

The adviser who posed a problem for Carter on the subject of Israel was in fact not Brzezinski but George Ball, who thought that the major powers should impose a peace settlement on Israel and its neighbors, including a return to the 1967 borders.[206] That controversial position led Carter to take Ball out of the running for the position of secretary of state. Carter's Southern Baptist religiosity, if it was used positively to emphasize his biblical attachment to Israel, was also seen negatively by certain Jews who associated it with the sectarianism and anti-Semitism of southern Christians (just as Brzezinski's Polish identity was associated with a suspicion of anti-Semitism). Thus in early summer some publications echoed the Jewish community's hesitations about Carter, even if that community finally gave him the benefit of the doubt.[207] Carter committed himself to continue to provide Israel with economic and military aid indefinitely, even in the absence of a peace agreement, and he envisioned using American military forces to guarantee a future territorial settlement.[208] In mid-July he chose Walter Mondale—close to Humphrey and benefiting from an excellent image among American Jews—as vice president. In the end, candidate Carter did not suffer from his positions on Israel—though the honeymoon would not last.

Beyond the special interests of certain segments of the electorate, the real question, for Carter, was the overall orientation of his foreign policy, given the context of deep division among the Democrats. The dilemma was not unique to the Democratic Party. The entire consensus on American foreign policy had imploded, and the challenge Reagan presented to Ford during the Republican primaries reflected a similar division between a realist wing that supported Kissinger and détente and a nationalist wing that rejected both and demanded a more moral and especially a more muscular foreign policy. Among the Democrats, a fault line had been created by the Vietnam War. On the one side were the liberals, who rejected the interventionism of the past, acknowledged America's mistakes, and saw a world in which new issues (interdependency, development, energy, the climate, and so on) would supplant the bipolar confrontation. On the other side were the Scoop Jackson Democrats, or nascent neoconservatives who thought that the reaction to Vietnam had gone too far and that both Kissinger's détente and the liberals' guilt-ridden isolationism posed increasing dangers, given the growing assertiveness of the Soviet Union.[209]

Carter's brilliance lay in his ability to be flexible and vague enough to avoid being rejected either by the party's base, which was liberal (Carter succeeded in defeating Udall on his left), or by the centrists or Cold War Democrats (he was ahead of Jackson on his right). Voters in the latter group were inclined to see him as a new McGovern in foreign policy. They tended to give him the benefit of the doubt, for diverse reasons: because he had no liabilities in foreign policy, because he was a former officer in the Marines and a nuclear engineer, because his speeches were reassuring, and because his chief adviser was Zbigniew Brzezinski, whose image as a hawk was well established. Kampelman, for example, confided that for him Carter was an unknown quality, but he wrote to Brzezinski: "What I do know, however, is that you are apparently associated with him, and this provides some encouragement to me."[210] Still, there were doubts. On April 30, 1976, Eugene Rostow, one of Kampelman's close associates, a founding member of the Coalition for a Democratic Majority (centrist Democrats close to Scoop Jackson) and creator of the Committee on the Present Danger (a hawkish bipartisan group), still chafing at the defeat of his hero Jackson in Pennsylvania, wrote to share his analysis with Brzezinski. The country's mood was on the hawkish side, he said; moreover, the McGovern wing was more or less out of steam after the primaries. The party needed to be purged of them, as had happened in 1948 with the Henry Wallace wing: "It would be a mistake for Carter to defer too visibly to the McGovern wing, either in what he says, or in the personnel he gathers around him. I think his overall position, both within our Party and among Republicans, would be *strengthened* if he began to lay down a foreign policy position that sounded more like that of the real Brzezinski, rather than one which sounds like an uneasy and contradictory combination of your views and Paul Warnke's [Warnke was a liberal foreign policy expert and official]."[211]

Nevertheless, that uncertain approach continued to dominate the campaign, judging by the internal debates over defense policy and the role that Paul Nitze played in them. Nitze was known even more than Brzezinski for his hawkish positions, from the NSC-68 to the Gaither report, and a little later in 1976, from Team B to the cofounding of the Committee on the Present Danger with Rostow.[212] Nitze had placed his bet on Carter early on, on the recommendation of his grandchildren, who loved the candidate, and after meeting with him Nitze joined his team of advisers.[213]

Throughout the campaign, Brzezinski seemed eager to get Nitze to participate; he was, after all, the only expert who was more hawkish than Brzezinski himself. On February 10, for example, after Nitze had been unable to attend a meeting, Brzezinski wrote to ask for his advice, assuring him that "we need it very badly."[214] On March 30, he passed along to his acolytes Henry Owen and Steve Stark an apocalyptic letter from Nitze: when he was in office, Nitze predicted, Carter would find himself facing a dangerous world. The military balance of power with the Soviets would be unfavorable almost everywhere; several European countries would have turned communist; Israel would be isolated; and so on. Carter might find some inefficient programs in the Pentagon to eliminate, but he would certainly want to spend more, not less, in particular in order to strengthen the nuclear arsenal. Carter's Chicago speech bothered him, Nitze added; it was too Wilsonian, inappropriately expressing guilt on America's part.[215] In transmitting that alarmist letter, Brzezinski said that even if he did not agree with all of Nitze's conclusions, several considerations absolutely had to appear in the candidate's speeches.[216]

Moreover, when the team discussed the content of a statement on defense, Brzezinski insisted on a strong America and on the fact that the recent expansion of Soviet military power gave the USSR a strategical and tactical global reach for the first time, and thus both capabilities and temptations that it had not had before. Finally, Brzezinski advised Carter not to make any pronouncements on the subject. "I am increasingly doubtful that Jimmy would gain much by giving a statement on defense in the near future. The country wants increasingly stronger defenses; the liberal community does not. He would simply lose and tie his hands unnecessarily by going out on a limb at this stage."[217]

Carter followed his advice, writing in the margin of the memorandum: "Stu, Steve, Jody: *No* statement on DEFENSE. JC."[218] Not revealing his position was a tactic that proved effective, but it could not be maintained until the end of the campaign. The debate quickly started up again among his advisers. The left wing was represented by Averell Harriman and Paul Warnke, who, in May 1976, wrote to Carter that the battles over numbers made no sense: the governor should speak rather of capabilities, of missions to accomplish, and of commensurability between the two. A review of objectives and missions might indeed lead to reductions. Henry Owen, for his part, emphasized that there needed to be reductions in certain programs, but that the budget should continue to grow.[219] Finally, Carter came out shortly afterward in favor of reductions of 5 percent to 7 percent in the $115 billion dollar budget projected by the Ford administration, which retained an increase with respect to the previous year.[220]

On July 26, Carter's advisers on defense issues met at his home in Plains, Georgia. Nitze came with his charts and graphs, and found himself quite isolated, personally and politically. Carter described the scene: " 'Nitze was typically know-it-all,' he said. 'He was arrogant and inflexible. His own ideas were sacred to him. He didn't seem to listen to others, and he had a doomsday approach.' "[221] This impression was reinforced in letters written by Warnke, Vance, and Brown after the meeting, all of whom refuted Nitze's hawkish approach.[222] In September, Nitze was the only one of Carter's advisers who wanted to join the Committee on the Present Danger, but Brzezinski advised him against it, because of the role he was playing on the Carter team.[223] Even if Carter continued to include him in the common effort in September and continued to take his remarks into account, the equilibrium among the advisers was broken, and the center of gravity was no longer situated between Warnke and Nitze, but closer to the former—and thus farther from Brzezinski.[224]

In early July a *New York Times* article had concluded, from an interview with the candidate and his advisers, that the foreign policy mapped out by Carter was clearly situated "in the liberal wing of the Democratic Party."[225] The quotations from Carter included in the article amounted to a summary of the leitmotifs proper to the liberal wing. The problems of war and peace were now more a function of economic and social questions than of military problems and security; America could "turn [its] attention more effectively towards matters like the world economy, freedom of the seas, environmental quality, food, population, peace, conservation of irreplaceable commodities and the reduction of world armaments." At this point, the centrist wing of the Democratic Party became alarmed. Seymour Martin Lipset offered a good example of this when he confided his anxieties to his friend Stuart Eizenstat on September 16, 1976:

> Carter's foreign policy advisors, particularly people on the payroll, are drawn too heavily from the *Foreign Policy* group.[226] Huntington apart, this

group may be described as the Establishment Left in foreign policy. Many of them were hawks when we first went into Vietnam. They all sharply reversed, and ultimately became relatively cynical and strong anti-cold warriors. They tend to favor a globalism [*sic*] approach, detente, though like Ford they reject the war, and show little evidence of strong support of our Mid-East policy. But if the *Foreign Policy* view is well represented in Atlanta and Washington among your foreign policy people, other foreign policy experts more sympathetic of the *Commentary* orientation (one I feel goes too strong in the other direction) are not visible among Carter advisors.

I am not suggesting that this latter group is right and that the *Foreign Policy* group is wrong . . . I think I would place myself in the middle . . . My main concern is the need to include among Carter advisers and staff now and particularly later in the Carter administration, people of both perspectives with the party, much as the Harriman-chaired advisory committee did. Such balance is relevant for many issues, but for Israel in particular, since most of those who were burned by Vietnam have taken up a neo-isolationist posture.[227]

What is interesting in this judgment, which was typical but somewhat removed from the heart of the action (Lipset taught at Stanford), is that he mentioned Huntington but not Brzezinski. Brzezinski supplied the element of balance at the heart of the Carter team, especially after Nitze's stock went down. In other respects, though, Brzezinski was no Nitze—an alarmist hawk, obsessed with the Cold War. After all, it was the author of the "technetronic era," the creator of the Trilateral Commission, who had been calling since the 1960s had advocated going beyond the narrow framework of the Cold War. He was a globalist, without being truly a liberal. He was a hawk, but not a neoconservative. In the chapter that follows (which sets the stage for the study of Brzezinski's White House years, in particular his opposition to Cyrus Vance and to the liberals in the State Department), the challenge is try to define his unique position, through a portrait that attempts to discover the origins of his worldview.

It is important to consider the following question: Why didn't Brzezinski recruit more hawkish advisers for Carter's team, so he would be less isolated and so the team would be better balanced? His answer: "I didn't need to have people supporting me because I felt comfortable with Carter, and Carter was relying on me a lot. And I wasn't inclined to pick a fight with the dominant group in the sort of Democrat establishment, because I don't think it would have anything to do with what would follow if he won. And a lot of them then fell by the side, but not that many, because Carter himself was rather peacenicky, in part—in part."[228]

5

Portrait of an Academic in Politics

"Any statesman is in part the prisoner of necessity," Henry Kissinger wrote. "He is confronted with an environment he did not create, and is shaped by a personal history he can no longer change. It is an illusion to believe that leaders gain in profundity while they gain experience. As I have said, the convictions that leaders have formed before reaching high office are the intellectual capital they will consume as long as they continue in office."[1]

Through a detailed portrait from various angles—intellectual, personal, political—this chapter addresses two basic questions. Where did Zbigniew Brzezinski's ideas originate? Was he simply a man of the Cold War, anti-Russian because he was born Polish, anti-communist because he was Catholic? His family background—that "personal history he [could] no longer change"—unquestionably conditioned part of his outlook, but it cannot account for his overall thinking. His personality, his moral convictions, his academic work, his encounters, his political itinerary, all these elements played a role in his worldview, and in a dynamic rather than a cumulative fashion.

The content of the "intellectual capital" that he drew on during his four years in the White House is worth exploring. For his part, Brzezinski preferred a more martial—or more sporting—metaphor. As he recalled in his memoirs regarding his service in the Carter administration, "I was very conscious of the degree to which my intellectual arsenal was becoming depleted in the course of a continuous race against time. There was hardly ever any time to think systematically, to reexamine views, or simply to reflect. A broader historical perspective and a sense of direction are the prerequisites for sound policy making, and both tend to [*sic*] gradually to become victims of in-house official doctrine and outlook and of the pressure toward compromise."[2]

With the progress of the social sciences and the need to administer large public policy programs, the 1960s saw an increased influence of academics and scientists in the formulation of American policies—including foreign policy, which brings up the question of the specific impact social sciences had on American national security. What conceptual weapons in Brzezinski's arsenal stemmed from his intellectual activity in earlier years, and what did they owe to the social sciences? Was the strategist indebted to the academic?

Concepts: Brzezinski the Intellectual

"Tell me what's right and I'll fight for it. Give me a guaranteed position," Woodrow Wilson asked of his researchers in The Inquiry.[3] Wilson sought a positivist peace, underwritten by the social sciences and based on disinterested analyses by experts. This faith in the ability of researchers to determine "the right policies" grew out of the progressive era. It also inspired the think tanks and foundations created in the first two decades of the twentieth century—most notably the Carnegie Endowment and the Brookings Institution—came back into favor with the Second World War, owing to the enormous need for competent managers and thinkers who could administer the war efforts. But it was the bipolar confrontation and the Cold War University that marked the golden age of the scholar armed with the certainties of the social sciences. As Michael Desch explained, "there is a rich history of academics influencing specific national security policies at particular periods in recent history. The three most significant areas in which social science has directly affected policy are nuclear deterrence theory, political development and nation-building, and the use of systems analysis to guide national security decision-making."[4]

According to Desch, during the 1950s and even more so during the 1960s, political decision makers relied heavily on the advice of scholars in those three areas. On the topic of nuclear dissuasion, the East Coast group, chiefly through a joint Harvard-MIT seminar (Bowie, Kissinger, Bundy, Rostow, Tom Schelling, Lincoln Bloomfield, and so on), was in competition with the West Coast group (RAND, in Santa Monica, with Bernard Brodie, Albert Wohlstetter, and Herman Kahn, among others). All these theoreticians had "a profound

influence on civilian leaders," according to one observer.[5] Lucian Pye, Daniel
Lerner, and Gabriel Almond all contributed to the theories of socioeconomic
and political evolution of developing countries. Walt Rostow's book theorizing
the stages of economic growth through which Third World countries had to
pass was most influential, until Samuel Huntington critiqued the excessive
optimism of theories of modernization, and left-wing observers criticized their
orientalism.[6] Systemic analysis had been imported from the world of business
management to the Pentagon by Robert McNamara and his "whiz kids" chiefly
to rationalize arms purchases.

Tom Schelling, Kissinger and Brzezinski's colleague at Harvard, was known
for developing game theory, among other things; he produced schematic analyses of conflicts that could be applied to war.[7] He was criticized most notably
by Fred Kaplan—in *The Wizards of Armageddon,* which dealt with the nuclear
strategies of the 1950s to the 1970s—for his role in inspiring the campaign of
graduated escalation of the bombing in Vietnam (Operation "Rolling Thunder"), which was a failure and which led to open conflict.[8] Schelling defended
the idea that war was only a form of negotiation, and that "rational signals" had
to be sent to persuade the enemy, gradually increasing the force of the signals,
if the message was not received, in a controlled escalation. "When, in the
early months of 1964, President Lyndon B. Johnson and Secretary of Defense
Robert McNamara were looking for ways to step up military action against
North Vietnam, they adopted Schelling's concept," Fred Kaplan explained.
In a text written on the occasion of Schelling's acceptance of the Nobel Prize,
Kaplan denounced his disastrous role in this episode: "This dark side of Tom
Schelling is also the dark side of social science—the brash assumption that
neat theories not only reflect the real world, but can change it as well, and in
ways that can be precisely measured."[9]

The question remains: was Schelling really necessary to Operation Rolling
Thunder? In a work with the explicit title *Blind Oracles,* refuting the claim that
academics had had the influence with which they were credited even in that
golden age, the historian Bruce Kuklick returns to the episode with derision:
"One did not have to be a strategic genius to come up with graduated escalation. It is encapsulated in advice such as, Don't use a tank to kill a flea."[10] Not
only did Schelling's theory not work—as it did not take into account either the
"fog of war" or Saigon's determined nationalism—but it was not the source of
Johnson's decision. Referring to memoranda written by McGeorge Bundy to

Johnson on the subject, Kuklick wrote: "For the president, Bundy repeatedly dressed up the decisions as graduated escalation—or flexible response, sustained reprisal or pressure, measured or proportionate response, controlled escalation, war-fighting, counterforce, and even covert operations or quasi-guerilla action. Johnson got a respectable label for what he was doing."[11]

But Kuklick did not stop there in his destruction of the myth. Rostow's stages of economic growth? They were chiefly useful to John F. Kennedy as a way of dressing up his initiative vis-à-vis the Third World and the elite of the developing countries so that they could ask for more development aid from Uncle Sam, dramatizing their needs under the pretext of their imminent "take-off"—the key stage identified by Rostow.[12] Systemic analyses at the Pentagon? Many commentators have said that they served only to lend a scientific patina to decisions McNamara had already made and was seeking to impose on the staff. Nuclear strategy? Looking back, in a long letter addressed to Michael Howard on November 6, 1968, Albert Wohlstetter concluded that the essential advances—in particular the vulnerability of the Strategic Air Command, the distinction between a first strike and a second, the precarious stability of dissuasion—owed nothing to theorists such as Brodie and Schelling; they owed everything, rather, to operational research and empirical analyses.[13] Paul Nitze reasoned, at the end of his life, that "most of what has been written and taught under the heading of 'political science' by Americans since World War II . . . has also been of limited value, if not counterproductive as a guide to the conduct of actual policy."[14] Kuklick concluded that not only did scholars most often operate in the dark, guided more by shifts in fashion than by truth, they were also superfluous. "At the same time, irrespective of the quality of their knowledge, in the usual case the ideas of the cerebral strategists had little causal impact. They served to legitimate but not to energize policies. Intellectuals were most effective when they showed, after the fact, that some endeavors had been desirable. Or they articulated schema that exculpated policymakers—or themselves—from responsibility for action later identified as bad. The basic though not the only function of strategic ideas was to provide politicians with the fictions used to give meaning to policies for the public."[15]

Although Kuklick's skepticism probably goes too far, it helps to relativize the image of academics directly applying their theories in the real world. At its core, the question is more complicated than it appears, and historian Marc Trachtenberg has proposed some relevant distinctions. When commentators evoke the influence of academics on US foreign policy, are they talking about those who simply possess a Ph.D.? Or do they mean those who teach and publish up to the moment when they take on an official role, or rather those who possess, in addition to the standard academic qualifications, a certain vision derived from the social sciences, a theory, and try to put it to work? Kissinger and Brzezinski both published books before they took on their government roles, but were these really academic works, or were they political essays? Both men exercised great influence on American diplomacy, but to what extent can this influence be attributed to their status as academics?[16]

Here is where Henry Kissinger's trajectory is worth recalling. For some, Kissinger stands as the model for professors who, once in Washington, put their theories to work. Even the skeptic Kuklick saw things this way: "Had Kissinger's ideas not been applied to Soviet-American relations in the early 1970s, the outcomes would have been different than they were."[17] Moreover, Kissinger had chosen his thesis topic—"Metternich, Castlereagh, and the Problems of Peace, 1812–1822"—with explicit reference to the contemporary period, where he found analogous problems entailing an insular power, the United Kingdom, bringing to mind the United States, and a revolutionary power, Napoleonic France, bringing to mind Soviet Russia.[18] Just as Castlereagh and Metternich had succeeded, through skillful diplomacy, in shaping a balance of power that could keep a lid on France's ambitions, Kissinger could be thought to have created a stable structure of peace, in particular by orchestrating the opening to China and détente with the USSR. In sum, he could be characterized simultaneously as a theorist and as a practitioner of realism.

This popular image, accentuated by Kissinger's professorial side, which always gave the impression of seeking to teach an immature America about the superior principles of European realism so it could realize its vocation as a great power, calls for some retouching. First, his realism was certainly not orthodox or classical, but eccentric, as the historian Mario Del Pero has suggested, crossed with the political culture of the Cold War (strategic globalism, insistence on the credibility of American hegemony, on interdependence, and so forth). Above all, Kissinger pursued initiatives begun by Johnson, and it is not certain that a Humphrey administration would have acted differently. Kissinger's preoccupation with domestic constraints was a much more important factor than the image of the statesman as a pure diplomat concerned solely with the raison d'état might suggest.[19] Other observers have concluded that the realist dressing was largely excessive, and that, rather than the creation of a subtle global peace structure, a stable framework for cooperation, the opening to China was above all designed to make the USSR fail. Further, détente kept that nation from reacting too energetically or even making a preemptive attack before a tacit alliance between Washington and Beijing was established.[20]

Kissinger's diplomatic practice was undoubtedly realist in its inspiration; certain of the principles on which it relied—and which served to present and justify it—are fully compatible with Kissinger's pre-1969 academic writings. Still, his diplomacy was not a faithful implementation of a theory, nor did it entail transposing Metternich and Bismarck into the world of the 1970s. Moreover, in his thesis Kissinger often described a practice of diplomacy that was almost an art (requiring specific qualities—skill, omniscience, determination, and so on) as much as a content, and adaptation to circumstances was set up as the primary value. To what extent can Kissinger's diplomatic practice be explained by his theorization of the Concert of Powers, or of Bismarckian politics?[21] And to what extent does it depend on other factors that shaped his worldview, such as his personal history (a preference for stability, pessimism about the future of Western democracies, fear of a reactionary groundswell as had happened in Nazi Germany, and so on), or his political position taking?

The conclusion that can be drawn from these assorted examples is twofold. On the one hand, it appears that the rise in power of academics in the American national security apparatus during the Cold War did not entail a sudden injection of theory into foreign policy. Academic inspiration was the exception rather than the rule. Ultimately, the era of the academic took on a primarily sociological meaning. It was characterized by the rise of men from universities rather than from the worlds of finance, industry, or public service, to the highest policy-making positions—rather than an intellectual meaning, for in the latter case it would be possible to point to decisions that directly reflected the concepts and theories developed by academics. In this sense, the two orders, that of academic reflection and that of political decision making, are undoubtedly separated in a more watertight fashion than they have generally appeared, even during that period. From another standpoint, that watertight separation means that considerations other than intellectual production can be brought to bear on the issues at stake, as the example of Kissinger shows. The challenge in this chapter is not only to present a portrait of Brzezinski as a thinker about international affairs and to summarize his academic theories on the subject, but also to explore both the multiple sources of his approach to the world and other facets of his personality that may give us a better understanding of his diplomatic practice between 1971 and 1981.

By profession, Brzezinski was a political scientist, but at no time in his career did he show any taste for theorizing or for excessively abstract considerations. The area of political science in which he worked—that of cultural zones, in the subfield of Sovietology—scarcely lends itself to such considerations; this subfield comes closer than any other to the descriptive, even encyclopedic, sciences of history and geography. It must be noted that in the 1950s and 1960s, both political science and the nascent discipline of international relations maintained close contact with reality and practice, something that they would later lose as excessive formalization and quantitative methods made headway. By the time this later development came about (starting in the 1970s and especially in the 1980s), Brzezinski had for the most part pulled away from a strict academic framework. He had begun to operate instead in the in-between world of think tanks and nonspecialized journals, zones whose development was facilitated by the fact that political science as a discipline was by and large losing contact with reality.

Brzezinski's university work in the 1950s and 1960s focused on developments that were taking place in the USSR and more generally in the Eastern bloc. In addition to description, the intellectual tools he used were simple ones: generalizations, paradigms, ideal types, comparisons, and so on, but he did not engage in formal model making or theorization. Good examples of this approach are found in the debates concerning the concept of totalitarianism, over the book he published with Carl Friedrich (1956), or the relations between ideology and political power (early 1960s), or the degeneration of the Soviet system, in connection with articles he published in 1966 and 1968.[22] Each time, the objective was to capture realities, and in some cases discuss the concepts that were most useful for interpreting those realities, but not focus on theories per se, or on the methodological debates of the discipline. Moreover, in Brzezinski's eyes, theory was necessarily retrospective. Thus, if a given theory failed to predict the future, or if measures were taken to avoid a development that was anticipated but not desired (such as measures to avoid a confrontation between the United States and China, a conflict that some analysts deemed inevitable), it was replaced by a different theory, demonstrating the limited utility of theories in general.[23]

In his scholarly writings and elsewhere, three modes of thought recur that he favored as ways of shedding light on reality: typologies, scenarios, and historical analogies. The book cowritten with Friedrich, for example, rests on an implicit typology of authoritarian regimes—Oriental despotism, absolute monarchy, military dictatorship, and so on—according to their political features: among these, totalitarianism stands out in that it presents a unique combination of six features. This approach differs from the more philosophical one adopted by Hannah Arendt, who was in some sense seeking the underlying principles of totalitarianism, its deep nature.[24] When Brzezinski analyzed the after-effects of de-Stalinization in the nations of Eastern Europe in 1957, he distinguished three categories among Marxists. These were idealistic Marxists, eager to alleviate human suffering; scientific Marxists, persuaded that their "human engineering" was the way of the future; and apparatchik Marxists, attracted by the power that Marxism procured—the latter were the ones who "translate[d] Marxism from an ethical appeal or from a social science into a political system."[25] One last example: when he evoked the internal divisions within the communist bloc in the early 1960s, he emphasized that the bloc had moved from unity under the iron rule of Moscow to diversity, offering a typology of "constellations" of which it would consist from then on. The solid Soviet bloc that continued to keep most of the satellite countries together was now confronted by the Sino-Albanian alignment, while Vietnam and North Korea stood out as neutralist communists, Cuba and Guinea were fellow travelers aligned with Moscow, and the communist parties that were not in power were divided.[26]

Since in his analyses of the present Brzezinski often tried to sketch what the future might have in store, it is not surprising that scenarios were another conceptual tool found frequently in his writings. In 1970, for example, he proposed five possible scenarios for the evolution of the Soviet regime: (1) oligarchic petrification, (2) pluralist evolution, (3) technological adaptation, (4) militant fundamentalism, and (5) political disintegration.[27] He added that what seemed to him most likely to occur in the years to come was a combination of scenario (1) with a dose of scenario (3). He saw this as the formula most apt to preserve the interests of the elite and the educated class while maintaining the means of rivalry with the United States—although this formula would not prevent decline. But he added, too, that, for the 1980s, the second scenario, an opening toward pluralism, might gain ground. His reasoning was the following: the first truly de-Stalinized leaders would be forty-five years old in 1980 and would find themselves blocked by their elders. But they would have more contacts with their global environment and a higher level of education; they would be neighbors of those Eastern European countries whose regimes would be potentially more flexible and consequently could decide to open up the political game. Taking into account the resistance that would spring up, a deliberate decision on the part of the leadership to change the rules and to lessen the ideological control of society would be necessary—but that might be a way of initiating change.[28] The aptness of this prediction is quite striking (Mikhail Gorbachev was forty-nine years old in 1980); the prediction was certainly not perfect, but it contained a large number of prescient elements.

It is much easier, in any case, to foresee the past, and Brzezinski made an extensive use of history in order to understand and explain the present.[29] He used historical analogies both in his scholarly writing and in his political analyses. During his interview with South Vietnamese president Nguyen Van Thieu in 1969, he did not hesitate to use a historical analogy to support the recommendation that he wanted his interlocutor to adopt, that of an offer of cease-fire. Ho Chi Minh had died two days earlier, and Brzezinski argued that it was essential to take advantage of the struggles for succession that were taking place: the United States had been patient and prudent when Stalin died, whereas they now knew that they could have pressed their advantage.[30] The year before, he had predicted territorial disputes between the United States and the Soviet Union during the 1970s, comparable to the late nineteenth-century Fashoda colonial clash in Africa between France and Britain, given the geographical extension of Soviet power in the Third World.[31]

Some of his historical analogies were more audacious. For instance, in a 1961 article for the *American Political Science Review,* he compared the doctrinal conflicts that were raging within the communist camp to those that had roiled the Catholic Church, in particular the conflict over Jansenism, or the struggle between Jesuits and Franciscans. He concluded that the control of "ideological deviants" had been successful, but at the price of a certain relativization of the dogma, which in the long run eroded its attractiveness and its militant energy.[32] Finally, certain analogies were too bold, and not very persuasive. He analyzed the "histrionics" of the new left as symptoms of the difficulty of the shift into the technotronic era. Going further still, he compared the students engaged in violent protests with the English Luddites of the early nineteenth century, those who smashed machines with "primitive passion, destroying that which they did not understand well enough to harness."[33] Here the analogy is crude; in reality, the Luddites had quite concrete reasons for smashing the machines, for they understood, correctly, that the machines were stealing their jobs. Overall, Brzezinski used this form for decoding reality in an opportunistic way, and without ever transforming it into an absolute; he always kept a critical distance with respect to these analogies and did not fall into a syndrome of the "No more Munichs" type.

Because the forms of his approach to the world did not vary over time, there is no doubt that the quality of his writing tended to decrease as he passed from the academic realm to the "between-two-worlds" space of informed political commentary. He himself was fully aware of this. In 1963, for example, Harvey Mansfield asked him, on behalf of the *American Political Science Review,* for an article he had written on the Soviet perception of the common market. Brzezinski declined the invitation, preferring to publish it in *Foreign Affairs;* he explained that he did not want to be judged by his political scientist colleagues on an article that was not very scholarly.[34] He later acknowledged that, from 1970 on, when he was largely detached from the academic world, he adopted the form of the political essay.[35] This tendency was accentuated by his lack of time: "Some of his recent work was not of very high quality because he tends to do too many things too fast," according to a comment made in 1972 by Miriam Camps, a former colleague on the Policy Planning Staff.[36] His friend Henry Rosovsky added, in 1977: "Zbig's stuff is like high-class journalism. I don't run it down at all, but it can be done pretty quickly. You dictate into a machine, and he's certainly done his share of that. Zbig also loves expressions, like the 'technetronic society'; he has an ear for that sort of stuff."[37] Stanley Hoffmann went even further: "Maybe the thing I am most mad at in the case of Zbig—he was a man who could have been an absolutely first-rate scholar. He had it in him. His first books were very good books. And to me he has a little bit prostituted that talent in order to get power. . . . It has been a willingness to follow intellectual fashions and present views, albeit always brilliantly argued, because he thought they would have an impact and be in the stream even if they were very flimsy or very derivative."[38]

The pressure of time, the lack of distance, and the need to make a strong impression undoubtedly accentuated two other flaws in his intellectual production in the 1970s. The first was the tendency to express himself verbosely, with vague terms and a certain confusion. In 1977, William Buckley reasoned that, after having been a model of clarity in his Cold War rhetoric and his anti-communism, Brzezinski became fuzzy with détente: "On a recent day he advised me that the United States foreign policy was based on 'the primacy of the individual and the centrality of pluralism.'"[39] Buckley went on to say, "and forsooth I gave up trying to understand ZB . . . In short, ZB is a very brilliant man who tends to say and write slightly more than he has to say and write."[40] This is more or less the impression created by reading certain of his post-1970 texts, such as the following passage, for example, from *Between Two Ages:* "The international equivalents of our domestic needs are similar: the gradual shaping of a community of the developed nations would be a realistic expression of our emerging global consciousness; concentration on disseminating scientific and technological knowledge would reflect a more functional approach to man's problems, emphasizing ecology rather than ideology; both the foregoing would help to encourage the spread of a more personalized rational humanist world outlook that would gradually replace the institutionalized religious, ideological, and intensely national perspectives that have dominated modern history."[41]

The second flaw in Brzezinski's production, going back to the 1960s and the famous, shifting "community of the developed nations," is his tendency to propose international contrivances. These included various multilateral structures or geopolitical constructions, cooperative triangles, communities, mechanisms, development projects, and so on, which were often somewhat hollow and seemed to be chiefly intended to constitute the concrete proposal or recommendation required for each of his articles. In 1972, he suggested creating a Pacific maritime triangle (Japan, Indonesia, Australia) and institutionalizing bilateral forms of consultation with Korea, Indonesia, and Australia.[42] The following year, he called for a development project for an enlarged Middle East, supported by the international community, in which Israel would become a technological center.[43] In *Between Two Ages,* he had proposed a veritable institutional Erector set: "through formal links in the economic sphere between OECD and the Council for Mutual Economic Assistance (CEMA); in the security sphere between NATO and the Warsaw Pact, and through United States-Soviet arms-control arrangements; or by the creation of an informal East-West political consultative body."[44]

These flaws should not be allowed to hide the fine qualities of most of his writing. In his effort to comprehend the Soviet bloc and other foreign countries he studied, Brzezinski demonstrated a taste for complexity, a subtle grasp of the mutual interactions of social factors, and attention to popular perceptions.[45] An experienced traveler, at ease in English, Polish, Russian, and French, he attended closely to the national particularities that could be glimpsed in numerous publications—nationalism being in his eyes an essential force, even in the technetronic age. The other aspect that added heft to his approach was his political orientation. He devised the best tools for analyzing the Soviet bloc, it was not out of passion for the discipline, it was because he sought to find the weak spots that would allow the bloc to be split open and destroyed to "help . . . the cause of Freedom."[46] This normativity did not lead to blindness, which would have been counterproductive; indeed, Brzezinski's judgment has generally been confirmed, but it implies a vision of history that is at once dynamic and positive.

This vision points out one of the major contrasts between Brzezinski and Kissinger. The latter, to go back to Mario del Pero's characterization, "explicitly rejected progressive and teleological visions of history, preferring the analysis of structure and stability to that of transformation and evolution."[47] Brzezinski, on the contrary, embraced and welcomed historical change, all the more so in that he often viewed it as playing out positively for America. He was a man of movement, not stability. His faith in America and his optimism offered a striking contrast to Kissinger's Spenglerian pessimism.

Behind that difference lay another fundamental difference in approach. Whereas Kissinger focused on the philosophy of history (in his master's thesis) and then on diplomacy (for his Ph.D.), Brzezinski studied living foreign societies, with all their complexities and contradictions. The former saw international affairs as a political game that was, if not abstract (he was not a structural realist of the Kenneth Waltz variety), then at least limited. That is, diplomatic and military affairs were the only ones that really counted; the Third World, beyond a perfunctory recognition, was neglected; this was also true of economies, ideologies, popular passions, and so on; and the central actor was the political leader who dominated his period (for instance Metternich, Bismarck, Churchill, de Gaulle, or Mao).[48] Brzezinski had a different view of the way the world worked. Without ever losing sight of the bipolar confrontation, he directed his gaze beyond diplomatic and military relations. He was interested in socio-political tensions, in technological disruptions, in the passions and ideologies that stirred up developed societies as well as those of the Third World, and that could affect international relations. In the 1970s in particular, through the Trilateral Commission, he paid attention to the new themes that were shaping international relations: energy and raw materials, the environment, demands for economic equality, economic interdependence, and so on.

That difference led to two worldviews, each of which could be said to present advantages and flaws. Kissinger's prose was in some sense timeless. It clung to the immutable rules of diplomacy, and it generally described diplomacy through nineteenth- and twentieth-century European history, interweaving considerations that could almost come from a moralist. Many of his books have held up over the years, becoming classics and even best-sellers.[49] Between 1980 and 2010, Kissinger came across as a political chameleon. He sought to stay as close as possible to the Republican power, over time transforming himself from a Realpolitiker into a Reaganite in the 1980s, then into a supporter of George W. Bush and especially of the Iraq war in the 2000s, lastly as an enabler of Donald Trump. Still, his thinking has shown somewhat greater resistance to the vicissitudes of politics, leaving a mark on history. But it has also neglected entire facets of international (and, it must be added, American) reality and of the ongoing processes of political change; it has offered a selective vision, often blind to the transformations announcing a new world, and it has been peculiarly reticent about—and ill-equipped for—predicting the future.

Brzezinski, for his part, wrote for his contemporaries, trying to shed light on the dynamics at play and to announce the contours of the world to come, always with a strong element of recommendation—prescriptions have rarely been absent from his publications, and have colored all his analyses. Why write, if not in the interest of action? He has sometimes been mistaken, but the accuracy of a number of his predictions is overwhelming. By the same token, though, his thought and his prose have suffered from two problems. On the one hand, his works have not aged as well as some of Kissinger's more atemporal writings, for Brzezinski's have been more deeply engaged with contemporary realities and their aftermath; thus they have inevitably been contradicted, at least in part, and have lost some of their validity for succeeding generations. This is not true of his early works, such as *The Soviet Bloc;* that book has remained a classic, recognized by *Foreign Affairs* as one of the most important books on the topic in the twentieth century.⁵⁰ On the other hand, his thinking is more versatile than Kissinger's; it has a considerable ability to adapt to new developments, which of course has left it susceptible to being influenced by trends and fashions. Brzezinski has thus often been accused of being an unoriginal thinker who falls for the latest concepts, yielding to a sort of intellectual and media-generated infatuation.⁵¹

There is no doubt that Brzezinski sought to be in the front of the pack in the analysis of international affairs, with the concomitant difficulty in distinguishing what is important from what is secondary or ephemeral. He also sought to translate his intuitions into formulas and catchy slogans that could be used in particular by politicians. It is true that he had a real gift for coming up with concise, catchy formulas. Examples include "France seeks reincarnation as Europe," while "Germany hopes for redemption through Europe."⁵² Vietnam was the "Waterloo of the WASP elite."⁵³ Owing to the growing important of the role of the nation-state throughout the world and owing to the new demands for equality, America should resign herself to "capitalism in one country."⁵⁴ He summed up the evolution of the USSR by explaining that "under Lenin the Soviet Union was like a religious revival, under Stalin like a prison, under Khrushchev like a circus, and under Brezhnev like the U.S. Post Office."⁵⁵ It is also certain that he was a talented political adviser; he had a subtle intuition of the needs of candidates and then of presidents, and an ability to formulate a frame of reference for them, an overall approach. As his adviser on Middle Eastern affairs at the NSC, William Quandt, remarked: "If Vance was the steady, patient negotiator, Brzezinski was a theoretician and a manipulator. He operated on two distinct levels. More than anyone else in Carter's entourage, he had a talent for providing a general frame of reference for policy debates. Formulation came easy to him, and Carter found this useful in integrating all the discrete pieces of information that flowed in his direction."⁵⁶

This taste for formulas and the ability to supply politicians with what they need sometimes made him look like an organic intellectual. But the image is reductive, and the accusation of yielding to the effects of fashion is largely unjust. It has often come from observers who could be reproached for their blindness to the changes in the international system. The 1970s provide a good case study. Starting in the mid-1960s, Brzezinski began to take an interest in developments other than the bipolar confrontation and started to define the nonmilitary challenges that awaited developed or developing societies.[57] This reflection led him to write *Between Two Ages* and to create the Trilateral Commission, which focused particularly on problems of development and the economy. In other words, he was a pioneer rather than a follower of the tendency to open up international relations to themes and actors other than those of the Cold War. Most important, he did not replace one view with another lightly; rather, he adjusted his conceptions to make room for the greater complexity of what was for the first time a "global" world in the 1970s.[58] It was also in this sense that he did not truly belong, despite his key role in the magazine, to the *Foreign Policy* group that abandoned the paradigm of the Cold War for that of "world order" and other new themes: in this respect, his position was close to Samuel Huntington's.

Moreover, Brzezinski was sensitive to the first signs of a cooling off in US-USSR relations, and as early as 1974 he perceived the limit of détente as practiced by Kissinger (Brzezinski's position as an opponent of Republican policy undoubtedly heightened his sensitivity). Without relinquishing his attention to global themes, he insisted more and more, in his analyses of the period 1975–1980, on the growing assertiveness of Soviet power and on the danger inherent in an American failure to respond; his warnings brought him into conflict with those who, in the State Department, denied the seriousness of these developments. It seems difficult, under these conditions, to accuse him of having yielded to a new fashion.

Moreover, Brzezinski was protective of his own intellectual independence. As an athlete of the mind, always ready to engage in debate and to defend his views in a very competitive way, he counted only on his own strengths, on what he actually knew and understood. Thus he was interested in economics and kept himself informed about developments in this area, although without ever venturing to write on the topic. Another example can be found in technical knowledge related to questions of strategy. Nitze, for example, often manifested an exaggerated faith in the Byzantine—and dubious—technical knowledge of certain experts and scientists, losing his political distance and his sense of proportion.[59] By contrast, Brzezinski, while he studied closely the scientific data related for example to antimissile defense or civilian antinuclear defense, maintained a skeptical distance in the face of assertions by experts, taking care to surround himself with contradictory opinions.[60] Thus in 1968 he protested against his inclusion in a group supporting anti-ballistic missiles (ABM) created by the Hudson Institute, explaining his position this way: "I really cannot argue *for* deployment, but I do not think that it would do any harm politically and, in fact, might even be helpful eventually to an arms control arrangement. The reason I do not feel competent to argue *for* (in spite of your excellent article) is that I am by now thoroughly confused by the conflicting scientific-military testimony."[61]

A year later, and despite his sympathy for the political orientation of that initiative, Brzezinski refused to participate in the Committee to Maintain a Prudent Defense Policy created by Dean Acheson, Paul Nitze, and Albert Wohlstetter to support the deployment of ABMS (a committee that employed two youngsters, Paul Wolfowitz and Richard Perle). Convinced that the committee, instead of proposing to examine the question in an impartial way, sought to defend a position defined in advance, Brzezinski thought the matter deserved a more in-depth examination, given its complexity.[62] He showed the same blend of pronounced interest and skeptical reserve on the question of civilian antinuclear defense during the 1960s and 1970s. The issue had to do with Soviet programs for protecting population in case of nuclear war (evacuation of cities, creation of bomb shelters, and so on), programs apt to reduce the number of victims significantly and thus to change the balance of terror. Brzezinski studied the question closely, searching for concrete evidence, because he was skeptical not only about the effectiveness of such programs but about their very existence, the predictions of some inventive Soviet strategists notwithstanding. (Nitze, on the contrary, took the programs seriously, and he had a bomb shelter at his farm in Maryland.) Brzezinski suggested, for example, to one specialist in the field that he should interview Soviet citizens who had recently immigrated to Israel in order to verify his speculations.[63]

Prophecies: Brzezinski the Visionary

To complete this presentation of Brzezinski's intellectual approach to the world, it is useful to consider an important aspect of his writing, one that belongs squarely within a reflection on the links between ideas and politics: the many predictions that Brzezinski formulated in the course of his career. Around 1965, a joke was circulating between his friends William Griffith and Pierre Hassner that reflects at once his sometimes categorical tone, his taste for predictions, his occasional mistakes, and his anti-communism:

"Why is Zbig always wrong?
"Not at all, it's the communists who are wrong not to act as Zbig predicted!"[64]

This joke notwithstanding, it seems that Brzezinski's judgments were often confirmed, sometimes quite strikingly. But the exercise of comparing his predictions with historical reality—the privilege of a retrospective analysis—poses three sets of questions.

First, what constitutes a prediction? Brzezinski always denied being a futurologist, even when he had explicitly expounded on the future. With him, prediction was consubstantial with the analysis of the present and with the political recommendations he addressed to decision makers. Indeed, how could action be advised in the absence of any prediction about what the future held in store? This was the underlying mission of the Policy Planning Staff created in 1947, where Brzezinski worked from 1966 to 1968. As he formulated it: "Planning . . . has a kinship to forecasting; but . . . it is also significantly different from it. It involves not only forecasting, but, more important, a response to it; in the process, the forecast is purposely altered in keeping with what the planner deems to be attainable and desirable. Implicit in this is the notion that the planner is conscious of certain national purposes, and the confrontation between what is likely and what is desirable results in the formulation of the deliberately attainable."[65]

With Brzezinski, then, prediction takes on the aspect of an intellectual exercise, and it seems to be part of an analyst's or a political adviser's routine. Brzezinski's correspondence and his articles swarm with predictions large and small, especially regarding political development and electoral results in various countries throughout the world. ("My gut feeling is that Giscard will make it, even though it will be touch and go," he predicted to Pierre Hassner in early May 1974.)[66]

Not every sentence written in the future tense needs to be considered a prediction, of course. In *The Fragile Blossom*, in passing, Brzezinski evokes a worst-case scenario that would have Japan exploring a warming of relations with China.[67] It is not clear what degree of probability he assigned to that scenario, and to what extent he can be reproached for the fact that it never came to pass. For example, in 1973 he tried to guess who would succeed Leonid Brezhnev. He boasted that he had identified the latter, in the 1950s, as a leader to whom attention should be paid, and then, in the early 1960s, as the man to watch among the Soviet leaders. But this time he went out on the wrong limb; he underestimated Brezhnev's determination to hang onto his position despite his illness. Thus his schematic portrait and the names of possible successors he had supplied were largely outdated when Yuri Andropov rose to power in 1982. Brzezinski had indeed listed him, but after thirteen other possibilities.[68] Finally, certain predictions were unverifiable, because they had been overtaken by events. Take, for example, his warning on the subject of Indochina, which would become a Chinese zone of influence if the dominos were allowed to fall. The dominos were not allowed to fall, thanks in particular to such predictions; this was in fact the point of policy planning.[69]

The second set of questions had to do with the very conditions of judgment. The starting point for any assessment is Pierre Dac's famous witticism: "Predicting is hard, especially when it concerns the future." It is impossible to recreate perfectly the context of cognitive destitution in which a prediction has been made, and thus to measure with any precision the difficulty of making pronouncements about future developments in the absence of reference points that appear crucial in retrospect—often without the observer's awareness—and lend a given event a deceptive appearance of inevitability. This is also the reason why the moment when the prediction is made is so important to the way it is assessed. Thus, for an election, a prediction verified immediately before the results are in does not have the same merit as one made a long time in advance. But even this result has an element of contingency (Ford could have won in the race against Carter had he not made his gaffe on Eastern Europe), so much so that a successful prediction necessarily rests in large part on luck, and, conversely, an erroneous prediction may contain a large share of truth. Brzezinski's predictions must be evaluated insofar as possible in context, and must be compared with those of his contemporaries. Thus the book Brzezinski wrote with Huntington, *Political Power: USA / USSR,* which refuted the theory according to which the two different socioeconomic models—the American and the Soviet—would inevitably converge, reminds us that in the 1960s there were indeed scholars who believed in that theory.[70]

The last set of questions has to do with the criteria for evaluating predictions and their author. It is obviously more important to have correctly anticipated major developments (the breakdown of the Soviet system) than developments at the level of detail (the identity of the next secretary general), and for good reasons rather than by chance. But it is also necessary to take into account the entire set of predictions that have been made, and not only those that have been verified. It is often said about economists, to make fun of their feeble performance as forecasters, that they have "correctly predicted seven of the last three recessions." In the 1970 article, which indicated scenarios for evolution in the USSR, alongside some remarkable intuitions, Brzezinski suggested several developments that did not come to pass, such as student unrest.[71] Overall, he did not have a tendency to multiply predictions, to cover all possible developments, so that he could then point triumphantly to the one that was verified while concealing all the others. On the contrary, he often identified situations in which uncertainty and the multiplicity of factors were such that it was useless to make any predictions at all.[72]

The last criterion for evaluation involves the margin of error. It is not the same thing to have predicted a development in an incomplete or partly erroneous way as to have predicted its opposite, or asserted that it could not occur. Similarly, a prediction error is more serious if it concerns the observer's area of specialization—for example, for Brzezinski, his error or at least his delayed prognosis about the Sino-Soviet split—than if it concerns an area that is largely foreign to him (the evolution of Africa). Finally, the temporal factor and the sense of proportion count. As Simon Serfaty suggests in his retrospective critique of Brzezinski's writings on the technetronic era, Brzezinski's mistake was "to force the future too quickly into the present. Some of the 'shift[s] of historic magnitude' that he wrote about did occur but did not add up to a new international system."[73] However, for the decision maker, such temporal considerations are often decisive.

Clearly, given all the factors that make judgment difficult, the assessments offered here can constitute only a sketch. Still, the sketch helps draw attention to some of Brzezinski's important qualities—his intuition, his sense of history—and to his particular intellectual approach to the world. Here Brzezinski's position on the Vietnam War is an example of a failed analysis and a mistaken prediction, even if it is impossible to assert that the principal goals he assigned to the intervention were not fulfilled. These were to protect the countries in the region (Thailand, Indonesia, and so on) from communist influence, to avoid siding with Beijing against Moscow, and to preserve American credibility. But Brzezinski no doubt overestimated China's role, and, like the other hawks, he did not perceive clearly enough that the struggle being waged by the Vietnamese was nationalistic rather than ideological in character. He also overestimated America's capacity to "contain" communism on this terrain. Thus, as journalists have emphasized, until February 1968 he defended the idea of staying there for "thirty years," chiefly in order not to damage American credibility; next, he defended a rapid end to the war in 1969, judging that the war's objectives had been accomplished.[74] In November 1970, in Tokyo, he predicted that the retreat of the American troops would be completed before the 1972 election (true), that there would not be peace with North Vietnam (false), that a survival of the regime for two or three years would be viewed as an American victory (true, even if the word victory is ambiguous). He also predicted that a fall of Saigon around 1975 would be attributed to the South Vietnamese regime rather than to Washington (largely false—the image of the helicopter on the roof of the US embassy in Saigon in 1975 has remained as the symbol of an American defeat).[75]

By contrast, concerning the bipolar confrontation in the 1970s, Brzezinski had good intuitions. As early as 1968, he realized that the Soviet Union's achievement of strategic parity was going to create an environment less stable than the asymmetrical situation that had prevailed until then. Instability in the Third World could then multiply the occasions for US-USSR rivalry and could lead the two countries, each one seeking to secure gains through preemption, into territorial disputes with no certainty, for example the skirmishes in the 1970s in southern Africa, in East Africa, in Central America, and also in Afghanistan.[76] During the next few years he observed the Soviet rearmament efforts very attentively, but with less paranoia than the neoconservatives. As early as November 1971, he recommended to Hubert Humphrey that the question be raised: "This is not a matter of flag waving or for calling 'wolf,' but there is room for an expression of earnest concern over the overall thrust of change in the American-Soviet strategic equation. Indeed, precisely because you have backed SALT, a warning from you may have the desired effect of galvanizing the Soviets into a more forthcoming posture in these critical talks. Unless there is some Soviet give, there may follow an American over-reaction, and we will all be paying the price for this in the years to come."[77]

In the years that followed, Brzezinski maintained the idea that it was necessary to react to the overly insistent questioning of the strategic balance by the USSR in order to avoid an American overreaction. He put this idea to work in the Carter administration, but the overreaction may be thought to have come in the form of the Reaganian build-up in the 1980s.

Was Brzezinski right in his predictions about the "technetronic age"? The diagnosis was not entirely new. Brzezinski's originality lay in his having attracted attention starting in 1966, the year he published the article that laid out what would be the themes of *Between Two Ages*.[78] He named the new subjects that, beyond the Cold War, would be on the international agenda in the 1970s, and described the consequences for American foreign policy in a coherent and convincing way. To be sure, the effects of the new information and communication technologies were felt later than he predicted (more in the 1990s than in the 1970s), and these technologies did not result in the creation of a new international system. The fact remains that the passage into the postindustrial era did indeed transform America, and it accentuated the economic lag in the insufficiently innovative Soviet Union. By contrast, the prediction in *Between Two Ages* regarding the Third World, the multiplication of global ghettos in which instability would be endemic, was exaggerated. Brzezinski was often excessively pessimistic as to the effects of underdevelopment and overpopulation. He predicted in 1970, for example, a possible national disintegration in India and the intensification of conflicts in Thailand, Malaysia, and Burma; more generally, he predicted that it would be difficult or even impossible to implant or to maintain democracy in the Third World.[79]

This error in perspective did not recur in other predictions made by Brzezinski outside his area of expertise. For example, the book about Africa he edited in the early 1960s led to conclusions that were verified. Moscow had difficulty penetrating Africa but did make opportunistic incursions; there was no truly communist regime in Africa; there were East-West tensions around the apartheid regimes; and so on.[80] Similarly, his book on Japan, after several months of residency and interviews, offered a remarkably accurate prognosis—from Japan's nuclear ambitions to skepticism about the idea, expressed by Herman Kahn, that the archipelago would become a super state, the leading economic power worldwide in the 1990s.[81] Brzezinski was in general overly optimistic about Europe's capacity to unify (this was a frequent distortion among Atlantic specialists), although there were isolated exceptions, as for example when he was pessimistic about Europe's potential in the area of space exploration.[82] Finally, regarding Latin America, the continent he certainly knew least well, Brzezinski nevertheless correctly sensed that the future would belong not to the Castro-style Marxist revolutionaries but rather to Peron-style nationalist and anti-American officers from the middle class.[83]

Let us now turn to Brzezinski's predictions about the future of the USSR, an area at the core of his expertise. Brzezinski did not believe that the USSR would survive indefinitely, or that the Soviet system could ever compete seriously with that of the United States. Moreover, he did not subscribe to the thesis of the decline of the West; on the contrary, he always proclaimed that the pillars of American power were solid, even in times of crisis, and sometimes even when the dominant opinion went in the other direction.[84] From early on, he accurately identified the problem of nationalities within the USSR and its devastating potential for the Soviet regime. During the Carter administration, for example, he opposed Marshall Shulman on the appropriateness of projects aimed at helping non-Russian minorities. Shulman defended the idea that there was a Soviet nationality that would make such plans ineffective. We now know how that turned out.[85]

Brzezinski's work during the first half of the 1950s on the role of purges in the Soviet system and on totalitarianism led to a first erroneous prediction. The concept of totalitarianism was a formalization of the Nazi and Stalinist (and fascist) experience, but the paradigm was too rigid to characterize the de-Stalinized USSR.[86] The prognosis according to which totalitarian regimes could not gradually move toward a softening of the forms of power has been discredited. Brzezinski's prediction that the Soviet purges would not disappear has been invalidated, even if considering the "quiet purges" that he thought he had detected as replacements for Stalin's trials. It is true that, unlike Friedrich, Brzezinski quickly became aware that the concept of totalitarianism was too rigid. He acknowledged, starting in late 1956, that the Soviet regime was going through a phase of rationalization.[87] He reformulated the concept of totalitarianism in 1961, then gradually abandoned it in the years that followed, declining, for example, to update the book written with Friedrich, who went ahead with the revision on his own.[88]

By that time, Brzezinski had already become known for his expertise on the divisions and tensions within the communist bloc, especially through *The Soviet Bloc: Unity and Conflict,* the pioneering book published in 1961 that quickly became a classic in the field of communist studies. *The Soviet Bloc* sold well, was widely translated, and came out in an updated second edition in 1967.[89] However, between the first edition and the revised version, there was a significant difference: the space allotted to China. The Sino-Soviet breach was foreshadowed by doctrinal differences in the second half of the 1950s, including differences in attitudes toward the United States (Mao challenged the Soviet idea of peaceful coexistence with the United States as much as he did that of de-Stalinization), then through increasing tensions in 1960 and 1961, in the communist congresses and through the intermediary of satellite nations. It finally took concrete form in 1962 when relations between the two giants were broken off. Brzezinski obviously cannot be reproached for not having referred to the breach in his 1960 book; however, he saw the schism coming only belatedly, after having firmly disputed its possibility. In an article in *Problems of Communism* in September 1960, he responded to an analysis by Donald Zagoria, who foresaw the schism, by stressing the fact that both countries operated within narrow limits, sharing the same ideology even if they might disagree on its interpretation, and they faced common enemies. In short, all that could happen—in the absence of reconciliation, though reconciliation was entirely possible—was a situation of "divergent unity." His conclusion: "Naïve and persistent talk about a Sino-Soviet split is not only senseless but may well have the effect of drawing the regimes closer together."[90]

In early 1961, during a lecture, as he was sketching a picture of the communist world, he scarcely mentioned the Sino-Soviet tensions, and he stated that he did not expect either splits within or disintegration of the communist bloc.[91] In April 1961, in *Foreign Affairs,* he maintained his position on the limits of the Sino-Soviet disagreements that made a break unlikely.[92] In July 1961, in a lengthy letter to the editor of the *New York Times,* he challenged the "exaggerated" analyses of journalists who hinted at an impending rupture where he himself saw only "admittedly serious Sino-Soviet disagreements."[93] Finally, it was in the fall that he revised the chapter of *The Soviet Bloc* that dealt with Sino-Soviet relations, and in December 1961 he published a detailed version of the new chapter, in *The New Republic,* finally evoking the possibility of a break, which materialized in the course of the following year.[94] His prescriptive vision then changed somewhat. Owing to the Sino-Soviet rivalry for communist leadership, he reasoned that it was crucial to contain China in order to avoid giving it an advantage in its policy of militant hostility toward the West in relation to a USSR that, without yielding at all on the fundamentals, at least respected a certain code of conduct.[95] One place to which this principle would be applied was Vietnam.[96]

During the 1960s, Brzezinski's perception of Soviet realities and the predictions that followed from that perception are striking in their accuracy, and they were for the most part confirmed by developments in the following decades.[97] He refuted the theories according to which the regime would become more liberal or would converge with the democracies. He also predicted the meltdown, the slow petrification or sclerosis of the USSR.[98] The 1968 schema, which summed up the debates launched by his 1966 article in *Problems of Communism*, shows where he was situated in relation to the predictions made by his colleagues, most of whom gravitated toward the prognosis of a "conservative adaptation" rather than a "melt-down."[99] More important, the reasons underlying his position—the "natural selection in reverse" that privileges the most conformist and the oldest leaders, bureaucratic and dogmatic constraints that put the brakes on innovation, the spread of power among several leaders that thus paralyzes reforms, the acute problem of the nationalities, and so on—were the ones that were able to account for the Soviet sclerosis. In 1970, in *Between Two Ages* and other publications, he sketched out the prospects for the next two decades. The portrait in which he highlighted the Soviet Union's technological lags, its catastrophic research policy, and its watertight separation between military research and civilian applications was right on target. "The Soviet lag is unmistakable in computers, transistors, lasers, pulsars, and plastics as well as in the equally important areas of management techniques, labor relations, psychology, sociology, economic theory, and systems analysis."[100] During the 1960s, Brzezinski focused less and less on analyzing a stagnant Soviet Union, a tendency that paralleled his gradual detachment from properly academic reflection and his increasing interest in other topics (Japan and the Trilateral Commission, the Middle East, the presidential campaign and his own move to the White House).

He returned to the question of the Soviet Union in the 1980s, after writing his memoirs as national security adviser, *Power and Principle*. Although his analytic framework remained unchanged (the Soviet system suffered from irreparable ills and was destined to disappear), at first he did not anticipate any disintegration in the short term. Moreover, from 1983 to 1986 his approach was much more prescriptive than predictive. He was interested in the strategy that

America should follow toward the USSR rather than in the future of the Soviet Union. In an International Institute for Strategic Studies (IISS) lecture in 1983, he spoke of an uneasy military coexistence with Moscow "for many decades to come . . . on the edge of the nuclear abyss."[101] Three years later, the preface of his book *Game Plan* opened with this assertion: "The American-Soviet contest is not some temporary aberration but a historical rivalry that will long endure. This rivalry is global in scope but it has clear geopolitical priorities, and to prevail the United States must wage it on the basis of a consistent and broad strategic perspective."[102] He maintained this line of thinking—even though he had already begun to analyze the entrance of the USSR into a terminal stage of its internal tensions—at least through June 1987, when he wrote: "My argument is based on the judgment that the American-Soviet conflict is an historical rivalry that will endure for as long as we live."[103]

Under these circumstances, how did Brzezinski resolve the contradiction between his description of a sclerotic USSR that had been left behind by the West, on the one hand, and the persistence for decades to come of a Soviet threat to the West, on the other? First, he specified that the threat was "one-dimensional." After having lost its ideological power of attraction in the 1950s, the Soviet Union had lost its wager that it could catch up with the West economically in the 1960 and 1970s, and the lag—with respect to Japan, for example—was increasing. The USSR had acquired its global military power only in the 1980s, and this was the sole area in which it could rival the United States. Still, it could not claim to replace America as a power capable of maintaining the world order.[104] "In the long run, unless military means prove historically decisive, it is social creativity that will determine the outcome of the American-Soviet contest."[105] In terms of creative innovation, the communist system remained far, far behind the liberal system.

It might endure, nevertheless, thanks to the weight of interests acquired by the network of accomplices and dependents that benefited from the communist system, and thanks to another, more surprising factor, Great Russian nationalism—an argument that presented an interesting paradox. On the one hand, the mosaic of nationalities that made up the Soviet Union put its own future at risk by its centripetal movement, as Brzezinski had been explaining for a long time. On the other hand, and precisely for that reason, Great Russian nationalism (with its militaristic tradition), which remained the soul of power in Moscow, would not allow the empire to be destroyed and would not accept pluralism among the non-Russians (the satellites) or even among the Russians themselves.[106] Thus an argument hinting at the end of the Soviet Union turned into an argument in favor of its persistence.

Brzezinski did not perceive Gorbachev's potential for reform when that leader took power in 1985. He described Gorbachev as chosen by his predecessors to embody continuity while rejuvenating and modernizing the system somewhat, but no far-reaching reforms could be expected any time soon, he predicted.[107] However, with the passing years, as Gorbachev imposed perestroika and glasnost, Brzezinski's view of him and of the Soviet Union began to change. At the end of December 1986, Brzezinski declared: "I think we could have some very major events happening in the Soviet Union in the next year or two . . . When you take a totalitarian system, which for 40 years dominated and controlled all of the society, and then you begin to open up, to introduce openness, try to tolerate some dissent, you set in motion forces which ultimately you cannot yourself control."[108] The definitive shift in his predictions came about in mid-1987. Between the summer of 1987 and August 1988, he undertook to write a book on worldwide communism, titled *The Grand Failure: The Birth and Death of Communism in the Twentieth Century.* The book was published, opportunely, in January 1989, the year that saw the fall of the Berlin Wall in November.[109] A year earlier, in a public lecture in London, after noting that the convergence of measures of political liberalization with a phase of economic regression generally produces explosive results, he correctly diagnosed a "prerevolutionary" situation in most of the Eastern European countries of the Warsaw Pact, while the USSR was anemic: under these conditions, he said, gradual change and not sudden eruption should be the goal.[110]

In *The Grand Failure,* he predicted that before the end of the century the inexorable decline of communism would have marginalized it, to the point that it would "be remembered largely as the twentieth century's most extraordinary political and intellectual aberration."[111] Although the fall of the Berlin Wall was only fifteen months away, this prediction of disintegration has to be placed in the context of uncertainty that prevailed at the time. It was not really a question of whether the Soviet system would disappear, but whether Gorbachev's reforms and his openings to the West were sincere or whether instead they presaged a new period of repression and of sudden aggressiveness abroad. Brzezinski considered that, if a real opening of the system could not be expected (because of the deadbolts put in place by the communist system and Great Russia nationalism), the possibility that Gorbachev could take the situation

in hand was limited, as an attempt on his part to do so would create a potentially revolutionary situation. Thus one had to expect a gradual breakdown
of the Soviet order that "could lead eventually lead to a coup at the center,
undertaken by the military with KGB backing"; as the Cold War historian
Mark Kramer points out, this was precisely what happened in August 1991.[112]
Kramer also notes the strong and weak points of the predictions in *The Grand
Failure*.[113] Brzezinski's overview of the death of communism, particularly the
link between the domestic crisis in the Soviet Union and the crisis in the satellites, is convincing, even if he underestimated the rapidity and the radical
nature of the dismantling that took place between 1989 and 1991. Brzezinski
correctly predicted the success of Deng Xiaoping's economic reforms in China,
but he was mistaken in thinking that these reforms would be accompanied
by a loosening of the power of the Chinese Communist Party; the repression
at Tiananmen Square, which occurred a few months after the publication of
The Grand Failure, was the first painful correction. Finally, Brzezinski stressed
the particular danger represented by multiethnic countries such as Russia or
Yugoslavia when they exploded. In the end, the book, reinforced by several
op-ed pieces after it came out in 1989, presented a rather prescient picture of
a very volatile situation.[114]

To this measured but overall positive summary of Brzezinski's "international prophecies" can be added some remarks about the domestic arena,
specifically his predictions about the political evolution of the two parties
and their electoral situation. Particularly memorable was his warning, issued
in September 1968—that is, even before Humphrey's defeat (but after the
convention in Chicago, which hinted at this development)—that a Goldwater
from the left could win the 1972 primaries before getting soundly defeated,
given the internal evolution of the Democratic Party. He repeated that prediction insistently during next few years, and rightly so; it corresponded closely
to George McGovern's profile. Similarly, some fifteen years later, he noted
that Michael Dukakis occupied a position too far to the left and, despite
George H.W. Bush's low ranking in the polls, Brzezinski predicted his victory
and committed himself to Bush's campaign. In 2007, Barack Obama was also
lagging behind Hillary Clinton, but Brzezinski placed his bet on the young
senator from Illinois.

The fact remains that this portrait of Brzezinski's intellectual approach to
the world gives only some of the keys necessary to a grasp of his overall vision;
personal elements are of greater weight in this respect.

Identity: Brzezinski the American

The child is the father of the man, but is he also the father of the thinker and of the strategist? To what extent did Brzezinski's national identity and his personality count in the genesis of his ideas, his approach to the world, and his exercise of political power? As was discussed in the introduction, Brzezinski was often attacked over his Americanness, or more precisely because he was deemed insufficiently American. For him, as for large numbers of immigrants who chose this nationality, the accusation was paradoxical. "I was a naturalized American, even though politically probably more intensely American than most," he explained in his memoirs on his service in the Carter administration.[115] This remark leads to the heart of the immigrant's bond with America. When Brzezinski arrived at Harvard in September 1950, he was a citizen of Canada. But his Canadian roots were superficial. First, the family shifted from a diplomatic status to the status of naturalized immigrants. At that time, "Canada was still pretty much a British entity: British number one, French Canadians were number 2, everybody else was kind of number 3."[116] The young Zbigniew kept up with the news from Poland and with current international affairs. While Canada, in that respect, was a provincial country, America, which had been the leader of the free world against Nazism, was now the leader of the democracies against Stalinism, and that was precisely what attracted him. "Yes, I had a sense of real pride that day," he says about his naturalization ceremony in 1958. "I remember walking through the Harvard yard and looking at an American flag, and saying to myself 'Well, I'm now part of this country, and this country really is carrying the torch of liberty for all.'"[117]

His commitment was reinforced by the openness of American society to new arrivals. Far from the cumbersome stratification that prevailed in Montreal, the fluidity he encountered in Cambridge and the possibilities of professional success and social ascension that were offered him at Harvard clinched his new self-identification as an American. Still, however open that society might be, could a Zbigniew Brzezinski really succeed where Putnams, Smiths, and Jacksons ruled?

> I contemplated very briefly perhaps changing my name or simplifying it to give it a more acceptable American ring, which by then of course meant only Anglo-Saxon names, Irish names, to some extent German names and Jewish names, were sort of "kosher" so to speak. But more

exotic names, especially one like mine, were immediately stamping you as an outsider. But I think I gave it one hour of thought. I didn't come up with any idea, because I decided against it. Actually, one thing I contemplated was eliminating the first z, maybe . . . Discussion with friends, who were joking about this, one hour max. . . . And I decided not to change my name.[118]

The future proved him right. In the early days of the Carter administration, twenty years later, the president sent a memo to the entire White House staff specifying the correct spelling and pronunciation of his national security adviser's name.[119] Despite the many jokes and the countless distortions to which his first name and especially his last name were subjected throughout his career, and that are echoed in the archives, Brzezinski continuously climbed the ladder of society and power. As a 1966 article notes, all this "would seem to justify a wisecrack cherished by Brzezinski's friends: 'America is a place where a man called Zbigniew Brzezinski can make a name for himself without even changing it.'"[120]

This does not mean that his Polish origin did not matter. Although Brzezinski celebrated the openness of the society that had welcomed him, and noted starting in the 1970s that the WASP elite was on the decline, he also reported that he had sometimes felt the effects of an implicit, subtle hierarchy. Speaking with a journalist who pointed out Kissinger's success despite his accent and his origins, Brzezinski explained: "I think it is a fact that WASPs, then Germans who have assimilated into a kind of superwaspishness, then Jews, then Irish, have become part, to a greater extent, of the accepted framework of Americanism than either Slavs or Greek or Italians, not to speak of Puerto Ricans or blacks. So while I don't want to put too much emphasis on my ethnic background, I think it subconsciously probably plays a bit of a role, so does the name."[121]

The fact remains that his feeling that he belonged to America had a strength that is often found among naturalized immigrants. This feeling was the source of his constant optimism and also of his activism, the unshakeable faith that it is possible to influence world events in a positive direction.[122]

The force of his patriotism and his loyalty to America notwithstanding, it is undeniable that Poland remained a central factor in his identity. After all, he was drawn to America partly because it was the country that counted the most in international relations, and thus for the future of Poland. Polish was his native language, and he never lost his accent. Although he spent only three years living in Warsaw, from 1935 to 1938, those were the important years of his childhood (from age seven to age ten). He felt very Polish when he lived in Montreal; he missed his country all the more in that it had been attacked, and the return home he had longed for was no longer possible.[123] When he met Jan Nowak, a hero of the Home Army, a writer and journalist who was the first director of the Polish branch of Radio Free Europe, Nowak was struck by the young man's patriotism and his knowledge of the history of the Polish Resistance. "I concluded after our first meeting: this is a man who will play a considerable role in the future, in the United States government and in the problems of East Central Europe."[124] In another interview, Nowak expressed that idea more directly: "His father later told me that since he was a child, his son was determined to play a personal role in liberating Poland from the Soviet Union."[125]

Taken to an extreme, the impression that emerges from this testimony leads to the idea of instrumentalization. Brzezinski might be thought to have become an American because it was the most powerful lever available for liberating Poland, and, on a personal level, as a way of compensating for his own powerlessness during the war. Although this notion may be oversimplistic, and may place too much emphasis on an elementary psychological and teleological explanation, it probably does contain some truth. To go back to the quote that introduced chapter 2, it is certain that Brzezinski wanted to do his part: "I wanted somehow to influence events—that I remember. But whether that would be by joining the foreign service, or dealing with foreign affairs in some capacity or being an academic, I hadn't really thought that through."[126] What counted above all else was his ambition to play a leading role—and to combat the USSR. This accounts for the fact that he abandoned his university career with no regrets once it had allowed him to enter the in-between zone of political influence.

Brzezinski did not hide the importance he attached to Poland, but he always considered it fully compatible with his Americanness, and even as an expression of that quality. "The thing which was really striking to me about America was that you had the right to be concerned not just about America, but also about some place you felt some special kinship for, and that was true of the Irish Americans, the Jewish Americans and their concern for Israel, the Polish Americans (many of whom volunteered for the Polish armed forces rather than the American armed forces)—that was why I was also attracted by America—that sound of universality."[127]

This acclamation of American pluralism and of the legitimacy of ethnic lobbying must not be misunderstood. Brzezinski was an immigrant, but he had never been an "émigré," a political refugee wholly focused on his country of origin, obsessed with returning. He had lived a fully American life, over time feeling less and less Polish. He described the experience of his first return to Warsaw, in 1957, as "a strange rediscovery of a past which is no longer a part of you and yet is an indelible part of your past. On subsequent visits, if anything, I realized how American I had become."[128] His interests diversified in the 1960s, shifting from the USSR and Eastern Europe toward other societies. Even if Poland constituted an important background, Brzezinski did not give it disproportionate attention. He did not play an active role in ethnic associations such as the Polish-American Congress (although he was a member of the advisory board of the Polish Institute of Arts and Sciences in America), and Poland did not occupy a privileged place in his correspondence. As for his political opinions, they were not necessarily different from those of other hawks.

This did not prevent outside observers from interpreting his opinions and his actions in the light of his origins. Thus, Brzezinski was branded as an anti-Soviet hawk and more specifically anti-Russian because he was Catholic and Polish. Brzezinski was determined not to allow prejudices to call into question his legitimacy as a political adviser or to diminish the credibility of the positions he took. The press often made a connection between his ethnic origins and his mobilization against Soviet expansionism, especially in 1978, and sometimes even made a connection with his positions on Israel, hinting at anti-Semitism.[129]

The accusation of anti-Semitism had no basis whatsoever; it was defamation, pure and simple. Was Brzezinski a hawk because he was Polish? That fact clearly played a role, but it does not explain much more than an overall stance; it tells us nothing about the strategy he recommended, and it leaves aside entire swaths of his worldview. Was he anti-Russian? There, the connection appears more direct, and his attitude after the Cold War might constitute a confirmation (support for Ukraine, for the expansion of NATO, and so on). On this question, the Soviet ambassador Anatoly Dobrynin recounts in his memoirs a very interesting discussion with Brzezinski that took place on October 30,

1980, a few days before the election that Carter lost. Brzezinski sought to correct the image that the press, especially the Moscow press, had of him; he was not the crude anti-Soviet he was said to be. Historically, relations between Russians and Poles had been complicated, and that tragic past had not been completely forgotten. "He admitted to some subconscious prejudice as well. But he insisted that his conscious conviction was different: he was well aware of the fact that the national destiny of the Poles was unbreakably connected to the Soviet Union, to Russia."[130] Thus if Germany were to reunify, Warsaw would have no choice but to ally itself with Moscow to counter Berlin. Finally, Brzezinski complained about the fact that, unlike Kissinger, he had been more or less confined to the White House by his role as adviser and had not been able to interact and negotiate with Soviet leaders, a situation that had undoubtedly accentuated his distance from Moscow.

Character: Brzezinski the Man

These questions of national identity and belonging are obviously not the only personal factors that have influenced Brzezinski's approach to the world. His personality, however, is not easy to grasp. Elizabeth Drew summed up the problem in a portrait she wrote for the *New Yorker* in 1987:

> Zbigniew Brzezinski's personality and style embrace a number of contradictions. He can be a man of charm, graciousness, cheerfulness, and vivacity, and he has a deep streak of fun in him. He has, for all his sophistication, a certain childlike quality that can be appealing. He can also be cold, arrogant, insensitive, peremptory with others; he has a combative nature, and, according to the testimony of a number of people who have observed him, he is often inclined toward debate rather than discussion, and enjoys putting people down and making jokes—sometimes unkind ones—at others' expense. People have observed him to be patient, controlled, and decent, and also impatient, mercurial and a bit mean. He is described as a person who can show equanimity and can be temperamental, as one who can be both stubborn and flexible.[131]

It appears that the origin of these contradictions lies in the particular alchemy produced between Brzezinski and his interlocutors. Sometimes the chemistry is right, as with Jimmy Carter, Robert Gates, William Odom, or Madeleine Albright. Sometimes it is not—as with the Establishment figures such as Harriman, Bohlen, and Lovett. Seemingly, he left no one indifferent, and often provoked sharp reactions of either aversion or admiration. Beyond these contradictions, five specific character traits stand out for what they tell us about Brzezinski as a politician, especially during his tenure in the Carter administration.

Brzezinski was endowed with a great deal of energy and with the ability to do things fast. A number of metaphors have been used over time to express this aspect of his personality: "a battery," "a dynamo," "in perpetual motion," and even "Vitamin Z," the nickname his secretaries at Columbia gave him.[132] That ability, of which he made much use for his own career, seems inseparable from a first important character trait, the taste for action. William Quandt recalls that Brzezinski "liked the game of political maneuver and was often frustrated by Vance's legalistic views and Carter's apolitical approach to problems. He was above all an activist."[133] Activist: the word here takes on a more etymological than political sense, going beyond the defense of a particular cause. In Brzezinski's case, it designates a tendency to want to bring about change rather than to accept the givens of a problem: a logic of action, as it were.

This propensity to act appears tied to a strong refusal of historical determinism: history is not written in advance; it is political. Concerning the crisis that toppled the Shah of Iran in 1978–1979, Brzezinski judged retrospectively, and with regret, that American should have done more to avoid the disaster. "Historical determinism is only true after the fact," he added.[134] In other words, supplementary American efforts could have changed the configuration of the problem and potentially its outcome, but those efforts were not made. In 1963, he offered what may well be one of the keys to his rejection of fatalism, when he evoked his interpretation of the Second World War: "My feeling that the war might have been avoided had the peoples of the West been more politically aware and less inclined to take the easy way out, namely postponing reactions to the threats of the aggressors, lead [*sic*] me to undertake the study of Soviet affairs and of Communism in general."[135]

This preference for action is related to a second character trait that is in a way an exaggerated version of the first; his impulsive, even imprudent, "hot-headed" side. Pierre Hassner has described going on a walk with Brzezinski and Stanley Hoffmann during a conference in Bellagio in March 1988, when a mudslide had destroyed the mountain path, and the group was divided about how to proceed. The alternatives reflected the character of the participants: Brzezinski, minimizing the danger, wanted to forge ahead, while Hoffmann wanted to turn back, and Hassner hesitated, seeing the advantages of each position.[136] Such a propensity to commit oneself may play out differently when it is applied to international affairs. For example, with respect to Cuba, he had recommended force, or a no-fly zone that implied the use of force. Concerning Vietnam, Hoffmann commented: "I think he is someone who needs very solid brakes on him. I mean, I remember him arguing about why don't we send countersubversion teams into North Vietnam . . . in 1965. The next day I'm sure he must have forgotten it. That's fine when you're not in power. But when you are, you might try and carry it out on the day itself."[137] In fact, in February 1978, to respond to the growing Soviet presence in Ethiopia, Brzezinski suggested sending an aircraft carrier off the Horn of Africa. Cyrus Vance, Harold Brown, and Jimmy Carter were opposed, stressing the absence of clarity as to what would happen in a second phase: would that signal be followed by inaction—suggesting impotence—or escalation?

This episode sheds light on one of the consequences of this feature of Brzezinski's character, the need to have a countervailing force to balance his impulsive side. As Carter explained: "Long before I ever was elected President I recognized Zbig's strengths and some of his possible weaknesses. Zbig put together a constant barrage of new ideas and suggestions and plans, and ninety percent of them in that totality would have to be rejected. Sometimes maybe fifty percent of them, I'm just estimating, would have some essence or benefit that if modified were good and some of them had to be rejected outright."[138]

Within the administration, Brzezinski himself acknowledged the usefulness of Vance's moderating influence, as Carter too was an activist by temperament, sometimes impulsive.[139] In late 1978, it was George Ball, called in as a consultant, who dissuaded Carter from sending Brzezinski to Tehran. The trip was Brzezinski's suggestion, but it appeared not to have been thought through, as any initiative on the part of the shah (a military coup, or his resignation) would have then been interpreted, after he had met with Carter's closest adviser, as having been ordered by the American president.[140] A tennis metaphor comes up often among those close to Brzezinski. For instance, Carter's press secretary Hamilton Jordan, who sometimes played with Brzezinski on the White House court, described his game as that of an athlete who hits hard, so every ball will win the point. Thus the volleys remain short, for either Brzezinski would score a point or the ball would go out of bounds or end up in the net. One day, Jordan called him on it: " 'Zbig, you play tennis like you conduct foreign policy.' 'You must mean that every shot is well-planned, crisply hit, low and hard.' 'Yes, I said, and usually out.' "[141]

Although Brzezinski sometimes acted impulsively, he was generally cool and collected in his everyday work, even in times of crisis. One night, William Odom, his military adviser, woke him up at 3:00 A.M. to tell him that 220 Soviet missiles had been launched against the United States. Brzezinski did not wake up the president, who would have had only a few minutes of reaction time. Determined to react, but skeptical about the alert, he verified that the bombers of the Strategic Air Command had indeed taken off so that they could drop their bombs on the USSR if it came to that, and then waited for confirmation of the attack before warning Carter. Confirmation arrived in a first phase, and it was alarming (2,200 missiles rather than 220 were said to be on their way), before it was confirmed that it was a false alarm. Brzezinski let out a sigh of relief, and verified that the American bombers had been recalled.[142]

The third character trait that contributes to our understanding of Brzezinski is his competitive spirit, which undoubtedly won him some unnecessary enemies. Here is Robert Gates's account:

> A lifelong professor, he relished verbal dueling and gave no quarter to the professional staff or others in government. He debated like he played tennis—to win and to win all the time. The intellectually weak or deficient or slow merited no sympathy. Sometimes his combative instincts overcame his good judgment and he would reject ideas or approaches simply in the course of winning a debater's point. Accordingly, whenever I had a controversial problem or issue to raise with him, I would do it in writing. . . . His reactions to the written word were always more considered, more reflective, and better balanced.[143]

After a debate at the Council on Foreign Relations in which they had both participated, for example, Averell Harriman came away with a negative image of Brzezinski. "I thought you were unrealistically hard line with a somewhat closed mind," he explained to Brzezinski later.[144] Leslie Gelb, a journalist with the *New York Times* who became assistant secretary of state for political and military affairs at the State Department under Vance, explained that, up to the 1990s, more or less, "Zbig had the mentality that unless you were with him completely, you were against him. . . . So a lot of people who would have become his allies had to oppose him because he was attacking them. . . . Eg, while working with Vance, I agreed with 80% of what Zbig was saying . . . but I was in the other camp. He could have easily 'recruited' me to advance his position, but I was enemy."[145] His difficulty in making allies has been pointed out by numerous observers. Inclined to be a loner in his modus operandi, Brzezinski had trouble using the register of seduction: "He simply doesn't know how to massage people," said one of his collaborators on the NSC with regret.[146] As Secretary of Defense Harold Brown commented, "He is not necessarily abrasive—but more willing to push things hard on a personal basis."[147]

This did not prevent him from having a group of colleagues and friends who were devoted to him, and who had a mixture of admiration for his quick intelligence and affinity for his lighter, almost playful side. He also knew how to create an esprit de corps and to make good use of his fondness for debate. At Columbia, for instance, he had set up a regular, much-appreciated lunchtime gathering at which guests came to discuss a specific topic with a group of students and colleagues. Between 2008 and 2010, Brzezinski organized a reprise of the Columbia lunch debate series at the School of Advanced International Studies (SAIS) in Washington, DC. He invited Charles and Toby Gati (from the Columbia period), Fritz Ermarth and Jessica Mathews (from the NSC), as well as friends accumulated over time. It is noteworthy that Brzezinski's correspondence shows him to have been a faithful friend, who was attentive to others; a fourth admirable character trait. This applied to both people close to him, such as Albert Mavrinac, and to acquaintances, such as Eze Ogueri, a Nigerian whom he sought out during his 1963 Africa trip and whom he helped later by sending him books after the war in Biafra.[148]

Moreover, Brzezinski had a certain high-mindedness and a courteous side. Robert Gates notes, for example, that he could be harsh with his equals and demanding with his advisers, but that he always treated lower-ranking personnel (secretaries, security guards, White House staff, and so on), with attention and dignity.[149] This leads us to a final aspect of Brzezinski's character, which had to do with his ego. A certain pride was of course intertwined with his ambition, and some observers pegged him as arrogant. He liked to make jokes, but rarely at his own expense. Gates describes an incident when, during a trip to Egypt, he protected Brzezinski from an ABC television crew so that he could have a moment of tranquility during his visit to the pyramids and the Sphinx at Giza. Afterward, Brzezinski told Gates that "he was a bright young man who would undoubtedly go far, but not if [he] ever again got between him and a TV news crew."[150] In short, Brzezinski liked publicity and sought notoriety; he held his own intellectual capacities in high regard.

What is striking, though, is that he retained a certain simplicity; he did not see himself as the center of the universe, and he did not court journalists. Far from being obsequious, he was frank with the presidents he served, including Johnson,—to whom Brzezinski declared that LBJ's popularity problem with academics arose from his personal style, and Carter, whom he often annoyed by insisting on giving his own opinion, no matter how negatively Carter reacted. On all these levels the contrast with Kissinger is striking, when considering the latter's attention to his own popularity, his obsession with the media, the time he spent maintaining his relations with journalists, a relation of servile submission to Richard Nixon, and memoirs longer than Winston Churchill's. In early 1978, the journalist Jim Hoagland noted this disparity through a significant detail. He had had lunch with Brzezinski without being noticed as there was no squadron of security agents like those with which Kissinger chose to be surrounded.[151] Where Brzezinski was famous for limiting the time of the interviews he granted, and sticking to it, Kissinger, from his Harvard days on, set up meetings at precise times, and arrived fifteen minutes late.[152]

But Kissinger also had a talent, at least from the 1960s on, that Brzezinski lacked—that of seduction. He knew how to make his interlocutors believe that they were important and that their opinions counted; this is perceptible even in his letters to Brzezinski. This skill produced real dividends; among journalists, in particular, he became a legend, a myth. Brzezinski, by contrast, had no such aptitude, and during the Carter administration he was sometimes treated harshly by the press.[153] When Jimmy Carter awarded him the Presidential Medal of Freedom, the president recognized that Brzezinski had been the target of unfair attacks, some of which were scandalous.[154] But this was one more aspect of Brzezinski's "well-regulated ego"; he had hardened himself to criticism. He did not pay too much attention to what the press was saying, and he had been able to build a protected familial universe that gave him great personal stability.

ZBIGNIEW BRZEZINSKI

Values: Brzezinski the Cold War Liberal

Beyond his national identity and his particular personality traits, Brzezinski's moral values need to be examined as well, because they played an important role in his approach to the world. His lifelong commitment to the Democratic Party—except for the period in 1988 when he supported George H.W. Bush for reasons related to foreign policy—counted less in itself than as a sign of his firm liberal convictions, which he sometimes displayed in public manifestations against racism or in favor of human rights. His friend Charles Gati declared that, "in European terms, for the 1950s, he is a right-wing social democrat, anti-Soviet and anticommunist, but social democratic or liberal on domestic issues. Look who he wrote for—*The New Leader* was a Menshevik paper! A bit of Christian democracy too."[155]

After Harvard, Brzezinski constantly positioned himself as a Cold War liberal, concerned with social justice but staunchly anti-communist, and mistrustful of the excesses of the New Left in the 1960s and 1970s. The most outspoken faction of the left with which he could reach an understanding was represented, for example, by Irving Howe's journal, *Dissent,* which Brzezinski supported occasionally.[156] As a lifelong Democrat, he felt particularly close to Kennedy, then to Hubert Humphrey. But whereas his attachment to Humphrey was rational, his enthusiasm for Kennedy had something irrational about it; he had succumbed in some sense to what became known as the Kennedy Camelot myth (the legend inspired by the tales of King Arthur and his court, revived in 1960 by a musical comedy).

We find evidence of this in his excitement and pride when he received a letter from JFK during the Cuban missile crisis—a letter that he kept on display in his office at Columbia.[157] A month after Kennedy's assassination, in a friendly exchange with Hoffmann, he lamented the fact that the inspiration and enthusiasm Kennedy had provided were in danger of being forgotten by history, although they were going to form the basis for Johnson's presidency, which might be quite successful for that very reason. Kennedy's image, he added, would be stronger if the Republicans won in 1964, "but then I wonder if we can afford to pay that price. In brief, his death is a tragedy on a personal, on a national and on an international level, and I find it very difficult to decide which is the most tragic of them all."[158] After a few years Brzezinski took some distance from the assassinated young president and became quite critical of the Kennedy family as the myth began to deflate. In 1976 he chose not to support Ted Kennedy's presidential bid to avoid the return of the "Camelot crowd" to Washington.[159]

It is possible that Kennedy's religion played a role in Brzezinski's initial infatuation. He himself was Catholic, and even though he did not attend Mass on a regular basis, he sometimes stopped at a church to pray during his travels.[160] He brought up his children as Catholics and attached a great deal of importance to his relations with Pope John Paul II. For example, the two men debated the teachings of Pierre Teilhard de Chardin—a Jesuit scholar, at once a paleontologist and a theologian—who had profoundly marked Brzezinski in his youth, especially through his reflections on the relations between the limits of human knowledge and the moral imperatives of human lives.[161] Nevertheless, he described the type of Catholicism to which he adhered as not very demanding, not dogmatic, and thus liberal. "My father was always very liberal—politically, socially, racially—and it really is more a part of your cultural background than part of any living social doctrine."[162] Moreover, when questioned about the origin of his struggle in favor of human rights, against racism and anti-Semitism, he refers to his family legacy rather than to religion:

> I don't think Catholicism has necessarily something to do with it. I think maybe it's just kind of a fundamental notion of what is right and what is wrong. I remember my mother in her Memoirs noted that she refused to shake Hitler's hand when there was some sort of diplomatic reception where my father had to go. And this was instinctive with her. And my father went to camps, in Saxony, to get Jews out. I got some letters, here, in America, from a woman and her husband, who was engaged to, it must have been the left-wing, socialist or maybe communist both of them Jews and my father gave them Polish passports, which might have been a serious violation not only of German interests but also of Polish government policy to get them out. And I remember as a child, my father attacking a demonstration of Polish anti-Semitic students with his cane. I was probably seven or eight.[163]

Far from leaving traces of Polish Catholic anti-Semitism in Brzezinski, his family heritage had in fact predisposed him to combat anti-Jewish prejudice. Although he did not deny the existence of such prejudice in Poland, he often highlighted the ravages of the official anti-Semitism of the Soviet Union. In his master's thesis, he specifically condemned the anti-Semitic facets of Stalinism through his denunciation of cosmopolitanism.[164] At Harvard, the two groups he associated with were the WASPs and the Jews, especially his close friend Henry Rosovsky, who had been a witness and groomsman at his wedding in 1955. To a journalist who interviewed Rosovsky during the Carter administration about possible signs of anti-Semitism in Brzezinski, the former replied seriously: "ZB even made me kneel in a church on cold marble!"[165] In the 1960s, Brzezinski became sensitized to the cause of Jews in the USSR thanks to Moshe Decter, who was at one point the editor-in-chief of *The New Leader* and who became the director of Jewish Minorities Research. This organization, created by the Nativ, later shown by historian Pauline Peretz to have been a secret Israeli agency, drew the attention of intellectual and journalistic milieus to the persecution of the Soviet Jews and sought to force Moscow to liberalize its immigration policy toward Israel. The 1975 Jackson-Vanik amendment to the Trade Act of 1974 would constitute a Pyrrhic but symbolically essential victory.[166] Brzezinski participated in the Conference on the Status of Soviet Jews held in October 1963. Other participants included Martin Luther King Jr., Norman Thomas, and the writers Saul Bellow and Arthur Miller. In December he signed a petition titled "An Appeal of Conscience for the Jews of the Soviet Union."[167]

In 1968, Brzezinski became alarmed about a wave of anti-Semitism sweeping throughout Poland, stirred up by the authorities. Thanking Decter for sending him documents on the subject, he said that he would be happy to participate in publishing a statement of protest. "I would be particularly anxious to draw a sharp distinction between the attitudes of the Polish youth and intellectuals, and even more generally the masses, and the deliberately fostered campaign, launched by the regime for internal partisan purposes."[168] In addition, Brzezinski proposed to the board of the Polish Institute of Arts and Sciences in America, of which he was a member, that it send a letter to the *New York Times* condemning the anti-Semitic outbreak. This was a controversial initiative. Because the victims were often communist Jews who had been in the vanguard of Stalinism, many Polish-Americans had reservations. But Brzezinski ended up convincing the board, and the letter was published.[169]

The moral values inherited from his parents were manifested in another area in which Brzezinski was active: the struggle for civil rights, or against racism. It all began with what he called his "embarrassing ignorance" on the subject when he was at Harvard: "You know when I was in Harvard, I had Blacks fellow students who lived on my floor, we were living there together, but it tended to be little kings from Nigeria or Ghana and stuff like that. Not African Americans. And I just had no realization of what was going on in the South until the Civil Rights thing, the Kennedy business arose, and I realized that it was just such an unbelievable shame, a violation of everything America stood for in my identification with America."[170] As he explained, what triggered his awareness were speeches made by his hero at the time, John F. Kennedy; televised images of demonstrations by hate-filled segregationists; and especially the murder by the Ku Klux Klan of three activists (two black and one white) in June 1964 in Mississippi, an episode that hastened the passage of the Civil Rights Act in July.

In 1965, Brzezinski thanked Daniel Patrick "Pat" Moynihan for sending him the now-famous and controversial study on the disintegration of the black family ("The Negro Family: The Case of National Action").[171] Brzezinski explained that he and Muska belonged to an "interracial committee" in their hometown of Englewood, New Jersey, and that the report would surely provide material for debate within the group.[172] In early 1967, Brzezinski received a prize from the Alfred Jurzykowski Foundation. He donated the entire award of $1,000 to three beneficiaries, providing a striking illustration of his preoccupations at the time: an orphanage for blind children run by nuns in Laski, near Warsaw; Project Concern, a hospital in the Montagnard region of Vietnam; and the NAACP, the civil rights organization to which he had belonged for several years.[173] In the years that followed, civil rights was almost the only topic other than international affairs on which he wrote letters to the editor or published op-ed pieces in newspapers. In 1968, for example, he proposed that April 4, the day of Martin Luther King's assassination, be officially declared a Day of National Reconciliation, and in 1969 he called for an investigation into the death of a Black Panther leader, Fred Hampton, because the official version struck him as suspect (Hampton was in fact assassinated by the Chicago police).[174]

On the question of civil rights, though, by far the most interesting and unusual initiative on Brzezinski's part took place in 1964–1965 in the Columbia context. Even if it did not amount to much in the end, it offers a revealing and fascinating glimpse into his personality. Shortly after the disappearance of the

three activists in Mississippi, Brzezinski talked with his colleagues Alexander
Dallin and Leopold Haimson about what they could do to contribute to deseg-
regation in America. He related their exchanges in a memorandum addressed
to departmental colleagues on July 20, 1964, under the title "Possible Lecture
Series in Negro Colleges in the South." It read: "We felt at the time that we
ought to do something in connection with civil rights, and we regretted that
Columbia, as an institution, was not taking a more active part in helping the
cause of Negro education in the South. As a result, we agreed that it would be
a good idea if at least our group, that is, those of us who teach in Russian and
Soviet affairs, attempted to do something on our own. Our present plan is to
approach a Negro college and to offer it our services in teaching an intensive
course on Russian and Soviet affairs."[175]

Brzezinski set forth the details of the project, sketching out a solid program
in several stages, along with the list of courses that could be offered. Columbia
professors would travel at their own expense and spend a week on campus;
the host college would provide lodging. The project would begin with a small
nucleus of Sovietologists but would seek to draw in other Columbia faculty;
thus it would become an informal initiative of the university.

What is striking in the memorandum is its mix of idealism and practical-
ity, with touches of paternalism and naïveté (this was in 1964, before the real
transformation of interracial perceptions began). Dallin responded that he was
more favorably disposed toward the project than ever and even gave the dates
when he would be available to participate, but he wondered about the appropriateness of the topic: were courses on the Soviet Union and communism
what students in the Negro colleges needed most? "I suspect that many of them
could do very well without that particular series of lectures, as they have in
the past, but that there are other things we could help provide that are more
essential for their development and adjustment and understanding."[176] He
proposed to participate in discussions of political science, sociology, and so
on, dealing with contemporary issues that engaged and aroused these students
more directly. In early 1965, he insisted on the need to remain a full week, so
that the experience would be meaningful, but also so they could avoid being
seen by the local professors as "self-styled VIPs" who would drop in only to
give a class.[177]

The project took time to materialize. In December 1964, Brzezinski was
contacted by George W. Jones, dean of Miles College in Birmingham, Alabama,

who expressed interest in the proposal.[178] Brzezinski collected information from his colleagues about their availability and sounded them out about the desirability of seeking foundation support to reimburse their travel expenses; the response was more or less positive, with scholars saying they were prepared to do without financial support. In early March, Brzezinski was in contact with Fisk University in Nashville, Tennessee, as well as with Miles College. But his Columbia colleagues were busy, and some, including Henry Roberts, no longer had the time. Still others, such as the historian Fritz Stern, had heard about the initiative and wanted to join.[179] On March 24, 1965, Brzezinski proposed to the administration at Fisk that Leo Haimson would go there in April and Alex Dallin at the beginning of May; Erlich could go in in October and he himself could follow soon afterward.[180] He indicated to the dean at Miles that he could not arrange for a series of courses, but he offered to come himself, alone, in May, to meet with students and perhaps give a lecture.[181]

In the end, the archives confirm that one Columbia professor, Leo Haimson, did indeed travel to Fisk on April 9–10, 1965; the dean wrote to thank Brzezinski on the day the visitor arrived, and Haimson came back quite happy with the experience. The three other visits (Dallin, Erlich, and Brzezinski) were set up, but there is no confirmation in the files that they actually took place.[182] The final tally is thus quite meager, and the enterprise did not lead to a broader movement within Columbia. Nevertheless, the project provides a revealing window into Brzezinski's idealism, the sincerity of his antiracist convictions, and his unmistakable membership in the liberal camp. It is, ultimately, a good example of the "activist" Brzezinski, with his inclination to forge ahead, to implement his ideas, to act—even when the course of action chosen is not necessarily the most appropriate one.

The same liberalism and the same strong moral convictions were present in the international realm, through the defense of human rights, all the more so as these values were generally aligned with Brzezinski's geopolitical preferences, that is anti-communism. In 1966, for example, he joined the newly created American branch of the young organization Amnesty International.,[183] He was also on the board of Freedom House, an organization devoted to the defense of human rights and democracy. In 1967, he recommended giving the Freedom House's annual prize to Pablo Casals, for the musician had opposed Franco's dictatorship and supported America's action in Vietnam.[184] In the

1980s and 1990s, Brzezinski served on the board of directors of the National Endowment for Democracy for a total of nine years.

For Brzezinski, then, the defense of human rights represented a genuine commitment, and also one of the key differences between the West and the communist bloc. For this reason, it was also an instrument of the Cold War. "In seeking that cooperation, the West should not adopt a posture of moral relativism. It is, above all, the West's political freedom—and not its material wealth—that is the real stake in competitive peace. It is also the fear of the contagion of this freedom that makes the Communist systems of the Leninist-Stalinist variety, which thrive on hostility, shrink away from unrestricted East-West collaboration. Western insistence on widening that collaboration beyond economic or formal political relations is hence desirable not only in order to avoid war. It is the means for eventually attaining a real peace."[185]

The idea that moral convictions such as those pertaining to human rights, or democracy, are aligned with the geopolitical interests of the West—since Western freedom has the power to introduce insidious fissures in the communist bloc, an idea that was at the root of "peaceful engagement" and then of détente—is not unproblematic. When Brzezinski recommended Casals for the Freedom House prize, one of his arguments was the latter's support for the Vietnam War. But here is the dilemma: can it be surmised that America's enterprises are all necessarily marked with the seal of respect for human rights and the defense of democracies? How can the defense of American interests be reconciled with the universalism of human rights? In the case of Vietnam, it is easy to point to the nondemocratic character of the Nguyen Van Thieu regime (installed after a coup d'état supported by Washington), as well as to the American abuses in the conduct of the war (the use of napalm, the bombing of civilians, and other war crimes). At least Brzezinski mentioned Casals's opposition to Franco, a US ally, as another reason for his support, restoring a more universalist interpretation of the struggle for human rights.

In 1976, in "America in a New World," a manuscript that was not published owing to the author's official position in the White House, Brzezinski evoked the moral dilemma raised by the cooperation of the United States with dictatorial regimes. "While from the standpoint of American values all dictatorial systems are abhorrent, it is still a political reality that some dictatorships pose a graver international challenge than others."[186] He set forth three distinctions: between dictatorships that were politically and ideologically aggressive and those that were not; between those that had fused ideology and bureaucracy and could thus carry on indefinitely and those that were apt to evolve toward more pluralism; finally, between those that served only the interests of a small elite and those that undertook useful social reforms. From the standpoint of foreign policy, he designated the first distinction (external aggression) as the most important, even if the other two have to be taken into account as well in order to adjust the American attitude.

One aspect of this attempt to reconcile morality and geopolitical interests is the extent to which Brzezinski foreshadowed the argument that Jeane Kirkpatrick made in 1979 in her article in *Commentary*, "Dictatorships and Double Standards." The similarity is surprising given that Kirkpatrick's piece, a straightforward critique of the Carter administration, included several attacks singling out Brzezinski for his *Between Two Ages*.[187] Kirkpatrick accused the administration of having destabilized allied dictatorships such as those of Iran and Nicaragua (which risked becoming even less democratic and fiercely anti-American), while it exempted from criticism countries that violated human rights even more seriously and threatened US interests, those of the Eastern bloc. She also implicitly borrowed the distinction between authoritarian regimes that could evolve and totalitarianisms incapable of transforming themselves from Hannah Arendt—and from the 1956 work by Brzezinski and Friedrich.

In fact, within the administration, Brzezinski was the one who, in human rights policy, pushed the hardest to exert pressure on the communist regimes and to relieve the pressure on friendly dictatorial regimes. He constantly urged either the restoration of the Shah of Iran to power or a military takeover, whatever the short-term costs in terms of values. His response to the dilemma was not that different from Kirkpatrick's. Both of them reasoned that simple distinctions ought to make it clear that priority should be given to putting pressure on communist regimes, given that, as Kirkpatrick put it, "liberal idealism need not be identical with masochism, and need not be incompatible with the defense of freedom and the national interest."[188]

Strategy: Brzezinski the Wily Anti-Communist

Was Brzezinski a realist, a liberal, or perhaps a neoconservative? "On the whole, my views are strategically consistent, tactically very fluid," he explained in

1978.[189] This strategic consistency refers to the objective, dating back to his youth, of destroying the Soviet empire, breaking its stranglehold on Eastern Europe, and provoking the implosion of the USSR. It may be possible to distinguish a series of four more "tactical" visions (although they are actually strategies): confrontation, peaceful engagement, the reinforcement of alliances, and then a return to confrontation; however, the fundamental elements of the Cold War, such as the necessity of military containment and the ideological confrontation, never disappeared.

In the early 1950s, Brzezinski thought—without leaving clear written traces of his view—that sooner or later a war would bring the two superpowers face to face, and he was certain that the United States would be victorious. In his master's thesis, he predicted that "Russo-Soviet nationalism and what we believe to be true Freedom will clash someday."[190] On the occasion of the 1956 Hungarian Uprising, his disappointment when the Republican rhetoric calling for a "rollback" of the Soviets from Eastern Europe did not lead to action left him persuaded that there would be no confrontation, and this conviction led him to change his position in the years that followed. His straightforward critique of the Eisenhower administration in 1957 opened the way to a more subtle and less direct vision of the struggle against the USSR, that of "peaceful engagement." This approach, articulated in the article he wrote with William Griffith for *Foreign Affairs* in 1961, was then spelled out in detail in his work for the Council on Foreign Relations, which appeared in book form in 1965, *Alternative to Partition.*[191]

The alternative to the status quo that Brzezinski was proposing was a kind of lure combining patience and ruse. The idea of peaceful engagement was to bring into play the natural tendency of Eastern Europeans to be attracted by the West by increasing their exposure to human, economic, and scientific exchanges while reducing political tensions. This would inevitably lead to distancing from Moscow and allow the West to enjoy the positive domestic and international image that accompanies every campaign for peace and dialogue. The project basically amounted to détente before its time, although with some differences. The Soviets were not fooled, however, and they did not respond favorably to peaceful engagement, whether in the form suggested by Brzezinski to Johnson in 1966 (the discourse of bridge building), or to Humphrey during the 1968 campaign. The events in Prague in 1968 had a paradoxical effect. They confirmed the general validity of Brzezinski's approach, in that the Czechs were among the most advanced of the Eastern European populations, but they were also a reminder that contacts with the Soviet bloc countries could go only so far. In short, the Cold War in Europe seemed to resist attempts to change the status quo, and paralysis set in.

In the meantime Brzezinski had begun to take an interest in other aspects of the international system and to distance himself from the East-West confrontation. This was the path that led him to "Tomorrow's Agenda" in *Foreign Affairs* in 1966, to *Between Two Ages* in 1970, and to a strategy of reinforcing alliances, embodied in the Trilateral Commission. The overall context was a world in which American power was perhaps temporarily weakened by the failure in Vietnam and by domestic unrest, but in which it was undergoing its transformation into a postindustrial power, whereas the USSR, immobilized by bureaucracy and a stagnant ideology, was failing to navigate the shift to the technetronic age. At that point, America's interest consisted in reducing tensions with the Soviet Union and in reinforcing its ties with the allies with which it had the most in common—Europe and Japan. The latter was done in order to face the shared internal and external challenges and manage world order as well as possible (with attention to the Third World, energy, commercial and monetary conflicts, and so on), given the growing tensions related to the rise in power of both Europe and Japan. This trilateral strategy was thus based on optimism and patience rather than on interaction with the Eastern bloc, although it did not recommend isolating the bloc.

The gradual decline of the USSR notwithstanding, starting in 1974–1975 it became obvious that the Soviets were beginning to reassert their international power, both in terms of strategic weapons and in terms of their presence in the Third World. They were apparently convinced that the "correlation of forces" was shifting in their favor. In fact, they had achieved strategic (nuclear) parity by the early 1970s. The result of that shift was a return to a more classical strategy of containment, which was sharply accentuated starting in 1978, leaving more room for playing the "Chinese card" and for tactics that included harassing the Soviet empire, most notably the support for the mujahedeen in Afghanistan through the intermediary—Pakistan.

Beyond these variations, it bears repeating that Brzezinski's overall vision remained consistent. He did not shift in a whimsical or arbitrary way from confrontation to ruse then to accommodation and back to confrontation. Each phase, even that of accommodation, was grounded in unchanged beliefs, those of the Cold War. The three pillars of his political discourse in particular remained constant from the 1950s to the 1980s. First, the role of the armed forces, which led him always to stress the need to maintain powerful military means. Second, the role of nationalisms and the divisions within the communist bloc, which led him to support any initiative that could heighten these centripetal tendencies. Finally, the role of ideology, which led him to support, decade after decade, the action of the American radio broadcasts aimed across the Iron Curtain (Radio Free Europe-Radio Liberty, or RFE-RL).

The first pillar—the need to maintain adequate armed forces—was included in all of Brzezinski's plans. In *Alternative to Partition* (1965), he spelled out three basic principles that had to be kept in mind in developing any new policies, the first being that "Western military strength must be maintained and Western interests vigorously protected."[192] In *Between Two Ages* (1970), he insisted less clearly on this principle, judging that the US military position would not suffer from a limited reduction in American military presence abroad (a presence that sometimes created needless resentment) and that the emergence of a "global consciousness" could lead to some arms control treaties and to "unilateral restraints on defense spending."[193] He made it clear that the bipolar confrontation would continue, and he warned Americans that conflicts with the USSR would become less intense but more extensive.[194] He was far from abandoning the Cold War framework. And in 1976, in "America in a New World," he evoked the need to regulate the East-West conflict and seek an accommodation, while specifying that "the maintenance of a strong American military deterrent is a necessary precondition for a stable, increasingly comprehensive as well as reciprocal détente—a détente which will remain both competitive as well as cooperative."[195]

The second pillar entailed encouraging divisions and nationalisms. The Soviet Union's vulnerability to centripetal forces was part of Brzezinski's vision starting with his master's thesis in 1950. It was the theme of his most important academic work—*The Soviet Bloc: Unity and Conflict*. Moreover, in all his analyses he insisted on the persistence of nationalisms, although he did not imply that there were powder kegs that could be ignited by the smallest spark. Although he did not predict the Sino-Soviet split and came to acknowledge its occurrence only gradually, he did perceive early on—in the fall of 1961—the political potential of that development. He remained prudent, in the early 1960s, about the possibilities of ties with Beijing, given the militant character of Mao's regime, but the "Chinese card" was included in his recommendations after the 1968 events in Prague.[196]

The third pillar was the role of ideology. Owing to his expertise regarding the Soviet system and totalitarianism, Brzezinski knew the importance of propaganda and information control. It is thus not surprising that he always vigorously supported the radio broadcasts RFE-RL; he knew how widely they were heard, and thus detested by the leaders of the Eastern bloc. This was true whatever his strategy of the moment may have been, although radio programming was an especially important component of his second strategic phrase, that of peaceful engagement, in which subversion played a considerable role.

Numerous examples exist of his support for RFE-RL, from his visit to Jan Nowak in the RFE offices in Munich in 1953 to his repeated references to the subject in exchanges with Kissinger during the Nixon administration. On April 6, 1970, for example, he mentioned to Kissinger his fear that their Östpolitik would lead the Germans to question the presence of RFE on their territory, at the request of their interlocutors. That prediction came true, and this led Brzezinski to speak out during a meeting with Kissinger a month later; he received the latter's assurance that he would keep a close watch on the situation.[197] That fall, Brzezinski expressed his concerns again to Kissinger, given the efforts—unprecedented, he asserted—made by the Soviet and East European leaders. Kissinger assured him that he was in agreement "on the importance of maintaining the radios," and he added in a handwritten note that "we were quite active in attempting to save RFE."[198] In 1972, Brzezinski slipped some words of support for RFE-RL into his advice to the presidential candidates. He indicated that the broadcasts "contribute positively to the gradual evolution of the Communist societies, and they are therefore positive instruments of promoting a détente"; he added that that position would be particularly well received by the Jewish community and the Slavic communities of the Midwest.[199] In early 1974, Brzezinski tried to make Senator Scoop Jackson aware of the implications of reduced funding for RFE-RL: "What is generally not recognized is that RFE-RL have become sources of fantastically important US leverage on internal developments in Eastern Europe and in the Soviet Union. For less than 15 cents per head per year the United States has direct access to the thinking of literally tens of millions of people, and it nullifies, day after day, the effects of Communist censorship and propaganda."[200]

In 1975, following threats of budget cuts and a State Department takeover of the editorial line on the radio broadcasts (and even censorship), not to mention the destabilizing operations directed at the RFE leadership by the Polish and Czech secret police (anonymous letters, defamations, and so on), Brzezinski wrote to Kissinger again. This time he was joined by Richard Pipes at Harvard and William Griffith at MIT. In April, the three men had submitted an official report about the Polish programing on Radio Free Europe and had had no criticisms of the station beyond a few minor mistakes; they deemed its impact very positive. Their letter to Kissinger stressed the fact that the radio broadcasts were a component of the equilibrium of détente; since the Soviets had not been prepared to show restraint on their side, it would be detrimental to carry out a sort of one-sided sabotage.[201] It is clear that Brzezinski was eminently deserving of the title Nowak bestowed on him, "Patron Saint of Radio Free Europe."[202]

It is easier to understand, with these three Cold War pillars as the constant support for Brzezinski's geopolitical vision, why the Soviets did not place Brzezinski into the group of liberals with dovish tendencies, unlike the neoconservatives who attacked Brzezinski in the late 1970s (Carl Gershman and Jeane Kirkpatrick) for being a globalist with a tendency to be too soft on the USSR.[203] This perception of Brzezinski as a hawk was true even at the time of his "peaceful engagement" phase, which they rightly read as a snare, and it remained true after his opening to the new themes marked by *Between Two Ages*. By contrast, the Moscow press attacked him quite frequently, starting in the early 1960s, and his image among the top Soviet leadership is revealed by a declassified report dating from 1978: "Dr. Brzezinski was seen as the arch enemy, a man not to be trusted. This perception was based on several factors: On what was seen as a past record in academic life of speaking and writing against the Soviets; on the fact that he was a Sovietologist and the view that Sovietologists as a genre are anti-Soviet; and on the fact that he was of Polish ancestry. He could thus be expected to continue to be anti-Soviet in his new position . . . Both Gromyko and Dobrynin interpreted the appointment of Dr. Brzezinski as an indication that an inexperienced President Carter might come under the influence of an anti-Soviet adviser."[204]

Brzezinski's position toward détente and toward the evolution of the world in the 1970s can be usefully compared to Kissinger's. Unlike Kissinger, who maintained a " 'maniacally bipolar' perspective," according to Mario Del Pero, a perspective that often prevented him from grasping the nuances and complexities of the international system or of countries in crisis, Brzezinski was able to entertain considerations that went beyond the East-West confrontation.[205] In *Between Two Ages* and later in "America in a New World," he showed that he was attentive to the implications for American foreign policy of the developments that were disrupting the Third World—economic problems, "global" questions such as those pertaining to energy or the environment, and also social upheavals in the developed societies. As a symbol of that evolution, in 1974–1975 he changed the name of the center he ran at Columbia from "Research Institute on Communist Affairs" to "Research Institute on International Change." And with the Trilateral Commission, he increasingly emphasized issues that transcended the East-West framework and necessitated global governance, or at least multilateral coordination, especially the North-South dialogue. For example, he recommended more American involvement in the Conference on International Economic Cooperation in Paris, or the North-South Conference, which first convened in 1975.[206]

But even as he developed a more complex vision of the international system than Kissinger's, he also became suspicious of détente more quickly than Kissinger did. There was an obvious political bias in Brzezinski's evolution. After all, Kissinger had constructed détente and it was part of his legacy, whereas it was in Brzezinski's interest to stress the failures of the Republican administration's foreign policy. In 1974, Kissinger found it easy to reproach Brzezinski, in an exchange about the second report card in *Foreign Policy,* which constituted Brzezinski's first attack against détente, for criticizing a policy that he had earlier recommended.[207] Was Kissinger right? Was Brzezinski's position indeed contradictory? There are three fundamental differences between "peaceful engagement" as advocated by Brzezinski and détente as implemented by Kissinger. Whereas the latter had a pessimistic foundation (it sought to limit the effects of the American decline), Brzezinski's approach was optimistic (his approach sought to put the assets of the West, its power of attraction, into play). The first, which aimed to stabilize the status quo, was "geopolitically conservative."[208] The second sought to go beyond the status quo. Finally, while the first minimized the ideological element, the second aimed to exert direct influence on the evolution of Eastern European societies.

Brzezinski continued to support the idea that accommodation was necessary, but from 1974 on, he saw the Soviets as the ones benefiting from détente, reaping both commercial and geopolitical advantages. Having more or less neutralized the bilateral relation and achieved political restraint on the part of the United States, they were advancing their pawns elsewhere (in the Third World, and through widespread propaganda), at the same time pressing their advantage in terms of weaponry. This tendency was accentuated by the fact that the Nixon and Ford administrations needed to collect the political benefits of détente on the home front, and this situation put Kissinger in a position of weakness, almost of dependency.[209] In June 1975, a visit to Moscow left Brzezinski even more pessimistic. He sensed a whiff of triumphalism there that reminded him of America in the 1950s or even of the Manifest Destiny belief. The Soviets seemed to consider that détente had worked to their advantage, and he thought that these gains could well precipitate a new era of Soviet assertiveness, owing to the Soviets' new confidence, their sense that the "correlation of forces" was working in their favor, along with the crisis that reigned in the West.[210] Détente thus had to become reciprocal and global; It had to give Americans the same access to the USSR as the Soviets enjoyed to the United States, and it had to encompass all aspects of the relationship, including a moderation of Soviet behavior in the Third World. Those two key terms of struggle against Kissinger's détente—reciprocal and global—quickly became stakes in Brzezinski's contest with Cyrus Vance over the definition of Carter's foreign policy.[211]

This struggle against a détente that would be to America's unwitting disadvantage offers an additional occasion to speculate about Brzezinski's position within the changing intellectual and political landscape of the 1970s. After all, on the Democratic side, the liberals who surrounded Carter in 1976 firmly supported détente as it was promoted by the realists who dominated the centrist wing of the Republican Party. Further to the right, the conservative wing represented by Ronald Reagan rejected détente and attacked Kissinger, but the latter's narrow nationalism and his exclusive focus on military issues contrasted strongly with Brzezinski's position. There was, however, a third group that rejected détente while maintaining liberal positions on the domestic front, a group constituted by Scoop Jackson Democrats—the neoconservatives.

A schematic portrait of Brzezinski would seem to make him a perfect neoconservative. He was a Cold War liberal close to Humphrey (like Max Kampelman), a supporter of civil rights (like Penn Kemble, Joshua Muravchik, or Paul Wolfowitz), and critical of the New Left and of McGovern (like Norman

Podhoretz). He was in favor of a strong defense (like Scoop Jackson and his assistant Richard Perle), in favor of an ideological vision of the Cold War and of a defense of American values (like Pat Moynihan), against Kissinger's détente (like the Coalition for a Democratic Majority and Eugene Rostow and Paul Nitze's Committee on the Present Danger), having made more or less the same distinctions as Jeane Kirkpatrick had made to resolve the dilemma of support for dictatorships, but four years earlier than she. The resemblance between his trajectory and hers is troubling. In reality, Brzezinski was in some sense a fellow traveler of the neoconservatives, but not a neoconservative himself. Closer attention to the details of his interactions with the principal neoconservative figures and organizations reveals the sometimes subtle distinctions that persisted.

For instance, in 1969 he refused to participate in an organization that many have seen as a precursor to neoconservatism, the Committee to Maintain a Prudent Defense Policy set up by Paul Nitze and Albert Wohlstetter—with Paul Wolfowitz, Richard Perle, and Edward Luttwak as the principal researchers—because he did not fully share their infatuation with antimissile defenses.[212] By contrast, he participated enthusiastically in the Coalition for a Democratic Majority, launched principally by Ben Wattenberg, Penn Kemble, and Max Kampelman, and he signed the 1972 anti-McGovern appeal, "Come Home, Democrats."[213] It was a matter of struggling, within the Democratic Party, against the ascendancy of the New Left. The effort was focused on avoiding the repeat of the 1972 disaster in 1976 and to reaffirm the Cold War liberal message, which combined a resolute anti-communism with a traditional progressive position on the domestic side (defense of unions, support for civil rights but not for quotas, patriotism, and so on).[214] Brzezinski also agreed to join the foreign policy task force of the Coalition for a Democratic Majority created by Eugene Rostow in 1974 (with Norman Podhoretz, Richard Pipes, Jeane Kirkpatrick, John Roche, and others). The Coalition published the first attack on the détente from the Democratic side. Brzezinski did not actively participate in its work, because he was absorbed in the Trilateral Commission in New York at the time.[215]

Brzezinski was also an active supporter of Senator Scoop Jackson, the key figure in the second phase of the neoconservative movement.[216] In particular, he stood with Jackson to support the emigration of Soviet Jews to the United States and Israel. In 1963, he congratulated Jackson for having gotten through one of the steps in the process leading to the adoption of the 1974 Jackson-Vanik

amendment, which made the opening of trade with the USSR—a key component of Kissinger's détente—contingent on the liberalization of immigration
policy. "A historic accomplishment," he commented, declaring that Jackson
had demonstrated that the Soviets were ready to make concrete concessions
that confirmed the need to be harder on them; a real "Jackson doctrine" was
emerging. The senator, pleased with Brzezinski's reaction, sought his counsel
on other issues and directed him to Perle as a point of contact.[217] Brzezinski
later spelled out his position: the amendment, if it were adopted, would make
it possible to bring things back into balance: "A true and lasting East-West
détente has to be across the board, and your amendment, as I understand it,
has that objective in mind. I see it, therefore, as an important contribution
to the process of ending the East-West conflict, and certainly not as an effort
to obstruct further growth in East-West trade, which I most assuredly do
strongly favor."[218]

Brzezinski also signed several petitions in favor of democracy. For example,
in 1975 he joined an appeal prepared by Norman Podhoretz, Bayard Rustin,
Martin Peretz, and Sol Chaikin for SDUSA (Social Democrats, USA) in favor
of "democracy, freedom of the press, and religious tolerance" in Portugal,
against the machinations of the communists and the USSR, a year after the
Carnation Revolution. He found himself in the company of intellectuals
such as Daniel Bell, Nathan Glazer, Midge Decter, Jeane Kirkpatrick, Lionel
Trilling, Elmo Zumwalt, and Sidney Hook.[219] A number of his friends, at
Columbia and elsewhere, belonged to the loosely affiliated Scoop Jackson
Democrats. By contrast, he was less involved than they in the issue of Israel.
In 1970, he did sign a petition protesting Egypt's installation of missile
sites in the cease-fire zone, which brought the strategic equilibrium back
into question and made Israel's security more fragile—thus putting at risk
the possibility of a future peace settlement.[220] But the cosigners were not
instinctive defenders of Israel like the Scoop Jackson Democrats; they were
liberals and realists (Hans Morgenthau, Stanley Hoffmann, Leslie Gelb, Sam
Huntington, and so on), and Brzezinski's conviction was more balanced than
that of his pro-Israeli friends (Kampelman or Rostow, for example).

His position on the danger represented by the Soviet armament efforts is yet
another element that illustrates his position as a "fellow traveler" of the neoconservatives. Brzezinski was unquestionably worried about the consequences
of the USSR achieving strategic parity, and his trip to Moscow in June 1975

reinforced his concern. After some hesitation, he refused to join the Committee on the Present Danger (CPD). From May 1976 on, Brzezinski felt that he was too closely identified with Carter to be able to participate in that group, which wanted to make America aware of the Soviet danger. He confirmed that refusal in the fall when the CPD was launched, recommending to Carter's other advisers that they not participate (only Nitze had already committed himself).[221] But that did not mean that Brzezinski disagreed with the CPD. He explained that the committee was useful to him starting in 1977 to counterbalance Vance and the McGovernist tendencies of the State Department. "So the views of the Committee on the Present Danger to me were helpful, although I did not embrace them totally and in any case I couldn't embrace them totally because they were very critical of President Carter. But tactically, they were useful; substantively, strategically, they were in part or in the main congenial, though I did not embrace some of the catastrophic packaging in which these views were presented."[222]

He adopted the same position with respect to "Team B," a group of hawks set up by CIA director George H.W. Bush in 1976. This group was challenging the analyses its members—including Nitze, Wolfowitz, Pipes, and other neoconservatives—deemed too reassuring on the part of the agency concerning the intentions and strategic capabilities of the USSR.[223] Brzezinski realized that Team B contributed a useful corrective, which drew attention to a phenomenon that he himself had identified, the Soviets' growing confidence in their military capabilities. But "what I didn't buy," he said later, "was its alarmist tone."[224] Moreover, when he put together his NSC team in late 1976 and early 1977, he briefly considered enlisting Perle, but that was impossible, given the antagonism between Carter and Scoop Jackson, Perle's patron and mentor.[225]

In the end, three elements probably account for the fact that Brzezinski was never more than a fellow traveler with the Scoop Jackson Democrats—beyond his support for Carter and then his position as Carter's adviser, which clearly distanced him from that group. For one thing, his reaction to the New Left and the liberals was doubtlessly not as strong as that of the neoconservatives, and it did not lead him into a forced march toward the right (unlike Jeane Kirkpatrick or Elliot Abrams, for example). Next, his position of support for Israel, sincere and never called into question, was more balanced and more directed toward the search for an ultimate settlement than that of the neoconservatives. Finally and most important, he never adopted the paranoia (authentic or calculated) or the Manichaeism, the famous "moral clarity," that tended to accompany the neoconservative vision. "Well, look, I did think that in a broad sense, we represented the right moral choice, and Stalinism, Hitlerism represented the wrong moral choice for people, but I'm not a Utopian, I'm not a Manichean, I don't think that our side was always right, and I've been increasingly critical for example of decisions to bomb Nagasaki and Hiroshima."[226] As a specialist on the Soviet Union, Brzezinski was too familiar with the weaknesses of the Russians to overemphasize their strengths, and he was sufficiently attentive to the complexities of the world order not to reduce it to two colors (black and white) or to a single dimension (military).

Rather than a risk of Soviet domination, which the neoconservatives feared but in which he did not believe for a moment, Brzezinski was concerned about the fact that the USSR could hamper the United States in its management of world order and could increase the tendency toward worldwide anarchy. He knew that the Soviet Union was too weak economically and not attractive enough politically to become a substitute for the United States. His position with respect to the neoconservatives is summed up well in a response he gave to *Commentary*, the neoconservative journal par excellence, during a debate in 1975. Criticizing the almost magical incantation of recourse to force, which was not adapted to the problems of the globalized world, he succeeded in synthesizing the "two Brzezinskis" by seeking to marry planetary humanism (the liberal side) with power realism (the neoconservative side).

> In that new setting, we must be responsive both to the more traditional political problems and to the new planetary issues—in effect, a combination of "power realism" and of "planetary humanism." Since we still live in a world in which some states possess enormous military power (and the Soviet Union is making enormous efforts to increase its power), we simply cannot abandon continued efforts to maintain military security on a scale capable not only of insuring American safety but also the safety and independence of our allies and friends, be they Western Europe, Japan, or Israel.
>
> At the same time, we must also try to exercise whatever leverage we have in our possession . . . to obtain greater cooperation from other major powers in dealing with the new global problems . . . [such as]

development, food, ecology, the future of the oceans, demography, and so forth.[227]

It was this Brzezinski, ultimately uncategorizable, fiercely independent, and irreducible to any particular school of thought, who became the head of the National Security Council on January 20, 1977. The time had come to put his vision of the world to the test of reality.

6

In the White House

The men who bore the principal responsibility for foreign policy in the Carter administration have all published their memoirs.[1] So have several subordinate figures who played important roles in the administration.[2] Brzezinski's amounts to more than 600 pages for that period alone.[3] There have been many studies of foreign policy under Carter (of variable quality, to be sure), as well as more general analyses of the Carter administration, supported by archival material along with firsthand testimony.[4] In other words, Brzezinski's role and his impact on American foreign policy during this crucial four-year period have been well documented. This chapter focuses on how Brzezinski's actions were inspired and nourished by the intellectual arsenal that he had acquired during the preceding thirty-five years, to show how the confrontation with the real world played out and how it changed him.

The personal diary in which he wrote almost daily during his four years at the White House remains inaccessible. Other sources, however, make it possible to describe the interactions between the national security adviser and the president he served, and to characterize the adviser's influence over the administration's foreign policy. In addition to the countless memoranda he addressed to Carter, Brzezinski wrote weekly reports for Carter's exclusive attention summing up the events of the week; by way of introduction, he included a sort of editorial presenting his own views and his political recommendations on the burning issue(s) of the moment.[5] These weekly reports, added to Brzezinski's own accounts and those of other actors in this story, including the president himself, make it possible to present the history of foreign policy during the Carter administration from the standpoint of one particularly privileged actor, Zbigniew Brzezinski.

The Political Landscape under Carter: A Shifting, Competitive Environment

Had he followed the advice that had been heaped on him, Carter would doubt-less not have enlisted Brzezinski. According to the Soviet ambassador Anatoly Dobrynin, Henry Kissinger went to see Jimmy Carter and Walter Mondale on November 20, 1976, accompanied by Lawrence Eagleburger, at the president-elect's residence in Georgia.[6] There he tried "to talk Carter out of appointing one of his advisers, Zbigniew Brzezinski of Columbia University, as secretary of state because he found the Polish-born professor excessively emotional and not able to think impassively in the long term."[7] Clark Clifford, a former secretary of defense under Johnson, went further; he deemed Brzezinski "too much of an advocate and not enough of an honest broker," so that he would inevitably come into conflict with the "gentle" Cyrus Vance.[8] It is hardly surprising that Averell Harriman gave the same advice to the president, urging him not to appoint either James Schlesinger or Brzezinski, both too "hawkish." Richard Holbrooke was of the same opinion.[9]

Many others recommended Brzezinski, beginning with Vance himself. Car-ter confirmed in his memoirs that numerous individuals had come to see him to warn him about Brzezinski's "aggressive" and "ambitious" side, which could bring him into conflict with Vance. "Knowing Zbig, I realized that some of these assessments were accurate, but they were in accord with what I wanted: the final decisions on basic foreign policy would be made by me in the Oval Office, and not in the State Department. I listened carefully to all the com-ments about him, considered the factors involved, and decided that I wanted him with me in the White House."[10]

The decision took time. Carter finally called Brzezinski to offer him the role of national security adviser on December 15, 1976, well after he had named Cyrus Vance and Harold Brown. He explained that he had had to go through all the formal steps in the selection process. Brzezinski, for his part, later con-firmed that no one else had been interviewed specifically for this role, but he had an idea about what had delayed his nomination. "[Carter] probably had to go through a process of digesting a lot of opposition to me, kind of rational-izing the reasons why he wouldn't accept the arguments against me, and I heard there were quite a few."[11]

All this highlights the very solid bond that existed between Carter and Brzezinski. Brzezinski had made significant contributions to the Georgia governor's international education through the Trilateral Commission, then as his principal adviser on foreign policy. "Zbig had an early record of being my supporter," Carter explained later.[12] Brzezinski also served as his sparring partner in preparation for the televised debate with Gerald Ford held on October 6, 1976. Brzezinski's early support and his role as adviser do not explain everything. Carter took real pleasure in listening to him and debating with him; he enjoyed his company, as he noted later, in many ways: "I really enjoyed Mr. Brzezinski explaining to me because he made it interesting." "I was an eager student of Zbig's and I enjoyed being around him." "Zbig and I had a relationship not nearly as close as Jody and I, but we joked with each other, we argued about issues, we were together four or five times every day. I started off my days meeting with Zbig." "Next to members of my family, Zbig would be my favorite seatmate on a long-distance trip; we might argue, but I would never be bored."[13]

Thus it was this blend of good personal chemistry and what some journalists called "Brzezinski University."[14] The "university" was attended by a president relatively unfamiliar with foreign affairs but eager to learn, devouring the memoranda and studying the files like no one before (overdoing it, even), which cemented the relationship between the two men. Brzezinski reported later that he was embarrassed when Carter had him take the oath of office, so effusive was Carter about his role as mentor, describing him as "the eyes and the ears through which he sees the world."[15] This did not mean that Carter turned everything over to Brzezinski. It was he who made the decisions, sometimes frustrating his national security adviser, and he had his own opinions, especially on nonproliferation of nuclear weapons (because of his training as an atomic engineer) and on civil rights (because of his religious convictions). In Carter's eyes, Brzezinski always remained an interesting professor.

As for the personal chemistry between the two men, Brzezinski understood it as stemming in part from their shared status as outsiders. He had come from Poland, and Carter from the American South, two cultures rooted in aristocracy, gallantry, and honor even in defeat. Brzezinski found the unexpected Polish-Southerner parallel in William Styron's *Sophie's Choice,* which he encouraged Jimmy and Rosalyn Carter to read.[16] Their affinity was manifested in many ways. On Saturday mornings, especially during the first year of Carter's presidency, they often plunged into lively, freewheeling discussions. They played tennis together and jogged together (but Carter went too fast).[17] Brzezinski noted in his memoirs that he and Carter generally had the same opinions of foreign leaders: neither liked the German chancellor Helmut Schmidt or the Mexican president Lopez Portillo, but both appreciated the Egyptian leader Anwar Sadat, France's Giscard d'Estaing, and China's Deng Xiaoping.[18] Carter was grateful to Brzezinski for always accepting the collective decisions made by administration members or by the president alone, and for his willingness to play the role of lightning rod for the administration.[19] On occasion, the president and his wife would invite themselves to dinner at the Brzezinskis' home, or would invite the Brzezinskis to come watch a movie at the White House. Mika, Brzezinski's daughter, came regularly to 1600 Pennsylvania Avenue and to Camp David to play with her contemporary Amy, the Carters' youngest child.[20] One day during the Israeli-Egyptian negotiations, when the adventurous teenagers were driving a golf cart around Camp David, Mika almost ran into Menachem Begin; Secret Service agents managed to intervene just in time to prevent an accident.[21]

This does not mean that the relationship between Brzezinski and Carter was all sweetness and light. On several issues the president did not share his adviser's opinion; the latter was often the bearer of bad news, and his standing was particularly low at the beginning of his discordant relations with Vance over the Soviet Union and during the events in Iran.[22] Brzezinski considered it his duty always to tell the president what he thought, without varnishing the truth. But he could sometimes be very insistent—too insistent, even, as when he wanted Carter to send him to China. One day the president's private secretary came in and made a show of presenting him with an envelope from the Oval Office. The letter, signed "Jimmy," contained a single sentence: "Zbig, don't you ever know when to stop?" Brzezinski was touched by the gesture: "There was the President of the United States, whom I was obviously annoying, and yet the delicacy of that message really struck me."[23] Indeed, the president never went further than that, never raised his voice with Brzezinski, never subjected him to the angry outbursts he reserved for Jody Powell or Hamilton Jordan, or to the occasional scolding delivered to his principal subordinates, including Vance and Harold Brown.

It was also the case that Powell and Jordan were much younger than the president, whereas Brzezinski was just four years his junior. While he treated the former like sons, Brzezinski was more his equal, his only peer in the White House environment. However, their cordial relations did not preclude a certain distance.[24] Despite the president's encouragement, Brzezinski could never bring himself to call him "Jimmy" in private. He kept his own communications with him on a strictly professional level and never brought up personal matters except when Carter invited him to do so. Over the years, as Brzezinski remarked later, the institution of the presidency came increasingly between him and Jimmy Carter the man, weakening the personal cement and creating a distance, a certain formality.[25]

On occasion the two men found themselves in substantive, even philosophical, disagreement. During the first three years, Brzezinski relentlessly argued in favor of adopting a harder line toward the Soviet Union; in 1980, he no longer needed to do so. In his weekly reports, during the second half of 1977 and in 1978, the national security adviser advised the president to demonstrate resolve, even toughness. He wanted Carter to be a President Truman before being a President Wilson. Most often, the president's annotations reflected his approval. But in an unprecedented way, on April 21, 1978, when Brzezinski contrasted a foreign policy of endless negotiation that was essentially contractual (the policy espoused by Vance and Warren Christopher, both lawyers) with a more flexible and more muscular approach, Carter reacted strongly to the Machiavellianism that Brzezinski was advocating. In the president's caustic and sarcastic annotations (see the right-hand column in Table 6.1) to the passages Brzezinski underlined (here in italics), one senses his moral repugnance toward practices he associated with Nixon and Kissinger.[26]

These occasional disagreements and the gradually increasing distance between the two men must not be allowed to obscure the human quality of the relationship. To make an extreme comparison, it is useful to consider the relationship between Kissinger and Nixon. As Jeremy Suri writes, these two "were more rivals than partners, more antagonists than friends."[27] He compared Nixon to a gangster boss and Kissinger to his obsequious right-hand man; he evoked "a marriage of convenience, filled with all the suspicion, hostility and jealousy that accompanies these dysfunctional alliances."[28] Nixon found it unbearable that Kissinger should be chosen as *Time Magazine*'s "Man of the Year" at the same time he achieved that honor, and he thought that the Nobel Prize should have been his rather than Kissinger's.[29] The latter had to endure the president's anti-Semitic outbursts, and had his phone tapped, as did the other White House staff members, by order of the president. Nothing of the sort was imaginable in the

Table 6.1.

Brzezinski's Weekly Report #55	Carter's Annotations
In some cases, what is needed is a <u>demonstration of force, to establish credibility</u> and determination and even to infuse fear; in some cases it requires <u>*saying publicly one thing*</u> and quietly *negotiating something else* . . . Examples of the foregoing would include quiet efforts to manipulate African leaders to obtain desired results; a willingness to back some friendly country very strongly, so that it in turn is prepared to use its force on our behalf (for example, I think there is a good chance that by <u>tangibly backing Morocco with arms</u> we could <u>get Hassan *to use its troops for us*</u> the way Castro is using <u>his on behalf of the Soviets</u>); readiness to use *black propaganda* to stimulate difficulties for our opponents, for example by <u>encouraging national sentiments among the non-Russian Soviet peoples</u> or by <u>*using deception*</u> to divide the Soviets and the Cubans on African policy. *I will be developing some ideas for you regarding the above.**	Like Malaguez?** Lying? Proxy war? ? ? You'll be wasting your time.

*That is, disinformation distilled by seemingly allied and trustworthy sources.
**Carter meant to write Mayaguez, the name of the American ship seized by the Khmer Rouge in May 1975, an incident that gave Ford the pretext, two months after the fall of Saigon, to undertake a military operation intended to rescue the hostages. The intervention was in fact useless, since the crew had been released, although Ford did not know this.

relations between Carter and Brzezinski, which were characterized by loyalty, respect, and trust.

It would be just as hard to imagine Brzezinski having his subordinates' phones tapped, as Kissinger did on a large scale, on the pretext of combating leaks. The relations between Brzezinski and his National Security Council (NSC) team were collegial and orderly, offering a certain contrast with the tense relations that developed, especially from 1978 on, between the NSC and the State Department. It is clear that Brzezinski had long since identified most of the advisers that he wanted to have working with him. "In 1968, I for the first time thought that maybe I would have a senior position at the very top in the US government. Not necessarily NSA, but as Deputy Secretary of State, something like that. . . . But I was conscious in any case, of something like this arising, and I remember, before leaving Washington, in '68, I started putting in my notebook names of people that struck me as people I would like to quickly mobilize if I got appointed."[30]

A good example is William Odom, a brilliant officer trained at West Point who was Brzezinski's student at Columbia in 1961 and a participant in his seminar on the dynamics of Soviet politics. Only four years younger than Brzezinski, after completing his master's degree Odom was assigned to a position in Germany; he went back to Columbia for his Ph.D. in 1967. Afterward, he served in Vietnam, before returning to Columbia once again when Brzezinski offered him a visiting position at the Research Institute on Communist Affairs in 1971–1972. His next assignment took him to the US embassy in Moscow for two years (where he managed among other things to get Aleksandr Solzhenitsyn's personal archives out of the country), and Brzezinski enlisted him as his military assistant on the NSC in 1977. Odom ended up with the rank of general, and he served as head of the National Security Agency under Reagan.

Odom was one of several whom Brzezinski had picked out in advance; the group made up a National Security Council that was very well supplied with gray matter. As Odom commented: "There was no lack of intellectual power and analytical power on the Brzezinski NSC staff. In fact, I'd say there was an enormous difference between Brzezinski's NSC staff and the two others [those of his predecessor Brent Scowcroft and his successor Richard Allen]."[31] Among the thirty-five people who worked as advisers (a reduction from about fifty during Kissinger's and Scowcroft's time), several of them came from universities—for example, Lincoln Bloomfield and also Sam Huntington, whom Brzezinski persuaded to lead a vast exercise to assess the US-USSR balance of power.

The other two groups that made up Brzezinski's team were, first, professional diplomats and, second, experts and advisers who were more liberal than he. This latter group was chosen, he explained later, in order to provide cover against the attacks he expected from the left, given his reputation as a hawk. One notable figure in this last category was Jessica Tuchman Mathews, who had been an adviser to Morris Udall, and to whom Brzezinski assigned a working group on "global affairs"—human rights and transborder issues. Brzezinski also recruited Robert Hunter, an adviser to Ted Kennedy, and Robert Pastor, from the Linowitz Commission on relations between the United States and Latin American countries. In 1976, that commission recommended negotiating an agreement on the Panama Canal.[32] But Brzezinski also covered his bases on the right: several advisers were viewed as more hawkish than he—for example, Fritz Ermarth, Huntington, and Odom. According to Odom, Brzezinski used them to send out trial balloons and to formulate extreme opinions, to be able to return to a more acceptable "centrist" position.[33] His principal deputy was David Aaron, a veteran of the NSC under Kissinger who had worked with Walter Mondale; his personal assistants—whom he "used up" one after another, so unrelenting was the pace he set—were Rick Inderfurth, Robert Gates (future secretary of defense), and Colonel Leslie Denend.

Madeleine Albright, who had also taken courses from Brzezinski at Columbia, joined the team in 1978, after leaving her position with Ed Muskie in the Senate. At her goodbye party, Muskie joked that she was going "from Pole to Pole," since he himself was of Polish origin; and a colleague enjoined her to keep in mind that her boss was "Zbig" but that she was "zmall."[34] She was in charge of the NSC's relations with Congress, at a time of mounting tension, delegated by Brzezinski, who did not take those relations seriously enough. Finally, as the latter notes in his memoirs, two of his recruits stirred up controversy. The pro-Israel lobby challenged the nomination of William Quandt, who was deemed too pro-Palestinian. That reputation followed him for the entire four years, contributing to the tensions between Brzezinski and the Jewish community. Beyond that, Brzezinski decided to name a spokesperson for the NSC, because Jody Powell—Carter's press attaché—was not very well versed in international questions and Brzezinski himself wanted to keep a low profile. But the press interpreted this nomination on the contrary as an act of self-assertion on Brzezinski's part, and saw Jerry Schecter from *Time Magazine*—the first person to hold the position—as a sort of impresario for the national security adviser, working to shape a favorable image of his boss.[35]

Whatever their origin, Brzezinski's thirty-five "team members" at the NSC all had equal access to him, owing to an innovation in the way the work was organized. Brzezinski did away with the distinction between "juniors" and "seniors," and he also abolished regional groupings, so that everyone could interact directly with him; this created extra work for him, but also attributed greater responsibility to everyone.[36] To accentuate this tendency, he tried to have the president meet each of his advisers, and on a weekly basis during those four years he gave them a detailed report on his exchanges with Carter. Albright remembers these exciting sessions as the symbol of an efficient and collegial NSC: "One of the best parts about my work was our weekly staff meeting, which was like a first-class seminar. It was a very smart group. Brzezinski said he would always tell us about his meetings with the President as long as there were no leaks. There weren't, and he did. . . . For those who only saw Brzezinski on television, he seemed an austere figure, with sharp features that cartoonists gleefully transformed into those of a hawk. He had frightened me as a professor, but as a boss he was warm. He didn't just talk about collegiality, he practiced it."[37]

Collegiality was a key concept that Brzezinski, in his role as the president's coordinator for the various agencies dealing with foreign affairs, wanted to see the major decision makers adopt. But this attitude did not last very long, and the relations between Brzezinski and Secretary of State Vance deteriorated, especially from 1978 on. A dark legend about the relation between the two men took shape in the press around that time, suggesting a sort of combat between Titans based on mutual loathing, an "all-out civil war."[38] It is important to bring the situation back to its real proportions.

Vance and Brzezinski did fundamentally disagree on the general orientation and priorities of American foreign policy. It is not surprising that this disagreement centered on interpretations of the Soviet attitude. Vance considered the USSR to be a conservative power whose advances in the Third World reflected opportunism rather than a plan for world domination; he thought that the Soviets' behavior could often be explained as a reaction to US initiatives. In his eyes, it was essential to pursue détente and to stabilize the relationship with the USSR, beginning with the SALT negotiations that were at the heart of the matter, and extending the effort to other topics such as the Middle East. Improving relations with China was desirable but secondary; in any event, it could not be allowed to imperil détente.

Brzezinski saw things differently. From his standpoint, the USSR, despite its domestic paralysis, was in a phase of geopolitical self-assertion, and he thought that the Soviets could use détente to stabilize the relationship on a bilateral level, in particular with regard to arms control, even as they pressed their advantage elsewhere, especially in the Third World. If the United States did not want Moscow to continue to grow bolder and to threaten American leadership, something that would sooner or later be condemned by public opinion and by America's allies, détente had to be made more balanced. In other words, it had to be reciprocal and global. For this, ties with the traditional allies had to be reinforced, and the United States had to react to Soviet and Cuban advances in the Horn of Africa and elsewhere, had to play the Chinese card, including on the military level, and had to oppose Soviet interference in the Near East and in West Africa.

President Carter's indecisiveness, his inability to choose between these two visions, accentuated the disagreement, giving it resonance and often creating the impression of an administration more divided than it was. That discord, in turn, fed Carter's indecisiveness, in a typical vicious circle. This unfortunate quality of Carter's reflected an increasingly polarized political environment (divisions were growing within the Democratic Party, among the elite, in public opinion, and elsewhere), in a changing geopolitical context, which in fact favored and in a sense justified Brzezinski's hard-line position.

From another standpoint, though, the limits of the struggle between Vance and Brzezinski need to be stressed. In the first place, their discord developed only gradually and did not involve all the issues of shared concern. It was during the second year, especially during the spring of 1978, that tensions really mounted, over the Soviet and Cuban presence in the Horn of Africa (how should the United States react? did the situation call détente into question?) and over the prospect of normalizing relations with China (could that endanger the ongoing SALT negotiations?). Starting at the end of that year, protests that led to the overthrow of the Shah of Iran became the second major locus of disagreement between the State Department and the NSC, especially after hostages were taken at the US embassy in Tehran. But Vance and Brzezinski cooperated on other crucial issues, from the Panama Canal treaties through the handling of crises in Southern Africa to the Camp David Accords. The two men had gotten to know each other through the Trilateral Commission, and each had recommended the nomination of the other to Jimmy Carter.[39] Throughout the four-year term they played tennis together regularly, and after Vance's resignation, when the new secretary of state Ed Muskie gave an interminable press conference that turned into a one-man show, they sat together in Brzezinski's office listening to him and could not help bursting out laughing.[40]

One of the principal factors that exacerbated the struggle between Vance and Brzezinski was the role that their subordinates played, especially in the State Department. The two men never criticized each other in the press, but a large number of leaks coming from the lower ranks served as the basis for attacks, sometimes violent ones, in the major newspapers. Leslie Gelb and Tony Lake implicitly admitted to leaks perpetrated against Brzezinski, followed by a reprimand by Vance.[41] Gelb and Lake, along with Hodding Carter and Richard Holbrooke, were indeed the ones Brzezinski accused of having spread rumors to the press, anonymously while they were in office and openly afterward (especially in Gelb's case, as he went back to work for the *New York Times*). The same accusation was made against members of the NSC and against Brzezinski himself, but it was not of comparable significance and was never as clearly proved.[42]

Carter was on Brzezinski's side against Vance's subordinates in condemning the leaks coming from the State Department during a lunch—the only one of its kind—intended to arbitrate between the secretary of state and the national security adviser, on December 19, 1978.[43] Vance acknowledged, in understated terms, that "the collegiality and the relative absence of interdepartmental jealousies which (at least in the beginning) prevailed among the cabinet members were not always shared by our staffs."[44] It should be noted that Vance was at the head of a huge organization, known for its bureaucratic culture, one that had been traumatized by its isolation during the Kissinger years. By contrast, Brzezinski headed a smaller, loyal team, while increasingly playing the role of inspiring and presenting policy, a domain that actually belonged to the secretary of state. Vance never really challenged the scope of Brzezinski's portfolio as national security adviser. Brzezinski's abrupt and peremptory way of expressing and defending his opinions played a counterproductive role in the matter. Carter ultimately summed things up well when he wrote in his diary in February 1979: "Zbig is a little too competitive and incisive. Cy is too easy on his subordinates. And the news media constantly aggravate the inevitable differences and competition between the two groups."[45]

Carter left out one crucial actor in this competitive dynamic: himself. Brzezinski's activism was only a reflection of his desire to see the White House play a key role in the formulation of American foreign policy, something that inevitably constituted a threat to the State Department. In the fall of 1976, when Brzezinski discussed candidates for the position of secretary of state with Carter, and commented with regard to one of them (probably George Ball), that he would be "the kind of Secretary of State who'd like to make and run American foreign policy," Carter exclaimed: "Well, he's not my type."[46] An active White House meant a powerful national security adviser. This was why Brzezinski was sincere when he insisted that he would rather have that job than be secretary of state, though he was suspected of coveting the latter position; he had sensed where the action would be. The support Carter offered him later also had to do with the low esteem in which he held the State Department; he described it as a vast bureaucracy incapable of sending him innovative proposals but quick to leak information. Moreover, during the December 19 "arbitration" lunch, when Vance complained of the secrecy Brzezinski had maintained about the normalization of relations with China (the State Department had been kept largely away from the negotiations between June and December 1978), Carter took full responsibility—it was he who had wanted to avoid any risk of leaks.[47] Vance did not deny the problems created by the leaks.[48]

Brzezinski thus served as "chief strategist," the architect of Carter's foreign policy, the one who set its overall directions. Vance, by contrast, appeared as the "chief negotiator," the one who handled America's external relations with excellent results; he was largely responsible for the success of the Camp David Accords, the SALT talks, and progress in Southern Africa. Starting in January 1977, the national security adviser was the one who drafted, at the president's request and with the help of Huntington and Odom, a detailed plan with ten major objectives (of which seven would be achieved) and with specific secondary objectives that would guide the administration.[49] He was also the one who found the slogans to describe the policy. These included "constructive global engagement" at the beginning of the Carter administration.[50] Then in December 1978, in one of the weekly reports, he coined the phrase "reciprocal restraint," which contrasted with other models such as Nixon and Kissinger's "condominium," Reagan's confrontation, or McGovern's partnership, and which was intended to create sound conditions for cooperating with the USSR.[51]

Carter pushed Brzezinski to center stage to present the administration's foreign policy. Before the inauguration, on January 12, 1977, Carter met Congressional leaders at the Smithsonian Institution. It was understood that he would give an introduction and that the session would then be led by Vance; but Carter asked Brzezinski to speak at several points.[52] Carter then asked him to make summary presentations to the Cabinet, and even to his family.[53] On numerous occasions Brzezinski found himself in charge of describing the overall thrust of the administration's policy, even in Vance's presence. For example, on July 1978, while the secretary of state and Brown were participating in a discussion of foreign policy with members of Congress, Carter asked Brzezinski—who was supposed to discuss only the trip he had made to China a few weeks before—to offer a general overview of the policy. Senator Adlai Stevenson congratulated him on his performance in private but stressed that the presentation ought to have been made by the secretary of state.[54]

Vance did not seem affected by these developments, but he did complain about Brzezinski's public pronouncements. In fact, this was one of the few explicit complaints he made about Brzezinski in his book. "In spite of repeated instructions from the president, Brzezinski would attempt increasingly to take on the role of policy spokesman. At first, his public appearances, press interviews, and anonymous 'backgrounders' to journalists were simply a source of confusion. Eventually, as divergences grew wider between my public statements and his policy utterances, Brzezinski's practice became a serious impediment to the conduct of our foreign policy."[55]

This version was contradicted by Carter. He explained that, "almost without exception," Brzezinski had spoken to the press with his approval and had accurately expressed the president's political position; the real underlying objection of the State Department, he added, had to do with the very idea that he should speak publicly at all.[56] And if Carter let his national security adviser give interviews and make the rounds of televised talk shows, it was because Vance did not do so, for it was not to his liking. "Secretary Vance was not particularly inclined to assume this task on a sustained basis," Carter explained, and in his view the administration really did need a spokesperson.[57] "In practice, it turned out that Vance, for all of his many gifts and personal qualities, was not an effective communicator," Brzezinski commented, "and the President started encouraging me to speak up more."[58] It must be said that Brzezinski himself excelled on television, and that he was always ready to talk to journalists. "Encouraged by the President," Carter's chief of staff Hamilton Jordan confirmed, "the proud Pole moved quietly into the vacuum that Vance left for explaining and defending the administration's foreign policy."[59] Ultimately, Brzezinski's power and his intellectual and media-based visibility were largely products of Vance's weaknesses, as much in the articulation of the principal directions of foreign policy as in the presentation of these directions to the public at large.

Brzezinski also showed himself to be a skilled maneuverer, and this allowed him to promote his own viewpoint and often to make it prevail. To this end he used his privileged access to the president and his control over the decision-making process as well as over the "paper" flow, and he also used more classic techniques of bureaucratic in-fighting, such as strategic alliances.

Brzezinski's decisive advantage was clearly his daily interaction with the president, whom he saw every morning in order to give him his briefing on security questions and whom he saw again several times in the course of the day. His appropriation of the security briefing was moreover one of Brzezinski's early bureaucratic victories: he presented to the president a document based on information supplied by the intelligence agencies but that he himself had composed. He did not allow Admiral Stansfield Turner, head of the CIA, or even an officer of the agency, to be present. When Turner protested against the exclusion, Brzezinski simply rechristened the "Morning Intelligence Briefing" as a "National Security Briefing." At the time, the CIA was under the strict control of the NSC, and Turner ended up having limited access to Jimmy Carter.[60]

In terms of access, Brzezinski enjoyed two exorbitant privileges that created an unbalanced situation with respect to Cyrus Vance. On the one hand, he could go see the president whenever he wanted to, unconstrained by another adviser or even a secretary. He was well aware of his good fortune, keeping in mind the frustration Kissinger had expressed as he confronted the strict control over access to Nixon exercised by H. R. Haldeman (nicknamed "the Berlin Wall"), and he tried not to abuse it or to compromise it.[61] On the other hand, he was systematically present at Carter's conversations with foreign dignitaries, and with American leaders who came to discuss international affairs; Harriman was memorably frustrated on this point. Most significant, Jimmy Carter never saw Secretary of State Cyrus Vance, Secretary of Defense Harold Brown, or CIA director Stansfield Turner without Brzezinski being present. Only toward the end of the Carter years did Vance occasionally seek to see the president one-on-one, mainly to complain about Brzezinski's bad manners.[62]

This omnipresence at Carter's side, which allowed Brzezinski to remain aware of the relations between the president and his chief subordinates, was paralleled by his preeminence wherever foreign policy was discussed and in the information flows that reached the Oval Office. The National Security Act of 1947 had created the NSC as a format for deliberation, but it had not spelled out the organization of the work that surrounded it, and each administration had to adopt its own decision-making procedures (the structure has become somewhat stabilized since then). Carter entrusted the task to Brzezinski, who, having met with rejection for an overly complex scheme that involved seven different councils, reduced his proposal to two principal models, the Policy Review Committee (PRC) and the Special Coordination Committee

(SCC). Carter formally accepted the plan on the eve of his inauguration, to Vance's great displeasure, although Vance did not turn his reservations into a casus belli.[63]

Three types of formal meetings were held that led to foreign policy decisions under Carter. The NSC, in the presence of the president, and with its format fixed by law (toward the end of the administration Carter included his advisers on domestic policy along with the officially designated members), was reserved for major decisions. These included the negotiating position on SALT, the response to the invasion of Afghanistan, and the raid to free the hostages in Iran. The most important legal actions of the executive branch, the presidential directives (sixty-three in all) came out of the NSC. The two new formats Brzezinski created, the PRC and the SCC, met without the president. They brought together the secretaries of state and defense, the national security adviser, and, depending on the topic, the CIA director, the secretaries of the treasury, agriculture, and so on. The relevant secretary presided over the PRC, which dealt with general issues of foreign policy, defense, and international economic affairs, but Brzezinski headed the SCC, which dealt with sensitive issues—intelligence matters, arms control strategy (most notably SALT), and crisis management. These two formats could lead to a unanimous recommendation; if there was disagreement, a set of options was presented to the president. In all cases, the president received a summary report on the meeting. And the NSC, said Brzezinski, always had the responsibility for preparing the reports and the notes presenting the options coming out of the PRC and the SCC.

In addition to these formal meetings, there were two types of informal ones. The Friday presidential breakfast brought Carter and Vice President Mondale together with their principal subordinates (Vance, Brown, Brzezinski). This weekly event took on growing importance in the deliberations of the administration—to such an extent that Carter soon began to include his political advisers (Hamilton Jordan, Jody Powell, Lloyd Cutler, and Hedley Donovan), and Vance brought along his deputy, Warren Christopher. As for the weekly "V-B-B" lunch (often on Wednesday), a more intimate gathering, it was an opportunity for Vance, Brown, and Brzezinski to come together to work on problems that did not require formal meetings; in this more relaxed context Vance, in the absence of his subordinates, could be more flexible. Brzezinski supplied reports on these meetings to the president, for Carter was very protective of his prerogatives and did not want to let anything get past him.[64]

Overall, Brzezinski exercised an exceptional degree of control. Not only was he present at all these meetings, but he presided over the SCC, which allowed him to control a significant portion of the foreign policy agenda. "Even if he didn't carry the day," Odom commented, "he would force the people who did carry the day to have a much clearer view of what they were doing and what the implications of it were."[65] Moreover, early in the Carter years the PRC meetings, especially when Vance presided, were the most numerous. Then, with time, Brzezinski multiplied the SCC meetings and used them to influence foreign policy in various domains (the Persian Gulf, European security, SALT, and so on).[66] He was the one who controlled the reports of both groups, and these were sent to the president without prior approval by Vance or Brown to avoid leaks. Here was a potential lever of power; Vance complained about it: "I found discrepancies, occasionally serious ones, from my own recollection of what had been said, agreed, or recommended."[67]

Betty Glad, in her book about foreign policy decision making under Carter, takes up that accusation, showing for example that, in his summary to the president of an SCC meeting on the Horn of Africa, Brzezinski mentioned that there were disagreements about sending an aircraft carrier, but he did not indicate their full scope. On another occasion, he included a recommendation to look into cooperation with the Chinese in a particular context, whereas Brown had only mentioned the idea in passing.[68] Brzezinski was accused of abusing his reporting power in order to advance his political vision. Was this actually the case? There is no doubt that he was able to give a personal twist to the accounts he submitted to Carter, but the scope of this "deceit" was certainly limited. As Robert Pastor explains, "Carter insisted that the memos that went to him included the views of the State Department and other interested agencies, and in the cases in which there were differences, he would often check directly with Vance or other departmental secretaries. Therefore, Brzezinski's credibility with Carter depended in part on the fairness in which he summarized other views. Glad found no evidence that Brzezinski abused his position to mis-characterize Vance's views."[69] Secretary of Defense Brown went further: "My belief is that he always correctly reflected other people's views, gave his own, but didn't try to force a compromise."[70]

Nevertheless, when Muskie replaced Vance as secretary of state he insisted on modifying the procedure, and on having access to the PRC and SCC minutes before they were sent to Carter. Brzezinski then used another of his powers, that of accompanying any transmission to the president with a cover note. Thus, when Muskie decided to alter the minutes, Brzezinski pointed out the changes to Carter and put them in perspective, indicating, for example, that they reflected a change of viewpoint that occurred after the meeting.[71] This anecdote illustrates the extent of Brzezinski's control: with the exception of the daily evening report from Vance and later from Muskie, which went directly to the president and which Carter read early in the morning, before his national security briefing), Brzezinski covered all the communications that reached Carter with his own thoughts. By contrast, his own notes could either be passed along through the normal White House circuit, and thus be read by other advisers, or sent directly to Carter.

To complete the picture of Brzezinski's grip on foreign policy, two further assets must be mentioned. For one thing, he controlled the process for drafting presidential speeches about foreign policy matters. For example, in January 1980 he prevailed on Vance and Cutler at the last minute to insert into the State of the Union address a reference to what was to become the Carter doctrine, the "regional security framework in the Middle East."[72] For another, on behalf of the president he drafted travel instructions for the secretaries of state and defense; but when he went to China, he wrote his own instructions, getting Carter to sign them.[73]

His power to influence the foreign travels of other members of the administration provides an example of the clever political and bureaucratic maneuvering of which he was capable. Once diplomatic relations with China had been normalized, to keep from letting Sino-American exchanges fall back into a routine, he promoted numerous trips to Beijing by members of the administration— Mondale, Blumenthal, Brown, Schlesinger, Turner, and others who were all eager to travel.[74] Earlier, in order to get control of the process of normalizing relations with China, he had used another subterfuge, having his adviser Michael Oksenberg suggest discreetly to the Chinese that they should send him an invitation; that way he could appear passive and simply respond, thus disarming the suspicions of the State Department.[75]

Forming alliances is the most classic bureaucratic maneuver, and Brzezinski knew how to play on that register in order to stand up to a State Department that was stronger than he on many levels. Carter's political advisers Powell and Jordan wanted the president to take on an image of strength and determination, which meant taking a harder line against the USSR; Brzezinski could count on using these advisers against Vance.[76] As for Brown, who disappointed him initially owing to his equivocations and the fact that Brown hewed closely to Vance's line, he became an ally in the second half of Carter's presidency, insisting on the need for a stronger defense.[77] Finally, this time with respect to Carter, Brzezinski had one additional card to play: his closeness to Rosalynn Carter, who appreciated him and whose positions were often more hawkish than her husband's.[78] This confirms the verdict issued both by Albright and by Brzezinski, despite the many criticisms that assailed him in late 1980. If Carter had been reelected, he would have invited Brzezinski to stay on and work with him, and if Muskie had protested, the matter would have been resolved in Brzezinski's favor.[79] Brzezinski won most of his battles on fundamental issues, given the clear hardening of the political line under Carter during the last year of his presidency. These observations thus constitute an interesting final testimony to Brzezinski's bureaucratic skills.

At the outset, the Carter administration was not confronted by any immediate dangers or major crises on the international level. Thus Carter's team could begin to implement the program prepared in advance. Over time, however, the administration had to react to an insidious type of challenge: the gradual return of the East-West confrontation. At the time Jimmy Carter took the oath of office, détente had been challenged, but it remained the dominant paradigm. When he left power, the new Cold War had begun. This uneasy context of transition constituted the background for Brzezinski's actions.[80] The new Cold War grew out of a vicious circle that involved four actors: a worried public; Congress, which accentuated the fears by responding strongly to that anxiety; the administration, which then had to make a show of strength; and finally the Soviets, who reacted negatively, thereby increasing public anxiety, and so on. The origin of this spiral, which led to the new era of tension in the early 1980s, lay in Soviet initiatives.

However much Team B may have exaggerated, the Soviets did in fact increase their strategic arsenal during the fifteen years that followed the Cuban crisis; they did so in a sustained way that was even more disturbing in that the CIA had underestimated their efforts.[81] Even if the increase in the Soviet nuclear arsenal were more quantitative than qualitative, it was a legitimate subject of concern. The historian Samuel Wells, a contemporary without hawkish inclinations, wrote in 1978 that one could indeed wonder about the Soviets' strategy and intentions in this area, especially their attitude toward dissuasion, given the proportion of national revenue, revised upward by analysts, that the USSR was devoting to military expenses, but also given their defensive projects (radar, hardening of silos, counterforce targeting, civil defense planning, and so on).[82]

However, the image that was troubling to the public, more than that of Soviet missiles, was that of the Soviet Union advancing its pawns on the worldwide geopolitical chessboard, while the United States seemed to be pulling back. During the Yom Kippur War in 1973, the Soviet Union, which had supplied arms to the Arab states, threatened to intervene directly to defend Egypt, and the United States put its strategic forces on alert to counterbalance that pressure. The oil embargo that followed the war demonstrated the West's dependency and plunged it into an economic crisis. In April 1975, South Vietnam and Cambodia fell to the communists, and the Soviets, privileged allies of Hanoi, did nothing to moderate their Vietnamese comrades. The image of the helicopter flying off the roof of the American embassy symbolized that ultimate humiliation. In early 1979, the Shah of Iran, a traditional ally of the United States in the region, was overthrown by a revolution soon dominated by the Islamist component, though many Americans suspected it had been secretly manipulated by Moscow. Such suspicions were reinforced by the fact that the USSR had been intervening frequently in neighboring Afghanistan, starting in 1978; it invaded that country in late December 1979.

On the African continent, in Angola, the communist party in power, the People's Movement for the Liberation of Angola (MPLA, requested Moscow's help in 1975 to push back an offensive by Jonas Savimbi's National Front for the Liberation of Angola (FNLA) and by the National Union for the Total Independence of Angola (UNITA), supported by South Africa; the Soviets referred the MPLA to Fidel Castro. Within a few months, tens of thousands of Cuban soldiers intervened in Angola, with Soviet logistical support. In May 1977, Lt. Colonel Mengistu's Ethiopia, until then an American ally, signed a treaty of military assistance with the Soviet Union. Cuban troops soon came in to train the Ethiopian forces in their confrontation with Somalia, at the Soviets' request. This created a great deal of tension within the Carter administration between Brzezinski, who wanted to react, and Vance, who minimized the matter. The Soviets were scoring points elsewhere in Africa as well: in Rhodesia, in the Maghreb (where Colonel Gaddafi's Libya was stirring up trouble with Egypt, Sudan, and Chad), and even beyond, on the Arabian Peninsula (where the Soviets supported South Yemen against the North). The situation in America's own backyard, Central America, was no better; the influence of the Cuban revolution was making itself felt, and in 1979 Grenada and—even more significantly—Nicaragua fell into the hands of Marxist forces. The risk of contagion, especially in El Salvador and Guatemala, was growing.

The Soviets reminded the Americans that the USSR had also undergone a number of reversals in the 1970s. It had lost Egypt, Sudan, Somalia, Guinea, Zaire, and Chile. It had also had to face the hostility of China, its rival in the communist camp and in the Third World, and that country's increasingly close alliance with the United States, even on the strategic level.[83] However, these arguments did nothing to lessen the impression produced among Americans that the USSR was expanding in a way that was creating an increasingly unfavorable balance of power. The rising anxiety led to a complex debate. Those who warned against the Soviet peril too quickly were accused of crying wolf and making self-fulfilling prophecies (since they urged Washington to respond strongly, and this in turn would provoke the Soviets), but they found their position gradually justified by the facts. Those who appealed to reason, kept cool heads, and minimized the Soviet threat were overtaken by events, little by little, in part because of the action-reaction interplay between the Soviet hawks and their American counterparts.

No wonder, then, that the problem for the White House, at this transitional moment, was as much domestic as international. American public opinion shifted during the second half of the 1970s from a desire for peace (embodied in support for détente) and a rejection of interventionism (the Vietnam syndrome) to a desire for nationalist self-assertion and renewal of American power. The latter phenomenon was accentuated by the 1979 energy crisis that led to long lines at gas stations and to a pronounced general discontent. The new themes that had appeared in the first half of the 1970s—interdependence, development, raw materials, the environment—gave way to a return of traditional political and military themes, and to a desire for a strong reaction to the international challenges.

This shift in public opinion was reflected and even heightened in Congress, where several members took alarmist positions. On August 30, 1979, for example, Democratic senator Frank Church, who knew that his image as a dove threatened to cost him reelection the following year, called a press conference on the notorious "Soviet brigade in Cuba," which had in fact been present on the island for a long time. Church called emphatically for an immediate withdrawal, counting on rebalancing his image with an electorate that had become more hawkish. But in the end, while the issue was fading away on its own, the ratification of the SALT II treaty was delayed and became more difficult, given the climate of greater hostility toward the USSR. (As for Church, he was defeated by a Republican in 1980.)[84]

This climate partly explains the difficult relations between the Carter administration and Congress. The president expended a good deal of political capital in order to get the Panama Canal treaties ratified in 1978, then to win acceptance of normalized relations with China the following year. At the same time, he was not very diplomatic with Congress, judging that the intrinsic merit of his own initiatives ought to suffice to convince its members, and he spent little time cultivating relationships with them (the same thing was true of Brzezinski, at least until he took on Madeleine Albright as a liaison in March 1978).[85] Once the hawkish shift in public opinion is added, it becomes clear why the Senate was not inclined to ratify the SALT II treaty, which was submitted to it in mid-1979. The hostage crisis in Iran, which added to the prevailing disquiet, and especially the invasion of Afghanistan, definitively sealed the fate of the treaty, which had little chance of ratification in the fall of 1979.

In the vicious circle of Soviet actions and public or Congressional perceptions, the next link was the attitude of the Carter administration, which found itself forced to react and show signs of firmness if it wanted to preserve its popularity and its chances of putting through treaties like SALT II. This constraint, expressed more and more clearly by the president's political advisers (Jody Powell and Hamilton Jordan in particular), obviously favored Brzezinski's position over that of Cyrus Vance. As Brzezinski recalled the situation: "I felt increasingly vindicated by events and encouraged by the growing national consensus in favor of a firmer handling of the Soviet challenge."[86]

However, the administration faced two problems. On the one hand, it was suffering from a deterioration in the means of American power, after the Vietnam War and especially the reaction that followed. Its military resources had stagnated, as it was painfully reminded by the poor performance of the helicopters during the hostage rescue mission in Iran. Following repeated budget cuts in the 1970s, its intelligence services were also in a poor state, as illustrated by the fiasco of the Soviet brigade in Cuba, whose existence was "discovered" by the CIA only in 1979 whereas it had been present on the island since 1962. The administration's diplomatic resources were not much better, as they too had sustained budget cuts, and the quality of political information about Iran, or Poland, was poor—a serious handicap for Carter and Brzezinski.[87] Overall, the Carter administration did not manage to project an image of resolution and strength; it did not succeed in holding to the "Brzezinski line." Until the Soviet invasion of Afghanistan, President Carter remained torn between his humanist convictions, his desire for peace, his wish to pursue détente, and the need to react more firmly to the Soviet challenge—if only to satisfy public opinion and Congress. This resulted in decisions made in fits and starts that did not satisfy the hawks but irritated the USSR. During the SALT negotiations, for example, the administration failed to gain the support of Paul Nitze and the Committee on the Present Danger by insisting on the right to deploy missiles in an unpredictable fashion (a "shell game" known as the Multiple Aim Points system), which provoked a crisis in the negotiations.[88]

For this game of upping the ante between public opinion, Congress, and the administration influenced perceptions on the Soviet side and made détente ever more fragile, provoking hostile reactions, which in turn fed American paranoia. On December 12, 1979, when Moscow made the decision to invade Afghanistan, the Soviet leaders did not seem to grasp the extent to which détente was threatened. Unless, on the contrary, they had concluded that the fruits of détente had become so meager (the chances of ratifying SALT II were virtually nil at that point) that it was no longer worth worrying about Western reactions.

This spiral in the new Cold War resulted in a split within the Democratic Party between a wing favorable to détente and a neoconservative wing, which soon defected to join the opposing camp (Ronald Reagan) in 1980. "Carter 1976" had been given the benefit of the doubt and was able to bring his party together by transcending the divisions between liberals and traditional Democrats, in a promising post-Watergate context. "Carter 1980" was no longer able to bridge that gap, losing the liberals to Ted Kennedy during the primaries and losing the centrists (for example, the Catholic vote) to Reagan in the general election. All this was taking place in the context of international crises (the hostages in Tehran, the Soviet occupation of Afghanistan), an energy crisis, and an economic crisis (inflation reached 13.5% in 1980, and a recession took hold in the spring).

Because of his image as a hawk, Brzezinski was an asset vis-à-vis centrist Democrats and Republicans worried about Reagan's extremism.[89] Conversely, he was a handicap during the Democratic primaries, when Ted Kennedy challenged Carter by turning to the liberal wing, to such an extent that Jody Powell suggested that Brzezinski should stay off television screens for a few weeks.[90] During his brief appearance at the Democratic National Convention in New York in August 1980, where the candidacy of the incumbent president was confirmed, Brzezinski was booed by numerous delegates.[91]

An Academic in Charge: Brzezinski's Impact on the Major Issues Facing the Carter Administration

Brzezinski's international opinions in 1976, on the eve of his move to the White House, are well known, as he had developed them in his writings and through his actions, especially from 1968 on (the texts "Peace and Power" and *Between Two Ages,* his critiques of détente as practiced by Kissinger, the Trilateral Commission, and so on).[92] Brzezinski also wrote an unpublished manuscript (although an abridged version of one of its chapters appeared in *Foreign Affairs*), titled "America in a New World."[93] Brzezinski wrote this political essay between the spring of 1975 and the summer of 1976, with the goal of recording his ideas and giving himself a guiding program if he were to be appointed to an executive position, or else as a way of participating in the debate over international affairs if he were to remain in the opposition.[94]

"America in a New World" continued the reflections put forth in *Between Two Ages.* In it Brzezinski focused on global social dynamics, especially in the Third World, and combined them with geopolitical considerations, and ended with recommendations for American foreign policy: the United States should maintain its firmness toward the USSR but should also open up to new themes, be alert to planet-wide changes. The technetronic revolution was not forgotten, but the motor of history was presented somewhat differently. In Brzezinski's eyes, the increase in literacy, the spread of technology, and the rapid population growth in certain regions were driving what he called "global populism," aspirations to political participation and social progress reflected in the demands of the developing countries at the United Nations. In that context, America, whose central message was that of freedom and pluralism rather than equality and the role of the state (which were the dominant tendencies among

294 ZBIGNIEW BRZEZINSKI

democracies such as Japan or France), risked experiencing hostility and isolation (the book's title was intended to stress the fact that America itself was no longer the "new world"). This would be the case if the United States did not build a cooperative framework that went beyond the Atlantic region and made it possible to respond to the new challenges to the world order.

According to Brzezinski, the United States was located at the intersection of three triangles, constituting the summit in each case: a West-West triangle (the trilateral), a North-South triangle (with the Third World and the Fourth World, the latter term designating the least advanced countries), and an East-West triangle (with the USSR and China). The United States thus had to have three priorities. First, it had to shape more cooperative relations among the democracies of Europe and Japan, a condition sine qua non for strengthening their power and for a good response to the other two priorities. Second, it had to increase North-South cooperation and encouraging development, seeking especially to separate the radical nations from the moderate ones. Finally, it had to find an accommodation with the Eastern bloc. "East-West accommodation should be a major purpose of American policy, for the East-West conflict bears directly on the problem of human survival. The ideological as well as political conflict between the West and the Soviet Union will go on but one should strive gradually to moderate it. To achieve that moderation both vigilance as well as cooperation will be necessary. Consequently, the maintenance of a strong American military deterrent is a necessary precondition for a stable, increasingly comprehensive as well as reciprocal détente."[95]

The manuscript was accepted for publication by Basic Books in May 1976.[96] Yet the book was never published, because Carter feared that it would be seen as the "bible" of his administration.[97] But the ideas it contained were distilled not only in documents prepared for Carter's presidential campaign but also in documents and speeches during the Carter administration, so that in the end it did constitute a reference work—at least for Brzezinski himself. When he arrived at the White House Brzezinski proposed to send Carter an overall strategic plan, in the form of a forty-three-page briefing book that contained ten general goals, with specific sub-goals and proposed dates for their realization, all this placed under the heading of "constructive global engagement."[98] These goals, which represent Brzezinski's inspiration but also Carter's aspirations (in point 8, for example), were the following:

1. Create more active and more solid cooperation with Europe and Japan.

2. Increase the density of the network of alliances and economic relations with the new regional poles (Venezuela, Brazil, Nigeria, Saudi Arabia, Iran, India, Indonesia) so as to complement the reliance on the transatlantic community.

3. Develop calmer North-South relations (settle the question of the Panama Canal, in particular) and encourage economic development.

4. Push SALT along (a treaty to be concluded and then ratified in early 1978) toward SART (Strategic Arms Reduction Talks), that is, toward a logic of reduction and not just limitation; seek a second treaty around 1980).[99]

5. Normalize Sino-American relations.

6. Achieve an overall solution to the Israeli-Palestinian problem, to avoid a radicalization of the Arab world and a return to the Middle East by the USSR.

7. Work toward a gradual, peaceful transition in South Africa to a biracial democracy, while favoring a coalition of moderate African leaders in order to avoid Cuban and Soviet involvement; do the same thing in Zimbabwe.

8. Limit the worldwide level of armaments, unilaterally and through international agreements. Reduce American arms sales. Encourage non-proliferation agreements.

9. Increase the importance and attention given to human rights, by underlining the respect for these rights in the United States and through initiatives designed to incite other nations to give them priority.

10. Maintain a defense posture designed to dissuade the Soviet Union from committing hostile acts.[100]

This list, with its overlapping themes, did not constitute an integrated policy or strategy, but Brzezinski, responding to those who criticized its lack of coherence, insisted that it entailed a priority order established at the outset (normalizing relations with China, for example, was seen as an objective to be accomplished during the first two years). In fact, the first year of Carter's presidency was devoted to the four issues deemed the most pressing.

Cyrus Vance was sent on a mission to the Middle East in February, while regional leaders were received by Carter between March and May. But the initial enthusiasm quickly turned into pessimism. The severity of the Israeli-Arab blockage was such that the idea of a major conference in Geneva was dropped, especially after Menachem Begin's new rightist party, the Likud, won the May 1977 elections, and after Carter's mention in March of a "Palestinian homeland," along with the joint memorandum with the USSR issued on October 1, 1977, had aroused strong domestic opposition. Thus the administration preferred to exploit the path offered by Anwar Sadat's surprise visit to Jerusalem in November. The idea of seeking an overall solution was abandoned in favor of a separate peace between Israel and Egypt, which could later be exploited to solve the other problems in the region.

The second priority in 1977 was to conclude the difficult negotiation over transferring control of the Panama Canal. This took place on August 10, opening an even more difficult second phase; Senate ratification was not achieved until March 18, 1978, in a close call. This may look like a secondary point, but it was crucial for US relations with Latin America and the Third World in general; if it had not been resolved, it would have remained a dangerous open wound in the 1980s. The third priority was clearly the SALT negotiation. The two proposals worked out by the new administration were flatly refused by Moscow on March 30, 1977, which led to internal tensions. The talks were relaunched when Carter and the Soviet leader Andrei Gromyko met on September 23, 1977, and pursued when Vance and Gromyko met in Moscow the following spring. Considerable progress was made, but the domestic political atmosphere was deteriorating, so that ratification seemed more and more difficult as the negotiations dragged on through 1978 and 1979. The fourth priority was the new stress on human rights, through Carter's now-famous speech at Notre Dame on May 22, 1977, and then its concrete translation in a presidential directive, PD-30, in February 1978.[101]

The year 1978 was marked both by the difficult quest for some success in the Near East, finally made concrete by the Camp David Accords (September 27, 1978), and by the intensification of the Vance-Brzezinski debates over relations with the USSR in general. The differences were particularly pronounced in early 1978 concerning the Horn of Africa, where Brzezinski's hard-line lost out. But this reversal led him to press tirelessly for normalizing the relationship with China, where Carter ended up sending him as an emissary (May 21–23)—a trip followed by a negotiation that led to the normalization announced on December 15, 1978. Deng's January 1979 trip to Washington, followed by an awkward moment of flux during the Chinese intervention against Vietnam in February, was prolonged by an intensification of the relationship in late 1979 and in 1980. The other significant developments in 1978 were commercial sanctions against the USSR in the area of advanced technology, adopted in order to protest against the trials of dissidents, and strategic tension over the European theater. Transatlantic relations, dominated by the issue of the Soviet ss20 missiles, suffered owing to Carter's hesitations and ultimately owing to the decision not to develop a neutron bomb (April 7, 1978). But a consensus gradually emerged within NATO over the upgrading of conventional forces, the increase in defense budgets, and, finally, the deployment of Pershing II missiles and cruise missiles coupled with an offer to negotiate at the NATO summit to be held on December 12, 1979.

In early 1979, President Carter invested heavily in following up on the Camp David Accords, managing after much effort to get the Egypt-Israel peace treaty signed on March 26, 1979, in Washington. Shortly afterward, the SALT accord was finally concluded; it was signed on June 18, 1979, in Vienna. It had been preceded by various shows of strength (an exchange of prisoners for Soviet dissidents, the decision to build the MX strategic missile). It was then followed by an intense, difficult campaign in favor of ratification, marked by the fiasco of the Soviet brigade in Cuba in September 1979 and abandoned following the Soviet invasion of Afghanistan on December 25, 1979.

The last months of 1978 and all of 1979 were marked by gradual deterioration of the situation in Iran, one of the pillars of the United States in the Middle East. At first the administration hesitated to follow Brzezinski's recommendation to act decisively, with a military coup d'état if necessary, but it was too late. The shah left the country on January 16, 1979, without having chosen to reassert his power by force. The shah's peregrinations, in the months that followed, became a thorny problem for the administration, which hesitated to receive him in the United States. Before long, the Iranian military no longer had the resources or the will to act: the revolutionary situation pushed the most radical elements into the foreground, and the American embassy was seized by Ayatollah Khomeini's militants on November 4, 1979; fifty-two American diplomats were taken hostage.

At the start of 1980, the situation was critical on both the Iranian and the Afghan fronts. The Carter administration adopted a considerably harder line, following Brzezinski's recommendations in this respect: the Carter doctrine on the Middle East, spelled out on January 23, was followed by concrete decisions (Rapid Deployment Force, designation of logistical support points, and so on), an embargo on grains, a boycott of the Olympic Games in Moscow, a reinforcement of ties with Pakistan and Saudi Arabia, transfer of advanced technology to China, a pronounced increase in the defense budget, an air raid in an attempt to free the hostages in Tehran (on April 24, a failure from the start), a new more flexible and more offensive doctrine of nuclear dissuasion (PD-59), and so on. Unfortunately, this new firmness did not pay off. Public opinion was not convinced; Carter was still seen as soft and hesitant, and his not-very-effective retaliatory measures against the Soviet Union provoked discontent in various quarters, contributing to the electoral failure on November 4. The hostages in Iran were not freed until after Carter left office (January 20, 1981). Only in Poland did the Carter administration, aware of Moscow's plans to invade, take measures to make the costs prohibitive by warning the leaders of the Solidarity union movement of the imminent risk and thus perhaps helping to avoid it (December 5–8, 1980).

The most important issue was that of US relations with the USSR. Brzezinski prompted Carter, especially from the second year of his mandate on, to adopt a firmer position toward Moscow. The critical episodes were the SALT II negotiations, the debate over the Horn of Africa, the fight for ratification of SALT II, and finally, in 1980, the vigorous responses to the invasion of Afghanistan and to the threat of an invasion of Poland—responses that prefigured Reagan's foreign policy. Here, it is important to mention two significant aspects of Brzezinski's action: his role as "guardian" of the US-USSR balance of power, and his support for actions intended to harass and destabilize the Soviet bloc. "Vienna in 1959 writ large," it could be called, with reference to the role Brzezinski played in the subversive infiltration of the World Youth Festival (for more on this, see Chapter 1).

The attack on détente, especially by right-wing conservatives and neo-conservatives from the Democratic Party, did not arise solely from a differing interpretation of Soviet intentions. It was also based on the idea that America had become, in Ronald Reagan's words, "Number 2" behind the Soviet Union;

this attack helped trigger the Team B episode.[102] To make sure the administration was on the right track and that its strategic policy would be on a solid footing, Brzezinski, in agreement with the other decision-makers, proposed to Carter that they undertake a large-scale study of the Soviet-American balance of power. Samuel Huntington, named coordinator of White House Security Planning, was assigned to head an exercise involving all the relevant agencies and twelve task forces, 175 people in all; the result was a document known as PRM-10 (*Presidential Review Memorandum* 10, "Comprehensive Net Assessment and Military Force Posture Review").[103] The angle of approach was not military but rather global. As explained by William Odom, who was Huntington's chief deputy on the project, it was a matter of comparing the two countries in all categories of power (economy, propaganda, alliances, and so forth); the model was more Nitze's NSC-68 from 1950 than Nixon-Kissinger's NSSM3, which was limited to military issues.[104] For example, as Huntington explained, "we analyzed what could be called the diplomatic balance and constructed a numerical way of analyzing the diplomatic balance which I thought would appeal to the president since he was an engineer (and we obviously did very well there)."[105] The PRM-10 exercise was completed by June 1977, and the executive summary alone ran to four hundred pages.

The conclusion was clear: America was dominant everywhere except in the military realm, where there were disturbing developments, which called for corrective measures, especially in the area of conventional weapons. Among the discoveries made in the PRM-10, two in particular deserve mention, because they soon became Brzezinski's key themes. First, Huntington developed the concept of "economic diplomacy," which consisted in using American technological and commercial advances for political purposes. After lengthy efforts to overcome strong bureaucratic resistance, which did not succeed until 1980, the NSC and Odom in particular placed advanced technologies for oil extraction—over which the United States had a quasi-monopoly—under a regime of export licensing, so that they could be used as currency in political exchanges with the USSR.[106] Huntington's second discovery was that the Persian Gulf and Iran in particular were identified as the most probable sites of coming geopolitical crises, and the projection capability of the American forces in the region had to be increased.[107] In January 1980, this proclamation became known as the Carter doctrine, materialized by the Rapid Deployment Force in the region.

What is interesting in this exercise conducted by the NSC is not only Huntington's application of the methodology of political science, but the fact that Brzezinski had largely anticipated this scenario in "America in a New World." In that text he offered a summary chart of the US-USSR balance of power (see Table 6.2), and he concluded by judging that "the only area where the Soviets are truly competitive with the US and where the trends could become ominous is in military power."[108] Although there was no direct relationship between the manuscript and the PRM-10 exercise, since the idea was not necessarily original and since the conclusions reached in the PRM-10 reflected a group effort, Brzezinski's views may well have contributed to them nonetheless.

The PRM-10 led organically to the presidential directive PD-18 of August 24, 1977. It established the goal of maintaining a military posture "of essential equivalence" between the conventional and strategic forces of the two superpowers; it reaffirmed the strategy concerning NATO (a "first line of defense" in Europe) and the maintenance of mobile deployment units for urgent situations, especially in the Persian Gulf and in Korea. Although the PRM-10 and PD-18 processes revealed the divisions between doves and hawks within the administration, they ended up strengthening Brzezinski's hand.[109] In December 1978, Brzezinski sent Carter a partial update of the PRM-10, the result of a more modest exercise that was limited to the NSC alone and that ultimately reinforced the conclusion of June 1977: "The trends in almost all non-military components of national power (except technology and covert action) now favor the U.S. The trends in the military components of national power, on the other hand, all favor the Soviet Union, except for a mixed trend in the NATO—Warsaw Pact military balance."[110] "Essential equivalence" was at issue, and it was imperative to react. In short, the approach and the conclusion are once again typical of Brzezinski: an expansive vision of the balance of power, overall optimism, but insistence on the need to reinforce American military power.

It comes as no surprise to see Brzezinski, once in the White House, go to work reinforcing the other two of the three Cold War pillars: the role of nationalism and the divisions within the communist bloc, and the role of ideology. In addition to military power, he attempted to launch a propaganda program destined for the various nationalities in the USSR, and he defended the actions of Radio Free Europe-Radio Liberty (RFE-RL). Thus at his instigation, on March 22, 1977, Carter submitted to Congress a "Report on International Broadcasting" in which he recommended the acquisition of more powerful transmitters to counter the interference introduced by the Soviets and Eastern

Table 6.2. The US-USSR Balance of Power:
Nonmilitary Aspects of American and Soviet Systems Compared

I. INTERNAL

Economic power:	1974 US GNP: $1,225 billion. Soviet GNP: $723 billion. US lead in key areas of frontier technology; US lead in food production and Soviet dependence on US exports.
Social infrastructure:	Communications: massive US lead in autos, trucks, highways, telephones. Social amenities: massive US lead in housing, per capita income, distribution of consumer goods. Social welfare: Soviet services more extensive but quality uneven; rough equivalence.
Social cohesion:	Soviet Union a multi-national society dominated by the Great Russians but with increasing political restlessness among the non-Russians who number approximately 50% of the population.
Political structure:	US leadership renovated regularly by infusion of new blood; Soviet leadership bureaucratically gerontocratic: average age of the Politburo is 67; average age of the Presidium of the Council of Ministers is 67.

II. EXTERNAL	*The Soviet World System*		*The American World System*	
direct control (ideological— political— economic ties)	5 East European states Mongolia	alliance ties	NATO Japan Australia	
dependent allies (ideological— political— economic ties)	Cuba Vietnam North Korea (?) Rumania (?)	dependent allies	Israel South Korea Taiwan	
collaborative states (political— economic ties)	India Afghanistan Finland (?) Libya	collaborative states (political— economic ties)	Brazil Iran Indonesia Saudi Arabia	
sympathizer states (ideological— political ties)	Algeria Angola Syria Yemen, People's Republic Guinea Bissau Mozambique Guinea Congo, People's Republic Somalia	sympathizer states (ideological or political ties)	Egypt Indonesia Malaysia Mexico Morocco Philippines Singapore Spain Switzerland China (?)	
		controlled states (political— economic ties)	Haiti Dominican Republic Central America (?)	

Source: Excerpted from Zbigniew Brzezinski, "America in a New World."

Europeans (sixteen new 250-kilowatt stations, five for the Voice of America and eleven for RFE-RL).[111] On several occasions, Brzezinski intervened to defend the radio broadcasts—for example, against the Stanton report, which had been ordered by Kissinger and which recommended that the Voice of America and RFE-RL be fused—and he tried to get their budgets increased.[112]

Starting in March 1977 he also sought to mobilize the administration to stir up trouble behind the Iron Curtain. He convoked a meeting of the SCC on May 10, 1977, to discuss support for dissidents, and another on June 20, 1978, to discuss nationalities (in particular Ukrainians and Muslims in the Soviet Union), but he was discovering America's timidity: neither the Soviet Union nor even Eastern Europe were primary fields of action for the clandestine operations of the CIA. Undaunted, Brzezinski pressed as hard as he could, but Robert Gates later reported that the strength of the inertia of the State Department and part of the CIA, which were opposed to such actions, got the better of Brzezinski's schemes—and even of Reagan's, in the 1980s. At the very most, Brzezinski's efforts led to a program for disseminating dissident literature and information (*samizdat*), but they produced nothing concrete in the direction of the nationalities, even though, as Gates noted, these would not need much encouragement when the Berlin Wall fell.[113]

Brzezinski also pressed for a shift in policy toward Eastern Europe to encourage the centripetal forces. The option that emerged from the April 1977 PRM-9 exercise consisted in increasing bilateral relations with all the countries of Eastern Europe, but with special attention to those that were most liberal on the domestic front (Poland, Hungary) or most independent of Moscow on the external front (Rumania)—this was presidential directive PD-21 of September 13, 1977. Moreover, Carter began his first major trip (aside from the trip to the G7 meeting in May 1977) with a visit to Poland in late December 1977. Brzezinski took the opportunity to pay a visit, accompanied by Rosalynn Carter, to Cardinal Wyszynski, the symbol of Polish resistance to Stalinism, while the president, on the recommendation of his national security adviser, laid a wreath on the memorial to the 1943 Warsaw Uprising (the Home Army), thus sending a signal of recognition to the Polish quest for independence.[114]

As soon as he arrived at the White House, Brzezinski prompted Carter to make direct contact with Leonid Brezhnev, and he supported the proposals regarding SALT II that Vance was to present to Moscow on March 30, for these undertakings were compatible with his vision of détente. His agreement with Vance did not stem from some dissimulation or calculation (Brzezinski as a "closet hawk"), but from an objective alliance based on an underlying disagreement.[115] Whereas Vance saw the SALT Accord as the heart of the Soviet-American relationship, designed to spur more cooperation, Brzezinski saw it as a useful way to curb the arms race on the Soviet side, but he did not consider it centrally important.[116] He especially encouraged Carter in his human rights policy, for example by prompting him to reply to the letter of congratulations from the dissident Andrei Sakharov, which enraged the Soviets, and which Brezhnev mentioned in his second, scathing letter of response to Carter.[117] Thus, unlike his colleagues, Brzezinski was not worried or bothered by the Soviet rejection of the American proposals on March 30, 1977. On the contrary, that evening he noted the following in his diary: "If the American public stands fast and we do not get clobbered with the SALT issue, I think we can really put a lot of pressure on the Soviets. We have developed an approach which is very forthcoming; on the one hand, we are urging reductions, with the other hand we are urging a freeze, and at the same time we are urging more recognition for human rights. All of that gives us a very appealing position, and I can well imagine that the Soviets feel in many respects hemmed in."[118]

During the months that followed, the administration had to soften its line, by toning down the issue of human rights, and by bringing the dovish expert Marshall Shulman into the State Department, and Brzezinski encouraged the resumption of negotiations. He also pressed his vision of a reciprocal and global détente by soliciting Soviet cooperation on other topics: the demilitarization of the Indian Ocean, the limitation on conventional arms sales to the Third World, the resumption of Mutual and Balanced Force Reductions (MBFR) negotiations in Vienna (on conventional forces), and of the Comprehensive Nuclear-Test-Ban Treaty (CTBT), a treaty prohibiting nuclear tests, to fight proliferation, and finally cooperation on the Middle East.[119] On this last issue, the Soviets responded favorably, and the high point of the warming of relations with Moscow was the joint memorandum with the USSR dated October 1, 1977, on settling the Israel-Palestine conflict. But the latter was so strongly criticized domestically that Washington had to beat a retreat, infuriating Moscow, and Sadat's initiative in November definitively excluded the Soviets. In short, during 1977, the administration's missteps and Carter's insistence on human rights (which provoked an angrier backlash than anticipated) led to a politics of détente entirely compatible with Brzezinski's vision.

This was no longer the case in 1978: Brzezinski thought that America had to react more decisively to the injection of Soviet and Cuban forces into the Horn of Africa, for that action represented a violation of the code of détente similar to the violation Kissinger had accepted, wrongly, in Angola. During the summer of 1977, the old territorial disputes in East Africa were complicated by a reversal of alliances. The Ethiopians, who had been allies of the United States up to that point, turned to Moscow for help in their struggle against the pro-Soviet Somalis who were trying to conquer the Ogaden (the eastern portion of Ethiopia) and, in reaction, the Somalis ended up turning to Washington. Several thousand Cuban soldiers were deployed in Ethiopia (as many as 15,000 in all); the Soviet Union provided them with weapons and military advisers. Bill Odom noted that the rapid supply of tanks and fighter-bombers shipped by plane or boat showed how much the USSR had progressed in its projections capability.[120] This situation worried allies such as France as well as those in the region (Egypt, Sudan, Saudi Arabia, and especially Iran), and, before long, American public opinion, which Brzezinski helped to alert via press briefings.[121]

Encouraged by the president, Brzezinski pressed for a more direct reaction, explaining that he was concerned about the implications that failing to react would have on foreign perceptions of America and about the effects those perceptions would have in turn on internal politics, especially regarding the ratification of a future SALT agreement. But on February 10, 1978, Harold Brown and Cyrus Vance rejected Brzezinski's suggestion that an aircraft carrier be deployed near the Horn of Africa to mark America's determination. Brown stressed that the deployment would just be a bluff without consequences, and it would reveal American weakness if Ethiopia invaded Somalia in reprisal. Vance refused to see the United States swept up in a local struggle (alongside the aggressors, to make things worse) that lacked any real strategic significance. Finally, the president took their side, which led Brzezinski to ruminate on his defeat and blame it on "the Vietnam bug."[122] Following this confrontation, a debate over "linkage" exacerbated the growing tension between Vance and Brzezinski. The latter, during a press conference on March 1, noted the existence of linkage: if Congress became worried about the Soviet attitude in the Horn of Africa, it would be less inclined to ratify SALT. The president repeated this the next day and the press transformed it into a policy statement (no concessions on SALT if support for Ethiopia continued), whereas Vance vehemently denied that this was the American policy.[123]

Since convincing Carter was the ultimate stake, late 1977 and early 1978 marked the moment when, in his communications with the president, Brzezinski grew increasingly insistent on the need to adopt a position of strength vis-à-vis the USSR. In his second annual performance report, in January 1978, he listed, in the negative column: "seeming softness in our policy regarding Soviet assertiveness."[124] The following month he told Carter that a president had to know how to make himself feared as well as loved.[125] On April 7, 1978, he stressed once again that détente had to be "reciprocal" and "global." To that end, it was necessary to adopt a harder line, give Vance instructions to negotiate SALT more forcefully, encourage the Yugoslavs and the Algerians (who were challenging Cuba's nonalignment, given Havana's involvement in Africa alongside the Soviets), accelerate the MX-Trident missile program in the budget discussions, reinforce the "technology package" that Brzezinski was going to offer the Chinese during his visit there the following month, and so on.[126] At the very least, he pleaded a week later, it was necessary to make one or two "hard" decisions in order to be certain that SALT would retain a chance to be ratified, given Carter's decision to cancel the construction of a neutron bomb the previous week, a decision that had projected an image of weakness.[127]

But Carter, while he gradually hardened his position, did not shift wholly to Brzezinski's side, and the latter saw his defeats during the first half of 1978 (over the Horn of Africa and the neutron bomb) as the historic turning point toward a new Cold War. In 1980, after the Soviet invasion of Afghanistan, he wondered whether a stronger American reaction on the Ethiopian question in 1978 might have led the Soviets to adopt more restraint in the aftermath, or even to refrain from going into Afghanistan. Such action would have prevented the increased hostility on the part of the public and of Congress, and would have permitted the ratification of SALT II and the preservation of détente. This is what was meant by his statement that "SALT lies buried in the sands of the Ogaden."[128] Some observers produced the opposite analysis: if the public had not been needlessly worked up by Brzezinski over the question of the Horn, the climate would not have deteriorated so badly. And the president would not have felt obliged to play the Chinese card by sending Brzezinski to Beijing in May 1978 to send a message of firmness and to counterbalance the USSR. This move considerably annoyed the Soviets—all the more so in that it led to a normalization of relations at the end of the year, and in that Brzezinski, during his trip to Beijing and in a televised interview upon his return, piled on anti-Soviet provocations. The situation that had developed around the Horn of Africa was at the heart of the debates over the new Cold War, in which Brzezinski was a committed participant.

The year 1979 was marked by the signing of the SALT II treaty in June, immediately followed by a campaign in favor of its ratification. Brzezinski supported the effort as much as he could. Because the treaty imposed limits on the growth of the Soviet arsenal, he believed that it was in America's interest, all the more so because, following the firm position taken by Harold Brown, Stansfield Turner, and Brzezinski himself, Washington had obtained the assurances it had sought from Moscow on the level of production of the new Soviet Backfire bomber and on the limits on data encryption during tests. Moreover, the national security adviser, owing to his reputation as a hawk, became the principal "briefer" for the Senate (the one who presented the details of the agreement) in support of the administration's efforts.[129] Brzezinski thought that things were looking good at the end of the summer with the main opponents, such as Henry Kissinger, concentrating their arguments on the need to mount a bigger defense effort and not on the treaty itself. Yet the climate changed with the revelation of the Soviet brigade in Cuba; that incident led to a month-long suspension of the debates.

This matter was the source of new tension between Brzezinski and Vance. The latter took a relatively hard-line (evoking a "combat" brigade and asserting that he would not be satisfied with the status quo). Brzezinski compared the situation to the Berlin crisis in order to stave off the more dangerous analogy with the missile crisis. He took advantage of the occasion to prompt the president to take additional strong measures (military cooperation with China, increase in the defense budget, and so on) rather than concentrating on Cuba, where any accommodation by the Soviets was impossible, since they had not created the problem.[130] Although he had Brown's support, he failed to prevent the summoning of a group of Wise Men—including Averell Harriman, John McCloy, Clark Clifford, George Ball, and Henry Kissinger—to consider the matter. The group concluded that the intelligence agencies had been wrong, thus adding to the administration's confusion and reinforcing its image as indecisive. The affair led even to tension between Brzezinski—who was unhappy with the appeasement that closed the incident and briefly considered submitting his resignation—and

President Carter.[131] When the debates over SALT resumed, the senators' reactions were heated, even more so because the Soviet Union was not putting any brakes on its activism in Vietnam or in Afghanistan, and the invasion of Afghanistan was the last straw as far as ratification was concerned. The administration ended up withdrawing the treaty from consideration by the Senate.

America's role in the Soviet decision to invade Afghanistan was subject to a great deal of commentary after Brzezinski was interviewed by French journalist Vincent Jauvert in *Le Nouvel Observateur.* Brzezinski's remarks were used as evidence for the "trap" thesis according to which he knowingly triggered a Soviet invasion by offering support to the mujahedeen who were fighting the communist government of Nur Muhammad Taraki and then that of Hafizullah Amin.[132] This thesis found fertile ground on the Internet, for it reinforced the ill-considered theory that the Americans were behind the creation of the Taliban and Al Qaeda and thus were, indirectly, behind the attacks of September 11, 2001.[133] But it was also taken up by more serious historians; for example, British historian Jonathan Haslam wrote that Brzezinski and Carter had been able to "trick Moscow into invading Afghanistan." According to Haslam, Odom—in the course of a friendly personal discussion after a hearty meal—told him that Brzezinski exclaimed, after the invasion: "They have taken the bait!"[134] Haslam cites the *Nouvel Observateur* interview but, strangely, in support of an uncontroversial element of the story: Brzezinski's November 26, 1979, memorandum to Carter evoking the possibility, deemed quite unlikely, moreover, that Afghanistan would turn into a "Soviet Vietnam."[135]

There are two more important elements in that interview. One is the headline: " 'Oui, la CIA est entrée en Afghanistan avant les Russes' . . ." (" 'Yes, the CIA went into Afghanistan before the Russians' . . ."). The statement appears in quotation marks and is followed by suspension points, leaving the impression that it is a direct quote from Brzezinski, according to which CIA agents were supposedly sent into Afghan territory before 1980—an initiative that does not fit with the historical context. Jaubert has indicated that the headline was invented by the editorial staff at *Le Nouvel Observateur,* and that it was not in fact a quote from Brzezinski.[136] The second element is Brzezinski's alleged remark to Jauvert that "this secret operation was an excellent idea. It succeeded into drawing the Russians into the Afghan trap." This would imply that Brzezinski saw a direct connection between the American initiative and the Soviet decision, and that he claimed a key role in the decision, which ended up bringing about the collapse of the Soviet

Union. Brzezinski, for his part, indicated later that the interview as whole was not reported verbatim, but that the article was a condensed and distorted version of his remarks; the translation from English to French was not submitted to him, as it was supposed to have been, and this casts doubt on the exact words used in this passage. Jauvert maintains that the interview was reported verbatim.[137]

This whole affair is less complicated than it seems, and it is partly a question of semantics. Brzezinski himself explains that he had not sought to draw the Soviets into a trap, with the underlying idea that Afghanistan would end up digging the grave of the USSR, but that he simply wanted to create difficulties for them, to heighten the dilemma they were going to have to face.

> We didn't really trap them, but we knew what they were doing, and they knew what we were doing. And what we knew was that they were inject-ing themselves into Afghanistan. . . . But anyway, what happened is we knew they were injecting their forces into Afghanistan, already in the summer, we also knew that the Mujahideen were resisting. So we first started to give them money, about six months before the Soviets went in. When we started to give them money, I told Carter that I think they'll go in, and they'll probably use that as an excuse in part, but that they're going in anyway, because they are taking over the regime. So we didn't suck them in but we knew what we were doing, namely we were in a sense engaging them in a preliminary skirmishing, prior to their more overt intervention.[138]

What would have happened if Brzezinski had claimed that he had antici-pated everything and calculated everything in advance? This would amount to crediting himself with a key role in the downfall of the USSR. Such a position would not be compatible with the archives. For example, on December 26, 1979, the day when Brzezinski purportedly rejoiced that the Soviets had "taken the bait," he wrote to Carter: "we should not be too optimistic about Afghani-stan becoming a Soviet Vietnam," for the historical analogy did not work out in favor of the mujahedeen.[139] The latter were poorly organized and poorly led; they had no territorial refuge, no formal army, no state, and no external support; they were going to face a degree of Soviet brutality that could not be compared to the American hesitations in Vietnam. During an SCC meeting on January 17, 1980, Brzezinski explained that a "massive insurgency" would doubtless not be in America's best interest and that it would be better to support a "low-level . . . insurgency" that would, above all, make it possible "to keep the Islamic states mobilized against the Soviets in Afghanistan."[140]

The pursuit of this counterfactual reasoning reveals a second contradiction with the archives, especially on the Soviet side; this one concerns the real influence of the American initiatives on Moscow's decision to invade Afghanistan. If Brzezinski claimed that he had drawn the Soviets into a fatal trap, it would be easy to retort that he was exaggerating his own role, that the American actions had only a marginal impact on the Soviet decision—and may have played no role at all. In other words, the chain of circumstances that led Moscow to intervene directly in December 1979 began with the gross incompetence of the Afghan communist leaders. They were so inept and violent that the Kremlin ended up intervening in order not to "lose" Afghanistan after "winning" it in 1978 through the communist coup d'état. Strategically situated between the Chinese and Pakistani enemies, Afghanistan was a country from which Islamic anger or "Khomeini fever" (as some Soviet documents of the time put it) might well spread. The money and propaganda sent from Washington in the summer of 1979 to the mujahedeen resistance reinforced Soviet fears as to the solidity of the regime and sent a worrying signal, but it is very unlikely that these interventions changed anything on the political or military level. As Brzezinski said, the invasion followed a certain logic and could be explained above all by incompetence on the part of Taraki and Amin.

The thesis according to which a trap was set having been dismissed, it is nevertheless important to specify what the Carter administration did to increase the Soviet dilemma in Afghanistan, and the personal role Brzezinski played. Once again, the veil was lifted by Robert Gates in his *From the Shadows* (1996), and then by the declassification of two of Jimmy Carter's "findings" (summaries of presidential decisions sent to Congress concerning secret operations) on support for the mujahedeen.[141] Brzezinski, in the memoirs he published in 1983, could obviously do no more than allude to the SCC meeting regarding Afghanistan held on April 6, 1979, during which he "pushed a decision through the SCC to be more sympathetic to those Afghans who were determined to preserve their country's independence."[142] Later, he confirmed the unfolding of events as Gates told the story, with many details.[143] In early 1979, the Afghan resistance to Taraki's communist government surprised the CIA by its solidity. And the question of support, raised in particular by the Pakistani allies, was evoked during a mini-SCC meeting (at the level of the deputies) on March 30, with arguments in favor of such support (Walter Slocombe, of the Pentagon, explicitly brought up the hypothesis of drawing the Soviets into a Vietnam-type morass) and opposing arguments (the risk of provoking the Soviets).[144] On April 6, the SCC, convoked by Brzezinski, examined various options and chose active but nonlethal support. The decision was approved by the president, who signed two findings, the first of which—dated July 3—authorized the United States to support the Afghan insurgents directly or through a third country with money, nonmilitary supplies, and propaganda, including radio broadcasts.[145] Ultimately, the Afghan resistance was supplied with a little more than $500,000 during the summer, but despite Pakistani pressure, the Americans did nothing more until the invasion (at most, they reiterated public warnings).[146] Under these conditions, American actions counted above all as a signal to Moscow, rather than through their concrete effects, which were very modest.

The invasion of Afghanistan marked a turning point in American perceptions, and particularly for the president, whose approach to the USSR hardened considerably. This explains why the last year of Carter's administration was marked by a triumph of the "Brzezinski line" over Vance's, thus accentuating the entry into the new Cold War. Several of Brzezinski's recommendations in favor of firmness in dealings with the USSR were implemented in 1980. The three principal measures in this shift were sanctions against the USSR, the Carter doctrine, and the new American nuclear strategy, all accompanied by a posture of firmness in Europe.[147]

The reaction to the invasion was immediate. The SCC, convoked by Brzezinski on December 26, 1979, decided to send a strong message to Brezhnev, warning him that the SALT treaty was henceforth threatened and that US cooperation with China would increase. It was also decided that Warren Christopher should be sent to Islamabad to assure the Pakistanis of American support despite the disagreements of recent years over nuclear nonproliferation. In the weeks that followed, the administration took several controversial retaliatory measures: a grain embargo, a symbolic return to registering young men for the draft, and a boycott of the Olympic Games in Moscow planned for July 1980. Brzezinski supported these measures, by and large; he insisted particularly on imposing an embargo on grain in addition to advanced technologies, to make it easier to resist pressure from domestic lobbies—agricultural and business interest. While he was struggling against the State Department's attempt to reopen a dialogue with Moscow, he encouraged a secret negotiation channel to explore the possibility of a Soviet retreat from Afghanistan—another element that undermines the "trap" theory.[148]

Beyond those measures, Brzezinski prompted Carter to carry out an authentic change of strategy vis-à-vis the USSR. In a memorandum on the long-term consequences of the invasion, he stressed the need to increase the defense budget massively and to reinforce the alliances with America's partners.[149] Concerning Afghanistan, it was less a matter of transforming the mujahedeen into a powerful military force than of maintaining their active resistance in order to mobilize the Muslim countries against the Soviet Union.[150] Pakistan was the most important ally, even if relations with General Zia were difficult; on November 21, 1979, the American embassy was burned down by angry students. In early February 1980, when Christopher went to Islamabad, Brzezinski accompanied him as a way of emphasizing that American assistance would also have a security component. The two men visited Afghan refugee camps, where they heard moving appeals for American assistance and arms delivery. Brzezinski also visited a Pakistani outpost on the Khyber Pass, where he was shown a Chinese version of an AK47 assault rifle; the photo of Brzezinski inspecting that weapon was interpreted as a symbol of Washington's bellicose new line with Moscow. Brzezinski and Christopher reinforced American ties with Islamabad and helped established cooperation between Pakistan and Saudi Arabia in view of supporting the mujahedeen.[151]

The Middle East was the other locus for applying the change in strategic posture. "Any attempt by an outside force to gain control of the Persian Gulf region will be regarded as an assault on the vital interests of the United States of America, and such an assault will be repelled by any means necessary, including military force."[152] The Carter doctrine, spelled out in his State of the Union address on January 23, 1980, was precipitated by the invasion of Afghanistan and the unrest in Iran, which provoked fear that the Soviets would take over the Gulf region. It was really a Brzezinski doctrine. The national security adviser relentlessly promoted the idea of a regional security framework for the Middle East, which he saw as the center of a crisis zone in which the Soviets were on the offensive, in military and political terms. Following the State of the Union address, Brzezinski worked tirelessly to turn the document into reality, by multiplying agreements with regional allies (Egypt, Somalia,

Kenya, Oman, and so on) for naval or air bases, arms and equipment supply depots, and joint exercises. He was also at the origin of the Rapid Deployment Joint Task Force, consisting in 100,000 men capable of autonomous deployment on short notice in the Gulf region, in order to come to the aid of an ally undergoing a subversive attack.

The final aspect of the strategic renewal largely inspired by Brzezinski was the strengthening of the US nuclear doctrine, which came to the support of the pronounced increase in the 1980 defense budget, this time well above the rate of inflation. On December 12, 1979, ironically on the day of the secret Soviet decision to invade Afghanistan, NATO voted to deploy medium-range and cruise missiles to counterbalance the Soviet SS-20 missiles. At the same time, NATO voted to negotiate arms control agreements with the Soviets. At the June 1980 summit in Venice, despite Chancellor Schmidt's efforts to soften that decision and propose a freeze on deployments on both sides, Carter, encouraged by Brzezinski, remained inflexible. On several occasions Schmidt suggested that Carter fire Brzezinski, declaring that the national security adviser had a detrimental influence on East-West relations.[153]

Ultimately, America's nuclear policy took up a major portion of Brzezinski's last year in the White House. Based on Odom's work and in partnership with Brown—but against the objections of Vance's State Department and then Muskie's—Brzezinski helped update the American deterrent through the presidential directive PD-59, with an approach known as "countervailing strategy."[154] The previous doctrine, based on mutual assured destruction, was implicitly based on American superiority: if there were escalation, America would prevail, forcing Moscow to pull back, as in Cuba, for example. The upgrading of the Soviet arsenal observed in the 1970s and in particular the preparations for conducting a nuclear war (increased capabilities in C3I ("command, communication, control, and intelligence"), civil defense, a hardening of command posts, all suggested that the Soviet calculation might have changed. Moscow seemed to be preparing to engage in a limited nuclear war or a combination of conventional and nuclear war—in short, mutual assured destruction might not prevent limited exchanges of fire. America's nuclear doctrine thus had to evolve. The United States had to acquire not only the ability to strike Soviet cities on a massive scale (which would be disproportionate, in certain cases, thus improbable), but also the ability to destroy political and military targets in a limited and flexible way, as well as

Soviet industrial capacities. As their use became more credible, American nuclear weapons would thus regain their full deterrent capacity.[155] Ironically, this doctrine was adopted by Carter, the president most committed to nuclear disarmament, and it was taken up by subsequent presidents, starting with Reagan.[156]

During the last months of the Carter administration, while the White House was preoccupied with the hostage crisis and the presidential campaign, the crisis in Poland gave Brzezinski a final opportunity to press for a harder political line toward the Soviet Union. In August 1980, after more than a year of deterioration in the economic and social situation and persistent resentment against Soviet domination, and after the historic visit in June of Pope John Paul II, discontent in Poland went up a notch, and thousands of workers began to occupy the shipyards at Gdansk, creating the Solidarnosc (Solidarity) Union. Brzezinski's main idea was to avoid allowing a repetition of the 1968 Prague repression. As he perceived it, Johnson had not adequately warned Moscow of the damage that a direct intervention in Czechoslovakia would cause to East-West relations, thus depriving himself of a means to weigh on the Kremlin's choices. The Carter administration multiplied its warnings during the fall; there was no expectation that the Soviets would give up, but there was hope of having some impact, nonetheless, on the internal deliberations of the Kremlin.

At the beginning of December, converging intelligence about the mobilization of Soviet resources pointed to an intervention planned for December 8. Brzezinski pressed Carter to send a clear warning to Brezhnev, along with assurance that America would not try to exploit the Soviet difficulties in Poland. He alerted the Solidarity leaders, communicated with the Pope and also with Lane Kirkland, the head of the American Federation of Labor and Congress of Industrial Organizations (AFL-CIO), which had supported the Polish union. The anticipated retaliatory measures included most prominently a worldwide boycott of freight shipments to the Soviet Union, orchestrated by the AFL-CIO, economic sanctions by Germany, and arms deliveries to China.[157] Brzezinski explained that it was difficult to know whether the American mobilization had changed the Kremlin's decision to intervene or whether it had simply contributed to the decision not to intervene. He could not keep from concluding that, if the lack of reaction by the White House regarding the Horn of Africa might have sent a permissive signal that then counted in the invasion of Afghanistan, then the strong reaction to the invasion of Afghanistan might have counted in the restraint regarding Poland.[158]

Brzezinski was no more predisposed to impose his mark on the US policy toward China than Kissinger was. "I could not help but think of the strange coincidence that the Sino-American relationship was being forged in the course of a single decade by two U.S. officials who were of immigrant birth and who approached this task with relatively little knowledge of or special sentiment for China, but with larger strategic concerns in mind. The opening of China in 1972 had been a bold stroke, of the greatest geopolitical significance, and I was determined to succeed in transforming that still-tenuous relationship into something more enduring and much more extensive."[159]

His deputy for China, Michael Oksenberg, recalled that, when Brzezinski arrived, he needed to be brought up to speed on China; after all, he was less familiar with the Middle Kingdom than with the USSR, Europe, or Japan.[160] Since 1968 he had been advocating an opening to China, mainly as a strategic counterweight to the Soviet Union. In "America in a New World," he stressed the need to cultivate relations with China, all the more so in that Mao's death, he predicted (writing before September 9, 1976), would surely be followed by an offer of reconciliation with the Soviet Union. He warned that a Sino-Soviet rapprochement would be unfavorable for the United States. However, he insisted just as strongly on the fact that intensifying relations with the most highly populated country in the world was justified in itself, as China had so much to contribute to solving the problems of the planet—in areas such as food, health, or population control.[161]

This balancing between power realism and planetary humanism resurfaced in Brzezinski's advice to President Carter. In Carter's speech at Notre Dame, the president reaffirmed his goal of normalizing relations with China, and he evoked Beijing's contribution to peace along with the creativity of the Chinese in responding to the challenges that faced the human race as a whole.[162] In the weekly report dated October 5, 1979, written during the period of debates over the shows of strength that could be organized in order to get beyond the fiasco of the Soviet brigade in Cuba and save the ratification of SALT II, Brzezinski clarified his position. "I do *not* favor playing *the* China card. For one thing, there is not a single 'China card,' but

many 'Chinese cards'—and you have just dealt one of them. More importantly, the long-range strategic significance of a cooperative U.S.-Chinese
relationship stands on its own feet, and thus is not a *tactical* matter."[163]
The long-term strategic interest of a cooperative Sino-American relationship sufficed in itself, he added, and in no case could it be summed up as a
merely incidental tactical advantage.

"Power realism" undeniably won out in his approach to China, so much
so that he wondered, during the early months of the administration, whether
it would not be desirable to intensify Sino-American relations in the area of
security but without normalizing diplomatic relations.[164] Despite normalization being among the ten goals set at the start of the administration, it
was not one of the top priorities. That goal was pursued seriously only when
Brzezinski considered it increasingly urgent to rebalance the Soviet-American
relationship, in the second half of 1977 and early 1978. Vance's trip to Beijing
in August had disappointed the Chinese, who wanted more rapid movement,
a more decisive and less inflexible America regarding Taiwan. They continued
to be concerned about the progress of détente with the USSR. Brzezinski
thus precipitated matters in November 1977, when he sought and received
an invitation from the head of the Chinese liaison mission to visit Beijing, to
the great displeasure of the State Department. Brzezinski then devoted several
months of "up close and personal" work on Carter to get the president to
send him to Beijing. He felt he was better positioned for the assignment than
either Vance or Mondale: the former was viewed by the Chinese as too soft
toward the Soviets, and the second was too high up in the hierarchy and thus
risked creating disproportionate expectations. Moreover, Brzezinski benefited
from the vice president's approval—Mondale thought that the administration needed to win a diplomatic success at any price—and he also had the
support of Harold Brown, who was interested in the strategic advantages of
such a relationship.[165]

Ultimately, Carter agreed to send Brzezinski to Beijing, with an important message: "The United States has made up its mind."[166] In other words,
Washington had come down in favor of opening negotiations intended to
normalize diplomatic relations. That explains why Brzezinski's trip to China
took on a historical importance that it was not meant to have. When he arrived
in Beijing on May 20, 1978, he led a small delegation of ten people, including his wife, his deputy Oksenberg; Huntington, who was to present to the

Chinese the results of PRM-10; and Holbrooke, who was to bring up the idea of expanding economic and cultural cooperation. Brzezinski gave an initial presentation of the administration's foreign policy, which lasted over three hours. He then negotiated with Prime Minister Hua Guofeng and First Vice-Premier Deng Xiaoping, to whom he addressed a personal invitation to pay him a visit at his home.

His trip was a success, in that it launched a secret negotiation about normalization, but it quickly took an anti-Soviet turn. Thus, during his visit to the Great Wall, this "polar bear tamer," as the Chinese had nicknamed him, threw out a challenge to his advisers that was repeated, amplified, and distorted by the press: the last one to reach the top of the Wall was to go fight the Cubans in Ethiopia. And when he offered toasts, he used the occasion to underline the Sino-American proximity and toss verbal darts at the Soviet Union.[167] Finally, when he returned, after a layover in Tokyo to keep the Japanese informed about his negotiations—in the interest of trilateral solidarity—he accepted an invitation to appear on *Meet the Press*, where he expected to talk about his China trip; instead, he was quizzed about Cuban activism in Africa. He then launched into an aggressive attack on the Soviets for breaking the "code of détente." Coming after his return from Beijing, this was interpreted as a hawkish turning point for the administration and an attempt on Brzezinski's part to get the upper hand over Vance. *Newsweek* headlined the story "A New Cold War?" and put Brzezinski on the cover.[168]

In Washington, he was warmly welcomed by the president. Carter was satisfied with the results achieved, but he also noted in his journal that "Zbig had come back from China. He was overwhelmed with the Chinese. I told him he had been seduced."[169] A few months later, in the margins of a weekly report in which he had waxed lyrical about the potentialities of an accord with China, the president noted: "Zbig—you have a tendency to exalt PRC issue."[170] There is little doubt that the personal role Brzezinski played in normalizing relations as well as the exceptional treatment he was granted by the Chinese in Beijing and afterward—a treatment specifically designed to create a solid point of support for themselves in the administration—had helped to "convert" him; it was a little like what had happened with Kissinger. The journalist and author James Mann has pointed out that, notwithstanding the intention to change things, the Carter team had finally slipped comfortably into the habits of the Nixon-Kissinger team: highly personalized relations around the national security adviser, partial exclusion of the State Department, negotiations kept largely secret from Congress, and so on.[171]

All this could be observed during the six months that followed Brzezinski's trip, as the negotiations were taking place. They were essentially conducted by Leonard Woodcock, the ambassador in Beijing; for his communications, he used the White House system rather than that of the State Department (although every cable was sent to Vance personally, as well as to Brzezinski). Brzezinski followed the negotiations closely, especially the details concerning US-Taiwan relations. He also resisted the attempts to normalize relations with Vietnam, which were being advanced by Vance and Holbrooke but which would not please the Chinese; in October, Carter came down in favor of China.[172] The final days of the negotiations were obviously the most eventful: at the last moment, the Chinese demanded confirmation that arms sales to Taiwan would be ended, whereas Washington intended to resume them after a year's break. However, the pro-Taiwan lobby could easily use this point to prevent Congress from normalizing relations. In the end, Brzezinski found a diplomatic formula that allowed the Chinese to register their disagreement on arms sales—which would indeed be resumed—without scuttling normalization (the Taiwan Relations Act was adopted in March 1979).[173]

Normalization was announced on December 15, 1978, by the president, after he had informed both Soviet ambassador Dobrynin, who was rather surprised, and Congressional leaders, who were unhappy to have been kept in the dark (except for Senate majority leader Robert Byrd) but who welcomed and approved the initiative. A controversy followed, for at that very moment Vance was winding up a trip designed to encourage the Israelis and the Egyptians to concretize the Camp David accord, and he had not expected that the negotiation with China would be completed so soon; he hastily returned to Washington.[174] But Carter and Brzezinski wanted to strike while the iron was hot and avoid any risk of leaks that might call the agreement into question. To avoid interference by Vance, Brzezinski also kept Christopher and Holbrooke in the dark. Oksenberg suggested that Carter could replace the signing of an Israeli-Egyptian peace agreement—announced as coming before Christmas, which did not happen—with this other foreign policy success.[175] At all events, the announcement was a success for the administration, and a personal victory for the national security adviser.

Brzezinski continued to play a major role in the administration's Chinese policy, most notably during Deng's visit to the United States on January 28–31, 1979. As soon as the Chinese leader arrived in Washington, he went as planned to McLean, Virginia, for a private informal dinner at Brzezinski's home. Brzezinski served vodka that Dobrynin had given him, and his children—Ian, Mark, and Mika—waited on the guests. At one point, with an awkward gesture, Mika spilled a dish of caviar on the Chinese leader, and began to clean it off with her hand. Vance, one of the guests along with Holbrooke and Woodcock, shook his head in disapproval.[176] This was not the only embarrassing incident. Just as the Chinese delegation was arriving, the chimney began to back up and filled the house with smoke; Muska and Oksenberg had to set up fans. But Deng was good-humored and showed a sense of repartee during dinner. For example, to his host, who referred to the obstacles he had had to overcome to get the Senate to approve the normalization of diplomatic relations, and asked him whether he too had had internal difficulties, Deng replied: "Yes, I did; there was some opposition in the province of Taiwan!"[177]

Beyond the dinner, Deng's visit was a welcome success for Carter, who was facing difficulties over Iran and the Egypt-Israel peace process in particular. The visit symbolized the administration's determination to go beyond merely normalizing diplomatic relations. Vance wanted to keep relations with China at a modest level to avoid worrying the Soviets. Conversely, Brzezinski felt that a closer relationship would force the Soviets to be more accommodating; Brown supported Brzezinski's approach. In fact, the relationship deepened in the area of security: James Mann has reported that, unable to sell weapons to Beijing, during his May 1978 trip, Brzezinski promised to let the Europeans do so, and he even took a "shopping list" from China to the French and to the British. During Deng's visit, an agreement was reached to replace the stations used for spying on the USSR—radars and listening posts that tracked nuclear—that had been lost because of the Iranian revolution. These would be replaced with stations set up in western China and managed jointly by CIA and NSA personnel along with staff from China. These stations became the eyes and ears of the West vis-à-vis the USSR—an extraordinary achievement.[178]

One of the most delicate points of the visit came up when Deng informed the Carter administration of the Chinese intent to "teach the Vietnamese a lesson." Vietnam had invaded China's ally Cambodia through a military operation of limited duration that would call a halt to the Soviets' activism in the region, through an interposed ally. Deng compared Vietnam to Cuba and predicted that Afghanistan was going to face the same fate as Cambodia. Unsurprisingly, Brzezinski's impulse was to protect the Chinese, and while Carter pushed Deng to reverse his decision, although he sent a more permissive signal by not threatening any consequences, as Brzezinski wished. This worried Vance, who reported the Soviets' displeasure, as the green light from Washington had been perceived as a threat in Moscow.[179] When war broke out on February 18, 1979, the administration demanded withdrawal of the Chinese troops from Vietnam and of the Vietnamese troops from Cambodia. Brzezinski managed to win out over Vance, who had sought to cancel Secretary of the Treasury Michael Blumenthal's planned trip to China.[180] The hostilities actually lasted only three weeks, and while they proved disappointing to the Beijing leadership, which had run into more resistance than it anticipated, they solidified relations between Washington and Beijing.

During the two years following Deng's visit, Brzezinski made sure that the Sino-American relationship continued to deepen and did not suffer from the inevitable tensions over Taiwan; or from the State Department's propensity to minimize that relationship in order to calm relations with Moscow. He thus defended a balanced Sino-American relationship rather than one of strict equivalence with its Soviet-American counterpart. In particular, he organized a kind of "travel diplomacy" with China, by arranging trips to Beijing for the principal US decision makers, in order to secure bureaucratic allies. Mondale's trip in August 1979 was the high point, for the vice president was able to offer China the status of most favored nation in trade. Above all, Brzezinski tried to reinforce ties in the area of security and advanced technology sales. In the fall of 1979, these efforts triggered a negative reaction from Vance, who was concerned about the imbalance with the Soviet-American relationship. But from that point on Brzezinski had a solid ally in Brown, whose trip to Beijing in January 1980, right after the invasion of Afghanistan, marked an acceleration of Sino-American cooperation. During the months that followed, China rapidly gained access to a whole gamut of advanced technologies and American military support equipment.[181]

Ultimately, the normalized relations with Beijing and the strengthened cooperation on security matters—which made China a true strategic ally of the United States—represented victories for the Carter administration. It is hard to imagine that a Republican administration could have done as much, owing to the sensitivity of the Taiwan issue on the right. It was also a personal success for Brzezinski. But this "Chinese card" was played at the cost of compromises (on human rights and on muting criticism on Cambodia, for example); ultimately, it reflected power realism rather than planetary humanism.

A similar phenomenon was observed in US relations with its European allies and with Japan. Attempts were made to give greater importance to the trilateral framework that had so preoccupied Brzezinski earlier. Other objectives had brought to light divergent interests among the allies, and more urgent issues (such as Panama and the Near East) had mobilized the administration before the mounting tensions with the USSR made it necessary to prioritize security considerations, thus reducing the preponderance of cooperation regarding the other issues that appeared during the 1970s.

The trilateral framework seems to have lost some of its importance in Brzezinski's eyes even before he entered the White House. Brzezinski maintained his role as animator of the Trilateral Commission in 1976, but he appeared disappointed by the way things were turning out. The Commission was interesting, but it never became sufficiently oriented toward action, in his view; it was never adequately prepared to commit itself to bold positions, for example by publishing regular columns on the major issues facing the world that would be jointly signed by the three presidents. It became too formal and too consensus-driven, and Brzezinski found the Japanese in particular overly passive.[182]

Even more significant, he gave the trilateral framework less emphasis in his writing, as reflected for example in "America in a New World." The reinforcement of ties with Europe and Japan remained a priority; the trilateral approach was a prerequisite for dealing with North-South and East-West issues. Behind this somewhat rote profession of faith, it became apparent that his perception had evolved. He stressed the rising strength of new regional powers, those that had more influence over their neighbors than the superpowers did, and whose growing role led to a pronounced shift in the international system. These "influentials" were China, Japan, India, Brazil, Iran, and Indonesia (the increasing importance of Algeria, Nigeria, and Zaire was also noted).[183] Elsewhere in the manuscript, he evoked other influential democracies that shared America's values (Canada, Australia, Venezuela, Israel), major economies (the three already mentioned plus Saudi Arabia and Mexico). He also specified that "in the context of some 150 states [the] United States should strive to create various cooperative webs, replacing its earlier Eurocentric emphasis with a more diversified pattern in which the ten or so leading non-European states become also more involved."[184]

These vast geopolitical schematizations, from the Trilateral to the influentials, did not count for much in the policies of the Carter administration, and they were entirely forgotten after the first year, supplanted by more urgent issues—most notably the rising tensions with Moscow. But traces of them are present in the early years of the administration. For example, when Ambassador Dobrynin sought to make contact with Carter a few days after his election, Harriman let him know that the president-elect wanted to meet European and Japanese leaders first.[185] To demonstrate his commitment to improving trilateral relations, Carter announced in early January 1977 that Vice President Mondale would travel to Europe and to Japan during the first week after the inauguration to present the new American foreign policy.[186] Among the ten goals set out by Brzezinski as the foreign policy work plan for the new administration, the first two concerned the relations with Europe and Japan, and with the influentials.

The first trip Carter made abroad was to London (May 7–8, 1977), for the G7 meetings—a trilateral format, in a way, since it brought together Americans, Europeans, and Japanese. Carter's most important trip that first year took him to Poland, Iran, India, Saudi Arabia, and Egypt (December 29, 1977–January 6, 1978), and the itinerary was explicitly built by Brzezinski around the idea of the influentials; the next major trip, three months later, took Carter to Venezuela, Brazil, and Nigeria. Brzezinski explained: "I developed the trip basically, in close conjunction with the Secretary of State. The President asked me back in March to start thinking about such a trip. It was designed to symbolize the larger and broader historical concerns that he expressed in his Notre Dame speech. . . . It also stresses the fact we are now moving into an age in which the scope of American relationships, worldwide, have to be wider than just the Atlanticists [sic] or even the Trilateral worlds."[187]

Starting in 1978, references to the Trilateral Commission or to the influentials disappeared, and the administration was too absorbed by various urgent dossiers to be able to implement any sort of grand geopolitical vision. It fell back, by and large, on preexisting formats, such as the G7 and NATO. From a certain standpoint, the informal and narrowly Atlantic summit meeting held in Guadeloupe (January 5–6, 1979), which brought together the United States, the German Federal Republic, France, and Great Britain, marked a step backward with respect to the trilateral architecture or the vast horizons Brzezinski had traced in earlier years. This format was not used again, because other allies that had been excluded—Italy, for instance—complained. Brzezinski remarked in this context that the proper formula would consist in transforming the G7 into a circle that would no longer focus exclusively on economic issues but would consider political and strategic matters as well. And at the Venice summit in June 1980, a half-day program was in fact devoted to the Soviet threat in the Persian Gulf.[188]

The relations between America and its European and Japanese allies did not receive as much attention during the Carter administration as might have been expected, and they fluctuated in relation to geopolitical vicissitudes during those four years. They also suffered from the failure to integrate the administration's various goals. Thus Carter's human rights policy at first surprised and disconcerted America's European allies, Germany in particular, because it created tensions with Östpolitik. Similarly, during that early period, the goal of nuclear nonproliferation so cherished by Carter quickly created friction—with Germany, for example, owing to Washington's opposition to exporting nuclear technologies to Brazil, and with Japan, concerned about American initiatives for its massive investments in the treatment of nuclear wastes.[189]

But it was on strategic questions, which quickly took priority, that relations with America's allies were most delicate. Although he got along well with European leaders and with his direct British and French counterparts, Brzezinski ran into particular difficulties with German chancellor Schmidt, even though he knew him already as a trilateralist, but whose relations with Carter were notoriously poor. Starting at the G7 summit in London, the chancellor took a patronizing tone and told Carter that he did not want to continue to house the radio broadcasts RFE-RL on German territory because he considered them antithetical to détente. Brzezinski, who was particularly attached to this Cold War tool replied that the matter could not be the object of a unilateral decision nor be considered apart from other aspects of European—and thus German—security.[190] But the difficulty went even deeper: Brzezinski had the feeling that German Östpolitik was developing in a direction that diverged increasingly from the détente, and especially the "reciprocal and global" détente that he advocated.

During Schmidt's visit to the White House in July 1977, the German chancellor wanted to encourage direct dialogue between Carter and "the good

Brezhnev who is promoting detente and who needs our help," and he offered his services as a secret go-between—an offer Carter did not pursue. Schmidt, annoyed, attributed the decision to Brzezinski's influence; the latter did not deny the charge, which could have been a factor in Schmidt's growing antagonism.[191] What followed was a set of more or less intertwined moves concerning the defense of Europe. On October 28, 1977, Schmidt gave a speech in London in which he emphasized that the Soviets' deployment of medium-range ss20 missiles was creating a regional asymmetry, at the very moment when the SALT negotiations were establishing a strategic global nuclear equilibrium. This was one of the starting points for a mobilization of NATO allies (a High Level group was set up in 1978) to envisage the modernization of their forces and develop a consensus on the question of Euromissiles.

In the meantime, a controversy had arisen over the neutron bomb—a nuclear weapon whose experimental development had been authorized by Gerald Ford, more lethal through the intense radiation it gave off than through its explosive power. It would kill people without damaging property, which accounts for its nickname, the "capitalist bomb." It was primarily designed to present less collateral danger for the allied troops. An article in the *Washington Post* in June 1977 disclosed its existence, triggering a broad debate in the United States and in Europe, where Moscow launched a big propaganda campaign, useful to distract attention from its own deployment of the ss20s or its production of enormous ss-22 missiles with an explosive power of 22,500 kilotons.[192] President Carter then asked for an investigation into the matter, and Brown recommended that the program to develop a neutron bomb be continued. Between June 1977 and April 7, 1978—when Carter announced that the program was being suspended and that the bomb would not be deployed in Europe—the discussions with the Europeans, especially with the German and British leaders, resembled a game of liars' poker. The Europeans preferred deployment, but were not ready to assume the political costs, even if the decision was dependent on the failure of the arms reduction agreement. The matter was complicated by internal confusion: the bureaucratic process had advanced without the president's full awareness, which complicated his decision and led to a rare moment of friction with Brzezinski. The latter was in favor of deployment, and he explained to Carter that American leadership sometimes meant making decisions that the Europeans would go to great lengths to avoid.[193]

Despite, but probably also in part because of, this setback, a month later (on May 30, 1978) NATO adopted an impressive program of conventional defenses, followed a year later by a common commitment to an annual 3 percent increase in defense funding until 1985. Following the debates over the Euromissiles that had been triggered primarily by Schmidt's speech in 1977, and taking into account the cooling of Soviet-American relations, Brzezinski pushed for the adoption of a high goal for the deployment of American missiles. This was announced to NATO in August 1979, and it set off a vigorous reaction in Moscow. But at its summit meeting on December 12, 1979, NATO adopted a robust deployment plan (108 Pershing II missiles and 464 cruise missiles), coupled with an offer to negotiate, which marked the starting point of an intense public debate in Europe over Euromissiles. Despite the deterioration of the East-West climate, in June 1980 Chancellor Schmidt advanced the idea of a moratorium on the deployment of nuclear weapons in the European theater. Brzezinski reasoned at the time that this would have resulted in encouraging the wave of pacifism and favoring the USSR de facto, since its missiles were already in place. He urged Carter to respond decisively to Schmidt, and to refrain from making such a proposal to Brezhnev. As a result, their meeting on the first day of the Venice summit was highly charged, and the tension rose in particular between the chancellor and Brzezinski; Carter finally had to ask the latter to calm down.[194]

US relations with Europe and Japan under the Carter administration, which, in its upper echelons, was made up exclusively of trilateralists, were certainly better than under Nixon, at the time of the disastrous "year of Europe." But the centripetal forces at work—greater economic equality among allies, the fallout from Vietnam and Watergate, the shift of the bipolar confrontation toward the Third World, the energy crises, and so on—continued to exert influence, and, as Brzezinski has noted, the transatlantic drift was only partially blocked. The decisiveness of NATO in December 1979 and its unanimity in condemning the invasion of Afghanistan must not obscure the substantial disagreements within NATO over the Soviet threat. Most notably this led to a disorganized response during the repression in Poland, to divergent policies toward the Middle East, and to continuing European sales of advanced technologies to the Soviets.[195] In addition, Washington's management of the 1979 energy crisis marked a retreat of American leadership vis-à-vis Europe (where the measures Carter took, especially on the domestic front, were deemed inadequate) and led to friction. Relations with Japan were somewhat better than those with Europe. Ultimately, in a world that had become less and less transatlantic and more and more chaotic, it was simply impossible to give the kind of priority to trilateral relations that Brzezinski had advocated before he arrived in the White House.

One of Brzezinski's principal themes of reflection before his White House years was America's growing isolation with respect to major changes in the world, especially in the developing regions. Unlike Kissinger, who concentrated on the balance of forces among the great powers and viewed international affairs through a narrowly bipolar prism, Brzezinski paid a great deal of attention to sociological, political, and ideological developments that were agitating the planet and could affect America's ability to maintain world order. His advice was well received by Carter who, beyond his desire to restore a certain morality in American foreign policy and to promote human rights, was sensitive to the urgent need to improve the image of the United States in the world.

America, Brzezinski observed, was isolated. Not only through its political system, which put the emphasis on freedom and pluralism when the worldwide tendency seemed to privilege a quest for equality and strong nation-states, but also through its disastrous image as a reactionary force in the Third World, one that supported authoritarian regimes, pursued a paternalistic policy in Latin America, was overly partial to the Israeli side in the conflict in the Near East, and defended the apartheid regimes in southern Africa in the name of the struggle against communism.[196] "America in a New World" was based on the hypothesis of the rise in power of "global populism" as a result of demographic and technological changes; in the global South, the masses, rapidly increasing in numbers and becoming more and more literate, wanted to participate in political life not only in their own countries but also, indirectly, in the international system. On this planet where technology was accelerating the circulation of information, America faced a growing hostility for its political choices, the impact of its multinationals, and the failures of its leadership in dealing with global problems (food and energy needs, environmental concerns, development issues, and so on). It thus had to change the course of its relations with the emerging countries and put human rights at the heart of its foreign policy.

This last objective rose to prominence after the Kissinger years when, as Jeremy Suri summed it up: "Personalized politics and a regional division of responsibilities transformed the United States from an inconsistent advocate of third-world political reform into a consistent supporter of local muscle."[197] The attacks on Kissinger by Carter and Brzezinski during the campaign were by no means artificial; they reflected the sincere opinion that America had become too Machiavellian and too preoccupied with the status quo, incapable of promoting peace in the Near East and deaf to the justified aspirations of the Africans or the South Americans.[198] The theme of human rights was also applicable to the USSR, and in "America in a New World" Brzezinski brought up the question of Jewish emigration from the Soviet Union and the need to set up mechanisms to verify the implementation of the Helsinki Accords.[199] Here Carter and Brzezinski were reflecting a growing moral aspiration of the American public after the experiences of Vietnam and also of Cambodia, Chile, and Watergate: an aspiration that was expressed, for example, in support for the 1974 Jackson-Vanik amendment, and in reforms in the regulations governing arms exports (the Arms Control Export Act of 1976). Putting forward human rights and freedom was also a direct reply, as Odom pointed out, to Soviet propaganda about class struggle and equality.[200] Finally, it made it possible to bring all Democrats into agreement: anti-Soviets from the Coalition for a Democratic Majority or from *Commentary*, Eastern Europeans, Jews, and so on—at least until the 1980 elections.[201]

As for the first objective, the establishment of better relations with the Third World, it relied both on the influentials and on a series of initiatives intended to reposition America on the right side of history. As Brzezinski wrote: "Progressive accommodation in the Middle East, normalization in Latin America, and rearrangements in Southern Africa would represent major steps within a wider redefinition of the American relationship with the Third and Fourth World."[202] After being an East-West problem, the conflict in the Near East had become a North-South problem, Brzezinski noted; America and Israel were facing hostility from most of the countries in the United Nations. For the long-term security of Israel and for America's image, it was essential to advocate resolving the conflict by spelling out the parameters of the final settlement, and this had to be done in an active way, not by taking "small steps." For the details, Brzezinski referred to the 1975 Brookings Institution study in which he had participated.[203] For Latin America, the idea of repudiating the Monroe Doctrine and treating the rest of the Western hemisphere in a normal fashion dates back to 1970. The year 1976 saw the addition of the Panama

Canal question—its retrocession, urgent on the political level, would offer an excellent symbol of the new course of American foreign policy.[204] Finally, regarding southern Africa and especially after the Angola fiasco, Brzezinski argued, Washington must use its influence to put an end to white supremacy in Southern Rhodesia (Zimbabwe) and encourage the creation of a more just South Africa.[205]

To what extent was Brzezinski able to promote that vision once he was part of the administration? Concerning his ambition to reconfigure America's external approach and open it to the developing world, the failure of the Conference on International Economic Cooperation—the North-South conference—quickly led him to recognize an impasse on the level of aid to development. Neither the rich countries nor the American Congress were ready to transfer significant resources toward the Third World. In early June 1977, Brzezinski advised Carter to place less stress on economic assistance and more on the quest for better political relations with the major emerging countries, the famous influentials (the president noted in the margin: "I agree").[206] This was a difficult quest despite the efforts made during the first year and especially the trip to visit several of the major emerging countries in late 1977 and early 1978. Not to mention that the multiple objectives pursued by the administration added tension to the relations with certain Third World allies, especially those concerning nuclear nonproliferation and human rights.

Where Latin America was concerned, Brzezinski participated indirectly in the negotiations that led to the success of the August 1977 agreements to organize the retrocession of the Panama Canal. He then played a much more active role in the effort to get the treaties ratified; this was finally achieved in March 1978—a close call. Regarding southern Africa, his role was secondary; Vance and the UN ambassador Andrew Young were on the front lines there, but Brzezinski followed the matter closely and worried about possible interference from the Soviets. He was relieved when an agreement was reached in Zimbabwe, which closed the door to the Soviets and the Cubans, but he remained concerned about the issues that had not been resolved in South Africa and in Namibia.[207]

A long and fascinating discussion could be devoted to the Israel-Palestine dossier, in which Brzezinski played an important role, including in the Camp David negotiations, even though he was always careful to specify that Carter and Vance were the key players. In his memoirs, the efforts to achieve a lasting peace in the Near East take up two full chapters.

The approach Brzezinski recommended to Carter on the Near East—an American affirmation proposing the parameters of a final settlement—quickly ran up against the reality on the ground. The initial idea of a major conference in Geneva that would lead to an overall agreement had to be given up in the fall of 1977. This decision was precipitated by the fiasco of the joint memorandum with the Soviets of October 1, which triggered vigorous domestic opposition and increased mistrust on the part of the Israelis, and then anger on the Soviet side when the initiative was abandoned. The irony, for Brzezinski, was that the second phase, which began with Sadat's visit to Jerusalem, was not very different in form from the "small steps" for which he had been criticizing Kissinger. From the outset, this was a question of proceeding in such a way that an eventual separate peace between Israel and Egypt would lead to a settlement of the other problems in the region. Brzezinski used the image of concentric circles to illustrate that hope. But the quest proved vain, and America found itself playing the role of active (and indispensable) intermediary, seeking to bring the viewpoints of Cairo and Jerusalem closer together. Brzezinski's and Carter's trips back and forth between the two capitals in the spring of 1979 were reminiscent of Kissinger's "shuttle diplomacy" a few years earlier.

On the personal level, Brzezinski had a somewhat unusual position with respect to Cyrus Vance and Jimmy Carter. On the one hand, he often urged the president to put his foot down, to come down hard on Begin. He believed that, given the nature of Israeli domestic politics, the leaders of the Jewish state could not make bold compromises in the peace process without being able to explain to their voters that Israeli-American relations were at stake; thus it was necessary to offer them this screen. On the other hand, his political line was often not as hard as that of the secretary of state and the president, especially on the question of the colonies. For example, in March 1978, Vance suggested that in the case of failure the United States would have to go to the UN and follow Secretary General Kurt Waldheim's suggestion to organize a conference that would include both the Soviets and the Palestine Liberation Organization (PLO). Brzezinski vigorously opposed that idea, emphasizing its electoral costs and the advantages it would give Moscow. If there had to be a test of strength with the Israelis, he added, it should occur at the right moment, and over the question of the settlements and Resolution 242.[208] The paradox was that at the same time, owing to his Polish Catholic origins, Brzezinski had to face accusations of anti-Semitism. Even the effective leader of the pro-Israel lobby, Rabbi Alexander Schindler, who presided over an association of major Jewish organizations, did not hesitate to encourage these accusations, if only implicitly.[209]

Brzezinski often stepped up as the administration's primary tactician on this issue. It was he, for example, who pressed in favor of linking the sales of F-15 planes to Saudi Arabia with sales to Israel and Egypt, which made it possible to defeat AIPAC (the pro-Israel lobby) when the issue came up for a vote in Congress. He also prompted the Egyptians to make maximalist proposals so that the Americans could then get the Israelis to accept a more reasonable version. And he was the first to suggest—in January 1978—the possibility of arranging a meeting at Camp David that would include Sadat, Begin, and Carter. Moreover, he was at the president's side throughout the Camp David negotiations (September 5–19, 1978), and it was he who announced their success to the media. The success was tarnished by the lack of a solution to the Palestine problem, and it required a great deal of follow-up work between the fall of 1978 and March 26, 1979, when the peace treaty between Israel and Egypt was signed in Washington.

Following Begin's visit to Washington in late February 1978, the Camp David Accords seemed on the verge of being abandoned, but Carter was shocked by the extremist stance of the Israeli leader, and Brzezinski reminded him once again that sometimes it was necessary to choose action, even confrontation. At that point Carter decided to go to Cairo, then to Jerusalem in order to get beyond the obstacles to concluding the peace treaty. Brzezinski made a preparatory trip, and succeeded in convincing Sadat to invite Begin to Cairo; he realized the symbolic importance of such a visit from Begin, with whom he had established a certain personal proximity.[210] Upon his return to Washington, Carter asked him to go to Saudi Arabia, to Jordan, and then to Cairo, to keep the Saudis and the Jordanians up to date (and in particular to appease the Saudis' anger at the Egyptians), then to inform Sadat about his talks. This was one of the few diplomatic missions Brzezinski carried out during his four years at the Carter White House. Before he landed in Amman he was informed of a possible assassination attempt against him on his way to the palace, which prompted his colleagues to avoid riding in his car.

In the end, the signing of the peace treaty on March 26, 1979, marked a striking success for the administration, and during the celebratory dinner that evening Brzezinski shared his table with Ezer Weizman, Mohammed Ali, and

Kissinger. From the standpoint of America's image, the result was mixed. To be sure, Washington had achieved peace. However, the Palestinian question that was mobilizing many Third World countries had not been resolved, and from a certain point of view settling it now seemed more complicated and more remote because it was less urgent for Israel. In keeping with the advice Brzezinski gave him a few days later, Jimmy Carter disengaged himself from the issue until the end of his mandate, in order to end up on a victorious note.[211]

As a sign of the importance he attached to a new objective—the promotion of human rights—Brzezinski created a working group in the NSC devoted to global topics. These included human rights along with nuclear nonproliferation and conventional arms export controls. He asked Jessica Tuchman Mathews and Colonel Leslie Denend, then, starting in 1979, Lincoln Bloomfield from MIT to lead the effort. Beyond the exchange of letters with Andrei Sakharov during the early weeks of the administration, it was Carter's Notre Dame speech that marked the launching of the human rights campaign. In that speech, the president introduced themes reminiscent of Brzezinski's, particularly those outlined in "America in a New World." His optimism, his confidence in America's solidity and its future were thus reaffirmed by contrast with the preceding administration, whose leaders were accused of "covert pessimism." His faith in democratic methods was underlined by the reference to the secret deals that his predecessors had made too often, leading to a precarious world order. Brzezinski's inspiration is also apparent in the insistence that America must adapt to the new geopolitical era marked by the lowering of tensions with the USSR in the early 1970s and the political awakening of "new peoples" owing to increased literacy. Cooperation with the Atlantic democracies needed to be oriented toward the new themes. Thus, at the G7 meeting in London, America and its allies had prepared proposals for the North-South summit to be held in Paris. All that did not preclude vigilance: Carter criticized the Cuban intervention in Angola as an attempt to impose a regime by force—one of Brzezinski's special concerns. But the Notre Dame speech also contained other inspirations, more liberal than Brzezinski's. The well-known disparaging reference to an "inordinate fear of communism"—which had too often led Americans to support anti-communist dictators, Carter explained—certainly did not come from Brzezinski, whose position on the subject was more or less critical.[212]

Nearly a year later, on February 17, 1978, the speech was codified in presidential directive PD-30, which prioritized civil and political liberties over the administration's other objectives. It put forward incentives (acknowledging progress rather than stigmatizing regression) and used positive instruments such as development aid. It ruled out American support for maintaining order in regimes that violated human rights, and it set keeping multilateral financial institutions in good working order as a condition for American economic interventions.[213] Brzezinski pressed regularly in favor of human rights. For instance, he discussed Carter's policies in this area with the newly elected pope John Paul II, who thanked him with a big smile.[214] In a weekly report in October 1978, Brzezinski commented: "I have no doubt that human rights is the genuine wave of the future, even if 'no one knows where it will lead.' Increased literacy and political activism makes the demand for human rights a growing political force in different parts of the world. Thus it would be good politics, as well as historically and morally right, for you to reaffirm at some point your general commitment." (The president's marginal comment: "I agree.")[215]

It is not surprising that Brzezinski pushed for greater assertiveness on America's part in the Conference on Security and Cooperation Europe, an organization that grew out of the August 1975 Helsinki Accords. He even suggested taking a hard line toward the Soviets, to the dismay of the State Department. It was he who suggested and obtained the nomination of Arthur Goldberg, a former Supreme Court justice and ambassador to the United Nations, as the US representative to the Belgrade conference where the third "basket" of issues from Helsinki was discussed, that of human rights; he knew that Goldberg would stand firm. Brzezinski's support for the radio broadcasts RFE-RL and Voice of America, for the circulation of information via samizdat, and for ethnic minorities was conceived as a way of supplying tools at the service of dissidents in the Eastern bloc and elsewhere.[216]

Brzezinski was also the first to recognize the limitations of the administration's human rights policy and to alert Jimmy Carter to the problems. There were two principal dilemmas: that of conflicting objectives, and that of unequal relations between America and the various authoritarian regimes. In March 1977 Brzezinski became concerned that the administration's initiatives in the areas of nuclear nonproliferation and human rights might produce a negative reaction, or even an anti-American front—in Latin America, and especially in Brazil. On August 7, 1978, he warned the president about the risk of "having bad relations simultaneously with Brazil, Chile, and Argentina."[217] He went as far as to blame the State Department for the way it was implementing the human rights policy. Brzezinski quickly noted that that policy was much more effective with pro-American right-wing regimes than with anti-communist regimes; Jeane Kirkpatrick formulated the same criticism of the Carter administration in late 1979.[218] Starting in the summer of 1977, the administration had to put a damper on its most acerbic criticisms of the USSR in that regard, owing to the strongly negative reaction on the part of the Soviets. The debates became less public, and Brzezinski negotiated with Ambassador Dobrynin to release some Soviet spies in exchange for the liberation or emigration of several dissidents, including Alexander Ginzburg, whom he received later at the White House.[219] In short, without abandoning the human rights policy, Brzezinski and Carter were obliged to reduce their ambitions for it.

The fact remains that the overall goals set by Brzezinski even before he took on his official position, goals aimed at restoring America's leadership in the Third World, especially "progressive accommodation in the Middle East, normalization in Latin America, and rearrangements in Southern Africa," were largely achieved. Admittedly, no major initiative toward the influentials was pursued, but America's image was somewhat improved in the rest of the world, ensuring better international support at the time of the shocks in 1979 and 1980, Afghanistan and Iran.

Iran was another example of the clash between the administration human rights policy and its other objectives. Most important, it was one of the tragedies of the Carter administration, and it contributed more than any other foreign policy matter to the president's defeat in 1980. Here, advanced policy planning was not at issue; the events in Iran called for crisis management.

The Carter team followed the path laid out by previous administrations by relying on Iran as one of the two policemen of the Persian Gulf, with Saudi Arabia being the other, but it linked its cooperation and its arms sales to encouragement for democratic reforms. It is by no means certain that this encouragement incited the opposition to assert itself, but it does seem to have contributed to the doubts of the Shah of Iran about the solidity of American support when the crisis hit.[220] For several years, dissatisfaction had existed with accelerated modernization accompanied by economic inefficiency, with the arbitrariness of the regime and the repressive actions of the secret police (Savak), and with the extravagant life style of the ruling

Pahlavi family. The situation got worse in 1978, so much so that strikes and demonstrations in the fall weakened the regime; the CIA and the US embassy in Tehran missed the warning signs and predicted political continuity. Gary Sick, the NSC adviser for Iran, was much more apprehensive; in the course of the year he alerted Brzezinski, who began a prolonged series of exchanges with Ardeshir Zahedi, the Iranian ambassador to the United States, in late August 1978.[221]

Between the first messages expressing American support for the shah in early November 1978 and the shah's departure from Tehran on January 16, 1979, President Carter went back and forth between two camps, the State Department and the National Security Council; and on a personal level between his conscience and his reason. On the one side, Vance and Christopher were preoccupied with the democratic evolution of Iran and with protecting the American residents of the country. The State Department did not like the dictatorship of Mohammad Reza Shah Pahlavi, and a number of diplomats thought it was possible to reach an understanding with the opposition figure on the rise, the Ayatollah Khomeini, who returned from exile on February 1, 1979. Among the scenarios he envisaged, US ambassador to Tehran William Sullivan even thought that he could play a Gandhi-like role and that elections would probably bring to power an Islamic republic favorable to the West.[222] It seems that the ambassador had continually diluted the strength of the messages of support from the White House to the shah; in other words, he had not followed his instructions. Retrospectively, Carter felt that he had been wrong not to insist more forcefully to Vance that Sullivan be relieved of his responsibilities after his acts of insubordination.[223]

On the other side, Brzezinski's vision was much less optimistic. At first, in November and December, he tried to send Tehran unequivocal messages of support: given the central role of the shah in the very personal power structure, he reasoned that any concession imposed by Washington would reinforce the opposition and could only lead to instability and chaos. He believed that the shah should articulate a project for Iranian society that would calm the tensions that had developed owing to an excessively rapid social and economic modernization. Yet he maintained that it would first be necessary to regain control of the situation by force, for the longer the authorities waited to act, the more difficult, politically costly, and violent their action would be. As for the idea that the shah would be replaced by a liberal alternative, Brzezinski did not give it much credence; the historical analogy that kept coming to mind was the revolutionary spiral. In his view, as had been the case in the French and Russian revolutions, the most radical protesters were the ones who would take over as the crises went from one stage to the next. In his defense of an iron-fisted government followed by a military coup d'état (when it became clear that the shah had become too weak), there was also an element of geopolitical anxiety: the Iranian communist party, the Tudeh, was active among the opposition groups, and the "loss" of Iran to the Soviets would be a disaster on all levels. On November 18, Brezhnev warned the United States against military intervention in Iran. Two weeks later, in his report to Jimmy Carter, Brzezinski evoked an "arc of crisis" that extended from Bangladesh through Islamabad to Aden.[224]

Brzezinski reasoned that political intelligence on Iran, whether from the CIA or from the embassy, was of poor quality, owing to budgetary restrictions and to the rules imposed on Americans by the shah that prohibited any contact with the opposition. This accounts for the contacts with Ambassador Zahedi; Brzezinski encouraged the latter to return to Iran in November 1978 to gather information, just as he was encouraging a businessman close to the shah to do the same thing.[225] This channel had given rise to accusations of secret parallel communications with the shah, which Brzezinski denied, stressing that only information was involved. Conversely, Vance wrote in his memoirs that he went to see Brzezinski to put an end to that communication, and even had to involve the president.[226] During the first half of December George Ball recommended an effective transfer of power to a civilian government, leaving the shah in control of the army and nothing else; a recommendation that Carter did not follow. This episode ended up mainly complicating things, but it also left Carter disinclined to send Brzezinski as an emissary to Tehran.[227]

By the end of December 1978, it was clear that the shah did not want to take responsibility for a large-scale repression and wanted Washington to make the decision for him. On December 28, Brzezinski insisted that the message to Tehran should indicate that a civilian government remained the preferred solution. However, if any uncertainty existed about the political orientations of that government or about its capacity to govern, or if the army was at risk of fragmenting, then the shah should choose a strong military option immediately, thus ending the disorder.[228] Instead, the shah asked Shapur Bakhtiar to take the reins of power while agreeing to leave the country himself, and during January Brzezinski pressed strongly for a military coup d'état if Bakhtiar failed, something he deemed inevitable, given the improbability of a democratic or even a moderate alternative. What he feared was the temporizing that would see Iran pass from one civilian government to another, each more radical than the one before, ending up either with a break-up of the country or a regime hostile to America. But his defense of a coup d'état supported by Washington brought him into a head-on clash with Vance, Mondale, and the president, all of whom found that solution repugnant, for it recalled all too well the events in Chile.[229] In addition, Brzezinski opposed direct contacts with Khomeini, who returned from exile in January, for that could sent a disastrous signal to the Iranian military; a secret indirect contact was established via the French.[230]

In early February, General Robert Huyser, who had been sent by Carter and Brown on a mission to the Iranian military leaders a month earlier to compensate for the limited information provided by Sullivan, reported that there was still time for a military coup. He also pointed out that the high command was demoralized, a large number of soldiers were defecting, and the situation was complicated overall.[231] Whereas Ambassador Sullivan assessed that an Islamic republic led by Khomeini would lead toward democracy and preached without restraint in favor of the latter, Huyser predicted that Iran was headed for takeover by the Tudeh Party.[232] The army soon submitted to the new regime of the Islamic Republic, instituted through a referendum, and it was gradually decapitated, putting a definitive end to the option of a coup d'état. The regime began in a moderate fashion under Mehdi Bazargan, named by Khomeini, but it quickly became radical following the incident on November 4, 1979, in which diplomats from the US embassy were taken hostage. Although the events seem to have justified Brzezinski's pessimism, it is impossible to know whether a coup d'état attempted earlier—by the shah, in January, or by the military in early 1979—would have succeeded and whether it would have resolved the underlying problems. Conversely, would early cooperation with Ayatollah Khomeini have led to the establishment of a pro-American regime? This question is just as impossible to answer, but the internal resistance to Khomeini and the difficulty he had in eliminating the other opposition groups (which led him most notably to launch the taking of hostages and to use the Iran-Iraq war begun by Saddam Hussein to consolidate the regime) may lead us to doubt that this would have helped.

The admission of the shah to the United States for medical treatment on October 23, 1979, served as a pretext for the seizure of the American embassy; the action was soon officially supported by Khomeini. The shah's peregrinations since January had been a source of embarrassment for Carter and his team. Prominent figures such as Henry Kissinger, David Rockefeller, and John McCloy were pressuring the administration to welcome the shah to the United States, and this was perceived as a provocation by the Islamic republic. On November 1, Brzezinski had gone to Algiers for the celebration of the twenty-fifth anniversary of Algerian independence, and he took advantage of the opportunity to meet with Prime Minister Bazargan, accompanied by other ministers. Their exchange was constructive, and allowed hope for an accommodation, for example over the possibility that Iranian doctors could examine the shah (the Iranians did not believe he was ill). But the seizure of the embassy three days later led Bazargan to resign (his meeting with Brzezinski, made public, may have contributed to his decision), and the revolution pursued its logic of radicalization.[233]

On November 6, during the second SCC meeting at which the possible options for liberating the fifty-two hostages were examined, Brzezinski presented three conceivable military scenarios. These included an operation that would rescue the hostages by force; an act of retaliation if the Americans were killed; and, in the case of Iran's disintegration, a military action centered on the oil fields in the southwestern part of the country. Brzezinski demonstrated his willingness to use action in order to change the configuration of a problem, especially given that the invasion of Afghanistan, on Christmas Day in 1979, had led the Soviets to the borders of Iran. The situation called for subtlety, in order to avoid fostering the perception of a fight between America and the Muslim world. Brzezinski was supported by Brown, who surmised that time was not on America's side, even if the priority was given to negotiations, as the State Department desired.[234] Under the circumstances, the tensions between Brzezinski and Vance surged up again, stronger than ever, as the path of negotiation—whether through the PLO or the Libyans—appeared unpromising; Khomeini was betting on the crisis to help consolidate the regime.

On December 21, 1979, recognizing that economic sanctions and the limited military operations proposed—mining of the Iranian waters, a naval blockade—had little chance of working, Brzezinski had suggested two other possible options to Carter. The first was a regime change; a military operation that would lead to Khomeini's downfall. The second was the imposition of a lasting humiliation on Khomeini, which he could reverse by releasing the hostages, for example taking part of Iran's territory. Jimmy Carter responded in the margins: "We need to list everything that Khomeini would not want to see occur and which would not incite condemnation of U.S. by other nations."[235] This exchange reinforces our impression of a Brzezinski inclined to create a new situation, to change the givens of the problem, even if the options he proposed might appear perplexing: what would be the international reaction to a large-scale American military operation aiming to change the Khomeini regime, and what would be the consequences for the hostages? Once a few Iranian islands had been seized, what would happen next, and then again, what would happen to the hostages?

On April 7, 1980, as the negotiations had completely ceased by then, the president decided to take stronger initiatives; he applied maximal economic sanctions and broke off diplomatic relations. This was also the time when the idea of rescuing the hostages by force took shape. Vance was opposed to the operation, but he said he preferred it to a generalized blockade of Iran, which was the other option envisaged. The decision was finally made on April 11, while Vance was on vacation in Florida. But when he returned, "stunned and angry" at what had been done in his absence, Brzezinski called a new NSC meeting to debate the matter so that Vance could make his objections known (April 15).[236]

The mission "Eagle Claw" was extraordinarily complex and daring on the logistical level. Eight helicopters were to meet three C-130 transport planes in the Iranian desert the first night, for refueling. The helicopters would then go on to a site near Tehran, hiding until the assault, which was scheduled to be carried out during the second night by soldiers transported in vehicles prepared in advance by the CIA. But on April 24, when the operation was launched, it could not be completed as planned: two of the eight helicopters were grounded by sandstorms, and a third had a hydraulic problem. It had been determined that a minimum of six helicopters would be required for the operation to succeed. Brzezinski wondered if he should advise Carter to continue the operation anyway. "Would I not be abusing my office by pressing this man into such a quick decision after months of meticulous planning? Would I not be giving in to a romantic idea?"[237] But he finally suggested that Carter should rely on the advice of Delta Force commander Charles Beckwith, who chose to interrupt the mission. In preparing for take-off, one of the helicopters collided with a C-130, killing eight men. In short, the operation turned into a humiliating disaster—in addition to the shattered hulls left in the desert, two of the remaining helicopters were abandoned to the Iranians, and the bodies of the eight marines killed were exposed in Tehran.[238]

Throughout this whole affair, Brzezinski and Carter surrounded themselves with the best historical metaphors. They took care not to interfere with the decisions of the military concerning the mission (as Kennedy had not interfered at the Bay of Pigs), even if they indicated their preference for a relatively modest mission (as the Israelis had done at Entebbe, an operation that had left a deep impression on Brzezinski). Neither had any regrets, and Brzezinski added that not to have made an attempt would have been unworthy of America, just as he had felt, at the end of 1979, that not to have received the shah on American soil would constitute an affront to national honor.[239] His opinion was not shared by Vance, who resigned at the end of April because of this disagreement, but also because of other points of friction with the president; and more generally because the geopolitical context of the new Cold War was increasingly incompatible with his own vision.[240] Brzezinski then offered to resign as well, but Carter refused, consulting him instead about the choice of Vance's successor (Brzezinski recommended Muskie).[241] As Kissinger had warned him, the media then took after Brzezinski, accusing him of having driven Vance to resign. This did not make the adjustment of his relations with Muskie any easier, but the national security adviser retained his essential prerogatives.

During the final months of the administration, Brzezinski played only an indirect role in the hostage negotiations. Instead, he concentrated on the implementation of the Carter doctrine, especially the development of a rapid response force and the issues surrounding nuclear deterrence (PD-59). The shah's death in late July 1980 facilitated the negotiations, which accelerated in September and October, owing especially to the Iranian need for American spare parts for the Iran-Iraq war. Brzezinski warned the president that this was probably a diversion on the part of the Iranians intended to dissuade the Americans from attempting another "October surprise" raid before the elections. Moreover, unlike his deputy Gary Sick, who supported the hypothesis of secret negotiations between the Reagan team (led by William Casey) and the Iranians to liberate the hostages only after the election, Brzezinski was skeptical.[242] In fact, despite a vote by the Majlis (the Iranian Parliament) on the conditions for liberating the hostages on November 2, nothing happened before the election on November 4. It was a few minutes after the Carter presidency had ended, on January 20, 1981, that the Iranians finally freed the hostages, following an agreement that anticipated the end of American sanctions, but did not include either apologies or restitution of the presumed fortune of the shah.[243] Brzezinski, bitter over this affair that had contributed to Carter's defeat, indicated later that the president could easily have increased his own popularity and saved the elections by launching punitive military actions against Iran; but the latter had given priority to negotiations in order to increase the chances of saving the hostages.[244]

The "Brzezinski Administration": A Balance Sheet

To sum up Brzezinski's four years at the White House requires adopting several perspectives, both political and personal. The first entails the paradox of an administration whose numerous successes contrast with the image it left behind, a remarkably negative one in the eyes of contemporaries as well as in the collective memory. The second column in the political balance sheet concerns Brzezinski's performance as national security adviser, charged with coordinating America's external activity and with guiding and "protecting" the president. As for the more personal summing-up, it consists especially of attempting to answer the question raised in the introduction: which of Brzezinski's ideas really counted in the exercise of power?

When he sought to criticize the Obama administration and warn it against the risk of "weakness and indecision," "incoherence and reversals," in an article published in early 2010, the historian Walter Russell Mead evoked the threat of a "Carter syndrome." His piece made the cover of *Foreign Policy*, on which the two presidents appeared with a disquieting equals sign between them, followed by a question mark.[245] However, few administrations have known so many tangible successes (Panama, Camp David, China) in only four years. Several factors make it possible to account for this paradox. The Soviet invasion of Afghanistan and then the Iran hostage affair weighed heavily on the image of weakness and impotence that the Carter administration projected, shoving the other issues, and the successes, onto the sidelines and then into oblivion. The electoral defeat itself, which can largely be attributed to this image, left an impression of failure that colored Carter's entire balance sheet—a defeat that also resulted from economic factors directly affecting Americans (inflation above 13 percent, plus the oil crisis) and thus exacerbating the negative image of the administration. Two other more complex factors on the external level played major roles.

Carter was unquestionably a victim of the historical transition between détente and the new Cold War. Elected with the support of the doves and with the benefit of the doubt on the part of the hawks, he could not help but disappoint the former with his shift to a stronger defense policy in 1980, without going far enough to satisfy the latter, who were little inclined to recognize his real change in posture between 1977 and 1980. Several decisions made in the area of security during the first two years of his administration had created an image of weakness. These were the initial lowering of the defense budget by $6 billion, the withdrawal of nuclear weapons and some troops from South Korea (a choice highly contested by the military and by Congress), the decision to stop the B-1 bomber program in June 1977, and then to stop production of the neutron bomb in April 1978 (two decisions strongly criticized by the Republican opposition), and the launching of new domains of arms control negotiations (conventional weapons, the Indian Ocean, and so on). Each time, as Robert Gates has noted, Carter had solid reasons for making particular choices, but he was incapable of measuring the overall effect produced by the accumulation of his decisions—which were often made against Brzezinski's advice.[246]

This explains why Carter's overall rating in defense matters remained negative, despite decisions that were often important for the future. These included the pursuit of the cruise missile program, the deployment of the MX missile, the decreased importance attributed to Minutemen missiles, the modernization of the Trident submarines and their SLBM missiles, and, most important for the wars to come in the 1990s and 2000s, the decision to finance the next generation of stealth bombers (the B-2, which explains the decision to cancel the B-1), and the new directive concerning the nuclear deterrent (PD-59), the Carter doctrine for the Middle East, and the Rapid Deployment Force. All of these decisions were either unknown to the public at the time or else deliberately minimized by the hawks and Ronald Reagan during the 1980 campaign, thus contributing to the image of Carter as a weak leader who had endangered the security of the United States.

The inability to promote the administration's decisions and achievements, highly honorable though they were, constitutes the second general explanation for the paradoxical balance sheet. The president and his team, at the outset, were very ambitious. They set maximally ambitious goals and in fact met a good number of them but not all, or not as fully as they had proclaimed, and this could not help but disappoint. The Carter administration set a trap for itself through its rhetoric, by creating expectations that no administration could have realistically expected to satisfy. Carter's ambition to eliminate nuclear weapons and thereby create a more humane world, announced at the start, could only give way to disappointment in the face of the modest steps taken toward realizing it. The rhetoric of human rights, even without hyperbole, contributed to the disillusionment when the inevitable compromises had to be made between values and national security. The administration promised too much in the areas of peace and disarmament, before promising too much in the area of containment; Destler, Gelb, and Lake argue that it fell into its own trap after alerting the public about the Cuban and Soviet intervention in the Horn of Africa. The same phenomenon of overoptimistic declarations from which the administration had to back down was also manifested in statements about the Soviet brigade in Cuba, the Soviet invasion of Afghanistan (described as "the most serious threat to world peace since the Second World War" but followed by largely symbolic retaliatory measures such as boycotting the Olympic Games), and also the Tehran hostage crisis, during which Jimmy Carter announced his decision to stay in the White House to concentrate on freeing the hostages rather than traveling to campaign for reelection (the "Rose Garden strategy"). He thus held himself hostage to the situation, and ultimately highlighted his own helplessness.[247]

Beyond these failures, many of which can be attributed to a poor political communications strategy and to a troubled geopolitical environment, the administration did have its share of successes. On January 20, 1981, Carter's team did not have to be embarrassed about the situation it was leaving to Ronald Reagan. The picture was somewhat smudged in Latin America owing to the rise of Marxist forces; the dictator Somoza fell in 1979, to be replaced by the Marxist Sandinistas. But the Panama Canal treaties—which Reagan had strongly opposed—had removed a major, truly explosive source of irritation for Washington's relations with the region, and set the stage for a better climate. The Soviets had invaded Afghanistan, but Washington had adopted a sturdier defense posture, including within NATO, and a significantly increased budget. Reagan maintained and expanded these measures, while respecting the SALT II treaty, even though it had not been ratified and even though he had opposed it. Reagan gradually pursued some of the policies that had been introduced largely under Brzezinski's influence, in particular, support for the mujahedeen, sanctions on trade and on advanced technologies, and insistence on the implementation of the Helsinki Accords. The Reagan administration could also count on normalized and stabilized relations with China, even in the realm of intelligence—an achievement that the Republicans could not have managed, given the importance of the Taiwan lobby in their ranks. In the Middle East, the huge advance at Camp David had helped stabilize the situation.[248] Further, the Tehran hostages were freed by Carter (who flew to bring them home on January 20, 1981), opening up the possibility of establishing new relations with Khomeini's Iran, at war with Saddam Hussein's Iraq at the time. The increasingly negative image of America in the post-Vietnam world and the Nixon era had begun to shift, owing to Carter's human rights policies and the efforts of Cyrus Vance and Andrew Young.

Many of these successes, which partially made up for America's strategic retreats in the 1970s (in Indochina, in Africa, in Iran, toward OPEC, and so on), were the result of courageous decisions that proved to be costly for Jimmy Carter in electoral terms. Nearly one-third of the senators voted against the ratification of the Panama Canal treaties, and 30 percent of those who voted in favor lost their seats in the next election. This allows us to glimpse the intensity of the opposition of elected officials to the campaign being waged by the White House, and thus the political capital Carter committed to that fight. Contrary to what might have been expected, given the success of the Camp David Accords, Carter's policy on the Israeli-Arab conflict won him no gratitude from the Jewish community. Instead, it abandoned him in favor of his opponents John Anderson and Ronald Reagan in November 1980 (for the first time, the Democratic candidate fell below the bar of 50 percent of the Jewish vote). In addition to political courage, Carter must be credited with honesty. When his White House is compared to Nixon's (Watergate) or to Reagan's (the Iran-Contra affair), it is striking how impeccable respect for the law prevailed.

The administration also experienced partial successes and several painful failures. It won the SALT II treaty, but too late, and, when the invasion of Afghanistan led it to withdraw the treaty from consideration by the Senate in late 1979, there was almost no chance of ratification, given the climate of suspicion exacerbated by the issue of the Soviet brigade in Cuba. On human rights, the results were also mixed.[249] On the one hand, the administration reoriented American foreign policy by giving unprecedented attention to human rights.

This was attested by the "global issues cluster" created by Brzezinski within the NSC and especially by the elevation of the head of the Office of Human Rights to the position of assistant secretary of state. It also obtained concrete albeit limited results with the freeing of a large number of political prisoners and a lessening of repression (for example, in Peru, Chile, Argentina, and Ecuador), and with its support for dissidents in the Eastern bloc in the wake of the Helsinki Accords. These moves enhanced the image of America among the populations and dissidents involved, often at the price of friction with their governments. On the other hand, the administration soon had to lower its ambitions, especially where the USSR was concerned. It also discovered that its policies were much more effective with the small authoritarian countries that were allies of the United States than with communist countries, and it was forced to make hard choices between American interests and moral values.[250] The example of El Salvador highlighted by Betty Glad seems questionable.[251] Cambodia also comes to mind, where China—an American ally—supported the criminal Khmer Rouge regime against Vietnam.[252] In southern Africa, the record is equally mixed. If American support for the British efforts to settle the crisis in southern Rhodesia (Zimbabwe) contributed to the final resolution, in 1980 the situation in Namibia and especially in South Africa remained critical.

Ultimately, the Carter administration met with several unmistakable failures. In Iran, the replacement of the shah's authoritarian but pro-American regime by Khomeini's Islamist and violently anti-Western regime marked a step backward on the geopolitical stage. This was followed by the interminable humiliation of the hostage situation, with American diplomats held captive for 444 days; the failure of the military raid to free them in April 1980 further exposed America's weakness. In 1979, the affair of the Soviet brigade in Cuba was costly for the administration on every level. More generally, relations with the Soviets took on more importance than the White House had wanted to give them in the beginning; and they suffered from the confrontation, within the Carter team, of the very different perceptions brought to bear by Vance and Brzezinski.

In this connection, it is important to mention the challenge brought to one aspect of Brzezinski's personal political scorecard by liberals, contemporaries, and historians alike: the national security adviser was accused of having, at the very least, helped to precipitate the new Cold War through his hard-line toward the USSR. This between-the-lines accusation appears both in Elizabeth Drew's 1978 portrait and in Betty Glad's 2009 book; the latter adopts a viewpoint close to that of Cyrus Vance.[253] The accusation is based on the implicit idea of a defensive, reactive, and opportunistic USSR that had been provoked by Brzezinski's uselessly aggressive initiatives. The latter, although he was well aware of the Soviet Union's fragility, was thought to have created a self-fulfilling prophecy, setting off the fatal mechanism of action and reaction.

When considering the various stages of the shift from détente to the new Cold War under Carter, especially in the light of what has been learned from the Kremlin archives, two elements stand out. One is the blindness of the Soviet leadership to the negative effect that their military adventures in the Third World had on the Americans. The second, on Washington's side, is the pressure of public opinion and from Congress, which made it necessary for the administration to harden its original political line considerably. In this sense, while it is true that Brzezinski and the hawks overreacted to the Soviet initiatives in the absolute, it is an illusion to think that the administration could have held out long against the public perception of an American decline amplified by Soviet gains. In other words, even if Vance's approach had prevailed, he would have quickly been forced to give up his conciliatory line, and he too would have had to offer evidence of firmness to public opinion and to Congress if he wanted to preserve the dialogue with Moscow and in particular the SALT negotiations.

Brzezinski's critics concentrate on the Horn of Africa issue (1977–early 1978), asserting that the national security adviser, through his numerous press briefings on the subject, helped alert public opinion for no good reason, whereas the affair was benign in strategic terms and could not in any case have led to an effective American reaction. His was a posture that necessarily put America in a position of failure even as it degraded the American-Soviet climate, especially in Washington. Dobrynin goes further, in his memoirs: the African incidents were not taken seriously by the Politburo, which did not think that they could really upset the United States (a country that was itself active throughout the globe)—and the Horn certainly did not represent a strategic base, as the hawks alleged.[254]

From a different standpoint, Cuban and Soviet support was substantial; it demonstrated new capacities of military projection, and it worried America's regional allies. All his briefings, as Brzezinski later emphasized, had been approved by Carter.[255] Would it have been better if the public had learned of these developments via a campaign by the hawks, accusing the administration of naïveté and blindness, leading potentially to a later American overreaction that would have been, at that point, fatal to détente? Brzezinski's calculation, during those years, led him to send signals of resolve to the USSR in order to counter what he perceived as a Soviet illusion, the conviction according to which Moscow could advance its pawns without threatening the framework of détente—a framework that Brzezinski sought to preserve. The doves saw the American overreaction with regard to the Horn of Africa as a damaging blow struck to bilateral relations, one that led Moscow to lose all interest in détente to the extent of abandoning its restraint toward Afghanistan. Brzezinski, by contrast, saw America's under-reaction as a signal of weakness that emboldened the Soviets and led them to decide that they could invade Afghanistan with impunity, since America was not reacting (hence his observation that "SALT lies buried in the sands of the Ogaden").

The next step was the normalization of relations with China on December 15, 1978. Vance, backed by the liberal observers, considered that Brzezinski had given an anti-Soviet nuance to the joint communiqué, which criticized the powers seeking "hegemony." Vance had accompanied it with declarations to the press that were hostile to the Soviets, leading the latter to stiffen their stance in the SALT negotiation (he invoked "a sudden surge of Soviet inflexibility in the winter 1978–1979").[256] It can only be speculated whether Moscow would really have reacted more favorably to the announcement of normalization if it had been made with more attention to Soviet sensibilities, and in December 1978, in any case, numerous points of negotiation on SALT remained unresolved.

The last phase in the accusations against Brzezinski was the interpretation of the Afghanistan affair. For Brzezinski, it was the absence of a decisive American reaction earlier that made the invasion more probable; for the doves, it was the idea that the Soviets had nothing more to gain from the détente, and thus nothing more to lose. This was the viewpoint defended by Marshall Shulman.[257] Vance was of the same opinion, stressing stressed the diverse Soviet motivations, in particular the fear of Islamist contagion and the desire not to pull back in the face of two enemy countries—Pakistan (where the United States briefly considered setting up listening posts to replace those lost in Iran) and China (where they did install listening posts).[258] To the underestimation of the American reaction and to the feeling that, at all events, Brezhnev had nothing to lose, Dobrynin added another factor—his irritation when he learned that NATO's had made its "two-track" decision regarding Euromissiles the same day that the Soviets had invaded Afghanistan.[259] Finally, the Soviet archives show that the decision was made by a small group in the Politburo, which had ignored all external opinions (those of the military, Dobrynin's, and those of the embassy in Kabul), moreover, for essentially defensive reasons: to avoid losing an important geopolitical pawn. But there was no question of a plan for regional domination, or a race to the warm seas, as Brzezinski suspected.[260] In his weekly report, titled "Afghanistan: An Aberration or a Symptom?," Brzezinski positioned himself clearly in the "symptom" camp, and he cited the Molotov-Ribbentrop Pact, which designated the south and the regions leading to the Indian Ocean as the natural zones of expansion for the USSR (an interpretation that has been challenged).[261]

On this specific point, the liberal doves were right when they insisted, countering Brzezinski, that the Soviet invasion was primarily defensive. The fact remains that it was disturbing, easy to interpret as a stage in a concerted project of Soviet self-assertion, one preceded by other advances since 1975 and announcing future offensives—all this in a climate of pessimism about America's declining power. In addition, it was always possible that the Soviet Union, even if it had no immediate designs beyond Afghanistan, would acquire some later, drawn along by the logic of its own expansion, according to the adage "the more you have the more you want." Even Vance insisted on reacting firmly to the invasion. Thus, a vicious circle emerges that grew out of mutual blindness and led to the new Cold War; in hindsight, there seems to have been no way out. As Brzezinski remarked: "I don't think I appreciated the extent to which the Soviet leadership at the top over time had become sclerotic, and prisoner almost of the institutional dynamics of their own system. Because if you read now, the transcripts of the discussions in the Politburo on Afghanistan, and also some of the warnings of the Soviet military, you realize that you were dealing with a leadership that was operating in some sort of world actually divorced from reality, and of very low intellectual capability."[262]

One final remark to complete the evidence for this less-than-convincing trial of Brzezinski as the one who launched a new Cold War. In hindsight, an essential element appears that counted for much more than the background briefings and other stentorious declarations made by the national security adviser to feed the vicious circle of the Cold War: it was Carter's human rights policies, whose destabilizing impact on the Soviet leadership has been considerably underestimated. A recently declassified American intelligence report from 1978, for example, indicates that the Soviets had been hoping for a Ford victory in 1976, for they had counted on being able to continue the direct secret discussions they had had with Nixon and then Kissinger, discussions that they counted among their main postwar successes. Not only were they irritated by the lower priority Carter and Brzezinski (but not Vance) gave the bilateral relation, they were also very annoyed by the interference in the area of human rights, which seemed to them a violation of the code of détente.[263] The letter to Sakharov and the launching of the human rights campaign were greeted with a mix of incomprehension and anger, and that is what contributed the most to changing the climate of bilateral relations. Robert Pastor, a former member of Brzezinski's NSC, explains:

> With the detachment of thirty years, it now appears that the late 1970s were a period when the Soviet Union was feeling as if it were on an upward trajectory and could begin to play the kind of global role that the United States had played before Vietnam. At the same time, Carter, who was viewed by the American public as more accommodating, was actually tougher on the Soviets than his predecessors, not just in buttressing NATO but in a new area—human rights—which was de-legitimizing and thus more threatening. Previous presidents had criticized the Communists for political repression, but Carter was the first U.S. President to enhance the credibility of the argument by applying human rights globally—against friendly, right-wing regimes as well as against unfriendly Communist regimes.[264]

The American president's national security adviser, who really appeared in the modern form only in the 1960s with McGeorge Bundy and Walt Rostow, has two fundamental missions. The first is to coordinate the formulation of American foreign policy by making sure that the president's decisions result from a process that has taken into account the viewpoints of all the major protagonists (defense, foreign affairs, intelligence, and so on) and that they are then actually implemented by each agency. The second is to advise and protect the president, by looking out for his political interests rather than those of a bureaucracy such as the State Department or the Pentagon. Thus the adviser's sole and unique "client" is the president. Beyond these two tasks, in which he is helped by the NSC team (about thirty-five people, under Brzezinski), the national security adviser can participate in the orientation of American foreign policy and give his opinion, can be the administration's spokesperson in this area, and can sometimes even negotiate himself—at which point he is impinging on the role of the secretary of state. In the continuum that goes from the role of simple coordinator and adviser to that of originator and even kingpin of American foreign policy, Kissinger represents the extreme point of activism, while Brzezinski is positioned a few notches behind—but still within the most activist part of the spectrum.

To draw up Brzezinski's personal balance sheet for the White House years thus amounts to evaluating his performance in carrying out his two principal missions and the related tasks that he chose to take on. An initial observation is called for: if the president is in fact the national security adviser's only "client," he is therefore the adviser's most important evaluator. By this measure, Brzezinski acquitted himself well, since Jimmy Carter appreciated his work and seemed prepared to reappoint him to his position for a second term.

There were certainly some glitches in the NSC's machinery, owing to a lack of vigilance for which Brzezinski reproached himself in his memoirs. The joint memorandum on the Israeli-Arab conflict with the USSR of October 1, 1977, provides one example. Brzezinski advised Carter to approve the text, which was based on an initial Soviet document that had been revised by the State Department, but he failed to show it to the internal NSC advisers (who would have had objections), and the affair had disastrous repercussion both at home and abroad.[265] The reversal on the production of a neutron bomb offers another example of a failure to protect the president, as Richard Neustadt points out.[266] In his memoirs, Brzezinski explained that he had not grasped the full extent of the president's reticence about that weapon, and he had allowed the bureaucratic processes and the negotiations with the Europeans to proceed between August 1977 and March 1978, by which point it had become much more awkward to back out.[267]

But these "glitches" in the NSC machine were rare, especially considering the high-pressure atmosphere in which Brzezinski worked during those years. There were two more serious problems at the core of the national security adviser's responsibilities for which Brzezinski can be reproached: the cacophony of the administration and a partial failure to integrate its various foreign policy objectives strategically: in short, the "failure of leadership" for which Carter has been criticized.

On June 8, 1978, ten days after Brzezinski returned from Beijing and after he had made his famous anti-Soviet pronouncements on *Meet the Press*, fourteen members of the House Foreign Relations Committee sent a letter to Secretary of State Vance asking him to dispel "the doubts and confusion" as to the administration's position on crucial foreign policy issues such as Soviet-American relations and the Horn of Africa: who really spoke for the administration?[268] Congress was not the only entity to be disoriented. " 'I just don't know what to report anymore,' said a prominent ambassador in Washington. 'Dr. Brzezinski is up, then down. Vance is up, then down. It all goes so fast, and we don't know what to expect.' "[269]

The disagreements within the Carter administration posed two sets of problems, one having to do with external communications, the other with the substance of American foreign policy. The paradox is that the tensions between Vance and Brzezinski were not as severe as the press suggested. Yet if the press described them that way, it was not solely in the interest of sensationalism; it was also because the spectacle offered by the administration was disconcerting for outside observers. There was no way to know that, despite the partial disagreements between his two subordinates, Carter was satisfied with the advice he was getting. Thus the image projected to the public and the world at large was the catastrophic one of an administration at war with itself, and this reinforced the negative image of Carter as hesitant, bouncing back and forth between advisers, incapable of making decisions.

The question, then, is what Brzezinski could have done to keep Carter from being perceived that way. The problem was that he himself was caught in a contradiction between defending the position he believed to be correct, which required him to stand up to Vance, and, on the other hand, protecting the president's interests, which could require him to keep a lower profile in order to give the administration a veneer of coherence. Yet he felt that it was precisely by defending a stronger line that he was really protecting the president (from an attack by the right, from an image of weakness, from the risk that the SALT agreement would not be ratified, and so on). To complicate things further, Carter asked him to intervene with the media, which exacerbated the rivalry with the State Department and the impression of cacophony. In short, the origin of the contradiction lay primarily in the very functions of a national security adviser, and only Jimmy Carter himself could really have put an end to the detrimental confusion.

Brzezinski himself faced the problem head on. On February 24, 1979, he explained to Carter that the press, fascinated by the alleged Vance-Brzezinski rivalry, had exploited and magnified it. Although such phenomena had occurred in previous administrations, for example among Franklin Roosevelt's advisers, the president had been seen as a manipulator of these divisions and as their beneficiary, rather than as a victim tottering between out-of-control advisers. Brzezinski advised Carter to follow Roosevelt's example and use his two advisers in a role-reversing way: he should send Vance to Beijing and Brzezinski to Moscow, thus demonstrating presidential authority and the fact that he was holding to a single political line, his own. In the absence of that sort of initiative, Brzezinski recommended having Vance make a major hawkish speech, while he himself would make a speech about the importance of détente and the interest of a SALT agreement.[270] Carter does not seem to have reacted to that proposal. Moreover, it appears that he never fully appreciated the extent of the damage caused by the outside perception of a divided administration, as he himself was satisfied with the way it was working, and even his memoirs minimize the problem.[271]

The problem went beyond questions of image. One of the dramas with Jimmy Carter was that he was often unable or unwilling to prioritize among the various foreign policy objectives, or even to make a decision, to choose in a timely fashion between the two options presented to him, often embodied by Vance and Brzezinski. Could the latter have done more to ensure more political coherence? After all, strategic integration was one of the national security adviser's essential tasks, whereas the secretary of state had the primary mission of ensuring good relations between America and the rest of the world. The fact was that the Carter administration's objectives were sometimes in conflict with one another, especially in the early stages.

Thus the policy of nuclear nonproliferation clashed with the desire to improve trilateral relations, and it suffered in addition from the lack of European and Japanese support; it was also burdened by the promotion of human rights. Odom has provided a concrete example: Pakistan, an ally, found itself confronted with the nuclear non-proliferation policy at the same time that the Carter administration was trying to establish controls on the export of conventional weapons—but the restriction on the possibility of buying conventional weapons only incited proliferation.[272] The effects of the administration's human rights policy on allied nondemocratic regimes (South Korea and Iran, for example), their rejection by allied regimes (France and Germany in particular), and their impact on the USSR were underestimated worldwide, and the ardor of the White House had to be tempered. But it was on the relations with the Soviet Union and with Iran that the lack of strategic integration was felt most powerfully. Carter's inability to arbitrate between Vance and Brzezinski led to the adoption of a confused and detrimental policy both in terms of the administration's image and in terms of the signals sent to the other international players.

In both cases, Brzezinski faced the same dilemma. Should he take on the role of simple foreign policy coordinator in order to reinforce the unity of the administration and the coherence of its political line, while betraying his own convictions and his responsibility to give the best possible advice to the president? Or should he actively defend his point of view even if that meant causing harmful friction, while failing in his responsibility to formulate a harmonious foreign policy? Through his clear choice of the second option, Brzezinski sometimes amplified the effects of Carter's indecisiveness. Because the president had trouble making up his mind, the presentation of stubbornly defended contrasting options may have exacerbated his dilemma, with lack of choice as the result. On Iran, for example, Brzezinski explains:

> The problem I think is that neither my strategy or Vance's strategy were ever given a full-scale trial, or maybe another way of putting it: neither one or the other was ever the choice. Much of the problem was that it was like this all the time. And I don't want to blame anybody, particularly for that, because I understand how difficult that was for the President but it just was never in my view, sharply enough decided which way to go. And so we were on the one hand, giving instructions to the Shah; I was [sic]: "toughen up, declare and impose martial law, and then after that make reforms," and at the same time there were messages to Sullivan or from Sullivan undercutting the credibility of that, and so forth.[273]

The source of the problem must be sought in the direction of the president himself, whether it was the juxtaposition of contradictory objectives or an inability to decide. Brzezinski confirmed the image of a Carter immersed in the technical details of all the issues, which he mastered like no president before him, but without ever managing to be decisive. He even compared him to a sculptor who does not know when to put his chisel down.[274] Brzezinski was powerful enough to have substantial influence on Carter, and he could dissuade him from following the path recommended by Vance, but he was not powerful enough to force him to make a decision or to adopt his own recommendations wholesale. Seweryn Bialer, Brzezinski's successor at Columbia's Research Institute on International Change, explained to *Time Magazine* in 1980 that he disagreed with many aspects of the administration's foreign policy, and especially its inability to formulate a clear, firm line, but he did not blame Brzezinski. "It's the President's fault. My disappointment with Brzezinski is that he cannot change the President to make him less spasmodic."[275]

Certain of Brzezinski's critics have gone further, judging that the national security adviser amplified the weaknesses in Carter's personality. Far from leading him to adopt a clearer line, far from stabilizing him, according to the historian John Lewis Gaddis: "Brzezinski played a role that was more eccentric than centralizing, jumping from one tactical move to another with a kind of frenetic superficiality that induced uneasiness more often than insight among those looking to him for a coherent world view."[276] The journalist Strobe Talbott went even further, in a portrait devoted to Brzezinski in 1980:

> While the National Security Adviser cannot be blamed for the recent misfortunes that have befallen the U.S. or for the President's own failures of leadership, Brzezinski is personally responsible for exacerbating institutional tensions within the Government, needlessly agitating foreign leaders with his penchant for braggadocio, and sowing confusion with pronouncements that too often sound like geostrategic gobbledygook. Thus he has contributed to the impression so widespread at home and abroad of an Administration that is impetuous and in disarray. In that sense, Brzezinski is unquestionably part of Carter's overall political problem, now as the President faces the election and later if he gets a second term.[277]

Talbott also explained that Brzezinski's taste for concepts and arresting formulas (the arc of crisis, the influentials, and so on), and his endless capacity for inventing new ones ultimately amplified the impression of a lack of direction and an absence of strategic integration. In short, instead of providing ballast, as the role of national security adviser demands, in Talbott's view Brzezinski accentuated the zigzags of the administration.

All these criticisms have some truth in them, but they exaggerate the situation. First, Carter was fully conscious of the character traits of his national security adviser, and he said explicitly that he had hired him for his creativity, which he felt able to manage and use to his own benefit.[278] Next, Brzezinski indeed occasionally made some outlandish proposals, but he also fulfilled his role as national security adviser by offering the administration a coherent overall framework and a plan of action—something that Vance did not do. Finally, this framework for action did in fact lead to several undeniable successes, so that in all fairness it must be said that, beyond the failures, most notably those of 1980 (above all Iran), the Carter White House defended American interests in an effective way in a troubled period, and the national security adviser—whatever his shortcomings—had considerable responsibility for this outcome.

This debate raises the question that has to do with the link between Brzezinski's concepts and his advice to Jimmy Carter during the four years in the White House. Did ideas matter? The solid base of opinions that Brzezinski had acquired prior to 1977 was indeed the one that served him well in his advice to the president. By contrast, the relative unimportance of his university work was confirmed: it was not Dr. Brzezinski who advised Jimmy Carter, it was the man Zbigniew Brzezinski, with his past, his origins, and his convictions. He himself, evoking the origins of his political ideas, stresses that the social sciences were not much help to him: "But, generally speaking, I was never particularly overwhelmed by what might be called the stars in the different disciplines of social sciences, I thought that was increasingly theorizing of an abstract, quasi-philosophical type, not really helpful in actual decisions. I liked more this sort of combination of experience, professionalism and some academic background but sort of a mixture of that. That's the kind of staff I tried to have, actually. Huntington was a good example of that."[279]

Rather than referring to his university studies, Brzezinski mentions several sources to account for his ideas: his childhood in the context of the Cold

War; his political education in the America of the 1950s, and especially his discovery of the limits of political slogans such as "rollback"; and his contact with various organizations such as the Congress for Cultural Freedom.[280] It was not his university past that served him in his bureaucratic struggles or in the domestic policy considerations that he had to incorporate into his recommendations.[281]

Nevertheless, his academic past shows up indirectly, in the remarkable continuity in terms of his approach, his grasp of the world, and his intellectual reflexes. Brzezinski's NSC represented a powerful concentration of gray matter, and it was organized with the hierarchical flexibility of a research center, even including a weekly seminar. Throughout those four years, Brzezinski himself used the intellectual tools evoked earlier: typologies, scenarios, historical analogies, and even constant assessments in the form of grade reports (he was much more indulgent than when he graded the Nixon administration, and Carter reproached him for this).[282]

Another aspect of Brzezinski's academic background came through in his insistence on political intelligence. He had always had an excellent knowledge of the countries in which he specialized, filling in gaps through books and the press and frequent travels, and he complained on many occasions about the poor quality of the reports he received from the CIA or from the embassies. In his way of thinking, only the most solid knowledge could lead to good political decisions. Chapter 5 discussed his opposition to Marshall Shulman, also a professor of Soviet studies from Columbia, on the subject of aid to the Soviet nationalities: it was not so much that he found Shulman too "dovish," but he considered the latter, who was after all an expert on the USSR, embarrassingly ignorant. Shulman believed in the idea of a "Soviet nationality" that had been created and was presumed to have supplanted the old nationalist and identitary allegiances.[283] In November 1978, for example, Brzezinski reacted very strongly to the flagrant failure of the CIA and the embassy in Tehran to predict the troubles that threatened the shah's regime. He asked his deputy Gary Sick for an assessment of the quality of the intelligence being received from Iran—Sick found it superficial—and he requested a meeting with Cyrus Vance and CIA director Stansfield Turner to take measures designed to increase the level of political intelligence; he also alerted the president.[284]

It is in this in-between zone, where the academic background plays a highly substantial intellectual role, that the origin of Brzezinski's ideas must

Table 6.3. First Six Months: An Academic Exercise in Self-Criticism

	Brzezinski's Grades	Carter's Marginal Annotations
Basic Spirit	A	
Fundamental Assumptions	A− / B+	
Specific policies		
U.S.–Soviet	B+	↓
Middle East	A−	↓
Trilateralism	B	
South Africa	B	↓
African Crises	A	
China	C+	
Nuclear Non-Proliferation	B	
Arms Transfers	B+	↓
Latin America	B+	
Eastern Europe	D	
South Asia	B	You're too generous—we must (a) have clear goals and (b) be tenacious
Korea	A−	
Defense Policy	A−	

Source: Weekly Report #23, July 29, 1977, Box 33–41, Brzezinski Collection, Carter Library.

be sought. This reflection can be concluded with a mention of two examples of important issues in which his approach was inspired by his reflections in earlier years—but for which he himself has pointed out the limits of his knowledge: Soviet strategy and the Iranian revolution. Recall the historical reminder he addressed to Carter, after the Soviets invaded Afghanistan, about the natural expansionist tendency of the USSR, basing his argument on an interpretation of the exchanges between Molotov and Ribbentrop.[285] In another weekly report, Brzezinski used a historical analogy. Whereas Bismarck had managed to keep Germany from being surrounded, his successors did not have his skills, and, through their provocations and their clumsiness they gave rise precisely to the alliances they wanted to avoid, first between France and Russia, then between France and Great Britain. This was exactly what the Soviets were in the process of doing, Brzezinski explained, pushing

China into the arms of the United States and Japan, and inciting Europe to close ranks within NATO.[286]

Similarly, his approach to the Iranian revolution, for want of specific information about the country, was largely informed by his reflections on the French and the Russian revolutions—and even the student revolt at Columbia. In an article written for *The New Republic* in 1968, he had proposed an analysis of revolutions and counterrevolutions, and in particular of the errors committed by the powers in place in their response to the revolutionaries. In particular, he mentioned the failure to respond quickly enough, engagement in negotiations that dragged on and led to radicalization, offering concessions without a political quid pro quo, using force in the short run without attacking the heart of the revolutionary movement, and failing to introduce immediate reforms after putting down the uprising.[287] The very same analytic grid can be found in his recommendations to Jimmy Carter and even in recommendations made directly to the shah of Iran. However, a number of murky areas remain. When asked what mattered in his vision of the case, he answered;

> Well, there is no doubt that from a historical point of view, my interest in the dynamics of the French Revolution and what they did on the populace level, the whole notion of global awakening, starting with the French Revolution and my understanding of the dynamics of the Bolshevik revolution, and how revolutions tend to move towards extremes. Also, my sense that some of them could have been averted had the Anciens Régimes in either case been more intelligent and more decisive. But then at the same time, some degree of ignorance. I wasn't really alert to the specificity particularly on the fanatical side of the Shia manifestation of Islam. I had generalized but not specialized knowledge of that, but I probably therefore underestimated the contagious and extremist aspect of that phenomenon. I probably also initially at least thought too much that the Tudeh party was as much as a danger as this and I didn't anticipate that it would fade as quickly when Khomeini took over.[288]

Beyond this chiaroscuro where knowledge is concerned, one of the intellectual resources that counted the most in Brzezinski's approach was the attention he paid to change. For example, he had renamed his Research Institute on Communist Affairs at Columbia the Research Institute on International Change in 1975. Then since the 1960s he had kept his eyes on the emerging tendencies of the international system—an attentiveness embodied in his books *Between Two Ages* and "America in a New World." Unlike Kissinger, who found himself increasingly out of step with the changing world of the 1970s, Brzezinski attempted to adapt his view of international affairs—even when that meant a return to the Cold War; and he was right, in a sense, before the rest of the administration caught up. Revisiting the intellectual lessons of those four years when he exercised power, he ultimately insisted on the importance of having reflected on "the subtleties and complexities of change, and the limits of our capacity to understand."[289]

7

The Age of Authority

A few minutes after noon on January 20, 1981, Zbigniew Brzezinski left his office in the White House to begin a new stage of his life. At the age of fifty-two, he found himself back in the "between-two-worlds" atmosphere of think tanks, universities, and political commentary, but this time as an established and influential actor in discussions of international affairs. In short, he was an authority.

The attention still accorded to him after 1981 was not won on the basis of his former glory alone. Brzezinski's regular publications, his interventions in the media, his participation in groups of experts or "Wise Men," his access to decision makers at the highest level, and his occasional official or semi-official missions confirmed him in the eyes of the public and of politicians, year after year, as an authority, a reference in the world of foreign affairs. Up until his death in May 2017, the question was routinely asked by observers of international crises: What does Brzezinski think about it?

This chapter covers the more than three decades that followed Brzezinski's departure from the White House, recounts the rest of his career, and tracks his role in the major debates over foreign affairs in which he participated: the fall of the USSR (a lifelong goal); the evolution of Europe, most markedly in the east (the fate of Poland, the expansion of NATO, relations with Russia) and in the south (the wars in the Balkans); the 9/11 attacks on US soil; the wars in Afghanistan and Iraq; the crises in the Near East; China's increasing power; and Russia's renewed assertiveness. Brzezinski's life remained closely identified with the international destiny of the United States, and thus with the larger story of our world.

A Hawkish Democrat during the Reagan Years

In *Power and Principle,* Brzezinski explained that as soon as he arrived at the White House he began preparing his return to ordinary life.

> During the preceding four years I had often reminded myself—deliberately—that being in the White House was an exceptional and very transitory period in my life. Frankly, I enjoyed it enormously but I also sensed how easy it would be to become attached to the trappings of power and to become totally enveloped in its aura. I was determined not to become the captive of my temporarily exalted status, or to take it for granted, or to yearn for it when it was over. I conditioned myself to view my White House experience as a unique chapter in my life, self-contained and not repeatable. This helped me to retain some sense of perspective about it all and to be detached about its end. "Decompression" was not a problem.[1]

After leaving the White House, he joined the Center for Strategic and International Studies (CSIS), which was housed in Georgetown University at the time; its founder David Abshire had succeeded in attracting Brzezinski as a "senior adviser" alongside Henry Kissinger, Harold Brown, and James Schlesinger (with the latter playing a crucial role in convincing him to accept). Until his final days, Brzezinski retained an office at CSIS; for more than three decades his active presence had accrued to the reputation of the think tank, including in its most difficult moments.[2] At CSIS he resumed the old habit of meeting with his friends and former associates from the NSC for a weekly "brown bag lunch," a practice he later observed at the Johns Hopkins School of Advanced International Studies (SAIS).[3]

His work at CSIS was only part-time. It allowed him to have an office in Washington; predictably, he served as a consultant and gave numerous talks; he was as highly valued a presence as Kissinger on the lecture circuit.[4] He also resumed his academic activities, slipping back into his position at Columbia—a smooth transition that was by no means guaranteed in advance. The relations between academics who had "gone over to the dark side"—to positions of authority—and their colleagues could be difficult. For example, Walt Rostow had not been able to return to his position at MIT in 1969, and Kissinger had given up a position at Columbia in 1977 because of student and faculty protests. In the fall of 1981, during a reunion at Columbia, Brzezinski had lunch with colleagues from the School of International and Public Affairs and then engaged in dialogue with students, who crowded into an auditorium to hear his stories and his analyses of the four years he had spent exercising power at the highest level.[5] During the fall semester that year he resumed teaching regularly at Columbia, commuting to New York every week. In 1989, SAIS founder Paul Nitze recruited him—against Georgetown's competing offer—to join the faculty at the SAIS campus in Washington. He taught there on a weekly basis until 1997, and after that continued to give regular lectures and participate in the intellectual life of SAIS.[6]

During the summer of 1981, the entire Brzezinski family made an extraordinary trip to China at the personal invitation of Deng Xiaoping. They traveled along the route of the Long March of Mao Zedong and the Chinese Red Army of 1934–1935—a route passing through provinces often closed to foreign visitors. Those two weeks offered an exceptional family experience: the Brzezinskis discovered remote regions in a China that had not yet opened up to modernity, but in which Deng's early reforms were beginning to take hold. In the villages of Guizhou Province, they were sometimes the first Westerners the locals had ever seen; the latest model Polaroid camera Brzezinski had brought along gave them instant popularity. They stopped at historic sites along the Long March, walked over suspension bridges, ate salamanders and dog stew, and avoided deadly floods and landslides in Sichuan Province. Brzezinski could not help collecting political impressions of the Chinese people he met; he wrote them up in an article for *Life Magazine* that was equal parts popular and political.[7]

He was not taken in by this glamorous adventure, however.[8] He knew perfectly well that the trip was part of a Chinese calculation that involved cultivating influential American figures (Kissinger, Brzezinski, and Alexander Haig, in particular). By offering privileged treatment to win their good graces, the Chinese hoped to turn them into linchpins of better relations with the United States.[9] The family was accompanied by the Chinese ambassador to Britain, who knew Brzezinski because he had been Deng Xiaoping's translator during the latter's visit to Washington, and in that capacity had been to dinner at the Brzezinskis'. (China's ambassador to the United States had flatly refused to play the role of guide because of the rustic nature of the Brzezinskis' trip.) An army escort also stayed with them throughout their travels.

The fact remains that throughout the 1980s Brzezinski continued to see China, with which he had normalized diplomatic relations, as an essential counterweight to the USSR—so much so that he was concerned about the Reagan administration's tentative moves toward semi-diplomatic relations with Taiwan. In June 1989, however, given the repression in Tiananmen Square and the fall of the Berlin Wall, a new inflection could be observed in his approach. He became more critical of the Beijing government and of its treatment of human rights; indeed, he was among those who demanded that China's most-favored-nation status be revoked.[10]

Back in Washington, Brzezinski plunged once again into the controversies that had accompanied his White House years. Before leaving office in 1981, he had faced attacks by administration members. Critics included, for example, Donald McHenry, the ambassador to the United Nations, who publicly criticized Brzezinski for having communicated too much and impinged on the role of the secretary of state. Hodding Carter, in an interview with *Playboy*, characterized Brzezinski as a "second-rate thinker" who took himself to be a Kissinger but was not cut from the same cloth.[11] Brzezinski faced a much larger reputational challenge, however. The image of the Carter administration, despite several tangible successes in foreign policy, suffered disproportionately from its failures (primarily, the Iranian hostage crisis and the impression of weakness it had fostered) and from Carter's inability to win reelection.

To fight off that dark legend and also to defend his own record, Brzezinski worked all through 1981 and 1982 on a memoir of his years as the president's national security adviser. He turned for support in particular to Madeleine Albright, who helped him structure the book and clarify his approach and his memories; it was an experience in friendship in the continuity of their shared NSC experience.[12] The book that resulted, *Power and Principle,* is substantial, precise, and complete. Drawing—sometimes verbatim—on Brzezinski's personal diary, it also excerpted original documents including the confidential weekly reports he prepared for the president. As an overall theme, Carter administration policies were presented under the overall theme of tension between realism and idealism (above all in the area of human rights), but Brzezinski, writing these memoirs with a strong sense of democratic duty to provide transparency, also developed other themes that shed light on the workings of power—in particular, the bureaucratic tensions between the NSC and the State Department.

On April 6, 1983, nearly three hundred people attended an elegant reception in the headquarters of the Organization of American States, in close proximity to the White House; they had been invited by Brzezinski and his editor to the launch of *Power and Principle*. But the reception was as notable for the absences as for the luminaries among the guests. Cyrus Vance, Edmund Muskie, and Walter Mondale stayed away, as did Hodding Carter, William Sullivan, Robert Strauss, and others skewered in the book.[13] Reviews, even the positive ones, all focused on the same aspect of the book—its personal attacks and revelations— and concluded that Brzezinski was going beyond a "kiss-and-tell" treatment. He was spitting in the soup and settling scores. Indeed, *Power and Principle* denigrated the WASP elite and Vance's legalistic approach; it mocked how Mondale took out his comb before every meeting (and, more substantially, described Mondale as taking foreign policy positions solely based on domestic calculations). Brzezinski recalled the president's negative impressions of various figures: Helmut Schmidt, for example, had been seen as "a bully and a hypocrite."[14] Of course, the book offered much more than this that was worthwhile, but the dismissive remarks and damning judgments obscured the rest. Stanley Hoffmann, who was familiar with Kissinger's *The White House Years* and *Years of Upheaval*, summed up how Brzezinski's approach differed: "Henry Kissinger's memoirs are a monument carefully erected as an appeal to history. Reading them is like following a proud architect who points out the grandeur of his conception, the vistas outside, the spacious rooms inside, a sumptuous gallery of portraits, and an odd philosophical library. Brzezinski's recollections are straight and swift. Indeed, they remind one of a fighter plane that flies much of the way on automatic pilot, strafing enemy targets, and also, here and there, in passing, hitting friendly positions."[15]

For the first few months, the book's reception in the press was rather negative. Leaving aside the scathing critiques by Brzezinski's known enemies (from George Ball to Gaddis Smith, who demolished the book in a few lines in *Foreign Affairs,* to the former secretary for human rights Patricia Derian, who called the book "ludicrous garbage"), the critiques mainly came in two flavors.[16] First, the candid narrative of Brzezinski's victories and failures in the bureaucratic game gave journalists (such as Flora Lewis of the *New York Times* and Jim Hoagland of the *Washington Post*) a powerful sense of justification. Whereas Brzezinski had always reproached the press for being interested only in the personal angle and for exaggerating his struggles with Vance, here he offered a chronicle showing that these things had indeed mattered to the conduct of American foreign policy. This in turn led some to hold the book up as evidence that the functions of the national security adviser really needed to be reformed—especially after the vagaries of Kissinger and Brzezinski, since they had not been able to serve as impartial arbiters. The mistakes that multiplied under Carter (the Soviet participation in the attempt to settle the Israeli-Arab conflict, the neutron bomb, the Soviet brigade in Cuba, the Iran hostage affair, and so on) made this seem all the more true.

The second criticism leveled by some commentators was that the book proved Brzezinski understood neither the American political system (since it said virtually nothing about Congress or the press) nor President Carter's profound moral aspirations. He simply plastered a falsely elaborate system made up of dubious concepts and slogans onto a complex international system. In retrospect, this decidedly cool reception is not surprising. In an atmosphere of strong political polarization, the author intentionally wrote with a fiery candor which was clearly not in his publisher's interest to dampen. After all, the *New York Times* published four articles on *Power and Principle* (including joint reviews of Brzezinski's book and one by Vance), and the *Washington Post* published three. If the goal was to attract attention, it was met.[17]

The book's reception was the mirror of what its author would experience from the Democrats at the end of Carter's term. At the Democratic Convention in New York, in August 1980, he was booed during his talk. But he held his own, maintaining his consistent political line despite the attacks. A few weeks after Carter's electoral defeat, at the end of November 1980, Brzezinski lambasted the "escapism" that marked the party's attitude toward questions of power and toward the USSR in general. In an interview with the *New York Times,* he said: "I think the Democratic Party damages itself when it moves excessively to the left and if it becomes excessively preoccupied with what might be called the do-gooders agenda in international affairs."[18]

This increased distancing from the Democrats does not mean that Brzezinski supported the Reagan administration. After a short period of silence on the subject, he sounded the alarm in December 1981: "If present trends continue, American foreign policy is likely to be in a state of general crisis by the spring of 1982. What makes matters potentially even worse is that this could coincide with a serious economic downturn, causing the overall global position of the United States to be placed in jeopardy."[19] He proceeded to make a wholesale critique of

Reagan diplomacy, starting with the abandonment of the Israel-Palestine peace process launched at Camp David, and continuing with the deterioration of ties with China, the wave of European pacifism around Euromissiles, the growing alienation of the Third World, the chaos in the decision-making process, and a worst-case policy toward Poland (by which the administration blocked its participation in the International Monetary Fund). He attributed the latter to the absence of a carefully thought-out strategy and to a "simple-minded anti-Communist perspective."

On December 13, 1981, only a few days after the article's publication, Wojciech Jaruzelski imposed martial law in Poland, and all the leaders of the Solidarity Movement were arrested.[20] Brzezinski condemned the Reagan administration, which had abandoned the policy he had followed with Carter of warning the Communist leaders (and the leaders of Solidarity) of rumored moves—a policy that could have warded off the coup d'état.[21] He could make this assertion with confidence in part because he knew that the American government had been kept very well informed by a mole within the Polish military staff. Since 1972, Colonel Ryszard Kuklinski, because he resented Soviet domination and feared that Poland would be the first victim of an American-Soviet nuclear exchange, risked his life by turning over thousands of pages of Warsaw Pact plans to the CIA. He kept the Americans up to date on all Moscow's and Warsaw's projects, as well as on Poland more generally and the repression of Solidarity. In 1981, shortly before the military coup, he realized that his activities had been discovered, and he and his family were spirited out to the United States on an emergency basis.[22] Five years later, in 1986, General Jaruzelski's government revealed the whole story, and profited from it to stress that the Reagan administration had in fact had in its possession the plans for a coup d'état, but had said nothing and had not warned the Solidarity leaders, which might have resulted in the failure of the operation.[23] Later, Jaruzelski asserted that that silence had in effect been interpreted as a green light, confirming Brzezinski's opinion that the Reagan administration had been indifferent to the fate of Poland and had preferred the worst-case scenario, the imposition of martial law, over support for Solidarity.[24] In 1997 Brzezinski made great efforts to rehabilitate Kuklinski, who was viewed as a traitor in Poland.

In the meantime, Brzezinski was not happy with Reagan's policy. He attacked the administration's incoherent stance toward the Middle East, and while he was not opposed to taking a firm line with the USSR, he found it dangerous not to have paths for dialogue with Moscow, all the more so because the West was divided, mostly on the question of Euromissiles. He went back to suggestions he had made in the 1970s. These included regular US-USSR summits (in fact, before Reagan's second term began in 1985, there were none), a serious resumption of negotiations over arms control, a plan for Western European support for Eastern Europe and Poland in particular, and a warming of relations with China to ensure that Moscow and Beijing did not reconcile at America's expense.[25] Drawing up a balance sheet in 1986, just before the revelation of the Iran-Contra affair, Brzezinski acknowledged that Reagan had achieved some successes, chief among them the restoration of America's confidence in itself. He was severe, however, in his criticism of Reagan's passivity on the Israeli-Arab negotiations and on the question of apartheid in South Africa. Similarly, he criticized Reagan on Central America, where Brzezinski recommended a harder line in Nicaragua. As for the deficits in the budget and in trade, these constituted a time bomb for the next president; they would weaken America's position in the world.[26]

Brzezinski's opposition to Reagan never reached the virulence of his opposition to George W. Bush in the 2000s. In an ironic role-reversal, that stance made him a hero of the left wing of the Democratic Party. In both cases, he opposed the overly Manichean vision of a Republican administration, especially of the neoconservatives at its heart, and he criticized unilateralism and the absence of a developed strategic vision that would make it possible, for example, to strengthen the hand of the United States toward Europe and the Third World. He had supported Reagan's general approach—that is, his firm line toward the USSR in a Cold War that needed to be won—and unlike many Democrats, he was not put off by Reagan personally. Yet he was only half-convinced by Bush's initial responses to the September 11 attacks, and he violently opposed the war in Iraq. He also had little respect for George W. Bush personally. The Reagan administration he considered less dogmatic and, behind its inflamed rhetoric, ultimately more cautious than Bush's—a reflection of America's less dominant position in the international system.

The distance between a Brzezinski moderately critical of the Reagan administration and a Democratic Party for which anti-Reaganism became a political passion can be perceived, for example, in Brzezinski's more or less favorable response to the Strategic Defense Initiative, the "Star Wars" project for antimissile protection of the American territory announced by President Reagan on March 23, 1983. To be sure, "launched without adequate preparation and formulated in vague and even utopian terms, the President's Strategic Defense Initiative (SDI) invited criticism," he conceded.[27] But he did not believe it warranted the avalanche of criticism that it drew from its Democratic adversaries, who, during Walter Mondale's 1984 campaign, advocated a nuclear freeze—an idea that Brzezinski considered "a hoax," given the vagueness and naïveté of the notion. In reality, he wrote, SDI offered the possibility of stabilizing the strategic American-Soviet relation in a potentially more effective way than the process of arms control alone. The idea was not to create an impenetrable shield above American cities and to move definitively beyond mutual assured destruction (MAD), but rather to use the SDI system to force Moscow to reduce its arsenal of offensive missiles in exchange for discussions about its deployment—without which the system would have to be deployed quickly in order to increase American security.[28]

For all the attacks launched by Republicans on Carter's foreign policy, Brzezinski was perceived by them as the voice of anti-communist reason among the Democrats, and as a hawk. It is not surprising then that President Reagan—himself a former Democrat—and some of his advisers sought Brzezinski's services. He was received at the White House on several occasions and appointed to several commissions, including the President's Chemical Warfare Commission (1985), the President's Intelligence Advisory Board (1985–1987), and the National Security Council–Defense Department Commission on Integrated Long-Term Strategy (1987–1988).

In 1986, after the Iran-Contra scandal broke out, the president's national security adviser, Admiral John Poindexter, was forced to resign. CIA director William Casey recommended that Brzezinski be appointed Poindexter's successor. Secretary of State George Schultz recalled the suggestion in his memoirs: "I respected Brzezinski, but I thought that bringing back the NSC adviser from the Carter Administration was a crazy idea," especially after a scandal and with the confusion that surrounded the decision-making process under Reagan.[29] On another occasion, Reagan thought of Brzezinski as a substitute for himself. Brzezinski got a call from Ed Meese, one of the president's most influential advisers, who told him that the president was going to participate in an exercise that involved a simulated nuclear crisis, but that he could only attend the first two hours and that he wanted a replacement for the rest of the exercise who had some experience with the presidential role; he had thought of Brzezinski. The latter was surprised, and recommended that Meese first verify that Secretary of State Schultz and Secretary of Defense Caspar Weinberger would accept the idea. It is not surprising that both proposed someone else for the role.[30]

During the summer of 1987, Brzezinski was consulted by Vice President George H.W. Bush, who had been a member of the Trilateral Commission, regarding a possible trip to Poland in view of his presidential campaign the following year. Brzezinski advised him to plan a trip resembling the one Carter had made ten years earlier, meeting some of the regime's opponents as well as government officials. He served as intermediary with the regime and secured Jaruzelski's consent that Bush could circulate freely and make contact with representatives of the Catholic Church and Solidarity, and also with the public at large. The trip, made in late September 1987, was a triumph. The vice president was met with acclamation by the Polish crowds. He visited the memorial to Father Jerzy Popieluszko (a dissident priest and a chaplain of Solidarity who had been assassinated by the regime three years earlier), then appeared on the balcony of the church alongside Solidarity leader Lech Wałesa, both making the "V" for victory sign in front of banners showing the union colors. It was a bonus for the imagery of Bush's campaign, and the message that Brzezinski wanted to get across had been transmitted: there could be no substantial economic support from the West without political reforms.[31]

The collaboration on the Polish trip undoubtedly encouraged Brzezinski to make a serious decision regarding the 1988 presidential election. He offered public support for the Republican candidate George H.W. Bush. He went as far as to be co-president of Bush's foreign policy task force, briefing the candidate regularly. Brzezinski made up his mind during the summer of 1988, when the Democratic candidate Michael Dukakis was leading by seventeen points in the polls; this was in no way a career-driven calculation. For Brzezinski, it was a matter of supporting the candidate who seemed most apt to ensure America's security. "I have misgivings about his fundamental impulses," he said about Dukakis. "His view of the world is out of touch with the difficult realities of the world." In his eyes, the Democratic candidate was a reincarnation of George McGovern: "a combination of extensive ignorance and very strong antimilitarist impulses."[32] The decision was made more painful by the fact that Madeleine Albright was Dukakis's chief foreign policy adviser. According to Albright, Brzezinski's decision took her by surprise just as she was trying discreetly to bring him into Dukakis's camp; he, by contrast, claimed that she had kept him away from the candidate. In any case, Dukakis was not upset at the loss. His assessment aligned with other liberals' views: "I was never a fan of his. I thought he was a lousy national security adviser, with an ego as big as a house."[33]

During the 1980s, Brzezinski published two books in addition to his memoirs. In 1983, he began work on an overall strategy for America to prevail in the Cold War. This became *Game Plan,* published in 1986.[34] Although he predicted in it that the American-Soviet rivalry would continue for decades, he nevertheless started by observing that over the previous twenty years Moscow had lost ground in two ways: it had suffered both an ideological defeat and a corresponding economic defeat. The USSR had lost its credibility in both domains, and world leaders did not perceive it as a model for transforming their societies or modernizing their economies.[35] By the same token, the Soviet Union was a one-dimensional power that was falling behind in other areas of competition and could impose itself only in the military domain—with the advantage that all it had to do was avoid losing, while the United States, as guarantor of the world order, had to prevail.[36] This meant care had to be taken in choosing the military arrangements that would allow the United States to stand up to the Soviets, whom Brzezinski saw as having the capacity, over time, either to carry out a successful first strike or to make Washington pull back in an area of vital interest. To this end, Brzezinski supplied concrete recommendations, most notably urging a combination of limited antimissile defenses and restraint in the number of offensive missiles. An alternative (or addition) to the latter could be an adjustment in the geographical distribution of the American forces in the world, placing fewer in Europe, where the allies had to be forced to take more responsibility for their own security, and placing more in the Middle East and even in Central America.[37]

In the late 1980s, he went back to the history of the USSR and communism, which he had largely set aside in the early 1970s, and published *The Grand Failure* in early 1989.[38] In this far-seeing book, he argued that communism was in its death throes, with no chance of remission. Gorbachev's economic reforms could not succeed, because they did not call into question the system created by Lenin and Stalin based on the monopoly of the Communist Party and the submission of the non-Russian populations—the famous "nationalities" with centripetal tendencies that Brzezinski had described in 1950 and later in his book *The Soviet Bloc.* The other communist systems would meet the same fate, beginning with multiethnic Yugoslavia. Meanwhile, certain countries such as Poland and Hungary would be the first to evolve toward democratic regimes and would lead the Soviet Union to its collapse, while China might succeed in its economic reforms because it did not insist on maintaining ideological orthodoxy.[39]

Brzezinski was clear about the general direction of history, affirming that "Gorbachev has unleashed forces that make historical discontinuity more likely than continuity."[40] He offered four scenarios, any of which he judged more probable than the success of perestroika: an inchoate systemic crisis that would remain inconclusive; a return to stagnation; a coup d'état by the KGB and the army; or an overturning of the communist regime that would lead to the fragmentation of the USSR as a nation-state, accompanied by large-scale interethnic violence. He deemed the fourth alternative the least probable, betting rather on a cross between scenarios one and two.[41] However, contrary to his usual practice, he did not accompany his trenchant conclusions with recommendations. While he was reproached for this by the critics, he had judged, rightly, that the situation was really too fluid for doing so.[42] In other position statements made in 1988 and 1989, he stressed that brutal evolution—revolution—was not in the interest of the West, for it would surely provoke an attempt to regain control by Moscow. America must not give the impression that it was seeking a new Yalta, and NATO must not give the impression that it sought to encompass Eastern Europe. On the contrary, an agreement with the Warsaw Pact countries was necessary to demilitarize the region gradually, and economic support (from Europe, Japan, and the United States) was needed, strictly tied to the implementation of economic and political reforms in the direction of pluralism.[43]

Beyond making general political recommendations, Brzezinski was able to engage closely in Polish political life, thanks to his connections with the various parties, especially after Jaruzelski's move in September 1988 to begin a dialogue with Solidarity. The historian Patrick Vaughan describes Brzezinski's role as that of an "unofficial" operator, a facilitator working in the wings to bring together the various protagonists. The dialogue led to the Round Table Agreement in the spring of 1989 (Brzezinski went to Warsaw as an observer), which made it possible for non-communist Tadeusz Mazowiecki to be named prime minister in August 1989. Brzezinski was exultant: "These changes are the most important upheavals in Eastern Europe and in the Soviet world since the death of Stalin," he said. "And they have enormous implications for the future of communism and the East-West relations . . . We are seeing the end of an entire era."[44]

A non-communist prime minister was not the last taboo to be shattered before Brzezinski's eyes. In late October 1989 he went to Moscow, invited to give the keynote speech at a Soviet-American conference at the Diplomatic Academy of the Ministry of Foreign Affairs. He listed the stages that would be required to build the "common house" (or "home") that Mikhail Gorbachev had evoked: self-determination for the countries of Eastern Europe; German unification; political and economic liberalization everywhere; a confederate structure for the USSR. The audience gave him a standing ovation, and in the exchanges that followed, he explained that the problem went back to Lenin, and not simply to Stalin.[45]

Immediately after this episode he visited the site of the Katyn massacre with historian Jack Matlock, the American ambassador to the USSR, and a few members of the delegation. Gorbachev had for the first time authorized Polish families to return to the site where the elite among Poland's officers and intelligentsia had been murdered (amounting to twenty-two thousand executions) in April and May 1940—not by the Nazis, as Russian propaganda would have it, but by the Soviets. During that visit, on November 1, Brzezinski pulled no punches: at the base of the monument marked "In memory of the Polish officers murdered by the Nazis in 1941," he laid a basket of flowers with a card inscribed "For the victims of Stalin and the NKVD." While Polish families celebrated masses for All Saints Day on the site, Brzezinski gave interviews in which he insisted on the responsibility of the Kremlin, even as he brought a message of reconciliation: "Russians and Poles, tortured to death, lie here together . . . All over Russia there are hidden cemeteries where Russians lie, killed by Stalin and the KGB . . . It seems very important to me that the truth should be spoken about what took place, for only with the truth can the new Soviet leadership distance itself from the crimes of Stalin and the NKVD."[46] Gorbachev knew what he was doing in authorizing Brzezinski to visit Katyn. That evening, when he returned to Moscow, Brzezinski was greeted with gratitude by Russians who had seen the extensive televised report on the trip, and had heard his words. Seemingly, the Kremlin had left him the task of beginning to reestablish the historical truth.[47]

As Brzezinski had predicted, but more suddenly than he had anticipated, the Berlin Wall fell a few days later, on November 9, and the populations of

Eastern Europe regained their freedom. Strobe Talbott—a senior *Time Maga-zine* reporter who had been unsparing in his criticism of Brzezinski when he was in power, and who had been part of the delegation to Katyn—asked for an interview. His subject could only have enjoyed the headline: "Zbigniew Brzezinski: Vindication of a Hard-Liner."[48]

After the Cold War: Consolidating Victory

Until late 1989, Brzezinski's entire adult life had been oriented toward a constant strategic goal: the dissolution of the Eastern bloc and the liberation of Poland. In the 1990s, the gains from the hoped-for but unexpected fall of the Berlin Wall had to be emulated on the European continent. At the same time, another grand strategy for the United States in the world had to be imagined, at a time when new geopolitical fault lines were opening up and when, paradoxically, America was experiencing self-doubt—a vigorous debate over its supposed decline was under way. Although Brzezinski sided with the doves regarding the Gulf War in 1991, he went on to adopt a hawkish position on the wars in the former Yugoslavia, and he played an important role in the expansion of NATO to include new countries in Eastern Europe—this was one facet of his support for Poland during that decade.

In 1990, the situation was murky: the Wall had fallen, but the USSR and the Warsaw Pact were still in place, and Germany was engaged in a forced march toward reunification in October. In a landscape changing so rapidly, every position became quickly outdated. In the spring, for example, Brzezinski rec-ommended a security framework featuring institutional cooperation between NATO and the Warsaw Pact (declaring that "for the foreseeable future, there is no alternative to the two existing alliances"), moving towards a "trans-European commonwealth" that would include Central Europe and that would be open to the USSR, which would have to become a confederation.[49] He also suggested that the world order would henceforth depend on Europe and "Amerippon" (a pan-Pacific alliance with Japan).[50] These published views placed him out of step with fast-evolving realities. A similar problem seemed to mark his responses to Saddam Hussein's invasion of Kuwait on August 2, 1990, and the forceful reaction to it ordered by President Bush in early 1991.

As early as August 16, 1990, Brzezinski expressed approval for the president's decision to deploy American forces around Iraq. After all, it represented an enforcement of the "Carter Doctrine" by which it was in the vital interest of the United States to prevent any hostile domination of the Gulf, including by military means, and it used the "Central Command" directly inherited from the Rapid Deployment Force instituted in 1979—two of Brzezinski's own initiatives. But in his view, if it was up to America to deter a second aggression (against Saudi Arabia, for example), it was up to the international community—in particular the USSR, Japan, and the Arab states—to drive Saddam Hussein out of Kuwait. America should not take that on as its own crusade; doing so might well alienate the Arab populations and incite other regional actors to go to war, thereby endangering the only objective he saw as truly vital, the security of the oil supply.[51]

It was hardly surprising then that when Bush assembled hundreds of thousands of American soldiers in the Gulf to prepare for war during the fall, Brzezinski recommended "patience and prudence." As he saw it, a war would produce a very large number of casualties, American troops included; it would destabilize the region and be perceived as an Israeli-American offensive; it would be extremely costly, in part owing to a rise in oil prices; and it would quickly become unpopular. He recommended rather a strategy of "punitive deterrence" against Iraq (in the form of UN sanctions), with mediation and an international conference that would also deal with the Israel-Palestine problem.[52] He maintained this position until the military offensive began on January 17, 1991, which contradicted all his predictions, thanks mainly to the superiority of the American forces and the successful effort to assemble a broad coalition that included Arab states.

In April 1991, Brzezinski acknowledged his error with good grace: the victory had been easier than anticipated, leading to tangible and easily identifiable gains. A pronounced aggression had been driven back. America had regained its lost military glory and established itself as the predominant power in the Middle East—a situation that could only reassure its allies, and all those who depended on moderate oil prices. Meanwhile, the USSR had been reduced to the role of onlooker. After noting these developments, Brzezinski went on to exhibit a renewed flair for predictions, pointing out the dangers for the future. First, because Iran had been strengthened, there would now be a need to maintain a substantial American military presence in Saudi Arabia, which could become the source of future instabilities. Indeed, this would become one of Osama bin Laden's charges against the Americans and the Saudi monarchy. Second,

problems would result because the image of America among the region's populations had suffered, both from the crushing of Iraq and from the abandonment of
the rebellious Shiites and Kurds. Third, this war might have unleashed a chain
reaction leading to a "Lebanonizing" of the entire region, in which the United
States could become enmeshed.[53] In a 1993 book, *Out of Control,* Brzezinski
developed these themes and while he may have underestimated the potential
of Islamism, he recognized its importance. "The United States is almost certain to remain, throughout this decade and into the next century, the central
arbiter of the power politics of the Persian Gulf/Middle Eastern region. The
long-range danger is that the United States could thereby become embroiled
in a protracted engagement in the region's almost endless list of trouble-spots,
with the additional risk of a dangerous cultural-philosophical cleavage with
the world of Islam, whose theocratic and fundamentalist tendencies the West
understandably fears."[54]

Written in 1991–1992, *Out of Control* is one of Brzezinski's most curious
books, and the most out of character; here, his usual optimism gave way to
very dark predictions. In it, he was responding implicitly to Francis Fukuyama's
The End of History by arguing that ethnic hatreds, xenophobia, religion, and
perhaps even "a new form of fascism" (in Russia, for example—which could
prove contagious for Central Europe) all threatened the supposedly inevitable
march toward liberal democracy. He referred to a forthcoming article by Samuel
Huntington on the "clash of civilizations," noting that Huntington's analysis was
close to his own.[55] Countries such as India and China, far from becoming stable
market democracies, could plunge into the kind of turbulence that previously
industrialized countries had experienced in the twentieth century. Meanwhile,
the developed countries, beginning with the United States, were weakening
their model and their message with levels of hedonism and consumerism that
were "out of control." A *New York Times* review noted that Brzezinski was beginning to sound "like Aleksandr Solzhenitsyn denouncing the spiritual malaise
of the West," as he criticized television for its glorification of sex and violence,
and mocked Americans' fondness for plastic surgery.[56] America, Brzezinski
concluded, would jeopardize its preeminence as the foremost world power if it
did not return to sounder moral values.

This diatribe is all the more striking given that Brzezinski had not sided
with the "declinist" camp in the great debate aroused by Paul Kennedy's *The
Rise and Fall of the Great Powers,* published in 1987. As shown by his article in

Foreign Affairs in the spring of 1988, he put himself in the same camp as Joseph Nye (in *Bound to Lead*), believing that America's potential power would remain intact despite the ups and downs of its economy—provided that sound political decisions were made.[57] This would be his position again in 2012 when, during a new epidemic of declinism, he published his last book, *Strategic Vision: America and the Crisis of Global Power.*[58]

Brzezinski found himself in direct disagreement with the Bush administration regarding the Gulf War, and increasingly unaligned on the issue of the Balkans. On other matters, especially regarding changes in Europe, developments in China, and the Israel-Palestine question, the winner of the 1988 election did not disappoint him. The president consulted him on various occasions, most notably regarding what stance to adopt during the Malta summit with Gorbachev in early December 1989. Yet Brzezinski had less access to the administration than he had hoped for, because Secretary of State James Baker never consulted him. This may have played a role in his decision not to support President Bush in his 1992 reelection campaign. He returned to the Democratic fold, judging that the campaign dealt essentially with domestic matters, and he claimed to be less worried about the leftist tendencies of the Clinton-Gore team on international affairs. Still, he was not very active in the campaign, which was directed in part by former members of the State Department with whom he had clashed under Carter (especially Tony Lake and Richard Holbrooke).[59]

His relations with the Clinton administration were mixed from the outset. On the one hand, he opposed with increasing impatience a policy toward the Balkans that he found too soft, and broadly criticized the president for his lack of leadership in foreign policy—a deficiency that was not compensated for by Secretary of State Warren Christopher, who had been Vance's second in command under Carter. On the other hand, he managed to find increasingly common ground with several members of the Clinton administration with whom he was not naturally close—for example, with Lake and Holbrooke on the expansion of NATO, and even with Strobe Talbott, after getting off to a rocky start, on the question of Russia and Ukraine.

The outbreak of hostilities in Yugoslavia came as no surprise to Brzezinski, who had predicted it in early 1989 in *The Grand Failure.* He resumed his critique of America's passivity toward the crisis as soon as Bill Clinton took office, pressing the administration to act forcefully against Slobodan Milošević's Serbs, whose fight to take over Bosnia at the expense of the Croats and the

Bosnian Muslims was devolving into ethnic cleansing. In an echo of his Carter administration struggle, Brzezinski the hawk opposed the Vance-Owen peace plan for Bosnia-Herzegovina, a plan put forward by Vance (who was then serving as a special envoy of the UN general secretary) and defended by Secretary of State Christopher during the first half of 1993. In April, Brzezinski assailed the administration in a *New York Times* opinion piece titled " 'Never Again'— Except for Bosnia." It skewered the statesmen who, despite being "retroactively 'Churchillian' " (convinced, that is, that they would have done just as Churchill did in the face of evil), were turning a blind eye to the atrocities being carried out by the Serbs. Faced with a crime that called for a forceful response, they were playing the part of the appeasement-like modern-day Chamberlains. Brzezinski had rarely come across as so idealistic, or so impassioned, as he did in condemning the Vance-Owen plan. "The feud, Defense Department spokesmen tell us, does not involve our national security interests. Neither did the slaughter of the Jews, some would have argued. Of course national interests dictate large defense budgets—but apparently not the use of force to defend justice and to assert morality. It follows that bombing the aggressors, providing arms to the defenseless and truly enforcing—rather than pretending to enforce—the no-fly zone is beyond the political courage and moral sensitivity of the West."[60]

After the failure of the Vance-Owen plan had been acknowledged, Brzezinski joined a hundred other prominent figures—including Margaret Thatcher, George Schultz, and Jeane Kirkpatrick—in calling on President Clinton and NATO to strike Serbian military targets in Bosnia and air bases in neighboring Serbia, and to help the Bosnian government arm itself so as to bring balance to the conflict. During the following year, Brzezinski continued to defend the option known as "lift and strike" (a unilateral lifting of the arms embargo in favor of the Bosnians and air strikes on Serbian targets), and he signed other appeals to that effect.[61] He assailed the administration, deploring the lack of leadership by a president excessively focused on domestic matters. "I am concerned by the fact that an America whose power has to be credible has been defied in the last few months by Milosevic, has been defied very successfully by Aidid—and today's liberation of the American prisoner [in Somalia] is no American victory, it follows in the wake of an American capitulation—and we have been defied by brigands in Haiti. This is devastating to American power."[62]

With the Srebrenica massacre perpetrated by Republika Srpska forces, killing more than eight thousand Bosnian men and boys on July 11, 1995, the impotence of the international community became glaringly clear. Brzezinski published a *New Republic* piece that had the structure and tone of a presidential address, and prefaced it with a withering line: "The following is the speech that might have been delivered immediately upon the fall of Srebrenica if the post of Leader of the Free World were not currently vacant."[63] He defended the "lift and strike" option more strongly than ever and criticized the UN's impotence, which encouraged the Serbs' aggressions. He insisted that if the United States left it up to the Bosnians to fight, which they would be quite ready to do if they had not been denied the means, then it had to accept responsibility for avoiding widespread massacres. He stressed that the international order and the defense of human rights were at stake. Subsequent responses—the NATO bombardments starting on August 30, and the Dayton Agreement negotiated by Holbrooke and signed in December—were more in line with his positions.

The dramas of the former Yugoslavia were not over, however, and the question of Kosovo soon arose. Kosovo, with its majority population of Albanian Kosovars, was another ex-Yugoslavian province under the authority of Belgrade, and considered by the Serbs to be a cradle of their civilization, where Milošević tried to crush a rebellion of independence seekers. In the fall of 1998 and in early 1999, while Holbrooke, eager to repeat the success of the Dayton Agreement, believed a solution could be negotiated with Milošević, Albright, who had become secretary of state for Clinton's second term, was tougher. After the failure of the Rambouillet negotiations (in February–March 1999), she pushed NATO toward a military intervention that began on March 24. Brzezinski strongly criticized American diplomacy, which had lost its credibility by multiplying threats but not following through where Milošević was concerned; this also made it more difficult for the Serbian leader to explain to his own people that the time had come to make concessions.[64]

The intervention, which entailed only aerial bombardments carried out at high altitudes to minimize the risks, worried Brzezinski. Indeed, it was slow to produce effects, for Milošević accepted a peace plan only at the beginning of June, and in the interval public opinion grew impatient. On March 30, Brzezinski criticized the limits of the air strategy and called not only for arming the Kosovo Liberation Army, but also for preparing an intervention on the ground—a move the Clinton administration had ruled out for domestic reasons, thus lessening its ability to put pressure on Milošević. In May, Brzezinski worried about the damage done to NATO's credibility, and to American leadership in general, if Milošević did not yield. He was critical of Bill Clinton's action, which he deemed inept: "His overeager diplomacy has undercut the credibility of his military campaign, while his timid military tactics are depriving his diplomacy of serious clout."[65] The only solution was to intervene on the ground, which would be necessary in any case to guarantee that the Albanian Kosovar refugees could return home. Finally, Brzezinski was irritated by the Clinton administration's benevolence toward Russia, whereas Russia's goal throughout the crisis had clearly been to discredit both NATO and American leadership.[66]

When victory came in the first weeks of June 1999, it brought an important lesson for Brzezinski: Russia had played a negative role throughout the crisis. A few months later, he even put forward a theory about Milošević's capitulation that gave Moscow a central role. According to him, the Serbian leader gave up not because of the bombing, which had not been effective either in reducing his military potential or in turning public opinion against him, and not because of the threat of intervention on the ground. Rather, it was because he had turned to the Russians to obtain a partition of Kosovo, under the pretext of accepting the G8 peace plan. When Russian forces took control of the Pristina airport on June 11, it was in order to carve out an occupation sector in the northeast, the heart of the Serbian part of Kosovo, which could in the long run be attached to Belgrade rather than becoming autonomous or even, eventually, independent. But the Europeans' determination to reject a Russian zone of occupation in addition to the Western zones, and especially the refusal of Hungary, Rumania, and Bulgaria to let the Russians use their airspace to send troops to Pristina, thwarted the Russian and Serbian plans. Clinton, Brzezinski pointed out mockingly in his conclusion, had warmly thanked the Kremlin for its aid in resolving the crisis.[67]

For the Russian question remained very much at the heart of Brzezinski's strategic thinking during the 1990s. Having declared early in the Gorbachev era that Moscow's road toward stability and democracy would be a hard one, Brzezinski was not surprised by the difficulties that arose on several fronts—the bilateral relation, Ukraine, Chechnya, and even the expansion of NATO. His overall approach grew out of a simple principle. By yielding too much to the

Russians, by seeking to spare their egos and closing its eyes to their excesses, the West only encouraged the extreme elements in their internal debates and delayed their indispensable adjustment to the new post-imperial reality. To encourage that adjustment, on the contrary, it would be necessary to consolidate the satellite countries that had emerged from the communist era, a move that would have the twofold effect of encouraging Russia itself to follow the path of modernization, and of cutting short any dreams of recreating a post-Soviet empire.

This explains why Brzezinski was so concerned about Ukraine during the 1990s: "It cannot be stressed strongly enough that without Ukraine, Russia ceases to be an empire, but with Ukraine suborned and then subordinated, Russia automatically becomes an empire."[68] He was consulted on several occasions by Ukrainian presidents Leonid Kravchuk and Leonid Kuchma, and he intervened with the administration in particular, in 1993, over the question of dismantling the nuclear weapons that had remained on Ukrainian territory.[69] The following year, he created the "American-Ukrainian Advisory Committee" within CSIS, bringing together observers from the two countries (including Jimmy Carter and Henry Kissinger) to make recommendations on the bilateral relation, especially in terms of economic development and energy independence vis-à-vis Russia.

At the beginning of the Clinton administration, Brzezinski vigorously opposed the political priority granted to Russia (the "Russia-first policy") embodied by Talbott, who soon became number two at the State Department. As Brzezinski saw it, the administration did have a grand strategy toward Moscow, but it was the wrong one. In order to avoid accusations of having "lost Russia" the way others had lost China in the late 1940s, the administration flattered Russia. It gave Russia tokens of respect (entry into the G7, first as an observer and then as a participant, 1996–1998), encouraged investments even while closing its eyes to the oligarchs' corruption, concentrated on nuclear disarmament and pretended to be unaware of the Russian interventions among its close neighbors (Moldavia, Croatia, Tajikistan, and so on). But democracy was slow to develop, while the imperialist temptation was quite manifest in Moscow's relations with its neighbors, where it used economic weapons and military intimidation. Brzezinski was particularly indignant about Washington's passivity and acquiescence in the face of the first Chechen war carried out by Boris Yeltsin (1995–1996), as he was to be in the face of the second one, conducted by Yeltsin and Vladimir Putin

(1999–2000). The latter incited him to create the "American Committee for Peace in Chechnya" with former secretary of state Haig.[70] Rather than accommodation, he recommended an overall strategy of "geopolitical pluralism" in the territories of the former Eastern bloc, which would force Moscow to acknowledge the post–Cold War reality and stop nourishing the post-imperial dream This strategy implied reinforcing the independence of countries such as Ukraine, encouraging regional integration in central Asia, and/or expanding NATO.[71]

These recommendations turned up again in the most important book Brzezinski produced in the 1990s, *The Grand Chessboard* (1997), an attempt to prescribe an American geopolitical strategy adapted to the post–Cold War world. The book had quite an effect on public opinion (and on conspiracy theorists in particular), given that Brzezinski recommended a foreign policy aimed at ensuring American control of the Eurasian continent, which was described, following the British geographer and politician Halford Mackinder, as the heart of the world. Brzezinski wrote:

> This huge, oddly shaped Eurasian chessboard—extending from Lisbon to Vladivostok—provides the setting for "the game." If the middle space can be drawn increasingly into the expanding orbit of the West (where America preponderates), if the southern region is not subjected to domination by a single player, and if the East is not unified in a manner that prompts the expulsion of America from its offshore bases, America can then be said to prevail. But if the middle space rebuffs the West, becomes an assertive single entity, and either gains control over the South or forms an alliance with the major Eastern actor, then America's primacy in Eurasia shrinks dramatically. The same would be the case if the two major Eastern players were somehow to unite. Finally, an ejection of America by its Western partners from its perch on the western periphery would automatically spell the end of America's participation in the game on the Eurasian chessboard, even though that would probably also mean the eventual subordination of the western extremity to a revived player occupying the middle space.[72]

What was interesting about Brzezinski during this period was his capacity to integrate concrete policies in a coherent way into an overall picture, as he did in *The Grand Chessboard*. A good portion of his activity continued to revolve not around reflection of the academic sort but rather around tangible initiatives and projects, many of which—no surprises here—involved Poland. In particular, he advised its leaders, and he sought above all to orient Washington's decisions in a favorable direction. The expansion of NATO was to crown his efforts.

When Wałesa was elected president of Poland in December 1990, Brzezinski made two recommendations: first, to look closely at the background of the tens of thousands of Poles hired by the Ministry of the Interior to spy on their compatriots, in order to prevent suspicions and revelations from continuing to poison social life in the future; and, second, not to adopt a constitution too quickly. In fact, Poland made only cosmetic changes in 1992, before adopting a definitive constitution in 1997.[73] Brzezinski made himself particularly useful from his vantage point in Washington. He intervened as a facilitator, as a sort of informal lobbyist, especially on the financial questions that were particularly troublesome for Poland at the time (on the convertibility of the zloty and the restructuring of the debt with the Club of Paris, he made sure that Washington played an active role). He also worked to set up a "Polish-American Enterprise Fund," a fund financed by the US Congress amounting to $240 million in the context of American support for the transitions in Eastern Europe (the SEED act) and intended to stimulate free enterprise in Poland.

In 1992, following his discussions with Wałesa and other leaders, Brzezinski created the "US-Poland Action Commission" at CSIS (which quickly grew to become the "America-Europe-Poland Action Commission"). As its name indicates, it was wholly oriented toward concrete endeavors rather than reflection.[74] The purpose was to help Poland make the transition to a market economy by bringing together officials and businessmen from the two countries. It resulted most notably in the creation of the position of ombudsman for foreign investment and of a council that would facilitate access to businesses for the ministers concerned. Another action group, focused on Russia, was created at CSIS shortly afterward by Kissinger and by the mayor of Saint Petersburg, Anatoly Sobchak, modeled on Brzezinski's Polish commission.[75]

Brzezinski's activism in favor of the country where he was born gave rise to an unexpected question, on two occasions: What if Brzezinski became president of Poland? In the context of the democratization of formerly communist countries, this hypothesis was far from being pure speculation, and one can find several cases in which Westerners from the diaspora, or immigrants from those countries, were elected to important positions during the 1990s and 2000s. For the November 1990 election, it was too early, and in any case it was out of the question for Brzezinski to run against the national hero. By contrast, for the November 1995 election, the hypothesis came up more often. Wałesa was not convincing as president, and would not be reelected. Brzezinski was urged to run by several prominent Polish leaders, among them the former prime minister Mazowiecki, who headed one of the principal opposition parties, and the former Solidarnosc militant Alexander Hall, who led a center-right group and wanted to put forward a consensus candidate as a replacement for Wałesa.[76] But Brzezinski did not hesitate for long: he was American, not Polish, and would he be capable of managing a country in the middle of a major transition, in all its dimensions?[77] He preferred to continue to play the role of a remote adviser, to help Poland become a Western-style liberal democracy.

He was not at all an untrammeled free-market ideologue, however; on the contrary, after a few years he became critical of the shock treatment that certain Americans recommended for the transformation of countries in the former communist bloc. In place of the dogmatism he observed, he recommended in 1991 that the varied experiences of the countries involved be taken into account, and above all, that changes not be made too hastily in a misguided attempt to achieve in a short time what had taken decades in Western Europe and in the United States. He summed up his advice in a schema consisting in three stages. The first, which was to last three to five years, depending on the country, would see political transformation and economic stabilization. The next stage, extending from the third to the tenth year, would see political stabilization and economic transformation. Finally, the third stage, open-ended, would see political consolidation and continued economic progress. In applying his schema, he distinguished the countries in which political evolution and economic evolution were mutually positive (citing Poland and Hungary as examples) from those in which only the political evolution (Russia) or the economic evolution (China) had been positive, and finally from those in which both had been problematic (Rumania).[78]

In the same article, addressing his advice to American and European decision makers, he insisted on the need for a more coordinated and more strategic approach on the part of the G7, and on the importance of Ukraine, which required a specific form of aid: "the needed strategy should be neither Russocentric nor Russo-phobic."[79] Given the growing instability in the territories of the ex-Eastern bloc, it was essential to think about new security arrangements that would see the gradual admission of the former communist states into NATO (the first ones could be admitted as early as 1996). The process was made more acceptable for Russia and Ukraine by the creation of a large Euro-Atlantic system of security that might one day include Moscow and Kiev.[80]

The expansion of NATO was indeed Brzezinski's major cause during the 1990s, even more than intervention in the Balkans. To achieve it, he lobbied intensively and finally became—according to James Goldgeier, the author of a book on NATO expansion—the external actor who had the most influence over the process.[81] Goldgeier explained that as compared to Kissinger, the other expert to whom the decision-makers listened on this topic, Brzezinski benefited from better access to the Democratic administration (despite his past friction with actors such as Lake, Albright, or Holbrooke), and that the strategy he proposed had the advantage of reserving a place for Russia. His op-ed column in the *New York Times* in December 1993 thus suggested a dual approach. He recommended admission, at the appropriate time, of three or four countries as full-fledged members of NATO, balanced with a formal treaty between NATO and Russia, to reassure the latter rather than claiming that it too could join NATO one day, an unrealistic hypothesis that would lead, if it were implemented, to diluting the organization.[82] During the following fall, the administration adopted that approach, which ended up prevailing in 1997.

But before reaching that point, let us look quickly at the protagonists and the stages in the battle. As supporters, Brzezinski had a sort of "Polish clan" consisting of Jan Nowak and the ambassador Jerzy Kozminski. Nowak was a hero of the Polish resistance who had played the role of emissary for the Home Army vis-à-vis the Allies, including Churchill, and he had become the animator of the Polish branch of Radio Free Europe after the war. The young Brzezinski, full of admiration, went to see him in Munich in 1953, and a lasting friendship was born. Nowak lived in Washington from 1976 on, and he soon became head of the Polish-American Congress, the lobby of the large Polish-American community, estimated at some ten million citizens. Kozminski, after having served in the highest echelons of the new Polish state, was named ambassador to Washington in 1994, a crucial year for the decision to expand NATO. At the height of the battle around this issue, these three compatriots spoke to one another by telephone every day to coordinate their actions on the various fronts.[83] They had allies within the administration. Lake, the president's national security adviser, did not always get along with Brzezinski, but he shared the latter's views on NATO expansion and worked closely with him. So did Holbrooke when he was recalled from his post as ambassador to Germany to join the State Department and take over Bill Clinton's vacillating European policy (focusing on the Balkans and NATO expansion). He carried this out in the face of direct opposition from a large group in the State Department that wanted to prioritize good relations with Russia. Talbott was responsible for the US policy toward the former Soviet Union; he believed that to ensure Europe's security, the first priority was to stabilize the former Soviet Union. Under these circumstances, it was out of the question to provoke Moscow. As for the Defense Department, the leaders in the Pentagon, military as well as civilian, did not look favorably on the extension of NATO security guarantees to new countries, a move that would dilute the military effectiveness of the organization, moreover; they tried simply to block expansion, or at least to postpone it indefinitely.

The idea of adding new members to NATO was born in 1991, with the dissolution of the Warsaw Pact. Brzezinski observed, during the fall of that year, that the liberated countries dreamed of joining the European community and NATO, and that Moscow wanted to prevent that development at all costs. Even as he noted that a certain form of guarantee by NATO began to extend, de facto, to countries such as Poland, Czechoslovakia, and Hungary, he did not yet call for their inclusion, and he hoped that Europe would respond to their aspirations.[84] By contrast, as early as February 1992 he declared to the Polish Senate that the time had come to put the question of their membership in NATO officially on the table.[85] In the spring he wrote in the *Washington Post* that in order to respond to their growing sense of precariousness "Hungary, Poland and Czechoslovakia should now be more formally included in binding security arrangements involving either NATO or the Western European Union."[86] When Clinton took office in January 1993, Brzezinski began to militate for their inclusion as full-fledged members of NATO.

Three months later, Clinton inaugurated the Holocaust Museum in Washington, in the presence of several East European leaders. Lech Wałesa and Vaclav Havel took advantage of the opportunity to ask for their country's admission to NATO, which made a powerful impression on the young president. However, in June, Secretary of State Christopher declared that expansion of NATO was not on the agenda, deferring the discussion to early 1994 in Brussels. The first round was played at this point: the Pentagon promoted a program for associating the former communist countries called "Partnership for Peace," which it envisaged in fact as a perpetual antechamber as a way of avoiding any expansion. Talbott supported that position, all the more so as the Russians were making their opposition to enlargement clear.

The partisans of expansion quickly mobilized. Nowak transmitted an article to the *Washington Post* that accused the Clinton administration of turning Eastern Europe over to Moscow.[87] He also coordinated a meeting of eighteen groups representing the ethnic communities of central Europe and the East for a common lobbying effort in favor of expansion; he organized a letter-writing campaign by Polish-Americans via the Polish-American Congress to protest against what he called "Yalta II." Brzezinski spoke out on radio and television and wrote two articles, including the op-ed piece in the *New York Times* cited earlier; he spoke to Lake several times and invited him to his home to meet leaders from Eastern Europe, which convinced Lake to push the political line beyond the Partnership for Peace.[88] On December 21, Brzezinski suggested to him that Clinton should adopt an authentic strategic vision for Europe: as Bush had brought about the entrance of a unified Germany into NATO, the president ought to bring in the countries of Eastern Europe. After that meeting, Lake took a harder line in the memos send by the NSC to the president, in favor of expansion.[89] Finally, Clinton sided with the partisans of expansion: in Brussels, he put forward the Partnership for Peace, but he also indicated that it was no longer a question of expanding or not: the question from now on was "not whether, but when and how."[90]

The game was still not over; the second round was played in 1994 around the implementation of the president's position. While Brzezinski, Nowak, and Kozminski kept the pressure on from the outside, Lake saw his position reinforced, within the government, by Holbrooke's arrival at the State Department. Holbrooke relied on the president's statements (as no formal decision had been made) to move things along and force the military to develop a concrete plan for access to the organization of candidate countries. In late 1994, Brzezinski's suggestion of a two-fold approach that would make it possible to minimize friction with Moscow was adopted by President Clinton. This approach led to the signing of the foundational NATO-Russia Act in May 1997, then to the invitation to join NATO tendered to Poland, Hungary, and the Czech Republic during the Madrid summit two months later. In the meantime, Clinton, during his reelection campaign, had announced his goal of welcoming the three former Warsaw Pact nations to the NATO summit in 1999 marking the fiftieth anniversary of the organization. He did this after the Russian presidential election, and in Detroit, a city with a high concentration of American voters with East European backgrounds, under Nowak's satisfied gaze.

The third round was the ratification of the decision by the Senate; a challenge, given the pronounced reticence of the Republican majority to the principle of expansion. And this reticence was exacerbated by continuing anxiety over Russia's reaction. Had not George Kennan deemed that enlarging NATO "would be the most fateful error of American policy in the whole post-cold-war era"?[91] Forty-six experts and former officials, including Marshall Shulman, Paul Nitze, and Robert McNamara, sent an open letter to the president against ratification, expressing particular concern about the future consequences for Russia's behavior. It was against this opposition that Brzezinski's intellectual campaign scored points. He wrote articles and opinion pieces, was interviewed in the media, testified before the Senate Foreign Relations Committee in favor of ratification, making an all-out effort.[92] The Senate finally ratified the enlargement on April 30, 1998, by a comfortable majority; the game was won.

An epilogue of sorts is needed to complete this saga of NATO expansion. Away from public view, and even in secret, with arrangements worthy of a spy novel, Brzezinski played another, semi-official role.[93] It was difficult for the Clinton administration to agree to Poland's entrance into NATO unless Kuklinski, the Polish spy, who had been spirited out of the country at the time of the 1981 coup d'état and who had rendered such great service to America and thus to NATO, could be rehabilitated. He had been condemned to death in absentia in 1984, then in 1989 his sentence had been commuted to twenty-five years in prison, but Wałesa had refused to pardon him, as public opinion was strongly opposed. The affair was undeniably complicated. If Kuklinski were recognized as a hero, it would mean that all the Polish officers that had not spied for NATO were traitors. But if the Polish legal system continued to view him as a traitor, it would mean that Poland was still a communist country. On the American side there was considerable pressure, even though an official intervention of the Clinton administration would be counter-productive, for it was up to Poland to decide how to interpret its own past.

In 1996, Ambassador Kozminski began to worry about the repercussions of this affair for Poland's membership in NATO, as the clock was ticking; the Kuklinski question had to be resolved before the 1997 Madrid summit. When Interior Minister Leszek Miller made an official visit to Washington, the ambassador had him meet with Brzezinski, who knew Kuklinski and had taken up his

THE AGE OF AUTHORITY

rehabilitation as a personal cause. Miller indicated to Brzezinski that the Polish president Aleksander Kwasniewski was determined to settle the matter, but within the framework of the Polish judicial system. Brzezinski replied, however, that Kuklinski did not wish to rely on the Polish judicial system. The two men finally reached a compromise: Brzezinski obtained a commitment from Miller that the affair would have a "satisfactory" outcome, and in exchange he took on the task of convincing Kuklinski, who was living quietly in Florida, to meet the Polish military prosecutors—but in Washington.

The meetings took place in Brzezinski's CSIS office, located on K Street at the time. Ambassador Kozminski had taken his precautions. He did not send official diplomatic telegrams about the matter, for fear of leaks on the Polish side, and when he spoke to Miller on the telephone, he used code names ("our friend" for Kuklinski, "the travelers" for the prosecutors, "the professor" for Brzezinski). As for Kuklinski, he was protected in his trips between the hotel and CSIS by his former contact in Warsaw, retired CIA agent David Forden, and one of his colleagues, with the help of an FBI agent. The questioning went well, and Kuklinski had the opportunity to account for his actions in detail; Brzezinski had made sure that the prosecutors would address him with respect, calling him "Colonel." But after the latter returned to Warsaw, nothing happened, while the date of the NATO summit in Madrid was fast approaching; Ambassador Kozminski was increasingly nervous. The Americans agreed to wait patiently. Finally, the affair was mentioned for the first time during a bilateral Clinton-Kwasniewski meeting in Warsaw immediately after the Madrid summit. Next, the White House sent Brzezinski at the end of July to bring up Kuklinski's fate once again with the president and the minister of the interior, both of whom indicated that there was still strong opposition at the highest levels of the Polish state.

Finally, in early September 1997, Kozminski received a call from the Polish minister of justice: Kuklinski had been exonerated of all charges, for he had acted "out of higher necessity." That decision was read to him solemnly in Brzezinski's CSIS office: Kuklinski could return to his homeland without fear of arrest, which he did soon thereafter. When Brzezinski went to a conference on the history of the Cold War some months later, Marshal Victor Kulikov, the former commander in chief of the Warsaw Pact, mocked Kuklinski and minimized the importance of the information that he had transmitted. Brzezinski retorted that, thanks to that information, had the Soviets attacked NATO, the entire Soviet command, which included Kulikov himself, would have been decimated three hours later. Kulikov dropped the subject.

In hindsight, a central question arises with regard to the outcome of NATO's expansion in the eyes of history. There is no doubt that Poland's security was reinforced by its membership in NATO—this was a central goal for Brzezinski—as was that of the eleven other countries that followed the same path in 1999, then in 2004 and 2009. But could this thousand-kilometer eastward shift of the dividing line between the Atlantic and the Russian zones of influence fail to make the Russian elite feel that they were surrounded, that they had lost geopolitical ground, and thus lead to the increased nationalist prickliness that has been visible in Moscow since Vladimir Putin took power? Russian rhetoric confirms this: the operations in Georgia, Crimea, and Ukraine from 2008 to 2014 constitute a response to NATO's advance toward the East; the enlargement of NATO may have been a self-realizing prophecy. In other words, were not those who opposed NATO's expansion in 1998 accurate in their criticism? Would it not have been wiser to dilute the borders in Europe rather than to reinforce them? "No," Brzezinski replies:

> I think I took into account the fact that it will be a difficult and complex and even potentially reversible process in Russia, and that therefore one should not confuse in terms of the expansion and deepening of Europe, the realities of Central Europe which was still Europe in some larger sense, if not quite like France and Italy, and that Russia really had to go to a process of accommodation and adjustment that would take longer and that there may be reverses. This is why I thought NATO was important and when sometimes this issue arises here I say to my critics who say "we shouldn't have pressed for NATO expansion" I say "what do you think our relation with Russia would be today if there was no NATO and there was this inter-mediate zone—like Ukraine, but in a much more contested fashion?"[94]

Against George W. Bush, against Iraq, for Barack Obama

On September 11, 2001, Brzezinski was dining in Beijing with former German chancellor Helmut Kohl when they learned that an attack had been carried out against the United States; the two towers of the World Trade Center had been struck by airplanes and were on fire. Given the transportation bottlenecks that ensued, it took him a week to get back to Washington. Meanwhile, his daughter Mika was proving to be an outstanding on-site journalist. CBS News sent her to Ground Zero, where she stood at the foot of the Twin Towers until they collapsed. She spent a week reporting almost around the clock on the chaos in Manhattan.[95] A new geopolitical era was beginning. Even so, some weeks later, Brzezinski made an effort to show that the underlying realities of the international system had not really changed. Europe remained disunited, Russia remained antagonistic despite protestations of solidarity, and the Middle East remained hostile to the United States, owing to the Palestinian conflict and the Iraq embargo. It was thus up to America to maneuver skillfully to draw the consequences from Al Qaeda's successful attacks.[96]

In the first opinion piece he published after the attacks, on September 25, 2001, Brzezinski outlined the strategy he advocated for the struggle against terrorism. In the long run, America had to ensure cooperation from as broad a coalition of nations as possible, in order to prevent terrorists from acting (through cooperation in intelligence, policing, finance, and so on), but also in order to deal with the political—rather than religious—resentments that motivated support for terrorists in a population, as with the Israel-Palestine conflict. In the short run, it was obviously appropriate to act vigorously against the terrorists themselves, especially in Afghanistan, through military operations that would demonstrate American determination, and not only by bombings carried out from afar. If the Taliban regime had to be targeted, it was still essential to avoid being drawn into a large-scale ground war; what was needed, instead, was to galvanize the Afghan opposition.[97] A month later, after operations in Afghanistan had begun, Brzezinski sent a fax to Secretary of Defense Donald Rumsfeld to share his concern: it would be a mistake, he explained, to plunge into an operation aimed at political reconstruction in Afghanistan, for that would lead sooner or later to a stalemate.[98]

Finally, within the next few months, it was essential to go after the nations that were presumably supporting the terrorist organizations: in this connection, if it were proven that Saddam Hussein's Iraq had provided support for the September 11 attacks, "direct U.S. military action to destroy such a regime would be not only justified, but required."[99] It is surprising to see this recommendation by someone who went on to become the most visible opponent to George W. Bush's war in Iraq. But Brzezinski remained convinced for a long time of the need to act against Hussein. On November 2, he even seemed ready to settle for a vague connection to September 11: "The explosive character of the Middle Eastern tinderbox, and the fact that Iraq has the motive, the means, and the psychopathology to provide truly dangerous aid to the terrorist underground, cannot be ignored on the legalistic grounds that conclusive 'evidence' is lacking of Iraq's involvement in Sept. 11."[100]

As James Mann notes, Brzezinski's hostility toward Bush's strategy came to light early in 2002.[101] Brzezinski was upset by the State of the Union Address, in which the president had cobbled together an "axis of evil," comprising Iran, Iraq, and North Korea. In Brzezinski's eyes, Bush's Manichean approach was precisely the one that had to be avoided. This was because it masked the real political stakes by substituting morality for strategic reality, and because it made it harder for America's political allies to go along—a phenomenon amplified by the alternative posed by Bush in the immediate aftermath of the attacks: "you're either with us or with the terrorists." The other essential development in the spring of 2002 was the resumption of the Israel-Palestine conflict, which Brzezinski viewed as central to the Middle East.[102] Against Secretary of State Colin Powell, who wanted to launch an initiative leading to a peace conference, Vice President Dick Cheney imposed his vision calling for regime change at the head of the Palestinian Authority as a prerequisite: Yasser Arafat had to go. Ultimately, by the time the plan to invade Iraq had taken shape, Washington was not in a position to recreate a coalition like the one formed in 1991.

Brzezinski's skepticism toward the Bush administration's foreign policy increased during the summer of 2002. Brent Scowcroft—who had been national security adviser under Ford and George H.W. Bush—launched a scathing critique of the projected invasion of Iraq from the Republican side; Brzezinski did the same thing a few days later.[103] The two men had worked together on US policy toward Iran and Iraq in the second half of the 1990s; they had urged a softening of the Clinton administration's "dual containment" policy and a more realistic reevaluation of the risk posed by Hussein's Iraq.[104] What Brzezinski said was quite simple: since America would be launching an optional war in an inflammable region, the intervention had to satisfy even stricter conditions—a well-established factual justification (weapons of mass destruction), an explicit violation of clearly stated rules for disarmament, a broad international coalition, preparation with that coalition for the after-Saddam phase, cost-sharing, and so on.

While the probability of intervention grew over the next few months, none of these conditions had been met, and in late December 2002 Brzezinski again insisted on the need to make America's word more credible than it had been. The world order was at stake. If America did not manage to convince other countries to join in the fight against terrorism and proliferation, if its leadership was not respected, the world risked falling, over time, into the law of the jungle. That would not happen if Saddam Hussein went along with the United Nations' demands, or if America undertook an intervention under UN auspices. But if a third scenario occurred, in which America intervened unilaterally, purely to bring about regime change, the consequences would be disastrous: generalized anti-Americanism, lasting political and financial costs for Washington, a threat to its global leadership.[105]

This third scenario was the one that prevailed when the offensive against Iraq began on March 19, 2003, despite Brzezinski's appeal to put off the intervention so that Saddam Hussein's attitude could be clarified.[106] Unlike what had happened with the Gulf War twelve years earlier, this time Brzezinski's predictions were verified point for point. The absence of weapons of mass destruction in particular, which became apparent to all in late spring, made him absolutely furious, since it invalidated the entire argument for starting the war and left the impression that the goal was indeed to bring about regime change. America's word was damaged. It was at this point that Brzezinski became a real embodiment of the antiwar movement, a hero for the Democrats and the anti-Bush camp. For the first time in his life he was a favorite of the party's liberal wing, hailed by *The American Prospect* and *The Nation*.[107]

Until the election of Barack Obama, Brzezinski assailed the ideas of the neoconservatives and the Manichean concept of the War on Terror that had created a climate of irrational fear and Islamophobia within the population and had at the same time given other leaders in Russia, in Israel, and elsewhere an unhoped-for tool for dressing up their own repressive policies. He also went after any notion of military intervention in Iran. As early as 2004, well before other opponents of the war had done so, and despite the risks of division between Sunnis, Shiites, and Kurds, he advocated setting a calendar for withdrawing American forces from Iraq. The withdrawal would take place at the conclusion of a regional conference that would include the Israeli-Palestine question, through a transfer of responsibility to the United Nations (with the support of American peace keeping troops), and support from Europeans, and even from NATO.[108]

In late 2006, Brzezinski supported the bipartisan report on Iraq prepared by James Baker and Lee H. Hamilton, cochairs of the Iraq Study Group that had been set up by Congress in March. The report's observation that the intervention had failed and its recommendations for action resembled his own: resume contacts with Syria and Iran, begin troop withdrawal, accelerate the transfer of power to the Iraqi leadership, and so on.[109] The Bush administration decided not to follow the report's recommendations, choosing instead to forge in virtually the opposite direction with a "surge" (an increase in the number of soldiers in Iraq, mainly to protect Baghdad); history proved it right against Brzezinski, as the situation improved in 2007. However, what made the difference was not so much the infusion of 20,000 additional soldiers but rather the skillful politics of General David Petraeus, who managed to enlist Sunni tribes in the fight against Al Qaeda. The fact remains that the spiral of violence in which Iraq had been mired was arrested, and this relative stabilization allowed President Obama to carry out the withdrawal of American troops. America's withdrawal did not prevent the return of sectarian struggles, owing to the partisan position of Prime Minister Nuri al-Maliki, whose role in the rising power of Daesh, or ISIS (the Islamic State) was significant.

During the Bush years, Zbigniew Brzezinski published two books. In the first, in 2004, he went back to his positions in the strategic debate that followed the September 11 attacks and the invasion of Iraq and Afghanistan. In *The Choice,* he took the opposite stance from Bush's unilateral approach and demonstrated that America's security was tied to that of other countries: Washington should thus act cautiously and seek adherents to its policies. The policy of the War on Terror was a major error (for the reasons set forth earlier); it was essential to attack the political roots of terrorism in the Middle East.[110] In 2007, he published *Second Chance,* in which he compared the three presidents who had had the opportunity to shape the post–Cold War world and define a new form of American leadership. Bush Sr. came off best, even if he had underestimated the nationalist energy liberated by the implosion of the USSR (hence his mistakes in the Balkans and his excessive support for Moscow) and had wasted the opportunity to settle the Israeli-Palestinian conflict. Clinton had the merit of understanding certain challenges of globalization—encouraging the birth of the World Trade Organization (WTO), for example—and opening NATO to new members, but his murky policies, from the Balkans to Iraq, or in the Israel-Palestine peace process, handicapped by virulent domestic opposition, were not convincing.

Bush Jr. received the lowest grade from Professor Brzezinski, a solid F, while Clinton earned a C and George Sr. a more honorable B. Under George W. Bush, one saw a spectacular weakening of American leadership, an encouragement of radicalization in the Muslim world, a transformation of the Afghan intervention into nation-building, an abandonment of attention to human rights and global warming. Fortunately, unlike emperors, presidents can serve only eight years, Brzezinski observed; otherwise the empire might disappear. And an exceptional president was now required to correct the nation's course.[111]

As it happened, this heaven-sent surprise seemed to appear in the form of a young African American senator from Illinois, Barack Obama, and in fact he appeared on Brzezinski's horizon precisely because of the publication of the book *Second Chance*. In the spring of 2007, the columnist David Ignatius published a favorable article about the book, suggesting that the path laid out by Brzezinski might constitute a foreign policy "manifesto" for Obama, a new face in American politics.[112] Intrigued, Obama called Brzezinski and invited him to lunch. Brzezinski came away from the meeting convinced: "And I was immensely impressed by him, I said to someone that after Kennedy this is the most politically intellectually impressive would-be candidate for president. We had a very good discussion about a range of issues, the Middle East, the Far East, etc. Shortly thereafter his office called and said he's planning to go to the Midwest I think to Iowa to give a major speech on Iraq, critical of Bush, and would I be willing to fly out with him and introduce him."[113]

Brzezinski gladly agreed, and during the plane ride he let Obama know that he was available to offer advice if he decided to seek the nomination of his party for the presidential election. But he added a caveat: he would not do it on an official basis, because he would then be attacked by the right wing of the Jewish community, and those attacks could end up harming Obama. The young senator agreed, though he seemed surprised. This is exactly what happened some months later when critics such as Alan Dershowitz and Abraham Foxman began to attack Brzezinski when they learned that he was close to Obama. They demanded that Obama repudiate a campaign adviser whose political views, they claimed, were anti-Israeli, and who seemed to have supported the very critical book by John Mearsheimer and Steve Walt on the pro-Israel lobby:

> He then sent me an e-mail or phoned me and said "Look, I'm going to confirm officially that you are not part of my staff, but we'll keep in touch."

And I have a whole folder of e-mails throughout the entire campaign, back and forth, back and forth, including shortly before the election, about four weeks before the election—he must have been very confident already by then—"Can you help me select the top people from my national security positions, etc.?" and I wrote him a memo on it, suggesting some people, and also suggesting how to organize it, the point of departure being you have to decide: "Are you going to be engaged in foreign policy deeply or are you gonna delegate to this very powerful strong secretary of State?" And then everything follows from that, different names came up, I forget exactly who they were.[114]

Once Obama took office, in January 2009, his contacts with Brzezinski became less frequent, but the president consulted him or called him to the White House on several occasions. Brzezinski kept his independence, since he was not part of Obama's foreign policy team, and his opinions often differed from those of the administration even if, at least during the early years, he supported administration policy in its basic thrust.

It was on the Israel-Palestine issue that he quickly became critical. This was also the issue that preoccupied him the most, almost more than Poland; from 2000 on, it became nearly an obsession. He devoted many articles to the subject and often referred to it in more general writings. But as David Ignatius—who published a dialogue on foreign policy with Brzezinski and Scowcroft in 2008—points out, his position had been quite consistent since the 1970s.[115] He rejected the method of "small steps" (Kissinger's approach and, under Obama, that of special envoy George Mitchell) in favor of a strategy that consists, for America, in defining the broad outlines of a peace settlement and then exercising a certain pressure on the protagonists to work out the details among themselves.[116] The parameters he advocated, in his articles or in talking with President Obama, were simple: a demilitarized Palestinian state, the 1967 borders with mutually agreed-on adjustments, no right of return for Palestinian refugees (but compensation), and Jerusalem as the capital of both nations.[117]

His stubborn insistence on this issue made him the target of the most virulent of Israel's defenders in the United States, just as he had been targeted during his White House years. The episode in 2007, centered on the publication of Mearsheimer and Walt's book on the influence of the pro-Israel lobby on

American foreign policy, is revealing.[118] In a debate for the journal *Foreign Policy*, Brzezinski, without associating himself with the shortcuts or with all the conclusions of the Mearsheimer-Walt volume, wrote that it had the merit of launching a necessary public debate. He added that, among the ethnic lobbies, which were legitimate in American political life, the pro-Israel lobby was the most effective, and that this situation really ought to invite questions on the way the US constructs its stance toward the rest of the world. Has Washington not passed from relative impartiality (at the time of Camp David) to a position as Israel's advocate? In particular, he criticized the conditions of the debate and the abusive use of the accusation of antisemitism; he also criticized those who had reacted strongly to the accusations contained in the book. It is not surprising, under these conditions, that the latter group attacked him, forcing Obama to distance himself from Brzezinski.[119]

Despite these early efforts, starting in 2009, and the hopes that Obama inspired in Brzezinski and others, the new president did not succeed in making progress toward settling the Israel-Palestine question. He was outdone by Benjamin Netanyahu, who relied on Israeli public opinion and on Israel's supporters in Congress—as well as on the disunity among the Palestinians. In the end, this issue is the one on which Brzezinski's disillusionment with Obama is the strongest. He referred to that disappointment in an interview in the fall of 2013:

> Once he made those speeches I felt the first term was the term in which he ought to apply maximum pressure to get his way and to see if some sort of settlement can be pushed through. The longer he hesitates, the more costly and difficult it would be, and I was quite disappointed that when he made his public commitment to the peace process and to an outcome, and Netanyahu then challenged him openly and confronted him first on the settlements and then more generally through this kind of humiliating experience with the US Congress, where Netanyahu is openly campaigning against him, in the Capitol of the United States, I was disappointed that he didn't reassert himself the way other presidents did. Carter was not the only one, Eisenhower did, Bush 1 did, very strongly. I felt that was the way the president should act, and I think that has cost the president time and some credibility, and probably made the pursuit of that outcome, because he's still dedicated to it, more difficult.[120]

If the divergence in viewpoints thus continued to grow between Brzezinski and the new president over the Israel-Palestine question, there was greater agreement about the rest of the US Middle East policy. On Iraq, in 2010 and 2011 Obama implemented the policy of withdrawal that Brzezinski had been advocating since 2004. This was not accompanied by measures that the latter had recommended: a residual force to help the Iraqi army defend itself against an external or internal threat; a frank dialogue with the Iraqi leaders to make sure there was political inclusiveness; a regional conference.[121] In hindsight, after seeing the assertiveness of ISIS in the region, it is doubtful these measures would have sufficed to prevent the sectarian policy of Prime Minister al-Maliki from leading the Sunnis to support ISIS or to keep the Iraqi army from collapsing (as it did during the seizure of Mosul and the surrounding region by ISIS in June 2014). This forced—as the Republicans mocked by Brzezinski during the 2008 campaign had rightly feared—America's embarrassing military return to Iraq in the form of air strikes and support for the Kurds and the Iraqi army to retake Mosul and other territories.

In the meantime, the Arab Spring events had changed the situation in the region, especially in Syria. In early 2011, mass demonstrations against authoritarian regimes arose first in Tunisia and then in Egypt. Brzezinski was skeptical about the degree to which the demonstrators in Tahrir Square were representative of the larger population and highly suspicious, as was Kissinger. Both saw this agitation more as the expression of a certain populism than the promise of an incipient democracy. For Brzezinski, it was an illustration of what he had been predicting since the 1970s in the form of a "global political awakening." In other words, populations demanding to participate in the political process, a movement that had begun with the French Revolution. But there is a long way to go between popular agitation and the establishment of a democracy. Brzezinski refused to see any parallels with Poland in the 1980s, for example: "In the case of Solidarity, you had an alliance between trade unions, intellectuals, the church. . . . So we knew what we were doing. The problem in Egypt is that we have an amorphous mass that is rebelling against a dictatorship. . . . Our sympathies are with them. But how do we translate that into a democratic takeover? . . . A political process of some sort [is needed] unless you want to have just bloodshed in the streets."[122]

Before Colonel Gaddafi's threat of large-scale massacres against Benghazi and the Libyan rebels in February and March 2011, Brzezinski supported

military action by the Western coalition—the French and the British supported by the Obama administration, then by NATO. In particular because
such action would find support in a resolution by the U.N. Security Council
and could rally Arab states to the cause. By contrast, his skeptical stance was
pronounced in the case of Syria. Like many others, he had hoped that Bashar
al-Assad would be a partner in the regional crises, and he had conducted
interviews in Damascus in 2007. Brzezinski refused to see the strictly peaceful
uprisings that took place from January to July 2011 as having an antiauthoritar-
ian and democratic inspiration, as in Tunisia or in Egypt, and interpreted them
instead as a mix of economic rebellion, owing to drought in certain regions in
Syria, and manipulation by Qatar and Saudi Arabia, determined to unleash
a religious war there.[123]

This highly debatable interpretation subtended Brzezinski's critique of the
Obama administration's approach.[124] On the one hand, he supported the
president in his position of non-intervention in Syria, despite the high moral
and diplomatic costs and the damaging consequences of the Syrian civil war
(contagion spreading to neighboring countries, reinforcement of the civil war in
Iraq through the intermediary of ISIS, and encouragement of jihadism). On
the other hand, he was critical of the White House rhetoric that called for al-
Assad to step down in August 2011 and referred to the "red lines" that he must
not cross in August 2012, even though the United States lacked the ability to
follow through on these threats. In other words, it failed to react forcefully
when Assad's use of chemical weapons was documented, in late August 2013.
Such inaction projected an image of weakness on America's part. A year later,
Brzezinski supported the return of American military forces to Iraq and to
Syria in the form of air strikes against ISIS. As he explained after a dinner at the
White House on September 8, 2014, it was necessary to act, on the condition
of doing so in a coalition with Arab states.[125]

On Iran, Brzezinski campaigned throughout the Bush and Obama years in
favor of negotiations on the nuclear program and especially against military
strikes, judging the consequences potentially catastrophic, or at least more so
than the possibility that Tehran would eventually reach the nuclear threshold.
After all, in that case, why would dissuasion not work? With Scowcroft and
other former government officials—including Anthony Zinni, Thomas Pick-
ering, and his former NSC collaborator Jessica Mathews, then president of the
Carnegie Endowment for International Peace—Brzezinski insisted tirelessly

on the importance of reaching a compromise and avoiding war. It was necessary to stop threatening the Iranians with regime change, to conclude an agreement authorizing them to enrich uranium for civilian purposes, and to lift the sanctions, in exchange for a commitment on their part to halt the military program.[126] In September 2009, he even suggested that if the Israelis were to launch a military operation against Iranian nuclear sites, American planes, which at the time controlled the Iraqi air space, should intercept their planes. That idea did nothing to improve Brzezinski's relations with the pro-Israel community.[127]

On Afghanistan, Brzezinski's position remained particularly consistent. Since his October 2001 fax to Secretary of Defense Rumsfeld recommending that American forces not linger indefinitely in the country after the defeat of the Taliban, he had regularly warned America about the danger of becoming perceived as an occupying power, as Russia was in the 1980s. This could well happen, he argued, if the United States and its European allies in NATO persisted in seeking to construct a centralized state where there had never been one before. He pleaded in favor of an orderly withdrawal, and was skeptical of Obama's move, beginning in 2009–2010, to send more troops into Afghanistan before beginning a withdrawal.[128] In the debate over Afghanistan, and over Al Qaeda more generally, Brzezinski was regularly attacked for his role in providing support to the mujahedeen starting in the spring of 1980, with the idea that he played the sorcerer's apprentice by supporting them in order to weaken the Soviets. He responded, of course, that such a reproach presupposed total clairvoyance on the part of the American leaders concerning the future implications of support for the Afghan resistance (namely, the constitution of Al Qaeda)—a capacity that the leadership obviously did not possess. His priority, at all events, was to weaken the USSR.[129]

During the 2000s and beyond, Brzezinski remained mistrustful of Russia's intentions. He strongly criticized the West's failure to react to the two wars in Chechnya (a failure that in his view encouraged a shift away from democracy in the country). He also criticized the Bush administration, which turned a blind eye to Moscow's interventions in the Caucasus or in its ex-satellites as part of the war against terrorism. He then developed an approach to Russia with two temporal horizons, an approach he maintained beyond the Ukrainian crisis in 2013–2014. He was persuaded that the process of modernization would gradually create—within the developing middle classes and especially among young people—pressure in favor of liberalizing the regime. He estimated that Russia would have no choice but to build ties with the European West, for the Chinese alternative was less favorable and less natural. However, in the short run, his analysis of Putin's power was much darker. He compared that power to Mussolini's or Stalin's, marked by centralization and hierarchization, repression of opponents, muzzling of the press, exaltation of a composite past in which orthodoxy, Slavophilia, and national grandeur served to ensure acceptance of the Kremlin's dominance.[130]

The resulting recommendation was a simple one: America had to support Russia's neighbors, for the more their political and economic health improved, the more Russia would be encouraged to follow their example even as it was being drawn into the European orbit—and the less it would be tempted to exploit their weaknesses in order to reconstitute an empire. Brzezinski spoke out during the color revolutions, especially the Orange Revolution in Ukraine in late 2004, which saw the pro-Western camp of candidate Viktor Yushchenko mount a successful challenge to the election fraud committed by Viktor Yanukovych, the candidate supported by Moscow.[131] Four years later, in August 2008, Vladimir Putin took advantage of provocations by Georgia to invade the provinces of South Ossetia and Abkhazia, creating two new frozen conflicts. Brzezinski reacted strongly, comparing the events to Hitler's annexation of the Sudetenland and to Stalin's invasion of Finland; he recommended imposing sanctions on Russia while inviting Georgia to join NATO. In his view, Russia's latest military intervention proved that the Kremlin was not accepting post-Soviet reality and that Putin was seeking to rebuild an empire.[132]

In relation to the presidential campaign, Obama's assumption of office, and the weakening of America following the Iraq war, Brzezinski's position was nevertheless not entirely confrontational. He recommended wagering on the reform-minded president Dmitry Medvedev and looking for zones of agreement where Russian and American interests coincided (Iran, a nuclear accord, Afghanistan, and so on), while avoiding useless provocations (an anti-missile shield); this was to be the basis for Obama's "reset" policy, of which Brzezinski approved. In fact, Russian-American relations grew somewhat warmer in 2009–2010, and this bright spot extended to Poland, after the tragic Smolensk plane crash in which Poland's president and dozens of Polish leaders were killed on the occasion of a commemorative visit to the Katyn massacre site.[133]

Alas, Russian-American relations became strained once again starting in 2011, owing in particular to the Western intervention in Libya, to Western support for the rebels in Syria (while the Russians were actively supporting Bashar al-Assad), and to the anti-Putin demonstrations in Moscow during the winter of 2011–2012, which seemed to illustrate Brzezinski's theory about the Russian middle classes. The real deterioration occurred in the fall of 2013 and especially in 2014, with the more serious crisis in Ukraine. Putin refused to allow Kiev to sign an agreement of association with the European Union (which ran counter to his plans for a Eurasian Union and would bring Ukraine closer to the European Union and perhaps to NATO). Ukrainian president Viktor Yanukovych yielded, but there were demonstrations objecting to that decision and protesting against a corrupt regime. Seeing that he was losing ground, Putin invaded and then annexed Crimea before supporting the separatists in eastern Ukraine, providing direct aid during the summer in order to inflict a military defeat on Kiev, which then had to negotiate. Throughout the crisis, in addition to supplying Ukraine with defensive weapons, Brzezinski recommended a solution of political appeasement that would take Moscow's interests into account and would see Ukraine adopt a plan for decentralization and an international formula similar to Finlandization (no open door to join NATO, but a distant European perspective).[134]

Although Russia continued to preoccupy Brzezinski, China received the most attention in his reflections, especially in his prognoses. He urged sanctioning Beijing after the repression of the demonstrators in Tiananmen Square and he supported Bill Clinton, who criticized "the butchers of Beijing" during his campaign. During the 1990s, geopolitical realism gained the upper hand. It was necessary to integrate China as much as possible into the international community to make it a responsible actor, for example by offering it a place within the G7, which it deserved more than Russia did, and of course in the WTO, while intensifying the dialogue with Beijing about security in East Asia.[135] Unlike Mearsheimer at the University of Chicago, who predicted an inevitable confrontation between China, a rising power, and America, an established power, Brzezinski judged that the clash would be avoided, owing as much to Beijing's realism—China was concentrating on its economic growth—as to the existence to nuclear weapons that limited the tensions—even if frictions could develop.[136]

China's increasing power reinforced Brzezinski's conviction that it would be useful to develop a broader partnership: starting in 2009, he argued for a veritable G-2, a "group of two that could change the world" by reaching agreement on major issues such as Iran, the financial crisis, or climate questions; even the Israeli-Palestinian conflict would benefit from a joint Sino-American position.[137] In the years that followed, and given the renewal of relations with Beijing starting in 2010, Brzezinski did not renew his appeal for a G-2, but he continued to insist on the importance of a cooperative relation with China. This is why he criticized Obama's "pivot to Asia"; he feared that it would be perceived by Beijing as the announcement of an anti-Chinese coalition. Similarly, he recommended not being too closely connected with other Eurasian powers such as India, whose potential he continued to doubt (as he did in the 1970s), in order to stand up to China.[138]

Zbigniew Brzezinski published his last book, *Strategic Vision,* in 2012. He used it to refute the declinist theories. America was suffering from quite real ills (its debt, its blocked partisan system, its failing infrastructures, and so on), and it had made serious errors (the Iraq war), but it also had unrivaled assets (economic power, technological innovation, demography, geography, and so on), and few countries could really claim to replace it in its role of foremost world power. America had to serve as the rallying point for the West—which it would be appropriate to enlarge so as to include Turkey and Russia—and as a balancing power in Asia. The task ahead was daunting, for the world was experiencing, simultaneously, a dispersal of power with the appearance of new poles, and a period of global political awakening on the part of its populations: in 2025, the world would no longer be American, but it would not be Chinese, either. It would be chaotic.[139]

The situation that prevailed in the following years seemed to support this prediction. In an interview in *Foreign Policy* in July, Zbigniew Brzezinski judged that the world was experiencing a period of instability that was "historically unprecedented, in the sense that simultaneously huge swaths of global territory are dominated by populist unrest, anger, and effective loss of state control." In short, "the kind of world in which there is enormous turmoil and fragmentation and uncertainty—not a single central threat to everybody, but a lot of diversified threats to almost everybody."[140] In the Middle East, a new thirty-years war had begun between Sunnis and Shiites, and except for a few true nation-states (Iran, Turkey, Israel, Egypt), the other countries were and would remain unstable. Under these conditions, America would have to reduce its footprint in the Middle East, while seeking the cooperation of the two powers that would be the most affected by the new disorders, Russia and China. In fact, given Russia's structural weakness and given its actions in Ukraine, that basically left only China, even if America refused to take on a real "G-2." As for the Europeans, they had marginalized themselves, owing to their ineffectiveness and the absence of a sense of a European identity among the populations. There remained China, then, with which America had the possibility of getting along, especially in the absence of ideological antagonism. It was up to Washington to take care in calibrating its reaction to China's advances in its own neighborhood or in common spaces—to reassure without provoking, and to know how to manage the great problems of the world in cooperation with Beijing.[141]

Conclusion
Brzezinski's Enduring Legacy

"My father passed away peacefully tonight," Mika Brzezinski announced on the evening of May 26, 2017. After decades of unbounded energy, which diminished little in the final years, Zbigniew Brzezinski died at age eighty-nine, at Inova Fairfax Hospital in Falls Church, Virginia. He was celebrated two weeks later in a memorial service where President Jimmy Carter, Secretary of State Madeleine Albright, Secretary of Defense Robert Gates, and other former officials added their voices to those of his family. Then, at the Center for Strategic and International Studies, his second family—the in-between world of academia, think tanks, journalism, and officialdom—celebrated the man who had been a mainstay of the Washington strategic community for so long.

His death coincided with a time of seeming strategic disarray in America, when the need to determine the country's role in the world felt more urgent than ever. The election of Donald J. Trump as US president in November 2016 added a layer of uncertainty to the upheavals of the international system, from Beijing's territorial expansion in the South China Sea to Pyongyang's race for a nuclear deterrent and the seizure of large swaths of territory by terrorist groups like ISIS. Trump was elected on a platform of isolationism, unilateralism, and protectionism, which seemed to upend all the principles that had guided US foreign policy since the end of World War II in 1945.

Zbigniew Brzezinski had reacted not by jumping on the anti-Trump bandwagon, but by requesting clarity and a sense of purpose from the new president. In his last op-ed, for the *New York Times* in February 2017, he stressed that "'Make America Great Again' and 'America First' are all very well as bumper stickers, but the foreign policy of the United States needs to be more than a campaign slogan." He asked the president for "an address that offers a bold statement of his vision, including his determination to provide America's leadership in the effort to shape a more stable world," adding that "a Trump Doctrine, any doctrine more or less, is sorely needed."[1] On his popular Twitter account, he was even pithier. The very last tweet he offered to his followers, just three weeks before passing away, read: "Sophisticated US leadership is the sine qua non of a stable world order. However, we lack the former while the latter is getting worse."[2]

The more substantive message and advice he left behind had come six months earlier, on December 11, 2016, during his last major public appearance, when he gave an extraordinary speech at the Nobel Peace Prize Forum in Oslo together with Henry Kissinger.[3] Sixty-six years after their first encounter at Harvard, the two grand masters of strategy dueled again on stage, arguing about great power politics and the role America should play. The sometimes nostalgic exchange included anecdotes from the past and marks of affection. Kissinger evoked his proximity with his "friend Zbigniew Brzezinski, whose life and career in our adopted country have so closely paralleled my own." The two had had their conflicts over sixty years, he allowed, "but what I know most about Zbig, is what I have learned from him, and how important a contribution he has made to our thinking as a nation and to my thinking as a public figure and professor."[4] Brzezinski responded in kind, telling the story of their first unfortunate encounter in the fall of 1950, when Kissinger, then a teaching assistant, presented a class heavy in German philosophers. Brzezinski, turned off, decided "rather impolitely" to skip it. "Our paths thereafter crossed systematically . . . A lot binds us. We often disagreed, but more significantly, on the larger issues, agreed."[5]

This mix of agreement and disagreement, and the different approaches to great power politics, were still on display in Oslo. Kissinger, who had maintained a line to all Republican presidents and publicly supported even their most hazardous initiatives in foreign policy, asked his audience to grant president-elect Trump the benefit of the doubt; indeed, as it would later become known, he had helped establish a secret channel between Trump and Chinese president Xi Jinping just two weeks earlier.[6] He characteristically focused on the need to reestablish a balance of power, a structure of international order that was key to world peace. This implied getting back to a strict Westphalian system of state sovereignty, legitimacy, and international law, a system that was under attack from several sources. Nonstate actors were pretending to address global issues; the concept of soft power was a retreat from the balance of power; extreme nationalism was leading to isolationism; and the rules-based system was accused to be a tool of Western domination.

Brzezinski's approach included points of convergence with Kissinger—on the continuing role and underappreciated relevance of nuclear weapons, for example, and on the need to educate the American public on international realities. He was less indulgent with Trump and more impatient to see some sort of articulation of purpose coming from the president-elect. His message, while focusing on great power politics, also paid attention to other factors of international life, including global warming and its potential to intensify political problems, as well as social mobilization in the Muslim world. It was less abstract than Kissinger's and more oriented toward policy recommendations.

In his Oslo address, Brzezinski returned to the balance of power on the Eurasian continent, which had been at the center of his 1997 best seller, *The Grand Chessboard*.[7] He pointed out the challenges confronting the three major players. Russia was faced with the reluctance of East European states to participate in any structure evocative of the defunct Soviet Union, a strategic expansion by Beijing into Central Asia, and an inviting imbalance in population and power with China in the Russian Far East. The United States had seen a deterioration of its relationship with Beijing, with the two no longer sharing a common strategic vision. To correct this, the United States must not treat China as if it were already an enemy and especially not favor India as America's principal ally in Asia, which would almost guarantee a closer connection between China and Russia. This scenario represented the most dangerous configuration of all for US interests. Washington had to be firm but cautious in its strategic reassurance of Japan and South Korea, while it had to be firm and assertive in its guarantees to Western Europe—even threatening a massive blockade of Russia's maritime access to the West in case of Russian military aggression against the Baltic states.

Ultimately, Brzezinski concluded that the "ideal geopolitical response is a trilateral connection between the United States, China, and then Russia." But what primarily emerged from this last major address was really an insistence on the China-US bilateral relationship to solve regional problems like North Korea as well as other global problems. This message was reminiscent of his 2009 writings on a "G-2 that could change the world," a concept reiterated in other interventions of 2015 and 2016.[8] At the end of his life, Brzezinski was still wary of Russia, which had to be engaged but carefully kept in check, while the United States had to be prepared to defer to China to keep a cooperative balance of power.

With the voices of Kissinger and Brzezinski fading away, many have remarked that no strategist has really stepped up to fill their shoes, while the need for thinking about America's role in the world remains acute. To be sure, they had pioneered a now-familiar model to which many have aspired after them—the academic shifting into politics, the adviser whispering into the ear of the White House candidate, the wise former official counseling generations of presidents. Many have followed their path and some have had impact or success for a time, but none has managed to reach the level of authority and longevity that these two immigrants attained, both at home and abroad.

What, then, made Brzezinski such a powerful and influential figure? After all, he exercised high-level responsibilities for only a brief period—just four years, while serving as national security adviser to a president who left a decidedly mixed impression on Americans—too little to attribute his influence to his experience as a former political leader. Similarly, although he had an extraordinary life as an immigrant who reached the commanding heights of US foreign policy, he did not cultivate journalists to create a favorable image of himself or try to become a legend; rather, he was almost negligent on that front. Certainly his prodigious intellectual output was an important factor; by articulating new concepts and visions, and getting the word out, he differentiated himself from other advisers who were more discreet and whose careers were more oriented toward public service (including his friend Brent Scowcroft, for example).[9] Most important, two qualities he exhibited from the start—strategic vision and political independence—yielded the respect and influence he enjoyed throughout his long career. They also form his enduring legacy.

Strategy is not really a profession; it is a discipline, an exercise that feeds on various fields of knowledge and requires specific talents. Brzezinski was a master strategist because he cultivated these talents and followed with great personal rigor some simple imperatives: substantial expertise, identification and hierarchization of goals, adequation of means to ends, integration of varied contextual elements and of the multiple dimensions of power, anticipation of possible evolutions of the geopolitical environment, and so on. Very early on, he expanded the boundaries of his field of knowledge (that is, of the USSR and the communist world) and started thinking about American foreign policy in general, considering the constraints on decision makers, formulating concrete recommendations, and presenting them in a coherent vision—a set of activities he kept up until the end of his life.

His strategic recommendations have not all been of equal value. Some have been too vague, and a few have been more than contestable. But by offering, for six decades, a structured and often compelling vision of international politics to policy makers and the general public, through books, articles, and other media appearances, he established himself as a mainstay in the American and global foreign policy debate, to the point of being heard as the voice of America itself.

Like Kissinger's, his strategic vision is inscribed in history, but two elements, at least, distinguish it from his Harvard comrade's. Brzezinski did not reduce the international scene to the play of great powers and great men alone. Beyond relations among states, he paid attention to other factors, such as underlying forces, public opinion, technology, and nongovernmental organizations. His Oslo speech was another illustration of that. He also thought in terms of dynamic change, whereas Kissinger tends toward static analysis, modeling international relations on the basis of the past. A thinker about international change, Brzezinski was very much a thinker about the future, always seeking to cast his recommendations in the world he anticipated—not for the sake of futurology, but out of intellectual honesty, to spell out the coherence of his vision. That he was the object of many conspiracy theories is ironic, because the lines of his strategic thinking were explicit and devoid of dissimulation or hidden agendas.

The second quality that distinguishes Brzezinski's legacy is political independence, sustained by professional positions that allowed him to avoid the appearance of dependence on any master. There are some quasi-invariants in his representation of the world, themes that can be traced all the way to the Oslo speech. These include a certain severity toward Russia, contrasting with a certain indulgence toward and even fascination with China; an insistence on the resolution of the Israel-Palestine conflict; persistent skepticism about India; and relative neglect of Latin America and Africa. But beyond these consistent threads, Brzezinski's opinions were constructed each time "from the bottom up," starting from a reckoning with the political realities on the ground as he interpreted them. In fact, he belonged to no identifiable school of thought in foreign policy. Close to the neoconservative Democrats during the 1970s, he was at the opposite extreme from the neoconservative Republicans in the 2000s, in his opposition to the Iraq War.

This independence of mind can also be discerned in his public affiliations: Brzezinski was not the man of a particular party. He never felt the need to identify with a clan or a coterie, to associate with a particular group, much less to settle there. Very much a Democrat at the beginning of his career, fascinated by the epic character of the Kennedy saga, he did not hesitate to distance himself from the party in 1972, condemning the leftist positions of candidate George McGovern. In 1988, judging once again that the Democratic Party was yielding to its idealist tendencies, he went further still by endorsing Republican George H.W. Bush for the presidency, before returning to the Democrats in 1992. In 2007, he chose an improbable candidate yet again, one ranked at the bottom of the polls, but one who, like Jimmy Carter, had convinced him and would end up convincing America: Barack Obama.

Brzezinski's positions on America's military interventions exhibited the same independence: he was neither a warmonger nor a pacifist; everything depended on the circumstances of the intervention under consideration. For example, initially a hawk toward the USSR, in the 1950s he quickly became aware that the "rollback" advocated by the Republicans was only a campaign slogan, and he became an owl—still aiming for the fall of the USSR, but through the long-term strategy of "peaceful engagement." He was very hawkish on Vietnam, a dove regarding the 1991 Gulf War, a hawk regarding Bosnia and Kosovo (1995 and 1999), a prudent hawk concerning Afghanistan (2001), a hesitant then an outspoken dove against George W. Bush concerning Iraq (2003), a hawk on Libya (2011), and a dove on Iran and Syria (two contemplated interventions that ultimately did not occur). His position on the Ukrainian issue starting in 2014 was nuanced: he defended federalization and Finlandization, while recommending that Kiev be supplied with defensive weapons.

Strategic vision, political independence, longevity, and abundant output explain Brzezinski's aura and influence. However, the fascination his work holds for so many and the reason his name will live on in history have to do with something larger than these qualities. What Brzezinski's life points to, above all, is the power of ideas in politics and in history. Indeed, a major theme in this biography has been to explore how Brzezinski's ideas were formed in specific contexts, where they originated, and how they were translated into action. This quest is aligned with the way he saw his own life: "I tried to act

upon my vocational call, my desire to pair ideas with action in the hope of
being able to serve a good cause."[10]

The debate over the exact role ideas play in politics in general and international relations in particular—that is, whether they have independent impact
or merely serve as a dressing for deeper material forces—will not be settled here.
But many episodes in Brzezinski's life point to his influence on the course of
history, and not only through decisions he made or advocated while in the
White House. Indeed, the belief that ideas rule the world, pushed to the extreme,
is the real fuel behind conspiracy theories. Brzezinski was often represented as
a mastermind who manipulated US foreign policy from behind the scenes,
not only through the Trilateral Commission but also through his books and
articles—through his ideas.

It is certain that Brzezinski's intellectual production made a difference to the
way the United States conducted its external relations. It is left to the reader to
conclude to what extent it did, and whether the influence was positive. What
remains when the name Brzezinski comes up is the image of an American foreign
policy sage. America, which welcomed Brzezinski as a student in 1950, made
him a citizen in 1958, and brought him all the way to the White House in 1976,
continued to listen to his foreign policy advice until his death in 2017. In what
other country would such a career have been possible? A grand master of strategy
and geopolitics, Zbigniew Brzezinski helped guide America's course through an
extraordinary century, the age in which it became an empire.

Notes

Acknowledgments

Index

Publications Index

Notes

Introduction

1. See the narrative in David Halberstam, *The Best and the Brightest* (New York: Random House, 1974), 3–10; Walter Isaacson and Evan Thomas, *The Wise Men: Six Friends and the World They Made* (New York: Simon & Schuster, 1986), 594ff.; and I. M. Destler, Leslie Gelb, and Anthony Lake, *Our Own Worst Enemy: The Unmaking of American Foreign Policy* (New York: Simon & Schuster, 1984), 2.

2. Isaacson and Thomas, *Wise Men.* To this group we can add the Bundy brothers (William and especially McGeorge), the Dulles brothers (John Foster and Allen), James Forrestal and also Paul Nitze. On the Bundy brothers, see Kai Bird, *The Color of Truth: McGeorge Bundy and William Bundy, Brothers in Arms* (New York: Simon & Schuster, 1998). On the Dulles brothers, see Stephen Kinzer, *The Brothers: John Foster Dulles, Allen Dulles, and Their Secret World War* (New York: New York Times Books, 2013). On Nitze, see especially Strobe Talbott, *The Master of the Game: Paul Nitze and the Nuclear Peace* (New York: Knopf, 1988).

3. See Dean Acheson, *Present at the Creation: My Years in the State Department* (New York: W. W. Norton, 1969).

4. The best analysis has been provided by three members of the new elite, Destler, Gelb, and Lake, in *Our Own Worst Enemy.*

5. Hans Morgenthau, *Politics among Nations: The Struggle for Power and Peace* (New York: Knopf, 1948).

6. Brzezinski to W. Averell Harriman, June 21, 1974, folder "Harriman, W. Averell, 1964, 1974–1976," Box I.12, Zbigniew Brzezinski Papers, Manuscript Division, Library of Congress, Washington, DC (hereafter, Brzezinski Papers, LoC). The attachments were not preserved with the letter, but, according to Harriman's response, they included an interview in the July 1, 1974, issue of *Newsweek* and an article by Harriman titled "The Framework of East-West Reconciliation" in *Foreign Affairs* 46, no. 2 (January 1968):256–275.

7. See Rudy Abramson, *Spanning the Century: The Life of W. Averell Harriman, 1891–1986* (New York: William Morrow, 1992).

8. W. Averell Harriman to Brzezinski, July 2, 1974, folder "Harriman, W. Averell 1964, 1974–1976," Box I.12, Brzezinski Papers, LoC.

9. On the Harriman-Brzezinski-Vance-Carter relations, see Abramson, *Spanning the Century,* 690–692; Betty Glad, *An Outsider in the White House: Jimmy Carter, His Advisors, and the Making of American Foreign Policy* (Ithaca, NY: Cornell University Press, 2009), 58; and Zbigniew Brzezinski, *Power and Principle: Memoirs of the National Security Adviser, 1977–1981* (New York: Farrar, Straus & Giroux, 1983), 74.

10. Abramson, *Spanning the Century,* 692.

11. Isaacson and Thomas, *Wise Men,* 736.

12. See especially Bruce Kuklick, *Blind Oracles: Intellectuals and War from Kennan to Kissinger* (Princeton, NJ: Princeton University Press, 2007); Fred Kaplan, *The Wizards of Armageddon* (New York: Simon & Schuster, 1983); Joseph Lepgold and Miroslav Nincic, *Beyond the Ivory Tower: International Relations Theory and the Issue of Policy Relevance* (New York: Columbia University Press, 2001).

13. Patrick Vaughan, *Zbigniew Brzeziński* (Warsaw: Świat Książki, 2010); an English-language version, *Zbigniew Brzezinski: A Life on the Grand Chessboard of Power,* is announced as forthcoming. Vaughan's work was titled "Zbigniew Brzezinski: The Political and Academic Life of a Cold War Visionary" (Ph.D. diss., West Virginia University, 2003). See also Patrick Vaughan: "Zbigniew Brzezinski and Afghanistan," in *The Policy Makers: Shaping American Foreign Policy from 1947 to the Present,* ed. Anna Kasten Nelson (Lanham, MD: Rowman & Littlefield, 2009), 107–130, and "Zbigniew Brzezinski and the *Helsinki Final Act,*" in *The Crisis of Détente in Europe: From Helsinki to Gorbachev 1975–1985,* ed. Leopoldo Nuti (New York: Routledge, 2009), 11–25.

14. Charles Gati, ed., *Zbig: The Strategy and Statecraft of Zbigniew Brzezinski* (Baltimore: Johns Hopkins University Press, 2013); Andrzej Lubowski, *Zbig: The Man Who Cracked the Kremlin* (Open Road Distribution and Kindle Edition), 2013). Gati's collective work contains many valuable contributions.

15. Hubert Humphrey to Brzezinski, December 7, 1956, folder "Humphrey, Hubert H. 1956–1957," Box I.12, Brzezinski Papers, LoC.

16. See David Ignatius, "Obama Weighs New Peace Plan for the Middle East," *Washington Post,* April 7, 2010.

17. See Brzezinski, *Power and Principle,* and Glad, *Outsider.*

1. A Brilliant Young Man in the Cold War University

1. Brzezinski tells the story in *Power and Principle: Memoirs of the National Security Adviser, 1977–1981* (New York: Farrar, Straus & Giroux, 1983), 100.

2. See Zbigniew Brzezinski, François Duchene, and Kiichi Saeki, "Peace in an International Framework," *Foreign Policy,* no. 19 (Summer 1975):3–17. The conclusions of the Brookings Institution report are reproduced in Brzezinski, *Power and Principle,* 85–86.

3. Nabil Mikhail, "Zbigniew Brzezinski: The Scholar and the Statesman: A Study of the Thoughts and Politics of the National Security Adviser and His Staff in the Carter Administration" (Ph.D. diss., University of Virginia, 1996), 64.

4. Mikhail, "Zbigniew Brzezinski," 52–53.

5. Patrick Vaughan, "Zbigniew Brzezinski: The Political and Academic Life of a Cold War Visionary" (Ph.D. diss., West Virginia University, 2003), 18.

6. Ibid., 19.

7. Patrick Vaughan, *Zbigniew Brzeziński* (Warsaw: Świat Książki, 2010), 11.

8. Mikhail, "Zbigniew Brzezinski," 55; Vaughan, "Zbigniew Brzezinski," 21.

9. Mary Allen, "Zbigniew Brzezinski Exit Interview," Jimmy Carter Library, Atlanta, GA (hereafter, Carter Library), February 20, 1981, 1, http://222.jimmycarterlibrary.gov/library /exitInt/Brzezinski.pdf.

10. Vaughan, *Zbigniew Brzeziński,* 14–15.

11. John Mitchell (Chief Counsel) to Brzezinski, March 1952, folder "Min-Miy" Miscellaneous 1952–1955, 1962–1977, Box I.21, Zbigniew Brzezinski Papers, Manuscript Division, Library of Congress, Washington, DC (hereafter, Brzezinski Papers, LoC).

12. See "World Notes HISTORY Judgment on Katyn," *Time Magazine* (November 13, 1989):57.

13. Benjamin Fischer, "The Katyn Controversy: Stalin's Killing Field," *Studies in Intelligence* (Winter 1999–2000): 61–70.

14. Patrick Vaughan, "Zbigniew Brzezinski and Afghanistan," in *The Policy Makers: Shaping American Foreign Policy from 1947 to the Present,* ed. Anna Kasten Nelson (Lanham, MD: Rowman & Littlefield, 2008), 112.

15. A copy of the thesis, titled "Russo-Soviet Nationalism," is available in Box I.84, Brzezinski Papers, LoC.

16. Brzezinski, "Russo-Soviet Nationalism," 142, Box I.84, Brzezinski Papers, LoC.

17. Mikhail, "Zbigniew Brzezinski," 59.

18. Interview with Zbigniew Brzezinski, June 2, 2011.

19. Mikhail, "Zbigniew Brzezinski," 55–56.

20. See Jeremy Suri, *Henry Kissinger and the American Century* (Cambridge, MA: Harvard University Press, 2007), 109–110.

21. Interview with Zbigniew Brzezinski, June 22, 2010.

22. Frederick Watkins to Brzezinski, July 30, 1950, folder "Harvard University 1950–1953, 1959–1960," Box I.12, Brzezinski Papers, LoC. The professor reported that Brzezinski's thesis was "quite satisfactory," but that the analysis was sometimes weak and the style left room for improvement.

23. Reginald Phelps to Brzezinski, August 17, 1950, folder "Harvard University 1950–1953, 1959–1960," Box I.12, Brzezinski Papers, LoC.

24. Brzezinski to Prof. William Langer, February 25, 1958 (actually 1959), folder "Harvard University 1950–1953, 1959–60," Box I.12, Brzezinski Papers, LoC.

25. Mikhail, "Zbigniew Brzezinski," 63.

26. Interview with Zbigniew Brzezinski, June 22, 2010.

27. Interviews with Stanley Hoffmann, December 1 and 4, 2009.

28. Mikhail, "Zbigniew Brzezinski," 60–61, and interviews with Stanley Hoffmann, December 1 and 4, 2009.

29. Emilie A. Benes, "Bay State Bride," *New York Times,* June 12, 1955.

30. Brzezinski to District Director, US Immigration and Naturalization Service, Boston, October 2, 1956, folder "United States and Immigration Service 1956–1958," Box I.32, Brzezinski

Papers, LoC. A picture of Brzezinski's "Petition for Naturalization," which allowed him to become an American, is available from the National Archives: http://arcweb.archives.gov/arc.

31. Interview with Zbigniew Brzezinski, June 22, 2010.

32. Robert Scheer, "Brzezinski: Activist Seeker of World Order," *Los Angeles Times,* January 24, 1977, B1 and B3.

33. Brzezinski, *Power and Principle,* 211.

34. Shirley M. Bender to Brzezinski, April 4, 1952, folder "Speeches and Events 1952–1955," Box I.52, Brzezinski Papers, LoC.

35. F. Bosworth, Director, Simmons College, to Brzezinski, October 8, 1954, folder "Speeches and Events 1952–1955," Box I.53, Brzezinski Papers, LoC.

36. I collected these phrases in the course of my research at the Library of Congress.

37. According to historian David Engerman, the term *Sovietologist* appeared in the late 1950s. It was generally a neutral descriptor, whereas the term Kremlinologist, which designated specialists in the intrigues at the heart of Soviet power (often émigrés and spies), was used pejoratively by scholars. Correspondence with David Engerman, July 27, 2011.

38. Interview with Abby Collins, December 3, 2009, Cambridge, MA; interviews with Stanley Hoffmann, December 1 and 4, 2009.

39. Interviews with Stanley Hoffmann, December 1 and 4, 2009.

40. Friedrich to Brzezinski, December 20, 1955, folder "Friedrich, Carl J. 1954–1958," Box I.9, Brzezinski Papers, LoC.

41. According to Charles Gati, quoted in Vaughan, *Zbigniew Brzeziński,* 48.

42. David Engerman, *Know Your Enemy: The Rise and Fall of America's Soviet Experts* (New York: Oxford University Press, 2009), 210–214.

43. Brzezinski to Albert Mavrinac, May 8, 1972, folder "Mavrinac, Albert A., 1966–1976," Box I.20, Brzezinski Papers, LoC.

44. Zbigniew Brezinski, "Merle Fainsod—Intellectual Creativity," *Harvard Library Bulletin* 20, no. 3 (July 1972):230–232.

45. Interview with Zbigniew Brzezinski, June 22, 2010.

46. Interview with Robert Bowie, July 7, 2009.

47. Zbigniew Brzezinski, "Party Controls in the Soviet Army," *Journal of Politics* 14, no. 4 (November 1952):565–591.

48. The thesis is available in the Harvard University Archives, HU90 6319.20 A. The book was published under the title *The Permanent Purge: Politics in Soviet Totalitarianism* (Cambridge, MA: Harvard University Press, Russian Research Center Studies 20, 1956).

49. Brzezinski, *Permanent Purge,* 8.

50. Ibid., 31.

51. Edward Taborsky, "Review," *American Political Science Review* 50, no. 3 (September 1956):873; see also W. W. Kulski, "Review," *Russian Review* 15, no. 4 (October 1956):280–281.

52. John Gillespie, "Review," *Journal of Politics* 19, no. 2 (1957):293–295.

53. Zbigniew Brzezinski and Carl Friedrich, *Totalitarian Dictatorship and Autocracy* (Cambridge, MA: Harvard University Press, 1956).

54. Hannah Arendt, *The Origins of Totalitarianism* (New York: Harcourt Brace, 1951).

55. This paragraph is largely inspired by the analysis in Engerman, *Know Your Enemy,* 207–209.

56. Their exchanges, from 1955 in particular, are found in folder "Friedrich, Carl J. 1954–1958," Box I.9, Brzezinski Papers, LoC.

57. Interview with Zbigniew Brzezinski, June 22, 2010.

58. Engerman, *Know Your Enemy,* 208.

59. Ibid., 214.

60. Zbigniew Brzezinski, "Totalitarianism and Rationality," *American Political Science Review* 50, no. 3 (September 1956):751–763.

61. Zbigniew Brzezinski, "Poland—A Political Glimpse," *Problems of Communism* 6, no. 5 (September-October 1957):26–30.

62. The theme of the Cold War University is addressed in the contextualization of Kissinger's agenda by Suri in *Henry Kissinger and the American Century.* There is an abundant bibliography on this theme; see especially Noam Chomsky, Richard Lewontin, Laura Nader, and Richard Ohmann, *The Cold War & The University: Toward an Intellectual History of the Postwar Years* (New York: New Press, 1997); Sigmund Diamond, *Compromised Campus: The Collaboration of Universities with the Intelligence Community, 1945–1955* (New York: Oxford University Press, 1992); Rebecca Lowen, *Creating the Cold War University: The Transformation of Stanford* (Berkeley: University of California Press, 1997); Ron Robin, *The Making of the Cold War Enemy: Culture and Politics in the Military-Industrial Complex* (Princeton, NJ: Princeton University Press, 2001); Christopher Simpson, *Universities and Enemies: Money and Politics in the Social Sciences during the Cold War* (New York: New Press, 1998); David Szanton, *The Politics of Knowledge: Area Studies and the Disciplines* (Berkeley: University of California Press, 2004). An article by David Engerman offers a useful overview: "Rethinking Cold War Universities, Some Recent Histories," *Journal of Cold War Studies* 5, no 3 (Summer 2003):80–95.

63. See Peter Grose, *Continuing the Inquiry: The Council on Foreign Relations from 1921 to 1996* (New York: Council on Foreign Relations Press, 2006).

64. David Atkinson, *In Theory and in Practice: Harvard's Center for International Affairs, 1958–1983* (Cambridge, MA: Harvard University Press, 2007), 3.

65. Diamond, *Compromised Campus,* 52.

66. Engerman, *Know Your Enemy,* 1.

67. Kennan to James Russell, October 11, 1950. George F. Kennan Papers 139 (Mudd Library, Princeton University):8; cited in Engerman, *Know Your Enemy,* 2.

68. Engerman, *Know Your Enemy,* 35.

69. Engerman, "Rethinking Cold War Universities," 85.

70. Ibid.

71. Engerman, *Know Your Enemy,* 35.

72. Engerman, "Rethinking Cold War Universities," citing figures from Clark Kerr, *The Uses of the University* (Cambridge, MA: Harvard University Press, 1963), 85.

73. Edward H. Berman, *The Influence of the Carnegie, Ford and Rockefeller Foundations on American Foreign Policy: The Ideology of Philanthropy* (Albany: State University of New York Press, 1983), 5.

74. Suri, *Henry Kissinger*, 121.

75. Engerman, *Know Your Enemy*, 72.

76. Ibid., 18.

77. Quoted in ibid., 26–27.

78. Atkinson, *Theory and Practice*, 5.

79. Lowen, *Creating the Cold War University*, mentioned in Engerman, "Rethinking Cold War Universities," 90–92.

80. Kerr, *The Uses of the University*.

81. Ibid.

82. Engerman, *Know Your Enemy*, 87.

83. Chomsky et al., *Cold War & the University;* Diamond, *Compromised Campus;* Robin, *Making of the Cold War Enemy.*

84. Dwight D. Eisenhower, "Farewell Address, 17 January 1961," https://www.ourdocuments .gov/doc.php??flash=true&doc=90&page=transcript.

85. Diamond, *Compromised Campus*, 59.

86. Simpson, *Universities and Enemies*, xvii.

87. Engermann, *Know Your Enemy*, 6.

88. See Donald Bailyn and Donald Fleming, *The Intellectual Migration: Europe and America, 1930–1960* (Cambridge, MA: Belknap Press of Harvard University Press, 1969).

89. Suri, *Henry Kissinger*, 96.

90. See James B. Conant, *My Several Lives: Memoirs of a Social Inventor* (New York: Harper & Row, 1970), and James Hershberg, *James B. Conant: Harvard to Hiroshima and the Making of the Nuclear Age* (New York: Knopf, 1993).

91. Lise Namikas, "The Committee to Defend America and the Debate between Internationalists and Interventionists, 1939–1941," *Historian* (Summer 1999):843.

92. Suri, *Henry Kissinger*, 102.

93. Samuel F. Wells, "Sounding the Tocsin: NSC-68 and the Soviet Threat," *International Security* 4, no. 2 (Fall 1979):116–158.

94. Diamond, *Compromised Campus*, 66–67.

95. Ibid., 73ff.

96. Ibid., quoting an internal memorandum of the Carnegie Corporation dated July 14, 1947.

97. Engerman, *Know Your Enemy*, 35.

98. Diamond, *Compromised Campus*, 71.

99. Engerman, *Know Your Enemy*, 48ff.

100. Walt Rostow, *The Dynamics of Soviet Society* (New York: W. W. Norton, 1953).

101. Engerman, *Know Your Enemy*, 49–50.

102. Raymond Bauer, Alex Inkeles, and Clyde Kluckhohn, *How the Soviet System Works: Cultural, Psychological, and Social Themes* (Cambridge, MA: Harvard University Press, 1956).

103. Ibid., 186.

104. Engerman, *Know Your Enemy*, 54 and 182–183.

105. On the International Seminar, see Walter Isaacson, *Kissinger: A Biography* (New York: Simon & Schuster, 1992), 70ff., where Isaacson offers an excessively negative description, and Suri, *Henry Kissinger,* 117ff. The authorization of the dean of the Summer School is required for access to the papers of the International Seminar, but in the Harvard University Archives (UAV 813.141.25 and UAV 813.141.75) I was able to find a large number of relevant documents, including Kissinger's correspondence, issues of *Confluence,* and annual reports, all of which allowed me to flesh out the context presented here.

106. Summaries of the contents of *Confluence* and the related correspondence are found in the Harvard Archives, series UAV 813.141.75, boxes 1–8.

107. Hugh Wilford, *The Mighty Wurlitzer: How the C.I.A. Played America* (Cambridge, MA: Harvard University Press, 2008), 126.

108. Isaacson, *Kissinger,* 70.

109. Interview with Abby Collins, December 3, 2009.

110. Brzezinski to Kissinger, February 28, 1956 and February 16, 1957; Kissinger to Brzezinski, March 15, 1957, all in folder "Kissinger, Henry 1956–1969," Box I.16, Brzezinski Papers, LoC.

111. Atkinson, *Theory and Practice,* 15. In addition to the archives (see the Works Cited list for details), Atkinson's book is the principal source on the WCFIA. There is another book, by Howard Wiarda, *Harvard and the Weatherhead Center for International Affairs (WCFIA): Foreign Policy Research Center and Incubator of Presidential Advisors* (Lanham, MD: Lexington Books, 2010), but it adds nothing of interest.

112. Their disputes took on a Homeric flavor; even fifty years later, in 2009, Bowie still asked that the recording device be turned off when he was describing them in an interview. Interview with Robert Bowie, July 7, 2009.

113. Atkinson, *Theory and Practice,* 47–49.

114. Zbigniew Brzezinski, *The Soviet Bloc: Unity and Conflict* (Cambridge, MA: Harvard University Press, 1960), xxii.

115. Henry Kissinger, *The Necessity for Choice* (New York: Harper and Brothers, 1961).

116. See "Risk Seen in Hope for Freer Soviet," *New York Times,* January 17, 1960, 17.

117. Atkinson, *Theory and Practice,* 117.

118. Interview with Stanley Hoffmann, December 1–4, 2009.

119. Zbigniew Brzezinski, "Shifts in the Satellites," *The New Republic* 134, no. 24 (June 11, 1956):37–41.

120. Interview with Zbigniew Brzezinski, June 2, 2011.

121. Brzezinski to Norman Birnbaum, September 10, 1976, folder " 'Bh-Bi' " Miscellaneous 1959–1977," Box 1.3, Brzezinski Papers, LoC.

122. Zbigniew Brzezinski, "U.S. Foreign Policy in East Central Europe: A Study in Contradiction," *Journal of International Affairs* 1, no. 1 (1957):60–71.

123. Ibid., 70–71.

124. Zbigniew Brzezinski, "Ideology and Power: Crisis in the Soviet Bloc," *Problems of Communism* 6, no. 1 (January-February 1957):12–17; Zbigniew Brzezinski, "Communist Ideology and Power: From Unity to Diversity," *Journal of Politics* 19, no. 4 (November 1957):549–590; Brzezinski, *Soviet Bloc.*

125. Alexander Dallin, "In Unity, Diversity," *New York Times,* July 3, 1960, Book Review, 10; Cyril Black, "Review," *Russian Review* 19, no. 4 (October 1960):399–400.

126. Brzezinski, *Soviet Bloc,* 25.

127. Ibid., 59.

128. Ibid., 157.

129. Ibid., 308. Tito was presented as the common enemy in order to recreate unity.

130. Ibid., 406.

131. Ibid., 408.

132. Zbigniew Brzezinski, "The Politics of Underdevelopment," *World Politics* 9, no. 1 (October 1956):55–75.

133. Brzezinski, "Politics of Underdevelopment," 74.

134. Senator Humphrey to Brzezinski, December 7, 1956, and Brzezinski to Humphrey, January 4, 1957, folder "Humphrey, Hubert H. 1956–1957," Box I.13, Brzezinski Papers, LoC.

135. "Remarks of Senator John F. Kennedy at the Annual Awards Dinner of the Overseas Press Club, New York City, May 6, 1957," http://findingcamelot.net/speeches/remarks-of-senator-john-f-kennedy-at-the-annual-awards-dinner-of-the-overseas-press-club-new-york-city-may-6-1957/.

136. See Brzezinski, "Poland—A Political Glimpse," 36.

137. Vaughan, *Zbigniew Brzeziński,* 71.

138. Kennedy, "Remarks," May 6, 1957.

139. John F. Kennedy to Brzezinski, August 23, 1957, folder "Kennedy, John F. 1957–1962," Box I.16, Brzezinski Papers, LoC.

140. See, for example, the unsigned article "The Team That Jack Built . . . Professional, Polished and Persistent," *Newsweek* (June 27, 1966):40–42, or Joseph Loftus, "Kennedy Is Given a Secret Briefing by CIA Director," *New York Times,* July 24, 1960, 1.

141. John Brademas to Brzezinski, September 24, 1963, folder "Brademas, John 1961–1976," Box I.2, Brzezinski Papers, LoC.

142. Leo Egan, "Kennedy Outlines Program to Court East Europe Bloc," *New York Times,* October 2, 1960, 1.

143. Robert Novak, "Kennedy's Brain Trust: More Professors Enlist but They Play Limited Policy-Making Role," *Wall Street Journal,* October 4, 1960, 1.

144. Interview with Zbigniew Brzezinski, June 22, 2010.

145. Ibid.

146. Brzezinski to Stanley Hoffmann, November 7, 1960, folder "Hoffmann, Stanley, 1960–1970," Box I.12, Brzezinski Papers, LoC.

147. Jean Pennar (American Committee for Liberation from Bolshevism, Inc.) to Brzezinski, May 20, 1955, folder "Am-Ap Miscellaneous, 1954–1976," Box I.1, Brzezinski Papers, LoC.

148. Brzezinski, *Soviet Bloc,* xxii.

149. "Notes taken in the course of the trip," folder "Speeches and Events 1952–1955," Box I.53, Brzezinski Papers, LoC.

150. Allen Ballard (notetaker), Government 215 Seminar, October 1, 1956, "Remarks by Professor Brzezinski on his trip to the Soviet Union," folder "Miscellany 1946–1949, 1956–1969," Box I.93, Brzezinski Papers, LoC.

151. Vaughan, *Zbigniew Brzeziński*, 73.

152. Brzezinski, "Poland—A Political Glimpse."

153. "Scattered Notes and Impressions from Poland," folder "Speeches and Events 1958," Box I.53, Brzezinski Papers, LoC.

154. Ibid.

155. Ibid.

156. Interview with Zbigniew Brzezinski, February 15, 2011.

157. Ibid.

158. Wilford, *Mighty Wurlitzer*, 144.

159. Elsie Carper, "U.S. Youth Countering a Red Gala," *Washington Post*, May 3, 1959, E3.

160. Philip Benjamin, "Youths Briefed on Red Festival," *New York Times*, July 4, 1959, 2.

161. Wilford, *Mighty Wurlitzer*, 144.

162. Ibid.

163. Interview with Zbigniew Brzezinski, June 17, 2011.

164. Interview with Zbigniew Brzezinski, June 2, 2011.

165. Wilford, *Mighty Wurlitzer*, 145.

166. Interview with Zbigniew Brzezinski, June 2, 2011.

167. Sydney Stern, *Gloria Steinem: Her Passions, Politics, and Mystique* (New York: Birch Lane Press, 1997), 119; quoted in Wilford, *Mighty Wurlitzer*, 145 and 146.

168. Stern, *Gloria Steinem*, 120.

169. Alfred Friendly, "Youth Festival Is Flop as Red-Line Showpiece," *Washington Post*, August 4, 1959, 14.

170. William Jordens, "Red Displeased with Youth Fete," *New York Times*, October 26, 1959, 2.

171. "CIA Subsidized Festival Trips," *New York Times*, February 21, 1967, 33.

172. Pincus in Wilford, *Mighty Wurlitzer*, 146; interview with Zbigniew Brzezinski, June 2, 2011.

173. Brzezinski to McGeorge Bundy, February 3, 1960, folder "Harvard University, 1950–1953, 1959–1960," Box I.12, Brzezinski Papers, LoC.

174. Brzezinski to Albert Mavrinac, February 13, 1959, folder "Mavrinac, Albert A., 1959–1965," Box I.20, Brzezinski Papers, LoC.

175. Ibid.

176. Brzezinski to Albert Mavrinac, February 28, 1959, folder "Mavrinac, Albert A., 1959–1965," Box I.20, Brzezinski Papers, LoC.

177. Brzezinski to Albert Mavrinac, March 16, 1959, folder "Mavrinac, Albert A., 1959–1965," Box I.20, Brzezinski Papers, LoC.

178. Brzezinski to Albert Mavrinac, April 21, 1959, folder "Mavrinac, Albert A., 1959–1965," Box I.20, Brzezinski Papers, LoC.

179. Brzezinski to Albert Mavrinac, February 28, 1959.

180. Interviews with Stanley Hoffmann, December 1 and 4, 2009;

181. Brzezinski's French: "I don't give a damn!" Interview with Zbigniew Brzezinski, June 22, 2010.

182. Interview with Zbigniew Brzezinski, June 2, 2011.

183. Brzezinski to Alexander Dallin, May 28, 1962, and July 29, 1962, folder "Dallin, Alexander, 1954–1966," Box 6, Brzezinski Papers, LoC.

184. Ibid.

185. Brzezinski to Grayson Kirk, March 30, 1965; Grayson Kirk to Brzezinski, April 2, 1965, folder "Columbia University 1961–1966," Box I.5, Brzezinski Papers, LoC.

2. A Political Adviser Is Born

1. David Truman to Brzezinski, December 21, 1959; Brzezinski to David Truman, January 14, 1960, folder "Columbia University 1959–1960," Box I.5, Zbigniew Brzezinski Papers, Manuscript Division, Library of Congress, Washington, DC (hereafter, Brzezinski Papers, LoC).

2. Brzezinski and Cyril Black to Brice Wood, Social Science Research Council, "Report on Third International Sovietological Conference," September 30, 1960, Box I.53, Brzezinski Papers, LoC.

3. Interview with Zbigniew Brzezinski, June 22, 2010.

4. Alexander Dallin to Brzezinski, September 6, 1963, folder "Reactions to Brzezinski 1960–66," Box I.100, LoC; and I.M. Krasnov, "American Research Centres at the Service of Anti-Communism," International Affairs (Moscow, August 1963):34–35.

5. Brzezinski to Alexander Dallin, July 29, 1962, folder "Dallin, Alexander 1954–1966," Box 6, Brzezinski Papers, LoC.

6. Dallin to Brzezinski, August 2, 1962, folder "Dallin, Alexander 1954–1966," Box 6, Brzezinski Papers, LoC.

7. Madeline Albright, with Bill Woodward, Madam Secretary: A Memoir, Madeleine Albright (New York: Miramax Books, 2003), 57.

8. Brzezinski to J. Kyle Goddard, U.S. Junior Chamber of Commerce, November 21, 1963, folder "Biographical Information 1956–1965," Box I.91, Brzezinski Papers, LoC.

9. Zbigniew Brzezinski, Ideology and Power in Soviet Politics (New York: Praeger, 1962).

10. Zbigniew Brzezinski, "The Nature of the Soviet System," Slavic Review 20, no. 3 (October 1961):351–368.

11. Ibid., 353.

12. Ibid., 359.

13. Ibid., 365.

14. Friedrich to Brzezinski, December 6, 1961, folder "Friedrich, Carl J. 1960–1965," Box I.9, Brzezinski Papers, LoC.

15. Brzezinski to Friedrich, December 12, 1961, folder "Friedrich, Carl J. 1960–1965," Box I.9, Brzezinski Papers, LoC.

16. Brzezinski to Friedrich, August 19, 1961, folder "Friedrich, Carl J. 1960–1965," Box I.9, Brzezinski Papers, LoC.

17. Friedrich to Brzezinski, January 15, 1962, folder "Friedrich, Carl J. 1960–1965," Box I.9, LoC. The book appeared as Zbigniew Brzezinski and Carl Friedrich, Totalitarian Dictatorship and Autocracy, second edition revised by Carl Friedrich (Cambridge, MA: Harvard University Press, 1965).

18. Zbigniew Brzezinski and Samuel Huntington, *Political Power: USA / USSR* (New York: Viking Press, 1964).

19. See also the discussion in David Engerman, *Know Your Enemy: The Rise and Fall of America's Soviet Experts* (New York: Oxford University Press, 2009), 222.

20. Brzezinski to Friedrich, May 12, 1966, folder "Friedrich, Carl J. 1960–1965," Box I.9, Brzezinski Papers, LoC.

21. Zbigniew Brzezinski, "The Soviet Political System: Transformation or Degeneration?" *Problems of Communism* 15 (January–February 1966):1–15.

22. Ibid., 7.

23. Zbigniew Brzezinski, "Reflections on the Soviet System," *Problems of Communism* 17 (May–June 1968):48.

24. Interview with Zbigniew Brzezinski, June 2, 2011.

25. Mary Allen, "Zbigniew Brzezinski Exit Interview," Jimmy Carter Library, Atlanta, GA (hereafter, Carter Library), February 20, 1981, http://222.jimmycarterlibrary.gov/library/exitInt/Brzezinski.pdf.

26. See Nabil Mikhail, "Zbigniew Brzezinski: The Scholar and the Statesman. A Study of the Thoughts and Policies of the National Security Adviser and His Staff in the Carter Administration" (Ph.D. diss., University of Virginia, 1996), 92–93.

27. Brzezinski to Bowie, May 8, 1961, folder "Bowie, Robert R. 1958–1975," Box I.2, Brzezinski Papers, LoC. The articles in question are Zbigniew Brzezinski, "The Challenge of Change in the Soviet Bloc," *Foreign Affairs* 39, no. 3 (April 1961):430–443, and Zbigniew Brzezinski and William Griffith, "Peaceful Engagement in Eastern Europe," *Foreign Affairs* 39, no. 4 (July 1961):642–654.

28. Henry Kissinger, *The Troubled Partnership: A Re-appraisal of the Atlantic Alliance* (New York: McGraw-Hill, 1965); Zbigniew Brzezinski, *Alternative to Partition: For a Broader Conception of America's Role in Europe* (New York: McGraw-Hill, 1965); Timothy Stanley, *NATO in Transition: The Future of the Atlantic Alliance* (New York: Praeger, 1965). All three publications were sponsored by the CFA as part of the Atlantic Policy Study Series.

29. Zbigniew Brzezinski, "Communist Disunity and the West," *New Republic* 14, no. 25 (December 18, 1961):14–17.

30. Letters, Joseph Alsop to Brzezinski, December 21, 1961, and January 2, 1962, folder "Joseph Alsop 1961–1964," Box I.1, Brzezinski Papers, LoC.

31. Roscoe Drummond, "Accidental War Propaganda, Soviets Hanging Themselves," *New York Herald Tribune*, December 7, 1964; Roscoe Drummond to Brzezinski, December 7, 1964; Brzezinski to Drummond, December 11, 1964, folder "Drummond, Roscoe 1964–1971," Box I.7, Brzezinski Papers, LoC.

32. Brzezinski to Charles Bartlett, August 25, 1961, folder "Ban-Bax, Miscellaneous 1957–1977, n.d.," Box I.3, Brzezinski Papers, LoC.

33. Brzezinski to McGeorge Bundy, February 1, 1961, folder "Bundy, McGeorge 1956–1973," Box I.3, Brzezinski Papers, LoC.

34. Brzezinski to McGeorge Bundy, August 25, 1961, and Bundy to Brzezinski, September 4, 1961, folder "Bundy, McGeorge 1956–1973," Box I.3, Brzezinski Papers, LoC.

35. Interviews with Pierre Flassner, March 7, 2009 and August 22, 2010; interview with Zbigniew Brzezinski, June 17, 2011.

36. Brzezinski to McGeorge Bundy, n.d. [Fall 1962], folder "Bundy, McGeorge 1956–1973," Box I.3, Brzezinski Papers, LoC.

37. John F. Kennedy to Brzezinski, November 6, 1962, folder "Kennedy, John F. 1957–1962," Box I.16, Brzezinski Papers, LoC.

38. Zbigniew Brzezinski, "Surprise a Key to Our Cuba Success," *Washington Post*, November 4, 1962.

39. Interview with Zbigniew Brzezinski, June 22, 2010; Brzezinski to Charles Hamilton, March 4, 1970, folder "Ham-Han," Box I.13, Brzezinski Papers, LoC.

40. Brzezinski to Humphrey, March 4, 1965, and memo, n.d., folder "Humphrey, Hubert H. 1963–1969," Box I.13, Brzezinski Papers, LoC.

41. Testimony before the House of Representatives Committee on Foreign Affairs, March 18, 1962, folder "Cooper, Chester L. 1962, 1968–1971," Box I.5, Brzezinski Papers, LoC.

42. Brzezinski to Fulbright, February 21, 1961, folder "Fulbright, J. William, 1957–1965," Box I.9, Brzezinski Papers, LoC; re the CIA, Chester Cooper to Brzezinski, March 1, 1962, folder "Cooper, Chester L. 1962, 1968–1971," Box I.5, Brzezinski Papers, LoC.

43. See the correspondence beginning on July 14, 1963, folder "Brademas, John 1961–1976," Box I.2, Brzezinski Papers, LoC.

44. On the Ford Foundation roundtable, see folder "Speeches and Events 1962 (3 of 10)," Box I.55, Brzezinski Papers, LoC.

45. Rudolf Rathaus and Alexis Coudert to Brzezinski, December 13, 1966, and Brzezinski to Alfred Jurzykowski Foundation, October 5, 1971, folder "Alfred Jurzykowski Foundation 1966–1972," Box I.1, Brzezinski Papers, LoC.

46. For the salary figures, see folder "Columbia University 1959–1960," Box I.5, Brzezinski Papers, LoC.

47. Brzezinski to Bill Burden, October 11, 1967, folder "Burden, William A. M. 1964–1976," Box I.3, Brzezinski Papers, LoC.

48. Robert Scheer, "Brzezinski: Profound or Banal?" *Los Angeles Times*, January 23, 1977, A1.

49. Brzezinski to J. Kyle Goddard, U.S. Junior Chamber of Commerce, November 21, 1963, folder "Biographical Information 1956–1965," Box I.91, Brzezinski Papers, LoC.

50. Zbigniew Brzezinski, ed., *Africa and the Communist World* (Stanford, CA: Stanford University Press, Hoover Institution on War, Revolution and Peace, 1963).

51. Ibid., 226.

52. Ibid., 228.

53. Brzezinski, "Peaceful Engagement," 654.

54. Brzezinski, *Alternative to Partition*, 169.

55. Ibid., 155, 165.

56. Zbigniew Brzezinski, "Don't Go Home Yanks," *Washington Post*, February 21, 1965.

57. Zbigniew Brzezinski, "De Gaulle and Europe to the Urals," *New Leader* (November 23, 1964):12–15.

58. Brzezinski to Bowie, October 30, 1963, folder "Bowie, Robert R. 1958–1975," Box I.2, Brzezinski Papers, LoC.

59. See Zbigniew Brzezinski, "Russia and Europe," *Foreign Affairs* 42, no. 3 (April 1964): 428–444; and "Moscow and the MLF: Hostility and Ambivalence," *Foreign Affairs* 43, no. 1 (October 1964):126–134.

60. Pierre Hassner to Brzezinski, n.d., and Brzezinski to Hassner, January 3, 1966, folder "Hassner, Pierre 1964–1968," Box I.12, LoC.

61. Brzezinski to Humphrey, July 14, 1967, folder "Humphrey, Hubert H. 1963–1969," Box I.13, Brzezinski Papers, LoC.

62. Zbigniew Brzezinski, "Cuba in Soviet Strategy," *New Republic* 147, no. 18 (November 3, 1962):7–8.

63. Ibid., 8.

64. Zbigniew Brzezinski, "'Neutral' Vietnam a Chinese Backyard," *Washington Post,* March 1, 1964, E1.

65. Ibid.

66. Zbigniew Brzezinski, "Threat and Opportunity in the Communist Schism," *Foreign Affairs* 41, no. 3 (April 1963):513–525.

67. Brzezinski to Bowie, March 3, 1964, and Bowie to Brzezinski, March 30, 1964, folder "Bowie, Robert R. 1958–1975," Box I.2, Brzezinski Papers, LoC.

68. Zbigniew Brzezinski, "The Communist World in a New Phase," *Proceedings of the Academy of Political Science* 28, no. 1 (April 1965):64–68.

69. Zbigniew Brzezinski, "Peace, Morality, and Vietnam," *New Leader* (April 12, 1965):8–9.

70. Brzezinski to John Brademas, July 14, 1963, folder "Brademas, John 1961–1976," Box I.2, Brzezinski Papers, LoC.

71. Brzezinski to J. Kyle Goddard, U.S. Junior Chamber of Commerce, November 21, 1963, folder "Biographical Information 1956–1965," Box I.91, Brzezinski Papers, LoC.

72. Brzezinski, "'Neutral' Vietnam a Chinese Backyard."

73. Brzezinski to Hassner, October 19, 1965, folder "Hassner, Pierre 1964–1968," Box I.12, Brzezinski Papers, LoC.

74. Brzezinski to Ashok Bhadkamkar, May 17, 1965, folder "Bh-Bi Miscellaneous 1959–1977," Box I.3, Brzezinski Papers, LoC.

75. Brzezinski to Bob Freedman, October 12, 1965, and July 14, 1967, folder "Freedman, Robert Owen, 1964–1969," Box I.9, Brzezinski Papers, LoC.

76. Interview with Zbigniew Brzezinski, February 15, 2011.

77. Paige E. Mulhollan, "Interview with Zbigniew Brzezinski," November 12, 1971, The Foreign Affairs Oral History Collection of the Association for Diplomatic Studies and Training, Courtesy of the National Archives and Records Service, Lyndon Baines Johnson Library, http://web2 .millercenter.org/lbj/oralhistory/brzezinski_zbigniew_1971_1112.pdf.

78. Ibid.

79. Ibid. See also Brzezinski to Christopher Emmet, June 3, 1970, folder "Emmet, Christopher, 1963–1971," Box I.8, Brzezinski Papers, LoC.

80. Lyndon Baines Johnson, "Remarks in New York City before the National Conference of Editorial Writers," *Public Papers of the President,* October 7, 1966 [503], 1125–1130, http://www.presidency.ucsb.edu/ws/index.php?pid=27908.

81. Thomas Schwartz, *Lyndon Johnson and Europe: In the Shadow of Vietnam* (Cambridge, MA: Harvard University Press, 2003), see especially 133ff. and 210ff.

82. See also Aaron Lobel, *Presidential Judgment: Foreign Policy Decision Making in the White House* (Hollis, NH: Hollis, 2001), 76n2, in which Bator gives his version of the facts, offering an explicit refutation: "stories about the origin of the speech started going around that I knew to be false"—Brzezinski's "stories," though Brzezinski was not named.

83. Johnson, "Remarks," October 7, 1966.

84. Ibid.

85. Brzezinski, *Alternative to Partition,* 165.

86. Mulhollan, "Interview."

87. Ibid.

88. Brzezinski to Daniel Bell, October 19, 1966, folder "Bell, Daniel, 1964–1975," Box I.2, Brzezinski Papers, LoC.

89. "Diplomacy: The Thinker," *Newsweek* (November 14, 1966):44.

90. Interview with Zbigniew Brzezinski, February 15, 2011.

91. Raymond Garthoff, *Détente and Confrontation: American Soviet Relations from Nixon to Reagan* (Washington, DC: Brookings Institution Press, 1985), 123.

92. Anecdote reported by Schwartz, email correspondence with the author, July 3, 2011.

93. In the interview with Mulhollan, Brzezinski declares: "I have the suspicion that [Johnson] wasn't fully aware of the extent to which his speech actually involved a reversal of hitherto fundamental tenets of our policy towards Europe, and I suspect that he was rather surprised by the extent to which some of the more conservative elements in West Germany, including the Chancellor, were shocked by that speech."

94. Bator in Lobel, *Presidential Judgment,* 76.

95. Schwartz, *Lyndon Johnson and Europe,* 211.

96. "Diplomacy: The Thinker," 44.

97. Mulhollan, "Interview."

98. Schwartz, *Lyndon Johnson,* 211–212. Once again, only the role of the Acheson Group was mentioned, not that of the PPS and certainly not Brzezinski's.

99. Mulhollan, "Interview."

100. See Judith Apter Klinghoffer, *Vietnam, Jews and the Middle East: Unintended Consequences* (New York: Macmillan, 1999).

101. Mulhollan, "Interview."

102. Brzezinski to Humphrey, July 14, 1967, folder "Humphrey, Hubert H. 1963–1969," Box I.13, Brzezinski Papers, LoC.

103. Mulhollan, "Interview."

104. On Humphrey and the 1968 campaign, see Hubert Humphrey, *Education of a Public Man: My Life and Politics* (Minneapolis: University of Minnesota Press, 1991); Carl Solbert, *Hubert*

Humphrey: A Biography (New York: W. W. Norton, 1984); and Dan Cohen, *Undefeated: The Life of Hubert M. Humphrey* (Minneapolis: Lerner, 1978).

105. David Halberstam, "The New Establishment: The Decline and Fall of the Eastern Empire," *Vanity Fair,* October 1994, http://www.vanityfair.com/news/1994/10/old-establishment-decline -199410.

106. Interview with Zbigniew Brzezinski, June 2, 2011.

107. Ibid.

108. Brzezinski to Robert Nathan (United Democrats for Humphrey), June 3, 1968, folder "Presidential Election Campaigns 1968, Humphrey, Hubert H. 1968, n.d. (1 of 4)," Box I.94, Brzezinski Papers, LoC.

109. John Rielly to Bob Nathan, June 19, 1968, folder "Presidential Election Campaigns 1968, Humphrey, Hubert H. 1968, n.d. (1 of 4)," Box I.94, Brzezinski Papers, LoC.

110. Press release, "Humphrey Task Forces on Issues Announced," June 30, 1968, folder "Presidential Election Campaigns 1968, Humphrey, Hubert H. 1968, n.d. (1 of 4)," Box I.94, Brzezinski Papers, LoC.

111. Brzezinski to Amb. John Gronouski, October 21, 1968 [in Polish]. See also Brzezinski, letter to the editor of the *New York Times,* folder "Presidential Election Campaigns 1968, Humphrey, Hubert H. 1968, n.d. (4 of 4)," Box I.94, Brzezinski Papers, LoC.

112. Brzezinski to Humphrey, July 19, 1968, folder "Presidential Election Campaigns 1968, Humphrey, Hubert H. 1968, n.d. (3 of 4)," Box I.94, Brzezinski Papers, LoC.

113. Ibid.

114. Humphrey to Brzezinski, August 6, 1968, folder "Presidential Election Campaigns 1968, Humphrey, Hubert H. 1968, n.d. (3 of 4)," Box I.94, Brzezinski Papers, LoC.

115. Brzezinski to Humphrey, September 11, 1968, folder "Presidential Election Campaigns 1968, Humphrey, Hubert H. 1968, n.d. (3 of 4)," Box I.94, Brzezinski Papers, LoC.

116. Roy Reed, "Humphrey Urges U.S. Stop Trying to Contain Red," *New York Times,* July 13, 1968, 1.

117. "Foreign Affairs section," draft, August 15, 1968, folder "Presidential Election Campaigns 1968, Humphrey, Hubert H. 1968, n.d. (3 of 4)," Box I.94, Brzezinski Papers, LoC.

118. Brzezinski to Humphrey, September 21, 1968, folder "Presidential Election Campaigns 1968, Humphrey, Hubert H. 1968, n.d. (3 of 4)," Box I.94, Brzezinski Papers, LoC.

119. R.W. Apple, "Humphrey Backs Allied 'Summits,'" *New York Times,* October 6, 1968, 74.

120. Brzezinski to Miss Violet Williams, office of the Vice President, September 11, 1968, folder "Presidential Election Campaigns 1968, Humphrey, Hubert H. 1968, n.d. (3 of 4)," Box I.94, Brzezinski Papers, LoC.

121. Brzezinski to Humphrey, September 11, 1968.

122. Brzezinski to Williams, September 11, 1968; Apple, "Humphrey Backs Allied 'Summits.'"

123. The memo is mentioned by Rowland Evans and Robert Novak, "False Alarm of Switch by HHH on Vietnam Punctures Optimism," *Washington Post,* June 20, 1968, A20. Unfortunately, the text is not in the archives.

124. Roy Reed, "Humphrey's Advisers Critical of War," *New York Times,* July 14, 1968, 51.

125. Reed, "Humphrey's Advisers"; Paul Hofman, "Moyers Says Humphrey Will Stress Own Policies," *New York Times,* June 17, 1968, 1.

126. Harrison Salisbury, "Humphrey Favors a Cease Fire Now," *New York Times,* June 23, 1968, 1; on the rejection, see Hedrick Smith, "Humphrey's Call Rebuffed by Thuy," *New York Times,* June 25, 1968, 1.

127. Brzezinski to Humphrey, July 16, 1968, folder "Presidential Election Campaigns 1968, Humphrey, Hubert H. 1968, n.d. (3 of 4)," Box I.94, Brzezinski Papers, LoC.

128. Ibid.

129. Joseph Loftus, "Humphrey Maps Position on War," *New York Times,* July 25, 1968, 20. According to Van Dyk, the task force met starting in June and proposed a troop reduction and a conditional halt in the bombing: see Ted Van Dyk, *Heroes, Hacks, and Fools: Memoirs from the Political Inside* (Seattle: University of Washington Press, 2007), 73. The task force was apparently divided: see James Reston, "Washington: The Savage Pressures of the Campaign," *New York Times,* July 26, 1968, 32.

130. Mulhollan, "Interview."

131. Van Dyk, *Heroes, Hacks, and Fools,* 73–74. But the dates in Van Dyk's book appear to be incorrect.

132. Brzezinski to Humphrey, August 14, 1968, folder "Presidential Election Campaigns 1968, Humphrey, Hubert H. 1968, n.d. (3 of 4)," Box I.94, Brzezinski Papers, LoC.

133. R. W. Apple, "Humphrey Vows Halt in Bombing if Hanoi Reacts," *New York Times,* October 1, 1968, 1.

134. Mulhollan, "Interview."

135. Brzezinski to Humphrey, October 16, 1968, folder "Presidential Election Campaigns 1968, Humphrey, Hubert H. 1968, n.d. (4 of 4)," Box I.94, Brzezinski Papers, LoC.

136. Brzezinski to Rielly, n.d. [November 1, 1968?], folder "Presidential Election Campaigns 1968, Humphrey, Hubert H. 1968, n.d. (4 of 4)," Box I.94, Brzezinski Papers, LoC.

137. Brzezinski-Jelenski correspondence on the Princeton Seminar, Spring 1968, folder "Jelenski, Constantin, 1964–1969," Box I.15, Brzezinski Papers, LoC.

138. Available in English as *The American Challenge,* trans. Ronald Steel (New York: Atheneum, 1969).

139. See, for example, A. C., "L'Amérique et le 'reste du monde.' Un colloque ambitieux à l'Université de Princeton," *Le Monde,* December 11, 1968.

140. Brzezinski to Shepard Stone, January 6, 1969, folder "Speeches and Events 1968 (8 of 8)," Box I.62, Brzezinski Papers, LoC.

141. Israel Shenker, "A Hit and Myth Gathering of Intellectuals," *New York Times,* December 8, 1968, 238.

142. Exchange reported by Pierre Hassner in interviews held on March 7, 2009, and August 22, 2010.

143. Israel Shenker, "6 Experts, Interviewed in Princeton, Urge Complete Review of U.S. Foreign Policy," *New York Times,* December 8, 1968, 76.

144. Shenker, "Hit and Myth Gathering," 238.

145. Israel Shenker, "Seminar Studies U.S. Woes," *New York Times,* December 3, 1968, 49.

146. Shenker, "Hit and Myth Gathering," 238; see also "Pondering the Problems," *Time,* December 13, 1968, and Israel Shenker, "Intellectuals Look at the World, the U.S., and Themselves, and Find All 3 in Trouble," *New York Times,* December 7, 1968, 52.

147. Quoted in Israel Shenker, "Kennan Analysis Coolly Received: Intellectuals at Princeton Seminar Criticize Speech," *New York Times,* December 4, 1968, 93.

148. Robert Stulberg, "Hilsman Supports Vietnam Pullout by All U.S. Troops—SDS Confronts Faculty at Door to McVickar," *Columbia Spectator,* October 25, 1968, 1.

149. Interview with Zbigniew Brzezinski, June 22, 2010.

150. Fred Schneider, "Radical Groups Plan 3 Separate Protests," *Columbia Spectator,* November 6, 1969.

151. Interview with Zbigniew Brzezinski, June 22, 2010.

152. Bruce Campbell, "Speech Interrupted," *McGill Daily* 62, no. 20 (October 17, 1972).

153. Brzezinski to Alistair Buchan, n.d., folder " 'Bu-By,' Miscellaneous 1955–1977," Box I.4, Brzezinski Papers, LoC.

154. Brzezinski to Huntington, May 7, 1968, folder "Huntington, Samuel P., 1964–1968," Box I.13, Brzezinski Papers, LoC.

155. Brzezinski to Huntington, April 28, 1969, folder "Huntington, Samuel P., 1964–1968," Box I.13, Brzezinski Papers, LoC.

156. Art Buchwald, "Professor's Stand Is Firm—But Brief," *Washington Post,* April 24, 1969, A21.

157. Interviews with Stanley Hoffmann, December 1 and 4, 2009.

158. Huntington to Brzezinski, May 6, 1969, folder "Huntington, Samuel P., 1964–1968," Box I.13, Brzezinski Papers, LoC.

159. Zbigniew Brzezinski, "Histrionics as History in Transition," *Survey,* nos. 74–75 (Winter–Spring 1970):225–236.

160. On the notion of citizen's committees, see Justin Vaïsse, "Typologie des organisations de la société civile américaine qui influencent la politique étrangère des États-Unis," in *La politique extérieure des États-Unis au XXe siècle: Le poids des déterminants intérieurs,* ed. Pierre Melandri and Serge Ricard (Paris: L'Harmattan, 2008).

161. Presentation brochure, "National Committee for a Political Settlement in Vietnam / Negotiations Now!" folder "National Committee for a Political Settlement in Vietnam 1967–1969," Box I.94, Brzezinski Papers, LoC.

162. Mary Temple to Kerr, Prosterman, Sacks, Kleiman, and Brzezinski, August 12, 1969, folder "National Committee for a Political Settlement in Vietnam 1967–1969," Box I.94, Brzezinski Papers, LoC.

163. "Meeting with President Nguyen Van Thieu," September 4, 1969, folder "National Committee for a Political Settlement in Vietnam 1967–1969," Box I.94, Brzezinski Papers, LoC.

164. "Prospects for Peace—A Report from Saigon," October 1969, folder "National Committee for a Political Settlement in Vietnam 1967–1969," Box I.94, Brzezinski Papers, LoC.

165. See, for example, Arthur Dommen, "Extended Viet Truce Suggested," *Washington Post,* September 6, 1969, A14.

166. Knowing "Henry," he took care to send the message also via Bryce Harlow, in the White House, and via Elliot Richardson, under secretary of state, whom he also knew.

167. Brzezinski to Kissinger, October 13, 1969, folder "Kissinger, Henry 1956–1969," Box I.16, Brzezinski Papers, LoC.

3. The Rise of a New Foreign Policy Elite

1. The expression is from I.M. Destler, Leslie Gelb, and Anthony Lake, *Our Own Worst Enemy: The Unmaking of American Foreign Policy* (New York: Simon & Schuster, 1984).

2. Karl Mannheim, *Essays on the Sociology of Knowledge,* ed. Paul Kecskemeti (London: Routledge & Kegan Paul, 1952, repr. 1997), 276, 303ff. (the quotation is on 303).

3. As Jean-François Sirinelli has shown in his book *Génération intellectuelle: Khâgneux et Normaliens dans l'entre-deux-guerres* (Paris: Fayard, 1988). On the notion of generation, see also Michel Winock, "Les générations intellectuelles," *Vingtième Siècle* 22, no. 1 (1989):17–38; and Jean-François Sirinelli, ed., "Générations intellectuelles," *Les Cahiers de l'Institut d'Histoire du Temps Présent* (*IHTP*) 6, special issue (November 1987).

4. Priscilla Roberts, "The Transatlantic American Foreign Policy Elite: Its Evolution in a Generational Perspective," *Journal of Transatlantic Studies* 7, no. 2 (June 2009):165–167.

5. Ibid., 178.

6. Henry Fairlie, "Political Commentary," *The Spectator,* September 23, 1955.

7. Godfrey Hodgson, "The Establishment," *Foreign Policy,* no. 10 (Spring 1973):4–5.

8. After his first article in *The American Scholar* in 1961, Rovere published *The American Establishment and Other Reports, Opinions, and Speculations* (New York: Harcourt, Brace & World, 1962).

9. Rovere, *American Establishment,* 11.

10. On McCloy, see Kai Bird, *The Chairman: John J. McCloy, the Making of an American Establishment* (New York: Simon & Schuster, 1992), and Max Holland, "Citizen McCloy," *Wilson Quarterly,* no. 15 (Fall 1991):22–42.

11. Rovere, *American Establishment,* 8.

12. David Halberstam, *The Best and the Brightest* (New York: Random House, 1974), 8.

13. Walter Isaacson and Evan Thomas, *The Wise Men: Six Friends and the World They Made* (New York: Simon & Schuster, 1986), 644.

14. Ibid., 700.

15. See Peter Grose, *Continuing the Inquiry: The Council on Foreign Relations from 1921 to 1996* (New York: Council on Foreign Relations Press, 2006), 8. On the CFR, see also Robert D. Shulzinger, *The Wise Men of Foreign Affairs* (New York: Columbia University Press, 1984).

16. Grose, *Continuing the Inquiry,* 15 and 22.

17. Destler, Gelb, and Lake, *Our Own Worst Enemy,* 107.

18. On Stimson, see his memoirs, written with McGeorge Bundy: *On Active Service in Peace and War,* 2 vols. (New York: Harper, 1948). See also two biographies: Godfrey Hodgson, *The Colonel: The Life and Wars of Henry Stimson, 1867–1950* (New York: Alfred A. Knopf, 1990), and David F. Schmitz, *Henry L. Stimson: The First Wise Man* (Wilmington, DE: Scholarly Resources, 2001).

19. On the shape, values, and role of the Establishment, see especially Arthur Schlesinger Jr., *A Thousand Days: John F. Kennedy in the White House* (Boston: Houghton Mifflin, 1965), especially 128–129; Joseph Kraft, *Profiles in Power: A Washington Insight* (New York: New American Library, 1966); Ernest May, *American Imperialism: A Speculative Essay* (New York: Atheneum, 1968); Richard Barnet, *Roots of War: The Men and Institutions behind U.S. Foreign Policy* (New York: Atheneum, 1972); John Donovan, *The Cold Warriors: A Policy-Making Elite* (New York: Heath, 1974); and Halberstam, *Best and Brightest.*

20. David Halberstam, "The New Establishment: The Decline and Fall of the Eastern Empire," *Vanity Fair,* October 1964, www.vanityfair.com/news/1994/10/old-establishment -decline-199410, dated 4/4/11.

21. Halberstam, "New Establishment."

22. Isaacson and Thomas, *Wise Men,* 31.

23. Ibid., 29

24. Ibid.

25. Halberstam, "New Establishment."

26. Henry Kissinger, *The Necessity for Choice* (New York: Harper and Brothers, 1961), 341.

27. Halberstam, *Best and Brightest,* xix.

28. On McGeorge Bundy, see Halberstam, *Best and Brightest,* chap. 4; Isaacson and Thomas, *Wise Men,* 598; Andrew Preston, *The War Council: McGeorge Bundy, the NSC, and Vietnam* (Cambridge, MA: Harvard University Press, 2006); Kai Bird, *The Color of Truth: McGeorge and William Bundy, Brothers in Arms* (New York: Simon & Schuster, 1998); and Gordon Goldstein, *Lessons in Disaster: McGeorge Bundy and the Push to War in Vietnam* (New York: Times Books/Henry Holt, 2008).

29. Bundy and Stimson, *On Active Service,* 1948.

30. Grose, *Continuing the Inquiry,* 49.

31. Hodgson, "Establishment," 17ff.

32. Ibid., 21.

33. Halberstam, "New Establishment."

34. For example, on the right, Kent Courtney and Phoebe Courtney, *America's Unelected Rulers* (New Orleans, LA: Conservative Society of America, 1962), and, on the left, Laurence Shoup and William Minter, *Imperial Brain Trust: The Council on Foreign Relations and United States Foreign Policy* (New York: Monthly Review Press, 1977).

35. Hodgson, "Establishment," 35.

36. Grose, *Continuing the Inquiry,* 51.

37. Isaacson and Thomas, *Wise Men,* 725.

38. Halberstam, "New Establishment."

39. Destler, Gelb, and Lake, *Our Own Worst Enemy,* 109.

40. Leslie Gelb, "The Secretary of State Sweepstakes," *New York Times,* May 23, 1976, SM4.

41. Halberstam, "New Establishment."

42. Ibid.

43. Interview with Zbigniew Brzezinski, June 17, 2011.

44. Halberstam, "New Establishment."

45. Zbigniew Brzezinski, *Power and Principle: Memoirs of the National Security Adviser, 1977–1981* (New York: Farrar, Straus & Giroux, 1983), 43.

46. Ibid., 42–43 and 254.

47. Isaacson and Thomas, *Wise Men,* 736.

48. Destler, Gelb, and Lake, *Our Own Worst Enemy,* 96; Brzezinski, *Power and Principle,* 40.

49. Interview with Zbigniew Brzezinski, June 19, 2011.

50. Destler, Gelb, and Lake, *Our Own Worst Enemy,* 106.

51. On the Brookings Institution, see James Allen Smith, *Brookings at Seventy-Five* (Washington, DC: Brookings Institution Press, 1991), and Donald Critchlow, *The Brookings Institution: Expertise and the Public Interest in a Democratic Society* (DeKalb: Northern Illinois University Press, 1985).

52. Brzezinski, *Power and Principle,* 84–85.

53. See James Allen Smith, *Strategic Calling: The Center for Strategic and International Studies, 1962–1992* (Washington, DC: CSIS, 1993).

54. On the last two organizations, see Justin Vaïsse, *Neoconservatism: The Biography of a Movement,* trans. Arthur Goldhammer (Cambridge, MA: Harvard University Press, 2010), chaps. 3–5.

55. See Marilyn Berger, "Professors' Flight from Washington: What Went Wrong?" *Los Angeles Times,* February 27, 1972, F1.

56. Paige E. Mulhollan, "Interview with Zbigniew Brzezinski," November 12, 1971, The Foreign Affairs Oral History Collection of the Association for Diplomatic Studies and Training, Courtesy of the National Archives and Records Service, Lyndon Baines Johnson Library, http://web2 .millercenter.org/lbj/oralhistory/brzezinski_zbigniew_1971_1112.pdf.

57. Harry McPherson, *A Political Education: A Washington Memoir* (Austin: University of Texas Press, 1994), 294.

58. William Fox to Brzezinski, May 31, 1967, folder "Fox, William T.R., 1961, 1967," Box I.9, Zbigniew Brzezinski Papers, Manuscript Division, Library of Congress, Washington, DC (hereafter, Brzezinski Papers, LoC). The article in question was by Max Frankel, "Intellectuals to Johnson: War's the Rub; Johnson Advised by Intellectuals' Constant Interchange," *New York Times,* May 22, 1967, 1.

59. Brzezinski to William Fox, June 1, 1967, folder "Fox, William T. R., 1961, 1967," Box I.9, Brzezinski Papers, LoC.

60. Mulhollan, "Interview."

61. Halberstam, "New Establishment."

62. Isaacson and Thomas, *Wise Men,* 32.

63. Samuel P. Huntington and Warren Demian Manshel, "Why 'Foreign Policy'?" *Foreign Policy* 1 (Winter 1970–1971):5.

64. Stanley Hoffmann, "Vietnam: An Algerian Solution?" *Foreign Policy,* no. 2 (Spring 1971): 3–37; Albert Wohlstetter, "Is There a Strategic Arms Race?" *Foreign Policy,* no. 15 (Summer 1974):3–20; and "Optimal Ways to Confuse Ourselves," *Foreign Policy,* no. 20 (Autumn 1975):170–198; Paul Nitze, "Deterring Our Deterrent," *Foreign Policy,* no. 25 (Winter, 1976–1977):195–210; Hodgson, "The Establishment"; Zbigniew Brzezinski, "Half Past

Nixon," *Foreign Policy*, no. 3 (Summer 1971):3–21, and "The Deceptive Structure of Peace," *Foreign Policy*, no. 14 (Spring 1974):35–55.

65. See the correspondence in folder "Zbigniew Brzezinski Chronological File: Foreign Policy Magazine [Apr. 1 74–5/13/75]," Box 33.6, Trilateral Commission File, Donated Historical Material, Zbigniew Brzezinski Collection (33), Jimmy Carter Library, Atlanta, GA (hereafter, Brzezinski Collection, Carter Library).

66. Charles Gati, "The Forgotten Region," *Foreign Policy*, no. 19 (Summer 1975):135–145.

67. See "Zbigniew Brzezinski," *Current Biography* (April 1970):8.

68. "Nation: The Debate," *Time Magazine* (July 2, 1965):24–25.

69. See, for example, Birch Bayh to Brzezinski, June 1, 1964, folder "Bayh, Birch, 1964–1977," Box I.1, Brzezinski Papers, LoC.

70. See Carl Gershman, "The Rise and Fall of the New Foreign-Policy Establishment," *Commentary* 70, no. 1 (July 1980):13–24.

71. The Notre Dame speech is available at http://www.presidency.ucsb.edu/ws/?pid=7552.

72. Gershman, "Rise and Fall," 24.

73. Richard Perle, cited in Stephen Klaidman, "The New Foreign Policy Crowd," *Washington Post*, June 17, 1976, 31.

74. Zbigniew Brzezinski, "America in a Hostile World," *Foreign Policy* 23 (Summer 1976):65–96.

75. Sidney Blumenthal, *The Rise of the Counter-Establishment: From Conservative Ideology to Political Power* (New York: Harper & Row, 1988).

76. Jeremy Suri, *Henry Kissinger and the American Century* (Cambridge, MA: Harvard University Press, 2007), 164.

77. Walter Isaacson, *Kissinger: A Biography* (New York: Simon & Schuster, 1992), 82.

78. Henry Kissinger, "Military Policy and Defense of the 'Grey Areas,'" *Foreign Affairs* 33 (April 1955):416–428.

79. Henry Kissinger, *Nuclear Weapons and Foreign Policy* (New York: Harper [for the CFR], 1957).

80. Ted Van Dyk, *Heroes, Hacks and Fools: Memoirs from the Political Inside* (Seattle: University of Washington Press, 2007), 101.

81. Isaacson, *Kissinger*, 133.

82. An article in the *New York Times* details the assertions made on all sides (it is difficult to follow Kissinger in his vehement denegations): see Terence Smith, "Kissinger Role in '68 Race Stirs Conflicting Views," *New York Times*, June 13, 1983.

83. Isaacson, *Kissinger*, 133. We can appreciate the ambiguity of the statement: Brzezinski does not say whether the help "offered" was actually delivered.

84. Halberstam, "New Establishment."

85. Seymour Hersh, *The Price of Power: Kissinger in the Nixon White House* (New York: Summit Books, 1983), 12–13.

86. Richard Nixon, *RN: The Memoirs of Richard Nixon* (New York: Grosset and Dunlap, 1978), 323ff.

87. Isaacson, *Kissinger*, 132.

88. Halberstam, "New Establishment."

89. Zbigniew Brzezinski, *Between Two Ages: America's Role in the Technetronic Era* (New York: Viking Press, 1970), and *The Fragile Blossom: Crisis and Change in Japan* (New York: Harper & Row, 1972).

90. Humphrey to Brzezinski, November 8, 1968, folder "Presidential Election Campaigns 1968, Humphrey, Hubert H. 1968 n.d. (4 of 4)," Box I.94, Brzezinski Papers, LoC.

91. Brzezinski to Humphrey, November 22, 1968, folder "Humphrey, Hubert H., 1963–1969," Box I.13, Brzezinski Papers, LoC.

92. Brzezinski to Humphrey, March 5, 1970, folder "Humphrey, Hubert H., 1970–1977," Box I.13, Brzezinski Papers, LoC.

93. Brzezinski to Humphrey, May 13, 1960, folder "Humphrey, Hubert H., 1963–1969," Box I.13, Brzezinski Papers, LoC.

94. Brzezinski to Humphrey, March 16, 1970, folder "Humphrey, Hubert H., 1970–1977," Box I.13, Brzezinski Papers, LoC.

95. See Kevin Phillips, *The Emerging Republican Majority* (New York: Arlington House, 1969); Richard M. Scammon and Ben J. Wattenberg, *The Real Majority* (New York: Coward-McCann, 1970). On the "vital center," see Arthur M. Schlesinger Jr., *The Vital Center: The Politics of Freedom* (New Brunswick, NJ: Transaction, [1949] 1998).

96. Humphrey to Brzezinski, April 13, 1970, folder "Humphrey, Hubert H., 1970–1977," Box I.13, Brzezinski Papers, LoC.

97. Brzezinski to Humphrey, April 27, 1970, folder "Humphrey, Hubert H., 1970–1977," Box I.13, Brzezinski Papers, LoC.

98. Brzezinski to Humphrey, May 25, 1970, folder "Humphrey, Hubert H., 1970–1977," Box I.13, Brzezinski Papers, LoC.

99. See Zbigniew Brzezinski, "A 2-Year Stint for Youth," *Washington Post*, September 27, 1970, 33.

100. Brzezinski to Humphrey, May 25, 1970.

101. Humphrey to Brzezinski, June 24, 1970, folder "Humphrey, Hubert H., 1970–1977," Box I.13, Brzezinski Papers, LoC.

102. Max Kampelman to Brzezinski, November 17, 1971 (including excerpt from memo written by Humphrey), folder "Presidential Election Campaigns 1972, Humphrey, Hubert H. 1971–71, n.d.," Box I.94, Brzezinski Papers, LoC.

103. Humphrey to Brzezinski, November 24, 1971, folder "Presidential Election Campaigns 1972, Humphrey, Hubert H. 1971–71, n.d.," Box I.94, Brzezinski Papers, LoC.

104. Humphrey to Brzezinski, July 17, 1972, folder "Presidential Election Campaigns 1972, Humphrey, Hubert H. 1971–71, n.d.," Box I.94, Brzezinski Papers, LoC.

105. Brzezinski to Muskie, May 26, 1970, folder "Muskie, Edmund S., 1969–1975," Box I.21, Brzezinski Papers, LoC.

106. Brzezinski to Edward Kennedy, June 3, 1970, folder "Kennedy, Edward Moore, 1964–1976," Box I.16, Brzezinski Papers, LoC.

107. Edward Kennedy to Brzezinski, July 1, 1970, folder "Kennedy, Edward Moore, 1964–1976," Box I.16, Brzezinski Papers, LoC.

108. See, for example, in Box I.94, Brzezinski Papers, LoC: Brzezinski to Max Kampelman, March 6, 1972, folder "Presidential Election Campaigns 1972, Humphrey, Hubert H. 1971–72, n.d.": Brzezinski to Tony Lake, folder "Presidential Election Campaigns 1972, Muskie,

Edmund M. 1972, n.d."; Brzezinski to Humphrey, April 13, 1972, folder "Presidential Election Campaigns 1972, Humphrey, Hubert H. 1971–72, n.d."; Brzezinski to Muskie, April 13, 1972, folder "Presidential Election Campaigns 1972, Muskie, Edmund M. 1972, n.d."

109. Richard Gardner to Cyrus Vance, December 10, 1970, folder "Gardner, Richard N. 1963–1965," Box I.10, Brzezinski Papers, LoC.

110. Brzezinski to Roscoe Drummond, December 22, 1970, folder "Drummond, Roscoe 1964–1971," Box I.7, Brzezinski Papers, LoC.

111. Brzezinski to Muskie, August 1, 1971, and Brzezinski to Dwight Perkins (Harvard), September 10, 1971, folder "Presidential Election Campaigns 1972, Muskie, Edmund M. 1972, n.d.," Box I.94, Brzezinski Papers, LoC.

112. Maynard Toll to Brzezinski, December 10, 1971, and Brzezinski to Maynard Toll, December 14, 1971, "Presidential Election Campaigns 1972, Muskie, Edmund M. 1972, n.d.," Box I.94, Brzezinski Papers, LoC.

113. Brzezinski to Albert Mavrinac, January 20, 1972, folder "Mavrinac, Albert A, 1966–1976," Box I.20, Brzezinski Papers, LoC.

114. Brzezinski to Muskie, January 20, 1972, folder "Presidential Election Campaigns 1972, Muskie, Edmund M. 1972, n.d.," Box I.94, Brzezinski Papers, LoC.

115. Maynard Toll to Brzezinski, February 11, 1972, and Brzezinski to Maynard Toll, February 16, 1972, folder "Presidential Election Campaigns 1972, Muskie, Edmund M. 1972, n.d.," Box I.94, Brzezinski Papers, LoC.

116. Muskie to Brzezinski, March 13, 1972, folder "Presidential Election Campaigns 1972, Muskie, Edmund M. 1972, n.d.," Box I.94, Brzezinski Papers, LoC.

117. Brzezinski to Mavrinac, May 8, 1972, folder "Mavrinac, Albert A, 1966–1976," Box I.20, Brzezinski Papers, LoC.

118. Muskie to Brzezinski, August 19, 1972, folder "Presidential Election Campaigns 1972, Muskie, Edmund M. 1972, n.d.," Box I.94, Brzezinski Papers, LoC.

119. Brzezinski to Ted Van Dyk, August 18, 1972, folder "Presidential Election Campaign 1972, Miscellany 1972, n.d.," Box I.94, Brzezinski Papers, LoC.

120. Ted Van Dyk to Brzezinski, August 25, 1972, folder "Presidential Election Campaign 1972, Miscellany 1972, n.d.," Box I.94, Brzezinski Papers, LoC.

121. Rowland Evans and Robert Novak, "McGovern's Odd Braintrust," and Zbigniew Brzezinski, "Not in Agreement (Letter to the Editor)," both in *Washington Post*, September 3, 1972, C7.

122. Brzezinski to Mavrinac, September 15, 1972, folder "Mavrinac, Albert A, 1966–1976," Box I.20, and Brzezinski to Cord Meyer, folder "Presidential Election Campaign 1972, Miscellany 1972, n.d.," Box I.94, Brzezinski Papers, LoC.

4. From the Trilateral Commission to the White House

1. Zbigniew Brzezinski, *Power and Principle: Memoirs of the National Security Adviser* (New York: Farrar, Straus & Giroux, 1983), 4.

2. Zbigniew Brzezinski, *The Soviet Bloc: Unity and Conflict,* Russian Research Studies Center no. 67, 2nd rev. ed. (Cambridge, MA: Harvard University Press, 1967).

3. Zbigniew Brzezinski, *Between Two Ages: America's Role in the Technetronic Era* (New York: Viking Press, 1970).

4. Ibid., xvi.

5. Zbigniew Brzezinski, "Tomorrow's Agenda," *Foreign Affairs* 44, no. 4 (July 1966): 662–670.

6. Zbigniew Brzezinski, "America in the Technetronic Age," *Encounter* (January 1968):16–26; see also Zbigniew Brzezinski, "The Implications of Change for United States Foreign Policy," *Department of State Bulletin* 35, no. 1462 (July 3, 1967):19–23; "Crises Blur Reality of Slow Basic Change," *Washington Post*, July 9, 1986, B2; "The American Transition," *The New Republic* 157, no. 26 (December 23, 1967):18–21; "Peace and Power," *Survival* 10, no. 12 (December 1968): 386–396; "Why the Alliance Is Fading?" *Interplay* 1, no. 10 (May 1968): 18–19; and "The Search for Meaning amid Change," *New York Times*, January 6, 1969, 141.

7. See Daniel Bell, "Notes on the Post-industrial Society," *The Public Interest*, no. 6 (Winter 1967):24–35 and no. 7 (Spring 1967):102–118; *The Coming of Post-Industrial Society: A Venture in Social Forecasting* (New York: Basic Books, 1973).

8. Brzezinski, *Between Two Ages*, 10–14.

9. Ibid., 195–196.

10. Ibid., 126–138.

11. Ibid., 238.

12. Ibid., 35.

13. Ibid., 282.

14. Ibid., 297.

15. Sanford Lakoff, "Review," *Administrative Science Quarterly* 17, no. 3 (September 1972): 433–434.

16. Alvin Toffler, *Future Shock* (New York: Random House, 1970); Nigel Calder, *Technopolis* (New York: Simon & Schuster, 1970); Victor Ferkiss, *Technological Man* (New York: George Braziller, 1969).

17. Thomas Stritch, "The Banality of Utopia," *Review of Politics* 34, no. 1 (January 1972):105.

18. John McCandlish Phillips, "Scholar Sees U.S. at a Turning Point," *New York Times*, August 12, 1970, 30; Elting Morison, "What to Do Today before Tomorrow Gets You: The Future," *New York Times*, July 26, 1970, 186.

19. John Stoessinger, "Recent Books on International Relations," *Foreign Affairs* 48, no. 4 (July 1970):78.

20. This "inverted Marxism" brings to mind that of Walt Rostow in *The Stages of Economic Growth: A Non-Communist Manifesto* (Cambridge, UK: Cambridge University Press, 1960).

21. Interview with Zbigniew Brzezinski, June 2, 2011.

22. Interview with Zbigniew Brzezinski, February 15, 2011.

23. Herman Kahn, *The Emerging Japanese Superstate: Challenge and Response* (Englewood Cliffs, NJ: Prentice-Hall, 1971).

24. Brzezinski was in Tokyo in early 1970 after a trip to Australia, but he then went back to New York. See Richard Gardner to Cyrus Vance, December 10, 1970, folder "Gardner, Richard N. 1963–1975," Box I.10, Brzezinski Papers, LoC.

25. Interview with Zbigniew Brzezinski, June 2, 2011.

26. Brzezinski, *The Fragile Blossom: Crisis and Change in Japan* (New York: Harper & Row, 1972).

27. Tong-Whan Park, "Review," *Journal of Politics* 35, no. 4 (November 1973):1014.

28. Henry Scott Stokes, "Say Sayonara to Certainty in Japanese Political Life," *New York Times,* April 9, 1972, BR6.

29. Brzezinski, *Fragile Blossom,* 2.

30. Ibid., 66–67, 134.

31. Ibid., 111, 135–136, 140.

32. Brzezinski to Humphrey, August 20, 1971, folder "Presidential Election Campaigns 1972, Muskie, Edmund M. 1971" [this letter is misplaced], Box I.94, Brzezinski Papers, LoC.

33. Ibid.; Humphrey to Brzezinski, October 19, 1971, folder "Humphrey, Hubert H. 190–1977"; and Press Release, "Humphrey Calls for Clarification of U.S. Ties with Japan," August 30, 1971, Box I.13, Zbigniew Brzezinski Papers, Manuscript Division, Library of Congress, Washington, DC (hereafter, Brzezinski Papers, LoC).

34. See, for example, the brief historical section on the Trilateral Commission site, , http://www.trilateral.org/go.cfm?do-Page.View&pid=9#1. See also the two chief references on the Trilateral Commission: Holly Sklar, ed., *Trilateralism: The Trilateral Commission and Elite Planning for World Management* (Boston: South End Press, 1980); Stephen Gill, *American Hegemony and the Trilateral Commission* (Cambridge, UK: Cambridge University Press, 1991). Gill writes, 140: "It is worth emphasizing here that initiating the Trilateral Commission without David Rockefeller is as unimaginable as Hamlet without the Prince. Without Rockefeller's imprimatur, the proposals of Bowie, Trezise and Brzezinski might well have disappeared."

35. Zbigniew Brzezinski, "New Guidelines for the West," *New Leader* (March 28, 1966):13: "To encourage the eventual emergence of a looser community of the more developed nations, including not only Japan but also most of the European communist states, and thereby gradually transform current conflicts into the beginnings of cooperation." See also "Tomorrow's Agenda," *Foreign Affairs* 44, no. 4 (July 1966):669.

36. In Zbigniew Brzezinski, "Crises Blur Reality of Slow Basic Change" (*Washington Post,* July 9, 1967, B52), the four pillars were the United States, Eastern Europe, Western Europe, and the USSR, and Brzezinski added: "such a community of the developed nations, of which Japan should naturally be a member." In "Toward a Community of the Developed Nations" (*Department of State Bulletin* 56, no. 1446 [March 13, 1967]:415), Japan is hardly mentioned.

37. Brzezinski, *Between Two Ages,* 297.

38. Zbigniew Brzezinski, "America and Europe," *Foreign Affairs* 49, no. 1 (October 1970):29: "A new and broader approach is needed—creation of a community of the developed nations which can effectively address itself to the larger concerns confronting mankind. In addition to the United States and Western Europe, Japan ought to be included. Its inclusion would be good both for Japan and for Western Europe, giving both a sense of participation in concerns of global dimensions, yet rooted in their own attainments as well as problems. A council representing the United States, Western Europe and Japan, with regular meetings of the heads of governments as well as some small standing machinery, would be a good start."

39. Brzezinski to Clifton Forster, September 29, 1971, folder "Forster, Clifton B., 1971–1976," Box I.8, Brzezinski Papers, LoC.

40. Brzezinski to Joseph Reed, April 26, 1972, folder "Zbigniew Brzezinski chronological file 4 / 26 / 71–4 / 30 / 73," Box 33.5, Brzezinski Collection, Carter Library. The letter is accompanied by a plan of action on the one hand (see below), and on the other a three-page memorandum titled simply: "Memorandum: A Proposal."

41. Ibid.

42. Interview with Zbigniew Brzezinski, June 2, 2011.

43. David Rockefeller, *Memoirs* (New York: Random House, 2002), 416. It seems that he also proposed the idea at the Chase Manhattan International Financial Forums that took place in London, Paris, and Brussels in March of that year; see "Minutes of the May 9th meeting on the proposed Commission for Peace and Prosperity," in George Franklin to Brzezinski et al., May 11, 1972, folder "Correspondence File: 5 / 11 / 72–2 / 28 / 73," Box 33.1, Brzezinski Collection, Carter Library.

44. Interview with Zbigniew Brzezinski, June 2, 2011.

45. Ibid.

46. Gill, *American Hegemony,* 138.

47. George Franklin to Brzezinski, Bowie, Bundy, Rockefeller, Owen, William Butler [absent], James Perkins, Joseph Verner Reed, and Max Kohnstamm [absent], "Minutes of the May 9th meeting on the proposed Commission for Peace and Prosperity," folder "Correspondence File: 5 / 11 / 72–2 / 28 / 73," Box 33.5, Brzezinski Collection, Carter Library.

48. Brzezinski to David Rockefeller, folder "Zbigniew Brzezinski chronological file 4 / 26 / 71–4 / 30 / 73," Box 33.5, Brzezinski Collection, Carter Library.

49. Interview with Zbigniew Brzezinski, June 2, 2011.

50. Zbigniew Brzezinski, "Japan in a Trilateral World," *New Leader* 55 (July 24, 1972):5–7.

51. Frederick Starr and Edward Morse prepared the reports.

52. "Meeting on Proposed Trilateral Commission," George Franklin, reporter, folder "Correspondence File: 5 / 11 / 72–2 / 28 / 73," Box 33.1, Brzezinski Collection, Carter Library.

53. Interview with Zbigniew Brzezinski, June 2, 2011.

54. See Mario Del Pero, "The Crisis of the 1970s, the Contradictions of US Hegemony, and the End of Atlantica," paper presented at a conference "The West and the Rest—The Atlantic Community in the Global Arena," Torino-Vercelli, May 27–28, 2010.

55. Jean Monnet, cited in Jean Boissonnat, *Journal de crise, 1973–1984* (Paris: J.-C. Lattès, 1984), 9.

56. Interview with Zbigniew Brzezinski, June 2, 2011.

57. Brzezinski, *Between Two Ages,* 297–298: "The inclusion of Japan would be particularly important, both to the internal development of Japanese life and to the vitality of such a community. Japan is a world power, and in a world of electronic and supersonic communications it is a psychological and political error to think of it as primarily an Asian nation. Japan needs an outlet commensurate with its own advanced development, not one that places it in the position of a giant among pygmies and that excludes it de facto from the councils of the real world power. The regular American-Japanese cabinet-level talks are a desirable bilateral arrangement, but Japan will become more fully and creatively involved in world affairs in a larger setting of equal partners."

58. Gerard Smith to Henry Owen, April 2, 1973, folder "Correspondence File: 5 / 11 / 72–2 / 28 / 73," Box 33.1, Brzezinski Collection, Carter Library.

59. See George Franklin to Members of the Planning Group, December 19, 1972, folder "Gerard Smith File—Chron File: 5 / 11 / 72–2 / 28 / 73," Box 33.1, Brzezinski Collection, Carter Library; David Rockefeller to William McGill (President of Columbia University), March 6, 1974, folder "Columbia University 1971–1977," Box I.5, Brzezinski Papers, LoC; and Brzezinski to Gerard Smith, Henry Owen, and George Franklin, December 12, 1974, folder "Zbigniew Brzezinski Correspondence: 12 / 1 / 74–12.31.74," Box 33.7, Brzezinski Collection, Carter Library.

60. Brzezinski and Owen to David Rockefeller, July 26, 1972, folder "Correspondence File: 5 / 11 / 72–2 / 28 / 73," Box 33.1, Brzezinski Collection, Carter Library.

61. George Franklin to Members of the Planning Group, December 19, 1972, folder "Gerard Smith File—Chron File: 5 / 11 / 72–2 / 28 / 73," Box 33.1, Brzezinski Collection, Carter Library.

62. See folder "Correspondence File: 5 / 1 / 73–5 / 31 / 73," Box 33.1, Brzezinski Collection, Carter Library.

63. George Franklin to Gerard Smith and Brzezinski, May 9, 1973, folder "Gerard Smith File—Chron File: 5 / 1 / 73–5 / 31 / 73," Box 33.2, Brzezinski Collection, Carter Library.

64. James Reston, "Japan Demands Equality," *New York Times,* March 2, 1973, 35.

65. George Franklin, Summary of discussion, September 11, 1972, folder "Zbigniew Brzezinski Correspondence, 9 / 11 / 71–12 / 31 / 73," Box 33.7, Brzezinski Collection, Carter Library.

66. "14. Want Tril.Cssn. policy proposals fed to him and be kept abreast," in Memo of conversation, April 17,1973, folder "Kissinger, Henry, 1970–1973," Box I.16, Brzezinski Papers, LoC.

67. "New Atlantic Charter speech" to an Associated Press panel, April 23, 1973, www.cvce.eu /content/publication/2002/9/30/dec472e3-9dff-4c06-ad8d-d3fab7e13f9f/publishable_en.pdf.

68. "Another Step Backward," *Newsweek,* June 4, 1973, 21.

69. Brzezinski to Gerard Smith, May 1, 1973, folder "Gerard Smith File—Chron File: 5 / 1 / 73–5 / 31 / 73," Box 33.2, Brzezinski Collection, Carter Library.

70. Zbigniew Brzezinski, "Impressions from a Recent Trip to Europe," June 12, 1973, folder "Gerald Smith File—Chron File: 5 / 1 / 73–5 / 31 / 73," Box 33.2, Brzezinski Collection, Carter Library.

71. Brzezinski to Gerard Smith, Takeshi Watanabe, and Max Kohnstamm, July 10, 1983, folder "Correspondence File 1 / 1 / 73–5 / 31 / 73," Box 33.2, Brzezinski Collection, Carter Library.

72. "Statement of Purpose," *Trialogue,* no. 2 (1973):1–2.

73. Richard Halloran, "U.S.-Japanese-European Body Off to a Shaky Start in Tokyo," *New York Times,* October 24, 1973, 4.

74. Zbigniew Brzezinski, "Conversation with professor Hassner," October 2, 1973, folder "Correspondence File: 10 / 1 / 73–9 / 30 / 73 [*sic*]," Box 33.1, Brzezinski Collection, Carter Library.

75. Brzezinski to Kohnstamm, February 28, 1974, folder "Zbigniew Brzezinski Correspondence: 2 / 1 / 74–2 / 28 / 74," Box 33.7, Brzezinski Collection, Carter Library.

76. Brzezinski to Tatu, March 4, 1974, folder "Zbigniew Brzezinski Correspondence: 2 / 1 / 74–2 / 28 / 74," Box 33.7, Brzezinski Collection, Carter Library.

77. Brzezinski to Kohnstamm, Smith, and Watanabe, November 2, 1973, folder "Zbigniew Brzezinski Correspondence: 2 / 1 / 74–2 / 28 / 74," Box 33.7, Brzezinski Collection, Carter Library.

78. Kohnstamm to Smith, Watanabe, Brzezinski, Franklin, Yamamoto, Hager, Colonna, Owen, and Bowie, December 9, 1973, folder "Gerard Smith File—Chron File: 9/1/73–9/30/74," Box 33.2, Brzezinski Collection, Carter Library.

79. "Collective Crisis, Collective Interest," *New York Times,* June 18, 1974.

80. Regional Chairmen and the Director to Trilateral Commissioners, "First Annual Progress Report," September 6, 1974, "Gerard Smith File—Chron File: 9/1/73–10/31/74," Box 33.3, Brzezinski Collection, Carter Library.

81. Brzezinski to Kissinger, December 12, 1984, "Zbigniew Brzezinski Correspondence: 12/1/74–12/31/74," Box 33.7, Brzezinski Collection, Carter Library.

82. Brzezinski to Smith, Owen, Franklin, "Some Brutal Reflections on the State of the Commission," December 16, 1974, folder "Gerard Smith file—Atlantic Institute 12/16/74–10/31/74," Box 33.7, Brzezinski Collection, Carter Library.

83. Ibid.

84. Board of Trustees of the Trilateral Commission—Summary of Meeting February 8, 1975, New York City, folder "Gerard Smith File—Atlantic Institute: [12/1674–4/7/75]," Box 33.1, Brzezinski Collection, Carter Library.

85. George Franklin to Gerard Smith, June 3, 1977, folder "Gerard Smith File—Chron File: 1/1/76–6/3/77," Box 33.4, Brzezinski Collection, Carter Library.

86. Interview with Zbigniew Brzezinski, June 2, 2011.

87. Brzezinski to Huntington, April 5, 1973, folder "Huntington, Samuel P., 1969–1986," Box I.13, Brzezinski Papers, LoC.

88. Brzezinski to Huntington, folder "Zbigniew Brzezinski Correspondence: 4/1/74–6/30/74," Box 33.7, Brzezinski Collection, Carter Library.

89. "Democratic Goals Upheld by Panel," *New York Times,* June 1, 1975.

90. Michel Crozier, Samuel Huntington, and Joji Watanuki, *The Crisis of Democracy. Report on the Governability of Democracies to the Trilateral Commission* (New York: New York University Press, 1975), 60.

91. Brzezinski to Crozier, Huntington, and Watanuki, June 18, 1975, folder "Zbigniew Brzezinski Chronological File: 6/1/75–6/30/75," Box 33.6, Brzezinski Collection, Carter Library.

92. Brzezinski to François Duchêne and Tadashi Yamamoto, June 27, 1975, folder "Zbigniew Brzezinski Chronological File: 6/1/75–6/30/75," Box 33.6, Brzezinski Collection, Carter Library; and Brzezinski to Kohnstamm, Duchêne, Watanabe, Yamamoto, Smith, Franklin, Aug 25, 1975, folder "Zbigniew Brzezinski Chronological File: 7/1/75–9/30/75," Box 33.6, Brzezinski Collection, Carter Library.

93. Brzezinski to Irving Kristol, n.d., folder "Zbigniew Brzezinski Chronological File: 6/1/75–6/30/75," Box 33.6, Brzezinski Collection, Carter Library.

94. Brzezinski to Executive Committee, September 9, 1975, folder "Zbigniew Brzezinski Chronological File: 6/1/75–6/30/75," Box 33.6, Brzezinski Collection, Carter Library.

95. "Democratic Goals Upheld by Panel."

96. Brzezinski to Michael Blumenthal, December 11, 1975, folder "Gerard Smith File—Chron File: 6/1/75–12/31/75," Box 33.4, Brzezinski Collection, Carter Library.

97. Geoffrey Barraclough, "Wealth and Power: The Politics of Food and Oil," *New York Review of Books,* August 7, 1975.

98. Zbigniew Brzezinski to Georges Berthoin, Gerard Smith, Takeshi Watanabe, and François Duchêne, December 8, 1975, folder "Gerard Smith File—Chron File: 6 / 1 / 75–12 / 31 / 75," Box 33.4, Brzezinski Collection, Carter Library.

99. George Franklin to Gerard Smith, June 3, 1977, folder "Gerard Smith File—Chron File: 1 / 1 / 76–6 / 3 / 77," Box 33.4, Brzezinski Collection, Carter Library.

100. William Greider, "Trilateralists: Big Tycoons on Defensive," *Washington Post,* June 19, 1978, A1.

101. "*Memorandum.* A Proposal," November 1971, in Brzezinski to Joseph Reed, April 26, 1972, folder "Zbigniew Brzezinski Chronological File: 4 / 26 / 72–4 / 30 / 73," Box 33.5, Brzezinski Collection, Carter Library.

102. Irving Kristol, "The Trilateral Commission Factor," *Wall Street Journal,* April 16, 1980.

103. Stephen Rosenfeld, "The New Multinational Establishment," *Washington Post,* June 6, 1975, A28.

104. There is even a book on this subject: Gerry Argyris Andrianopoulos, *Kissinger and Brzezinski: The NSC and the Struggle for Control of US National Security Policy* (London: Macmillan, 1991).

105. For a caricature of this stereotype, see Howard Wiarda, *Harvard and the Weatherhead Center for International Affairs (WCFIA): Foreign Policy Research Center and Incubator of Presidential Advisors* (Lanham, MD: Lexington Books, 2010), 43: "Kissinger and Brzezinski came to Harvard at just about the same time. Kissinger was given tenure and promoted while Brzezinski was not. This is the origin of the famous rivalry between them, why Brzezinski had to go to Columbia instead of staying in Cambridge, and why ever since then and in whatever pursuit, Brzezinski has always felt he has to outdo and outshine Kissinger." But even Walter Isaacson, in his biography of Kissinger, characterizes Brzezinski as "Kissinger's old nemesis at Harvard" and mentions "a long-standing mutual coolness" (Walter Isaacson, *Kissinger: A Biography* [New York: Simon & Schuster, 1992], 699 and 715).

106. Interview with Henry Kissinger, January 27, 2012.

107. "Memo of conversation, 'Meeting with Secretary of State, luncheon given by Henry Kissinger, December 6, 1973, 1pm3:15 pm,'" folder "Kissinger, Henry 190–1973," Box I.16, Brzezinski Papers, LoC. The nine academics were Stanley Hoffmann, Marshall Shulman, David Landes, Nick Wahl, Richard Ullmann, Stephen Graubard, Robert Pfaltzgraff, Walter Laqueur, and Brzezinski.

108. Interview with Zbigniew Brzezinski, February 15, 2011.

109. Interview with Inge Hoffman, December 4, 2009; see also Isaacson, *Kissinger: A Biography,* 61.

110. Brzezinski to Albert Mavrinac, February 13 and 28, 1959, folder "Mavrinac, Albert A., 1959–1965," Box I.20, Brzezinski Papers, LoC.

111. Kissinger to Brzezinski, April 15, 1961 and July 24, 1961, folder "Kissinger, Henry 1956–1959," Box. I.16, Brzezinski Papers, LoC. For the articles, see Zbigniew Brzezinski, "The Challenge of Change in the Soviet Bloc," *Foreign Affairs* 39, no. 3 (April 1961):430–443, and Zbigniew Brzezinski and William Griffith, "Peaceful Engagement in Eastern Europe," *Foreign Affairs* 39, no. 4 (July 1961):642–654.

112. Kissinger to Brzezinski, October 24, 1963, and Brzezinski to Kissinger, October 30, 1963, folder "Kissinger, Henry 1957–1959," Box I.16, Brzezinski Papers, LoC.

113. Kissinger to Brzezinski, January 23, 1964, folder "Kissinger, Henry 1957–1959," Box I.16, Brzezinski Papers, LoC.

114. Brzezinski to Kissinger, January 30, 1964, folder "Kissinger, Henry 1957–1959," Box I.16, Brzezinski Papers, LoC. For the following years, see, for example, the welcome offered by Kissinger to Brzezinski's new recommendations for the International Seminar, or Brzezinski's comments on Kissinger's article on Bismarck: Kissinger to Brzezinski, November 21, 1967, and Brzezinski to Kissinger, July 17, 1968, folder "Kissinger, Henry 1957–1959," Box I.16, Brzezinski Papers, LoC.

115. Interviews with Pierre Hassner, March 7, 2009, and August 22, 2010.

116. See William Marvel (President, Education and World Affairs) to Brzezinski, March 24, 1969, and Kissinger to Brzezinski, April 3, 1969, folder "Kissinger, Henry 1957–1959," Box I.16, Brzezinski Papers, LoC.

117. "Talk + dinner with Henry Kissinger," July 14, 1969, folder "Kissinger, Henry 1957–1959," Box I.16, Brzezinski Papers, LoC.

118. Brzezinski to Kissinger, July 15, 1969, and Kissinger to Brzezinski, July 22, 1969, folder "Kissinger, Henry 1957–1959," Box I.16, Brzezinski Papers, LoC.

119. Brzezinski to Kissinger, Brzezinski to Elliott Richardson, Brzezinski to Bryce Harlow, and Brzezinski to Rosemary Woods, October 23, 1969, folder "Kissinger, Henry 1957–1959," Box I.16, Brzezinski Papers, LoC.

120. Kissinger to Brzezinski, November 17, 1969, folder "Kissinger, Henry 1957–1959," Box I.16, Brzezinski Papers, LoC.

121. Memo on conversation with Henry Kissinger, May 23, 1970, folder "Kissinger, Henry 1970–1973," Box I.16, Brzezinski Papers, LoC.

122. Zbigniew Brzezinski, "The Cambodian Crisis," May 25, 1970, folder "Kissinger, Henry 1970–1973," Box I.16, Brzezinski Papers, LoC.

123. Kissinger to Brzezinski, June 22, 1970, folder "Kissinger, Henry 1970–1973," Box I.16, Brzezinski Papers, LoC.

124. Zbigniew Brzezinski, "Cambodia Has Undermined Our Vital Credibility," *Washington Post,* May 24, 1970, 35.

125. See once again Kissinger's assurances to Brzezinski (added by hand) regarding RFE-RL: Kissinger to Brzezinski, November 14, 1970, folder "Kissinger, Henry 1970–1973," Box I.16, Brzezinski Papers, LoC.

126. Zbigniew Brzezinski, "Half Past Nixon," *Foreign Policy,* no. 3 (Summer 1971):3–21, and "The Balance of Power Delusion," *Foreign Policy.* no. 7 (Summer 1972):54–59.

127. Brzezinski to Kissinger, April 11, 1972; Kissinger to Brzezinski, May 19, 1972 (two letters); and Brzezinski to Kissinger, May 4, 1972, folder "Kissinger, Henry 1970–1973," Box I.16, Brzezinski Papers, LoC.

128. Kissinger to Brzezinski, October 19, 1973, folder "Kissinger, Henry 1970–1973," Box I.16, Brzezinski Papers, LoC.

129. Brzezinski to Kissinger, January 7, 1974, folder "Kissinger, Henry 1974–1975," n.d., Box I.16, Brzezinski Papers, LoC.

130. Zbigniew Brzezinski, "The Deceptive Structure of Peace," *Foreign Policy* 14 (Spring 1974):49.

131. Ibid.

132. Statement by Zbigniew Brzezinski before the Subcommittee on Multinational Corporations, Committee on Foreign Relations, US Senate, July 17, 1974, folder "Détente 1974," Box I.92, Brzezinski Papers, LoC.

133. Kissinger to Brzezinski, March 23, 1974, folder "Kissinger, Henry 1974–1975," n.d., Box I.16, Brzezinski Papers, LoC.

134. Brzezinski to Kissinger, April 16, 1974, folder "Kissinger, Henry 1974–1975," n.d., Box I.16, Brzezinski Papers, LoC.

135. Brzezinski to Kissinger, December 12, 1974, folder "Zbigniew Brzezinski Correspondence: 12/1/74–12/31/74," Box 33.7, Brzezinski Collection, Carter Library.

136. Brzezinski to Kissinger, February 20, 1975 and April 4, 1975, folder "Kissinger, Henry 1974–1975," n.d., Box I.16, Brzezinski Papers, LoC.

137. Kissinger to Brzezinski, April 21, 1975, folder "Kissinger, Henry 1974–1975," n.d., Box I.16, Brzezinski Papers, LoC.

138. Kissinger to Brzezinski, May 30, 1975, folder "Kissinger, Henry 1974–1975," n.d., Box I.16, Brzezinski Papers, LoC.

139. Brzezinski to Kissinger, September 18 1975, folder "Zbigniew Brzezinski chronological file: 7/1/75–9/30/75," Box 33.6, Brzezinski Collection, Carter Library.

140. Sewalyn Bialer, Zbigniew Brzezinski, Richard Löwenthal, and Donald Zagoria to Kissinger, October 22, 1975, folder "Kissinger, Henry 1974–1975," n.d., Box I.16, Brzezinski Papers, LoC.

141. Brzezinski to Carter, folder "Internal memoranda 1975," Box I.38, Brzezinski Papers, LoC.

142. George Franklin to Gerard Smith, June 7, 1977, folder "Gerard Smith file—Chron File: 1/1/76–6/3/77," Box 33.4, Brzezinski Collection, Carter Library.

143. "Zbigniew Brzezinski, along with William Odom, Leslie G. Denend and Madeleine K. Albright," interview by the Miller Center (University of Virginia) for the Carter Presidency Project, February 18, 1982, 58, http://web1.millercenter.org/poh/transcripts/ohp_1982_0218 _brzezinski.pdf (hereafter, Brzezinski et al., Miller Center interview).

144. Carter to Brzezinski, December 15, 1973, and Brzezinski to Carter, December 21, 1973, folder "Zbigniew Brzezinski chronological file: 11/1/73–4/1/74," Box 33.5, Brzezinski Collection, Carter Library.

145. Brzezinski to Carter, December 17, 1974, folder "Zbigniew Brzezinski correspondence: 12/1/74–12/31/74," Box 33.7, Brzezinski Collection, Carter Library.

146. Letter mentioned in Brzezinski, *Power and Principle,* 5.

147. Brzezinski to Carter, January 7, 1975, folder "Zbigniew Brzezinski chronological file: 1/1/75–1/31/75," Box 33.5, Brzezinski Collection, Carter Library.

148. George Franklin to Gerard Smith, June 3, 1977, folder "Gerard Smith file—Chron File: 1/1/76–6/3/77," Box 33.4, Brzezinski Collection, Carter Library.

149. Interview with Zbigniew Brzezinski, February 15, 2011, Washington, DC.

150. Brzezinski et al., Miller Center interview, 58; see also Brzezinski, *Power and Principle,* 6.

151. Brzezinski, *Power and Principle*, 6.

152. See Brzezinski's correspondence with these prominent figures in the archives, folder "Zbigniew Brzezinski chronological file: 6/1/75–6/30/75," Box 33.6, Brzezinski Collection, Carter Library.

153. Brzezinski to Carter, June 17, 1975, "Zbigniew Brzezinski chronological file: 6/1/75–6/30/75," Box 33.6, Brzezinski Collection, Carter Library.

154. See, for example, Brzezinski to Humphrey, September 26, 1974, folder "Humphrey, Hubert H. 1970–1977," Box I.13, Brzezinski Papers, LoC; Brzezinski to Humphrey, January 24, 1975, folder "Zbigniew Brzezinski chronological file: 1/1/75–1/31/75," Box 33.5, Brzezinski Collection, Carter Library; Brzezinski to Humphrey, June 24, 1975, and November 3, 1975, folder "Humphrey, Hubert H. 1970–1977," Box I.13, Brzezinski Papers, LoC.

155. Brzezinski to Dan Spiegel, January 20, 1976, and Humphrey to Brzezinski, January 28, 1976, "Humphrey, Hubert H. 1970–1977," Box I.13, Brzezinski Papers, LoC.

156. Brzezinski to Carter, July 31, 1975, folder "Zbigniew Brzezinski chronological file: 6/1/75–6/30/75," Box 33.6, Brzezinski Collection, Carter Library.

157. Brzezinski to Carter, December 11, 1975, folder "Zbigniew Brzezinski chronological file: 10/1/75–12/31/75," Box 33.6, Brzezinski Collection, Carter Library.

158. Brzezinski, *Power and Principle*, 7.

159. Brzezinski to Gardner, January 26, 1976, "Zbigniew Brzezinski chronological file: 1/1/76–4/30/76," Box 33.6, Brzezinski Collection, Carter Library.

160. Interview with Zbigniew Brzezinski, June 2, 2011, Washington, DC.

161. Jimmy Carter, interview at the Miller Center, University of Virginia, for the Carter Presidency Project, February 18, 1982, 5, http://web1.millercenter.org/poh/transcripts/ohp_1982_1129_carter.pdf.

162. Jimmy Carter, *Why Not the Best?* (Nashville, TN: Broadman Press, 1975), 127 and 140.

163. Cited in Betty Glad, *An Outsider in the White House: Jimmy Carter, His Advisors, and the Making of American Foreign Policy* (Ithaca, NY: Cornell University Press, 2009), 7.

164. Walter Isaacson and Evan Thomas, *The Wise Men: Six Friends and the World They Made* (New York: Simon & Schuster, 1986), 726.

165. Quoted in David Rockefeller, *Memoirs*, 418.

166. E.J. Dionne, *Why Americans Hate Politics* (New York: Simon & Schuster, 1992), 126.

167. James Reston, "When Jimmy Pretends," *New York Times*, March 19, 1976, 32; and see Clayton Fritchley, "And on Détente and Diplomacy," *Washington Post*, March 27, 1976, A15.

168. Brzezinski to Carter, March 23, 1976, folder "Zbigniew Brzezinski chronological file: 1/1/76–4/30/76," Box 33.6, Brzezinski Collection, Carter Library.

169. "Memorandum of Conversation, Washington, March 13, 1976, 10 A.M. Office of the Historian, Department of State," *Foreign Relations of the United States, 1969–1976*, vol. 37: *Energy Crisis*, 2012, 336, http:///static.history.state.gov/frus/frus1969-76v37/pdf/frus1969-76v37.pdf.

170. Stuart Eizenstat to Carter, June 1, 1976, folder "Foreign Policy, 4/76–6/76," Box 124.17, Jimmy Carter Pre-Presidential—1976 Presidential Campaign, Issues Office—Stuart Eizenstat (124), Jimmy Carter Library, Atlanta, GA (hereafter, Carter Library).

171. See https://history.state.gov/historicaldocuments/frus1977-80v01/d6.

172. Brzezinski, *Power and Principle,* 8, confirmed most notably by Richard Gardner in *Mission Italy: On the Front Lines of the Cold War* (Lanham, MD: Rowman & Littlefield, 2005), 19.

173. See James Wooten, "Carter Pledges an Open Foreign Policy," *New York Times,* June 24, 1976, 1; James Reston, "Hi-Ho, Silver!" *New York Times,* June 25, 1976, 22.

174. See Stephen Rosenfeld, "Secretary of State Scoop Jackson?" *Washington Post,* June 18, 1976. The complete text of the 1976 platform is available on the site of the American Presidency Project, http://www.presidency.ucsb.edu/platforms.php; see the chapter titled "International Relations."

175. See Brzezinski to Carter, June 3, 1976, folder "Zbigniew Brzezinski chronological file: 5/1/76–12/31/76," Box 33.6, Brzezinski Collection, Carter Library.

176. JBA [John Brian Atwood] to TFE [?], "Carter and the Soviet Threat in Europe," September 10, 1976; Atwood to Brzezinski, September 16, 1976; and Brzezinski to Eizenstat, September 21, 1976, folder "Speeches East-West Relations Correspondence and Memoranda 1976," Box I.40, Brzezinski Papers, LoC.

177. Brzezinski, *Power and Principle,* 9; Commission on Presidential Debates, October 6, 1976; "Presidential Campaign Debate, October 6, 1976, San Francisco," http://www.presidency.ucsb .edu/ws/inde.php?pid=6414#axzzWAvjWfs1.

178. "Presidential Campaign Debate, October 6, 1976, San Francisco."

179. Quoted in Isaacson, *Kissinger: A Biography,* 703.

180. Here is a statement listing the contributors to Carter's "Briefing Book" for the televised debate on October 6: "The books were produced by Richard Holbrooke, Robert Hunter, David Aaron and Nicholas McNeil, and reviewed in detail by Zbigniew Brzezinski. In addition, we consulted as appropriate, Les Aspin, George Ball, Fred Bergsten, Barry Bechman, Harold Brown, Jerome Cohen, Dick Gardner, Larry Hargrove, Milton Katz, Tony Lake, Paul Nitze, Mike Oksenberg, Henry Owen, Dean Rusk, Ted Sorensen, Ben Stefansky, Cyrus Vance, Paul Vance, Paul Warnke, and Jim Woolsey." Briefing Book, folder "Debate Briefing—Foreign Policy [1]," Box 34, Carter Family Papers, 1976 Campaign Files, Carter Library.

181. Brzezinski to Carter, March 1, 1976, folder "Internal memoranda 1975," Box I.38, Brzezinski Papers, LoC.

182. Brzezinski to Carter, March 29, 1976, folder "Internal memoranda 1975," Box I.38, Brzezinski Papers, LoC.

183. New Release, "Foreign Policy and Defense Task Force," April 22, 1976; John Kotch, "Additional members, Foreign Policy and Defense Task Force," May 11, 1976, folder "Carter Administration—Campaign—Miscellany 1974–1976, n.d.," Box I.39, Brzezinski Papers, LoC. The first nineteen were Fred Bergsten, Barry Blechman, Harold Brown, Zbigniew Brzezinski, Abram Chayes, Jerome Cohen, Richard Gardner, Richard Holbrooke, Milton Katz, Anthony Lake, Leonard Meeker, Ruth Morgenthau, Paul Nitze, William Overholt, Henry Owen, Theodore Sorensen, Cyrus Vance, Paul Warnke, and Charles Yost. The ten names added on May 11 were Goler Butcher, Larry Hargrove, Sam Huntington, James Moreley, Michael Oksenberg, Robert Pastor, William Roth, and Ben Stefansky, plus Bayless Manning and Don McHenry as "informal participants."

184. Brzezinski and Gardner to Carter, June 2, 1976, folder "Carter Administration—Campaign—Internal Memoranda June 1976," Box I.39, Brzezinski Papers, LoC.

185. Brzezinski to Carter, July 24, 1976, "Foreign Policy Briefing of July 29," folder "Carter Administration—Campaign—Internal Memoranda July 1976"; Jack Watson to "Contributors of Policy Planning Papers," August 24, 1976; and Bob Hunter to Stu Eizenstat, Dick Holbrooke, Al Stern, Tony Lake, October 29, 1976, folder "Carter Administration—Campaign—Internal Memoranda Aug.-Oct. 1976," Box I.39, Brzezinski Papers, LoC.

186. Holbrooke to Carter, May 5, 1976, folder "Foreign Policy, 4/76-6/76," Box 124.17, Jimmy Carter Pre-Presidential—1976 Presidential Campaign, Issues Office—Stuart Eizenstat (124), Carter Library.

187. Brzezinski to Carter, May 5, 1976, folder "Carter Administration—Campaign—Internal Memoranda Apr.–May 1976," Box I.38, Brzezinski Papers, LoC.

188. Brzezinski to Carter, May 13, 1976, folder "Zbigniew Brzezinski chronological file: 5/1/76-12/31/76," Box 33.6, Brzezinski Collection, Carter Library.

189. Brzezinski to Carter, June 21, 1976, "Carter Administration—Campaign—Internal Memoranda July 1976," Box I.39, Brzezinski Papers, LoC.

190. Brzezinski to Carter, April 15, 1976, folder "Zbigniew Brzezinski chronological file: 1/1/76-4/30/76," Box 33.6, Brzezinski Collection, Carter Library; Brzezinski to Peter Bourne and Jody Powell, April 23, 1976, folder "Carter Administration—Campaign—Internal Memoranda April-May 1976," Box I.38, Brzezinski Papers, LoC; Brzezinski to Peter Bourne and Jody Powell, June 21, 1976, folder "Carter Administration—Campaign—Internal Memoranda July 1976," Box I.39, Brzezinski Papers, LoC.

191. Briefing Book, folder "Debate Briefing—Foreign Policy [1]," Box 34, Carter Family Papers, 1976 Campaign Files, Carter Library.

192. Kissinger's advisor Helmut Sonnenfeldt, a high-ranking State Department official, discussed the situation in Europe with ambassadors in 1976 and the press interpreted what he said as justifying or at least accepting Russia's domination over Eastern Europe and discontinuing efforts to contest it.

193. Brzezinski to Carter, April 14, 1976, folder "Carter Administration—Campaign—Internal Memoranda April-May 1976," Box I.38, Brzezinski Papers, LoC.

194. Brzezinski to Al Stern, October 8, 1976, folder "Foreign Policy, 10/76," Box 124.18, Jimmy Carter Pre-Presidential—1976 Presidential Campaign, Issues Office—Stuart Eizenstat (124), Carter Library.

195. Leslie Gelb, "Presidential Challengers Diverge on Foreign Policy," *New York Times,* April 6, 1976, 21.

196. Brzezinski to Carter, April 6, 1976, folder "Carter Administration—Campaign—Internal Memoranda Apr.–May 1976," Box I.38, Brzezinski Papers, LoC.

197. Ibid.

198. Zbigniew Brzezinski, "A Plan for Peace in the Middle East," *New Leader* (January 7, 1974):7–9.

199. A summary of the Brookings report is reproduced in Brzezinski, *Power and Principle,* 84–85.

200. Brzezinski to Carter, January 6, 1976, folder "Carter Administration—Campaign—Internal Memoranda January–February 1976," and May 18, 1976, "Carter Administration—Campaign—Internal Memoranda Apr.–May 1976," Box I.38, Brzezinski Papers, LoC.

201. Brzezinski to Carter, May 17, 1976, "Carter Administration—Campaign—Internal Memoranda Apr.–May 1976," Box I.38, Brzezinski Papers, LoC.

202. Stuart Eizenstat to Carter, June 1, 1976, folder "Foreign Policy, 4/76–6/76," Box 124.17, Jimmy Carter Pre-Presidential—1976 Presidential Campaign, Issues Office—Stuart Eizenstat (124), Carter Library.

203. See Professor Brzezinski program, folder "Speeches and events 1976 (3 of 4)," Box I.67, Brzezinski Papers, LoC.

204. Brzezinski, *Power and Principle*, 84.

205. Ibid. Brzezinski indicated that he learned about the raid the next morning, but he left Israel the morning of Saturday, July 3, and the raid took place on July 4.

206. See, for example, "A Carter Foreign Adviser: Ball Would Impose Mideast Plan," *Sun*, June 18, 1976, A4.

207. See Richard Reeves, "Is Jimmy Carter Good for the Jews?" *New York Magazine*, May 24, 1976; James Reston, "Jimmy Carter, Evangelism, and Jews," *New York Times*, June 6, 1976, 165; Milton Himmelfarb, "Carter and the Jews," *Commentary*, August 1, 1976, https://www.commentarymagazine.com/articles/carter-and-the-jews/.

208. Leslie Gelb, "Carter's Foreign Views Fit Liberal Democratic Mold," *New York Times*, July 7, 1976, 1.

209. On this point, see Justin Vaïsse, *Neoconservatism: The Biography of a Movement* (Cambridge, MA: Harvard University Press, 2010).

210. Max Kampelman to Brzezinski, April 16, 1976, folder "Kampelman, Max M. 1972–1977," Box I.15, Brzezinski Papers, LoC.

211. Eugene Rostow to Brzezinski, April 30, 1976, folder "Foreign Policy Specialists 'R' 1976," Box I.38, Brzezinski Papers, LoC.

212. On Nitze, see Paul H. Nitze, *From Hiroshima to Glasnost: At the Center of Decision—A Memoir* (New York: Grove Weidenfeld, 1989); David Callahan, *Dangerous Capabilities—Paul Nitze and the Cold War* (New York: HarperCollins, 1990); Strobe Talbott, *The Master of the Game: Paul Nitze and the Nuclear Peace* (New York: Knopf, 1988).

213. Talbott, *Master of the Game*, 148.

214. Brzezinski to Nitze, folder "Carter Administration—Campaign—Internal Memoranda Mar. 1976," Box I.38, Brzezinski Papers, LoC.

215. Nitze to Brzezinski, March 26, 1976, folder "Carter Administration—Campaign—Internal Memoranda Mar. 1976," Box I.38, Brzezinski Papers, LoC.

216. Brzezinski to Owen and Stark, March 31, 1976, folder "Carter Administration—Campaign—Internal Memoranda Mar. 1976," Box I.38, Brzezinski Papers, LoC.

217. Ibid.

218. Brzezinski to Stark, March 31, 1976, folder "Foreign Policy, Defense—Correspondence/Recommendations/Analysis [1]," Box 34, Carter Family Papers, 1976 Campaign Files, Carter Library.

219. Averell Harriman and Paul Warnke to Carter, May 11, 1976, and Henry Owen to Carter, May 20, 1976, folder "Foreign Policy, Defense—Correspondence/Recommendations/Analysis [1]," Box 34, Carter Family Papers, 1976 Campaign Files, Carter Library.

220. Gelb, "Carter's Foreign Views," 1.

221. Cited in Talbott, *Master of the Game,* 149. The other participants in the meeting were Cyrus Vance, Harold Brown, Paul Warnke, James Woolsey, Walter Slocombe, Lynn Davis, and Barry Blechman.

222. Paul Warnke to Carter, July 29, 1976; Cyrus Vance to Carter, July 31, 1976; Harold Brown to Carter, August 25, 1976, folder "Foreign Policy, Defense—Correspondence/Recommendations/Analysis [1]," Box 34, Carter Family Papers, 1976 Campaign Files, Carter Library.

223. Dick Holbrooke and Stu Eizenstat to Governor Carter, September 1, 1976, folder "Foreign Policy, Defense—Correspondence/Recommendations/Analysis [2]," Box 37, Carter Family Papers, 1976 Campaign Files, Carter Library.

224. Brzezinski to Holbrooke and Anderson, September 13, 1976, folder "Speeches East-West Drafts Comments 1976," Box I.40, Brzezinski Papers, LoC.

225. Gelb, "Carter's Foreign Views," 69.

226. Lipset later acknowledged that the magazine *Foreign Policy* was not as monolithic as he had made it out to be here.

227. Seymour Martin Lipset and Stu Eizenstat to Governor Carter, September 16, 1976, folder "Foreign Policy, Defense—Correspondence/Recommendations/Analysis [2]," Box 37, Carter Family Papers, 1976 Campaign Files, Carter Library.

228. Interview with Zbigniew Brzezinski, June 17, 2001.

5. Portrait of an Academic in Politics

1. Henry Kissinger, *White House Years* (Boston, MA: Little, Brown, 1979), 54.

2. Zbigniew Brzezinski, *Power and Principle: Memoirs of the National Security Adviser, 1977–1981* (New York: Farrar, Straus & Giroux, 1983), 514.

3. Cited by Bruce Kublick, *Blind Oracles: Intellectuals and War from Kennan to Kissinger* (Princeton, NJ: Princeton University Press, 2007), 5.

4. Michael Desch, "Professor Smith Goes to Washington," *Notre-Dame Magazine,* Spring 2009, http://magazine.nd.edu/news/11174-professor-smith-goes-to-washington/.

5. Richard Betts, "Should Strategic Studies Survive?" *World Politics* 50, no. 1 (1997):14, cited by Marc Trachtenberg, in "Social Scientists and National Security Policymaking. Text prepared for a mini-conference sponsored by the Notre Dame International Security Program," Notre-Dame, April 23, 2010, http://n.d.edu/-ndisp/images/Trachtenberg_N.=D.10.pdf.

6. Walt Rostow, *The Stages of Economic Growth: A Non-Communist Manifesto* (Cambridge, UK: Cambridge University Press, 1990); Samuel Huntington, *Political Order in Changing Societies* (New Haven, CT: Yale University Press, 1968).

7. Thomas Schelling, *The Strategy of Conflict* (Cambridge, MA: Harvard University Press, 1960), and *Arms and Influence* (New Haven, CT: Yale University Press, 1966).

8. Fred Kaplan, *The Wizards of Armageddon* (New York: Simon & Schuster, 1983), 332–334, and "All Pain, No Gain: Nobel Laureate Thomas Schelling's Little-Known Role in the Vietnam War," Slate.com, October 11, 2005, http://www.slate.com/id/2127862/.

9. Kaplan, "All Pain, No Gain."

10. Kuklick, *Blind Oracles,* 143.

11. Ibid., 144.

12. Ibid., 149.

13. See Albert Wohlstatter in Robert Zarate and Henry Sokolski, eds., *Nuclear Heuristics: Selected Writings of Albert and Roberta Wohlstatter,* January 9, 245–246, http://www.strategicstudiesinstitute.army.mil/pdffiles/PUB893.pdf. I thank Marc Trachtenberg for directing me to this source.

14. Paul Nitze, *Tensions between Opposites: Reflections on the Practice and Theory of Politics* (New York: Scribner, 1993), 15, cited in Stephen Walt, "The Relationship between Theory and Policy in International Relations," *Annual Review of Political Science* 8 (2005):24.

15. Kuklick, *Blind Oracles,* 15.

16. Trachtenberg, "Social Scientists and National Security Policymaking," 2.

17. Kuklick, *Blind Oracles,* 226.

18. See Henry Kissinger, *A World Restored: Metternich, Castlereagh and the Problems of Peace, 1818–1822* (Boston: Houghton Mifflin, 1957).

19. Mario Del Pero, *The Eccentric Realist: Henry Kissinger and the Shaping of American Foreign Policy* (Ithaca, NY: Cornell University Press, 2010), see especially 66ff., 78ff., and 100ff.

20. Marc Trachtenberg, "The Structure of Great Power Politics, 1963–1975," 27, http://www.polisci.ucla.edu/faculty/trachtenberg/cv/chcw(long).doc.

21. On Bismarck, see Henry Kissinger, "The White Revolutionary: Reflections on Bismarck," *Daedalus* 97, no. 3 (Summer 1968):888–924.

22. Zbigniew Brzezinski and Carl Friedrich, *Totalitarian Dictatorship and Autocracy* (Cambridge, MA: Harvard University Press, 1956); Zbigniew Brzezinski, *Ideology and Power in Soviet Politics* (New York: Praeger, 1962); Zbigniew Brzezinski, "The Soviet Political System: Transformation or Degeneration?" *Problems of Communism* 15 (January–February 1966): 1–15, and "Reflections on the Soviet System," *Problems of Communism* 17 (May–June 1968):44–48.

23. See Stephen S. Szabo, "The Professor," in *Zbig: The Strategy and Statecraft of Zbigniew Brzezinski,* ed. Charles Gati (Baltimore: Johns Hopkins University Press, 2013), 208.

24. Brzezinski and Friedrich, *Totalitarian Democracy;* Hannah Arendt, *The Origins of Totalitarianism* (New York: Harcourt, Brace, 1951).

25. Zbigniew Brzezinski, "Communist Ideology and Power: From Unity to Diversity," *Journal of Politics* 19, no. 4 (November 1957):589.

26. Zbigniew Brzezinski, "Communist Disunity and the West," *New Republic* 145, no. 25 (December 18, 1961):14–17.

27. Zbigniew Brzezinski, "For Lenin's Centenary: Soviet Past and Future," *Encounter* 34, no. 3 (March 1970):3–16 (the scenarios are spelled out on 12–13); repeated in *Between Two Ages: America's Role in the Technetronic Era* (New York: Viking Press, 1970), 164–172.

28. Brzezinski, "For Lenin's Centenary," 16.

29. On this topic, see Ernest May and Richard Neustadt, *Thinking in Time: The Uses of History for Decision-Makers* (New York: Free Press, 1986).

30. "Meeting with President Nguyen Van Thieu," September 4, 1969, folder "National Committee for a Political Settlement in Vietnam 1967–1969," Box I.94, Zbigniew Brzezinski Papers,

Manuscript Division, Library of Congress, Washington, DC (hereafter, Brzezinski Papers, LoC).

31. Zbigniew Brzezinski, "America in the Technetronic Age," *Encounter* 30, no. 1 (January 1968):16–26.

32. Zbigniew Brzezinski, "Deviation Control: The Dynamics of Doctrinal Conflict," *American Political Science Review* 56, no. 1 (March 1961):5–22.

33. *Between Two Ages,* 108; more generally, see 94–110. This section also appeared as "Histrionics as History in Transition," *Survey* 74–75 (Winter–Spring 1970):225–236.

34. Brzezinski to Mansfield, December 9, 1963, folder "American Political Science Review 1952–1970," Box I.1, Brzezinski Papers, LoC; cf. Zbigniew Brzezinski, "Russia and Europe," *Foreign Affairs* 42, no. 3 (April 1964):428–444.

35. Interview with Zbigniew Brzezinski, June 22, 2010.

36. Memo "Re: Conversations with John Campbell and Miriam Camps about Professor Brzezinski and Mr. Owen as possible heads of staff of proposed commission," n.d., folder "Zbigniew Brzezinski chronological file: 4/26/72–4/30/73, Box 33.5, Donated Historical Material, Zbigniew Brzezinski Collection (33), Jimmy Carter Library, Atlanta, GA (hereafter, Brzezinski Collection, Carter Library).

37. Quoted in Robert Scheer, "Brzezinski: Profound or Banal?" *Los Angeles Times,* January 23, 1977, 23.

38. Ibid., 25.

39. Brzezinski used the same expression in a chapter of the unpublished manuscript "America in a New World," 103, and again when the chapter was published in article form as "America in a Hostile World," *Foreign Policy,* no. 23 (Summer 1976):94: "The basic message of the American experience was the primacy of liberty. But inherent in that was also the centrality of pluralism."

40. William Buckley, "And Who Is Brzezinski?" *National Review,* n.d. (early 1977?); cf. *Las Cruces Sun,* January 15, 1977, 4.

41. Brzezinski, *Between Two Ages,* 308–309.

42. Zbigniew Brzezinski, "Japan's Global Engagement," *Foreign Affairs* 50, no. 2 (January 1972): 270–282.

43. Zbigniew Brzezinski, "The Middle East: Who Won?" *Washington Post,* November 21, 1973, A18.

44. *Between Two Ages,* 302.

45. These points are highlighted in a good thesis on Brzezinski's approach to the world: Nisha Jain, "The Evolution of Zbigniew Brzezinski's Concept of International Politics and American Foreign Policy" (Ph.D. diss., University of Kansas, 1981); see especially 5.

46. MA thesis, "Russo-Soviet Nationalism," 142, Box I.84, Brzezinski Papers, LoC.

47. Del Pero, *Eccentric Realist,* 59.

48. Ibid.

49. See, for example, Henry Kissinger, *Diplomacy* (New York: Simon & Schuster, 1994).

50. Zbigniew Brzezinski, *The Soviet Bloc Unity and Conflict,* rev. ed., Russian Research Studies Center no. 37 (Cambridge, MA: Harvard University Press, 1967). See also Robert Legvold, capsule reviews on Eastern Europe and former Soviet Republics, *Foreign Affairs* 76, no. 5

(September–October 1997):231. (A section of the journal was devoted to "Significant Books of the Last 75 Years," a listing of the five best books published about each of various regions of the world since 1922, the year *Foreign Affairs* was founded.)

51. See Simon Serfaty, "Brzezinski: Play It Again, Zbig," *Foreign Policy,* no. 32 (Fall 1978): "Rereading Brzezinski with the invaluable assistance of historical hindsight (not only what happened where, but also what happened to whom) reveals his enduring penchant for fashionable issues and concepts that are adopted or discarded in the light of changing circumstances" (6).

52. Zbigniew Brzezinski, *The Grand Chessboard: American Primacy and Its Geostrategic Imperatives* (New York: Basic Books, 1997), 31.

53. Zbigniew Brzezinski, "America in a Hostile World," *Foreign Policy,* no. 23 (Summer 1976):83.

54. Ibid., 75.

55. Noted by Carter in his "diary"; see Jimmy Carter, *Keeping Faith: Memoirs of a President* (New York: Bantam Books, 1982), 223 (more generally, see 223–229).

56. William B. Quandt, *Camp David: Peacemaking and Politics* (Washington, DC: Brookings Institution Press, 1986), 35.

57. Zbigniew Brzezinski, "Tomorrow's Agenda," *Foreign Affairs* 44, no. 4 (July 1966):662–670.

58. See Niall Ferguson, Erez Manela, Charles Maier, and Daniel Sargent, *The Shock of the Global: The 1970s in Perspective* (Cambridge, MA: Harvard University Press, 2010).

59. See Strobe Talbott, *The Master of the Game: Paul Nitze and the Nuclear Peace* (New York: Knopf, 1988), 244. Talbott offers several examples of Nitze's "credulity" vis-à-vis scientists (Teller and the H-bomb in 1949, the CIA and possible Soviet superiority in 1950, and so on), to which can be added Nitze's belief in the elucubrations of Thomas K. "TK" Jones about what civil defense could do in the face of a nuclear attack.

60. For example, he had lengthy discussions with Jeremy Stone, an opponent of anti-ballistic missiles. See Brzezinski to David Ingles (SANE), July 5, 1968, folder " 'I' Miscellaneous 1956–1976, n.d.," Box I.14, Brzezinski Papers, LoC.

61. Brzezinski to D. Brennan, May 19, 1969, folder "Brennan, Donald G. 1969–1972," Box I.2. Brzezinski Papers, LoC.

62. Dean Acheson, Paul Nitze, and Albert Wohlstetter to Brzezinski, May 26, 1969, and Brzezinski to Acheson, June 3, 1969, folder "Ab-Ad" Miscellaneous 1952, 1960–1976, Box I.1, Brzezinski Papers, LoC.

63. Brzezinski to Cresson Kearny, June 16, 1971, folder "Kearny, Cresson H. 1971–1977," Box I.16, Brzezinski Papers, LoC.

64. Interview with Pierre Hassner, March 7, 2009, and August 22, 2010.

65. Zbigniew Brzezinski, "Purpose and Planning in Foreign Policy," *Public Interest* 14 (Winter 1969):59.

66. Brzezinski to Hassner, May 7, 1974, folder "Zbigniew Brzezinski Correspondence: 4/1/74–6/30/74," Box 33.7, Brzezinski Collection, Carter Library.

67. Zbigniew Brzezinski, *The Fragile Blossom: Crisis and Change in Japan* (New York: Harper & Row, 1972), 116.

68. Zbigniew Brzezinski, "Who Will Succeed Brezhnev?" *New Leader* (March 19, 1973):6–9.

69. Zbigniew Brzezinski, " 'Neutral' Vietnam a Chinese Backyard," *Washington Post,* March 1, 1964, E1.

70. Zbigniew Brzezinski, *Political Power: USA / USSR* (New York: Viking Press, 1964).

71. Brzezinski, "For Lenin's Centenary," 15.

72. See, for example, Brzezinski, *Soviet Bloc,* 404.

73. Serfaty, "Brzezinski: Play It Again, Zbig," 21.

74. Scheer, "Brzezinski: Profound or Banal?"

75. Samuel Jameson, "Viet Peace Is Unlikely, Expert Says," *Chicago Tribune,* November 9, 1970.

76. Brzezinski, "America in the Technetronic Age," 16–26.

77. Brzezinski to Humphrey, November 3, 1971, folder "Humphrey, Hubert H. 1970–1977," Box I.13, Brzezinski Papers, LoC.

78. Brzezinski, "Tomorrow's Agenda."

79. Jameson, "Viet Peace Is Unlikely"; and Brzezinski, *Between Two Ages,* 52.

80. Zbigniew Brzezinski, ed., *Africa and the Communist World,* Hoover Institution on War, Revolution, and Peace (Stanford, CA: Stanford University Press, 1963).

81. Brzezinski, *Fragile Blossom.*

82. Zbigniew Brzezinski, "Why the Alliance Is Fading?" *Interplay* 1, no. 10 (May 1968):18–19.

83. Zbigniew Brzezinski, "We Need a Latin Divorce," *Washington Post,* September 6, 1970, 36.

84. This is particularly clear in *Between Two Ages,* xvi.

85. Interview with Zbigniew Brzezinski, June 17, 2011.

86. Zbigniew Brzezinski, *The Permanent Purge: Politics in Soviet Totalitarianism,* Russian Research Center Studies 20 (Cambridge, MA: Harvard University Press, 1956); Zbigniew Brzezinski and Carl Friedrich, *Totalitarian Dictatorship and Autocracy,* second edition revised by Carl Friedrich (Cambridge, MA: Harvard University Press, 1965).

87. Zbigniew Brzezinski, "Totalitarianism and Rationality," *American Political Science Review* 50, no. 3 (September 1956):751–763.

88. Zbigniew Brzezinski, "The Nature of the Soviet System," *Slavic Review* 20, no. 3 (October 1961):351–368.

89. Brzezinski, *Soviet Bloc.*

90. Zbigniew Brzezinski, "Patterns and Limits of the Sino-Soviet Dispute," *Problems of Communism* 9, no. 5 (September–October 1960):7.

91. Zbigniew Brzezinski, "Political Development in the Sino-Soviet Bloc," *Annals of the American Academy of Political and Social Science* 336 (July 1961):40–52.

92. Zbigniew Brzezinski, "The Challenge of Change in the Soviet Bloc," *Foreign Affairs* 39, no. 3 (April 1961):30–43.

93. Zbigniew Brzezinski, "Sino-Soviet Relations," *New York Times,* July 16, 1961, E8.

94. Brzezinski, "Communist Disunity."

95. See in particular Zbigniew Brzezinski, "Threat and Opportunity in the Communist Schism," *Foreign Affairs* 41, no. 3 (April 1963):513–525.

96. Zbigniew Brzezinski, " 'Neutral' Vietnam a Chinese Backyard," *Washington Post,* March 1, 1964, E1.

97. On this topic, see Mark Kramer, "Anticipating the Grand Failure," in Gati, ed., *Zbig,* 42–59.

98. Brzezinski and Huntington, *Political Power.*

99. Brzezinski, "Soviet Political System," and "Reflections on the Soviet System."

100. Brzezinski, *Between Two Ages,* 157.

101. Zbigniew Brzezinski, "The Soviet Union: World Power of a New Type," *Proceedings of the Academy of Political Science* 35, no. 3 (1984):151, presented at the International Institute of Strategic Studies, Silver Jubilee Annual Conference, Ottowa, Canada, September 8–11, 1983.

102. Zbigniew Brzezinski, *Game Plan: A Geostrategic Framework for the Conduct of the U.S.-Soviet Contest* (Boston: Atlantic Monthly Press, 1986), xiii.

103. Zbigniew Brzezinski, "We Need More Muscle in the Gulf, Less in NATO," *Washington Post,* June 7, 1987.

104. "Soviet Union: World Power of a New Type, " 155.

105. Brzezinski, *Game Plan,* 130.

106. See, for example, ibid., 127–128.

107. Zbigniew Brzezinski, "Overview of East-West Relations—1985," *Washington Quarterly* 8, no. 4 (Fall 1985):31–37.

108. "For the Record: From Remarks by Former National Security Adviser Zbigniew Brzezinski on 'This Week with David Brinkley' Sunday," *Washington Post,* December 30, 1986, A20.

109. Zbigniew Brzezinski, *The Grand Failure: The Birth and Death of Communism in the Twentieth Century* (New York: Scribner, 1989).

110. Zbigniew Brzezinski, *A Year in the Life of Glasnost: The Hugh Seton-Watson Memorial Lecture and Other Essays* (London: Center for Policy Studies, 1988), 6–18.

111. Brzezinski, *Grand Failure,* 1.

112. Kramer, "Anticipating the Grand Failure," 54.

113. Ibid., 55–56.

114. See especially Zbigniew Brzezinski, "Will the Soviet Empire Self-Destruct? Four Scenarios for Failure," *New York Times,* February 26, 1989; "A Proposition the Soviets Shouldn't Refuse," *New York Times,* March 13, 1989, A19; "This Is the Big Moment in Eastern Europe—and It Is Dangerous," *Washington Post,* August 20, 1989, B7.

115. Brzezinski, *Power and Principle,* 20.

116. Interview with Zbigniew Brzezinski, June 22, 2010.

117. Ibid.

118. Ibid.

119. Interview with Zbigniew Brzezinski, June 17, 2011.

120. "Diplomacy: The Thinker," *Newsweek* (November 14, 1966):44.

121. Cited in Scheer, "Brzezinski: Profound or Banal?" 24–25.

122. In *Between Two Ages,* 208, he added a comment in a footnote: "One related and intriguing aspect of this development is the increasing entrance into the country's political elite of

previously nonparticipating ethnic and racial groups. Jews, Negroes, Italians, and, to a lesser extent, Poles and Greeks, have been making an appearance in the national government on levels and on a scale previously rarely attained by non-'WASPS.' While precise statistics are not available, these new 'elites'—whose Americanism is sometimes as intense as it is new—may have had something to do with the reappearance of [an] activist, nationalist, dynamic orientation."

123. Interview with Zbigniew Brzezinski, June 22, 2010.

124. Quoted by Nabil Mikhail in "Zbigniew Brzezinski: The Scholar and the Statesman. A Study of the Thoughts and Politics of the National Security Adviser and His Staff in the Carter Administration" (Ph.D. diss., University of Virginia, 1996), 64.

125. Quoted by Patrick Vaughan, "Zbigniew Brzezinski and Afghanistan," in *The Policy Makers: Shaping American Foreign Policy from 1947 to the Present,* ed. Anna Kasten Nelson (Lanham, MD: Rowman & Littlefield, 2009), 114.

126. Interview with Zbigniew Brzezinski, June 22, 2010.

127. Ibid.

128. Patrick Vaughan, "Zbigniew Brzezinski: The Political and Academic Life of a Cold War Visionary" (Ph.D. diss., West Virginia University, 2003), 47.

129. Brzezinski, *Power and Principle,* 321 and 98. See also Bernard Gwertzman, "Jewish Leader Says Mideast Policy Makes a 'Question Mark' of Carter," *New York Times,* March 10, 1978, A1.

130. Anatoly Dobrynin, *In Confidence: Moscow's Ambassador to America's Six Cold War Presidents (1962–1986)* (New York: New York Times Books, 1995), 463.

131. Elizabeth Drew, "Brzezinski," *New Yorker* (May 1, 1978):90.

132. "Nation: A Top Job for 'Vitamin Z,'" *Time Magazine* 108, no. 26 (December 27, 1976):15.

133. Quandt, *Camp David,* 35.

134. Brzezinski, *Power and Principle,* 354.

135. Brzezinski to J. Kyle Goddard, US Junior Chamber of Commerce, November 21, 1963, folder "Biographical Information 1956–1965," Box I.91, Brzezinski Papers, LoC.

136. Interviews with Pierre Hassner, March 7, 2009 and August 22, 2010, Paris, France.

137. Interviews with Stanley Hoffmann, December 1 and 4, 2009.

138. Jimmy Carter, interview at the Miller Center, University of Virginia, for the Carter Presidency Project, February 18, 1982, 5, http://web1.millercenter.org/poh/transcripts/ohp _1982_1129_carter.pdf.

139. Brzezinski, *Power and Principle,* 42.

140. George Ball, *The Past Has Another Pattern: Memoirs* (New York: W. W. Norton, 1982), 462.

141. Hamilton Jordan, *Crisis: The Last Year of the Carter Presidency* (New York: Putnam, 1982), 461.

142. Robert Gates, *From the Shadows: The Ultimate Insider's Story of Five Presidents and How They Won the Cold War* (New York: Simon & Schuster, 1997), 114.

143. Gates, *From the Shadows,* 70.

144. W. Averell Harriman to Brzezinski, July 2, 1974, folder "Harriman, W. Averell 1964, 1974–1976," Box I.12, Brzezinski Papers, LoC.

145. Interview with Leslie Gelb, September 10, 2010.

146. Quoted in Drew, "Brzezinski," 108.

147. Harold Brown, quoted by David Rothkopf in *Running the World: The Inside Story of the National Security Council and the Architects of American Power* (New York: Public Affairs, 2004), 188.

148. Correspondence, folder "Ogueri, Eze 1970–1973," Box I.23, Brzezinski Papers, LoC.

149. Gates, *From the Shadows,* 70.

150. Ibid., 71.

151. Jim Hoagland, "Brzezinski: An Eagerness to Show 'Resolve,'" *Washington Post,* March 14, 1978, A1.

152. Walter Isaacson, *Kissinger: A Biography* (New York: Simon & Schuster, 1992), 80.

153. See "Soviet Perception of US Foreign Policy and US Leaders," n.d. (after June 1978), declassified document NLC 33-6-15-11-1, 13, Brzezinski Collection, Carter Library.

154. The worst episode was the unfounded accusation by Sally Quinn that he had unzipped his fly in the presence of a female journalist from the *Washington Post;* see Sally Quinn, "The Politics of the Power Grab: Nine Rules of Notoriety; Brzezinski: Seeking the Limelight in the Shadow of State," *Washington Post,* December 19, 1979, C1; and Sally Quinn, "Courting the White House and Sniping at State: Gentle Strokes and Power Plays by Brzezinski," *Washington Post,* December 20, 1979, C1. For a review and analysis of the incident, see "Press: Brzezinski's Zipper Was Up," *Time Magazine* 114, no. 27 (December 31, 1979):15.

155. Interview with Charles Gati, April 26, 2011.

156. See Brzezinski to Irving Howe, February 21, 1972, folder "'Hom-How' Miscellaneous," Box I.14, Brzezinski Papers, LoC. See also Brzezinski's commentary on an article by Lewis Coser for *Dissent* in 1965 (in the same folder).

157. Interview with Zbigniew Brzezinski, June 22, 2010.

158. Brzezinski to Hoffmann, December 5, 1963, folder "Hoffmann, Stanley 1960–1970," Box I.12, Brzezinski Papers, LoC.

159. Interview with Zbigniew Brzezinski, June 22, 2010; Brzezinski, *Power and Principle,* 6.

160. Interview with Pierre Hassner, March 7, 2009, and August 22, 2010.

161. Interview with Zbigniew Brzezinski, June 22, 2010.

162. Scheer, "Brzezinski: Activist Seeker of World Order," *Los Angeles Times,* January 24, 1977, B3.

163. Interview with Zbigniew Brzezinski, June 22, 2010.

164. Zbigniew Brzezinski, "Russo-Soviet Nationalism," MA thesis, 140, Box I.84, Brzezinski Papers, LoC.

165. Anecdote related by Brzezinski, e-mail correspondence, September 5, 2011.

166. See Pauline Peretz, *Washington-Moscou-Jérusalem: Le combat pour les Juifs soviétiques* (Paris: Armand Colin, 2006).

167. See Brzezinski to Decter, December 30, 1963, folder "Speeches and events 1963 (2 of 4)," and Decter to Brzezinski, September 13, 1965, folder "Decter, Moshe, 1963–1977)," Box I.56, Brzezinki Papers, LoC.

168. Brzezinski to Decter, December 20, 1968, folder "Decter, Moshe, 1963–1967," Box I.6, Brzezinski Papers, LoC.

169. Theodore Abel, Zbigniew Brzezinski, Jan Fryling, Feliks Gross, Ludwik Krzyzanowski, Jerzy Krzywicki, and Damian S. Wandycz, "Events in Poland" (letter to the editor by the members of the board of directors of the Polish Institute of Arts and Sciences in America, dated April 15, 1968), *New York Times,* April 19, 1968.

170. Interview with Zbigniew Brzezinski, June 22, 2010.

171. Daniel Patrick Moynihan, "The Negro Family: The Case for National Action," Washington, DC: Office of Policy Planning and Research, United States Department of Labor, 1965, http://www.blackpast.org/q=primary/moynihan-report-1965.

172. Brzezinski to Pat Moynihan, November 18, 1965, folder "Moynihan, Daniel P. 1965, 1973–1975," Box I.21, Brzezinski Papers, LoC.

173. Brzezinski to Coudert and Rathaus, January 23, 1967, folder "Alfred Jurzykowski Foundation, 1966–1972," Box I.1, Brzezinski Papers, LoC.

174. Zbigniew Brzezinski, "Reconciliation Day," *Washington Post,* April 17, 1968, A1, and "Probing Panther Attack," *New York Times,* December 21, 1969, E15.

175. Brzezinski, Interdepartmental Memorandum, "Possible Lecture Series in Negro Colleges in the South," July 20, 1964, folder "Columbia University 1961–1966," Box I.5, Brzezinski Papers, LoC.

176. Dallin to Brzezinski, August 25, 1964 and January 12, 1965, folder "Lecture Series for Negro Colleges 1964–1965, n.d.," Box I.93, Brzezinski Papers, LoC.

177. Dallin to Brzezinski, January 12, 1965, folder "Lecture Series for Negro Colleges 1964–1965, n.d.," Box I.93, Brzezinski Papers, LoC.

178. George W. Jones to Brzezinski, December 10, 1964, folder "Lecture Series for Negro Colleges 1964–1965, n.d.," Box I.93, Brzezinski Papers, LoC.

179. Henry Roberts to Brzezinski, March 8, 1965; Fritz Stern to Brzezinski, March 23, 1965, folder "Lecture Series for Negro Colleges 1964–1965, n.d.," Box I.93, Brzezinski Papers, LoC.

180. Brzezinski to President Wright (Fisk University), March 24, 1985, folder "Lecture Series for Negro Colleges 1964–1965, n.d.," Box I.93, Brzezinski Papers, LoC.

181. Brzezinski to George Jones, March 26, 1965, folder "Lecture Series for Negro Colleges 1964–1965, n.d.," Box I.93, Brzezinski Papers, LoC.

182. S. J. Wright (Fisk University) to Brzezinski, April 9, 1965; Brzezinski to Wright, April 15, 1965; Christine Dodson to L. DeVinney, Rockefeller Foundation, May 3, 1965, folder "Lecture Series for Negro Colleges 1964–1965, n.d.," Box I.93, Brzezinski Papers, LoC.

183. See folder " 'Bu-By,' Miscellaneous 1955–1977," Box I.4, Brzezinski Papers, LoC.

184. Folder "Freedom House," Box I.9, Brzezinski Papers, LoC.

185. Zbigniew Brzezinski, "This Peace Is as Peaceful as Cold War Was Martial," *Washington Post,* July 26, 1970, 34.

186. Zbigniew Brzezinski, "America in a New World," folder " 'America in a New World,' (unpublished) Draft III 1976 (1, 2, and 3 of 3)," Box I.71, Brzezinski Papers, LoC.

187. Jeane Kirkpatrick, "Dictatorships and Double Standards," *Commentary* 68, no. 5 (November 1979):39.

188. Ibid., 45.

189. Cited by Jim Hoagland in "Brzezinski: An Eagerness to Show 'Resolve,'" *Washington Post,* March 14, 1978, A1.

190. Brzezinski, "Russo-Soviet Nationalism," 142.

191. Zbigniew Brzezinski, "U.S. Foreign Policy in East Central Europe: A Study in Contradiction," *Journal of International Affairs* 11, no. 1 (1957): 60–71; Zbigniew Brzezinski and William Griffith, "Peaceful Engagement in Eastern Europe," *Foreign Affairs* 39, no. 4 (July 1961):642–654; Zbigniew Brzezinski, *Alternative to Partition: For a Broader Conception of America's Role in Europe,* Council on Foreign Relations Atlantic Policy Studies Series (New York: McGraw-Hill, 1965).

192. Brzezinski, *Alternative to Partition,* 134–135.

193. Brzezinski, *Between Two Ages,* 275.

194. Ibid., 282.

195. Brzezinski, "America in a New World," 110.

196. Zbigniew Brzezinski, "Tougher Dealings by USSR Expected," *Washington Post,* November 17, 1968, B1; "Peace and Power," *Survival* 10, no.12 (December 1968):386–396; "Meeting Moscow's 'Limited Coexistence,'" *New Leader* (December 16, 1968):11–13.

197. Brzezinski to Kissinger, April 6, 1970, "Memo on Conversation with Henry Kissinger May 23, 1970," folder "Kissinger, Henry 1970–1973," Box I.16, Brzezinski Papers, LoC.

198. Brzezinski to Kissinger, October 13, 1970, and Kissinger to Brzezinski, November 14, 1970, folder "Kissinger, Henry 1970–1973," Box I.16, Brzezinski Papers, LoC.

199. Brzezinski to Muskie, March 1, 1972, folder "Muskie, Edmund S., 1969–1975," Box I.21, Brzezinski Papers, LoC; Brzezinski to Max Kampelman, February 29, 1972, folder "Presidential Election Campaigns 1972, Humphrey, Hubert H., 1971–72, n.d.," Box I.94, Brzezinski Papers, LoC.

200. Brzezinski to Scoop Jackson, January 9, 1974, folder "Jackson, Henry M. 1963, 1970–1974," Box I.14, Brzezinski Papers, LoC.

201. Brzezinski, Pipes, and Griffith to Kissinger, April 23, 1975; Report, "The Polish Broadcasts of Radio Free Europe," April 23, 1975, folder "Radio Free Europe 1975, n.d. (2 of 3)," Box I.100, Brzezinski Papers, LoC.

202. Cited in Patrick Vaughan, *Zbigniew Brzeziński* (Warsaw: Świat Książki, 2010), 68.

203. See Carl Gershman, "The Rise and Fall of the New Foreign-Policy Establishment," *Commentary* 70, no. 1 (July 1980):13–24, and Kirkpatrick, "Dictatorships."

204. "Soviet Perceptions of US Foreign Policy and US leaders," Brzezinski Collection, Carter Library. The passage omitted was marked as classified.

205. Del Pero, *Eccentric Realist.*

206. Brzezinski, "America in a Hostile World" (a chapter excerpted from the manuscript "America in a New World").

207. Zbigniew Brzezinski, "The Deceptive Structure of Peace," *Foreign Policy,* no. 14 (Spring 1974):35–55; Kissinger to Brzezinski, March 23, 1974, folder "Kissinger, Henry 1974–1975, n.d.," Box I.16, Brzezinski Papers, LoC.

208. Del Pero, *Eccentric Realist,* 10.

209. See especially Zbigniew Brzezinski, "A U.S. Portfolio in the USSR?," *New Leader* (August 5, 1974):5–7.

210. "Confidential Personnel Memorandum—Visit to Moscow: Broad Impressions," June 18, 1975, folder "Détente 1975–1976, n.d.," Box I.92, Brzezinski Papers, LoC.

211. Brzezinski, *Power and Principle,* 147.

212. Dean Acheson, Paul Nitze, and Albert Wohlstetter to Brzezinski, May 26, 1969, and Brzezinski to Acheson, June 3, 1969, folder " 'Ab-Ad' Miscellaneous 1952, 1960–1976," Box I.1, Brzezinski Papers, LoC.

213. See Justin Vaïsse, *Neoconservatism: The Biography of a Movement* (Cambridge, MA: Harvard University Press, 2010), chaps. 3 and 4. "Come Home, Democrats" is available at http://neoconservatism.Vaïsse.net/doku.php?id=come_home_democrats_1972.

214. Brzezinski to Max Kampelman, November 13, 1972, folder "Kampelman, Max M. 1972–1977," Box I.15, Brzezinski Papers, LoC.

215. Brzezinski to Eugene Rostow, March 18, 1974, folder "Rostow, Eugene V., 1958, 1964–1977," Box. I.26, Brzezinski Papers, LoC. Cf. "The Quest for Détente," a statement by the Foreign Policy Task Force (Eugene Rostow, chairman) of the Coalition for a Democratic Majority, July 31, 1974, http://neoconservatism.Vaïsse.net/doku.php?id=the_quest_for_detente.

216. See Vaïsse, *Neoconservatism.*

217. Brzezinski to Jackson, April 24, 1973, and Jackson to Brzezinski, May 18, 1973, folder "Jackson, Henry M. 1963, 1970–1974," Box I.14, Brzezinski Papers, LoC.

218. Brzezinski to Jackson, June 11, 1973, folder "Jackson, Henry M. 1963, 1970–1974," Box I.14, Brzezinski Papers, LoC.

219. "An Appeal for Democracy in Portugal," *New York Times,* July 13, 1975, 164.

220. "A Statement on the Middle East," *New York Times,* September 20, 1970, 188.

221. Brzezinski to Eugene Rostow, May 6, 1976, folder "Foreign Policy Specialists 'R' 1976," Brzezinski Papers, Box I.38; Dick Holbrooke and Stu Eizenstat to Governor Carter, September 1, 1976, folder "Foreign Policy Defense—Correspondence / Recommendations / Analysis [2]," Box 37, Carter Family Papers, 1976 Campaign Files, Carter Library.

222. Interview with Zbigniew Brzezinski, July 23, 2001, Washington, DC.

223. On Team B, see Anne Hessing Cahn, *Killing Détente: The Right Attacks the CIA* (University Park: Pennsylvania State University Press, 1998); the book follows up on Cahn's article, "Team B: The Trillion Dollar Experiment," *Bulletin of the Atomic Scientists* (April 1993):22–27. See also Raymond Garthoff, "Estimating Soviet Military Intentions and Capabilities," chap. 5 in Gerald K. Haines and Robert E. Leggett, *Watching the Bear: Essays on CIA's Analysis of the Soviet Union* (Langley, VA: Center for the Study of Intelligence, Central Intelligence Agency, 2003); the communications from the colloquium on which this volume is based are available at http://www.odci.gov/csi/books/watchingthebear/index.html.

224. E-mail from Zbigniew Brzezinski to Justin Vaïsse dated July 24, 2001.

225. Interview with Zbigniew Brzezinski, June 17, 2011.

226. Interview with Zbigniew Brzezinski, June 22, 2011.

227. Zbigniew Brzezinski, interview in Josiah Lee Auspitz, "America Now: A Failure of Nerve? A Symposium," *Commentary* 60, no. 1 (July 1975):27.

6. In the White House

1. See Jimmy Carter, *Keeping Faith: Memoirs of a President* (New York: Bantam Books, 1982), and *White House Diary* (New York: Farrar, Straus and Giroux, 2010); Walter Mondale, *The Good Fight: A Life in Liberal Politics* (New York: Scribner, 2010); Cyrus Vance, *Hard Choices: Critical Years in America's Foreign Policy* (New York: Simon & Schuster, 1983); Harold Brown, *Thinking About National Security: Defense and Foreign Policy in a Dangerous World* (Boulder, CO: Westview Press, 1983).

2. See especially Richard Gardner, *Mission Italy: On the Front Lines of the Cold War* (Lanham, MD: Rowman & Littlefield, 2005); William Quandt, *Camp David: Peacemaking and Politics* (Washington, DC: Brookings Institution Press, 1986); Robert Gates, *From the Shadows: The Ultimate Insider's Story of Five Presidents and How They Won the Cold War* (New York: Simon & Schuster, 1997); Gary Sick, *All Fall Down: America's Tragic Encounter with Iran* (New York: Penguin Books, 1986).

3. Zbigniew Brzezinski, *Power and Principle: Memoirs of the National Security Adviser, 1977–1981* (New York: Farrar, Straus and Giroux, 1983).

4. See, among others, Robert A. Strong, *Working in the World: Jimmy Carter and the Making of American Foreign Policy* (Baton Rouge: Louisiana State University Press, 2000); Betty Glad, *An Outsider in the White House: Jimmy Carter, His Advisors, and the Making of American Foreign Policy* (Ithaca, NY: Cornell University Press, 2009); Brian Auten, *Carter's Conversion: The Hardening of American Defense Policy* (Columbia: University of Missouri Press, 2008); Julian Zelizer, *Jimmy Carter* (New York: Henry Holt, 2010).

5. The series of Weekly Reports can be found in Boxes 41 and 42 of Collection 33 in the Jimmy Carter Presidential Library; reports 8, 21, 26, 30, 52, 70, 73, 113, 120, 143, and 152 are missing. A summary prepared by one of Brzezinski's advisers in late 1980 is included: Summary Listing of Opinion Items, folder "Weekly Reports [to the President]—Summary Listing of Opinion Items: [11 / 80]," Box 33.42, Donated Historical Material, Zbigniew Brzezinski Collection (33), Jimmy Carter Library, Atlanta, GA (hereafter, Brzezinski Collection, Carter Library). The second annex in *Power and Principle*, 556–569, provides a summary of more than a third of these reports (61 of 161).

6. Glad, *Outsider in the White House*, 47. Glad cites a document available at Yale that I was not able to consult, but which probably does not contain highly personal elements: Memo of conversation, Jimmy Carter, Walter Mondale, Henry Kissinger, Lawrence Eagleburger, and David Aaron, November 20, 1976, Vance Mss, Box 8, F:6, Yale University Library, New Haven, CT.

7. Anatoly Dobrynin, *In Confidence: Moscow's Ambassador to America's Six Cold War Presidents (1962–1986)* (New York: Times Books, 1995), 368.

8. Clark Clifford, *Counsel to the President: A Memoir* (New York: Random House, 1991), 620.

9. Rudy Abramson, *Spanning the Century: The Life of W. Averell Harriman, 1891–1986* (New York: William Morrow, 1992), 690; Patrick Tyler, "The (Ab)-Normalization of U.S.-Chinese Relations," *Foreign Affairs* 78, no. 5 (September–October 1999):95.

10. Carter, *Keeping Faith*, 52.

11. "Zbigniew Brzezinski, along with William Odom, Leslie G. Denend and Madeleine K. Albright," interview conducted at the Miller Center (University of Virginia) for the Carter Presidency Project, February 18, 1982, 60, http://web1.millercenter.org/poh/transcripts/ohp_1982_0218_brzezinski.pdf (hereafter, Brzezinski et al., Miller Center interview).

12. Jimmy Carter, interview at the Miller Center, University of Virginia, for the Carter Presidency Project, 38, http://web1.millercenter.org/poh/transcripts/ohp_1982_1129_carter.pdf (hereafter, Carter, Miller Center interview).

13. The third quotation is from Carter, *Keeping Faith,* 54; the others are from Carter, Miller Center interview, 20, 38.

14. See Russell Watson, Hal Bruno, and Scott Sullivan, "Life at Brzezinski U," *Newsweek,* May 9, 1977, 55.

15. Brzezinski et al., Miller Center interview, 72.

16. Brzezinski, *Power and Principle,* 21.

17. Brzezinski et al., Miller Center interview, 78.

18. Brzezinski, *Power and Principle,* 23.

19. Carter, *Keeping Faith,* 54.

20. Interview with Zbigniew Brzezinski, June 17, 2011.

21. Mika Brzezinski, *All Things at Once* (New York: Weinstein Books, 2009); Zbigniew Brzezinski, *Power and Principle,* 254.

22. Brzezinski et al., Miller Center interview, 72.

23. Interview with Zbigniew Brzezinski, February 15, 2011.

24. Brzezinski, *Power and Principle,* 18, 21.

25. Brzezinski et al., Miller Center interview, 72.

26. Weekly Report #55, April 21, 1978, Box 33–41, Brzezinski Collection, Carter Library.

27. Jeremy Suri, *Henry Kissinger and the American Century* (Cambridge, MA: Harvard University Press, 2007), 210.

28. Ibid., 202.

29. David Halberstam, "The New Establishment: The Decline and Fall of the Eastern Empire," *Vanity Fair,* October 1964, http://www.vanityfair.com/news/1994/10/old-establishment-decline-199410.

30. Interview with Zbigniew Brzezinski, June 17, 2011.

31. Quoted in Brzezinski et al., Miller Center interview, 45.

32. Brzezinski, *Power and Principle,* 74.

33. Brzezinski et al., Miller Center interview, 49.

34. Michael Dobbs, *Madeleine Albright: A Twentieth-Century Odyssey* (New York: Henry Holt, 1999), 258.

35. Brzezinski, *Power and Principle,* 501.

36. Dom Bonafede, "Brzezinski—Stepping Out of His Backstage Role," *National Journal* 9, no. 42 (October 15, 1977):1596.

37. Madeleine Albright, with Bill Woodward, *Madam Secretary: A Memoir, Madeleine Albright* (New York: Miramax Books, 2003), 84.

38. See Tyler, "(Ab)-Normalization," 94.

39. Carter, *Keeping Faith,* 52.

40. Brzezinski, *Power and Principle,* 501

41. I.M. Destler, Leslie Gelb, and Anthony Lake, *Our Own Worst Enemy: The Unmaking of American Foreign Policy* (New York: Simon & Schuster, 1984), 96.

42. See, for example, Glad, *Outsider in the White House,* 129, See also 344n76, which, refers to David Rothkopf, *Running the World: The Inside Story of the National Security Council and the Architects of American Power* (New York: Public Affairs, 2004), 190. Vance's entourage accused Brzezinski of a supposed leak concerning the result of a trip Vance had made to China; see also Tyler, "(Ab)-Normalization," 101.

43. Brzezinski, *Power and Principle,* 40; Carter, *Keeping Faith,* 53.

44. Vance, *Hard Choices,* 38.

45. Carter, *Keeping Faith,* 450.

46. Brzezinski et al., Miller Center interview, 62; Brzezinski, *Power and Principle,* 11.

47. See Carter, *Keeping Faith,* 53, and Brzezinski, *Power and Principle,* 41.

48. Vance, *Hard Choices,* 37.

49. Brzezinski et al., Miller Center interview, 66. The ten objectives are listed in Brzezinski, *Power and Principle,* 53–55.

50. Brzezinski, *Power and Principle,* 52.

51. Weekly Report #83, December 18, 1978, Box 33–42, Subject File, Brzezinski Collection, Carter Library.

52. Brzezinski, *Power and Principle,* 37.

53. Brzezinski et al., Miller Center interview, 65.

54. Brzezinski, *Power and Principle,* 37.

55. Vance, *Hard Choices,* 35.

56. Carter, *Keeping Faith,* 53.

57. Ibid., 54.

58. Brzezinski, *Power and Principle,* 29.

59. Hamilton Jordan, *Crisis: The Last Year of the Carter Presidency* (New York: Putnam, 1982), 49.

60. Brzezinski, *Power and Principle,* 64.

61. Ibid., 62.

62. Brzezinski et al., Miller Center interview, 77.

63. Brzezinski, *Power and Principle,* 64.

64. Ibid., 68–70.

65. Brzezinski et al., Miller Center interview, 53.

66. Brzezinski, *Power and Principle,* 66.

67. Vance, *Hard Choices,* 37.

68. Betty Glad, *Outsider,* 84.

69. "Review [of Glad, *Outsider*] by Robert A. Pastor, American University," *H-Diplo Roundtable* 11, no. 6 (2011), https://issforum.org/roundtables/PDF/Roundtable-XII-6.pdf.

70. Quoted in Rothkopf, *Running the World,* 188.

71. Brzezinski et al., Miller Center interview, 73.

72. *Power and Principle*, 445.

73. Glad, *Outsider*, 138.

74. Brzezinski, *Power and Principle*, 417.

75. Glad, *Outsider*, 124.

76. Brzezinski, *Power and Principle*, 73.

77. Ibid., 44ff.

78. Interview with Zbigniew Brzezinski, June 17, 2011; Brzezinski et al., Miller Center interview, 73.

79. Albright, *Madam Secretary,* 56; Brzezinski, *Power and Principle,* 69.

80. On the new Cold War, see especially Odd Arne Westad, ed., *The Fall of Détente: Soviet-American Relations during the Carter Years* (Oslo: Scandinavian University Press, 1997), and Odd Arne Westad, *The Global Cold War: Third World Interventions and the Making of Our Times* (Cambridge: Cambridge University Press, 2005). See also Leopoldo Nuti, ed., *The Crisis of Détente in Europe: From Helsinki to Gorbachev, 1975–1985* (London: Routledge, 2008).

81. On this debate, see in particular Colin S. Gray and Jeffrey G. Barlow, "Inexcusable Restraint: The Decline of American Military Power in the 1970s," *International Security* 10, no. 2 (Fall 1985):27–69; Raymond Garthoff, "Estimating Soviet Military Intentions and Capabilities," in *Watching the Bear: Essay on CIA's Analysis of the Soviet Union,* ed. Gerald K. Haines and Robert E. Leggett (Langley, VA, Center for the Study of Intelligence, Central Intelligence Agency, 2003), chap. 5. For a definitive judgment, see Steven J. Zaloga, *The Kremlin's Nuclear Sword: The Rise and Fall of Russia's Strategic Nuclear Forces, 1945–2000* (Washington, DC: Smithsonian Institution Press, 2002), and Pavel Podvig, ed., *Russian Strategic Nuclear Forces* (Cambridge, MA: MIT Press, 2001).

82. Samuel Wells, "Reviewing the Arms Race," *World Issues* 3, no. 3 (June–July 1978).

83. Dobrynin, *In Confidence,* 410.

84. Gates, *From the Shadows,* 157ff.

85. Brzezinski et al., Miller Center interview, 51 and 12.

86. Brzezinski, *Power and Principle,* 414.

87. Gates, *From the Shadows,* 160 and 163.

88. See Justin Vaïsse, *Neoconservatism: The Biography of a Movement* (Cambridge, MA: Harvard University Press, 2010), 176.

89. Brzezinski himself proposed to play that role: see Weekly Report #151, August 19, 1980, Box 33.42, SUBJECT FILE, Brzezinski Collection, Carter Library.

90. Glad, *Outsider,* 216.

91. Strobe Talbott, Gregory H. Wierzynski, and Roberto Suro, "Almost Everyone vs. Zbig But the National Security Adviser Hangs Tough," *Time Magazine* 116, no. 12 (September 22, 1980):16–19.

92. See Zbigniew Brzezinski, "Peace and Power," *Survival* 10, no. 12 (December 1968):386–396; *Between Two Ages: America's Role in the Technetronic Era* (New York: Viking Press, 1970), and "The Deceptive Structure of Peace," *Foreign Policy,* no. 14 (Spring 1974):35–55.

93. In folder " 'America in a New World' (unpublished) Draft III 1976, 1, 2, and 3 of 3," Box I.71, Zbigniew Brzezinski Papers, Manuscript Division, Library of Congress, Washington, DC (hereafter, Brzezinski Papers, LoC). See also Zbigniew Brzezinski, "America in a Hostile World," *Foreign Policy*, no. 23 (Summer 1976):65–96, which corresponds to a chapter in the unpublished book titled "The Changing World and America," 68ff.

94. Interview with Zbigniew Brzezinski, June 17, 2011.

95. Brzezinski, "America in a New World," 110.

96. Brzezinski to Irwin Glickes, November 10, 1976, folder " 'America in a New World' (unpublished) Correspondence 1975–1977," Box I.71, Brzezinski Papers, LoC.

97. Interview with Zbigniew Brzezinski, June 17, 2011.

98. Brzezinski, *Power and Principle*, 52–53.

99. This would be the logic of the future START negotiations, as we know with the advantage of hindsight.

100. Brzezinski, *Power and Principle*, 53–56.

101. The Notre Dame speech is available at http://www.presidency.ucsb.edu/ws/?pid=7552; a number of nonclassified presidential directives are available at http://www.fas.org/irp/offdocs /pd/index.html.

102. See Murrey Marder, "US as 2d Best Is Fairy Tale, Kissinger Says," *Washington Post*, April 12, 1976.

103. See http://www.fas.org/irp/offdocs/prm/prm10.pdf. All the unclassified PRMs from the Carter administration are available at the site of the Federation of American Scientists, https://fas.org.

104. Brzezinski et al., Miller Center interview, 31.

105. Interview with Sam Huntington, June 19, 2004.

106. Brzezinski et al., Miller Center interview, 33, 37.

107. Ibid., 32, 40; see also Brzezinski, *Power and Principle*, 177ff.

108. Brzezinski, "America in a New World," 180–181.

109. Brzezinski, *Power and Principle*, 177.

110. Weekly Report #92, March 30, 1979, Box 33–42, Subject File, Brzezinski Collection, Carter Library.

111. Gates, *From the Shadows*, 94.

112. See, for example, Brzezinski to Carter, "Stanton Report, Board of International Broadcasting and Related Issues," NLC-126-6-30-1-1, Carter Library.

113. Gates, *From the Shadows*, 91–95.

114. Brzezinski, *Power and Principle*, 196ff.

115. This hypothesis was advanced by Steven Campbell in "Brzezinski's Image of the USSR: Inferring Foreign Policy Beliefs from Multiple Sources Over Time" (Ph.D. diss., University of South Carolina, 2003), 113 and 134.

116. Brzezinski, *Power and Principle*, 146.

117. Ibid., 151–156.

118. Ibid., 162.

119. Ibid., 171.

120. Brzezinski et al., Miller Center interview, 39.

121. Brzezinski, *Power and Principle,* 178–187.

122. Ibid., 183.

123. Vance, *Hard Choices,* 75 and 86–88.

124. Weekly Report #42, January 13, 1978, Box 33–41, Subject File, Brzezinski Collection, Carter Library.

125. Weekly Report #48, February 24, 1978, Box 33–41, Subject File, Brzezinski Collection, Carter Library.

126. Weekly Report #53, April 7, 1978, Box 33–41, Subject File, Brzezinski Collection, Carter Library.

127. Weekly Report #54, April 14, 1978, Box 33–41, Subject File, Brzezinski Collection, Carter Library.

128. Brzezinski, *Power and Principle,* 189.

129. Ibid., 329 and 344.

130. Weekly Report #109, September 13, 1978, Box 33–41, Subject File, Brzezinski Collection, Carter Library.

131. Glad, *Outsider,* 192; Vance, *Hard Choices,* 362; Brzezinski, *Power and Principle,* 350.

132. Presented as the revelations of a former adviser to Carter: "Oui, la CIA est entrée en Afghanistan avant les Russes," interview with Zbigniew Brzezinski by Vincent Jauvert, *Le Nouvel Observateur* (January 15, 1998):76.

133. See an exploration of the question by Eric Alterman, " 'Blowback,' the Prequel," *Nation* 273, no. 15 (November 12, 2001):12, http://www.thenation.com/article/blowback-prequel.

134. Jonathan Haslam, *Russia's Cold War: From the October Revolution to the Fall of the Wall* (New Haven, CT: Yale University Press, 2011), 319, 326; see 472n217, where in note 217, 472, the author identifies Odom as his source. Professor Haslam gives the details: "I did not record Odom. I did a series of debriefings after hefty dinners in college. . . . We were talking about the Cold War during his period in government and it all slipped out by accident. I wrote it down immediately. Bill suddenly realized what he had said and hurriedly clarified that it was entirely off the record, which it was until he died." Email from Jonathan Haslam to Justin Vaïsse, September 15, 2011.

135. Brzezinski to Carter, "Reflections on Soviet Intervention in Afghanistan," December 26, 1979, declassified document, www.dlt.ncssm.edu/lmtm/ . . . /Presidential_memos _on_Afghanistan.doc.

136. Email message from Vincent Jauvert to Justin Vaïsse, July 18, 2011.

137. Email message from Vincent Jauvert to Justin Vaïsse, July 20, 2011; interview with Zbigniew Brzezinski, June 22, 2010.

138. Interview with Zbigniew Brzezinski, June 22, 2010.

139. Brzezinski to Carter, "Reflections on Soviet Intervention in Afghanistan."

140. "Special Coordination Committee Meeting," January 17, 1980, declassified document NLS-33-5-12-1-6, Brzezinski Collection, Carter Library.

141. Gates, *From the Shadows,* 143–149.

142. Brzezinski, *Power and Principle,* 427.

143. See especially Glad, *Outsider,* 198.

144. Gates, *From the Shadows,* 144–145.

145. Declassified document, Presidential finding, July 3, 1979, Staff Offices, Counsel Cutler, folder "CIA Charter 2/9–25/80," Box 60, http://www.activistmagazine.com/images/stories/government/carter-79-1581.jpg. The second finding, a few days later, concerned the propaganda efforts http://www.activistmagazine.com/images/stories/government/carter-79-1579.jpg.

146. Gates, *From the Shadows,* 146.

147. Brzezinski, *Power and Principle,* 430.

148. Ibid., 434.

149. Brzezinski to Carter, January 9, 1980, Declassified document NLC-33-6-2-8-9, Brzezinski Collection, Carter Library.

150. "Special Coordination Committee Meeting," January 17, 1980.

151. Brzezinski, *Power and Principle,* 449.

152. President Jimmy Carter, State of the Union address January 23, 1980, http://www.presidency.ucsb.edu/ws/?pid=33079.

153. Ibid., 463.

154. See http://www.fas.org/irp/offdocs/pd/index.html, along with other non-classified documents from the Carter administration at https://fas.org..

155. Brzezinski, *Power and Principle,* 459.

156. On Carter's position, see the chapter on nuclear issues in his *Keeping Faith,* 212ff.

157. Brzezinski, *Power and Principle,* 466–468.

158. Ibid., 468.

159. Brzezinski, *Power and Principle,* 209.

160. Transcript of Woodcock-Oksenberg Interview, Tape 4, November 2, 1981, in the possession of Mrs. Leonard (Sharon) Woodcock, cited by Breck Walker, "Friends, but Not Allies: Cyrus Vance and the Normalization of Relations with China," *Diplomatic History* 33, no. 4 (September 2009):579–594.

161. "America in a New World," 178–179.

162. Carter, Notre Dame speech, May 22, 1977.

163. Weekly Report #111, October 5, 1979, Box 33–42, Subject File, Brzezinski Collection, Carter Library.

164. Brzezinski, *Power and Principle,* 198; Vance, *Hard Choices,* 78.

165. Brzezinski, *Power and Principle,* 202.

166. Ibid., 208.

167. See Fox Butterfield, "Brzezinski in China: The Stress Was on Common Concerns," *New York Times,* May 24, 1978, A2.

168. Angus Deming, "A New Cold War?" *Newsweek* (June 12, 1978):26. In the same issue, see also David Butler, "Zbig on the Rise," 26.

169. Carter, *Keeping Faith,* 196.

170. Weekly Report #75, October 13, 1978, Box 33–42, Subject File, Brzezinski Collection, Carter Library.

171. James Mann, *About Face: A History of America's Curious Relationship with China from Nixon to Clinton* (New York: Alfred Knopf, 1999), 79–80.

172. Brzezinski, *Power and Principle*, 228.

173. Ibid., 231.

174. Vance, *Hard Choices,* 118.

175. Transcript of Oral History Project, Conversations between Leonard Woodcock and Michael Oksenberg, March 2, 1982, cited in Walker, "Friends, but Not Allies," 592.

176. Mika Brzezinski, *All Things at Once,* 21.

177. Brzezinski, *Power and Principle,* 405–406.

178. Mann, *About Face,* 86 and 97; see also Gates, *From the Shadows,* 116.

179. Brzezinski, *Power and Principle,* 408ff.; Vance, *Hard Choices,* 121–122.

180. Brzezinski, *Power and Principle,* 413.

181. Ibid., 422ff.

182. Interview with Zbigniew Brzezinski, June 17, 2011.

183. "America in a New World," 38–39.

184. Ibid., 144.

185. Dobrynin, *In Confidence,* 378.

186. Brzezinski, *Power and Principle,* 292.

187. Bonafede, "Brzezinski—Stepping Out of His Backstage Role," 1596.

188. Brzezinski, *Power and Principle,* 295.

189. Ibid., 193, and Weekly Report #5, March 18, 1977, Box 33–41, Brzezinski Collection, Carter Library.

190. Brzezinski, *Power and Principle,* 293.

191. Ibid., 307.

192. See Walter Pincus, "Neutron Killer Warhead Buried in ERDA Budget," *Washington Post,* June 6, 1977, 1.

193. Vance, *Hard Choices,* 68ff.; Brzezinski, *Power and Principle,* 301ff.; Carter, *Keeping Faith,* 225ff.

194. Brzezinski, *Power and Principle,* 310; Carter, *Keeping Faith,* 537.

195. Brzezinski, *Power and Principle,* 311.

196. Brzezinski, "America in a New World," 68 and 105; and the entire chapter reprinted as "America in a Hostile World," in *Foreign Policy* no. 23 (Summer 1976):65–96.

197. Suri, *Henry Kissinger,* 242.

198. Brzezinski, *Power and Principle,* 49.

199. Brzezinski, "America in a New World," 174–175.

200. Brzezinski et al., Miller Center interview, 49.

201. Glad, *Outsider,* 72.

202. Brzezinski, "America in the New World," 152.

203. Ibid., 148.

204. Zbigniew Brzezinski, "We Need a Latin Divorce," *Washington Post,* September 6, 1970, 36; Brzezinski, "America in a New World," 151.

205. Brzezinski, "America in a New World," 152.

206. Weekly Report #15, June 3, 1977, Box 33–41, Brzezinski Collection, Carter Library.

207. Brzezinski, *Power and Principle,* 143.

208. Ibid., 245.

209. Bernard Gwertzman, "Jewish Leader Says Mideast Policy Makes a 'Question Mark' of Carter," *New York Times,* March 10, 1978.

210. Brzezinski, *Power and Principle,* 282.

211. Weekly Report #91, March 23, 1979, Box 33–42, Brzezinski Collection, Carter Library.

212. Carter, Notre Dame speech, May 22, 1977.

213. PD-30 is available at https://www.jimmycarterlibrary.gov/documents/pddirectives/pd30.pdf; see also Brzezinski, *Power and Principle,* 126.

214. KGB propaganda would have it that the election of this pope had been concocted by Brzezinski, who was alleged to have asked the archbishop of Philadelphia, John Krol—of Polish origin himself—to organize the American and German cardinals in a coalition. Patrick Vaughan, "Brzezinski, the Pope, and the 'Plot' to Free Poland," in *Zbig: The Strategy and Statecraft of Zbigniew Brzezinski,* ed. Charles Gati (Baltimore: Johns Hopkins University Press, 2013), 127.

215. Weekly Report #77, October 27, 1978, Box 33–42, Brzezinski Collection, Carter Library.

216. Brzezinski, *Power and Principle,* 297 and 300.

217. Ibid., 128.

218. See Jeane Kirkpatrick, "Dictatorships and Double Standards," *Commentary* (November 1979):34–45.

219. Brzezinski, *Power and Principle,* 338.

220. On this point, see Vance, *Hard Choices,* 316.

221. See Sick, *All Fall Down.*

222. Brzezinski, *Power and Principle,* 354 and 368. For William Sullivan's defense, see his book, *Mission to Iran* (New York: W. W. Norton, 1981).

223. Carter, Miller Center interview, 15.

224. Weekly Report #81, December 2, 1978, Box 33–42, Brzezinski Collection, Carter Library.

225. Brzezinski, *Power and Principle,* 367.

226. Vance, *Hard Choices,* 328. On Brzezinski's denegation, see Talbott, Wierzynski, and Suro, "Almost Everyone vs. Zbig," 16.

227. George Ball, *The Past Has Another Pattern: Memoirs* (New York: W. W. Norton, 1982), 461.

228. See Vance, *Hard Choices,* 333.

229. See Carter's harsh annotation on Weekly Report #84, January 12, 1979, Box 33–42, Brzezinski Collection, Carter Library: "Zbig—after we make joint decisions, deploring them for the record doesn't help me."

230. Brzezinski, *Power and Principle*, 380ff.

231. Carter, *Keeping Faith*, 443; see also Robert Huyser, *Mission to Tehran* (Southwold, U.K.: Bookthrift, 1990).

232. Carter, *Keeping Faith*, 446; Brzezinski, *Power and Principle*, 393.

233. Brzezinski, *Power and Principle*, 476.

234. Ibid., 484.

235. Weekly Report #122, December 21, 1979, Box 33–42, Brzezinski Collection, Carter Library.

236. Vance, *Hard Choices*, 609; Brzezinski, *Power and Principle*, 494.

237. Ibid., 498.

238. Glad, *Outsider*, 266.

239. Brzezinski, *Power and Principle*, 500; Carter, *Keeping Faith*, 518ff.

240. Vance, *Hard Choices*, 411.

241. Brzezinski, *Power and Principle*, 501.

242. Interview with Zbigniew Brzezinski, June 17, 2011. See also Sick, *All Fall Down*.

243. Sick, *All Fall Down*, 507; Glad, *Outsider*, 272–273.

244. Sick, *All Fall Down*, 509.

245. Walter Russell Mead, "The Carter Syndrome," *Foreign Policy* (January–February 2010), http://www.foreignpolicy.com/articles/2009/12/18/the_carter_syndrome. For responses by Carter and Brzezinski, see "Presidential Debate," *Foreign Policy* (March–April 2010), http://www.foreignpolicy.com/articles/2010/02/22/presidential_debate.

246. Gates, *From the Shadows*, 110–111.

247. Destler, Gelb, and Lake, *Our Own Worst Enemy*, 72–76.

248. Conversely, the decoupling of the Israel-Egypt question from the Palestinian question, which Carter accepted and which stabilized the region, can also be understood as having contributed to the lack of a settlement concerning the dispute over land distribution that had arisen in 1967.

249. See a document written by Lincoln Bloomfield, "The Carter Human Rights Policy: A Provisional Appraisal," January 11, 1981, folder "NSC Accomplishments—Human Rights: 1/81," Box 33–34, Brzezinski Collection, Carter Library.

250. Brzezinski, *Power and Principle*, 144.

251. Glad devotes a full chapter of her book to El Salvador and the death of Archbishop Romero; see Glad, *Outsider*, chap. 24. See also Robert Pastor's response in a review of Glad's book: "Review by Robert A. Pastor, American University," *H-Diplo Roundtable* 12, no. 6 (March 2001):14–20, http://www.h-net.org-diplo/roundtables/PDF/Roundtable-XII-6.pdf.

252. On the Pol Pot regime, see Weekly Report #84, January 12, 1979, Box 33–42, Subject File, Brzezinski Collection, Carter Library.

253. Drew, "Brzezinski"; Glad, *Outsider*.

254. Dobrynin, *In Confidence*, 405.

255. Brzezinski, *Power and Principle*, 180.

256. Vance, *Hard Choices*, 112.

257. Marshall Shulman to Cyrus Vance, December 14, 1979, VF, USSR-US Conf., BBII, 2–3, Carter Library, cited in Glad, *Outsider,* 199.

258. Vance, *Hard Choices,* 388.

259. Dobyrnin, *In Confidence,* 439.

260. Glad, *Outsider,* 212–213.

261. Weekly Report #134, March 28, 1980, Box 33–42, Subject File, Brzezinski Collection, Carter Library. For the challenge to the interpretation of the Molotov-Ribbentrop exchanges, see Raymond Garthoff, *Détente and Confrontation: American Soviet Relations from Nixon to Reagan* (Washington, DC: Brookings Institution Press, 1985), 1050. It was the German draft that suggested the south as a zone of natural expansion for Moscow.

262. Interview with Zbigniew Brzezinski, June 17, 2011.

263. "Soviet Perception of US Foreign Policy and US Leaders," n.d. (after June 1978), Declassified document NLC 33-6-15-11-1, Brzezinski Collection, Carter Library.

264. Pastor, "Review by Robert Pastor."

265. Brzezinski, *Power and Principle,* 108.

266. Jimmy Carter, Miller Center interview, February 18, 1979, Box 33–42, Brzezinski Collection, Carter Library.

267. Brzezinski, *Power and Principle,* 306.

268. Glad, *Outsider,* 77.

269. Cited in Butler, "Zbig on the Rise," 26.

270. Weekly Report #89, February 24, 1979, box 33–42, Brzezinski Collection, Carter Library.

271. Carter, *Keeping Faith,* 53–54 and 450.

272. William Odom in Brzezinski et al., Miller Center interview, 58; see also Brzezinski, *Power and Principle,* 34.

273. Interview with Zbigniew Brzezinski, June 17, 2011.

274. Brzezinski, *Power and Principle,* 522.

275. Talbott, Wierzynski, and Suro, "Almost Everyone vs. Zbig."

276. John Lewis Gaddis, *Strategies of Containment. A Critical Appraisal of American National Security Policy During the Cold War* (New York, Oxford : Oxford University Press, 1982), 349, cited by Nabil Mikhail, in "Zbigniew Brzezinski: The Scholar and the Statesman. A Study of the Thoughts and Politics of the National Security Adviser and His Staff in the Carter Administration" (Ph.D. diss., University of Virginia, 1996), 31.

277. Talbott, Wierzynski, and Suro, "Almost Everyone vs. Zbig."

278. Carter, *Keeping Faith,* 52–53.

279. Interview with Zbigniew Brzezinski, June 17, 2011.

280. Ibid.

281. See, for example, Weekly Report #94, April 12, 1979, Box 33–42, Brzezinski Collection, Carter Library.

282. See, for example, Weekly Report #7, April 1, 1977, and Weekly Report #23, July 29, 1977, Box 33–41, Brzezinski Collection, Carter Library.

283. Interview with Zbigniew Brzezinski, June 17, 2011.

284. See Gary Sick to Zbigniew Brzezinski, November 17, 1978, NLC-33-8-16-21-7; Samuel Hoskinson to Zbigniew Brzezinski, November 17, 1978, NLC 38-8-16-22-6; and Brzezinski to Carter, November 20, 1978, NLC 33-8-15-2-9, Carter Library.

285. Weekly Report #134, March 28, 1980, Box 33–42, Brzezinski Collection, Carter Library.

286. Weekly Report #111, October 5, 1979, Box 33–42, Brzezinski Collection, Carter Library.

287. Zbigniew Brzezinski, "Revolution and Counter-Revolution," *New Republic* 158, no. 22 (June 1, 1968):23–26.

288. Interview with Zbigniew Brzezinski, June 17, 2011.

289. Ibid.

7. The Age of Authority

1. Zbigniew Brzezinski, *Power and Principle: Memoirs of the National Security Adviser, 1977–1981* (New York: Farrar, Straus and Giroux, 1983), 513–514.

2. On the CSIS, see James Allen Smith, *Strategic Calling: The Center for Strategic and International Studies, 1962–1992* (Washington, DC: CSIS, 1993).

3. Rudy Maxa, "A Foreign Policy for Lunch Bunch at Z. B.'s Office," *Washington Post Magazine,* March 14, 1982.

4. Lynn Rosellini, "What Washingtonians Get on the Lecture Circuit," *New York Times,* December 15, 1982.

5. Deirdre Carmody, "Brzezinski Renews His Columbia Ties," *New York Times,* April 2, 1981.

6. Nabil Mikhail, "Zbigniew Brzezinski: The Scholar and the Statesman: A Study of the Thoughts and Policies of the National Security Adviser and His Staff in the Carter Administration" (Ph.D. diss., University of Virginia, 1996), 825; and Stephen Szabo, "The Professor," in *Zbig: The Strategy and Statecraft of Zbigniew Brzezinski,* ed. Charles Gati (Baltimore: Johns Hopkins University Press, 2013), 213.

7. The article, supplemented with family photos, describes the trip: Zbigniew Brzezinski, "An American Family Retraces Mao's Long March through China," *Life Magazine* (October 1981): 88–93.

8. Interview with Zbigniew Brzezinski, November 21, 2013, Washington, DC.

9. See James Mann, *About Face: A History of America's Curious Relationship with China from Nixon to Clinton* (New York: Alfred Knopf, 1999), 80.

10. See, for example, Zbigniew Brzezinski, "Convincing Europe and China," *New York Times,* January 31, 1983. On Brzezinski's relations with China, see Warren Cohen and Nancy Bernkopf Tucker, "Beijing's Friend, Moscow's Foe," in Gati, ed., *Zbig,* 98–101.

11. "Brzezinski Defends Role After McHenry's Attack," *New York Times,* January 3, 1981, 4; Hedrick Smith, "Brzezinski Says Critics Are Irked by His Accuracy," *New York Times,* January 18, 1981, 3.

12. Brzezinski, *Power and Principle,* xvi; Madeleine Albright, with Bill Woodward, *Madam Secretary: A Memoir, Madeleine Albright* (New York: Miramax Books, 2003).

13. Carla Hall, "Brzezinski's Index: The Shows & No-Shows at His Book Party," *Washington Post,* April 7, 1983.

14. Brzezinski, *Power and Principle*, 26.

15. Stanley Hoffmann, "In Search of a Foreign Policy," *New York Review of Books* 29 (September 1983), http://www.nybooks.com.proxy.library.cornell.edu/articles/1983/09/29/in-search-of-a-foreign-policy/.

16. George Ball, Book review, *Political Science Quarterly* (March 1, 1984):96; Elisabeth Bumiller, "The Principals of Power: Brzezinski on Friends, Enemies, and Himself," *Washington Post*, April 1, 1983; Gaddis Smith, Book review, *Foreign Affairs* (June 1983):1199.

17. In the *New York Times:* Walter Goodman, "Books of the Times," March 21, 1983; Flora Lewis, "The Adviser's Advice," April 17, 1983; Bernard Gwertzman, "Vance and Brzezinski: Feuding Chapter by Chapter," May 29, 1983; Walter Goodman, "The War of the Memoirs," May 29, 1983. See also Stanley Hoffmann, "In Search of a Foreign Policy," *New York Review of Books* (September 29, 1983); James Hoagland, "The President's Right-Hand Hawk," *Washington Post*, April 3, 1983; Strobe Talbott, "Zbig-Think," *Time Magazine* (May 2, 1983):108.

18. Richard Burt, "Brzezinski Calls Democrats Soft toward Moscow," *New York Times*, November 30, 1980, 1.

19. Zbigniew Brzezinski, "What's Wrong with Reagan's Foreign Policy?" *New York Times Magazine* (December 6, 1981).

20. Patrick Vaughan, "Brzezinski, the Pope, and the 'Plot' to Free Poland," in Gati, ed., "Zbig," 134–135.

21. "Brzezinski Seeks Loud Outcry," *New York Times*, December 15, 1981.

22. On Kuklinski, see Benjamin Weiser, *A Secret Life: The Polish Colonel, His Covert Mission, and the Price He Paid to Save His Country* (New York: Public Affairs, 2004).

23. Michael Dobbs, and Robert Woodward, "CIA Had Secret Agent on Polish General Staff; Warsaw Aide Says U.S. Received Plans for Martial Law but Kept Them Quiet," *Washington Post*, June 4, 1986.

24. Vaughan, "Brzezinski, the Pope . . . ," 134.

25. See especially Zbigniew Brzezinski, "America's Mideast Policy Is in Shambles," *New York Times*, October 9, 1983, 19; "Peace at an Impasse," *Journal of Palestine Studies* 14, no. 1 (Fall 1984):3–15; "Rethinking East-West Relations," *Bulletin of the Atomic Scientists* 38, no. 5 (May 1982):5–8; "For a Broader Western Strategy," *Wall Street Journal*, February 19, 1982, 28; "A Deal for Andropov," *New Republic* 187, no. 24 (December 13, 1982):11–15; and "If the Russians and the Chinese Make Up . . . ," *Washington Post*, November 22, 1982.

26. Zbigniew Brzezinski, "Reagan Is Leaving an Ominous Legacy in Foreign Policy," *Washington Post*, October 5, 1986.

27. Zbigniew Brzezinski, "The Trap of Arms Control," *U.S. News and World Report* 101, no. 1 (July 7, 1986):46.

28. Zbigniew Brzezinski, "A Star Wars Solution," *New Republic* 193, no. 2 (July 8, 1985):16.

29. George Schultz, *Turmoil and Triumph: Diplomacy, Power, and the Victory of the American Deal* (New York: Scribner, 2010; Kindle edition).

30. Interview with Zbigniew Brzezinski, February 15, 2011.

31. David Hoffman, "Chanting Polish Crowds Provide Bush with Footage for '88 Campaign," *Washington Post*, October 4, 1987.

32. "Ex-Carter Adviser Joins Bush Group on Defence," *Financial Post* (Toronto), September 13, 1988; David Lynch, "Jimmy Carter Confidant Brzezinski Tells Why He Jumped Ship for Bush," *Defense Week,* October 3, 1988.

33. Patrick Vaughan, "Zbigniew Brzezinski: The Political and Academic Life of a Cold War Visionary" (Ph.D. diss., West Virginia University, 2003), 342–343. The citation from Dukakis on page 343 is excerpted from Michael Dobbs, *Madeleine Albright: A Twentieth-Century Odyssey* (New York: Henry Holt, 1999), 332–333.

34. Zbigniew Brzezinski, *Game Plan: A Geostrategic Framework for the Conduct of the U.S.-Soviet Contest* (Boston: Atlantic Monthly Press, 1986).

35. Ibid., 195.

36. Ibid., 349.

37. Ibid., 175; see also Zbigniew Brzezinski, "We Need More Muscle in the Gulf, Less in NATO," *Washington Post,* June 7, 1987.

38. Zbigniew Brzezinski, *The Grand Failure: The Birth and Death of Communism in the Twentieth Century* (New York: Scribner, 1989).

39. Ibid., 245–251.

40. Ibid., 243.

41. Ibid., 244; see also the op-ed piece drawn from the book: Zbigniew Brzezinski, "Will the Soviet Empire Self-Destruct? Four Scenarios for Failure," *New York Times,* February 26, 1989.

42. Gail Lapidus, "Writing as Communism Burns," *New York Times,* March 26, 1989.

43. Zbigniew Brzezinski, *A Year in the Life of Glasnost: The Hugh Seton-Watson Memorial Lecture and Other Essays* (London: Center for Policy Studies, 1988), 16; Mark Kramer, "Anticipating the Grand Failure," in Gati, ed., *Zbig,* 55; Zbigniew Brzezinski, "A Proposition the Soviets Shouldn't Refuse," *New York Times,* March 13, 1989.

44. Quoted in Patrick Vaughan, "Brzezinski, the Pope, and the 'Plot' to Free Poland," in Gati, ed., *Zbig,* 140.

45. Marin Strmecki, "Witnessing the Grand Failure in Moscow," in Gati, ed., *Zbig,* 153–155. For an adapted version of the speech, see Zbigniew Brzezinski, "A Common House, a Common Home," *New York Times,* November 15, 1989, A29.

46. Strmecki, "Witnessing the Grand Failure," 156; interview with Zbigniew Brzezinski, November 21, 2013.

47. Strmecki, "Witnessing the Grand Failure," 156.

48. See Strobe Talbott and Robert T. Zintl, "Zbigniew Brzezinski: Vindication of a Hard-Liner" (interview), *Time Magazine* 134, no. 25 (December 18, 1989):10–11.

49. Zbigniew Brzezinski, "Beyond Chaos: A Policy for the West," *National Interest,* no. 19 (Spring 1990):10 and 12.

50. Zbigniew Brzezinski, "Europe and Amerippon: Pillars of the Next World Order," *New Perspectives Quarterly* 7, no. 2 (1990):18–22.

51. Zbigniew Brzezinski, "The True U.S. Interest in the Gulf," *Washington Post,* August 16, 1990.

52. Zbigniew Brzezinski, "Patience in the Persian Gulf, Not War," *New York Times,* October 7, 1990, E19.

53. Zbigniew Brzezinski, "Three R's for the Middle East," *New York Times,* April 21, 1991, E17.

54. Zbigniew Brzezinski, *Out of Control: Global Turmoil on the Eve of the 21st Century* (New York: Scribner, 1993), 209.

55. Francis Fukuyama, *The End of History and the Last Man* (New York: Free Press, 1992); Samuel Huntington, "The Clash of Civilizations?," *Foreign Affairs* 72, no. 3 (Summer 1993): 22–49.

56. Michiko Kakutani, "An Antidote for Optimism after the Cold War," *New York Times,* April 9, 1993.

57. Paul Kennedy, *The Rise and Fall of the Great Powers: Economic Change and Military Conflict from 1500 to 2000* (New York: Random House, 1987); Zbigniew Brzezinski, "America's New Geostrategy," *Foreign Affairs* 66, no. 4 (Spring 1988):690–699.

58. Joseph Nye, *Bound to Lead: The Changing Nature of American Power* (New York: Basic Books, 1990); Zbigniew Brzezinski, *Strategic Vision: America and the Crisis of Global Power* (New York: Basic Books, 2012).

59. Mikhail, "Zbigniew Brzezinski," 835 and 845.

60. Zbigniew Brzezinski, " 'Never Again'—Except for Bosnia," *New York Times,* April 22, 1993, A25.

61. Daniel Williams, "Ex-Statesmen Urge Strikes against Serbs," *Washington Post,* September 2, 1993; Eric Schmitt, "Some Senators Renew Call to Lift Bosnian Arms Ban," *New York Times,* April 18, 1994.

62. Brzezinski on the *McNeil-Lehrer News Hour,* quoted in Mikhail, "Zbigniew Brzezinski," 847.

63. Zbigniew Brzezinski, "After Srebrenica," *New Republic* 213, no. 6 (August 7, 1995):20.

64. Zbigniew Brzezinski, "In Kosovo, U.S. Cannot Avoid Grim Choices," *Wall Street Journal,* March 24, 1999.

65. Zbigniew Brzezinski, "Compromise over Kosovo Means Defeat," *Wall Street Journal,* May 24, 1999.

66. Zbigniew Brzezinski, "To Stop the Serbs," *Washington Post,* March 30, 1999.

67. Zbigniew Brzezinski, "The Failed Double-Cross," *New Perspectives Quarterly* 16, no. 5 (Fall 1999):43.

68. Zbigniew Brzezinski, "The Premature Partnership," *Foreign Affairs* 73, no. 2 (March–April 1994):80.

69. Mikhail, "Zbigniew Brzezinski," 846.

70. See, for example, Zbigniew Brzezinski, "A Genocide, a Political Coup. Some Democracy," *Wall Street Journal,* January 4, 2000; "Indulging Russia Is a Risky Business," *New York Times,* May 31, 2000; "Living with Russia," *National Interest,* no. 61 (Fall 2000):5–16.

71. Brzezinski, "Premature Partnership."

72. Zbigniew Brzezinski, *The Grand Chessboard: American Primacy and Its Geostrategic Imperatives* (New York: Basic Books, 1997). For a summary, see Zbigniew Brzezinski, "A Geostrategy for Eurasia," *Foreign Affairs* 76, no. 5 (September–October 1997):50–64.

73. Mikhail, "Zbigniew Brzezinski," 832.

74. Interview with Jerzy Kozminski, November 10, 2011.

75. Smith, *Strategic Calling,* 100–101.

76. Tom Hundley, "Ex-Carter Aide May Seek Presidency—in Poland," *Chicago Tribune,* October 13, 1994.

77. Vaughan, "Zbigniew Brzezinski," 352; Mikhail, "Zbigniew Brzezinski," 31–832.

78. Zbigniew Brzezinski, "The Great Transformation," *National Interest,* no. 33 (Fall 1993):3–13.

79. Ibid., 12.

80. Ibid., 13.

81. James Goldgeier, *Not Whether but When: The U.S. Decision to Enlarge NATO* (Washington, DC: Brookings Institution Press, 1999), 48.

82. Zbigniew Brzezinski, "A Bigger—and Safer—Europe," *New York Times,* December 1, 1993.

83. Interview with Jerzy Kozminski, November 10, 2011.

84. Zbigniew Brzezinski, "Selective Global Commitment," *Foreign Affairs* 70, no. 4 (Fall 1991):1–20.

85. Ronald Asmus, *Opening NATO's Door: How the Alliance Remade Itself for a New Era* (New York: Columbia University Press, 2002), 17.

86. Zbigniew Brzezinski, "The West Adrift: Vision in Search of a Strategy," *Washington Post,* March 1, 1992.

87. Rowland Evans and Robert Novak, "Ghost of Yalta," *Washington Post,* November 22, 1993.

88. James Goldgeier, "NATO Expansion: The Anatomy of a Decision," *Washington Quarterly* 21, no. 1 (Winter 1998):48.

89. Asmus, "Opening NATO's Door," 56.

90. Goldgeier, *Not Whether But When,* 52ff.

91. Quoted in Alison Mitchell, "NATO Debate: From Big Risk to Sure Thing," *New York Times,* March 20, 1998.

92. See especially Zbigniew Brzezinski and Anthony Lake, "For a New World, a New NATO," *New York Times,* June 30, 1997; the deposition to the Senate Foreign Relations Committee on October 9, 1997; Zbigniew Brzezinski, "Global Implications for NATO Enlargement," *Officer* 73, no. 12 (December 1, 1997):28; "Stretching NATO," *New Perspectives Quarterly* 14, no. 2 (1997): 28–33; "NATO: The Dilemmas of Expansion," *National Interest,* no. 53 (Fall 1998):13–17; "On to Russia," *Washington Post,* May 3, 1998.

93. The account that follows is based on an interview with Jerzy Kozminski (November 10, 2011) and on Weiser, *Secret Life,* 318–328.

94. Interview with Zbigniew Brzezinski, November 21, 2013.

95. Mika Brzezinski, *All Things at Once* (New York: Weinstein Books, 2009), 149–150.

96. Zbigniew Brzezinski, "A New Age of Solidarity? Don't Count on It," *Washington Post,* November 2, 2001.

97. Zbigniew Brzezinski, "A Plan for Political Warfare," *Wall Street Journal,* September 25, 2001.

98. Andrzej Lubowski, *Zbig: The Man Who Cracked the Kremlin* (Kindle Edition, 2013).

99. Brzezinski, "A Plan for Political Warfare."

100. Brzezinski, "A New Age of Solidarity?"

101. James Mann, "Brzezinski and Iraq: The Makings of a Dove," in Gati, ed., *Zbig*, 169–170.

102. See Zbigniew Brzezinski, "Moral Duty, National Interest," *New York Times,* April 7, 2002.

103. Brent Scowcroft, "Don't Attack Saddam," *Wall Street Journal,* August 15, 2002; Zbigniew Brzezinski, "If We Must Fight . . . ," *Washington Post,* August 18, 2002.

104. Zbigniew Brzezinski, Brent Scowcroft, and Richard Murphy, "Differentiated Containment," *Foreign Affairs* 76, no. 3 (May–June 1997):20–30.

105. Zbigniew Brzezinski, "The End Game," *Wall Street Journal,* December 23, 2002.

106. Zbigniew Brzezinski, "Why Unity Is Essential," *Washington Post,* February 19, 2003.

107. Mann, "Brzezinski and Iraq," 176.

108. Zbigniew Brzezinski, "Know Thine Enemies," *American Prospect* 15 (August 2004):37–38; "Terrorized by 'War on Terror': How a Three-Word Mantra Has Undermined America," *Washington Post,* March 25, 2007; "Lowered Vision," *The New Republic* 230, nos. 21–22 (June 7, 2004):16–18; and "Where Do We Go from Here?" *Military Technology* 28, no. 1, January 2004):14–16.

109. See Zbigniew Brzezinski, "There Is Much More at Stake for America than Iraq," *Financial Times,* December 5, 2006.

110. Zbigniew Brzezinski, *The Choice: Global Domination or Global Leadership* (New York: Basic Books, 2004).

111. Zbigniew Brzezinski, *Second Chance: Three Presidents and the Crisis of American Superpower* (New York: Basic Books, 2007).

112. David Ignatius, "A Manifesto for the Next President," *Washington Post,* March 14, 2007.

113. Interview with Zbigniew Brzezinski, November 21, 2013.

114. Ibid.

115. Zbigniew Brzezinski, David Ignatius, and Brent Scowcroft, *"America and the World: Conversations on the Future of American Foreign Policy* (New York: Basic Books, 2008).

116. David Ignatius, "Solving the Arab-Israeli Conflict," in Gati, ed. *Zbig,* 181.

117. For Brzezinski's defense in the argument with Obama, see David Ignatius, "Obama Weighs New Peace Plans for the Middle East," *Washington Post,* April 7, 2010.

118. John Mearsheimer and Steve Walt, *The Israel Lobby and U.S. Foreign Policy* (New York: Farrar, Straus and Giroux, 2007).

119. John J. Mearsheimer and Stephen M. Walt, respondents Aaron Friedberg, Dennis Ross, Shlomo Ben-Ami, and Zbigniew Brzezinski, FP Roundtable, "The War over Israel's Influence," *Foreign Policy,* no. 155 (July–August 2006):55–66.

120. Interview with Zbigniew Brzezinski, November 21, 2013.

121. Zbigniew Brzezinski, "The Smart Way Out of a Foolish War," *Washington Post,* March 20, 2008.

122. Q&A with former national security adviser Zbigniew Brzezinski, *The Christian Science Monitor,* February 19, 2011.

123. Jacob Heilbrunn, "Brzezinski on the Syria Crisis," *National Interest,* June 24, 2013, http://nationalinterest.org/commentary/brzezinski-the-syria-crisis-8636; interview with Zbigniew Brzezinski, November 21, 2013.

124. Emile El Hokayem, *Syria's Uprising and the Fracturing of the Levant*, Adelphi Series (London: Routledge, 2013).

125. David Ignatius, "Proceeding with Caution," *Washington Post*, September 10, 2014.

126. Zbigniew Brzezinski, "A Sensible Path on Iran," *Washington Post*, May 27, 2008; "No Rush to War," *New York Times*, September 15, 2012 (a *New York Times* editorial citing The Iran Project); Zbigniew Brzezinski, "The 'Stupidest' War?" *Washington Post*, January 4, 2013.

127. Zbigniew Brzezinski, "US Should Shoot Down IAF Jets," *Jerusalem Post*, September 22, 2009; Zbigniew Brzezinski, "What Richard Cohen Got Wrong About My Views on Iran," *Washington Post*, February 24, 2010.

128. Interview with Zbigniew Brzezinski, "Dim Prospects in Afghanistan," *Christian Science Monitor*, September 8, 2009.

129. Adam Garfinkle, "'I'd Do It Again'—Talking Afghanistan with Zbigniew Brzezinski," *American Interest* (May–June 2008):51, 53–55.

130. Zbigniew Brzezinski, "Moscow's Mussolini," *Wall Street Journal*, September 20, 2004; "Russia, Like Ukraine, Will Become a Real Democracy," *Financial Times*, December 20, 2013.

131. Zbigniew Brzezinski, "Imperial Russia, Vassal Ukraine," *Wall Street Journal*, December 1, 2004.

132. Zbigniew Brzezinski, "Putin's Imperial Designs Are Reminiscent of Stalin's," *New Perspectives Quarterly* 25, no. 4 (Fall 2008):50–52; "Staring Down the Russians," *Time Magazine* 172, no. 8 (August 25, 2008):26.

133. Zbigniew Brzezinski, "How to Avoid a New Cold War," *Time Magazine* 169, no. 25 (June 18, 2007):44; "Russia Must Re-Focus with Post-Imperial Eyes," *Time Magazine* 175, no. 16 (April 26, 2010):1.

134. Zbigniew Brzezinski, "Russia Needs a 'Finland Option' for Ukraine," *Financial Times*, February 23, 2014; "Confronting Russian Chauvinism," remarks presented on a panel at the Woodrow Wilson Center on June 16, *American Interest* (June 27, 2014), http://www.the-american-interest.com/2014/06/27/confronting-russian-chauvinism/; and "Putin's Three Choices," *Washington* Post, July 8, 2014.

135. Zbigniew Brzezinski, "If Russia Joins the G-7, Why Not China?" *New Perspectives Quarterly* 13, no. 1 (Winter 1996):39–41; see also "Living with China," *National Interest*, no. 59 (Spring 2000):5–21.

136. Zbigniew Brzezinski and John Mearsheimer, "The Clash of the Titans," *Foreign Policy*, no. 146 (February 2005):48–49. See also Zbigniew Brzezinski, "Avoiding a New Cold War with China," *New Perspectives Quarterly* 18, no. 3 (Summer 2001):13.

137. Zbigniew Brzezinski, "The Group of Two That Could Change the World," *Financial Times*, January 14, 2009, 9; "How to Stay Friends with China," *Washington Post*, January 3, 2011; and "Giants, but Not Hegemons," *New York Times*, February 14, 2013.

138. Interview by Zachary Keck, September 10, 2012, "The Interview: Zbigniew Brzezinski," *Diplomat*, http://thediplomat.com/2012/09/10/the-interview-zbigniew-brzezinski.

139. Zbigniew Brzezinski, *Strategic Vision: America and the Crisis of Global Power* (New York: Basic Books, 2012). See also "Balancing the East, Upgrading the West: U.S. Grand Strategy in an Age of Upheaval," *Foreign Affairs* 91, no. 1 (January–February 2012):97–104.

140. David Rothkopf, "A Time of Unprecedented Instability? A Conversation with Zbigniew Brzezinski," *Foreign Policy,* July 21, 2014, http://foreignpolicy.com/2014/07/21/a-time-of-unprecedented-instability/.

141. Ibid.

Conclusion

1. Zbigniew Brzezinski and Paul Wasserman, "Why We Need a Trump Doctrine," *New York Times,* February 20, 2017, A19.

2. Zbigniew Brzezinski (@zbig), https://twitter.com/zbig/status/860177803194630144, Twitter, May 4, 2017.

3. The footage of the Nobel Peace Prize Forum Oslo 2016 with Dr. Henry Kissinger and Dr. Zbigniew Brzezinski is available at https://www.csis.org/events/nobel-peace-prize-forum-oslo.

4. Kissinger's prepared remarks are available at http://www.henryakissinger.com/speeches/121116.html. Brzezinski's remarks are not available, but they formed the basis for his article, "How to Address Strategic Insecurity in a Turbulent Age," *Huffington Post,* January 3, 2017, http://www.huffingtonpost.com/entry/us-china-russia-relations_us_586955dbe4b0de3a08f8e3e0.

5. Nobel Peace Prize Forum, https://www.csis.org/events/nobel-peace-prize-forum-oslo.

6. Josh Rogin, "Inside the Kushner Channel to China," *Washington Post,* April 2, 2017.

7. Zbigniew Brzezinski, *The Grand Chessboard: American Primacy and Its Geostrategic Imperatives* (New York: Basic Books, 1997).

8. Zbigniew Brzezinski, "The Group of Two That Could Change the World," *Financial Times,* January 14, 2009, 9. See also Brzezinski, "Toward a Global Realignment," *National Interest* 11, no. (April 2016), https://www.the-american-interest.com/2016/04/17/toward-a-global-realignment/; Nathan Gardels, "Zbigniew Brzezinski: Cooperation on Iran Deal Boosts US-China Ties," *World Post,* April 9, 2015, http://www.huffingtonpost.com/2015/04/09/zbigniew-brzezinski-iran-deal-us-china_n_7036070.html?1428613883.

9. See Bartholomew Sparrow, *The Strategist: Brent Scowcroft and the Call of National Security* (New York: Public Affairs, 2015).

10. Aleksandra Ziółkowska-Boehm, "A Conversation with Zbigniew Brzezinski," in *The Roots Are Polish,* 2nd ed. (Toronto: Canadian-Polish Institute, 2004), http://freepages.genealogy.rootsweb.ancestry.com/~atpc/heritage/articles/aleksandra/roots-brzezinski.html.

Acknowledgments

This book had its origin in a series of discussions with Stanley Hoffmann in 1998. That was when I became aware that Hoffmann had worked side by side at Harvard in the 1950s with Zbigniew Brzezinski, Henry Kissinger, and Samuel Huntington, as well as older figures including McGeorge Bundy and younger ones such as Joseph Nye. Hoffmann's colleagues and friends embodied the intellectual, sociological, and political renewal of American foreign policy during the Cold War. Ten years later, when I was a senior fellow at the Brookings Institution, I received an invitation from Zbigniew Brzezinski to speak about French foreign policy at the monthly lunch on international affairs he hosted at SAIS—a practice he had maintained since his days at Columbia in the 1960s. From that meeting and the many others that followed, a relationship of trust developed between us. Brzezinski agreed to grant me access to his personal archives, which had been deposited in the Library of Congress, and these supplied the foundation for this biography.

Thus it is to Zbigniew Brzezinski himself that I owe thanks first and foremost. This is by no means an "authorized biography," and its subject let me know about his occasional disagreements with my interpretations. But it would not have been as rich had he not opened his archives to me and agreed to be interviewed on many occasions, without asking to review my notes or seeking to impose his way of seeing things. I remain very grateful to him for this. Sam Huntington and Henry Kissinger also agreed to share memories and analyses, as did Stanley Hoffmann and Pierre Hassner, whose friendly support has been precious throughout this project. I cannot list here the dozens of other witnesses who granted me interviews, but I thank them all for their availability. I also benefited from the help of excellent archivists, including Laura Mooney and Sarah Chilton at the Brookings Institution.

Among my own colleagues, I express particular gratitude to David Engerman, a historian at Brandeis who helped me with the Sovietologist Brzezinski of the 1950s and 1960s, and to Jason Rockett and Niall Ferguson at Harvard, with whom I was able to exchange information regarding the biography of Henry Kissinger they were preparing. But many other historians also helped me: David Atkinson on the CFIA, Dino Knudsen on the Trilateral Commission, Jonathan Haslam on the Afghan episode, Nancy Walbridge Collins on the transatlantic aspects, Mark Kramer on Brzezinski during the Cold War, James Mann on the "Chinese" Brzezinski, and Charles Gati on Brzezinski's ties to Eastern Europe. The members of a jury for my *habilitation* (a step in academic careers in France)—Antoine Coppolani, Mario del Pero, Denis Lacorne, Pierre Melandri, Vincent Michelot, and Marc Trachtenberg—all offered extremely valuable remarks on the first version of this work, as did my father, Maurice Vaïsse, on several occasions, and I thank them all.

My interns are the colleagues I am most intent on thanking. They did not all expect to become experts on Zbigniew Brzezinski, but each brought fresh eyes and contributed hard work that helped me write this biography. At the Brookings Institution, I thank Emmanuelle Maitre, Martin Michelot, Hannah Dönges, Rémy Haentjens, and Antonia Doncheva. In Paris, my thanks go to Daniel Montin, Mahaut Chaudouët, and Jean-François Hardy. Their contributions have been extraordinary. I have additionally benefited a great deal from discussions with all the colleagues who took an interest in my work, especially at the Brookings Institution between 2009 and 2011, and most notably Fiona Hill and Jeremy Shapiro.

These acknowledgments would not be complete without a word of affectionate thanks to Marie, Timothée, Alice, and Eleanor. While the family was growing steadily, it also made room for an extra guest who sometimes took up a good deal of space in our universe, but who nevertheless was always well received. Their support allowed me to write this book. Lastly, if the words are mine, they are also, for this English version, those chosen by my translator, Catherine Porter, whom I thank very warmly for our fruitful cooperation and the heavy task she undertook with rigor and good grace.

Index

Aaron, David, 278
Abrams, Elliott, 3, 120
Abshire, David, 360
academia: Cold War University, 4–6, 32–47, 214–215; Brzezinski's professorial positions in, 6, 24–25, 54–55, 63–65, 67–70, 361; student militancy, 8, 21, 108–113, 136; Brzezinski's student years, 19–25; Sovietology as discipline, 25, 27, 35, 40, 68, 74–76, 416n37; federal research grants for, 35–40. *See also* professional elite
Acheson, Dean, 3, 119, 122, 128, 228
Adams, Creighton, 114
Afghanistan: Brzezinski on, 8, 398; Soviet invasion and US support of, 11, 259, 289, 292, 307–310, 346; US strategy post-9 / 11, 389, 393
"Afghanistan: An Aberration or a Symptom?" (Brzezinski), 346
AFL-CIO, 313
Africa. *See specific nations*
Africa and the Communist World (ed. by Brzezinski), 81
AIPAC, 329
Albright, Madeleine: support of Brzezinski, 69–70, 362, 403; on Carter's NSC team, 278; as congressional liaison, 291; on Dukakis's team, 368–369; as Clinton's Secretary of State, 377

Alfred Jurzykowski Foundation prize, 80, 253
Ali, Mohammed, 329
Allen, Richard, 146
Allon, Yigal, 205
Almond, Gabriel, 215
Al Qaeda, 307, 388–389, 392, 398
Alsop, Joseph, 77
Alternative to Partition (Brzezinski), 77, 82–83, 84, 85, 95, 158, 258
"America and Europe" (Brzezinski), 166, 437n38
"America in a Hostile World" (Brzezinski), 450n39
"America in a New World" (Brzezinski), 256–257, 263, 293–294, 300, 314, 325, 450n39
"America in the Technetronic Age" (Brzezinski), 166
American Committee for Peace in Chechnya, 380
American Council of Learned Societies, 36
American Enterprise Institute (AEI), 135
American Federation of Labor and Congress of Industrial Organizations (AFL-CIO), 313
American Political Science Review, 30, 221, 222
American Prospect, The, 391
American-Ukrainian Advisory Committee, 379

American University, 37, 39
Amin, Hafizullah, 307–309
Amnesty International, 255
Andrew W. Mellon Foundation, 40
Angola, 195, 289, 304, 330
Arab Spring, 396
Arafat, Yassar, 390
area studies, as discipline, 4, 5, 34, 35–40.
    See also Cold War University
Arendt, Hannah, 30, 31, 220, 257
Arms Control Export Act (1976), 326
Armstrong, Hamilton Fish, 76
Al-Assad, Bashar, 397
Atlantic Council, 135
atomic weapons. See nuclear weapons
    program
Atwood, Brian, 199
Avineri, Shlomo, 205

Baker, James, 375, 392
Bakhtiar, Shapur, 334–335
Balkan wars, 13, 359, 375, 383, 384, 392
Ball, George, 106, 107, 122, 206, 334
Banfield, Edward, 63, 64
Bartlett, Charles, 77–78
Basic Books, 294
Bator, Francis, 93, 94, 426n82
Bazargan, Mehdi, 335, 336
BBC News, 77
Beckwith, Charles, 337
Beer, Samuel, 25–26, 64
Begin, Menachem, 15–16, 206, 274,
    328–329. See also Camp David Accords
    (1978)
Bell, Daniel, 43–44, 95, 106, 113, 161
Bellow, Saul, 106, 113, 252
Benes, Emilie. See Brzezinski, Emilie Anna
    "Muska" Benes (wife)
Bergsten, C. Fred, 169
Berlin Wall crisis (Germany), 78, 238, 284,
    302, 362, 371–372
Berman, Edward, 36
Berthoin, George, 181
Best and the Brightest, The (Halberstam),
    126

Between Two Ages (Brzezinski), 147, 151,
    158–159, 161–163, 223, 227, 233, 438n57
Bialer, Seweryn, 352
Bilderberg Group, 80, 168–169
Bin Laden, Osama, 373
Black Panther movement, 107–108
Blind Oracles (Kuklick), 215
Bloomfield, Lincoln, 120, 277, 330
Blumenthal, Michael, 319
Blumenthal, Sidney, 142
Bodie, Bernard, 10
Bohlen, Charles, 3, 117, 245
Bondy, François, 106
Bosnia-Herzegovina, 375–377
Boston Globe, 198
Bound to Lead (Nye), 375
Bowie, Robert: as director of CFIA, 5, 23,
    28, 120; at Harvard, 26, 46; relationship
    with Brzezinski, 28–29, 90; relationship
    with Kissinger, 46, 419n112; on Policy
    Planning Council, 92; and Trilateral
    Commission, 165, 169
Brademas, John, 80
Brazil, 331
Brezhnev, Leonid, 74, 230, 302–303, 313, 334
Brookings Institution, 134, 169, 204–205,
    214, 326
Brown, Harold, 248, 274, 286, 288. See also
    Carter administration
Brown, Sam, 108
Bryn Mawr College, 36
Brzezinski, Emilie Anna "Muska" Benes
    (wife), 23–24, 55, 80, 318
Brzezinski, Ian (son), 24, 80, 81, 318
Brzezinski, Mark (son), 24, 80, 81, 318
Brzezinski, Mika (daughter), 139, 274,
    318, 389
Brzezinski, Tadeusz (father), 1, 8, 15,
    16–18, 28
Brzezinski, Zbigniew
—career: overview, 1–2, 147, 408–411; as
    Johnson adviser, 5, 76, 79–80, 92–98,
    426n93; on Policy Planning Council, 5,
    76, 91, 98, 136, 158; at Russian Research
    Center, 5, 42; discrimination against, 5–7,

93, 117, 133, 243; professorial positions of, 6, 24–25, 54–55, 63–65, 67–70, 361; relationship with Pope John Paul II, 8, 251, 313, 331, 467n214; creation of Trilateral Commission by, 11, 12–13, 28, 136, 147, 157, 165–171; as Humphrey adviser, 11, 12, 53, 79, 86, 98, 140; as Obama adviser, 11, 13, 393–394; work for electoral campaigns, 11, 12, 13, 15, 47, 54, 147–156, 368; relationship with Fainsod, 22, 27–28, 48; oratory skills of, 24–25; academic relationships of, 25–29; work on Smolensk archives, 27, 32; as Kennedy adviser, 53–55, 140; and Hoffmann, 55, 107; travels of, 55–59, 67–68, 81, 198, 287, 302, 329; at World Festival of Youth and Students, 60–62; at CFR, 76–77, 84; television appearances of, 77, 139, 283, 316; awards for, 80, 249, 253; on Africa, 81–82, 289, 327; political development of, 117–118; relationship with Vance, 126, 272, 279–285, 287–288, 306, 349–350; Japan residency of, 136, 147, 163–165, 173, 436n24; relationship with Kissinger, 183–192, 404–406, 441n105; anti-Semitism accusations against, 206, 243, 251–252, 328–329; difference between Kissinger and, 224–227, 249, 409; lecture program in Southern colleges, 254–255; criticisms of Trilateral Commission, 320; political intelligence of, 353–357; as Reagan adviser, 360, 367; as SAIS professor and lecturer, 360–361; and Kuklinski, 365, 386–387; at 2016 Nobel Peace Prize Forum, 404–406; as national security adviser for Carter (see Brzezinski, Zbigniew: as national security adviser for Carter)
—correspondence: with Harriman, 5–7; with Hoffmann, 55; with Sorensen, 55; with Bundy, 63; with Kissinger, 114, 183–185; with Humphrey, 148–150, 151, 232; with Carter, 193
—as national security adviser for Carter, 271–357; summary of, 1–2, 10, 157,

339–357; memoirs and record of, 13, 271; role in Israel–Palestine peace negotiations, 15–16, 327–330; relationship with Carter, 246, 272, 273–275, 284; relationship with Vance, 272, 279–285, 287–288, 307, 349–350; National Security Council (NSC) team, 276–279, 348; and Tehran hostage crisis, 280, 291, 292, 297–298, 335–339, 343; major objectives of, 282–283, 294–295, 321; NSC management by, 284–287; and China–US relations, 287, 290, 296–297, 314–320; and new Cold War, 288–293, 343–347; and Soviet-Afghanistan invasion, 289, 292, 307–310, 345–346; human rights policies, 296, 303–304, 322, 330–332, 341–343, 346–351; and Iranian transition of power, 332–335; criticisms of, 348–353. See also Brzezinski, Zbigniew: political opinions; Carter administration
—personal life: early life and education of, 1, 3, 4, 8, 17–19, 240; father of, 1, 8, 15, 16–18, 28; national identity of, 1, 3, 240–244; name of, 3, 17, 55, 109, 131–132, 240–241; birth and death of, 13, 17, 405; and Katyn massacre, 18–19, 371; language skills of, 19, 56; higher education of, 19–25; wife of, 23–24, 55, 80, 318; children of, 24, 80, 81, 251, 274, 318; US citizenship of, 24, 58, 240; Fainsod's eulogy by, 27–28; travels of, 55–59, 67–68, 81, 198; finances of, 80; character of, 244–249, 272, 273, 279; scandal accusations against, 249, 455n154; religion of, 251–252; assassination attempt on, 329; family trip to China, 361
—political opinions: on development of political thought, 8–10, 47, 52, 67; importance and influence of, 10–13; on Iraq War, 13, 373–374, 389–392, 396; on Israel-Palestine conflict, 15–16, 327–330, 394; on Soviet nationalism, 19–21, 237, 258, 260–261, 399; on totalitarianism, 31–32, 70–76; on peaceful engagement policy, 50, 54, 78, 82–87, 258; on Soviet

political opinions (*continued*)
degenerative phases, 73–76, 236; on technetronic revolution, 74–75, 112, 158–163, 233; on Cuban Missile crisis, 78–79, 87–88; on China–US relations, 89–90, 195, 239, 314–320, 362, 400–402, 405; on China–Soviet relations, 89–91, 195, 235, 260–261; on Democratic Party, 101, 106, 148, 149–150, 364; and student protests, 108–113; on Vietnam War, 113–114, 231–232; on Nixon administration policies, 187–188; intellectual arsenal of, 213, 219–228; political predictions by, 228–239, 451n51; Cold War liberal values of, 250–257; on Civil Rights movement, 252–254; geopolitical anti-communist strategy of, 257–269; on America's global engagement, 293–295, 324–328; on Radio Free Europe–Radio Liberty, 300–302, 331; on Afghanistan, 307–311, 398; on Middle East security, 311–312; on Carter's decision making process, 351–352; on global change, 356–357, 407; on Reagan administration, 364–366; on Islamism, 374; on Clinton administration, 375–379; on Poland's democratic transition, 381–383; on NATO expansion, 383–385; on Iran intervention, 391, 397–398; on Trump administration, 403–405; reasons for influence, 406–409. See also *specific regions*
—publications, 12, 77, 222; works about, 10, 11, 95, 161, 244, 372; "Russo-Soviet Nationalism" (thesis), 19–21, 22, 28, 43, 48, 415n22; *The Permanent Purge,* 28–30, 416n48; *The Soviet Bloc,* 46, 50, 56, 77, 158, 226; "Shifts in the Satellites," 48; "U.S. Foreign Policy in East Central Europe," 49–50; "The Politics of Underdevelopment," 52; "Poland—A Political Glimpse," 58; *Ideology and Power in Soviet Politics,* 70; "The Nature of the Soviet System," 71; *Political Power: USA/USSR,* 72–73, 230; "The Soviet Political System," 73–74; *Foreign Affairs*

articles, 76–77, 82, 83, 90, 158, 166, 183, 235, 259, 375; *Alternative to Partition,* 77, 82–83, 84, 85, 95, 158, 258; *Africa and the Communist World,* 81; "Peaceful Engagement in Eastern Europe," 82–84, 94, 185; " 'Neutral' Vietnam a Chinese Backyard," 89; "Threat and Opportunity in the Communist Schism," 90; "Histrionics as History in Transition," 112; *Power and Principle,* 132, 135, 271, 360, 362–364; *Newsweek* articles, 138; *Between Two Ages,* 147, 151, 158–159, 161–163, 223, 227, 233, 438n57; *The Fragile Blossom,* 147, 163–164, 229–230; "America and Europe," 166, 437n38; "America in the Technetronic Age," 166; "New Guidelines for the West," 166, 437n35; "Japan in a Trilateral World," 171; "Cambodia Has Undermined our Vital Credibility," 187; "The Deceptive Structure of Peace," 189; *Foreign Policy* articles, 189, 395, 401, 450n39; *New York Times* articles, 235, 376, 385, 403; *Game Plan,* 237, 369; *The Grand Failure,* 238–239, 369, 375; "America in a New World," 256–257, 263, 293–294, 300, 314, 325; "Tomorrow's Agenda," 259; "Afghanistan: An Aberration or a Symptom?," 346; "Revolution and Counter-Revolution," 356; *Out of Control,* 374; *Strategic Vision,* 375, 401; " 'Never Again'—Except for Bosnia," 376; *The Grand Chessboard,* 380–381, 405; *The Choice,* 392; *Second Chance,* 392, 393; "America in a Hostile World," 450n39; *Totalitarian Dictatorship and Autocracy* [see *Totalitarian Dictatorship and Autocracy* (Brzezinski and Friedrich)]
Buchan, Alastair, 106, 111
Buckley, William, 223
Bundy, McGeorge "Mac": establishment of CFIA and, 5, 23, 46, 127; at Ford Foundation, 5, 106, 147, 163; academic career of, 26; correspondence with Brzezinski, 63; political career of, 78, 122; credentials of, 127

Bundy, William, 105, 119, 129

Bunker, Ellsworth, 114

Burden, William, 80

Bush (G.H.W.) administration, 372–373, 375, 390, 392–393

Bush (G.W.) administration, 390–393

Bush, George H.W., 120, 196–197, 239, 368

Bush, George W., 13, 225, 366

Bush, Vannevar, 41

Calder, Nigel, 161

Cambodia, 187, 289, 318–319, 320, 343

"Cambodia Has Undermined our Vital Credibility" (Brzezinski), 187

Camp David Accords (1978), 280, 282, 296–297, 318, 329. See also Israel–Palestine conflict and negotiations

Camps, Miriam, 222

Canada, 1, 8, 17, 171, 240

Captain's Daughter, The (Pushkin), 19

Carnegie Endowment for International Peace New York, 135, 214, 397

Carnegie Foundation, 5, 36, 41, 42

Carter, Amy, 274

Carter, Hodding, 280–281, 362

Carter, Jimmy: 1976 campaign of, 13, 148, 156, 193–211; as Trilateral Commission member, 192–193, 196, 272–273; correspondence with Brzezinski, 193; Why Not the Best?, 196; relationship with Brzezinski, 246, 272, 273–275, 284, 405; Keeping Faith: Memoirs of a President, 272; family of, 273, 274, 288, 302; on Brzezinski-Vance relations, 281, 283; opinion of State Department, 281–282; 1980 presidential defeat of, 339; Brzezinski on decision making process of, 351–352; on American-Ukrainian Advisory Committee, 379

Carter, Rosalynn, 273, 288, 302

Carter administration: perceived failures and weaknesses of, 10, 339–341, 343–346, 349–353, 362; Panama Canal treaty, 11, 279, 280, 291, 296, 326–327, 341, 342; on Israeli-Palestinian peace negotiations,

194, 202, 204–206; appointments of, 196; Afghanistan support by, 259, 307–309; indecision on Soviet strategy, 279–280, 306–307, 350–351; and Tehran hostage crisis, 280, 291, 292, 297–298, 335–339, 343; leaks of, 280–282, 286; major objectives of, 282–283, 294–295, 321; China–US relations under, 287, 290, 296–297, 314–320, 342; missile program of, 288–293, 340; overview of new Cold War under, 288–293, 306, 343–344; —Congress relations, 291, 344, 349; on human rights, 296, 303–304, 322, 330–332, 341–343, 346–351; PD-30, 296, 330–331; on nuclear weapons development, 297, 305, 312–313, 323, 348, 364; PD-59, 298, 312, 338; Rapid Deployment Joint Task Force, 298, 299, 312, 340, 373; 1980 doctrine of, 299, 310, 311; PRM-10, 299–300, 316; PD-18, 300; PD-21, 302; PRM-9, 302; initial presidential travels of, 321–322; European defensive policies of, 322–324; on Iranian transition of power, 332–335; successes of, 341–343; Brzezinski in (see Brzezinski, Zbigniew: as national security adviser for Carter). See also National Security Council (NSC); SALT (Strategic Arms Limitation Talks)

Carter Doctrine (1980), 299, 310, 311

Casals, Pablo, 255

Casey, William, 338, 367

Castro, Fidel, 78–79, 87, 88, 289

Center for Communist Studies, Columbia University, 65

Center for Strategic and International Studies (CSIS), 135, 360, 381, 405

Central Intelligence Agency. See CIA (Central Intelligence Agency)

CFIA (Center for International Affairs): establishment of, 5, 23, 28, 37, 46, 127; Kissinger's work at, 45–46, 63–64, 144; publications of, 46, 120

CFR. See Council on Foreign Relations (CFR)

Chayes, Abram, 155

Chechnya, 378, 379–380, 398

Chemical Warfare Commission, 367

Cheney, Dick, 390

China:—Vietnam relations, 89, 318–319; —US relations, 89–90, 287, 296–297, 314–320, 342, 345, 400–402, 405; —Cambodia relations, 187, 289, 318; —Soviet relations, 235, 260–261, 290, 407; Tiananmen Square protests, 239, 362, 400; 1972 political transition of, 314; and Taiwan, 317, 319, 362; 1981 Brzezinski family trip in, 361

Choice, The (Brzezinski), 392

Chomsky, Noam, 39

Christopher, Warren, 132, 310, 311, 375

Church, Frank, 290–291

CIA (Central Intelligence Agency): Bowie at, 28; Directorate of Intelligence, 34; establishment of, 35; research funding by, 42, 45; 1956 request to Brzezinski, 59; on Vienna Youth Festival, 60–62; under Carter administration, 284, 291–292, 309–310, 333

Ciolkosz, Adam, 45

Civil Affairs Training Program, 37

Civil Rights movement, 252–254

"The Clash of Civilizations?" (Huntington), 374

Clifford, Clark, 122, 272

Clinton administration: Brzezinski's criticisms of, 375–379, 390, 392–393; foreign policy strategy of, 379–383; on NATO expansion, 383–386, 388; and Kuklinski situation, 386–388

Coalition for a Democratic Majority, 136, 207, 265, 326

Cold War University, 4–6, 32–47, 214–215. See also area studies, as discipline; professional elite

Columbia University: Research Institute on Communist Affairs, 12, 22, 68, 109, 263; and research funding, 36; Brzezinski's position at, 65, 67–68, 361; Center for Communist Studies, 65; student protests at, 108–112; Research Institute on International

Change, 263, 352; Russian Institute (see Russian Institute, Columbia University)

Commentary (journal): prominence of, 106, 138; Gershman in, 140; political stance of, 210, 326; Kirkpatrick in, 257; Brzezinski in, 268–269

Committee on the Present Danger (CPD), 41–42, 136, 207–208, 267

Committee to Defend America by Aiding the Allies, 41

Committee to Maintain a Prudent Defense Policy, 142, 228, 265

communism: Brzezinski on phases of, 50–51, 369–370; and World Festival of Youth and Students, 59–60; in Africa, 81–82. See also totalitarianism

Communist Party, 74

"Comprehensive Net Assessment and Military Force Posture Review" (PRM-10), 299

Comprehensive Nuclear-Test-Ban Treaty (CTBT), 303

Compromised Campus (Diamond), 39–40

Conant, James Bryant, 41

Conference on International Economic Cooperation, 327

Conference on Security and Cooperation Europe, 331

Conference on the Status of Soviet Jews, 252

Confluence (journal), 44–45, 144

Congress for Cultural Freedom, 39, 45, 106, 354

Convergence (theory of convergence between the USA and the USSR), 72–73

Cooper, Richard, 169, 176

Council for Mutual Economic Assistance (CEMA), 223

Council on Foreign Relations (CFR): Brzezinski's connections with, 76–77; establishment of, 118–119, 123; influence of, 121–124; distrust of, 125; and new professional elite, 131, 134. See also Foreign Affairs (journal)

Crimea, 400

Croatia, 375–376

Crozier, Michel, 106

cruise missile program, 297, 312, 324, 340

Cruse, Howard, 107–108

Cuba: US policy on, 72, 246; Cuban Missile Crisis (1962), 78–79, 87–88; Angola interference by, 289, 304, 330; Somalian interference by, 304; Soviet brigade in, 343

Cuban Air Space Peace Patrol, 78–79

Czechoslovakia, 23, 55, 258–259, 313

Czech Republic, 385

Dac, Pierre, 230

Daesh, 392

Dallin, Alexander, 68–69, 109, 254

Dartmouth College, 36

Dayan, Moshe, 205

Dayton Agreement (1995), 377

"The Deceptive Structure of Peace" (Brzezinski), 189

Decter, Moshe, 252

De Gaulle, Charles, 79, 85, 89

Del Pero, Mario, 224, 262–263

Democratic Party: Brzezinski's opinion of, 101, 106, 148, 149–150, 364; partisanship vs. pragmatism, 125–126; in 1972 presidential campaign, 147–156; 1979 split of, 292. See also specific leaders

Denend, Leslie, 278, 330

Deng Xaoping, 239, 274, 297, 316, 318–319, 361

Derian, Patricia, 363

Dershowitz, Alan, 393

Desch, Michael, 214

Détente and Confrontation (Garthoff), 95

Deutscher, Isaac, 32

Diamond, Sigmund, 39

"Dictatorships and Double Standards" (Kirkpatrick), 257

Dillon, Douglas, 2

Dissent (journal), 250

Dobell, Peter, 178

Dobrynin, Anatoly, 202, 243–244, 272, 318, 344

Drew, Elizabeth, 244, 343

Drummond, Roscoe, 77

Dubcek, Alexander, 148

Duchêne, François, 171, 176

Dukakis, Michael, 239, 368–369

Dulles, John Foster, 49–50

Dynamics of Soviet Society, The (Rostow), 35, 43

Eagleburger, Lawrence, 190, 272

"East-West Discourse" (Johnson), 93–94

Eban, Abba, 205

Eckstein, Harry, 63, 64

economic crises, 292

Egypt, 248–249, 321, 329, 396. See also Camp David Accords (1978)

Eisenhower, Dwight, 39, 49, 68

Eisenhower administration, 54, 258, 395

Eizenstat, Stuart, 197, 200, 205

electoral campaigns, 143–156. See also specific candidates and advisers

Elliott, William Yandell, 25–26, 44, 46, 144

Ellsberg, Daniel, 40

El Salvador, 290, 343

Encounter (journal), 166

End of History, The (Fukuyama), 374

energy crisis, 292, 324

Engerman, David, 40

Erhard, Ludwig, 95

Ermarth, Fritz, 248, 277

Establishment, 2–3, 121–130. See also professional elite

Ethiopia, 246, 289, 304

Euromissiles program, 323–324, 346, 365, 366

Evans, Daniel, 192

Fainsod, Merle, 22, 27–28, 43, 48

Fairlie, Henry, 121

Ferkiss, Victor, 161

Fisk University, 255

Fletcher School, Tufts University, 37

Ford, Gerald, 177, 199–200

Ford administration, 139, 323, 390

Forden, David, 387

Ford Foundation: Bundy at, 5, 106, 147, 163; research funding by, 36, 37, 40, 163

Foreign Affairs (journal): Brzezinski in, 76–77, 82, 83, 90, 158, 166, 183, 259, 375; founding of, 123; Kissinger in, 144, 183; review of books by Brzezinski, 161, 363. *See also* Council on Foreign Relations (CFR)

Foreign Policy (magazine): establishment and coverage of, 135, 138, 141–142; Brzezinski in, 189, 395, 401; on "Carter syndrome," 339

"The Forgotten Region" (Gati), 139

Fourteen Points, 33

Fox, William, 137

Foxman, Abraham, 393

Fragile Blossom, The (Brzezinski), 147, 163–164, 229–230

France, 79, 85, 89, 181

Franklin, George, 170

Freedom House, 135, 142, 255

French Revolution, 356

Fried, Edward, 134

Friedrich, Carl, 26; relationship with Brzezinski, 26–27; positions of, 28, 37, 41; political opinions of, 31, 46; correspondence with Brzezinski, 71; *Totalitarian Dictatorship and Autocracy* [see *Totalitarian Dictatorship and Autocracy* (Brzezinski and Friedrich)]

From the Shadows (Gates), 309

Fukuyama, Francis, 374

Fulbright grant program, 45

Furet, François, 106

G7 Summit, 321, 330, 379, 382

G8 Summit, 378

Gaddafi, Muammar, 289, 396

Gaddis, John Lewis, 352

Galbraith, John Kenneth, 106, 113, 121

Game Plan (Brzezinski), 237, 369

game theory, 215

Gardner, Richard, 100, 152, 169, 195–196, 201

Garthoff, Raymond, 95

Gates, Robert, 247, 248–249, 278, 302, 405; *From the Shadows,* 309

Gati, Charles, 139, 248, 250

Gati, Toby, 248

Gelb, Leslie: political opinions of, 3, 120; on new professional elite, 130, 133, 142; and Brzezinski, 247–248, 266, 280–281

generational approach to historical interpretation, 118–122

Georgetown University, 360

German Marshall Fund of the United States, 135–136

Germany: in WWII, 16; armament of, 53; Berlin Wall crisis, 78, 238, 302, 362, 371–372; Östpolitik, 82, 96, 187, 190, 261, 322; US policy on reunification of, 87, 93–96, 244; on US human rights policies, 322

Gerschenkron, Alexander, 26, 41, 112

Gershman, Carl, 140–141, 262

G.I. Bill of Rights (1944), 131

Gillespie, John, 30

Ginzburg, Alexander, 332

Glad, Betty, 286, 343, 468n251

Goldberg, Arthur, 331

Goldgeier, James, 383

Goldman, Guido, 136

Goldwater, Barry, 130, 201

Gomułka, Władysław, 32, 53

Gorbachev, Mikhail, 19, 238, 369

Governability of Democracies, The (1975 report), 180

government research funding, 35–43

Grand Chessboard, The (Brzezinski), 380–381, 405

Grand Failure, The (Brzezinski), 238–239, 369, 375

Grass, Günter, 106

Grenada, 290

Griffith, William, 81, 83–84, 191, 228, 258, 262

Gromyko, Andrei, 296

Groton ethic, 126

Grudzinski, Gustaw Herling, 45

Guatemala, 290

Guggenheim Foundation, 72
Gulf War (1990–1991), 372–373, 375
Gullion, Ed, 136

Haganah (Defense), 16
Haig, Alexander, 380
Haimson, Leopold, 254, 255
Halberstam, David, 99–100, 122, 131, 146;
    The Best and the Brightest, 126
Haldeman, H. R., 284
Halperin, Morton, 46, 120, 134, 139, 153
Hamilton, Lee H., 392
Harriman, Averell: in *The Wise Men,* 3;
    correspondence and discrimination
    against Brzezinski, 5–7, 93, 133; as Carter's
    adviser, 208–209, 284; description of
    Brzezinski, 247
Harrington, Michael, 60, 113
Harvard University: international affairs
    department of, 4, 5; Brzezinski's student
    years at, 21–25; as a Cold War University,
    33, 35, 37, 40–41; and research funding,
    35, 36; military training programs at, 41;
    International Seminar program, 44–45,
    144; Russian Research Center (*see* Russian
    Research Center, Harvard University)
Haslam, Jonathan, 307, 464n134
Hassner, Pierre, 86, 91, 106, 176, 228–229,
    245–246
Havel, Vaclav, 384
Helms, Jesse, 130
Helsinki Accords (1975), 342
Helsinki Youth Festival (1962), 62
Heritage Foundation, 135
Hilsman, Roger, 109
"Histrionics as History in Transition"
    (Brzezinski), 112
Hitler, Adolf, 18, 40. *See also* Nazi Germany
Hoagland, Jim, 249, 363
Hodgson, Godfrey, 128, 138
Hoffmann, Stanley: early life and education
    of, 4, 9; at CFIA, 46; and Brzezinski, 55,
    107, 222; academic career of, 63,
    112; political career of, 120; description
    of, 246

Hofstadter, Richard, 68
Holborn, Fred, 53
Holbrooke, Richard, 139, 202, 272, 281, 316,
    383–385
Holocaust Museum, 384
Hoover Institution, Stanford University,
    36, 135
Horn of Africa. *See specific nations*
Howard, Michael, 216
Howe, Irving, 106, 250
How Russia Is Ruled (Fainsod), 27
How the Soviet System Works (Refugee
    Interview Project report), 43–44
Hua Guofeng, 316
Hua Huang, 24–25
Hughes, Emmet, 99, 185
Hughes, Thomas, 135
humanism *vs.* power realism, 268,
    314–315, 320
human rights policies of Carter, 296,
    303–304, 322, 330–332, 341–343,
    346–351
Humphrey, Hubert: Brzezinski as adviser
    to, 11, 12, 53, 79, 86, 98–103; presidential
    campaigns of, 99–102, 106, 147–148,
    151–152, 195; on Vietnam War, 103–105;
    correspondence with Brzezinski, 148–150,
    151, 232
Hungary: Soviet rule of, 49, 73; Hungarian
    Uprising (1956), 51, 62, 258; as
    independent nation, 302, 370, 378; in
    NATO, 384, 385
Hunter, Robert, 277
Huntington, Samuel: education of, 4;
    political career of, 10, 120, 179, 277, 315;
    Brzezinski's friendship and work with,
    12, 23, 111–112, 353; academic career of,
    23, 26, 63, 65–66; and Friedrich, 26; *The
    Soldier and the State,* 26; at CFIA, 46,
    100; *Political Power: USA/USSR,* 72–73;
    and PRM-10, 299, 315–316; "The Clash
    of Civilizations?," 374
Husak, Gustav, 148
Hussein, Saddam, 335, 372, 389–391
Huyser, Robert, 335

Ideology and Foreign Affairs (CFIA report), 46
Ideology and Power in Soviet Politics
    (Brzezinski), 70
Ignatius, David, 393, 394
Ikota, Saburo, 169
Independent Research Service, 39, 62
Independent Service for Information on the
    Vienna Youth Festival (ISI), 60–63
Inderfurth, Rick, 278
India, 401, 407
Inkeles, Alex, 31, 43
Innis, Roy, 108
"The Inquiry" project (Wilson), 4, 33,
    123, 214. *See also* Cold War University;
    Establishment
Institute for Applied Systems Analysis, 97
Institute for Policy Studies (IPS), 135
Intelligence Advisory Board, 367
International Association for Cultural
    Freedom, 106
International Institute for Strategic Studies
    (IISS), 170, 237
international relations, as discipline, 3,
    4–5
International Seminar program (Harvard),
    44–45, 144
Interplay (journal), 169–170
Iran: 1978–1979 Revolution, 111, 297, 318,
    333; US embassy hostage crisis in, 280,
    291, 292, 297–298, 335–339, 343; transition
    of power in, 333–335, 351; Brzezinski on
    US intervention in, 391, 397–398; nuclear
    weapons program of, 397–398
Iran-Contra affair (1986), 342, 366, 367
Iran-Iraq War, 335, 338
Iraq: Iraq War (2003–2011), 13, 391–392,
    396;—Iran War, 335, 338; US invasion of,
    373–374, 389–391
Irgun, 16, 206
Isaacson, Walter, 3, 122, 129
ISIS (the Islamic State), 392, 396, 397
Islamism, 374, 392, 397
Israel: Likud party in, 15, 296; pro-Israel
    lobby, 204, 266, 278, 328–329, 393–395;
    US military aid for, 329

Israel–Egypt peace process. *See* Camp
    David Accords (1978)
Israel–Palestine conflict and negotiations:
    Brzezinski's position on, 15–16,
    327–330, 394; Johnson administration
    on, 97; Yom Kippur War, 177, 289;
    Carter administration on, 194, 202,
    204–206, 296, 327–330; Bush (G.W.)
    administration on, 390, 391; Clinton
    administration on, 390, 392; Bush
    (G.H.W.) administration on, 392; Obama
    administration on, 394; decoupling from
    Israel–Egypt process, 468n248. *See also*
    Camp David Accords (1978)

Jabotinsky, Vladimir, 16
Jackson, Henry "Scoop," 135, 195, 261,
    265–266
Jackson-Vanik amendment to the Trade Act
    (1974), 265–266, 326
Japan: Brzezinski's residency and work on,
    136, 147, 163–165, 173, 436n24; *The Fragile
    Blossom*, 147, 163–164; nuclear weapons
    program of, 164;—US relations, 164–165,
    325; Brzezinski's political opinions
    on, 320, 438n57. *See also* Trilateral
    Commission
"Japan in a Trilateral World" (Brzezinski),
    171
Jauvert, Vincent, 307–308
Jelenski, Constantin, 106
Jervis, Robert, 46
John Paul II (pope), 8, 251, 313, 331, 467n214
Johns Hopkins University, 37, 360
Johnson, Hewlett, 21
Johnson, Lyndon B.: "East-West Discourse"
    speech by, 93–96, 426n93; presidential
    campaign of, 122, 140
Johnson administration: Brzezinski and, 5,
    76, 79–80, 91, 92–98, 136, 158; Rostow as
    national security adviser in, 35, 123; on
    Germany reunification, 87, 93–96, 244;
    Vietnam policy of, 89, 91, 98–99, 215–216
Joji Watanuke, 180
Jones, George W., 254–255

Jordan, Hamilton, 196, 197, 200, 246–247
Journal of International Affairs, 49
Journal of Politics, 30, 163

Kahn, Herman, 163, 233
Kahn, Tom, 113
Kaiser, Karl, 46
Kakuei Tanaka, 176
Kalb, Marvin, 16
Kampelman, Max, 150, 152, 207, 264, 265, 266
Kaplan, Fred, 215
Karpovich, Michael, 31
Katyn massacre (1941), 18–19, 371, 399
Katz, Barry, 37
Katz, Milton, 58
Kaysen, Karl, 106
Keeping Faith: Memoirs of a President (Carter), 272
Kemble, Penn, 113, 265
Kennan, George, 3, 31, 35, 50, 92, 107
Kennedy, Edward "Ted," 100–101, 154, 194, 250–251, 292–293
Kennedy, John F., 47, 53–55, 140, 250
Kennedy, Paul, 374
Kennedy, Robert, 62, 99
Kennedy administration: appointments by, 2, 5, 122; on aid to Poland, 53; national security advisers of, 78; and Cuban Missile Crisis, 78–79, 87–88
"Kennedy's Brain Trust" (Novak), 54–55
Kerr, Clark, 38, 113–114
KGB (Komitet Gosudarstvennoy Bezopasnosti), 60. *See also* Soviet Union (1922–1991)
Khomeini, Ayatollah, 333, 335–337, 343
Khrushchev, Nikita, 51, 54, 58, 78–79, 87–88
Kiel Institute for World Economics, 169
King, Martin Luther, Jr., 252, 253
Kinhide Mushakoji, 171, 176
Kirk, Grayson, 68
Kirkland, Lane, 313
Kirkpatrick, Jeane, 257, 262, 332, 376
Kissinger, Henry: positions of, 3, 5, 10, 23; early life and education of, 4, 9;

importance and influence of, 10–11, 130, 132, 348; academic relationships of, 26, 28, 360; and International Seminar program, 44, 45; as editor of *Confluence,* 44–45; at CFIA, 45–46, 63–64, 84, 120; *The Necessity for Choice,* 46, 126; relationship with Bowie, 46, 419n112; mutual accommodation policy, 50; *Troubled Partnership,* 77, 87; description of, 99–100, 217–218; correspondence with Brzezinski, 114, 183–185; in Wise Men group, 120, 128–129; and 1968 electoral campaign, 143–147, 154; *Nuclear Weapons and Foreign Policy,* 144; relationship with Nixon, 145, 275–276, 284; "year of Europe" speech by, 174–175; relationship with Brzezinski, 183–192, 404–406, 441n105; on personal politics and office, 213, 306; "Metternich, Castlereagh, and the Problems of Peace, 1812–1822," 217; difference between Brzezinski and, 224–227, 249, 407; *The White House Years,* 363; *Years of Upheaval,* 363; on American-Ukrainian Advisory Committee, 379; as Trump aid, 404; at 2016 Nobel Peace Prize Forum, 404–406
Kleiman, Robert, 114
Kluckhohn, Clyde, 39, 43
Kohl, Helmut, 388
Kohnstamm, Max, 169, 174, 176–177
Kosovo, 377–378
Kosygin, Alexei, 74
Kozminski, Jerzy, 383, 385, 386–387
Kravchuk, Leonid, 379
Kristol, Irving, 181, 182
Kuchma, Leonid, 379
Kuklick, Bruce, 215–216, 217
Kuklinski, Ryszard, 365, 386–387
Kulikov, Marshal Victor, 387–388
Kuwait, 372–373

Lake, Anthony, 133, 152, 153, 383, 385
Laqueur, Walter, 46
leaks, 280–282, 286
Lehman, Herbert, 55

Lenin, Vladimir, 160, 226, 369, 371. *See also* Marxist-Leninist ideology
Leontief, Wassily, 26, 41, 54
Lerner, Daniel, 215
Lewis, Flora, 363
Life Magazine, 361
Likud party, 15, 296
Linowitz Commission, 277
Lipset, Seymour Martin, 113, 209–210
Lodge, Henry Cabot, 122
Long March of Mao Zedong, 361
Lovett, Robert: description of, 2; in Wise Men group, 3, 119, 122, 124, 125, 245; on Brzezinski, 7
Lowen Rebecca, 38
Lublin, Poland, 58–59

Maariv (newspaper), 205
Mackinder, Halford, 380
Madden Commission, 19
Majdamek concentration camp, Poland, 58–59
Malenkov, Georgy, 51
Al-Maliki, Nuri, 392, 396
Manhattan Project, 4, 34, 41, 124
Mann, James, 316, 318, 390
Mannheim, Karl, 118
Manshel, Warren Demian, 138
Mao Zedong, 260–261, 361
Marshall, George, 92
Marshall Plan, 52, 134
Marxist-Leninist ideology, 19, 24, 50, 52, 160, 162. *See also* communism; Lenin, Vladimir
Mathews, Jessica Tuchman, 248, 277, 330, 397
Matlock, Jack, 371
Mavrinac, Albert, 64, 248
Mazowiecki, Tadeusz, 370
McCarthy, Eugene, 99
McCloy, John, 3, 28, 121
McGill University, 8, 19–21
McGovern, George, 120, 151, 154–155, 201–202
McHenry, Donald, 362
McLuhan, Marshall, 160

McNamara, Robert, 2, 39, 92, 127, 215, 216
McPherson, Harry, 92–93
Mead, Walter Russell, 339
Mearsheimer, John, 393–394, 400
Meese, Ed, 367
Meet the Press (television show), 77, 316
"Metternich, Castlereagh, and the Problems of Peace, 1812–1822" (thesis by Kissinger), 217
Meyer, Cord, 61
Miles College, 254–255
military training programs, 36–37, 41
Miller, Arthur, 252
Milošević, Slobodan, 375–378
Minutemen missiles, 340
MIT (Massachusetts Institute of Technology), 35, 42–43
Mitchell, George, 394
Molotov-Ribbentrop Pact, 346, 355
Mondale, Walter, 206, 272, 315, 363. *See also* Carter administration
Monde, Le, 176
Monnet, Jean, 172, 181
Monroe Doctrine (1823), 326
Moore, Barrington, 26, 31, 43
Morgenthau, Hans, 4–5, 139
Morning Joe (television show), 139
Moscow. *See* Soviet Union (1922–1991)
Moscow Youth Festival, 59–60
Motoo Kaji, 176
Moyers, Bill, 92–93
Moynihan, Daniel Patrick "Pat," 199, 253
MSNBC, 139
Multiple Aim Points system, 292
Murphy, Robert, 122
Muskie, Edmund, 151–154, 194, 286–287, 338
Mutual and Balanced Force Reductions (MBFR), 303, 312
MX-Trident missile program, 305, 340

Namibia, 327, 343
Nation, The, 391
National Committee for a Political Settlement in Vietnam, 113–114

National Endowment for Democracy, 140, 256

National Front for the Liberation of Angola (FNLA), 289

National Security Act (1947), 284

national security adviser, overview of position, 347–348

National Security Council (NSC): NSC-68, 41–42, 207, 299; under Nixon administration, 132, 198; Brzezinski's management of, 276–279, 284–287, 348; creation of, 284; role of national security adviser, 347–348

National Security Council–Defense Department Commission on Integrated Long-Term Strategy, 367

National Student Association, 60

National Union for the Total Independence of Angola (UNITA), 289

NATO: expansion of, 11, 45, 383–386, 388; Eastern European participation in, 13, 372, 399, 400; creation of, 198; on Euromissiles and defense program of, 300, 312, 323–324, 346, 365, 366; and Serbian incidents, 375–378; Brzezinski on support of Iraq War, 391

NATO in Transition (Stanley), 77

NATO-Russia Act (1997), 385

"The Nature of the Soviet System" (Brzezinski), 71

Nazi Germany, 16

Necessity for Choice, The (Kissinger), 46, 126

Netanyahu, Benjamin, 395

Netanyahu, Yonatan, 206

Neumann, Sigmund, 31

Neustadt, Richard, 79, 348

" 'Neutral' Vietnam a Chinese Backyard" (Brzezinski), 89

neutron bomb development, 297, 305, 323, 348, 364

" 'Never Again'—Except for Bosnia" (Brzezinski), 376

New Deal (FDR), 33

"New Guidelines for the West" (Brzezinski), 166, 437n35

New Leader, The (journal), 171, 204, 252

New Republic, The (magazine), 48, 77, 108, 235, 356, 377

Newsweek, 95, 138, 151, 175, 316

New Yorker, 244

New York Herald Tribune, 77

New York Review of Books, 181

New York Times: on Brzezinski's books, 50, 163, 363, 364, 374; Brzezinski in, 77, 235, 376, 385, 405; on Johnson, 102, 136–137; on Princeton Seminar program, 106; influence of, 138; on Brzezinski, 161; on Trilateral Commission, 174, 176, 177; on Carter, 199, 202, 204, 209

Nicaragua, 290, 366

Niebuhr, Reinhold, 113

Nitze, Paul, 92, 138, 207–210, 227, 451n59

Nixon, Richard: relationship with Kissinger, 3, 275–276, 284; presidential campaign of, 101–102, 105–106, 145

Nixon administration: NSC under, 132; and Watergate, 155–156, 177; policies on Asia, 165, 174–175, 186–188; NSSM3, 299. See also Kissinger, Henry

Nobel Peace Prize Forum (2016), 406–408

Nora, Simon, 106

Nouvel Observateur, Le, 307

Novak, Robert, 54–55

Nowak, Jan, 16, 242, 261, 262, 383, 385–386

NSC-68 (Nitze), 41–42, 207, 299

NSSM3 (Nixon-Kissinger), 299

Nuclear Weapons and Foreign Policy (Kissinger), 144

nuclear weapons program: development of, 4, 34, 41, 124; of NATO, 85, 300, 312, 323–324, 346, 365, 366; of Japan, 164; of Carter administration, 288–293, 340, 343–344; neutron bomb development, 297, 305, 323, 340, 348, 364; PD-59, 298, 312; CTBT, 303; of Reagan administration, 313, 366–367; of Ford administration, 323; of Soviet Union, 323; of Iran, 397–398. See also SALT (Strategic Arms Limitation Talks)

Nye, Joseph, 46, 375

Oakes, John, 108

Obama, Barack, 239, 391, 393, 408

Obama administration: Brzezinski as adviser to, 11, 13, 393–394; Mead on, 339; conclusion of Iraq War, 392, 396; Middle East policy of, 394, 395–397; US-Russia relations under, 398–400

Odom, William, 247, 276–278, 299, 304, 326

Ogueri, Eze, 248

oil industry, 177, 198, 298, 299, 373

Oksenberg, Michael, 287, 314, 317

Olympic Games boycott (Moscow), 298, 310, 341

Operation Eagle Claw (1980), 337–338

Operation Rolling Thunder (1965–1968), 99, 103–105, 146, 215

Operation Thunderbolt (1976), 205–206, 338

Organization for Economic Co-operation and Development (OECD), 85, 223

Organization of American States, 78–79

Origins of Totalitarianism, The (Arendt), 30, 31

OSS (Office of Strategic Services), 34, 37

Östpolitik, 82, 96, 187, 190, 261, 322

Out of Control (Brzezinski), 374

Owen, Henry, 92, 134, 165, 169, 208–209

Oxford University, 21–22

Pahlavi, Mohammad Reza Shah, Shah of Iran, 333

Pakistan, 259, 310, 311, 345, 350

Panama Canal treaty, 11, 279, 280, 291, 296, 326–327, 341, 342

Papandreou, Andreas, 107

partisanship vs. pragmatism, 125–126

Pastor, Robert, 286, 347

PD-18 (Carter), 300

PD-21 (Carter), 302

PD-30 (Carter), 296, 330–331

PD-59 (Carter), 298, 312, 338

Peace Corps, 198

"Peaceful Engagement in Eastern Europe" (Brzezinski), 82–84, 94, 185

peaceful engagement policy with Eastern Europe, 50, 54, 78, 82–87, 94, 258

Pentagon Papers, 129

People's Movement for the Liberation of Angola (MPLA), 289

Peres, Shimon, 205–206

Peretz, Martin, 106, 108

Perle, Richard, 141–142, 228

Permanent Purge, The (Brzezinski), 28–30, 416n48

Petraeus, David, 392

Phillips, Kevin, 149

Pilsudski, Joseph, 17, 18

Pincus, Walter, 62, 63

Pipes, Richard, 41, 43

Playboy, 362

pluralism, 31, 71, 159, 221, 223, 243, 293, 450n39

Podhoretz, Norman, 106, 113

Poindexter, John, 367

Poland: Brzezinski's heritage from, 1, 3, 240–244; WWII violence in, 16, 18–19; as post-communist nation, 32, 48; 1956 political uprisings in, 51; Brzezinski's visits to, 58–59; Brzezinski's changing opinion on, 72, 370, 372, 381; anti-Semitism in, 252; Solidarity union movement, 298, 313, 365, 368, 370, 396; US support of, 298, 313–314, 381, 386; 1981 military coup in, 365; 1987 G.H.W. Bush trip to, 368; support of Brzezinski as president of, 381–382; in NATO, 385; 2010 plane crash, 399

"Poland—A Political Glimpse" (Brzezinski), 58

Polish-American Congress, 243, 383, 385

Polish-American Enterprise Fund, 381

Polish Institute of Arts and Sciences in America, 243, 252

Politburo, 40, 79, 88, 344, 346

Political Power: USA/USSR (Brzezinski and Huntington), 72–73, 230

Politics among Nations (Morgenthau), 4

"The Politics of Underdevelopment" (Brzezinski), 52

Popieluszko, Jerzy, 368
Portugal, 266
Powell, Colin, 390
Powell, Jody, 200, 274, 278
Power and Principle (Brzezinski), 132, 135,
    271, 360, 362–364
power realism *vs.* planetary humanism, 268,
    314–315, 320
pragmatism, 125–126
Pravda (newspaper), 55
Princeton University, 64, 124; 1968
    Seminars, 106–107, 108, 185
PRM-9, 302
PRM-10, 299–300, 316
Problems of Communism (journal), 32, 73,
    74, 236
professional elite: Cold War University,
    4–6, 32–47, 214–215; emergence
    of, 120–122, 128–129; new class of,
    130–140, 453n122; as "foreign policy
    establishment," 140–143; and electoral
    campaigns, 143–156. *See also* academia;
    Establishment
Project Camelot, 38–39
Project Troy, 42–43
Prosterman, Roy, 114
Public Interest, The, 138, 181
purges, Brzezinski on, 28–29
Putin, Vladimir, 379–380, 388, 399–400
Pye, Lucian, 120, 215

Quandt, William, 135, 245, 278
Quinn, Sally, 455n154

Rabi, Isidor, 68
Rabin, Yitzhak, 205
racism, 107–108
Radio Berlin, 18
Radio Free Europe, 16, 83; Radio Liberty,
    8, 187, 188, 191, 260–262, 300–302, 322,
    331; Polish branch, 383. *See also* Voice of
    America
RAND Corporation, 27, 35, 139, 144, 214
Rapid Deployment Joint Task Force, 298,
    299, 312, 340, 373

Reagan, Ronald, 225, 264, 292–293, 298
Reagan administration: nuclear weapons
    program of, 313, 366–367; early
    presidential program of, 341–342; Iran-
    Contra affair, 342, 366, 367; —China
    relations, 362; Brzezinski on, 364–367
Redmon, Hayes, 92
Refugee Interview Project, 28, 43–44
Reischauer, Edwin, 104, 178
Republican Party, 125–126, 147–156. *See also
    specific leaders*
Research Institute on Communist Affairs
    (RICA), Columbia University, 12, 22, 68,
    109, 263
Research Institute on International Change,
    Columbia University, 263, 352
Reuther, Walter, 113
"Revolution and Counter-Revolution"
    (Brzezinski), 356
Revolutionary Youth Movement, 109–110
Rhodesia (Zimbabwe), 289, 327, 343
Rielly, John, 100, 105
Rise and Fall of the Great Powers, The
    (Kennedy), 374
Roberts, Henry, 68, 255
Roberts, Priscilla, 118
Robin, Ron, 39
Robinson, Geroid, 31, 34, 42
Roche, John, 92–93, 136
Rockefeller, David: role in Trilateral
    Commission, 6, 125, 157, 165–166, 168–169,
    437n34; as friend of Brzezinski, 80
Rockefeller, Nelson, 99–100, 120, 144
Rockefeller Brothers Fund, 144
Rockefeller Foundation, 5, 36
Rogers, William, 128–129, 132
Roosevelt (FDR) administration, 6, 18,
    33, 41
Root, Elihu, 123
Rosovsky, Henry, 23, 24, 222, 252
Rostow, Eugene, 58, 207, 265
Rostow, Walt: education of, 4; *The
    Dynamics of Soviet Society,* 35, 43; political
    career of, 35, 120, 123, 216; academic
    career of, 136, 360

Round Table Agreement (1989), 370

Rovere, Richard, 121, 430n8

Rumania, 200, 302, 378, 382

Rumsfeld, Donald, 389, 398

Rusk, Dean, 2, 92, 93, 96, 119, 128, 144

Russia: Brzezinski's prejudice against, 8, 213, 243; and Chechnya, 378, 379–380, 398; and Ukraine, 378, 379, 382, 398, 399; inclusion in NATO, 386; Obama–Putin era of relations, 398–400; —China relations, 407. *See also* Soviet Union (1922–1991)

Russian Institute, Columbia University: leaders of, 22, 31, 34, 35; establishment of, 36, 42; research funding by, 67; Brzezinski's description of, 68–69

Russian Research Center, Harvard University: establishment of, 5, 27, 42; Brzezinski's work at, 22–23; Refugee Interview Project, 28, 43–44; funding and direction of, 39–40, 42

Russian Review, 50

"Russo-Soviet Nationalism" (thesis by Brzezinski), 19–21, 22, 28, 43, 48, 415n22

Rustin, Bayard, 113

Sacks, Milton, 114

Sadat, Anwar, 274, 296, 303, 328, 329. *See also* Camp David Accords (1978)

Sakharov, Andrei, 303, 330, 347

SALT (Strategic Arms Limitation Talks): ratification of SALT II, 11, 291, 306, 314; and Smith, 169; Kissinger on, 190; as 1978 critical issue, 279, 295, 296, 298; and Vance, 279, 282, 302–303, 344–345; and NSC management, 285; challenges to ratifications of, 291–292, 305–307, 323, 349–350; 1979 conclusion of, 297, 342; Brezhnev on, 302; linkages of, 304–305; Reagan's respect of, 341

Salzburg Seminars, 45

SART (Strategic Arms Reduction Talks), 295

Saudi Arabia:—Pakistan relations, 311; economic power of, 320;—US relations, 329, 332; Persian Gulf security by, 332, 373

Savimbi, Jonas, 289

Scammon, Richard, 149

Schecter, Jerry, 278

Scheer, Robert, 80–81

Schelling, Thomas, 4, 46, 100, 120, 215

Schindler, Alexander, 329

Schlesinger, Arthur, 25

Schlesinger, Arthur, Jr., 25, 45, 106, 107, 108, 113, 127, 144

Schlesinger, James, 23, 135, 272, 287, 360

Schmidt, Helmut, 203, 312, 322–323, 324

School of Advanced International Studies (SAIS), Johns Hopkins University, 37, 360, 361

School of International Service, American University, 37

Schultz, George, 366, 367, 376

Scowcroft, Brent, 198, 390

Second Chance (Brzezinski), 392, 393

Segre, Claudio, 176

Senate Commission on External Relations, 46

Senate Foreign Relations Committee, 53, 79

September 11, 2001 attacks, 307, 366, 388–389

Serbia, 375–378

Serfaty, Simon, 231

Servan-Schreiber, Jean-Jacques, 106

Shelepin, Alexander, 60

"Shifts in the Satellites" (Brzezinski), 48

Shulman, Marshall: academic career of, 7, 100; reputation of, 141, 151; political opinions of, 234, 303, 345, 354, 386

Sick, Gary, 333, 338, 354

Sigmund, Paul, 61

Simmons College, 25

Slavic Review, 71

Slocombe, Walter, 310

Smith, Gerard C., 169–170, 172, 173

Smolensk archives, 27, 32

Smolensk under Soviet Rule (Fainsod), 27

Social Democrats, USA (SDUSA), 142, 266

Soldier and the State, The (Huntington), 26

Solidarity Union (Poland), 298, 313, 365, 368, 370, 396

Somalia, 289, 290, 304, 311, 376

Sonnenfeldt, Helmut, 446n192
Sorensen, Ted, 54–55
South Africa, 289, 327, 343, 366
Southern Rhodesia (Zimbabwe), 289, 327, 343
Soviet Bloc, The (Brzezinski), 46, 50, 56, 77, 158, 226, 234–235
Sovietology as discipline, 25, 27, 35, 40, 68, 74–76, 416n37
"The Soviet Political System" (Brzezinski), 73–74
Soviet Union (1922–1991): Katyn massacre by, 18–19, 371; Brzezinski's on nationalism in, 19–21, 237, 258, 260–261; Stalin's death and de-Stalinization policy of, 30, 31–32, 48, 71; Politburo, 40, 79, 88, 344, 346; World Festival of Youth and Students, 59–60; degenerative phase of, 73–76, 236, 369–371; and Cuban Missile Crisis, 78–79, 87–88; US elections influence of, 202–203; and new Cold War, 288–293; Afghanistan invasion of, 289, 292, 307–310, 346; military assistance by, 289, 304; Olympic Games boycott, 298, 310, 341; US sanctions against, 310; nuclear program of, 323; Molotov-Ribbentrop Pact, 346, 355. *See also* Russia; SALT (Strategic Arms Limitation Talks); *and specific leaders*
Soviet Vulnerability Project, 43
Spectator, The (journal), 121
Sperber, Manès, 106
Srebrenica massacre (1995), 377
SS20 missile program, 323
Stalin, Joseph: purges by, 17; -US relations, 18; war crimes by, 18–19; death and de-Stalinization policy of Soviet Union, 30, 31–32, 48, 71
Stanford University, 36, 38, 42, 135
Stanley, Timothy, 77
Steinem, Gloria, 60, 62
Stern, Fritz, 255
Stevenson, Adlai, 23, 282–283
Stimson, Henry, 2, 124
Stone, Shepard, 80, 106

Strategic Arms Limitation Talks. *See* SALT (Strategic Arms Limitation Talks)
Strategic Defense Initiative, 366–367
Strategic Vision: America and the Crisis of Global Power (Brzezinski), 375, 401
student militancy, 8, 21, 108–113, 136
Students for a Democratic Society, 108, 109
Sullivan, William, 333, 351
Suri, Jeremy, 40, 275, 325
surveillance, 275–276, 318, 345
Svodboda, Ludvik, 148
Syria, 396–397

Taborsky, Edward, 30
Taiwan, 317, 319, 362
Taiwan Relations Act (1979), 317
Takeo Miki, 181
Takeshi Watanabe, 174, 176
Talbott, Strobe, 352–353, 372, 375, 384, 385, 451n59
Taliban, 307, 389
Tamir, Avraham, 205
Taraki, Nur Muhammad, 307–310
Tatu, Michel, 74, 176, 177
technetronic revolution, 74–75, 112, 158–163, 233. *See also* *Between Two Ages* (Brzezinski)
Tehran Embassy hostage crisis, 280, 291, 292, 297–298, 335–339, 343
telephone tapping, 275, 276
Temple, Mary, 114
tennis metaphor, 246–247
terrorism, 388–392, 397
Thatcher, Margaret, 40, 376
think tanks, 134–135, 142, 214, 219, 359. *See also specific institutions*
Thomas, Evan, 3, 122, 129
"Threat and Opportunity in the Communist Schism" (Brzezinski), 90
Tiananmen Square, China, 239, 362, 400
Time Magazine, 138, 275, 352
Tito, Josip, 51
Toffler, Alvin, 161
"Tomorrow's Agenda" (Brzezinski), 259

Totalitarian Dictatorship and Autocracy (Brzezinski and Friedrich): drafting and release of, 26–27, 30, 48; reception of, 31; book revisions and, 70–72, 73; core concepts in, 219–220, 234, 257

totalitarianism: purges in, 28–30; Brzezinski's changing views on, 31–32, 70–76; stage of rationalization in, 32; degenerative process of, 73–74; Kirkpatrick on, 257. *See also* communism; *Totalitarian Dictatorship and Autocracy* (Brzezinski and Friedrich)

Trachtenberg, Marc, 216

Treaty of Versailles (1919), 33

Trezise, Philip, 169

Trialogue (newsletter), 177

Trilateral Commission, 6; Rockefeller's role in, 6, 125, 157, 165–166, 168–169, 437n34; creation of, 11, 12–13, 28, 136, 147, 157, 165–171; criticisms of, 125, 173, 176–177, 181–182, 320; initiatives of, 171–173; projects and relationships of, 173–178; impact of, 178, 179–183, 196; *The Governability of Democracies* report, 180

Trilling, Lionel, 68

Troubled Partnership (Kissinger), 77, 87

Troy Plus Project, 43

Truman administration, 2, 6

Trump, Donald, 225, 403–405

Tufts University, 37

Turner, Stansfield, 284, 287, 306, 354

U-2 spy plane incident, 54

Udall, Morris, 194

Ukraine, 17, 378, 379, 382, 398, 399

Ulam, Adam, 37, 41, 43

United Nations, 134, 391

United States. *See specific administrations and agencies*

University of California, Berkeley, 36, 38, 113

US Air Force, 27, 34, 35, 42, 43

US Army, 27, 36–37

US Congress: investigations of, 43, 392; relationship with executive branch,

84–85, 278; political influence of, 180, 288; —Carter administration relations, 291, 344, 349

US Department of State: Policy Planning Council, 5, 76, 91, 92–98, 136, 158; research funding by, 42; Tehran Embassy hostage crisis, 280, 291, 292, 297–298, 335–339, 343; under Carter administration, 280–281, 349. *See also specific leaders*

US embassy hostage crisis (Tehran, 1979–1981), 333

"U.S. Foreign Policy in East Central Europe" (Brzezinski), 49–50

US Navy, 36

US Office of Education, 34

US-Poland Action Commission, 381

USSR. *See* Soviet Union (1922–1991)

Vance, Cyrus: relationship with Harriman, 7; description of, 122, 132; relationship with Brzezinski, 126, 272, 279–285, 287–288, 306, 349–350; and SALT negotiations, 282, 302–303; on Afghanistan invasion, 310, 345; on China-US relations, 317, 318, 319, 345; on Brzezinski's communication with Iran, 334; and Iranian hostage crisis, 337; and human rights policies, 342; as Clinton's special envoy, 376. *See also* Carter administration

Van Dyk, Ted, 100, 105, 145, 155, 185, 428n129

Van Thieu, Nguyen, 114, 146, 221, 256

Vaughan, Patrick, 53, 370

Vernon, Raymond, 45, 46, 100, 120

Vienna Youth Festival (1959), 59–63

Vietnam, 89, 291, 318–319

Vietnam War: US policy on, 89, 91, 98–99, 103–105, 122–123, 146, 215, 428n129; protests against, 99, 106–107, 109, 112, 187; Brzezinski on, 113–114, 231–232; divisions and Soviet interference in, 289

Voice of America, 42–43, 302, 331. *See also* Radio Free Europe

Waldheim, Kurt, 328
Wałesa, Lech, 368, 381, 384
Wallace, George, 99, 105–106
Wallace, Schuyler, 68
Wall Street Journal, 54–55
Walt, Steve, 393–394
Waltz, Kenneth, 46
Warnke, Paul, 128, 138, 208–209
War on Terror, 388–392
Warsaw Ghetto Uprising (1943), monument
   for, 58, 302
Warsaw Pact, 8, 300, 372, 384
Wartime Commission, 34
Washington Post: journalists of, 62;
   Brzezinski in, 77, 79, 89, 90–91, 187;
   influence of, 138; on Carter's speech, 198;
   on neutron bomb, 323; on Brzezinski's
   books, 363, 364; on NATO expansion,
   384, 385
Watergate, 155–156, 177
Watkins, Frederick, 19, 22
Wattenberg, Ben, 149, 265
WCFIA. *See* CFIA (Center for
   International Affairs)
weapons development, 4, 34
Wehrkunde Transatlantic Conference, 80
Weinberger, Caspar, 368
Weizman, Ezer, 329
Wells, Samuel, 288–289
White House Years, The (Kissinger), 363
Why Not the Best? (Carter), 196
Wilbur, Martin, 68
William Allen White Committee, 41

Wilson, Woodrow, "The Inquiry" project
   by, 4, 33, 123, 214
wire-tapping, 275–276, 318, 345
Wise Men, The (Isaacson and Thomas), 2–3,
   122, 129
Wise Men group. *See* Establishment
Wizards of Armageddon, The (Kaplan), 215
Wohlstetter, Albert, 216, 228
Wolfowitz, Paul, 228
Woodcock, Leonard, 317
World Festival of Youth and Students,
   59–63
World Trade Organization (WTO), 392
World War I, "The Inquiry" project, 4, 33,
   123, 214
World War II, 17–18, 33–34
Wyszynski, Stefan, 302

Xi Jinping, 406

Yanukovych, Viktor, 399, 400
Years of Upheaval (Kissinger), 363
Yeltsin, Boris, 379
Yom Kippur War (1973), 177, 289
Young, Andrew, 327, 342
Yugoslavia, 370, 372, 375, 377
Yushchenko, Viktor, 399

Zahedi, Ardeshir, 333, 334
"Zbigniew Brzezinski: Vindication of a
   Hard-Liner" (Talbott), 372
Zimbabwe, 289, 327, 343
Zionist militia. *See* Irgun

Publications Index

Works written by Zbigniew Brzezinski

"After Srebrenica," 473n63
Alternative to Partition: For a Broader Conception of America's Role in Europe, 77, 82, 84–85, 94–95, 122, 158, 166, 258, 260, 423n28, 424n54, 426n85, 457nn191–192
"America and Europe," 166, 437n38
"America in a Hostile World," 433n74, 450n39, 451n53, 457n206, 463n93, 466n196
"America in the Technetronic Age," 166, 436n6, 450n31, 452n76
"An American Family Retraces Mao's Long March Through China," 470n7
"The American Transition," 436n6
"America's Mideast Policy Is in Shambles," 471n25
"America's New Geostrategy," 473n57
"Avoiding a New Cold War with China," 476n136

"The Balance of Power Delusion," 442n126
"Balancing the East, Upgrading the West: U.S. Grand Strategy in an Age of Upheaval," 476n139
Between Two Ages: America's Role in the Technetronic Era, 147, 151, 158–159, 161–162, 166, 172, 182, 223, 227, 233, 236, 257, 259, 260, 262, 263, 293, 357, 434n89, 436n3, 436n8, 437n37, 438n57,

449n27, 450n33, 450n41, 450n44, 452n79, 453n100, 453n122, 457n193, 462n92
"Beyond Chaos: A Policy for the West," 472n49
"A Bigger—and Safer—Europe," 474n82

"Cambodia Has Undermined Our Vital Credibility,"187, 442n124
"The Challenge of Change in the Soviet Bloc," *Foreign Affairs* 39, no. 3 (April 1961), 430–443
The Choice: Global Domination or Global Leadership, 475n110
"A Common House, a Common Home," 472n45
"Communist Disunity and the West," 423n29, 449n26, 452n94
"Communist Ideology and Power: From Unity to Diversity," 419n124, 449n25
"The Communist World in a New Phase," 425n68
"Compromise over Kosovo Means Defeat," 473n65
"Confronting Russian Chauvinism," 476n134
"Convincing Europe and China," 470n10

"Crises Blur Reality of Slow Basic Change," 436n6, 437n36

"Cuba in Soviet Strategy," 425n61

"A Deal for Andropov," 471n25

"The Deceptive Structure of Peace," 189 433n64, 443n130, 457n207, 462n92

"De Gaulle and Europe to the Urals," 424n57

"Deviation Control: The Dynamics of Doctrinal Conflict," 450n32

"Dim Prospects in Afghanistan" (interview), 476n128

"The End Game," 475n105

"Europe and Amerippon: Pillars of the Next World Order," 472n50

"The Failed Double-Cross," 473n67

"For a Broader Western Strategy," 471n25

"For Lenin's Centenary: Soviet Past and Future," 449nn27–28, 452n71

The Fragile Blossom: Crisis and Change in Japan, 147, 163, 165, 229, 434n89, 437n26, 437nn29–31, 451n67, 452n81

Game Plan: A Geostrategic Framework for the Conduct of the U.S.-Soviet Contest, 237, 369, 453n102, 453n105, 472n34

"A Genocide, a Political Coup. Some Democracy," 473n70

"A Geostrategy for Eurasia," 473n72

"Giants, but Not Hegemons," 476n137

"Global Implications for NATO Enlargement," 474n92

The Grand Chessboard: American Primacy and Its Geostrategic Imperatives, 380, 407, 414n13, 451n52, 473n72, 477n7

The Grand Failure: The Birth and Death of Communism in the Twentieth Century, 238–239, 269, 375, 453n97, 453n109, 453n111, 472n38, 472n43

"The Great Transformation," 474n78

"The Group of Two That Could Change the World," 476n137, 477n8

"Half Past Nixon," 442n136

"Histrionics as History in Transition," 112, 429n159, 450n33

"How to Avoid a New Cold War," 476n133

"How to Stay Friends with China," 476n137

"Ideology and Power: Crisis in the Soviet Bloc," 419n124

Ideology and Power in Soviet Politics, 422n9, 449n22

"If Russia Joins the G-7, Why Not China?," 476n135

"If the Russians and the Chinese Make Up . . ," 471n25

"If We Must Fight . . ," 475n103

"Imperial Russia, Vassal Ukraine," 476n131

"The Implications of Change for United States Foreign Policy," 436n6

"Indulging Russia Is a Risky Business," 473n70

"In Kosovo, U.S. Cannot Avoid Grim Choices," 473n64

"Japan in a Trilateral World," 171, 438n50

"Japan's Global Engagement," 450n42

"Know Thine Enemies," 475n108

"Living with China," 476n135

"Living with Russia," 473n70

"Lowered Vision," 475n108

"Meeting Moscow's 'Limited Coexistence,'" 457n196

"Merle Fainsod—Intellectual Creativity," 416n44

"The Middle East: Who Won?," 450n43

"Moral Duty, National Interest," 475n102

"Moscow and the MLF: Hostility and Ambivalence," 425n59

"Moscow's Mussolini," 476n130

"NATO: The Dilemmas of Expansion," 474n92

"The Nature of the Soviet System," 71, 422n10, 452n88

" 'Neutral' Vietnam a Chinese Backyard," 425n64, 425n72, 452n69, 453n96

" 'Never Again'—Except for Bosnia," 376, 473n60

"A New Age of Solidarity? Don't Count on It," 474n96, 475n100

"New Guidelines for the West," 166, 437n35

"Not in Agreement (Letter to the Editor)," 435n121

"On to Russia," 474n92

Out of Control: Global Turmoil on the Eve of the 21st Century, 374, 473n54

"Overview of East-West Relations—1985," 453n107

"Party Controls in the Soviet Army," 416n47

"Patience in the Persian Gulf, Not War," 472n52

"Patterns and Limits of the Sino-Soviet Dispute," 452n90

"Peace, Morality, and Vietnam," 425n69

"Peace and Power," 293, 436n6, 457n196, 462n92

"Peace at an Impasse," 471n25

The Permanent Purge: Politics in Soviet Totalitarianism, 28, 416nn48–49, 452n96

"A Plan for Peace in the Middle East," 446n198

"A Plan for Political Warfare," 474n97, 474n99

"Poland—A Political Glimpse," 58, 417n61, 420n136, 421n152

"Political Development in the Sino-Soviet Bloc," 452n91

"The Politics of Underdevelopment," 52, 420nn132–133

Power and Principle: Memoirs of the National Security Adviser, 1977–1981, 132, 135, 236, 360, 362–364, 414n9, 414n17, 414nn1–2 (chap. 1), 416n33, 432n45, 432n48, 432n52, 435n1, 443n146, 443n150,
444n151, 444n158, 445n172, 445n177, 446n199, 447n204, 448n2, 453n115, 454n129, 454n134, 454n139, 455n159, 458n211, 459n3, 459n5, 460n16, 460n18, 460n21, 460n24, 460n32, 460n35, 460n40, 461n43, 461nn46–47, 461nn49–50, 461n52, 461n54, 461n58, 461nn60–61, 461nn63–64, 461n66, 462n72, 462n74, 462n76, 462n79, 462n86, 463n98, 463n100, 463n107, 463n109, 463n114, 463–464nn116–119, 464nn121–122, 464nn128–129, 464n131, 465n141, 465n147, 465n151, 465n155, 465n157, 465n159, 465nn164–166, 466nn172–173, 466n177, 466nn179–181, 466n186, 466n188, 466nn190–191, 466nn194–195, 466n198, 467nn207–208, 467n210, 467n213, 467nn216–217, 467n219, 467n222, 467n225, 468n230, 468nn232–234, 468n239, 468n241, 468n250, 468n255, 469n265, 469n267, 469n272, 469n274, 470n1, 470n12, 471n14

"The Premature Partnership," 473n68, 473n71

"Probing Panther Attack," 456n174

"A Proposition the Soviets Shouldn't Refuse," 453n114, 472n43

"Purpose and Planning in Foreign Policy," 451n65

"Putin's Imperial Designs Are Reminiscent of Stalin's," 476n132

"Putin's Three Choices," 476n134

"Reagan Is Leaving an Ominous Legacy in Foreign Policy," 471n26

"Reconciliation Day," 456n174

"Reflections on the Soviet System," 423n23, 449n22, 453n99

"Rethinking East-West Relations," 471n25

"Revolution and Counter-Revolution," 470n287

"Russia, Like Ukraine, Will Become a Real Democracy," 476n130

"Russia and Europe," 425n59, 450n34

"Russia Must Re-Focus with Post-Imperial Eyes," 476n133

"Russia Needs a 'Finland Option' for Ukraine," 476n134

"Russo-Soviet Nationalism," 415nn15–16, 450n46, 455n164, 457n190

"The Search for Meaning Amid Change," 436n6

Second Chance: Three Presidents and the Crisis of American Superpower, 392–393, 475n111

"Selective Global Commitment," 474n84

"A Sensible Path on Iran," 476n126

"Shifts in the Satellites," 48, 419n119

"Sino-Soviet Relations," 452n93

"The Smart Way Out of a Foolish War," 475n121

The Soviet Bloc: Unity and Conflict, 46, 50, 56, 68, 69, 71, 77, 147, 158, 226, 234–235, 269, 369, 419n114, 419n124, 420nn126–131, 420n148, 435n2, 450n50, 452n72, 452n89

"The Soviet Political System: Transformation or Degeneration?," 423n21, 449n22, 453n99

"The Soviet Union: World Power of a New Type," 453n101, 453n104

"Staring Down the Russians," 476n132

"A Star Wars Solution," 471n28

Strategic Vision: America and the Crisis of Global Power, 375, 401, 473n58, 476n139

"Stretching NATO," 474n92

"The 'Stupidest' War?," 476n126

"Surprise a Key to Our Cuba Success," 424n38

"Terrorized by 'War on Terror': How a Three-Word Mantra Has Undermined America," 475n108

"There Is Much More at Stake for America than Iraq," 475n109

"This Is the Big Moment in Eastern Europe—and It Is Dangerous," 453n114

"This Peace Is as Peaceful as Cold War Was Martial," 456n185

"Threat and Opportunity in the Communist Schism," 425n66, 452n95

"Three R's for the Middle East," 473n53

"Tomorrow's Agenda," 259, 436n5, 437n35, 451n57, 452n78

"To Stop the Serbs," 473n66

"Totalitarianism and Rationality," 32, 417n60, 452n87

"Tougher Dealings by USSR Expected," 457n196

"Toward a Community of the Developed Nations," 437n36

"The Trap of Arms Control," 471n27

"The True U.S. Interest in the Gulf," 472n51

"A 2-Year Stint for Youth," 434n19

"U.S. Foreign Policy in East Central Europe: A Study in Contradiction," 419n122, 457n191

"A U.S. Portfolio in the USSR?," 458n109

"US Should Shoot Down IAF Jets," 476n127

"We Need a Latin Divorce," 452n83, 467n204

"We Need More Muscle in the Gulf, Less in NATO," 453n103, 472n37

"The West Adrift: Vision in Search of a Strategy," 474n86

"What Richard Cohen Got Wrong About My Views on Iran," 476n127

"What's Wrong with Reagan's Foreign Policy?," 471n19

"Where Do We Go from Here?," 475n108

"Who Will Succeed Brezhnev?," 451n68

"Why the Alliance Is Fading," 436n6, 452n82

"Why Unity Is Essential," 475n106

"Will the Soviet Empire Self-Destruct? Four Scenarios for Failure," 453n114, 472n41

A Year in the Life of Glasnost: The Hugh Seton-Watson Memorial Lecture and Other Essays, 453n110, 472n43

Works edited or co-authored by Zbigniew Brzezinski

Brzezinski, Zbigniew, ed. *Africa and the Communist World,* 81, 424n50, 452n80

Brzezinski, Zbigniew, and Anthony Lake. "For a New World, a New NATO," 474n92

Brzezinski, Zbigniew, and Carl Friedrich. *Totalitarian Dictatorship and Autocracy,* 30, 71–73, 416n53, 422n17, 449n22, 452n86

Brzezinski, Zbigniew, and John Mearsheimer. "The Clash of the Titans," 476n136

Brzezinski, Zbigniew, and Samuel Huntington. *Political Power:*

USA/USSR, 72, 230, 423n18, 433n75, 452n70, 453n98

Brzezinski, Zbigniew, and William Griffith. "Peaceful Engagement in Eastern Europe," 82, 94, 185, 423n27, 441n111, 457n191

Brzezinski, Zbigniew, Brent Scowcroft, and Richard Murphy. "Differentiated Containment," 475n104

Brzezinski, Zbigniew, David Ignatius, and Brent Scowcroft. *America and the World: Conversations on the Future of American Foreign Policy,* 475n115

Brzezinski, Zbigniew, François Duchene, and Kiichi Saeki. "Peace in an International Framework," 414n2